GOING
GLOBAL

GOING GLOBAL

The Textile and Apparel Industry

THIRD EDITION

GRACE I. KUNZ

Iowa State University

ELENA KARPOVA

Iowa State University

MYRNA B. GARNER

Illinois State University

Fairchild Books
An imprint of Bloomsbury Publishing Inc

BLOOMSBURY

NEW YORK · LONDON · OXFORD · NEW DELHI · SYDNEY

Fairchild Books

An imprint of Bloomsbury Publishing Inc

1385 Broadway	50 Bedford Square
New York	London
NY 10018	WC1B 3DP
USA	UK

www.bloomsbury.com

**FAIRCHILD BOOKS, BLOOMSBURY and the Diana logo
are trademarks of Bloomsbury Publishing Plc**

First edition published 2006

Second edition published 2011

This edition published 2016

Library of Congress Cataloging-in-Publication Data

Names: Kunz, Grace I. | Garner, Myrna B.

Title: Going global : the textile and apparel industry / Grace I. Kunz, Elena
Karpova, Myrna B. Garner.

Description: Third Edition. | New York : Fairchild Books, 2016. | Revised
edition of Going global, 2011.

Identifiers: LCCN 2015039451 | ISBN 9781501307300 (paperback)

Subjects: LCSH: Textile industry. | Clothing trade. | Globalization. | BISAC:
BUSINESS & ECONOMICS / Industries / Fashion & Textile Industry. | BUSINESS
& ECONOMICS / Industries / Retailing.

Classification: LCC HD9850.5 .K857 2016 | DDC 338.8/877—dc23 LC record available at
http://lccn.loc.gov/2015039451

ISBN: PB 978-1-5013-0730-0
ePDF 978-1-5013-0731-7

Typeset by Lachina
Printed and bound in the United States of America

CONTENTS

EXTENDED CONTENTS

PREFACE

Everyone who buys and wears apparel in the United States knows that by far the majority of garments sold in this country are produced in other countries. Since the turn of the twenty-first century, Chinese-made apparel has dominated the US market. However, in the 1990s, Mexico was the number one supplier of garments to the United States. In the early 1980s, Korea, Taiwan, and Hong Kong supplied more apparel than any other country. Prior to that, the majority of imported clothes in the United States was Japanese-made.

Even though relatively little apparel is now produced domestically, most imported clothes are still designed, developed, and sourced by US companies. How do these companies decide where their garments will be produced and where all input materials, such as fabrics, trims, and packaging, will come from? Why and how do some countries become major producers and exporters of textiles and/or apparel? What trends affect textile and apparel production, trade, and consumption in the global marketplace? *Every* successful textile, apparel, and fashion professional must have the knowledge to answer these questions and many more. A primary purpose of this book is to equip readers with the knowledge that is essential for any apparel industry professional, regardless if she or he is a designer, product developer, merchandiser, buyer, or manufacturer.

We developed a comprehensive framework for understanding how and why the global textile and apparel industry's trade and markets function. The framework is used to holistically examine the global sourcing of textiles and apparel in the context of sustainability of the supply chain. To facilitate learning, this text introduces the language and concepts essential to the global textile and apparel industry without overwhelming the reader. This understanding of the global textile and apparel industry is essential to not only make everyday professional decisions but also to forecast its development in the future and secure a competitive advantage in the highly volatile wholesale and retail markets. The discussions apply to any products related to fashion, including textiles, apparel, shoes, accessories, and home furnishings, although the primary discussion is focused on apparel.

China remains the undisputed apparel manufacturing leader and supplies over 40 percent of the world market (World Trade Organization, 2014). However, that country's fast-rising production costs have necessitated exploration of new garment assembly locations by apparel companies around the world. This, coupled with new trade regulations and agreements, has resulted in shifts in sourcing strategies and the emergence of new players in the global apparel marketplace.

In addition to tightening environmental regulations, the fickle consumer of the 2010s demands not only the latest fashions at affordable prices delivered overnight but also would like them to be produced responsibly and sustainably. Apparel professionals have been under the greatest pressure ever to stay on top of these and other changes in the global environment. This new edition of the book addresses major developments in the global textile and apparel industry as well as trade strategies to help companies remain competitive and grow.

NEW TO THIS EDITION

This edition of *Going Global* updates discussions of ethics and social, economic, and environmental responsibility as well as trade agreements. The role and specialization of regions of the world as well as selected countries that are major players in the textile and apparel marketplace are featured. We significantly expanded and reframed the sustainability discussion in the context of textile and apparel production, distribution, and consumption with current and relevant examples. Specifically, a Sustainability Matrix for Textile-Based Product Life Cycle was developed by the authors to systematically examine the environmental impact of textile and apparel production and consumption. The matrix incorporates major stages in the textile and apparel life cycle and strategies for minimizing the environmental impact of textile and apparel products and production processes.

To address the growing importance of sourcing in the strategic success of apparel businesses, we developed two new chapters that provide an in-depth examination of strategies apparel companies employ when choosing countries and vendors for sourcing apparel production in the new global environment. The refocused discussion of the role of regulations, barriers, and politics in trade reflects the current state of the industries. This edition has all new cases to illustrate the latest developments and trends in the global textile and apparel industries and trade and facilitate the learning process. To ensure relevance and applicability, some cases for the new edition were exclusively developed for the text by the authors or contributed by industry professionals. New, relevant, and current photos (some taken by the authors) are included to help readers understand the concepts and engage in learning.

FEATURES

Each chapter begins with objectives that identify its primary goals and content. For readers' convenience, a "Global Lexicon" is presented at the beginning of each chapter that lists and defines the relevant new vocabulary and concepts. Reviewing the lexicon before proceeding with a chapter is an *active learning approach* that can speed progress and enhance understanding of the topics discussed.

Critical thinking is the type of *thought* involved in solving problems, formulating inferences, calculating likelihoods, and making decisions. It is useful in all aspects of our lives, and it will be valuable in the reading of this text as well as in making use of the information presented. Investing time, attention, and critical thinking to the topics will optimize learning processes as well as the opportunity for long-term application of the principles gained.

To encourage critical thinking, concepts and principles related to globalization of the textile and apparel business are presented in many forms; for example, as maps and main text as well as in tables, diagrams, cases, and pictures. Each form of information provides a different perspective, emphasis, and comparative food for thought. The tables provide an opportunity for comparisons among regions and countries to draw conclusions and create insights about levels of development, activity in the textiles and apparel business, as well as comparisons of labor productivity and costs among countries and regions. Amazing insights can be gained, but it takes a special bit of time and attention to appreciate the opportunities the multiple forms of information have to offer.

To help readers gain an understanding of supply chains as well as global sourcing concepts and practices, two to four cases are presented in each chapter to provide the opportunity to experience the application of academic concepts to real-world scenarios. Thought and discussion questions or other relevant activities are offered after each case to help deepen the understanding of the presented topic. It is important to keep in mind that many topics presented in the text are very complex and multifaceted and rarely can be judged as "good" or "bad" and "wrong" or "right." Often they can be looked at from multiple perspectives, so be prepared that your point of view might differ from your classmates or professor, and realize that people in other parts of the world might have even more different opinions than those around you.

Hands-on learning activities are positioned at the end of each chapter to help address the chapter's objectives and provide an opportunity to apply the concepts introduced. To generate long-term retention as well as the ability to apply what is learned to new situations, students are asked to research multiple perspectives, recognize assumptions, analyze relationships, and give reasons to support conclusions. This is critical thinking at its best.

COVERAGE AND ORGANIZATION OF THE TEXT

Achieving effective presentation of such complex and wide-ranging topics requires careful consideration of ways to present fundamental concepts and build on them. In this case it requires an introduction to the world that includes a globally pervasive textile and apparel industry that trades multinationally. To accomplish this, *Going Global* is divided into three parts.

Part One. Embarking on a Global Adventure

The focus is on establishing a foundation for effective learning about the global textile and apparel industry by developing an understanding of the organization and operation of the textile complex. Learning is dependent on developing some understanding of the fundamentals of globalization and how the textile and apparel industry operates within it. Examples of challenges to students include assessing levels of trade among countries, interpreting levels of development, and the concept of sustainability. The major components of the worldwide textile complex are introduced along with the role of the many supply chains that operate around the world. These are some of the concepts developed in Chapter 1.

During the last century, huge changes have emerged in the world's textile and apparel trade because of improved technology, equipment, machinery, transportation, and collaborative trade agreements between and among countries. Both apparel manufacturers and retailers are dependent on the world's consumers. The apparel business wraps around the world but it cannot continue to operate without satisfied customers for the products produced and retailed. One of the outcomes is the immensity of textile waste by both manufacturers and consumers. The foundation of successful business relies on understanding how target consumers make choices, how much they want to buy, how much they will spend, and when. This is the focus of Chapter 2.

Beginning in the late 1950s, retail buying offices in developed countries began seeking international business relationships. Their purpose was to supply US and European apparel retailers with finished garments *different from or at a lower cost than* what was being offered by domestic apparel firms. Buying offices grew in number and popularity until the late 1980s, when merchandisers and designers got involved in product development for private label lines. The race then began for development of supply chains that included the lowest-cost labor with the highest efficiency to make the garments somewhere in the world. This led to the development of the standardized merchandise identification systems essential for processing goods that are transported from one country to another. This is the focus of Chapter 3.

Supply chains for textiles and apparel, more often than not, are now global in scope and may involve a few, dozens, or even hundreds of different companies and governments. The interaction of all of the components of supply chains takes place in countries with different priorities, cultural values, and methods of communication and making decisions. Now, a primary challenge is incorporating social, economic, and environmental dimensions of sustainability into the supply chains. These priorities have the power to reduce waste of resources, improve the health and comfort of populations, and improve the welfare of people around the world. This is the focus of Chapter 4.

Part Two. The Global Supply Chain

Chapters 5 through 8 introduce, explain, and examine the flow of materials, products, and services that make worldwide sourcing in the textile and apparel industry possible. Trade involves exchange of goods and services across political boundaries. Governments establish regulations regarding the transfer of products from one country to another as well as to verify their origin, ownership, quality, and safety. Some regulations are developed to encourage trade, whereas others aim at restricting trade to control the amount of imports or exports of an economy. Politics frequently intervene, often in pursuit of self-interest. It is very important for apparel professionals to understand what effect different trade regulations might have on sourcing products and services from vendors in countries around the world. Textile and apparel trade barriers, regulations, and politics are the topics of Chapter 5.

As global industries like textiles and apparel develop, opportunities also develop for illegal and unethical activities. Trade regulations and trade barriers are put in place to protect ownership of brands, technology, production methods, and so on. Consumer protection activities by governments sometimes result in illegal attempts to get around them. Trade restrictions, requirements for customs compliance, intellectual property law, and social responsibility are ongoing sources of controversy and illegal activity in the global market. These are the topics of Chapter 6.

Global sourcing involves determining the most cost-efficient locations of services, materials, production, finished goods, or a combination of these at a specified quality and service level for delivery to specified locations within an identified time frame. Consideration of what countries to source involves political, economic, social, and cultural forces in the context of government regulations. Geographic locations of production can be a primary factor in efficiency and speed of delivery. These are the topics of Chapter 7.

Selecting vendors for global sourcing involves a complex combination of considerations and trade-offs. There is a variety of types of companies that provide textile and apparel manufacturing services, so matching the services needed with an efficient and effective vendor is an ongoing challenge. Multiple factors must be taken into account when selecting partners for designing a competitive and sustainable supply chain. Chapter 8 walks the reader through the decision-making process of vendor selection, explaining advantages and disadvantages of various options available in the marketplace.

Part Three. Trading Partners

Chapters 9 to 12 examine textile and apparel industries in countries in four major parts of the world, which are defined as Europe and the European Union, the Americas and the Caribbean Basin, Asia and Oceania, and the Middle East and Africa. This new edition introduces the Global Competitiveness Index (GCI), which determines the level of a country's productivity (World Economic Forum, 2015). The index is very useful in helping keep track of how developed countries are and whether each country is more likely to be more involved in the textile industry, the apparel industry, or both. Each chapter includes maps, a political and economic overview, and the role of textiles and apparel in each region.

Many countries that are major players in textile and apparel production and consumption are discussed in each of the regions, so there is a lot of geography involved to be able to keep track of where in the world you are. We sincerely hope you find your global adventure challenging, insightful, and rewarding.

References

World Economic Forum. (2015). "The Global Competitiveness Report 2014–2015." Retrieved April 28, 2015, from www.weforum.org/reports/global-competitiness-report-2014-2015

World Trade Organization. (2014). "Textile Exports of Selected Regions and Economies by Destination, 2013." Statistics: International Trade Statistics 2014. Merchandise Trade. Retrieved November 15, 2015, from www.wto.org/english/res_e/statis_e/its14_merch_trade_product_e.htm

INSTRUCTOR AND STUDENT RESOURCES

GOING GLOBAL STUDIO

New for this edition is an online multimedia resource, *Going Global STUDIO*. The online *STUDIO* is specially developed to complement this book with rich media ancillaries that students can adapt to their visual learning styles to better master concepts and improve grades. Within the *STUDIO*, students will be able to:

- Study smarter with self-quizzes featuring scored results and personalized study tips
- Review concepts with flashcards of essential vocabulary

STUDIO access cards are offered free with new book purchases and also sold separately through Bloomsbury Fashion Central (www.BloomsburyFashionCentral.com).

INSTRUCTOR RESOURCES

- The Instructor's Guide provides suggestions for planning the course and using the text in the classroom, supplemental assignments, and lecture notes
- The Test Bank includes sample test questions for each chapter
- PowerPoint® presentations include images from the book and provide a framework for lecture and discussion

Instructor's Resources may be accessed through Bloomsbury Fashion Central (www.BloomsburyFashionCentral.com).

ACKNOWLEDGMENTS

The authors thank Susan Maxwell and Kyle Madson for contributing original cases to the book and providing invaluable insights on industry developments and practices. We are grateful for Ana Correia's help with some tables in Chapters 9–12. Many thanks to Rona Tuccillo for her patience and persistence in finding appropriate pictures to illustrate many key concepts described in chapters. Also special thanks to Elena Karpova for sharing photos collected on her intercontinental travels.

EMBARKING ON A GLOBAL ADVENTURE

CHAPTER 1
INTRODUCTION TO GLOBALIZATION

OBJECTIVES

- Discuss perspectives for the examination of global issues and the critical thinking required for understanding of those issues.
- Examine relationships between a country's level of economic development and its role in the textile and apparel industry.
- Introduce the concept of a supply chain for textiles and/or apparel.
- Examine the nature of firms in the textile and apparel complex.

No other form of commerce can claim to be as pervasive throughout the globe as the textile and apparel business. This business provides employment for more people than any other business segment, directly affording a livelihood to many people in every country in the world. Globally, in 2013 compared to 2012, the apparel trade rose by 8 percent, four times higher than the 2 percent average growth of all other industries. India led the top ten exporters by posting an impressive 23 percent growth in textiles and apparel exports (Adendorff, 2014). This text explores the complexities involved in where textile and apparel products come from and how these products are distributed in today's global marketplace. The core of the discussion is examination of economic, political, and social issues that textile and apparel professionals face when making decisions.

Investing time, attention, and critical thinking to the topics addressed by this text will optimize the learning process and the opportunity for long-term application of principles gained. Critical thinking is the type of thinking involved in solving problems, formulating inferences, calculating likelihoods, and making decisions. It is useful in all aspects of our lives, and it will be valuable in the reading of this text as well as in making use of the information presented.

accessories handbags, jewelry, purses, wallets, tote bags, and belts as well as eyeglass frames

apparel clothing, accessories, and/or other attire that covers, adorns, and sometimes protects the human body

apparel firm a commercial or industrial business that is engaged in some aspects of designing, merchandising, marketing, producing, and/or retailing garments and/or other attire

apparel industry combination of trades and businesses that contribute to designing, developing, producing, and retailing garments and other attire that covers, protects, and/or adorns the human body

apparel manufacturer firm engaged in the entire process of apparel manufacturing; might also be involved in sourcing materials and/or retailing

apparel manufacturing processes involving division of labor for designing, merchandising, developing, producing, and often wholesale marketing garments and/or other attire that adorn the human body

apparel production part of the process of apparel manufacturing that actually converts materials—including fabrics, findings, trims, and usually thread—into garments; also known as apparel assembly

apparel production vendor firm that takes orders for apparel products from other firms and that either produces or arranges for the production of those specific garments; historically called production contractors

apparel sourcing determining the most cost efficient vendor of services, materials, production, and/or finished goods at a specified quality and service level, for delivery within an identified time frame

brand manager a former apparel manufacturer that is engaged in design and product development but owns little or no production facilities and sources garment assembly from vendors located elsewhere in the world

clothing wearing apparel including men's, women's, and children's garments as well as gloves, footwear, and headgear

conglomerate business formed when firms serving multiple markets join together with common ownership

contractor firm that provides services for other businesses, often used for selected apparel manufacturing processes; in today's sourcing language these firms are called vendors

country of origin the location where an article was wholly obtained; when more than one country is involved, the location where the last substantial transformation was carried out; the location where there is a change in the product designation number, according to the Harmonized Commodity Code and Designation System (HS)

cut-make-trim (CMT) factory or vendor apparel contractors that commonly provide apparel assembly as their primary service

department store retailer that provides a variety of product lines, including apparel for men, women, and children; soft goods for the home; and home furnishings, usually at moderate-to-higher price levels

developed country nation whose gross domestic product per capita and other measures of well-being fall well above the world average

developing country nation whose gross domestic product per capita and other measures of well-being fall near or slightly below the world average

e-commerce electronic business transactions conducted by systems such as the internet

e-tailing retailers providing opportunities for ultimate consumers to purchase products or services, using electronic systems such as the internet

exports goods shipped to another country for import in exchange for money, other goods, or jobs

findings materials other than face fabric used to construct garments: interlinings, pocket bags, linings, closures, and trims

firm any for-profit business, corporation, proprietorship, or partnership

full-package factory or vendor apparel production firms that not only provide production services but also assist with and finance materials sourcing and some phases of product development

garment a piece of clothing

GDP per capita (PPP) abbreviation for gross domestic product per capita adjusted by purchasing power parity

global trade interactive participation of many groups, cultures, and nations in the merchandising, design, development, production, and distribution of products and services

globalization process whereby the world's people, their firms, and their countries become increasingly interconnected in all facets of their lives

gross domestic product (GDP) market value of the output of products and services produced within a country in a year

gross domestic product (GDP) per capita gross domestic product (GDP) of a country divided by the number of people in the population after GDP has been adjusted by purchasing power parity (PPP); hereafter referred to as GDP per capita (PPP)

gross national product (GNP) value of the average output produced by domestic residents of a nation as they labor within that nation

gross national product (GNP) per capita gross national product of a country divided by the number of people in the population

horizontal integration when previously competitive enterprises engaged in offering similar goods or services join together under a single management organization

import and export trading recently developed type of enterprise that assists textile and apparel firms in satisfying customer demand for goods and services from the global market

imports goods available for domestic consumption or materials available for domestic production because of exports of other countries

international trade any exchange of goods involving two or more countries

lean retailing effective management of inventory, based on accurate and timely information and frequent resupply

market week calendar time set aside for trade shows featuring manufacturers' and brand managers' lines of textile materials, apparel, or machinery, presented at wholesale to other manufacturers or retail buyers

mass retailer firm that offers a wide variety of consumer goods in a self-service environment with broad appeal across income ranges, ethnic groups, occupations, and lifestyles

merger combining two business entities into one larger business

newly developing country nation whose gross domestic product per capita and other measures of well-being fall well below the world average; just beginning to be engaged in industrial development, likely to involve apparel production; some sources use term "least developed country"

nonstore retailer firm that sells goods to the ultimate consumer without use of traditional "brick-and-mortar" store presentation

origin-conferring operations processes that determine what a label on a product will state as country of origin

outsourcing contracting out specific operations outside the company to a domestic or foreign vendor with the goal to perform these operations more efficiently and/or at a lower cost; outsourced operations might include manufacturing, product development, logistics, IT, accounting, customer service, etc.

outward processing temporary exporting of goods for manufacturing processes or repair purposes; the goods are then re-imported back into the country with partial or total exemption from import duty or taxes; primarily used in European Union

per capita by or for each individual; total is divided by the number of individuals involved and all share equally

per capita purchasing power parity measure that allows comparison of well-being among populations in different countries, as indicated by GDP; determined by adjusting GDP of a country by the buying power of its currency using the Consumer Price Index and dividing the total by the number of people in the population

politics methods or tactics involved in managing an organization, business, state, or government, often in a pursuit of self-interest; sometimes includes crafty or unprincipled methods, or both

product development design and engineering of products to be serviceable, producible, salable, and profitable (Glock & Kunz, 2005)

purchasing power parity (PPP) measure that allows comparison of well-being among populations in different countries, as indicated by GDP; determined by adjusting GDP of a country by the buying power of its currency using Consumer Price Index

quota method used to restrict quantities of certain types of goods that can be imported or exported; limit on the quantity of products allowed to enter or exit a country

retail product developer individual or team that creates product designs and develops merchandise plans and specifications for a retailer's private brands, which are ultimately sourced from production vendors

retailing sale of merchandise or services, or both, to ultimate consumers

soft goods products made of textiles or other flexible materials: fabrics, apparel, linens, towels, upholstery, and small fashion accessories

sourcing process of finding, evaluating, and partnering with a vendor to secure services, materials, production, or finished goods, or a combination of these, at a specified cost, quality, and service level, for delivery within an identified time frame

specialty retailer retailers that focus on specific classes of merchandise to the exclusion of other products

supply chain total sequence of business processes involving single or multiple companies and countries that enables demand for products or services to be satisfied; an apparel supply chain might include some or all of the following: design and product development agencies, material suppliers, manufacturers, transporters, warehouses, retailers, and consumers

sustainability involves the corporate, government, and consumer responsibility to integrate economic, political, environmental, and cultural dimensions to promote cooperation and solidarity among people and generations

takeover absorption of a weaker firm into a more successful operation

textile complex combination of textile-related industries that supply soft goods to the world population; includes firms engaged in man-made fiber production, textile manufacturing (knit, woven, and nonwoven fabrics), apparel manufacturing, retailing, and product consumption and disposal

textile industry combination of trades and businesses that contribute to production, manufacturing, and retailing of fibers, yarns, fabrics, and related materials

textile materials sourcing identifying appropriate countries of origin and vendors of fabric, thread, or findings at a specified quantity, quality, and service level, for delivery within a designated time frame

trade exchange of goods, services, or both; can be domestic, international, or global

trade agreement means of encouraging, regulating, or restricting elements of trade among countries

trade balance quantitative relationship between exports and imports of a country

trade barriers means of regulating or restricting trade; examples include state trading, tariffs, quotas, and limits on foreign investment

trade deficit negative trade balance; value of imports exceeds value of exports

trade surplus positive trade balance; value of exports exceeds value of imports

vertical integration combining firms that perform different stages of the manufacturing and/or retailing of similar and/or compatible types of products

wearing apparel garments that adorn the human body for comfort, protection, and adornment

World Trade Organization (WTO) an institution with more than 160 countries as members; deals with the global rules of trade among nations

Concepts and principles related to globalization of the textile and apparel business are presented in many forms: as main text; in cases; and in pictures, diagrams, and tables. Each form provides a different perspective and emphasis and different food for thought. Numbers in tables provide amazing insights, but it takes a special bit of time and attention to appreciate what they have to offer. In addition, cases presented in each chapter provide the opportunity to apply what is learned to "real-world" scenarios. Each chapter includes cases representing current, real-life issues in the apparel industry. Discussion and reflection questions are considered after each case and "Learning Activities" are positioned at the end of each chapter. To generate long-term retention as well as the ability to apply what is learned to new situations, students are asked to research multiple perspectives, recognize assumptions, analyze relationships, and give reasons to support conclusions. This is critical thinking at its best.

We encourage delving into the complexity of the global textile and apparel market and appreciating the challenges that are likely to be a part of a professional career in the field. For Chapter 1, the primary purposes are to (1) introduce perspectives for examining globalization, (2) present the global lexicon, (3) explain a system for classifying countries according to levels of development, and (4) examine the nature of firms in the textile complex.

From the perspective of some consumers, textile and apparel products are simply something they purchase in the marketplace with their monetary resources to satisfy their personal needs. Many of these consumers have little understanding of or a particular interest in where these products originate or how they arrive at their favorite stores. At the opposite end of the consumer continuum are individuals who are concerned about unethical business practices, for example, labor exploitation and environmental issues. These consumers may attempt to force the textile and apparel businesses to employ fair and sustainable business practices, both domestically and abroad. These viewpoints, related to labor and the environment, represent social, environmental, and economic perspectives of globalization issues.

Throughout this exploration of global business and trade involving textiles and apparel, both participants and observers use multiple legitimate perspectives to reach diverse justifiable conclusions. The appropriate viewpoint is dependent upon content and context. The synergy among these perspectives is complex, challenging, and constantly changing. Case 1.1 and Case 1.2 present two global trade scenarios with an array of different economic, political, and social perspectives. The questions that follow these cases will help you think through their relationships.

PERSPECTIVES FOR CONSIDERATION OF GLOBALIZATION

Because of globalization, the world's people have become increasingly connected and interdependent in all facets of their lives. For example, in the last thirty years the sources and methods used by textile and apparel professionals for procuring textile and apparel products for their customers have undergone profound changes. Until the 1980s and 1990s, the vast majority of textile and apparel products available to consumers in developed countries were produced domestically. As we progressed into the twenty-first century, however, the source of these products changed from domestic to global as textile and apparel professionals sought the ever-elusive supplies

FOR BANGLADESHI WOMEN, FACTORY WORK IS WORTH THE RISKS[1]

To give her daughter opportunities neither she nor her mother had, Nazma Akhter made the only choices possible for a poor, illiterate woman in Bangladesh. She fled her village, bolting the door behind her so her mother couldn't chase her down. She moved to Dhaka, the capital, and began living in a shed the size of a parking space. She worked 12-hour days making jeans, T-shirts, and dresses, earning no more than $98 a month. The income was just enough to allow Akhter to bring her family to Dhaka and put her daughter, Riza, in school. Then, on Nov. 24, 2012, a fire broke out in the Tazreen Fashions factory where Akhter worked. The blaze killed 112 of her co-workers. A worse disaster followed. On April 24 last year, 1,129 perished when the Rana Plaza factory complex collapsed.

For Akhter, who guesses she's in her early thirties, the fallout from Tazreen has been severe. She unravels her sari to show the scar on her back from hours of surgery after she jumped out of the building, falling two stories, to escape the fire. She still can't work. But she says she'd do it all again if it meant that Riza, now 10 and an excellent student, could get a good education and a shot at an office job—the girl's dream. Nothing could be further from the life lived by Akhter's mother, who still pulls stalks of rice in paddy fields. "God, she worked so hard," says Akhter, whispering in the shed as her three children sleep in the afternoon heat. "My mother couldn't stand straight anymore. I couldn't live like that. I couldn't make my daughter live like that."

The paradox of Bangladesh's $20 billion garment industry, where substandard practices have resulted in the deaths of at least 2,000 people since 2005, is that it's virtually the only way for the nation's women and girls to claw their way out of poverty and illiteracy. For some 3.5 million Bangladeshis,

Figure Case 1.1
Akhter with her daughter, Riza, next to the shed they call home

mostly women, the 10-hour shifts spent hunched over a sewing machine offer a once-in-a-generation chance to better their lives.

In 2011 about 12 percent of Bangladeshi women ages 15 to 30 worked in the garment industry, according to a study by Rachel Heath of the University of Washington and Ahmed Mushfiq Mobarak of Yale University's School of Management. Pay was 13 percent greater than in other industries that rely on manual labor. Perhaps most important, the researchers found, 27 percent more young girls were attending school than before the garment industry existed.

Young as she is, Riza, a poetry-obsessed math whiz, understands that her mother's job was an essential step in her family's quest for security and prosperity. "Tell me something," she asks. "Do offices catch fire like factories do? Because I want to work in an office someday."

For Bangladesh, a nation dismissed by Henry Kissinger as a "basket case" after its violent birth in 1971, and which has since endured several political coups and uprisings, garment making has been a godsend. It now accounts for 6 percent of gross domestic product (GDP) [the market value of the output of products and services produced within a country in a year] and last year made up almost 80 percent of exports. "Don't forget that this industry has allowed Bangladesh to cut poverty by a third. Don't forget that it has created millions of jobs. Don't forget that it has helped put more young girls in school than ever before," says Gilbert Houngbo, deputy director general of the International Labour Organization, which has funneled millions of dollars in the past year into inspections of Bangladeshi factories. "On the other hand, you can't do that at the expense of women's basic rights—the right to feel safe, to be safe, to have decent work environments."

On a steamy afternoon, Akhter relives the day she almost died. She waves with her hands as she describes the smoke filling the air on her floor of the factory. She feigns a limp to demonstrate how her leg was stuck in a pile of bodies. Suddenly she starts howling, the memories still sharp. The cries awaken Riza as neighbors crowd into the shed to hear the story. The girl slips off of a thin sheet on the floor and starts putting things in her school bag, even though classes are over for the day. Three notebooks, a small box with a pencil, a sharpener and half an eraser, a book of Bengali grammar, and an empty lunchbox barely fit into her used Hannah Montana backpack.

[1]Srivastava, Mehul. (n.d.). "For Bangladeshi Women, Factory Work Is Worth the Risks." http://bloomberg.com/bw/articles/2014-04-24/for-bangladeshi-women-factory-work-is-worth-the-risks

1. What are the primary messages that you get from Case 1.1?

---

of merchandise that would both satisfy their customers and generate profit necessary to sustain their businesses.

The **textile complex** incorporates firms around the world to accomplish fiber production, textile manufacturing (for example, knit, woven, and nonwoven fabrics), apparel manufacturing, retailing, product use, and disposal. The apparel portion of the textile complex is the primary focus of this book. The term **apparel** is defined as follows: Apparel is wearing apparel and accessories with the primary focus on wearing apparel. Wearing apparel means men's, women's, and children's clothing including gloves, footwear, and headgear. Accessories include handbags, purses, wallets, tote bags, and belts as well as eyeglass frames and other devices that are attached to the body in some way for comfort or convenience. Examination of the operation of the textile complex in the global market involves language drawn from economic, political, and social perspectives and utilizes global business, government, and labor language.

The primary focus of this text is on the apparel supply chain portion of the textile complex, the sequence of business processes involving single or multiple businesses and countries that enables demand for products and/or services to be satisfied. You probably noticed the term "value chain" was used in Case 1.2. The focus of the **value chain** is on how each stage of the supply chain adds value (worth) to apparel products. The supply chain is

STUDY SAYS MOST APPAREL JOBS ARE IN UNITED STATES EVEN IF LABEL SAYS "MADE IN CHINA"[2]

A new study conducted by NRF (National Retail Federation) says the majority of jobs behind apparel sold in the United States are held by American workers even if the product is manufactured overseas.

"This study shatters several wide-spread myths about imports and trade," NRF president and CEO Mathews Shay said. "Labels identifying clothing or any other product as made outside the United States are largely meaningless. *Regardless of where the factory might be located*, these products support a huge number of good blue-collar and white-collar American jobs in retail and many other industries."

The study, conducted by Seattle economist Susan Hester for the Trans-Pacific Partnership Apparel Coalition, found an average of 70 percent of the final selling price of garments examined went to US workers. While clothing might be produced in an overseas factory, it is after it was designed and developed by American workers, and is transported, marketed and sold by US workers once it arrives on US soil, the study said. Only the lowest-skill, lowest-wage jobs in the "value chain" of the garment are typically done overseas.

"American consumers and policy makers tend to look at clothes and finished products and put them into one of two categories—either imported or made in America," Hester said. "This approach is outdated and inaccurate."

Hester's study looked at 20 categories of garments from underwear to shirts, pants, and coats. It found US apparel employment from design through sales totals 2.9 million workers. Jobs include design, research and development, transportation, logistics, distribution, quality assurance, marketing, merchandising, sales, and compliance with legal, labor, and environmental standards.

[2]Craig, Shearman J. (2013, Feb 13). Study Says Most Apparel Jobs Are in United States Even If Label Says "Made in China." https://nrf.com/news/public-policy/study-says-most-apparel-jobs-are-U.S.-even-if-label-says-made-in-China. Copyright, National Retail Federation.

1. What are the primary messages that you get from Case 1.2?
2. How do the scenarios in Cases 1.1 and 1.2 relate to each other?

the organizational structure that the value chain operates within. Thus, while value chain is a useful concept, the supply chain is used as the organizational structure for this text book.

For your convenience, a **Global Lexicon** is presented at the beginning of each chapter. It lists and defines the new vocabulary and concepts relevant in each chapter. You may be familiar with many of these terms in a different context, but reviewing the lexicon before you proceed through a chapter is an *active learning approach* that can speed your progress and enhance your understanding of the topics discussed. Referring back to the Global Lexicon to remind yourself of definitions as you work your way through is a strategic means of building your vocabulary and developing an understanding of the concepts introduced in each chapter. Note: The Global Lexicon in Chapter 1 is "loaded"; they will become less so as the chapters progress.

LEVELS OF TRADE

Trade refers to exchange of goods, services, or both and can be domestic, international, or global. **Domestic trade** refers to exchange of goods, services, or both within the boundaries of a specified state or country. **International trade** is any exchange of goods involving two or more countries. **Global trade** goes beyond the concept of international trade to include the potential interactive participation of many groups, cultures, and nations in the manufacturing and distribution of products. Although the terms *international* and *global* are sometimes used interchangeably, most people understand *global* to mean a universal, comprehensive perspective that pertains to the whole world. The terms *internationalization* and *globalization* are also sometimes used in relation to these same definitions used above. The discussion in this text is focused primarily on international and global trade.

International Trade

International trade in textiles and apparel is not a new phenomenon. Since the centuries-old trade routes brought silk out of China by way of camel caravans that crossed the Middle East to Europe, international trade in textile products has prevailed. The silk trade involved silk fiber, silk yarn, silk fabric, and some silk garments produced domestically in China and transported to Italy for exchange for other goods and services. Ships crossing the Mediterranean Sea from Asia to Europe invariably included textiles in their cargoes. The first ships that arrived in the Americas carried textiles as items for trade with the natives. One of the reasons the South was unable to win the US Civil War was because of the loss of revenue from the cotton trade with Great Britain. In today's markets, large and small textile and apparel firms import materials, finished goods, or both through international trade with firms in countries where supplies are available. Many of these same firms are using international trade to export their products and make them available for sale in multiple countries.

A primary driver of the growth of international trade of textiles and apparel into global trade is the outsourcing of apparel assembly and other services by firms based in **developed countries** from firms based in **developing countries** and **newly developing countries**, where lower labor costs are usually available. **Outsourcing** is contracting specific operations outside the company to a domestic or foreign vendor with the goal of acquiring more efficient operations and/or a lower cost. Outsourced operations might include manufacturing, product development, logistics, IT, accounting, customer service, etc. The term "outsourcing" is often used interchangeably with **sourcing**, which is the process of finding, evaluating, and partnering with a vendor to secure services, materials, production, or finished goods, or a combination of these, at a specified cost, quality, and service level, for delivery within an identified time frame. In this text, the term "sourcing" will be used primarily as its definition here can include apparel assembly along with selecting and buying materials, product development, and even design and logistics. Apparel sourcing priorities have contributed to the globalization of trade by driving the apparel manufacturing industry around the world.

Global Trade

Lodge (1995) provided a generalized definition of the **globalization** concept, stating that "globalization is the process whereby the world's people are becoming increasingly interconnected in all facets of their lives—cultural, economic, political, technological, and environmental" (p. 1). To further explain global business and the process of globalization, we must clarify the nature of global business transactions. The following three types of integration are occurring in the global business environment:

- financial, which tends to be globally integrated
- trade and investment, which tends to be regionally integrated
- labor, which tends to be nationally regulated

Businesses involved with the development, production, and distribution of textile and apparel products in a global market potentially deal with a combination of financial, trade and investment, and labor transactions. These transactions incorporate the operation of businesses, labor, and governments in the global context. See and think about Figure 1.1.

Seen from a pragmatic viewpoint, an example of global trade might simply involve 10,000 pairs of khaki pants. These pants, sold in department stores in towns in the rural and suburban United States, could have been designed and developed in Chicago, made with fabric woven in South Korea out of cotton fiber from Pakistan and polyester fiber from Taiwan, and cut and sewn somewhere in Honduras. In each country, individuals of different cultural backgrounds are employed; different languages are spoken; diverse tasks requiring different sets of performance skills are performed; and resources, from pesticides and petrochemicals to water and machinery, are required to produce the product. This simple pair of pants becomes a microcosm of globalization, involving many complex and potentially problematic issues

Measuring Levels of Trade

Trade is often described in terms of exports and imports. **Exports** are goods shipped for import to another country in exchange for money, other goods, or jobs. Exports result in the accruing of revenue to the firms in the countries where the goods originated. **Imports** make goods available for domestic consumption or materials available for domestic production. The difference between the quantity of exports and imports for a region or a country is called the **trade balance**. The trade balance is calculated as follows:

exports – imports = trade balance

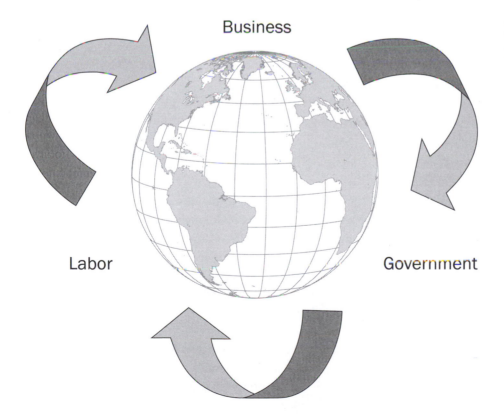

Figure 1.1
Business decisions in a global market.

A **trade surplus** means there is a positive trade balance; the value of exports exceeds the value of imports. A trade surplus is sometimes regarded as desirable, because, cumulatively, the firms and/or the government of the country in question has gained more revenue from the sale of exported goods than it gave up to other countries for the purchase of imported goods. There is a net gain in revenue that can be invested in domestic resources. It is important to note that a trade surplus does not necessarily mean that more products are available for trade than can be consumed domestically. In newly developing countries it is common that goods produced for export are not made available to or affordable for domestic consumers. A **trade deficit** means there is a negative trade balance; the value of imports exceeds the value of exports. A negative trade balance may be regarded as undesirable, because greater revenue is accrued to foreign countries as the result of trade than to the domestic country in question.

CLASSIFICATION OF COUNTRIES BY LEVELS OF ECONOMIC DEVELOPMENT

To understand what role countries play in the global textile complex in relation to trade and why some countries are primarily textile and apparel exporters while other countries import more textile and/or apparel products than they export, it is necessary to consider a country's level of economic development. The level of economic development is of particular interest to us because location of different parts of the textile and apparel supply chain is largely determined by level of development of the countries involved. Academic researchers and economists from major world organizations, such as the United Nations and the International Monetary Fund, typically classify all world countries into three groups: developed countries, developing countries, and newly developing countries.

- Developed countries are comprised of economically advanced nations where citizens enjoy a relatively high level of well-being.
- Developing countries are the group in the middle that have made some progress out of poverty and are striving for better lives.
- Newly developing countries are the poorest nations in the world that have the lowest level of economic development but are beginning to find ways to improve well-being.

See Figure 1.2 and focus on the clusters of developed, developing, and newly developing countries.

In general, the production portion of the textile and apparel industry takes place primarily in countries at the middle level, in developing countries, whereas most of the consumption takes place in developed countries. Many newly developing countries face ongoing political disruptions and social unrest that tend to discourage development of any kind of industry. The apparel industry is often the first form of industrial development in newly developing countries and therefore it is extremely important for apparel industries to contribute to establishing a culture that includes fair treatment with ongoing levels of employment.

Many interesting observations can be made related to the economic status of the textile and clothing industry. Some of these are revealed by the top portion of Table 1.1, which reports the total values of imports and exports by twenty-seven member countries of the European Union in 2012 in two parts:

Figure 1.2

World map showing locations of developed, developing, and newly developing countries in 2013 based on gross domestic product per capita adjusted by purchasing power parity (GDP per capita PPP) among nations.

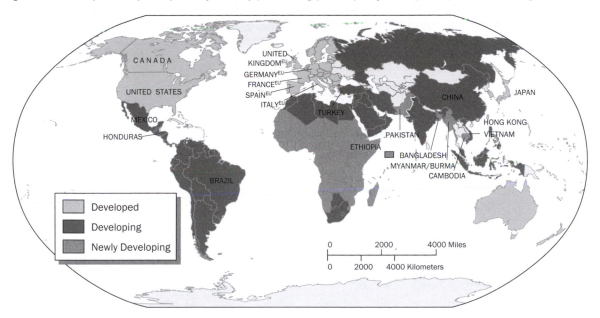

- Intra EU 27: trade within the members of EU
- Extra EU 27: trade between member countries and countries outside the EU 27

The EU has some of the same growth and development goals as the United States. However, each member country has more independence than the states within the United States. At the time this table was developed, all EU members were in the developed country category. The EU countries included in the lower part of the table are marked with the ᴱᵁ symbol.

The lower three parts of Table 1.1 have individual countries grouped into the levels of economic development. The categories are developed, developing, and newly developing. World average gross domestic product (GDP), the market value of the output of products and services produced in the world in a year per capita, is employed to classify a country as developed, developing, or newly developing. In 2012, the world average GDP per capita was $13,100. Level of development of countries is typically described as follows:

- When a country's GDP per capita is significantly higher than the world average, the country is called "developed."
- When a country's GDP per capita is significantly lower than the world average, the country is called "newly developing."
- The countries in the middle are called "developing."

To compare countries by **level of development**, it is necessary to consider three things:

- each country's gross domestic product (GDP);
- the size of each country's population; and
- the population's purchasing power parity.

Thus, GDP per capita is GDP divided by the number of people in a country's population but only *after GDP has been adjusted by purchasing power parity*. **Per capita**

TABLE 1.1

VALUES IN MILLIONS OF U.S. DOLLARS OF TEXTILES AND CLOTHING IMPORTS AND EXPORTS IN 2012 FOR EUROPEAN UNION AND SELECTED COUNTRIES RANKED BY GDP PER CAPITA PURCHASING POWER PARITY[1]

	Textile Imports	Textile Exports	Clothing Imports	Clothing Exports	GDP Per Capita (PPP)
European Union (Intra EU 27)[2]	74,118	46,992	170,058	80,356	NA[4]
European Union (Extra EU 27)[3]	27,118	22,374	89,702	28,540	NA[4]
Developed Countries					
United States	27,056.0	13,924.5	91,028.3	5,614.0	52,800
Hong Kong	10,419.7	10,718.5	16,457.7	23,737.0	52,700
Canada	4,591.0	2,018.0	9,948.7	———[5]	43,100
Germany[EU]	13,693.2	14,909.0	35,482.5	18,409.0	37,500
United Kingdom[EU]	7,377.5	———[5]	22,841.9	15,497.9	37,300
Japan	8,766.0	7,819.0	33,631.7	559.0	37,100
France[EU]	7,441.1	———[5]	23,369.0	11,045.8	35,700
Spain[EU]	———[5]	———[5]	14,993.2	11,543.3	30,100
Italy[EU]	8,514.4	13,459.4	15,734.0	23,735.4	29,600
Developing Countries					
Mexico	6,180.1	2,236.0	2,965.0	4,449.0	16,316
Turkey	6,789.2	12,156.9	2,677.0	15,409.9	15,300
Brazil	4,300.0	996.0	2,556.0	167.0	11,703
China	21,536.3	106,578.0	522.0	177,434.9	9,800
Honduras	1,566.0	———[5]	400.0	3,018.0	4,800
Vietnam	10,643.2	4,117.0	603.0	17,230.1	4,000
Newly Developing Countries					
Pakistan	1,077.0	9,341.4	———[5]	4,214.0	3,100
Cambodia	2,387.0	———[5]	———[5]	4,294.0	2,600
Bangladesh	6,217.0	1,634.0	276.0	23,501.0	2,100
Myanmar (Burma)	———[5]	———[5]	———[5]	868.0	1,700
Ethiopia	———[5]	———[5]	———[5]	———[5]	1,300

[1]Data gathered from World Trade Organization, International Trade and Market Access Data, at http://www.wto.org
[2]Refers to trade with countries within the European Union
[3]Refers to trade with countries that are not part of the European Union
[4]Purchasing power parity was not available for the two parts of the European Union
[5]The symbol ——— means imports or exports were less than $1 million

purchasing power parity (PPP) is a measure that allows comparisons of well-being among populations in different countries.

PPP is determined by adjusting GDP of a country by the buying power of its currency using the Consumer Price Index and dividing the total GDP by the number of people in the population. It provides insight into how total market value of products and services produced in a country relates to the number of individuals and their well-being. It is important not to drown in acronyms, so try to get a handle on them from the beginning. Hereafter, the combination of GDP and PP is indicated as **GDP per capita (PPP)**.

Focus on the last column of the table. The range among nations' GDP per capita is astounding! The countries listed in the table by developed, developing, and newly developing portions are organized based on GDP per capita purchasing power parity, the relative buying power of people in each nation. It is also important to remember that the United States is not the richest country in the world, but it has the highest per capita purchasing power (PPP) among countries strongly engaged in the textiles and clothing business. GDP per capita (PPP) is usually a factor in determining on what components of the industry a country is most actively engaged.

For textile imports, the United States, Germany, China, Hong Kong, and Vietnam are the leaders, while China dominates the value of textile exports. The United States dominates clothing imports, but the other developed countries are also very active. Clothing exports are dominated by developing country China followed by developed country Hong Kong (which primarily re-export apparel imported from China that was finished and packed in Hong Kong; more on this in Chapter 11) and newly developing country Bangladesh (featured in Case 1.1). Notice that Japan, Brazil, and Myanmar have the lowest clothing exports from each level of development. China dominates in the clothing exports category. Obviously, there are stories to be told about the world of clothing imports and exports.

Other Indicators of Economic Development

While GDP per capita is the primary indicator for determining a country's level of economic development, in some cases GDP per capita might be misleading. For this reason, it is important to consider other indicators of well-being. For countries selected from developed, developing, and newly developing groups in Table 1.1, Table 1.2 presents three well-being indicators along with the world average indicator for each:

- **Literacy rates** for males and females indicate the number of people in a country who are fifteen years old and older that can read and write; it is indicative of the level of education accessibility such as free primary education systems.
- **Infant mortality** measures how many babies die within the first year from birth and reflects availability of healthcare.
- **Life expectancy** indicates how long a newborn is expected to live on average and reflects levels of nutrition and healthy lifestyle.
- World average for each indicator reflects the overall living conditions related to levels of development.

In general, these variables present changes in a positive direction as countries become more developed.

In Table 1.2, literacy rates for developed countries United States and Japan are at 99 percent for both males and females, while Spain's are slightly lower. This means that in these nations almost all people who are fifteen years old and older can read and write, regardless of gender. In developing countries, literacy rates have a wider range from 97.5 percent for males in China to 50.8 percent for females in India. Half of females age fifteen and over in India cannot read and write. In newly developing countries, the highest literacy rate is in Pakistan, where nearly two-thirds of adult males but under

TABLE 1.2

INDICATORS OF LEVELS OF DEVELOPMENT FOR SELECTED COUNTRIES CLASSIFIED AS DEVELOPED, DEVELOPING, AND NEWLY DEVELOPING[1]

Country	Literacy Rate Male	Literacy Rate Female	Infant Mortality (in Thousands of Live Births)	Life Expectancy at Birth (in Years)
Developed				
United States	99.0%	99.0%	6.17	79
Japan	99.0%	99.0%	2.13	85
Spain	98.5%	97.0%	3.33	82
Developing				
Honduras	85.3%	84.9%	18.72	71
China	97.5%	92.7%	14.89	75
India	75.2%	50.8%	43.19	68
Newly Developing				
Pakistan	68.6%	40.1%	57.48	67
Bangladesh	62.0%	53.4%	45.67	71
Ethiopia	49.1%	28.9%	55.77	61
World Average	88.6%	79.7%	36.58	68

[1]*Based on estimates of 2009 data from the Central Intelligence Agency (CIA), "The World Factbook." Retrieved November 2009 from https://www.cia.gov/library/publications/the-world-factbook/*

half of adult females can read and write. The lowest rates are in Ethiopia where less than half of adult males and less than one-third of adult females can read and write.

In developed countries, infant mortality is low. Considering the countries listed in Table 1.2, out of 1,000 births in developed countries, between two and seven babies die. In developing countries, infant mortality is much higher and ranges from fifteen to forty-three babies for China, Honduras, and India. Newly developing countries have by far the highest infant mortality rates. Life expectancy tends to be higher in more advanced economies because of better health care systems, nutrition, and overall quality of life. In countries that are less developed and that have lower well-being levels, people are expected to have shorter lives. The highest life expectancy is in Japan (85 years), the lowest in Ethiopia (61 years), and the world average is 68 years. This implies that the majority of the world's population lives in conditions with less than average life expectancy.

When looking at data like these, it is important to assess the reliability of the source of data and to read the footnotes, which often explain peculiarities related to the reliability of the numbers. It is also important to consider several indicators. The examples in Table 1.2 illustrate that every indicator has to be considered together with other economic data and placed in appropriate context. We will be using demographics and other data like these throughout this text to examine the well-being of populations in relation to where the textile and apparel industry is located and how it works.

You should now have a good understanding of some of the indicators used to determine a country's level of economic development and be able to explain some differences among developed, developing, and newly developing countries. How does level of economic development relate to the textile and apparel industries and trade? For an apparel professional, why is it important to know how developed (or not) a country is? The answers to some of these questions now begin, after discussing major characteristics of the textile and apparel industries and reviewing the basics of trade.

TEXTILE AND APPAREL INDUSTRIES

Historically, both the textile and apparel industries were labor intensive and according to many measures, they still are. Materials that are used tend to be very pliable and delicate; fibers, yarns, and fabrics can be easily overstretched or shrunk during processing and machinery tends to be relatively crude. In contrast, many other industries use assembly components made of sturdy plastic, wood, glass, or metal that can hold a shape and can be handled and manipulated more easily. In addition, a great variety of types of materials are used to make textiles and apparel.

For example, the same top can be made of silk organza, cotton calico, polyester jersey, or wool crepe, not to mention leather or its substitutes. A combination of different fibers and blends with dozens of fabric weaves and structures for the relevant garment designs results in different sewing properties that have to be accounted for when assembling a garment as well as the equipment required for making it. Next, there is even a greater variety in products; hundreds if not thousands of styles are developed and produced by each company every year. Finally, each apparel product comes in many different sizes. An assembly line has to accommodate all the changes in materials, product styles, and sizes very quickly and frequently, which makes it nearly impossible or prohibitively expensive to use robots for sewing. This is why "despite millions of dollars invested in research in mechanization [and technology], people are still required to piece together fabric and feed it in the sewing machine" (Rivoli, 2009, p. 86). There has been lots of new technology developed since 2009 but the majority of the time the key event that makes apparel assembly possible is human hands running fabric under the needle (Figure 1.3).

Figure 1.3
Apparel assembly line with people operating sewing machines, illustrating the labor-intensive nature of the industry.

Another unique characteristic of the apparel industry is it has **low entry barriers**, which means it is easy to enter the industry by starting a new apparel business. Entry barriers are low because if, for example, you compare apparel production with manufacturing of electronics or cars:

- Relatively simple machinery and equipment is needed for apparel production.
- Machinery is relatively simple to operate; apparel assembly does not require highly skilled workers and training times tend to be short.
- Comparatively little capital is needed for a startup because machinery and equipment is comparatively less expensive than for other industries that are more technology-intensive.
- Developing and newly developing countries have lower wages than developed countries and an abundance of low cost, available labor.

These low entry barriers are the reason why practically all countries in the world began their industrialization with apparel manufacturing. Low wages are regarded as critical for labor-intensive apparel production. Labor cost depends on a country's level of development. In contrast to the apparel industry, the **textile industry**, which includes production of man-made fibers, yarns, and fabrics, is more **capital-intensive** and **technology-intensive** than labor-intensive. Modern textile mills are run by computers and look comparatively empty; there are a few operators who are there to adjust computer settings and address any machinery and process problems (Figure 1.4). Today, manufacturing of textiles requires little physical labor but workers need to be educated enough to operate complex computerized looms. Machinery for textile production is very expensive. In addition, textile finishing mills require compliance with environmental standards for using water for dyeing and finishing processes, and this equipment is also expensive. Typically textile mills rely on economy of scale and require a relatively large operation to produce competitively priced fabrics, which makes the textile industry more capital-intensive and technology-intensive than the apparel industry.

Figure 1.4

Modern textile mill in operation showing some of the machinery and technology required for producing textiles (notice: no human beings are on site).

As indicated in Table 1.2, the level of a country's development determines availability of educated and skilled human capital as well as financial resources, both required for textile production. Developed countries tend to have textile industries as a result of sufficient investments in production and research as well as development of innovative products and processes. In some developing countries it is possible for textile industries to produce basic yarns and fabrics, but that is very unlikely in newly developing countries.

As shown in Table 1.1, in 2012, the United States had by far the most textile and clothing imports with over $27 billion textile imports and $91 billion apparel imports. Because of high rates of consumption and low rates of production, the United States has dramatic trade deficits in both textiles and apparel. China ranked second in textile imports (about $22 billion), had the highest textile exports with about $107 billion, and had by far the most clothing exports at over $177 billion. Since the early 1990s, China has developed a textile and apparel production industry second to none in efficiency even though it no longer has the lowest labor costs. The net effect is the Chinese economy benefits more from textile and clothing trade than any other country in the world.

Developed Countries

Beginning in the late 1700s, with the start of the Industrial Revolution, production of textile and apparel products formed the foundation of the economies in developed countries. In every case, the developed nations listed in Table 1.1 plus many others have at one time or another utilized textile and clothing production as a major means of achieving industrial and economic growth. As the countries became developed and labor cost increased, there was a shift from producing textiles and clothing to consuming them. For example, recently, South Korea moved into this group because the country readily embraced industrialization in the 1970s and open trade policies as a means of building economic development. As the economy improves, industry evolves from a primary focus on industrial production to creative and technological aspects of business.

Due to high cost of labor, developed countries have relatively little domestic clothing manufacturing; as a result, developed countries have a deficit in clothing trade. All developed countries in Table 1.1 import significantly more clothing than they export. One exception is Hong Kong, which exported more clothing (nearly $24 billion) than it imported ($16 billion). This is a lot of clothing trade for a small island with a population of 7 million. Because it is a special administrative region of China, Hong Kong imports semi-manufactured clothing from China that is finished and exported to the world.

Most developed nations still have firms that are actively involved in clothing design, product development, sourcing, and brand management. In many cases, these firms employ significant numbers of workers and are leaders of the global fashion market. Some of these firms continue to produce high-end branded goods domestically. The United States imports by far the most clothing, followed by Germany, Japan, and France. Developed countries are more likely to import a high value of clothing as compared to developing countries like Mexico, Turkey, or Vietnam.

Many developed countries have advanced textile industries and produce a lot of man-made fibers, yarns, and fabrics. Because most of these countries have limited clothing production, they export a lot of their domestically produced textiles. For example, Italy and Germany have positive balance known as a textile trade surplus, where textile exports exceed imports. Other developed countries in Table 1.1—United States, Japan, and France—each have a negative trade balance in textiles; however, the textile trade deficit is much smaller than the clothing trade deficit.

Developing Countries

Through industrialization, developing countries have significantly improved their overall economic conditions and well-being. Many developing nations have embraced the production of textile and apparel products as a way to compete in the global marketplace and in some cases they are involved in producing many other types of products as well. However, developing countries are no longer the lowest-cost labor sources for textiles, apparel, and many other products. Thus, several of these countries, like Mexico, have struggled to maintain textile and apparel manufacturing in the face of lower labor costs in newly developing countries. Generally, developing countries are in a transition phase between focusing primarily on production for export and increasing focus on production for domestic consumption while facing increasing imports from lower-wage countries. The domestic demand for low- to moderately priced goods becomes satisfied by low-cost imports, but there may still be opportunity for upscale, high-quality goods both in domestic markets and abroad. Review textile and apparel imports and exports by developing countries in Table 1.1.

Being active players in the global apparel supply chain, some developing countries import and export a significant amount of textiles. They typically export natural fiber-based basic textiles to newly developing countries and import man-made fiber-based high-tech textiles from developed countries. For example, Turkey exports twice as much textiles as it imports and seven times more apparel than it imports. China exports over five times more textiles than it imports while exporting over 340 times more apparel than it imports. Those are extremely positive trade balances from the perspective of growing the country's economy. In contrast, Brazil has negative trade balances in both textiles and apparel. Mexico has a negative trade balance in textiles and a positive trade balance in apparel, implying that textiles are being imported for apparel manufacturing. In general, developing countries, over time, tend to upgrade apparel production to develop and manufacture higher-quality goods positioned at better and designer price points. This becomes necessary because, over time, wages increase because of a country's domestic development and there is still competition on low-cost goods from lower wages being paid in newly developing countries.

For example, as shown in Table 1.1, among developing countries, Mexico has the highest measure of per capita purchasing power parity (GDP per capita [PPP]) in the developing countries group, but, if we had data comparing it to previous years, we would see it is now assembling much less apparel for export than it was ten years ago. However, it has become a successful exporter to the European Union and other developed countries of better-quality natural fiber apparel, fur coats, and leather accessories. As the Chinese economy has developed in the 2000s and early 2010s at astonishing double-digit rates, the labor cost in the country has been increasing. As a result, apparel production in the country has been migrating inland, where wages are lower, as well as to other developing and newly developing countries in Asia and Africa, such as Bangladesh and Ethiopia. Vietnam is sometimes still considered a newly developing nation. The country has greatly benefited from apparel production and exports and was able to attract more business from North American and European companies in recent years because of lower wages in comparison to other developing countries.

Newly Developing Countries

Newly developing countries tend to be nations that have been slow in changing their way of life from agrarian or basic sustenance to the industrial age, although some of the countries have begun the process and made some progress. These countries have the highest poverty rates and lowest wages in the world. Many nations suffer from civil wars, social unrest, corrupt and inefficient government, and lack of appropriate laws and regulations, and/or their enforcement necessary for supporting business activity. Because the apparel industry has the lowest entry barriers in the industrial sector and labor-intensive production, newly developing countries can be ideal locations, as one of their most available resources is a low-wage workforce. As you learned from Case 1.1., in many newly developing economies apparel manufacturing often provides the only industrial employment option, especially for women, to support their families and afford education for children. Newly developing countries tend to focus more on production for export, rather than on production for domestic consumption.

All newly developing countries in Table 1.1 have apparel trade surplus as they export more apparel than they import. Many newly developing countries, such as Pakistan, Myanmar, and Ethiopia, have apparel manufacturing but have struggled to develop the support systems that would allow the business to thrive. Even though African countries, most of which belong to the group of newly developing countries, have attractive low wages and a large pool of labor, these countries tend to have low literacy rates and education, like Ethiopia in Table 1.2, and insufficient infrastructure for communication and trade. Newly developing countries tend to have very little textile production as they do not have sufficient capital, technology, and education levels to support the industry. As a result, these countries have to import the textiles needed for apparel production and therefore typically have a trade deficit.

ORGANIZATION AND OPERATION OF THE TEXTILE COMPLEX

The **textile complex** is the combination of textile-related firms that supply soft goods to the world population. A **firm** is any business, be it corporation, proprietorship, or partnership. In the textile complex a firm could be engaged in (1) manufacturing; (2) sourcing; (3) supplying materials, equipment, or technology; (4) retailing; or (5) some combination of these activities. It may also be any other organization that conducts business related to soft goods. **Soft goods** are products made of textiles or other flexible materials, including batting, fabrics, apparel, linens, towels, upholstery, draperies, and fashion accessories. There are three primary end uses for soft goods: apparel, household goods, and industrial products. The primary focus of discussion here is on the apparel component of the textile complex, although textile products, such as bedding, drapes, and towels, and industrial products, such as medical materials, roadbeds, and building materials, are growing components of the textile complex.

In the mid-twentieth century, textile and apparel firms were frequently small and family owned. As such, some of these companies tended to be slower to confront changes occurring in the overall business environment. Their reticence to modernize, inflexibility, and lack of response to markets condemned some of them to compromising product quality and even to failure (Underhill, 1998). To survive in the changing business climate, many firms found they had to join forces through horizontal integration. **Horizontal integration** brings change through **mergers** (firms with similar functions joining forces to form one larger business) and **takeovers** (strong firms absorbing weaker firms to form one larger business). Another method of change that has proven successful for the survival and growth of textile and apparel businesses is vertical integration. **Vertical integration** occurs when firms that perform different stages in the planning, design, production, and distribution of products unite to form one larger business. Takeovers are also a means used to create a vertically integrated textile or apparel firm, especially if supply of essential material or equipment is involved.

Mergers and acquisitions have been at an all-time high since the 1990s. However, today there are more alternatives to survival than merely increasing in size. One alternative is to have companies concentrate on core competencies and outsource specific operations that prove too costly to do in-house to firms that specialize in those activities. Many firms located in developed countries have looked to partnering with or sourcing from offshore firms to support their continued growth. These activities involve the complexity of the entire textile complex.

Structure of the Textile Complex

Figure 1.5 presents a conceptual model showing the four levels that are the primary components of the textile complex, from fiber and other materials supply through retailing of finished goods. The four levels of the model are linked together by a loop representing a supply chain supporting global sourcing. A dominant firm involved in managing hundreds of supply chains is Li & Fung, based in Hong Kong. The type and quantity of goods to source are commonly determined by a sourcing firm, often a retailer, based in one of the developed countries. Then Li & Fung, or one of many other firms offering similar services, determines where goods will be sourced and how they will arrive at the required destination on time, in the defined quantity and quality, and at a specified price.

Figure 1.6 shows a Li & Fung conceptual model of a global supply chain. Carefully examine the figure, noting all the different dimensions involved in operating a supply chain, beginning with customer demand, followed by developing and acquiring goods from the global market and then delivering them to a wholesaler or directly to a vertically integrated retailer, who sells the goods to consumers, who immediately develop more, different needs. Import and export trading firms provide services essential to the entire textile and apparel manufacturing and distribution process.

If you turn Li & Fung's model (Figure 1.6) on end with the consumer at the top, you can visualize it in place of the supply chain loop in Figure 1.5. This will help you to see the complexities of today's supply chains in relation to the textile and apparel trade matrix. The supply chain components relate to the levels of the textile and apparel complex and the inputs required to plan, design, produce, and deliver the products desired. These elements make up the sequence of events that are typically included in what now is often called **sourcing**.

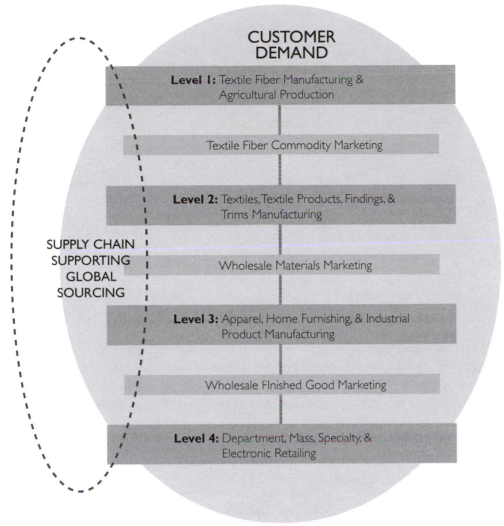

Each of the four levels of the textile complex in Figure 1.5 represent different but related areas of specialization necessary to convert raw materials into finished goods for the ultimate consumers. Each also has multiple categories, subcategories, and auxiliary activities that contribute to the necessary functions in each area of specialization. Between each of the levels is often a wholesale marketing function for transferring ownership of goods to the next level in the textile complex. In the model, think of the four levels as floating over a sea of customer demand that constantly requires redefinition of the products being conceptualized, planned, designed, developed, and produced for the next retail selling period. Ultimate consumers make the final decisions that determine who and what are the winners and the losers. Now, consider the activities that are necessary components of each level of the textile complex.

Level 1—Textile Fiber Manufacturing and Agricultural Production

Natural textile fibers derived from plants and animals are two basic types: cellulose and protein. Common examples of cellulose fibers from plants include cotton, flax (commonly called linen), and ramie; examples of protein fibers are wool (from sheep), cashmere (from goats), and silk (from silk worms). Manufactured fibers, including rayon and acetate, are made from cellulosic sources, such as wood pulp and cotton

Figure 1.6

Li & Fung supply chain model.

linters that contain naturally occurring polymers; rayon and acetate are two examples. Bamboo has recently become a popular source of wood pulp for making rayon. Many synthetic fibers, including nylon, polyester, and acrylic, have polymers made from petrochemicals, so their characteristics differ greatly from those of natural and manufactured cellulosic fibers. Whether the fibers come from the farm, the forest, or the laboratory, once they are harvested or generated, many are sold in commodity markets, where prices change on a daily basis, depending on supply and demand. Other fibers might be purchased directly from the producer or manufacturer.

Level 2—Textiles, Textile Products, and Findings Manufacturing: Wholesale Materials Marketing

Level 2 of the textile complex comprises all the activities related to textile manufacturing, including yarns, fabrics, fabric finishing, and the production of findings. Historically, in the United States, beginning in the mid-1800s as textile production became commercialized, each of the stages of textile production was completed by individual, family-owned businesses. Some companies specialized in yarns, others in weaving or knitting, and still others in fabric finishing. The products were bought and sold in each stage of textile development. Now, many firms are vertically integrated, so they make yarn, weave fabric, and finish fabric by dyeing or printing and applying wrinkle resistance, water resistance, and other finishes so that the fabrics are ready to be cut and sewn. In addition to being vertically integrated, some textile fabric mills are now also horizontally integrated and perform both weaving and knitting. An example of horizontal and vertical integration within Level 2 of the textile complex would be the merging of smaller mills into a massive textile conglomerate, such as Milliken, one of the largest privately owned producers of textile products in the United States. A **conglomerate** is a business formed when firms serving multiple markets join together with common ownership.

Findings are all the materials used in apparel products in addition to the face fabrics. Major categories of findings are as follows:

- thread, a special type of yarn that holds pieces of sewn products together

- closures, including zippers, snaps, hooks, hook and loop fasteners, and buttons
- support materials, including interlining, shoulder pads, adhesives, tapes, sleeve headers, and collar stays
- trims, including ribbon, lace, bindings, edging, and anything else that might be used to ornament or enhance garments
- labels, permanently attached information related to brand names, trademarks, fiber content, and care information

Because fabric and findings decisions need to be made very early in the apparel design process, wholesale textile product marketing (Figure 1.7) must occur early in the apparel product development cycle. Traditionally, fabrics were designed, marketed to product designers and stylists, and produced on a calendar scheduled up to a year in advance of apparel manufacturing. The present trend is to move wholesale markets and textile manufacturers closer to apparel producers in whatever country is most appropriate. Fabrics are more readily available for the finished goods manufacturing process; this shortening and simplifying of the supply chain can cut weeks off the apparel production process, making it possible to respond more quickly to changes in fashion-related customer demand. One of the major international market fairs for textile products is Première Vision, held in Paris, France.

Figure 1.7
Textile product trade show.

Level 3—Apparel Manufacturing: Wholesale Finished Goods Marketing

Apparel manufacturing encompasses processes involved with merchandising, design, product development, production, and often wholesale marketing. Apparel manufacturing includes three different, but often overlapping, categories of business structure: apparel manufacturers, apparel production vendors, and retail product developers. **Apparel manufacturers** traditionally were firms that engaged in the entire manufacturing process, including merchandising (line planning, design, and product development), production, and wholesale marketing of apparel, using the yarns and fabrics produced in Level 1.

However, in today's global market, few firms engaged in the apparel manufacturing business own all the technology, equipment, and expertise to complete the process from the beginning to the end. Manufacturers that were formerly vertically integrated may now specialize only in product development and wholesale marketing. The production process itself—those processes actually required to cut materials and assemble and finish garments—is usually sourced from firms called apparel production vendors that, at this point in time, are primarily located in developing and newly developing countries. Thus, the term "apparel manufacturer" in developed economies has been replaced by apparel firm or brand manager because of the emphasis on marketing nationally and internationally known brands of merchandise.

Apparel production vendors, historically called contractors, are firms that take orders for apparel products from other firms and that either produce or arrange for the production of those specific garments. Apparel production includes processes required to convert materials into finished garments: cutting, sewing, pressing, inspecting, packaging, and shipping. An apparel vendor can be located anywhere as long as there are transportation and power and communication systems and a relatively low-cost labor supply. There are two primary forms of production vendors: CMT and full package. CMT (cut, make, trim) apparel vendors commonly offer apparel assembly services. CMT vendors are paid to provide machines, labor, and thread to sew specified garments. The sourcing company provides product specifications and fabric and findings. However, because many of the retailers engaged in private brand development depend on vendors for both product development and production expertise, full-package vendors are very much in demand. "Full package" requires that the vendor not only provide production expertise but also engage in product development and materials sourcing. Apparel vendors in Hong Kong have provided full-package services since the 1970s, and now many vendors in other countries do the same. An example of a firm that has integrated many stages in production, from the manufacturing of fabric in Level 2 to the sale of garments at retail in Level 4, is the brand manager VF Corporation. VF now produces major brands of everything from hosiery to jeans, although it has elected to spin off some of its textile production. VF also operates a chain of outlet stores that retails a significant portion of its business. VF is ranked sixth in the list of most profitable firms (see Table 1.3).

Level 3 also includes retail product developers. Retail product developers are individuals or teams who create designs and develop merchandise plans and specifications for retailers' private brands, which are ultimately sourced from CMT or full-package vendors. Retail product developers usually perform the merchandising and design functions of the product development process and therefore avoid the costs of buying finished goods from brand managers.

Wholesale finished goods marketing connects Level 3, apparel manufacturing, with Level 4, retailing, when firms are not vertically integrated. In Level 3, two to five to sometimes twelve times a year, firms engaged in apparel manufacturing plan, design, and develop their product lines. The relatively recent development of "fast fashion" has multiplied the number of times these product development processes are repeated in a single year. Firms only engaged in apparel manufacturing have sales forces that sell their product lines to retailers either at wholesale markets, at a retail buyer's office, through sourcing fairs, or on the internet. An example of the traditional wholesale market method is the prêt-à-porter (ready-to-wear) market weeks in the major cities of Europe. During market weeks, formal presentations, such as fashion shows and personal presentations of styles to buyers by manufacturers' sales representatives, are made to encourage sales (Figure 1.8). Most retail buyers view the options among dozens

Figure 1.8
Manufacturer's sales representative showing finished merchandise to retail buyers at a wholesale trade show.

of product lines and return home to examine their merchandise plans and place orders to translate the line plans into styles, sizes, and colors of real merchandise. The product orders put the desired merchandise selections into production.

Because textiles and garments were most often sold at wholesale based on samples before they were mass-produced, market weeks were traditionally scheduled several months before the selling period in retail stores. However, with current technologies, the time between order placement and receipt of merchandise can now be weeks instead of months for some products, depending on a firm's supply chain strategies. For example, Tommy Hilfiger moved his traditional March market week for fall delivery of menswear to May, making the retail commitment for merchandise closer to point of sale at retail.

Major apparel market centers in the United States are located in New York, Los Angeles, Atlanta, Dallas, and Chicago. Major offshore apparel market centers include Milan, Paris, and London in Europe, and Tokyo, Hong Kong, and Singapore in Asia. One of the major market centers for knitwear is Florence, Italy. Today, global wholesale market activities are found on the calendar year-round, at various times of the year, depending on the categories of products, and in locations that include developing countries, such as India, China, and Turkey.

Level 4—Department, Mass, Specialty, Electronic, and Other Forms of Retailing

Retailing is the sale of merchandise or services, or both, to ultimate consumers. The face of retail in the United States and elsewhere has changed significantly in the first decade of the 2000s, and the traditional definitions and recognized classifications of these businesses and their product lines have become blurred. In the United States and some other developed countries, traditional brick-and-mortar type retailing has grown to such an extent that experts believe we are now "over-stored." The United States has more retail establishments than the consumer market can possibly support. Yet, new stores continue to open, while other retail businesses are closing their doors because of economic failure.

The most common type of store is a **specialty retailer**, one that focuses on selling only groceries, or shoes, or sportswear, or cars, or other specific types of products. Figure 1.9a shows an Ann Taylor store with visual merchandising and signs in the windows. The specialty chain focuses on business and business casual wear for career women. For well over 100 years, **department stores** have also been part of the retail scene, offering multiple classifications of goods grouped together in different parts of a store. Figure 1.9b shows the front entrance of Dillard's, a well-known US-based department store that began in Arkansas in 1938. The company now operates about 300 stores in twenty-nine states (Dillard's Inc., n.d.). Dillards is ranked forty-sixth in the Global Powers of Retailing, an annual ranking according to retail sales of the top 250 retailers in the world market (Deloitte, 2015). Many companies focused on textiles and apparel appear in the top 250 retailers and many of those companies are also now engaged in apparel manufacturing.

Over the past 40 years, discount stores became an important component of the retail scene. In 1977 T.J. Maxx came into being offering off-price, but upscale apparel for the whole family (Figure 1.9c). A key factor for T.J. Maxx was the reasonable prices with ever-changing fresh assortments. In 2012, T.J. Maxx opened its thousandth store and became number thirty-six in the Global Powers of Retailing (Deloitte, 2015).

More recently, **mass retailers** arrived on the scene. Mass retailers have large numbers of huge stores, often in multiple countries, that offer a wide variety of goods for home and family while featuring low to moderate prices. Target, classified as a discount department store, is number ten in net retail revenue in the Global Powers of Retailing (Deloitte, 2015). Target is a primary example of a mass retailer where the stores are huge in size and widely available to shoppers (Figure 1.9d). Target is now experimenting with smaller stores that can be available in crowded downtown areas.

Figure 1.9b

The impressive front door of a Dillard's department store.

Figure 1.9a

Ann Taylor, an example of specialty apparel retail chain for women.

Figure 1.9c

T.J. Maxx, one of the off-price and powerful US-based discount retailers.

Figure 1.9c

T.J. Maxx, one of the off-price and powerful US-based discount retailers.

Figure 1.9d

Target's classic symbol on the front of each store means "expect more, pay less."

The assortments offered cover nearly everything a family could want and more. Target is also experimenting with offering short runs of unique, moderately priced, designer-made casual and sportswear and is seriously considering increasing that assortment.

Traditional retailers are being severely challenged by the over-stored scenario as well as by the advent of many nonstore retail sectors, such as direct marketing, including catalog and television sales, and **e-tailing** on the internet. In October 2013, Forrester Research Inc. forecast that "by 2017, 60 percent of all retail sales will involve the Internet in some way, either as a direct E-commerce transaction or as part of a shopper's research on a laptop or mobile device.. . .[T]he categories that will be most influenced by Internet research in five years will be grocery, apparel and accessories, home improvement, and consumer electronics" (Dusto, 2013).

When the retail environment in one area of the world becomes saturated, retail firms look to other countries as a solution to their need for growth. The National Retail Federation (NRF), the largest retail trade association in the United States, created a subsidiary, the International Retail Federation (IRF). The IRF, in association with *Stores* magazine, developed a new publication, which is available on the internet, titled *Global Powers of Retailing*. It is updated annually, and it lists the 250 largest retailers in the world. Many of these are globalized retail conglomerates that consist of firms involved in unrelated markets but that are joined together because of common ownership. Retailing has become truly globalized; most global retailers are based in developed countries, and most are vertically integrated back into manufacturing processes. US retailers dominate (35 percent), followed by Japan (10 percent), Germany and United Kingdom (8 percent), France (5 percent), and other European countries (18 percent). Asian countries have only 6 percent of global retailers based there. Canada (Other N. American) has 4 percent. In the following discussion, retailers that were ranked among the top 250 in 2013 are noted.

Role of Apparel Firms in the Textile Complex

According to the Global Lexicon, an apparel firm is a commercial or industrial business that is engaged in some aspects of designing, merchandising, marketing, producing, and/or retailing garments or other attire. The operation of these apparel firms is the primary reason you can get dressed every morning. Apparel firms organize, operate, and fund the operation of supply chains that make it possible to deliver finished goods to retail stores and, if they are vertically integrated, also operate the retail stores. Some apparel firms are also becoming backward vertically integrated into the textile manufacturing business. As apparel firms merge and integrate, they may assume the names of the brands they own or become best known by the names of their retail stores.

Examine Table 1.3 to get a picture of where in the world the top 250 apparel retailers are based and how revenue from sales is distributed around the world. Take a few minutes to absorb the magnitude and complexity of the role of countries and companies, worldwide, that are involved in the textiles and apparel business. *Keep in mind that many of the "retailers" represented by these numbers are vertically integrated backward into some aspects of apparel manufacturing.* Then read Case 1.3, which provides an example of the magnitude of one apparel firm and what is required to run a vertically integrated apparel firm that is involved in the current trend toward fast fashion.

The Role of Retailing in the Textile Complex

The major categories of retail stores addressed in this book include what are commonly known as

- specialty stores, which focus on selected categories of merchandise;
- department stores, which present multiple categories of merchandise in designated areas of the store; and

TABLE 1.3

REGIONS OF THE WORLD WHERE TOP 250 RETAILERS ARE BASED PRESENTED IN ALPHABETICAL ORDER[1]

Top 250	Number of Companies 250	Share of Top 250 Retailers	Share of Top 250 Revenue
		100%	100%
Africa/Middle East	7	2.8%	1.0%
Asia/Pacific	55	**22.0%**	14.0%
Japan	31	12.4%	7.0%
Other Asia/Pacific	24	9.6%	14.0%
Europe	50	**36.0%**	38.9%
France	14	5.6%	9.4%
Germany	17	6.8%	10.6%
U.K.	14	5.6%	6.2%
Other Europe	45	18.0%	12.7%
Latin America	10	**4.0%**	1.8%
North America	88	**35.2%**	44.2%
United States	79	31.6%	41.9%
Canada	9	3.6%	2.3%

[1]National Retail Federation. "Regions of the World Where Top 250 Retailers Are Based." Retrieved January 28, 2015, from https://nrf.com/news/2015-top-250-global-powers-of-retailing

- hypermarket/supercenter/superstores, which provide a combination of department, specialty, grocery, and other merchandise to satisfy multiple consumer needs.

Then there are subcategory retail stores like off-price department and specialty stores, which always show mark-downs on the signs and/or the price ticket. Luxury department and specialty stores use open, elaborate displays and lighting to enhance the attraction and appeal of the merchandise with the price tag as the last thing you see. Mid-price type stores often use a combination of off-price and luxury presentation and also may present obvious mark-downs. Fast fashion presentation features crowded racks of short-lived styles that come and go on a weekly basis.

Regardless of the type of retail presentation, every store has to make a profit in order to stay in business. The Global Powers of Retailing is an annual trade report based on the largest apparel companies in the world. This publication uses annual net retail revenue in US dollars to rank the performance of global retailers in relation to apparel and accessories. See Table 1.4 for the 2013 top ten apparel companies in the world. You might be surprised at the location of their home bases as well as their spectacular

CASE 1.3

H&M: FASHION AT THE BEST PRICE[1]

Since 1947, H&M, the Sweden-based vertically integrated apparel manufacturer and retailer, has made its mark on the apparel industry, mixing the latest trends with fashion classics. H&M (Hennes & Mauritz AB) has cut a swath across the supply chain, successfully managing 3,300 stores in 54 countries employing 116,000 people. The company manages six independent brands: H&M, COS, Monki, Weekday, Cheap Monday, and Other Stores. The latest fashion at an affordable price is the "key" for H&M—from initial design to final product.[2] H&M offers everything from the hottest trends to the basics for women, men, teenagers, and children complete with shoes, accessories, cosmetics, and home interiors concepts. The collections are created by 160 in-house designers and 100 patternmakers. H&M works with about 900 suppliers representing 1,900 factories that produce for H&M in 30 different countries. In 2013, H&M's turnover (income) including VAT (value added tax) increased to SEK 150 billion. One dollar = 7.18 Swedish Krona (SEK), so H&M's income in US dollars was almost $20 billion. H&M's growth target is to increase the number of stores by 10 to 15 percent per year and at the same time increase sales in comparable units. Their growth is entirely self-financed.

Sustainability is an integral part of H&M's operations and it says it works actively to ensure a more sustainable chain of design, manufacturing, and product handling for both people and the environment. However, according to cleanclothes.org, H&M has approximately 675 suppliers in 30 countries but none of those factories pay a "living wage"; apparently there is still work to be done.[3] H&M has been working with the International Labor Association (ILO) since 2001 when the company joined the ILO's Better Factories program in Cambodia. In 2013, H&M and ILO signed a unique agreement on sustainable supply chains in the garment industry. The cooperation with ILO was expanded to specifically address industrial relations and wages, including actions at the government level. The more comprehensive and strategic partnership, designed to be active until 2018, will promote a wide range of activities at the global, national, and enterprise level in a larger number of countries.[4]

[1]Note, H&M is one of the major contributors to Europe's share of top 250 retailers as well as Europe's share of the revenue produced.

[2]http://about.hm.com/en/About/Facts-about-h.html

[3]http://cleanclothes.org/resolved/publication/cc-clec-betterfactories-29-8.pdf

[4]http://www.ilo.org/global/about-the-ilo/media-centre/press-releases/wcms_30605/lang-en/index

1. Where is H&M represented in Table 1.3? How does that description fit the company?

2. What are a few key things that make it possible for a complex apparel firm like H&M to operate in today's global markets?

ranking in the world market. Some of the companies listed in the table are probably familiar to but you might not know their size or country of origin.

Classification of Retail Stores

Specialty stores focus on specific classes of merchandise to the exclusion of other products. Specialty store variations include the off-price specialty retailers, such as T.J. Maxx (which is owned by TJX Companies and ranked 44th), which focus their merchandise mix on distressed items acquired from manufacturers and other retailers, including broken lots, end-of-season goods, and overruns. Specialty stores also make up the majority of thousands of independent, single-unit retailers. For example, within the moderate price point range that is found in many malls around the world, Foot Locker ranked 147th in the Global Powers of Retailing report. Foot Locker operates in thirty countries and offers apparel and footwear with an emphasis on athletic shoes. An example of the higher price point store that is commonly found in major US cities, but not in other countries, is Nordstrom, which ranked 80th in 2013.

Department stores provide a variety of product lines, such as apparel for men, women, and children; soft goods for the home; and home furnishings. Products are priced at or near the middle- to upper-middle price point ranges. Since the mid-1990s, department stores, like the main street specialty stores, have also lost market share. US department store groups are trying to maintain their current market share of retail apparel sales by expanding their private label programs and through expansion into e-commerce. An example of a department store is US-based Kohl's Corporation, which ranked 47th among worldwide retailers in 2013.

Among broad line **mass retailers**, Walmart ranked first, with over 11,000 stores in twenty-six countries. Target ranked 10th, with almost 2,000 stores, and provides serious

---

TABLE 1.4

TOP TEN WORLDWIDE APPAREL AND ACCESSORIES FIRMS IN 2013 BASED ON RETAIL REVENUE[1]

Rank	Company	Country of Origin	2013 Retail Revenue in millions of USD	2013 Revenue Growth[2]	Retail Classification
1	Macy's, Inc.	U.S.	$27,931	0.9%	department
2	TJX Companies	U.S.	$27,423	6.0%	off-price department
3	LVMH Moet Hennesey-Louis Vuitton S.A.	France	$24,392	3.7%	luxury department
4	Inditex, S.A.	Spain	$22,265	4.9%	fast fashion specialty
5	H&M; Hennes & Mauritz AB	Sweden	$19,729	6.4%	fast fashion specialty
6	Kohl's Corporation	U.S.	$19,031	−1.3%	mid-price department
7	The Gap, Inc.	U.S.	$16,148	3.2%	multi-brand specialty
8	Isetan Mitsukoshi Holdings Ltd.	Japan	$12,856	6.7%	department and specialty
9	Fast Retailing Co. Ltd.	Japan	$12,639	23.2%	fast fashion specialty
10	Nordstrom, Inc.	U.S.	$12,166	3.4%	luxury department

[1] Deloitte. (2015). "Global Powers of Retailing." Retrieved from www2.deloitte.com/content/dam/Deloitte/global/Documents/Consumer-Business/gx-cb-global-powers-of-retailing.pdf. (Note: 2015 is the publication date of the data but the data actually represents the year 2013.)
[2] Difference in millions of dollars from 2012 to 2013.

competition for Walmart primarily in the United States. These retailers sell in great volume at the lower-moderate and budget price points. They have both established significant private label programs, but Target has a much greater fashion focus with labels like Mossimo and Liz Lange brands for casual and Lilly Pulitzer for resort wear. Target has enhanced its fashion image in recent years by introducing new designers to do seasonal collections at moderate prices.

During the first decade of the twenty-first century, the **nonstore retailer** category of the apparel business really expanded. It is now common for customers to use internet sites for gathering product and pricing information and sometimes compare prices while shopping in stores before completing their purchase transactions. Product offerings for this venue change with great rapidity. For all forms of nonstore retailing, the issue of sizing and fit remains one of the most significant costs of doing business because of the high rate of consumer returns of ill-fitting garments and other unacceptable products.

Most forms of retailing have adopted practices now known as lean retailing. **Lean retailing** is the effective management of inventory based on accurate and timely information. The technology available to keep track of inventory levels in multiple locations is now regarded as essential to run a retail store. The fundamental goal is to maximize sales and gross margins while maintaining a minimum quantity of inventory in stock. Lean retailing practices have forced suppliers to hold inventory for frequent delivery to retailers. Replacement shipments are determined by electronically transmitted sales data.

Customer Demand

As represented by the "sea of customer demand" in the model of the textile complex (refer back to Figure 1.3), the primary purpose and driving force behind the entire apparel business is satisfying the needs of customers so that profits can be made. A business cannot survive without profits because businesses have to grow to break even. In today's marketplace the needs and desires of each customer are what fuels the demand for products, keeping the production and distribution cycle moving. Intensive competition drives marketing departments to generate pressure for consumption of products consumers did not even know they wanted or needed—and they respond.

Probably the biggest challenge in the textile and apparel business is forecasting what customers want to buy. Reliable consumer preference forecasts are essential for success at all levels of the textile complex. Major shifts in consumer demographics affect the acceptance of products offered in the marketplace. Recent changes in the cultural makeup of the overall population of the United States include significant growth of the Hispanic population, inclusion of larger and more diverse Asian populations, and a more visible Muslim population. The apparel preferences of these ethnic groups are influencing the styling and sizing of products being made available to all American consumers and increasing the focus on niche marketing by retailers.

Other consumer demographics are creating changes in the marketplace as well. Increased educational levels and higher incomes are influencing the apparel choices and expenditures of consumers. More and more people, especially in developed countries, are becoming aware of the impact of consumerism including the growing effects of the textile complex on the global environment. These consumers demand textile and apparel businesses employ sustainable materials and processes when designing, manufacturing, delivering, and even disposing products.

An increasingly aging demographic is causing a need for changes in product styling. Populations in most countries are living longer because of increases in income as well as more sophisticated medical care. Changes in lifestyle, such as participation in fitness programs, bring changes not only in physique, but in products desired as well. Conversely, the epidemic of obesity within the United States and other developed countries results in a need for changes in product sizes and in the sheer volume of fabric required for production of individual garments.

The most significant change affecting consumer apparel choices may be the greater availability of electronic communication worldwide. Consumers throughout the globe are able to compare available apparel choices by exploring hundreds of retailer websites, social media, television programs, etc., instantly seeing styles from around the world. A consumer in Jordan can watch an episode of a popular soap opera today, look on the internet to find a product he or she has seen on the program, and have that product delivered within days. (That consumer can also spend a day flying to Australia and turn on the TV to pick up where his or her favorite soap opera left off.)

The results of all these changes are causing something of a dichotomy. On one hand, there are more ethnically diverse ideas of what is beautiful and appropriate or fashionable to wear, and these ideas are made available to more consumers more quickly than at any time in history. However, more cultures are seeing and being influenced by what they see on television from the United States and Europe. Some cultures love it and others hate it. Much of the business climate worldwide is embracing western economic methods and being influenced by Westerners' methods of conducting business, both legal and illegal.

This increased visibility creates a homogenization of design ideas, with consumers from other cultures beginning to adapt their local choices in order to look like, as well as dress like, the people they see from the United States and Western Europe. A prime example of this homogenization over the last hundred years is the almost universal adoption of the tailored business suit. Another is the acceptance of jeans anytime and anywhere. This dichotomy of cultural differences versus universal sameness presents great challenges to the industry. One reality is that ultimate consumers still determine the winners. Textile and apparel consumption and the ability of consumers to consume is the topic of Chapter 2. Customer demand is the reason there are supply chains.

ESTABLISHING SUSTAINABLE SUPPLY CHAINS USING GLOBAL SOURCING

Beginning in the late 1950s, buying offices offered services that involved international business relationships, then mostly with firms based in Hong Kong, to supply US and European apparel retail buyers with finished garments different from or at a lower cost than what was being offered by domestic apparel manufacturers. In the United States most of the buying offices for domestic retailers were located in New York, and some of them still are. The buying offices also assisted buyers with the development of merchandise plans and the selection of domestically produced merchandise. Buying offices grew in number and popularity until the late 1980s, when vertical and horizontal mergers concentrated merchandising divisions and merchandisers got involved in product development for private label lines. The race then began in earnest to find the lowest-cost labor to make the garments. This led to the development of the standardized merchandise identification systems essential for processing goods that are transported from one country to another. This is the topic of Chapter 3.

A new category of textile and apparel business developed that is now called **import and export trading**. Based on a contract, import and export trading companies will merchandise, design, develop, source, or distribute textile and apparel products, or a combination of these, for customers anywhere in the world. Part of import and export trading responsibility is to develop and manage supply chains to assure that the desired goods will be delivered in a timely manner, in appropriate quantity and quality, and using sustainable methods. A **supply chain** is a total sequence of business processes within a single or multiple firms and countries that enables demand for products or services to be satisfied. Supply chains for textiles and apparel, more often than not, are global in scope and may involve a few, dozens, or even hundreds of different companies and governments. **Sustainability** involves the corporate, government, and consumer responsibility to integrate economic, political, environmental, and cultural dimensions to promote cooperation and solidarity among people and generations (Birnbaum, 2010). This is the focus of Chapter 4.

Governments establish regulations regarding the transfer of products from one country to another as well as verify their origin, ownership, quality, and safety. Some regulations are developed to encourage trade, whereas others aim at restricting trade to control amount of imports in an economy. Trade is encouraged with favorable terms and simplified processes. There are many types of regulations employed by governments to restrict trade. It is very important for apparel professionals to understand what effect different trade regulations might have on sourcing products and services from vendors in countries around the world. The interaction of all of the components of the supply chain takes place in countries with different political systems and among firms with divergent priorities, cultural values, and methods of communication and decision making. **Politics** are the methods, or tactics, involved in managing an organization, business, state, or government—sometimes including crafty, unprincipled politics. Politics as related to the textile and apparel global market and trade are the topic of Chapter 5. Trade regulations of all kinds of activities by governments result in attempts to get around them. Free trade, trade restrictions, requirements for customs compliance, intellectual property law, and social responsibility are ongoing sources of controversy and illegal activity in the global market. Illegal and unethical activity is rampant in the textile and apparel world. This is the topic of Chapter 6.

As you now know, sourcing means determining the most cost-efficient vendors of services, materials, production, or finished goods, or a combination of these, at a specified quality and service level, for delivery within an identified time frame. Sourcing also entails the process of selecting countries and vendors when building supply chains. These are the topics of Chapters 7 and 8. Chapters 9 to 12 examine countries in four major parts of the world, which we have defined as Europe and the European Union, the Americas and the Caribbean Basin, Asia and Oceania, and the Middle East and Africa. We sincerely hope you find your global adventure challenging, insightful, and rewarding.

Summary

A primary purpose of this chapter was to introduce perspectives central to the study of the textile and apparel trade from a global perspective. There are many valid ways to view and analyze the operations of global production and distribution. Perspectives include economic and business, political and governmental, as well as sociological and labor. These viewpoints commonly result in conflicts among options for resolution of issues. The conflicts are part of the context we wish to address.

Countries around the world can be viewed as newly developing, developing, or developed, based on the trade balance of each in relation to textiles and apparel and gross domestic product per capita. Gross domestic product per capita is gross domestic product of a country divided by the number of people in the population. Other related measures include literacy, poverty, infant mortality, and life expectancy. Newly developing and developing countries tend to focus on production and export of textiles and apparel to provide jobs to fuel industrial development. Developed countries have higher production costs, so they focus on product development and then skip to consumption of finished products. Goods produced in developed countries are less labor-intensive and much more technology intensive, such as for production of synthetic yarns.

The textile complex incorporates firms around the world to accomplish textile manufacturing, apparel manufacturing, retailing, and consumption of textile products. Import and export trading and sourcing companies are new types of firms that have responded to the demand for sourcing apparel in many countries around the world. Development of sustainable global supply chains involves many areas of expertise to navigate successfully and is currently a priority in the textile and apparel industries.

Learning Activities

1. Develop a list of positives and negatives that global trade brought to the textile and apparel industries in each of the three groups of countries by level of development: (a) developed countries; (b) developing countries; and (c) newly developing countries. Make sure to include the textile and apparel industries separately for every group of countries.

2. To comprehend the pervasiveness of imported apparel in our marketplace, conduct this class survey:

   - Make a list of all the countries represented in the labels of your clothing, and state the type of garment (e.g., jeans, Mexico; T-shirt, Haiti).
   - Compare your list with those of your classmates, and tally the list of countries and types of garments to see which countries are represented most frequently and what types of garments come from the countries identified.
   - Do some types of garments seem more likely to come from certain countries? Describe your results. Be alert in future chapters to why specific garments may come from certain countries.

3. What evidence has been presented so far that would explain why one-third of the world's largest retailers are based in the United States? Hint: Consider the data in Tables 1.1, 1.2, and 1.3 to help with your answer.

4. Considering the Li & Fung model, draw an example of what a supply chain might look like when only domestic sourcing is used to acquire all the products and services necessary to develop and sell to consumers an apparel product line. Explain your thinking about the process.

5. Based on Table 1.4, your personal shopping experience at H&M, and/or browsing an H&M online store, identify two or three retailers that seem to be in direct competition with H&M. What do you think makes it possible for H&M to continue to be successful in the over-stored and highly competitive US market?

References

Adendorff, L. (December 14, 2014). "Year in Review: Sourcing Winners and Losers." Retrieved from http://www.just-style.com

American Apparel and Footwear Association. (January 5, 2014). "AAFA Releases ApparelStats 2013 and ShoesStats 2013 Reports." Retrieved April 29, 2015, from https://www.wewear.org/aafa-releases-apparelstats-2013-and-shoestats-2013-reports/

Birnbaum, D. (March 9, 2010). "Comment: Garment Sector Well-Placed to Sell Sustainability." Retrieved November 15, 2015, from http://www.just-style.com/comment/garment-sector-well-placed-to-sell-sustainability_id106993.aspx

Central Intelligence Agency. (2009). "The World Factbook." Retrieved November 2009, from https://www.cia.gov/library/publications/ the-world-factbook/index.html

Craig, Shearman J. (February 13, 2013). "Study Says Most Apparel Jobs Are in US Even If Label Says 'Made in China.'" Retrieved October 24, 2015, from https://nrf.com/news/public-policy/study-says-most-apparel-jobs-are-us-even-if-label-says-%E2%80%98made-china%E2%80%99

Deloitte. (2015). "Global Powers of Retailing 2015: Embracing Innovation." Retrieved November 5, 2015, from www2.deloitte.com/content/dam/Deloitte/global/Documents/Consumer-Business/gx-cb/global-powers-of-retailing.pdf

Dillard's Inc. (n.d.). "Dillard's: The Style of Your Life." Retrieved September 16, 2015, from http://www.investor.shareholder.com/dillards/history.cfm

Dusto, A. (October 30, 2013). "60% of U.S. Retail Sales Will Involve the Web by 2017." *Internet Retailer*. Retrieved October 24, 2015, from https://www.internetretailer.com/2013/10/30/60-us-retail-sales-will-involve-web-2017

Glock, R., & Kunz, G. I. (2005). *Apparel Manufacturing: Sewn Product Analysis* (4th ed.). Upper Saddle River, NJ: Prentice Hall.

Lodge, G. (1995). *Managing Globalization in the Age of Interdependence*. San Diego, CA: Pfeiffer.

Srivastava, Mehul. (n.d.). "For Bangladeshi Women, Factory Work Is Worth the Risks." Retrieved April 24, 2014, from http://www.businessweek.com/articles/2014-04-24/for-bangladeshi-women-factory-work-is-worth-the-risk

Underhill, G. (1998). *Industrial Crisis and the Open Economy: Politics, Global Trade and the Textile Industry in the Advanced Economies*. New York, NY: St. Martin's Press.

World Trade Organization (WTO). (n.d.). "International Trade Statistics 2009: Top 15 Countries in Textiles and Apparel Trade in 2008." Retrieved November 14, 2009, from http://www.wto.org/english/res_e/statis_e/its2009

CHAPTER 2
CONSUMERS, CONSUMPTION, AND WELL-BEING

//

NOT SO FUN FACT

Inequality of opportunity is created by the lottery of birth: Gender, economic circumstances, geography, and ethnicity can trap large groups of people into poverty. (World Bank, n.d.)

OBJECTIVES

- Discuss the foundations of apparel choices in relation to the clothing consumption process.
- Explore the relationships between standards of living and apparel consumption patterns around the world.
- Provide a foundation for interpreting consumption expenditure data related to developed, developing, and newly developing countries.

Clothing styles and the materials with which the clothes are made may differ from place to place in the world, but some forms of many of these products are present everywhere and regarded as essential components of the clothing consumption process. For example, because of electronic communication, people in many parts of the world are readily aware of and follow current fashion. **Fashion** is the style of dress accepted by the majority of a group of people at a particular time. At the same time, in other parts of the world, religious doctrines and/or strong cultural customs do not allow exposure of the body or elaborate use of colors to enhance personal appeal. The unique nature of the textiles and apparel business can be attributed to many things, from their seemingly incompatible uses as both protection and adornment to the unpredictability of demand for and acceptance of new styles—the fashion factor. Regardless of where people live around the globe, in what culture or income, they all are consumers of textiles and apparel. Clothing is a very basic human need, right after food and shelter. Consumer demand drives the entire apparel industry.

This chapter examines concepts associated with human well-being, a state of being comfortable, healthy, and happy, and explores common methods of measuring it. One

acquisition the act of making products available for personal use; increases inventory of goods available for consumption

active inventory garments used within a one-year period

basic goods goods that are standardized and utilitarian, with infrequent demand for changes in styling

buying power *see* purchasing power

clothing renovation brushing, laundering, dry cleaning, ironing, and any other method used to restore garments to what is regarded as wearable condition after wearing

clothing standards criteria determining styles, sizes, and colors of garments regarded as suitable for specific occasions

complement a product purchased and used along with another; for example, shoes and socks

Consumer Price Index (CPI) a measure of the impact of inflation on consumer purchasing power in the United States

consumption commodities (goods and services), their uses, and services consumed by an individual or a family

consumption expenditure money used to support the level of consumption during a specified period

discard the act of giving up possession and ownership of a garment; reducing inventory

discretionary income the amount of money available after all current obligations are covered

disposable income take-home pay; the amount available to an individual or family to support the level of consumption, savings, and investment at a particular time

elastic demand demand for a product changes with the change in the product price: demand increases (decreases) as the product price goes down (up)

fashion a style of dress accepted by the majority of a group at a particular time

fashion goods individualized, differentiated by style, color, and fit; characterized by frequent changes in styling

inactive inventory garments that have not been used for at least one year

inelastic demand when income increases consumer demand decreases; when income decreases consumer demand increases; products with inelastic demand are called normal goods

inflation an increase of general price level, causing a decline in purchasing power

income elasticity the relationship between change in income and resulting change in expenditure

inventory the entire stock of garments owned by and/or available for use by an individual, family, or group of people that could be used as clothing at a given time

level of consumption the quantity and quality of goods and services that are available to be used by an individual or group during a given time period

level of living the combined benefits of goods and services and the overall well-being which is actually experienced, enjoyed, or suffered by an individual or group during a given period of time

minimum needs the essentials of life, defined by levels and standards of consumption and living; vary according to place and time

nonverbal communication uses appearance to communicate perspective, identity, age, sexual orientation, educational level, occupation, economic status, or marital status

poverty a lack of enough income or resources, or both, to satisfy minimum needs

price elasticity demand for a product does not change correspondingly with the product price (e. g., if price goes up, demand for the product does not decrease substantially); gasoline is an example of product with inelastic demand

primary source the most frequent means of clothing acquisition; purchased new ready-to-wear in developed countries, purchased secondhand or handed down in newly developing countries

product obsolescence discard of products owing to lack of interest in them rather than lack of their fundamental usability

progressive tax an increase in tax rate as income rises

purchasing power the amount of goods or services that can be acquired with a specified amount of currency at a given time and place; the value of money in terms of what it could buy during a specified period of time; also sometimes called buying power

real expenditure spending adjusted to reflect purchasing power, considering rate of inflation

real income earnings adjusted to reflect purchasing power, considering rate of inflation

regressive tax requires lower-income people to pay higher rates than higher-income people

secondary source a means of acquiring clothing other than the primary source: gifts, purchased used, handed down, rental, home sewing, custom-made, and others

standard of consumption or living a level that is urgently desired and strived for, substantial success yielding special gratification, and substantial failure yielding bitter frustration (Davis, 1945)

substitute a product purchased and used in place of another; for example, pants rather than skirts

temporary possession a means of momentary clothing acquisition from sources such as rental, borrowing, and clothing provided by an employer

total income gross income or personal income

well-being a good or satisfactory condition of existence; a state of being comfortable, healthy, and happy

unique thing about this chapter is that many of the citations are more than 20 to 40 years old because the authors of the works cited are the originators or early interpreters of the concepts and theories discussed.

FUNDAMENTALS OF THE CLOTHING CONSUMPTION PROCESS

The major parts of the clothing consumption process are as follows:

- acquisition
- inventory
- use
- renovation
- discarding

Acquisition is the act of making garments available for personal use; it provides possession and/or ownership, depending on the source of clothing. Acquisition creates the **inventory** of goods available for consumption and may or may not involve monetary expenditure (Winakor, 1969). When garments are acquired as gifts, handed down from friends or family members, or from charity organizations, monetary expenditures from the new consumer are not required. Garment use is the actual wearing of garments as apparel. Garment **renovation** might include brushing, laundering, folding, pressing, dry cleaning, ironing, mending, and any other methods used to restore garments into what is regarded as wearable condition. **Discard** is making a garment no longer available for wearing by current owner(s)/user(s) including things like throwing away, giving to charity, or destroying the item. Note: Sometimes more than one person claims ownership of an item. A scenario of shared ownership often leads to competition and/or disagreement related to who uses it and when as well as who renovates it or whether it gets renovated for or is available for the next use.

The majority of garments acquired by individuals in developed countries are purchased new from one **primary source**, such as when retailers offer imported, ready-to-wear garments. However, with recent increased popularity of vintage apparel as well as growing sustainability concerns, some consumers use multiple primary sources to acquire clothing, including used and repurposed apparel and shoes. **Secondary sources** of clothing include gifts, purchased used, handed down, home sewing, and others (Britton, 1969). Items acquired for **temporary possession** come from sources such as rental, borrowing, and perhaps clothing provided by an employer. Such items are available for use by the individual, are possessed by the individual, but are not owned by the individual. The intent is that these items will be returned to the owner when the individual no longer uses them (Winakor, 1969).

Clothing inventory is the entire stock of garments owned by an individual or group that could be used as clothing at a given time. Items that are temporarily in the possession of another person, such as borrowed or loaned garments, are considered part of the inventory of the owner, not the borrower. Inventory may have two parts: active inventory and inactive inventory. **Active inventory** may be defined as garments used within a one-year period (Winakor, 1969). This means **inactive inventory** is garments that have not been used for at least one year. However, definitions of active and inactive inventory by today's consumers may vary greatly. Consumers in developed countries sometimes have large quantities of inactive inventory, because these consumers have the ability to acquire more clothing than they can use at a particular time. Consumers in newly developing countries may have only a small amount of active inventory that gets very frequent use.

Clothing use is the actual wearing of garments for beauty, protection, comfort, and/or fashion acceptance. Each consumer is likely to have a set of priorities that determines personal choices among these four reasons for wearing clothes. Sometimes it is possible for all four priorities to apply but, for clothing, fashion often outweighs the others. **Clothing renovation** is the restoring of a garment, after a period of use or storage, into a condition that is regarded by the owner/user as suitable for wearing in public. The renovation process appropriate to the garment may be determined by the materials included in the garment, the style's complexity, the frequency of use, and/or the experience and standards of the restorer.

The majority of garments acquired by individuals in newly developing countries are likely to come from what are regarded in developed countries as secondary sources. Discard is the act of giving up possession and/or ownership of a garment; there is no longer intent for the item to be used as clothing by that individual or group. Discard reduces the inventory available for use by the current owner(s). Sale of garments at a consignment shop or garage sale can result in monetary gain for the owner. Some garments are destroyed or used as something other than clothing, such as rags. Garments may be cut into parts for quilts; jeans may be converted into a purse or carry-all bag. When items are discarded by handing down, donating, or selling, discard becomes a form of acquisition for someone else. Contributions of clothing to a charitable organization can sometimes result in income tax deductions for the donators.

Clothing standards of an individual or group can determine the types and quantities of garments desired in the clothing inventory. These standards might include the following:

- number of styles and colors
- variety of garments needed to address personal activities and fashion priorities
- acceptable frequency of wearing each garment
- compromises adopted to accommodate financial restrictions

The owner's intent for the use of a garment determines the use-life of a garment. For example, a garment that is acquired with the intended use for everyday wear, whether at work or at home, might have a use-life cycle as follows:

1. acquisition
2. frequent interchange of active storage, use, renovation
3. less frequent interchange of active storage, use, renovation
4. continuous inactive storage
5. discard

The movement of a garment through the use-life cycle from steps 2 to 4 may be caused by acquisition of substitutes for the garment or lack of suitable complements for the garment, or products that can be used along with it like scarves. An example of a garment **substitute** might be acquisition of new red T-shirt when a red T-shirt is already in inventory. An example of a **complement** for the red T-shirts might be a pair of black slacks to wear with the red shirts. Acquisition of another T-shirt may result in the less frequent use of a T-shirt already owned (because of an available substitute) and the more frequent use of the black slacks (complement). The more complements a garment has, the slower it may move through the use-life cycle. The acquisition of a complement may move an item back from step 4 into step 2, where it will go through the process a second time.

In contrast, garments that are acquired for special occasions, such as wedding dresses, may have a short or infrequent use-life and a long storage life, as follows:

1. acquisition
2. active storage, one or a few uses, renovation
3. continuous inactive storage

The position of garments in the use-life cycle and the type of use-lives of garments seem to be determined by the following:

- clothing standards of the owner(s) including number of garments owned, frequency of wear, and effectiveness of renovation
- intent of the owner(s) toward the garments in inventory including frequency of use and how many days, weeks, or years the garments will be actively used
- length of time garments have been possessed and/or owned
- condition of the garments in inventory relative to wear, fashion, and repair
- number of substitutes and complements that are available in inventory (Kunz, 1987)

There are extreme differences in average levels of clothing expenditure among consumers in developed, developing, and newly developing countries, due in part to frequent acquisition of overpriced branded apparel sold in developed countries. At the other extreme, use of handed down, purchased used, and home sewing are likely to be more important sources for clothing in developing and newly developing countries. Individual ownership of garments may also be less defined with garments drawn from a common inventory possessed by the household.

THE NATURE OF APPAREL CHOICES

Every human culture uses textiles and apparel for aesthetics and protection. Another important function of textiles and apparel is for **nonverbal communication**. By simply watching a neighbor walk out the front door, it is often easy to tell if he/she is going to work, for a walk or a run, to a sports event, shopping, to church, or to a formal party. The more mysterious component of clothing selection is fashion. Fashion is a powerful force in that it influences the types of garments people choose to wear during a particular time period and/or for particular occasions. This temporal quality of a garment's acceptance means that many of those who can afford to acquire new garments will continue to seek new and different items, whether it is physically necessary or not. This makes textile and apparel products different from many other consumer products.

Thus, the definition of the "need" for clothing extends well beyond adequate garments for physical comfort and protection. The "need" for clothing often includes the "want" for clothing based on the current fashion influence. Fashion helps define what is preferred in relation to fabrics, colors, patterns, textures, and shapes of garments. The intended function of a garment or accessory is also often an important factor, for example for active sportswear, strength of fabric, elasticity, resistance to snagging, etc. becomes a priority. But fashion still maintains a role in garment design, fabric patterns and colors, and garment cut and fit. All of these factors may play a role in the selection of a garment for a particular use.

What is in fashion? Fashion in apparel makes the textile and apparel business much less predictable than most other consumer products. The factors of unpredictability and ongoing change make the textiles and apparel business a vital but sometimes fickle field of employment. Firms that specialize in the manufacturing and retailing of apparel offer great varieties in locations, modes of operation, and types of product offerings with the intent to appeal to potential new employees and customers. Potential professionals in the apparel field must understand the underlying nature of consumer product choices:

- first to make a viable choice of employment in the apparel field, and
- second to make essential business decisions in the professional marketplace

Basic, Fashion, and Fast Fashion Goods

Apparel professionals have long thought of apparel products in three categories: basics, fashions, and fads. These three broad classifications of apparel differ in product characteristics, product presentation, inventory control, and appeal to customers as well as shelf life in retail stores. More specifically, **basic goods** tend to be standardized and utilitarian and have infrequent demand for changes in styling. The same styles, sizes, and colors can be sold for a year or longer, with relatively consistent levels of demand. Inventories in basic goods are steady, predictable, and refillable. Automated replenishment based on point-of-sale (POS) data can be used to keep products in stock.

Fashion goods are individualized, differentiated by style, color, and fit. Styles of one brand are distinct from styles of another brand, at least until another designer copies the design. Fashion goods go through a fashion cycle that includes a bell-shaped curve that involves introduction, early acceptance, and peak acceptance, followed by early obsolescence based on the use-life cycle of garments. Merchandisers plan for zero-to-zero inventories in fashion categories. Merchandise is bought, stocked, sold, and cleared from the retail sales floor during each selling period—extended selling times for basic goods and short periods for fashion goods that are immediately replaced with new styles. It is often difficult or impossible to restock fashion goods in the middle of a selling period, especially when they come from distant suppliers.

Historically, a **fad** was defined as a "temporary fashion," something that was extremely popular for a short period of time and quickly abandoned for something "newer." Fast fashion, introduced in Chapter 1, is now somewhat similar to what fads used to be.

Fast fashion goods are like fashion goods on steroids. The products are conceptualized by designers and pass through the entire manufacturing and distribution process in a matter of weeks instead of months. New designs arrive in retail stores nearly every week or two. High levels of efficiency are essential throughout the entire fast fashion supply chain. For fast fashion to continue to work for the retailer, customers have to be willing to shop very frequently to keep merchandise moving off the sales floor. The contrasts in the merchandising of basic, fashion, and fast fashion goods not only require staying ahead of the fashion cycle of each but also require significantly different timing and management of their textile and apparel supply chains. See Figures 2.1a through c and Table 2.1.

TABLE 2.1

FUNDAMENTAL CHARACTERISTICS OF BASIC, FASHION, AND FAST FASHION MERCHANDISE

	Basic	Fashion	Fast Fashion
Product characteristics	Standardized	Individualized (differentiated)	Focus on unique
	Utilitarian	Romanced with atmosphere	Romanced with new
	Infrequent changes in styling	Frequent changes in styling	Incessant changes in styling
	More common in menswear	Very common in women's wear	Focus on young men's and women's wear
Type of production	Partially to fully automated production processes	More labor-intensive production processes	Highly efficient supply chains
Product presentation	Individual items/related sets	Coordinated groups	Great variety of unique items
	Simple presentation	Project a fashion image	Represent immediate fashion image
Inventory control	Steady, predictable demand	Demand peaks followed by obsolescence	Immediate success or total failure
	Predictable selection	Seasonal changes of stocks	Biweekly replacement with new styles
	Automated replenishment	Selection limited by current fashion	Selection limited by immediate replacement with new styles
	Similar inventory consistently	Zero-to-zero inventory in stock	Zero-to-zero inventory in stock
Selection process	Easy price comparisons	Value difficult to assess	Value difficult to assess but it may not matter
	Comparative shopping	Impulse shopping	Dedication to shopping
Appeal to customer	Logical	Emotional	Passionate
	Tangible product	Intangible fashion image	Unexplainable fashion image
	Intrinsic value	Extrinsic; externally created value	Extrinsic; externally created value
	Meeting a need	Creating or directing a need	Creating or directing a more frequent need
	Replacement	Adding variety to a wardrobe	Adding endless variety to a wardrobe
	Price may be the major consideration	Appearance is a major selection factor	Appearance is the primary selection factor

a

b

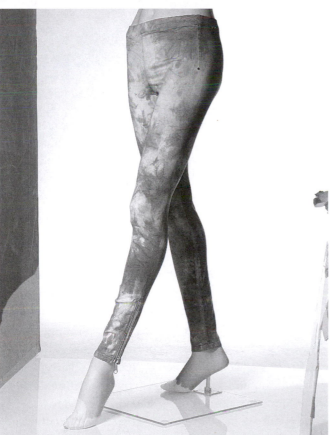

c

Figure 2.1a
Basic garments are products for men, women, and children that tend to be practical, everyday wear that are presented by retailers with relatively little change in style and fit over time.

Figure 2.1b
Fashion goods have frequent changes in textures, styles, and colors as well as fit over time and are often more frivolous in character.

Figure 2.1c
Fast fashion is like fashion goods on steroids; relatively inexpensive new designs appear on store shelves on a biweekly to monthly basis for rapid turnover in retail stores and frequent changes in the appearance of the new owners.

Figure 2.2
The life cycle of secondhand clothing.

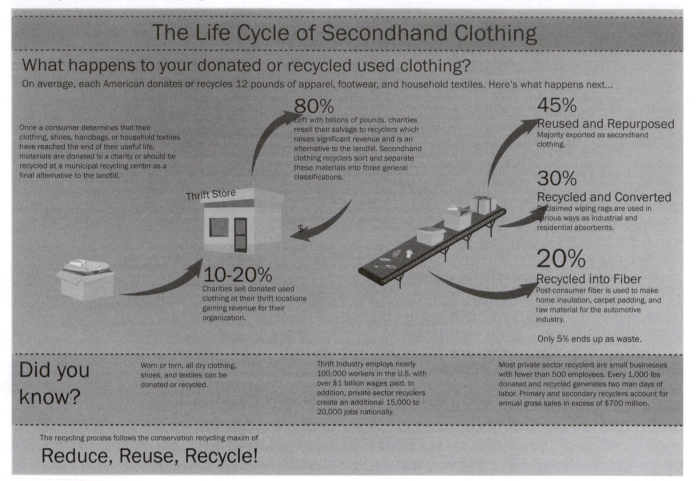

The Life Cycle of Secondhand Clothing

What happens to your donated or recycled used clothing?

On average, each American donates or recycles 12 pounds of apparel, footwear, and household textiles. Here's what happens next...

Once a consumer determines that their clothing, shoes, handbags, or household textiles have reached the end of their useful life, materials are donated to a charity or should be recycled at a municipal recycling center as a final alternative to the landfill.

Thrift Store

80%
Left with billions of pounds, charities resell their salvage to recyclers which raises significant revenue and is an alternative to the landfill. Secondhand clothing recyclers sort and separate these materials into three general classifications.

45%
Reused and Repurposed
Majority exported as secondhand clothing.

30%
Recycled and Converted
Reclaimed wiping rags are used in various ways as industrial and residential absorbents.

10-20%
Charities sell donated used clothing at their thrift locations gaining revenue for their organization.

20%
Recycled into Fiber
Post-consumer fiber is used to make home insulation, carpet padding, and raw material for the automotive industry.

Only 5% ends up as waste.

Did you know?

Worn or torn, all dry clothing, shoes, and textiles can be donated or recycled.

Thrift Industry employs nearly 100,000 workers in the U.S. with over $1 billion wages paid. In addition, private sector recyclers create an additional 15,000 to 20,000 jobs nationally.

Most private sector recyclers are small businesses with fewer than 500 employees. Every 1,000 lbs donated and recycled generates two man days of labor. Primary and secondary recyclers account for annual gross sales in excess of $700 million.

The recycling process follows the conservation recycling maxim of

Reduce, Reuse, Recycle!

The appeal of basic goods tends to be in meeting a new need and/or in replacing a product already owned. Price is often a major selection factor. The appeal of fashion goods is more emotional, as the customer acquires not only the garment, but also its associated fashion image. Appearance is the major selection factor with fashion goods. Table 2.1 organizes the fundamental differences between basic and fashion goods from the perspective of apparel professionals and consumers. Fast fashion creates an everyday runway fashion show that customers display every few weeks in their newly acquired fast fashion clothes. Color, cut, fit, fabric, accessories, and short wear life are all essential aspects of successful fast fashion.

It may be obvious by now that the characteristics of **firms** that produce and distribute basic, fashion, and fast fashion products differ. Basic goods can be manufactured using mass production and often automated techniques for large quantities of goods. Mass retailers and department stores can retail basic goods by replenishing similar merchandise on a daily or weekly basis over long periods of time. In contrast, fashion goods are produced by manufacturers or vendors who can produce relatively small quantities of styles, with frequent shutdown and start-up of production lines to introduce new styles. Because fashion customers want to see new merchandise every time they enter the store, fashion goods are more likely to be offered by specialty stores for short time periods in smaller quantities.

FACTS ABOUT TEXTILE WASTE AND THE LIFE CYCLE OF SECONDHAND CLOTHING[1]

Postconsumer wastes are products, materials, food, etc., discarded while still able to provide service to an owner. Of the 25 billion pounds of postconsumer waste generated per year in the United States, 85 percent goes into landfills while only 15 percent of the waste (70 pounds per US citizen) is donated or recycled. According to the US Environmental Protection Agency, postconsumer wastes consist of the following:

- Paper   28.2 percent
- Food scraps   14.1 percent
- Metals and glass 13.4 percent
- Plastics   12.3 percent
- Textile waste   5.2 percent
- Other   26.7 percent

It appears that the waste of textile products and materials is the least of our waste problems. While the 5.2 percent of total waste looks small compared with other sources of waste, the US textile industry creates about 130 million pounds of postconsumer textile wastes annually. According to the Council for Textile Recycling, postconsumer textile waste (PCTW) consists of clothing, footwear, accessories, towels, bedding, and draperies totalling about 82 pounds per US resident per year—and this amount is growing. Between 1999 and 2009, the volume of postconsumer textile waste grew by 40 percent while the diversion rate to recycling only increased by 2 percent. Thus, the amount being discarded increased greatly but the amount being recycled did not. Why?

Charities and thrift shops retail only 10 to 20 percent of textile wastes from consumers, businesses, and manufacturers while 80 to 90 percent is sold as salvage to recyclers commonly known as the "thrift industry." Recyclers sort and separate the materials into three classifications:

- 45 percent is reused and/or repurposed, the majority being exported as secondhand clothing
- 30 percent is recycled and converted, made into wiping rags used in various ways as industrial and residential absorbents
- 20 percent is recycled into postconsumer fiber used to make home insulation, carpet padding, and raw materials for the automotive industry
- 5 percent goes to the landfill

The thrift industry employs nearly 100,000 workers in the United States with over $1 billion wages paid. In addition, private sector recyclers create an additional 15,000 to 20,000 jobs nationally. Most private sector recyclers are small businesses with fewer than 500 employees. Every 1,000 lbs. of textiles donated and recycled equals two man days of labor. Primary and secondary recyclers account for annual gross sales in excess of $700 million. Charities and private sector combined handle 3.8 billion pounds of textiles annually. These items are recycled and processed quickly due to a highly efficient and well-organized recycling industry. Your donated textiles and clothing and other textile items go through this entire recycling process in just 30 to 60 days.

[1] Council for Textile Recycling. (n.d.). "The Facts about Textile Waste." Retrieved from http://www.weardonaterecycle.org/about/issue.html

1. What do you think is most troublesome about textile and apparel "waste"? Why?

2. Should more effort be made to reduce textile and apparel waste? Explain your answer.

However, given the pervasiveness of communication technology, particularly cell phones and other handheld research and communication devices, newly developed fashions are known by potential consumers almost instantaneously throughout the world. These potential consumers can see new fashions on a daily basis and buy them without going to a store. They also may be discarded after a few wearings in favor of new "fast fashion" opportunities. With fashion goods, in most economies, consumer obsolescence is a factor, because any individual with sufficient purchasing power may discard, hand off, or donate products from lack of interest in them rather than out of some other need of a replacement. **Purchasing power** is the amount of goods or services that can be acquired with a specified amount of currency at a particular time.

Large quantities of both secondhand and distressed new ready-to-wear are exported by charitable organizations and some retailers. These garments may become important sources of "new" clothing to those in less-developed nations. Current fashions not only influence consumers' purchase preferences when they are economically able to acquire new clothes but also guide choices in secondhand clothing markets and beyond. Study Figure 2.2 and then read Case 2.1.

LEVELS AND STANDARDS OF CONSUMPTION

To some, the greatest shortcoming of the western capitalist model of global business is the ownership advantage provided to some participants to the detriment of others. Critics of capitalism report that the gap between rich and poor is widening across the world. Unfortunately, the measure of rich and poor is tricky. To do it well, it is essential to develop a method of measuring consumption so that useful comparisons can be made across countries and across time. Each method introduces different types of biases into the conclusions drawn from the data. This section focuses on basic measures defined by levels and standards of consumption, including consumption expenditure, gross national product, gross domestic product, and purchasing power parity.

The survival of global capitalism as a model of economic exchange depends on the ability of participants to cope with some very real problems. One of these problems is the skewed distribution of economic development among participating nations. Another problem is the deterioration of the environment. A third is the decline of nonrenewable natural resources. A variation of this issue emerges when host governments lack the power to impose rules on the owners of foreign-owned business enterprises. These are fundamental problems related to the sustainability of apparel supply chains.

The well-being of individuals, together with the potential exploitation of citizens living in the countries involved with the textile and apparel supply chains, is a primary global issue. Levels and standards of consumption and living are commonly used measures of well-being. The types and amounts of products that people consume are used as indicators. Although many researchers regard it as too simplistic, consumption expenditure may be the most available measure of rate of consumption. To be effective, however, things like inflation must be accounted for, because inflation reduces purchasing power and distorts comparisons of different places and points in time. To compare across countries, monetary exchange rates also have to be considered.

To understand consumption patterns, the first challenge is developing and understanding a system of language to define concepts and clarify relationships. Joseph Stancliffe Davis (1945) laid out a system of language for describing well-being that is still used today. The four terms he used were *consumption*, *living*, *level*, and *standard*. The term **consumption** means commodities (goods and services), their uses, and services consumed. Consumption includes goods purchased in the market as well as in-kind gifts and those provided through home production. **Living** includes consumption and other dimensions of life, such as levels of remuneration, comfort, job security, and safe working conditions. Living also includes freedom of movement and association, security of personal and financial well-being, and environmental and political atmosphere (Davis, 1945). In this context, the term **level** implies that which is actually experienced, enjoyed, or suffered by an individual or group. Level is what a person or family actually has, whereas a standard is what is desired. The term **standard** is what "is urgently desired and striven for, special gratification attending substantial success and substantial failure yielding bitter frustration" (Davis, 1945, pp. 3–4). Typically, the standard is higher than the level. It is common for human beings to want more things or to want things that are different from what we actually have.

Teaming the terms *level* and *standard* with *consumption* and *living* provides additional distinctions and a better understanding of the concepts. A **level of consumption** includes

- the overall amount of food, fuel, and other nondurable goods consumed
- the use of houses, automobiles, clothing, and other durable and semidurable goods
- the services of people used by an individual or group in a given period of time (Davis, 1945)

A decline in the level of consumption means a reduction in the quantity or quality of goods and services consumed. A rise in the level of consumption means an increase in volume or improvement in its quality. The term *standard of living* is sometimes misapplied to the level of consumption as defined above. A **standard of living** is the level of consumption urgently desired and strived for, as mentioned above, plus the following additional components:

- working conditions
- freedom of movement and association
- safety and security
- political and environmental atmosphere

Standards of living are based on multiple aspects of our lives; the levels of consumption and other aspects of living that we strive for are founded on a variety of sources and experiences. For some people, religious faith or spirituality is first priority. For others, social acceptance is of primary importance—"What would the neighbors think?" For still others, providing evidence of conspicuous consumption (having more, better, newer designer clothes, homes, furniture, pools, electronic devices, automobiles, and so on) is the greatest goal. It seems to be inherent in the human intellect to continually want to improve our state of being, but what we think will make us better off varies with gender, age, culture, weather, income, education, religion, occupation, and life experience. Thus, our individual standard of living, in this sense, is more complex and abstract than our level of consumption and more difficult to measure in its entirety. For this reason, simpler measures are commonly used to determine well-being, such as monetary income.

It is common for standard of living to exceed level of living and standard of consumption to exceed level of consumption. Even at high levels of consumption, "more" is commonly perceived as "better." Higher-quality, more fashionable products—products that are regarded as more aesthetically pleasing but are more expensive—are commonly included in the level of living to which individuals or families aspire but are not yet included in their level of consumption because of budget constraints. When income increases, some components of the standard of living may be added to the level of consumption, increasing perceived well-being, but at the same time, *new aspirations are commonly added to the standard of living*. Thus, there is constant pressure to increase levels of consumption and living to achieve an ever-increasing standard of living. The standard and level of living provide a framework to guide the standard and level of consumption.

Standards of living commonly include the desire for increased quantities of textiles and apparel products. From an economic perspective, these products are what are sometimes called normal goods, and the demand for them tends to be inelastic. That is, when incomes increase, expenditures for soft goods increase; when incomes decrease, expenditures decrease, but the increases and decreases are proportionally less than the change in income. **Income elasticity** describes the relationship between consumers' change in income and resulting change in consumers' expenditures. **Price elasticity** describes the relationship between the change in price of a product and the related change in demand for that product, that is, the quantity of that product sold at the store. Income elasticity is more relevant to the well-being of the consumer; price elasticity is more relevant to the well-being of the retailer.

Income and Price Elasticity of Demand

The economic classifications of superior, normal, and inferior goods are based on income elasticity, technically known as **income elasticity of demand**. It is determined by relative changes in income and expenditures over a defined time period.

income elasticity of demand = percentage change in expenditures ÷ percentage change in income

An income elasticity of 1 means elasticity is unitary; that is, both income and expenditures are changing at the same rate and in the same direction. For example, when income and expenditure are changing at the same rate, an increase of 15 percent in income is associated with an increase of 15 percent in expenditure for a particular good. Percentage variation in expenditure is the same as percentage variation in income. When elasticity is greater than 1 for a particular product, the relationship is described as elastic. When elasticity is less than 1, the relationship is described as inelastic. Superior and normal goods have a positive income elasticity of demand. Inferior goods have a negative income elasticity of demand. The income elasticity of superior goods is greater than 1, income elasticity of normal goods is between 0 and 1.0, and income elasticity of inferior goods is a negative number.

- **Superior goods** (economic luxury): Expenditure increases as income increases and decreases as income decreases but at a faster rate than income. *Elasticity of superior goods is greater than 1.*
- **Normal goods** (economic necessity): Expenditure increases as income increases and decreases as income decreases but at a slower rate than income. *Elasticity of normal goods is between 0 and 1.*
- **Inferior goods** (inadequate income): Expenditure decreases as income increases and increases as income decreases. *Elasticity of inferior goods is less than zero.*

Definitions of Consumer Income

The apparel industry's employees must receive fair pay for their time at work. Based on the assumption that people are better off when income is higher, evaluation of the well-being of citizens of cities, states, and countries is often gauged by levels of income and consumption expenditures. In developed countries, levels of consumption at a given time are primarily dependent on levels of income, because the majority of citizens are employed and purchase rather than produce most of their own goods and services. However, there are many different definitions of income, and they are used in different ways. For a defined time period, these four definitions of income are related as follows:

total income (also known as gross income) – income tax and other taxes =

disposable income (also known as take-home pay) – savings and investment =

consumption expenditures (also known as consumption level) – necessary
consumption expenditures =

discretionary income = uncommitted income that can be used as needed
(Schwenk, 1985)

Total income is sometimes called gross income or personal income. It is the total amount earned in a given period of time. Many people never see or have their total income in hand, because employers deduct income taxes and other taxes and contributions to benefits before paychecks are written. Thus, the amount most people receive on a weekly or monthly basis is disposable income:

disposable income = total income – income tax and other taxes
and contributions

Disposable income is commonly known as take-home pay, the amount available to an individual or family to support the level of consumption, savings, and investments.

consumption expenditure = disposable income – savings and investment

Consumption expenditure is the money used to support the level of consumption during a specified period. When disposable income exceeds levels of savings, investments, and previously committed and other necessary consumption expenditures, discretionary income is available. If consumption expenditure exceeds disposable income, discretionary income is negative, resulting in obligations against future income.

discretionary income = disposable income – consumption expenditure

Discretionary income is the amount available about which new decisions can be made when some income remains after all current obligations have been covered with disposable income. Discretionary income can be saved toward future expenditure, invested, or spent as desired. Discretionary income may be used to move the family or household closer to its desired standard of living. This may involve increases in savings or investments, opportunities for impulse purchases, or a vacation, depending on the current standards of consumption and living. Discretionary income is often associated with fashionable clothing purchases, because fashionable clothing may be regarded as desirable according to standards but not necessary according to levels of consumption. Careful applications of these definitions can assist in analyzing past consumption levels and forecasting future consumption expenditures.

When reading and evaluating descriptions of well-being, it is essential to pay particular attention to the measures of income and consumption that are being used. If one study uses disposable income, another uses discretionary income, and a third uses consumption expenditure, their conclusions cannot be directly compared even though each may be valid in its own right. All may be interesting and useful, but remembering the definitions of these terms is essential for interpreting the findings.

Definitions of Poverty

Poverty is the lack of enough income or resources, or both, to satisfy a person's minimum needs. The **poverty line** is the point at which income or resources are inadequate to maintain life and health at a subsistence level. However, minimum needs for subsistence are not the same everywhere. **Minimum needs**, as defined by standards and levels of consumption and living, vary according to place and time. For example, in developed countries, the Internet and a variety of electronic devices are used regularly by the majority of people, both personally and professionally. For people in developed countries who do not have access to the Internet, gaining access has become a common component of the standard of living. In contrast, in least developed countries, electronic communication devices may be unknown to the majority of people and inaccessible even to most of those who do know about them. Electronic devices are unlikely to be a part of the standard of living in these least developed nations, because basic necessities are often unavailable including clean water, adequate food, and medical attention. Read Case 2.2 to learn more about definitions of poverty.

CASE 2.2

WORLD BANK GROUP'S MISSION—"OUR DREAM IS A WORLD FREE OF POVERTY"[1]

The World Bank's mission is carved in stone at the Washington, DC headquarters: "Our Dream Is a World Free of Poverty." This mission, alongside a focus on the welfare of the least well-off, drives its analytical, operational, and convening work in more than 145 client countries striving to end extreme poverty and promote shared prosperity. Five years ahead of the World Bank's target schedule, in 2010, the world attained the first World Bank Millennium goal target—to cut the 1990 poverty rate in half by 2015.

- According to the most recent estimates, in 2011, 17 percent of people in the developing world lived at or below $1.25 a day. That's down from 43 percent in 1990 and 52 percent in 1981.

- This means that in 2011, just over 1 billion people lived on less than $1.25 a day, compared with 1.91 billion in 1990, and 1.93 billion in 1981.

Even if the current rate of progress is to be maintained, some 1 billion people will still live in extreme poverty in 2015—and progress has been slower at higher poverty lines. In all, 2.2 billion people lived on less than $2 a day in 2011, the average poverty line in developing countries and another common measurement of deep deprivation. That is only a slight decline from 2.59 billion in 1981.

In some developing countries, we continue to see a wide gap, or in some cases, a widening gap between rich and poor, and between those who can and cannot access opportunities. This means that access to good schools, healthcare, electricity, safe water, and other critical services remains elusive for many people who live in developing economies. Other challenges such as economic shocks, food insecurity, and climate change threaten to undermine the progress made in recent years.

[1]The World Bank. (n.d.). "Poverty Overview." Retrieved October 7, 2014 from www.worldbank.org/en/topic/poverty/overview.print

1. When textile and apparel firms based in developed countries seek production in developing countries, in what ways might the firms exploit the developing countries' populations?

2. When textile and apparel firms based in developed countries seek production in developing countries, in what ways might they assist the developing countries' populations?

THE MEANING OF CONSUMPTION EXPENDITURE DATA

In general, when income increases, consumption expenditures increase. From the perspective of determining overall well-being or forecasting retail sales, one enlightening aspect is the relative rate of increase for different types of goods. The best known of early theorists of income–consumption relationships is Ernst Engel, who in 1857 proposed the famous law of food consumption: the poorer a family is, the greater the proportion of total expenditure it must use to procure food (Monroe, 1974). When income is lower, total expenditure is lower, but a larger proportion of income is required to have enough food. For example, in newly developing countries it is not unusual for families to spend 60 to 80 percent of income on food. In the same environment, when income is higher, a smaller proportion is required to buy the same amount of food and therefore more income is available for other goods and services.

Interpreting the Well-Being of Families

It is well documented that overall well-being has not been achieved in many countries of the world and especially in newly developing countries. For example, in China, life is much better in urban areas than in rural areas. Well-being in rural areas still includes high rates of poverty and sometimes extreme poverty. According to Lu and Peng (2000), a study of consumption expenditures of families in rural China found that in 1978 food expenditures were about 68 percent of total consumption expenditures. In China this represented a starvation level of poverty. In 1978, China began economic reform in rural areas where farm households became independent production and accounting units. The changes were enthusiastically received by the rural population of nearly 800 million. According to world news in 2015, China is an economic power, surpassing Japan for the world's second largest economy, and is soon to be recognized as the largest economy, surpassing the United States. But how well off are the families that live there? See Case 2.3 for the background on China's growth in economic power.

Expenditure Patterns in the United States

A fundamental theory related to consumption expenditures, which became known as Engel's Law, is as follows: the proportion of income spent on food decreases as income increases. Engel's Law is often applied in analysis of US expenditure patterns, as follows: When food expenditure is one-third or less of total consumption expenditure, a person's ability to consume may be regarded as adequate for general well-being. When food expenditure is greater than one-third of total expenditure, the person is regarded as living in poverty.

In the United States the **Consumer Price Index (CPI)** is used to measure the impact of inflation on consumer well-being considering purchasing power. **Inflation** is an increase in prices creating a decrease in the purchasing power of a monetary unit like the dollar. CPI is based on the Consumer Expenditure Survey program, which began in 1979 and was adjusted in 1984 so that consumer purchasing power in 1984 = 100. This is still the foundation for the CPI today. The CPI in 2011 was about 220, meaning that prices had more than doubled for consumer goods in the United States since 1984. The CPI in 2014 was about 237, indicating that prices of consumer goods had continued

CHINA'S ECONOMY OVERTAKING THE UNITED STATES DOES NOT TELL THE WHOLE STORY

A century of American economy is about to come to an end. China is on the point of overtaking the United States as the world's biggest economy. If Washington, DC, called the shots in the twentieth century, Beijing will be doing the same in the twenty-first century. These are the bold conclusions from reports showing that China is hard on the heels of the United States in terms of its share of global GDP (gross domestic product) and that it won't be long—given current trends in growth rates—before the positions at the top are reversed.

China, by virtue of its population, was the world's biggest economy at the dawn of the industrial revolution but lagged behind as countries in Europe and North America industrialized rapidly. As soon as China started its period of catch-up at the end of the 1970s, it was only a matter of time before its sheer size would make it number one (that is, the largest economy in the world). What has been surprising is the speed at which that transformation has taken place. The date at which the United States loses its top dog status is constantly being moved forward. John Hawksworth, chief economist at Pricewaterhouse Coopers, has estimated that the big moment will arrive in 2020; the latest data suggests it could be as soon as 2014.

There are two other points to bear in mind. The first is that the calculations rely on using purchasing power parity (PPP) to assess the comparative size of the economies. PPP allows for the fact that prices tend to be a lot lower in poor countries than they are in rich countries, so incomes stretch further. But the PPP measure can never be 100 percent reliable given the problems of comparing prices across the world, so it is impossible to be precise about when China will actually become the world's biggest economy.

The second—more significant—point is that even with the use of the PPP method, real living standards in China remain well behind those of the US. Per capita incomes in China, according to the OECD (Organization for Economic Cooperation and Development) are 75 percent of the global average, whilst those in the United States are 370 percent of the global average. China's sheer size and its rapid growth rate mean that it is now a global force to be reckoned with when it comes to talks about economic management, trade, and climate change. But on the measure that really matters to people—living standards—it remains a poor country.

[1]Elliott, Larry. (April 30, 2014). "China's Economy Overtaking the US Does Not Tell the Whole Story." *The Guardian*. Retrieved from http://www.theguardian.com/business/economics-blog/2014/apr/30/china-overake-us-economy-living

1. How does your interpretation of China becoming the largest economy change when purchasing power parity is brought into the discussion?
2. How can the concept of purchasing power parity (PPP) help us understand well-being among families in different countries?

to increase because of inflation, but not as rapidly as in the past. The monthly research to update the CPI provides a continuous flow of data on the buying habits of US consumers. It has two components:

1. an interview panel survey, in which the expenditures of consumer units are obtained in five interviews, conducted every 3 months, and
2. a diary, or record-keeping survey, completed by participating households for two consecutive one-week periods. Each component of the survey queries an independent sample of consumer units representative of the US population.

Ten thousand diaries are provided by 5,000 consumers each year, and 5,000 other consumers participate in panels each quarter. Data are collected in eighty-eight urban and sixteen rural areas of the country. Results are published monthly (Bureau of Labor Statistics, 2014). The CPI demonstrates that inflation has declined a lot since the 1970s, and the general trend has been toward lower rates of inflation annually:

- 1970s—7.0 percent increase in inflation annually
- 1980s—5.5 percent increase in inflation annually

- 1990s—3.0 percent increase in inflation annually
- 2000s—2.8 percent increase in inflation annually
- 2010s—1.3 percent increase in inflation annually

Since the mid-1990s, medical care and fuel have been responsible for a significant portion of price increases. By 2011, textile home furnishings increased in price about 8 percent, but apparel decreased in price by 10 percent and apparel has continued to decrease very slowly since 2011. As a consumer, it is unlikely that you are aware that, overall, apparel prices have decreased in recent years, but apparel may be the best bargain in consumer goods right now. Why have apparel prices decreased in the United States? As mentioned previously, the US retail condition is often described as being "over-stored" and "overmalled." The availability of apparel at retail has increased at a faster rate than overall apparel retail sales. Therefore, there are a lot of competitive price reductions on slow-moving merchandise.

Another major contributor to reduction of retail prices of apparel is the increased percentage of apparel being imported from developing countries. The price competition at retail has forced sourcers and vendors of apparel to seek lower-cost goods. Because apparel is a labor-intensive product, a lower-cost labor supply reduces production costs and allows retailers to use lower retail prices and still make the necessary gross margins to achieve profitability and stay in business (Figure 2.3a). However, these business practices have also resulted in many over-inventoried retailers and lots of markdowns on excess merchandise.

US consumers have financially benefited from the competition among retailers and the explosion of imports of textiles and apparel (Figure 2.3b). During the first decade of the twenty-first century and into the second decade, in spite of a situation of improving overall well-being in the population, apparel expenditures averaged a modest 3 percent increase per year. Most consumers could afford to buy what they wanted with very little more money compared to what they paid last year.

Figure 2.3a
Low apparel prices have benefited huge retailers like Macy's as well as locally owned retailers across the US.

Figure 2.3b

Strong spending power has also fuelled interest in multiple retail venues and recreational activities that inspire still more shopping activities.

Other Factors Affecting Consumption Expenditure Patterns

Taxes are another factor that can have a profound effect on consumption expenditures. Most of us face taxes in various forms every day: income taxes, sales taxes, excise taxes, real estate taxes, automobile license taxes, city service taxes, etc. Setting and applying tax rates can have a profound effect on how much consumers have available to spend on the goods and services that determine their level of living.

Taxes are often described as being progressive or regressive. **Progressive taxes** have an increase in tax rate as income rises; higher-income consumers pay higher rates than lower-income consumers. The US income tax is an example of a progressive tax. With **regressive taxes**, lower-income people pay higher rates than higher-income people. For example, a sales tax is regressive, because a sales tax takes a higher proportion of a low-income consumer's total income than a high-income person's total income when they make the same purchases. Low-income individuals and families commonly spend all or even more than all of their current income, whereas for high-income people, only half or less is spent on current consumption, with the rest going into savings or investments. That is why, in some states, sales taxes are not applied to food and sometimes not to clothing as well.

For example, in the state of Minnesota, neither clothing nor food is subject to sales tax. The well-known Mall of America in Minneapolis credits the tax-free status of clothing for bringing many buyers to its exclusive stores from out of state as well as from out of the country. For policymakers in Minnesota, food and clothing are regarded as a necessity and should not be subject to regressive taxes. Many other taxes are also regressive; for example, property taxes on rental units are regressive because the property owner, who usually has more income than the renter, passes the cost of the taxes on to the renter as part of the fee paid for use of the property.

A recent study conducted a distributional analysis of the tax systems in all fifty US states. The report assessed the fairness of state and local tax systems. The study measured taxes paid by different income groups in 2013 (at 2010 income levels including the impact of tax changes enacted through January 2, 2013) as share of income of every state and the District of Columbia. The report discussed state tax policy features and includes detailed state-by-state profiles providing essential baseline data for lawmakers seeking to understand the effect tax reform proposals will have on constituents at all income levels.

The main finding of the report is that every state's tax system is fundamentally regressive, taking a much greater share of income from middle- and low-income families than from wealthy families. In many states, the absence of a graduated personal income tax and the over reliance on consumption taxes exacerbate this problem (Institute of Taxation and Economic Policy, 2015). Additional findings of the study of tax systems in all 50 US states included the following:

- Combining all of the state and local income, property, sales, and excise taxes state residents pay, the average overall effective tax rates by income group nationwide are 11.1 percent for the bottom 20 percent, 9.4 percent for the middle 20 percent, and 5.6 percent for the top 1 percent.

- Ten states were ranked as having the most regressive overall tax systems. In the "Terrible Ten" states, the bottom 20 percent pay up to six times as much of their income in taxes as their wealthy counterparts. Washington State is the most regressive, followed by Florida, South Dakota, Illinois, Texas, Tennessee, Arizona, Pennsylvania, Indiana, and Alabama.

- Five of the ten most regressive states derive roughly half to two-thirds of their tax revenue from sales and excise taxes, compared to a national average of roughly one-third. Five of these ten most regressive states do not levy a broad-based personal income tax (four do not have any taxes on personal income and one state only applies its personal income tax to interest and dividends) while the other five have a personal income tax rate that is flat or virtually flat.

- Of the three broad kinds of taxes states levy (income, property, consumption), the income tax is the only one that is typically progressive in that its rate rises with income levels. Property taxes are usually somewhat regressive. Sales and excise taxes are the most regressive, with poor families paying eight times more of their income in these taxes than wealthy families, and middle-income families paying five times more.

- Personal income taxes varied in their fairness not only because of rate but because of deductions and exemptions. For example, the earned income tax credit improves progressivity.

Another form of taxation, import duties, has a strong influence on how much Americans and citizens in other countries pay for imported garments. For US citizens, given the billions of dollars worth of imported apparel that is purchased at retail stores every year, import duties on shoes are a serious problem. With 99 percent of the footwear sold in the United States being imported, US-based footwear firms pay the US Treasury over $2 billion in import duties every year. With markups at the wholesale and retail level, that $2 billion in duties amounts to a $6 billion tax on American families.

In an effort to relieve some of the costs of imports duties that are passed on to consumers, the American Apparel and Footwear Association initiated and drafted The Affordable Footwear Act,[1] which began moving through US Congress in 2014. It sought to end the expensive import duties (otherwise known as the shoe tax) on low- to moderately priced shoes and other children's footwear that is no longer made in the US. This act was intended to provide direct and immediate relief to hardworking American families in the form of a tax cut on the shoes they buy for themselves and their children, while at the same time keeping protections in place for remaining US domestic footwear manufacturers. As a result, it was intended to be truly noncontroversial legislation that could be supported by the entire US footwear industry (American Apparel and Footwear Association, 2014). Unfortunately, at the time of this writing, the act had not yet been acted upon by Congress.

It is clear that the clothing choices made by consumers around the world on a daily basis drive the decisions made by apparel professionals. The challenge is to figure out what consumers want before they do—so the goods can be in the store or online when those consumers go shopping.

Summary

Textiles and apparel are unique consumer goods because of their contributions to both aesthetics and necessities in the lives of human beings. Fashion has a powerful influence on clothing consumption. Fashion's influence is commonly described in the form of a fashion cycle, meaning a bell-shaped curve representing introduction, early acceptance, and peak acceptance, followed by early obsolescence, all related to the use-life cycles of fashion and basic clothing. Fashion trends help determine what apparel professionals present in the market and consumers decide what, when, and how much of it will be profitably sold. However, not all facets of apparel are fashion driven. Some apparel products are basics and there are major differences in both producing and consuming these different categories of apparel. The clothing consumption process involves different types of use-life cycles, depending on the perceived purpose of a garment.

The overall well-being of different populations around the world is the primary indicator of the ability of people to acquire and consume textiles and apparel. Measures of overall well-being include levels and standards of consumption, levels of consumption expenditures, gross national product, and purchasing power parity. Proportion of total consumption expenditures spent on food is sometimes used as a measure of overall well-being of families in a particular population.

Standards of living commonly include desires for increased quality and quantities of textiles and apparel products. When incomes increase, expenditures for soft goods increase; when incomes decrease, expenditures decrease, but the increases and decreases are proportionally less than the change in income. Income elasticity describes the relationship between change in income and the related change in expenditure. Price elasticity describes the relationship between change in price and the related change in demand. Income elasticity is more relevant to the well-being of the consumer; price elasticity is more relevant to the well-being of the retailer.

In the United States, clothing expenditures are currently close to 4 percent of total consumption expenditures. Clothing expenditures as a percentage of total expenditures has declined about 3 percent over the past ten years. According to the CPI, clothing prices have declined about 10 percent. Because of the decline in prices, US citizens have been able to increase clothing expenditures even though the proportion of total consumption expenditures has declined.

Learning Activities

1. Think through the clothing use-life cycle described in Case 2.1. How does the use-life cycle of your clothes compare with use-life described in the case? How do your parents' use-life cycles of apparel relate to Case 2.1? Explain how and why your use-life cycles are similar to and/or different from your parents'.
2. What is the relationship between a standard of living and a level of consumption? How do those concepts relate to consumption of apparel?

3. The level of consumption is used as a measure of poverty level. Why is the level of consumption more appropriate than the standard of living as a measure of poverty?
4. Explain why a sales tax is often regarded as an unfair method for states and countries to gather revenue.
5. What is the relationship between price elasticity and income elasticity in relation to clothing acquisition and use?
6. How do consumers' levels and standards of consumption and living contribute to postconsumer waste?

References

American Apparel and Footwear Association. (December 28, 2014). "Affordable Footwear Act: The Issue." Retrieved October 24, 2015, from http://www.wewear.org/aafa-on-the-issues/category /?CategoryId=96&print=y

Britton, V. (September 1969). "Gifts and Handed Down Clothing Important in Family Wardrobes." *Family Economics Review*, 3–5.

Bureau of Labor Statistics. (2014). "Consumer Price Index Frequently Asked Questions (FAQs)." Retrieved February 12, 2014, from http://www.bls.gov/dolfaq/blsfaqtoc.htm

Council for Textile Recycling. (n.d.). "The Life Cycle of Secondhand Clothing." Retrieved December 20, 2014, from http://www.weardonaterecycle.org/about/cloting-life-cycle.html

Council for Textile Recycling. (n.d.). "The Facts about Textile Waste." Retrieved December 20, 2014, from http://www.weardonaterrecycle.org/about/issue.html

Davis, J. S. (March 1945). "Standards and Content of Living." *American Economic Review*, 35(1), 1–15.

Elliott, Larry. (April 30, 2014). "China's Economy Overtaking the US Does Not Tell the Whole Story: China Is an Economic Giant but on the Measure That Really Matters to People—Living Standards—It Remains a Poor Country." *The Guardian*. Retrieved October 24, 2015, from http:// www.thegauardian.com/business/economics-blog/2014/apr/30/china-overake-us-economy -living

Institute of Taxation and Economic Policy. (January 2015). "Who Pays? A Distributional Analysis of Tax Systems in All 50 States." Retrieved February 15, 2015, from www.itep.org/pdf/whopays report.pdf

Kunz, G. I. (1987). "Clothing Consumption Process: Use-Life of Garments." Unpublished dissertation, Iowa State University.

Lu, J., & Peng, A. (2000). "Evolution of Rural Consumption Pattern in China." *Consumer Interests Annual*, 46, 222–225.

Monroe, D. (September 1974). "Pre-Engel Studies and the Work of Engel: The Origins of Consumption Research." *Home Economics Research Journal*, 3(1), 43-65.

Schwenk, N. E. (1985). "Measurements of Family Income." *Family Economics Review*, 1–4.

Winakor, G. (October 1969). "The Process of Clothing Consumption." *Journal of Home Economics*, 61(8), 629–634.

World Bank. (n.d.). "The Data Minute: What Is Inequity of Opportunity?" Retrieved February 15, 2015, from http://youtu.be/-ZzvicG-LHS

World Bank. (n.d.). "Poverty Overview." Retrieved February 17, 2015, from http://Worldbank.org/en /tropic/poverty/overview.print

CHAPTER 3

TEXTILE AND APPAREL SUPPLY MATRIX

NOT SO FUN FACT

Each year, over 2 billion T-shirts are sold worldwide and 520 million pairs of jeans are sold in the United States.

Production of one T-shirt takes 700 gallons of water and one pair of jeans takes 1,500 gallons. (Wallander, 2012)

OBJECTIVES

- Explain how textile materials and apparel are classified for the purpose of documenting items as they proceed through complex international supply chains.
- Examine the technology development and low-cost labor paradox that frustrates supply chain managers.
- Explore trade issues in the textiles and apparel business.

Today's textile and apparel professionals work in supply chains made up of an interwoven complex of firms, ranging from individual cotton growers to global business conglomerates. Many view the textile and apparel business from a linear perspective, comparing the industry with a pipeline of connected processes from growing or producing fibers used as raw material for textiles to distributing finished apparel products to the ultimate consumer. However, in today's marketplace this linear view is too simplistic. The magnitude and the complexity of the business defy such a singular orientation. Today's global textile complex may be better described as a matrix of interconnected structures and activities that provides multiple venues for designing, producing, marketing, merchandising, and distributing textiles and apparel and that begins and ends with consumers. In this chapter we introduce the Harmonized System for identifying textiles and apparel products, utilize the NAICS system of industry classification to understand the product flow of the apparel component of the textile complex, move on to the paradox of technology development and demand for low-cost labor, and complete the industry overview with an introduction to trade issues associated with textiles and apparel.

apparel knitting mill a manufacturing facility that interloops yarns to produce garments without producing the fabric first; can produce sweaters, tops, scarves, hats, dresses, and underwear

apparent consumption an estimation of domestic consumption of people in a country or region based on levels of domestic production, imports, and exports (production + imports – exports)

converter fabric mill that specializes in application of yarn and fabric finishes

cut-and-sew apparel manufacturing a cut-and-sew apparel production that performs both preproduction and production processes

distressed goods merchandise that is not saleable at the intended price; seconds, overruns, samples, last season's goods, retailer returns, and so on

domestic production products made in the same country in which they are sold

dyeing the process of combining fibers, yarns, or fabrics with a coloring substance and creating a bond

fabric finishing processes that convert greige goods into completed fabric

fiberweb fabrics made directly from fibers; traditionally called nonwovens

flexible production system quickly and efficiently producing a variety of styles at low volume per style, with zero defects; often uses single-ply cutters and modular systems with stand-up sewing

floor ready garment producers attach retailer-specified tickets and labels to garments that are ready for display before shipping them out

greige goods fabrics whose fibers are still their natural color and texture; usually require additional processes to improve aesthetics and performance

Harmonized System (HS) the international Harmonized Commodity Description and Classification System, developed by the World Customs Organization

Harmonized Tariff Schedule of the United States (HTS) the classifications of goods used to determine tariffs on specific products imported into the United States

import penetration the amount of consumption in a country or region that is provided by imports (imports ÷ consumption)

knit fabric fabric made by intertwining yarn or thread in a series of connected loops rather than by weaving

knit outerwear sweaters (jumpers), jackets, and coats

layette complete outfit of apparel for babies from birth until he or she begins walking; may also include bedding

logistics the process of planning, implementing, and controlling the efficient, effective flow and storage of goods, services, and related information from point of origin to point of consumption for the purpose of conforming to customer requirements

manufactured fibers made from chemical compounds; examples include nylon, polyester, acrylic, polypropylene, and spandex; also known as man-made fibers

mass customization the integration of information technology, automation, and team-based flexible manufacturing to produce a variety of products and services based on individual customer demand

Multifiber Arrangement (MFA) international trade agreement that allowed the quantity of textile and apparel trade to be regulated through quotas established in bilateral agreements between nations

natural fibers cotton, wool, silk, and linen as well as other vegetable and animal fibers

nano used loosely means "small" or "short-time"; nano in technology means application of extremely small things to make changes that can be used across many science fields

nanotechnology application of extremely small item, entity, or thing to make changes in performance or behavior that can be used across many science fields

North American Industry Classification System (NAICS) a standardized system for collecting, analyzing, and publishing statistical data involving trade among Canada, Mexico, and the United States; NAICS data includes textiles and apparel and many other products

Office of Textiles and Apparel (OTEXA) a division of US Department of Commerce that monitors textile trade throughout the globe in terms of both quantity and value

printing the localized application of color to the surface of a yarn or fabric

productivity a ratio of the outputs of a production process to the inputs; a measure of performance toward an established goal

radio frequency identification (RFID) a new generation of wireless tracking bar code systems being used for identifying and tracking products, cartons, and containers with tags attached to the objects

real-time immediately available when data are collected

square meter equivalent (SME) a means of measuring quantities of fabric and garments that are being exported or imported

sweatshop a firm with poor working conditions, very low pay, safety violations, and often inhumane treatment of employees

textile mill a manufacturing facility where yarns or fabrics are produced

textile product mill a manufacturing facility that produces fabric and uses it to create consumable goods, including carpets, rugs, curtains, draperies, and bed and bath products

thread a special form of yarn designed for use in sewing cut fabric pieces together to form garments or other products

transparency of information open communication among all participants within a system

underwear and sleepwear knitting mill a manufacturing facility in which products are produced by cutting and sewing knit fabrics

Universal Product Code (UPC) a bar code system for identifying and tracking products or containers

woven fabrics produced by interlocking two or more sets of yarns at right angles

yarn a continuous strand produced by twisting fibers together

BACKGROUND OF THE TEXTILE AND APPAREL SUPPLY MATRIX

As shown in the supply chain model in Chapter 1, the textile and apparel business is driven by consumer response to fashion and technology. When economies grow, consumer well-being usually improves, and the potential to satisfy consumer fashion wants and needs increases, causing growth for business firms within the soft goods industry. Technology not only creates the demand for styling change through rapid communications of fashion ideas, but also provides some of the tools for satisfying product demands through integration of new production processes.

National economies that have been slower to develop have looked to developed nations and adopted some of the practices that enabled the growth of the stronger industries. In many cases, participation in the textile and apparel industry has provided an avenue for economic growth. For example, the relatively low requirements for capital investment to start up a small apparel production facility and the availability of quantities of low-cost labor around the world have long provided the climate for developing nations to enter the global market. Shifts in the locations of textile and apparel production and the quantity of that production are tracked carefully as indicators of the economic health of individual nations.

The World Trade Organization (WTO) is the only global organization that deals with the rules of trade among nations. The WTO's main purpose "is to ensure that trade flows as smoothly, predictably, and freely as possible" (World Trade Organization, 2010). As of July 2014, WTO had 160 member countries and 24 observer governments, for a total of 184 countries addressing macro- and micro-issues of trade. At the center of the multilateral trading system are the WTO's agreements, negotiated and accepted by participating nations. These agreements are essentially contracts for international commerce among member nations. The system began as a series of negotiations, called rounds, held under GATT (General Agreement on Tariffs and Trade). They dealt mostly with quota and tariff reductions and other areas, such as antidumping. The Uruguay Round led to the WTO's creation in 1995. Additional rounds of talks began in 2000 in Doha, Qatar, and are still ongoing.

The WTO and the **Office of Textiles and Apparel (OTEXA)** in the US Department of Commerce monitor textile trade throughout the globe, using both quantitative amounts and dollar value to measure and compare production from country to country and from year to year. The Bureau of Industry and Security (BIS), in the Department of Commerce, also monitors the health and competitiveness of the US textile and apparel business.

Throughout this text, measures of trade and levels of production were selected and rigorously edited to facilitate your comprehension of the magnitude of and the business activity within the textile and apparel complex without throwing an overwhelming volume of data at you. Because the figures are constantly changing and may quickly become outdated, readers are encouraged to seek updated information that is readily available on the Internet. Using sources cited in tables and discussion can often lead to updated information. However, it is important to put on your critical thinking hat before interpreting, applying, or reporting the information. Also, be sure you understand the definitions of terms as they are used in the source so that you can use the data appropriately.

The quantity of trade between nations may be measured in number of units or in monetary value. Number of units may be determined by weight, size, or number of pieces or cartons, depending on the product. The number of units of woven fabrics is usually measured in square yards or square meters, whereas narrow fabrics used for trims, such as ribbon, are measured in linear yards or meters. Square yard or square meter measurements are used rather than linear meters or linear yards to measure woven fabrics, because the width of frequently used fabrics can vary from 27-inch silk brocades, to 72-inch polyester suiting, to 144-inch sheeting and drapery fabrics. Number of units of yarns and knit fabrics may be measured by weight, in pounds or kilograms. Findings, such as buttons, are measured in dozens or by the gross, or they may be sold by weight.

Apparel is measured in units (number of garments and/or accessories) and in monetary value. Data may also report total value or number of products in a shipment, or both. The only time apparel is likely to be measured by weight is for export of used garments from developed countries to be put on sale in newly developing countries. Monetary value is often determined by the cost of the product at the point ownership changes; in the case of international trade, ownership usually changes when it is shipped to the buyer.

US dollars have different value from Australian dollars and Canadian dollars, and most other countries also have their own currencies. For reporting purposes in the United States, international monetary values are usually converted to dollars via exchange rates. The reader is cautioned to be vigilant in interpreting data, because there has been some movement toward the use of the euro instead of the US dollar as the base currency by some record-keeping agencies.

The interaction between domestic production and imports on actual consumption within developed countries continues to this day to be a concern. Textile and apparel firms in the United States and other developed countries seek products from other parts of the world for multiple reasons, including securing products at lower costs and providing consumers with an increased array of product choices. However, the sheer volume of apparel products being imported into developed countries is causing grave concerns for some parts of the textile and apparel complex.

Increasing imports creates more competition for domestic production. Many imported products often have lower prices (because of lower labor costs) than similar domestically produced goods. The result in developed countries is usually reduction in **domestically produced goods**. This puts blue-collar workers within the developed nation out of their jobs, leaving them with no income to purchase any product, let alone apparel. At the same time, sourcing materials and production offshore and managing complex supply chain and logistics creates more white-collar professional jobs in the industry, not to mention jobs that involve global brand management, including design and product development for different markets (Asia, North America, Europe, etc.).

Considering wages relative to productivity during the 1980s, the United States and Italy were found to be the most competitive with developing countries. At that time, Hong Kong, South Korea, and Taiwan were the "big three" textile and apparel exporters. It has been normal for developing countries to be less productive per hour of labor than developed countries, given lower levels of literacy, technology, and infrastructure. Thus, for apparel producers with higher labor rates to compete with low-wage countries making similar products, they must have higher productivity per hour. Germany, France, the United Kingdom (UK), and the Netherlands felt the effects of low-cost imports as early as the late 1960s. Between 1965 and 1985, employment in textiles and apparel in these countries declined 51 percent, from 4.1 million to 2 million workers. Japan experienced similar declines, and the United States and Italy had declines between 15 and 20 percent (Cline, 1990). These declines in employment were not entirely due to imports. In Europe and Japan, textile and apparel firms were increasing **productivity** through additional investment in technology. As a result, workers produced more goods each hour of each day. Productivity was increasing faster than markets were expanding. In contrast, US and Italian consumers continued to increase demand, supporting ongoing growth in output into the 1990s (Cline, 1990).

During the 1980s a specialized team initiated by the **American Apparel Manufacturers Association (AAMA)** also helped develop the methods and technology for what came to be known as **Quick Response (QR)**. Quick Response became a comprehensive business strategy incorporating time-based competition, agility, and partnering to optimize apparel production systems, distribution systems, and service to customers. QR business systems were a stimulus toward improving applications of technology, production efficiency, and customer service to help compensate for higher wage rates being paid in developed countries. The AAMA also formed a Supply Chain Leadership Committee made up of AAMA members, college and university faculty members, executives of apparel firms, and leaders in the then-developing world of computer technology. Part of this committee's role was to spread the word about new methods of operation for planning, developing, and presenting textiles and apparel. The methods and strategies developed and publicized by AAMA and other similar organizations in other countries were important foundation pieces to the fast and efficient supply chains that are in use today.

These systems came into use in the 1980s and 1990s when the US apparel industry began suffering from imports of textiles and apparel from developing countries. The focus of QR was to *reduce lead times* while improving quality, reducing cost, and eliminating non-value-added waste of time while simultaneously increasing market competitiveness and market share by serving customers better and faster. These systems used what now are considered to be "simple" computer applications to improve speed of production as well as to facilitate record keeping and communication throughout the supply chain to reduce time required for product development, production, and distribution. Much more elaborate electronic systems are now used throughout the world, for example, adaptations of PLM, ERP, and Gerber with more elaborate computer applications continually being developed.

For the United States and several other developed countries, output of textiles and apparel continued to increase as employment decreased until the mid-1990s because of improvement in methods and technology. At the same time, however, imports from developing countries were increasing much faster than domestic production. The textile component of the US industry was regarded as more internationally competitive than the apparel component. It was not until the late 1990s that the textiles suffered declines in production because of import competition. Since then, the value of US apparel exports to the rest of the world decreased from $6,540.4 million in 2001 to $3,761.7 million in 2008 and then increased again to $6,080.9 million in 2014 stimulated by trade agreements that went into effect.

Table 3.1 presents statistics on US apparel exports and imports. Apparel exports decreased slowly from 2001 to 2007 and then nearly regained the loss by 2014. Some

TABLE 3.1

VALUE OF US APPAREL EXPORTS AND IMPORTS IN MILLIONS OF DOLLARS

	Exports	Imports
2001	$ 6,540.4	$ 56,460.4
2002	$ 5,643.1	$ 56,963.0
2003	$ 5,162.9	$ 61,162.1
2004	$ 4,629.7	$ 64,767.7
2005	$ 4,471.2	$ 68,713.3
2006	$ 4,317.0	$ 71,629.8
2007	$ 3,664.9	$ 73,922.6
2008	$ 3,761.7	$ 71,568.4
2009	$ 3,945.9	$ 63,104.7
2010	$ 4,519.9	$ 71,398.8
2011	$ 5,153.9	$ 77,659.1
2012	$ 5,539.1	$ 76,811.5
2013	$ 5,863.3	$ 79,797.3
2014	$ 6,080.9	$ 81,781.0

Source: Based on Office of Textiles and Apparel. (2013). "U.S. Imports of Textiles and Apparel." Retrieved February 20, 2015, from http://otexa.trade.gov/msrpoint.htm

of that recovery was related to new trade agreements. During the same time period the value of US apparel imports increased steadily from $56,460.4 million in 2001 to $81,781 million in 2014. The US population was growing but not as fast as the apparel imports, so consumers, on average, were spending more on clothes each year throughout the time period.

Now consider consumption. With **apparent consumption** (production + imports – exports), the assumption is that everything that is produced and imported and is not exported is consumed (that is why it is called *apparent* consumption). This is not likely the case. One of the serious problems in the retail community is excess inventory. That is what keeps off-price stores, such as Marshall's and T.J. Maxx, in business. The source of their inventory is primarily **distressed goods** that became distressed because they were not sold on clearance by the retailer that contracted, produced, or imported the apparel. Sometimes, the merchandise never even left the distribution center of the original retail owner. The amount of retail inventory that goes unsold to customers is not a published number, but it could be as much as 10 to 20 percent. The excess inventory originates in part from foreign sourcing of garments, in which resupplying is not an option. Many retail buyers believe they are financially better off with excess inventory when the product has a low price per unit than with lost sales because of stock outs. A country's or an industry's **import penetration** (imports ÷ apparent consumption × 100) is the amount of consumption that is provided by imports. Import penetration can be calculated based either on number of units or value. Although the results would be different, these figures would be similar enough to report with confidence that apparent import penetration of apparel is now more than 95 percent and has been creeping ever higher each year.

So which number best represents the level of import penetration? The number calculated based on units or the number calculated based on value? Both are mathematically acceptable, but they provide different kinds of information. Either could be useful, depending on the situation. In general, if you want to make a case for the successful survival of domestic industry in the face of import competition, the value figures might suit your purpose. If you want to make a case to Congress for import protection, use the unit-based numbers, because those figures emphasize the magnitude of the import problem. Is it unethical to use data in this way? That is another matter. For now, the point is that a data set can tell many stories, and it is up to the reader and the listener to analyze critically what assumptions are being made, what is being said, and what is being omitted or ignored.

Every textile and apparel professional has to communicate information about specific textile and apparel products. This has to be done in a systematic manner for multiple businesses in multiple countries so that everyone involved in the supply chain understands exactly the quantities and types of garments involved, including styles, sizes, and colors. Changes in the methods of doing business, along with the necessity of establishing record-keeping methods that are compatible for all global partners, have precipitated new ways of identifying products and classifying them.

SYSTEMS FOR PRODUCT CLASSIFICATION

The Harmonized Commodity Description and Code System generally referred to as **Harmonized System or HS** is a multipurpose international product nomenclature developed by the World Customs Organization (WCO). The system is used by more than 200 countries as a basis for the collection of international trade statistics and as a foundation for their tariff schedules. The system is also used for harmonization of customs and trade procedures. The HS is a universal economic language and code for goods and an indispensable tool for international trade. More than 98 percent of the merchandise in international trade, including textiles and apparel, has long been classified in terms of HS (United States Trade Representative (n.d.)).

The World Customs Organization's HS classifies a product by assigning it a six-digit tariff classification number, based on its name, use, the material used in its construction, or a combination of these. In addition to providing a means of identifying specific products, the HS is used to collect data on country of origin, quantity, and monetary value of specific textile and apparel imports. For the United States, which expands the numbering system to ten digits, the information regarding exports varies significantly from that of imports and is maintained on a separate schedule within the **Harmonized Tariff Schedule of the United States (HTS)**. The HTS is based on the HS and is the primary resource for determining tariff classifications for goods imported into and exported from the United States (Harmonized Tariff Schedule of the United States, 2008). The HTS is divided into 99 chapters and contains numerous appendices and indexes. Textile products are assigned to Chapters 50 through 60 while apparel products are identified in Chapters 61 (knit) and 62 (woven). The system is maintained by the US International Trade Commission (USITC). Tariffs on the products imported are collected by US Customs and Border Protection (CBP), an agency within the Department of Homeland Security. Annual updates of specific information in this system can be found online, and anyone who considers using the schedules for calculating tariff costs is strongly encouraged to make use of these updates.

When the United States, Canada, and Mexico joined to form the North American Free Trade Agreement (NAFTA) in 1994, they had a serious problem documenting the types and quantities of products they produced and traded in the supply chains linking the countries. Mexico and Canada use the metric system, and the United States is the only country in the world that uses the English system of measurement. Therefore, based on HS, the three countries developed the **North American Industry Classification System (NAICS)** to standardize the identification of textiles and apparel and other products in a manner consistent with the world market. Figure 3.1 gives examples of NAICS codes for the manufacturing sector of textiles and apparel.

The NAICS classification system facilitates communication between firms and agencies and provides the record-keeping capabilities needed to make many business decisions, especially those related to measuring productivity levels and unit labor costs. NAICS also explains why some job categories are defined as they are within the industry. For example, because hosiery and sweaters can be produced directly from yarn into finished apparel products, knit goods designers can skip the fabric production level; in fact, they are often hired and trained separately from designers for other apparel product categories. The rationale is that some knit products are produced by different methods, in different environments and require business practices that are different from those for other apparel products. NAICS was designed to accommodate the similar needs of three countries: Canada, Mexico, and the United States. It was updated in 2007 and 2012, and an update is in progress for 2017. See Case 3.1.

Figure 3.1

Graph of the components of NAICS. NAICS is an example of an industry classification system used by a trading bloc to identify imported and exported products. NAICS is compatible with the Harmonized System (HS), which is used in global trade. *Source: US Census Bureau (n.d.). 2007 Numerical List of Manufactured and Mineral Products. Retrieved December 28, 2015 from https://www.census.gov/prod/ec07/07numlist/07numlist.html.*

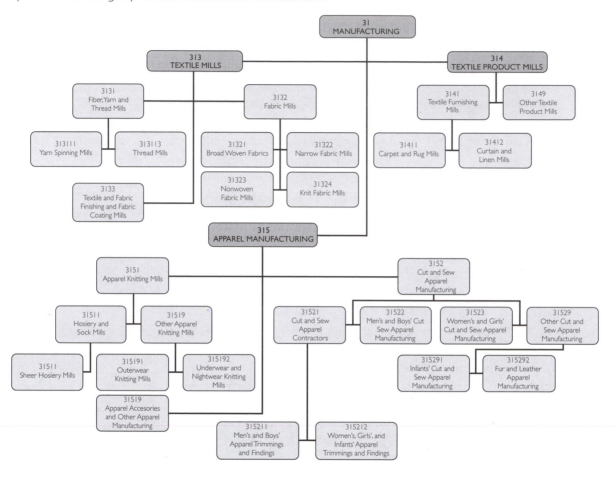

TEXTILE MILLS (NAICS 313)

Textile mills are manufacturing facilities of different types that process and produce fibers, yarns, fabrics, and finishes. Textile mills are businesses that own their own machinery. The following discussion is organized according to types of production processes and products, as reflected by NAICS codes.

Fiber, Yarn, and Thread Mills (NAICS 3131)

As mentioned in Chapter 1, the raw material in textiles is *fiber*. Fibers are divided into two basic categories: natural and manufactured. **Natural fibers** include cotton, wool, silk, and flax as well as a number of less widely used fibers, such as ramie, jute, cashmere, and mohair. Natural fibers are grown as vegetable or animal agricultural products and have been important to agricultural trade throughout the globe for centuries; NAICS classifies natural fibers under agriculture rather than manufacturing. Of these fibers, only cotton and wool are produced in significant quantities in the United States, so garments made domestically of other natural fibers are typically made of imported fibers.

THE DEVELOPMENT OF NAICS

The United States began using a new industry classification system on April 9, 1997, when the Office of Management and Budget (OMB) announced its decision to adopt the North American Industry Classification System (NAICS; pronounced "nayks") as the industry classification system used by the statistical agencies of the United States. NAICS replaced the 1987 US Standard Industrial Classification (SIC). The SIC was established in the 1930s to promote uniformity and compatibility of data collected and published by agencies within the US government, state agencies, trade associations, and research organizations. The SIC was revised periodically to reflect changes in the economic structure of the United States, the last revision having taken place in 1987. NAICS was designed to accommodate the similar needs of three countries: Canada, Mexico, and the United States. NAICS includes descriptions of more than 20,000 industries, including manufacturers and retailers. NAICS was updated in 2007 and 2012, and an update is in progress for 2017.

NAICS is the first-ever North American industry classification system. Representatives from Canada, Mexico, and the United States collaborated to develop a system to provide comparable statistics across the three countries. NAICS also allows for increased comparability with the International Standard Industrial Classification System (ISIC, Revision 3), developed and maintained by the United Nations. NAICS has a unique system for classifying business establishments. This production-oriented, industry-based system means that statistical agencies produce data that can be used for measuring productivity, unit labor costs, and the capital intensity of production, constructing input–output relationships and estimating employment–output relationships and other statistics. This method reflects the structure of today's global economy, including the emergence and growth of the service sector and new and advanced technologies.

NAICS is a six- to ten-digit system. It provides comparability among the three countries at the five-digit level. Additional digits are used to refine the definition of the industries involved. Ten digits are required to identify individual products. Examples of the meaning of the ten digits include the following:

- 2-digit = manufacturing sector (31)
- 3-digit = subsectors, including textile mills (313), textile product mills (314), and apparel manufacturing (315)
- 4-digit = industry groups, including fabric mills (3132), textile furnishing mills (3141), apparel knitting mills (3151), and cut-and-sew apparel manufacturing (3152)
- 5-digit = industry, including broad-woven fabric (31321), curtain and linen mills (31412), hosiery and sock mills (31511), and cut-and-sew apparel contractors (also called vendors; 31521)
- 6-digit = national, including sheer hosiery mills (315111) and infant cut-and-sew manufacturing (315291)
- 10-digit = required to identify individual products

With practice, the logic of the numbering system becomes second nature. Apparel professionals can read numbers as if they were words on the page.

Source: US Bureau of the Census. (2014). "North American Industry Classification System." Retrieved January 2, 2014, from http://www.census.gov/eos/www/naics

1. Why is it necessary to have an industry classification system like NAICS?
2. Would facing the need of learning a system as complex as NAICS discourage you from becoming a part of the importing and exporting component of the North American apparel industry?

Concentrations of agriculture producing natural fiber are found in diverse pockets throughout the globe. For example, significant quantities of cotton are grown in China and India (6,000 metric tons), the United States (3,000 metric tons), as well as Pakistan, Brazil, and several other countries. Silk fiber is produced in areas such as China, India, Japan, Brazil, and Korea, where mulberry leaves required for feeding the silk larva are readily available. Silk represents less than 0.2 percent of the textile fiber market. Wool harvested from sheep is produced primarily in Australia, Argentina, the United States, the United Kingdom, and South Africa.

Manufactured fibers, both cellulosic (acetate and rayon) and synthetic (nylon, polyester, acrylic, polypropylene, and spandex), are produced in many areas of the world. Production of manufactured fibers requires significant investment of capital and access to technology. These fibers are relatively new to the marketplace; much of their development as consumer products did not occur until the late 1940s, after World War II. The use of these fibers has skyrocketed since their introduction, both in volume and value.

Bamboo is natural fiber that was introduced into global trade nearly ten years ago. It is now used in forestry, the wood industry, the paper industry, and the textile industry. Although bamboo is itself a natural fiber, it is produced as a textile product in the form of manufactured rayon. Therefore, the United States now requires that bamboo be labelled as "rayon" or "rayon from bamboo" when used for producing outerwear, underwear, socks, and bulletproof vests. The biggest use of bamboo may be in disposable diapers and related items that are now available in a variety of brands but it is also used in towels and blankets. The US Federal Trade Commission has been charging some companies of being deceptive in their claims of bamboo's environmental friendliness, because some of the processes required to make it usable as a textile product are not environmentally friendly.

Among synthetic fiber producers, horizontal integration (mergers between companies with the same target market) has continued to concentrate technical expertise into fewer larger companies, many of them located in China and a few in Vietnam. It has also concentrated corporate assets and the ability to do fundamental research for new product development, which has been especially important to the development of synthetic fibers. Mergers among already known global textile companies have produced the largest textile companies ever known. For example, "INVISTA is an independently managed, wholly owned subsidiary of Koch Industries, Inc. In 2004, subsidiaries of Koch Industries acquired INVISTA from E.I. duPont de Nemours and Company. Invista, formerly DuPont Textiles and Interiors, was combined with KoSa, a producer of commodity and specialty polyester fibers, polymers, and intermediates. KoSa had been a Koch affiliate since 1998. One of the largest privately held companies in the world, Koch Industries is primarily a family owned company, built on values such as integrity, humility and a desire to add real, long-term value to society. Koch companies have a presence in about 60 countries and employ more than 100,000 people worldwide with about 60,000 of those in the United States" (INVISTA, n.d.).

Koch had already owned KoSa, which had purchased the worldwide Trevira polyester business from the German manufacturer Hoechst in 1998, and by forming a consortium between KoSa and Grupo Xtra, of Mexico City, Koch became the world's largest polyester producers by 1998 (Koch Industries, 1998). When Koch merged that consortium business into INVISTA, it became one of the largest textile firms in the world.

Two other textile firms that survived the turmoil of the development of the synthetic textiles business include the following:

- Formosa Plastics Group of Taiwan is one of the largest textile fiber producers in the world and has now diversified into other related products.
- Far East Textile Group Co. Inc., based in Hong Kong, is a producer of high-grade garment materials as well as production equipment.

Yarn-Spinning Mills (NAICS 313111)

Yarns are the basic building blocks of woven and knit fabrics and other products. Staple yarn is produced by twisting fibers together; filament yarns are produced by extrusion. Pure, natural fiber yarns are produced to make things like 100 percent cotton fabrics and 100 percent wool fabrics. Natural and manufactured fibers are also mixed together to form blended yarns. The most common blend today is a mixture of cotton and polyester, used extensively in fabrics for apparel and home use. A quick search on the Internet came up with the following blends that might be found in "partially cotton" yarns and fabrics:

- Cotton and ramie
- Bamboo and cotton
- Cotton and Lycra
- Cotton and silk
- Linen and cotton
- Hemp and cotton
- Soy and organic cotton

(Note: The product listed first in the description usually represents the highest percentage component in the fabric.)

The cotton-and-ramie yarns, found sometimes in sweaters and woven fabrics, came into use during the latter part of the twentieth century, when quota limits were set on the amount of cotton that could be brought into the United States from China. Because there were no quota limits on ramie (a rather stiff cellulose fiber) at that time, blends of cotton and ramie were used to avoid going over the cotton quota on imports; thus, with the blends, more sweaters could be imported. The result was the development of ramie as a widely used textile fiber for apparel. Before that time, ramie was rarely seen in the United States.

Some fibers are spun into yarns in mills close to where the fibers are produced, but most are shipped in raw form to areas where production machinery is readily available. Yarns are spun at thread mills. Major factors in the determination of where the thread mills are located include access to ease of transport, intended end use of the yarns, and economic conditions related to technology.

Thread Mills (NAICS 313113)

Thread is a special form of yarn. It is produced by treating and finishing the yarn to make it strong, even with the fine diameter that is used in sewing cut fabric pieces together to form garments or other products. Although seemingly insignificant to the outsider, thread is a critical component related to the quality and durability of finished textile and apparel products.

One major manufacturer of thread products is American & Efird, Inc., better known as A&E. A&E's headquarters are located in Mount Holly, North Carolina. In 2015, its supply network included manufacturing centers in twenty countries and service centers in forty-four countries with thread products sold in ninety countries (American & Efird, 2009). A&E produces a variety of thread and related products for use in apparel, upholstery, home furnishings, and footwear. Variations of their thread products are packaged in numerous formats, for example, on bobbins, spools, and cones suitable for commercial production and home sewing use (e.g., Mettler and Maxi-Lock consumer products).

Fabric Mills (NAICS 3132)

Fabrics are produced by interlocking yarns made of fiber using mechanical and chemical means. **Woven fabrics** and **knit fabrics** constitute a significant portion of fabric production destined for use in apparel, although **fiberweb fabrics**, traditionally called **nonwovens**, continue to be a fast-growing category. Broad-woven fabrics for apparel range in width from approximately 27 inches to 144 inches. Narrow-woven fabrics include laces, ribbons, and braids used for trim. Fiberweb nonwoven fabrics are now widely used for garment interfacings, gloves, industrial apparel, protective clothing, shoe components, and for disposable products, such as diapers and single-use hospital gowns, scrubs, and other protective garments. Fiberweb fabrics made from manufactured (synthetic) materials are chemically inert, easy to sew, have good dimensional stability, and have nonravelling edges. Knit-fabric mills often make either filling-knit or warp-knit fabrics, because each requires different types of machinery and yarns.

Since the advent of manufactured fiber products in the mid-twentieth century, fabrics are produced in more areas of the globe than was possible when the industry was hampered by geographical limitations in agricultural production, transportation, and power sources to run the looms. Over time, fabric production has tended to follow the growth patterns of the industrialization of nations and has contributed heavily to the early growth of many national economies. For example, during the 1700s, England imported cotton and wool from its colonies India and Australia and flax for linen from Ireland to produce enough fabric not only to supply its own population but also to sell to settlers in the United States and other places. As the United States began to move from an agrarian society to industrialization during the 1800s, the textile industry led the way. At the same time, Italy has long imported silk from China for production of fabrics for apparel and home furnishings that are still highly sought throughout the world.

More recently, as apparel production has increased in developing countries, fabric production has followed; therefore, there have been decreases in apparel fabric production in developed countries. For example, during the 1990s, much of jeans production moved from the United States to Mexico. Many denim mills followed, including Cone Mills, whose goal was to be the largest denim producer in the world (Figure 3.2). By 2014, Cone Mills operated facilities in the United States, Mexico, and China. Cone

Figure 3.2

Processing denim to achieve fashionable color and texture effects.

Mills functions as part of International Textile Group, owned by WL Ross & Co., which also owns Cone's former competitor Burlington Industries. In the United States, denim production increased until 1989, when it peaked, and has since declined to below the 1989 level but had some recovery in 2014.

Textile and Fabric Finishing and Fabric Coating Mills (NAICS 3133)

A majority of fabrics used in apparel tend to be produced as greige goods. **Greige goods** are made up of fibers that are still their natural color and texture and that require additional processes to improve aesthetics and performance. Whereas mills that make yarn and fabric and convert greige goods to finished textiles are considered vertically integrated textile mills, those that specialize in fabric finishing processes only may be referred to as converters. **Converters** buy greige goods from a fabric mill and apply the finishes, such as dyeing and printing.

Dyeing and **printing** produce colors, and **fabric finishing** processes change hand or simplify product care. The transition from natural to chemical dyes and the development of finishes to improve the comfort and ease of care of textile products have contributed heavily to more recent changes within the textile industry. Many finishing processes require complex manufacturing techniques or significant investment of capital in the technology used to produce them, or both. Another consideration is the need for large quantities of fresh water for these processes. For these reasons, more economically developed nations tend to excel in new dyeing and finishing techniques. Countries such as the United States, Germany, and Japan led the way, but Taiwan and South Korea moved into these areas of specialization as their economies improved in the latter part of the twentieth century. See Case 3.2 for a few examples of the newest forms of technology for textiles and apparel.

TEXTILE PRODUCT MILLS (NAICS 314)

Textile product mills that produce home furnishing textiles—including carpets and rugs, curtains and draperies, and bed and bath products—are important components of the textile business. A unique aspect of textile product mills is that they usually produce finished goods instead of materials for other firms to convert into finished goods. For example, a mill producing sheets or towels generally cuts and hems the fabric and then packages the finished goods ready for sale to ultimate consumers.

The rates of sale of home furnishing textiles tend to reflect rates of sale of homes. During the 1990s, when textile production was decreasing in developed countries, carpet production increased in the United States by 46 percent. The 1990s was a very active period of home building in the United States. Bedding and bath textile production peaked during the mid-1990s and declined as the country experienced a corresponding increase in imports, making towels and bedding from distant nations more visible in the US marketplace (ATMI, 2004). By the late 2000s overall carpet sales were down anywhere from 20 percent to 30 percent as the market faced a weakening economy, with declining new home sales and increasing foreclosures of existing homes (Floor Biz, 2009). By late 2012, however, there was a beginning of improvement in housing sales and some improvement in carpet sales in 2013. The carpet industry is the largest collector and recycler of plastic drinking bottles, accounting for more than 25 percent

NANOTECHNOLOGY APPLICATIONS FOR TEXTILES AND APPAREL

Nanotechnology can be used across many science fields. The application of nanotechnology to modify the behavior and serviceability of textiles has been around for about ten years, but only recently has it become common for it to be found in textiles and apparel now found in retail stores. **Nanotechnology** can modify characteristics of fibers and fabrics to make them perform in selected desirable ways.[1]

Nano used loosely means "small" or "short-time." Nano involves application of extremely small items, entities, or things to make changes in performance or behavior.[2] Conventional methods used to modify textile performance were not durable so they had to be frequently reapplied, for example, starching and ironing a dress shirt. Historically, nanotechnology was used in textiles mainly to impart stain-resistance or antibacterial properties. Garments made from nano textiles can now be purchased with many special properties described on the attached tags, though they may not mention the words "nano" or "nanotechnologies."

Teflon-like nano coatings can bond with a textile because *molecular hooks* of the coating can attach to fabric that can be used for garments. These new nano applications address the challenge of keeping clothes from getting dirty or smelly, for example, by using what is called the "lotus effect." Many plants, animals, and insects have tiny "nano-sized" hairs on their bodies that shed water, dirt, and contaminants. The tiny hairs protect them and keep them clean. These hairs were first discovered on lotus leaves, so this form of protection has become known as the "lotus effect."

The lotus effect is achieved by using teflon-like nano coatings that can bond with a textile because *molecular hooks* in the coating can attach to a variety of fabrics that can be used in garments. The hair-like structures in the coating repel water like a lotus leaf does. But because they are nano-sized, they don't make the fabric stiff. They keep the texture of whatever fabric is coated. A spill on a nano-enhanced garment can be renewed by simply shaking it or wiping it off. This is the lotus effect at work.

The lotus effect is now also being used to apply antibacterial agents to things like pillows, bedding, socks, shoes, and many other textile products. This is achieved by using silver nanoparticles in the nano coatings. These treatments can keep worn garments clean and odor free, thus greatly reducing the need for dry cleaning of garments such as suits, ties, coats, and protective overcoats.[2]

[1]Nano and Me. (n.d.). "Nano in Textiles and Clothing." Retrieved August 28, 2015, from www.nanoandme.org/nano-products/textiles-and-clothing/

[2]Kiron, M. I. (n.d.). "Application of Nanotechnology in Textile Industry." Retrieved September 2, 2015, from www.fibre2fashion.com/industry-article/printarticle.asp?article_id=4944&page=1

1. How might improved fitness, comfort, and care of nano fabrics be valued from the seller's and the buyer's perspectives?
2. How might nano fabrics contribute to efficiency in apparel production processes?

of the plastic bottle discards in the United States. The next challenge is to make the carpet-face fiber, namely polyester, even more sustainable (Spieler, 2013).

Yarns and fabrics are the basic materials used in the production of the two major categories of apparel: knit products and cut-and-sew apparel. The NAICS classifications of knit products are "hosiery and socks" and "other" knit apparel, containing the subcategories "outerwear," "underwear," and "sleepwear." Cut-and-sew products reflect the classification of all garments made by cutting knit or woven fabric into garment components and sewing garment components into finished apparel.

Apparel Knitting Mills (NAICS 3151)

Specialized knitting machines can produce jersey, tricot, or double-knit fabrics or finished knit garments made directly from yarns, including sweaters and socks. Growth in the production and use of knit-apparel products has been fueled by the introduction of new technology in knitting. It has significantly increased the capability of **apparel knitting mills** to produce a wide variety of finished products.

Hosiery-and-Sock Mills (NAICS 31511) and Sheer Hosiery Mills (NAICS 315111)

The line between the two areas of this category—hosiery and socks—seems blurred because of the vocabulary used to define the products. By 2011, pantyhose sales had been going down for 15 years, responding to more casual dress codes, leg tanners, open toe shoes, etc. The sources of hosiery products are also in a state of flux. Previously, the greatest quantities of socks sold in the United States were produced domestically or in Central America. Today, significantly greater quantities of socks are being imported from China and Taiwan. However, there are still some sock producers in the US, for example the Darn Tough Sock Factory in Northfield, Vermont. Darn Tough's best sock has 1,441 stitches per square inch and can stand 30,000 "rubs" from a machine (Martin, 2013). There also may be more than 100 other companies, mostly based in the US, that are now focused on using nanotechnology to make socks that do not smell, reduce bunions and blisters, and sell for about $25 dollars a pair.

By 2013, leggings took on a new role by using seamless apparel technology. "No sewing, no seams, no stitches. That's seamless. A specific knitting technology that uses specialized circular looms to develop garments that adapt perfectly to the body, making people forget they are actually wearing them. By eliminating the fabric cutting and sewing process, there is an optimization of the production process making seamless production a lot faster than conventional. There are also fewer product failures since most garment failures are due to seam failure, which translates into better quality pieces" (Bhosale, Jadhav, Pareek, & Eklahare, 2013).

For example, Leg Resource, Inc., a leading manufacturer and brand marketer of legwear categories, joined with Well Hosiery and Apparel, a leading US-based manufacturer of hosiery and seamless body wear as well as cut-and-sew apparel. Their goal was to address a new set of expectations related to "bodywear." Many other companies joined the trend. The result by 2015 was the rapidly developing new category of clothing called "seamless body wear" in a wide variety of applications including formal wear. It will be interesting to watch the fashion impact of this trend.

Other Apparel Knitting Mills (NAICS 31519)

All other apparel products made by the knitting process tend to fall into this loosely defined and encompassing category. The category includes products knitted directly from yarns and garments made from knitted fabrics.

Outerwear Knitting Mills (NAICS 315191)

Knit outerwear might be best identified as sweaters. Britain and its former colonies refer to sweaters as jumpers, which confuses some Americans, because in the United States a jumper is a completely different article of clothing. Therefore, the category for sweaters is "outerwear" so that everyone in the global community is clear on what is being discussed.

Figure 3.3

Workers in a knitting mill set up yarns by hand to make complex, beautiful knitted fabrics.

The category contains products of diverse styling and value, depending not only on their design but also on the fibers used for the yarns and whether the garment is made by machine or requires many hand operations. Today, the majority of sweaters marketed in the United States are machine made, with yarn composed of cotton, wool, or man-made fiber (such as acrylic), or a combination of these. In smaller quantities we find sweaters made of expensive natural fibers, such as cashmere and alpaca (Figure 3.3).

When evaluating the value of knit outerwear products, it becomes clear that the economic value of a large quantity of inexpensive cotton-ramie blend, machine-made (automatic, as opposed to manual) sweaters from China may be similar in dollar value to a small number of very expensive handmade or manually machine-made alpaca sweaters from Peru. When making comparisons of production from different parts of the world, it is critical to have an accurate description of the category and the products involved as well as figures of the overall volume and value of the products.

Underwear and Sleepwear Knitting Mills (NAICS 315192)

Products made in **underwear and sleepwear knitting mills** are manufactured by cutting and sewing knit fabrics. Because many of the products found in this category today are basic products that are sold year-round and considered staples in the overall wardrobe, they lend themselves well to mass-production methods, including the significant use of automation to reduce labor costs. The construction methods used to produce T-shirts and shorts or underpants are also quite simple, so these items tend to be relatively inexpensive to produce and market when compared with tailored suits or coats made of woven fabrics.

The major producers of branded men's underwear have long included Fruit of the Loom, Hanes, Calvin Klein, and Jockey, and there are now many more men's fashion brands. Great quantities of this product category are sourced by US retailers and manufacturers from Mexico, Central America, and China and sold by retailers in the United States. The rationale, as with many other products, is that merchandise costs are less if the product is manufactured offshore and shipped to the United States rather than if it is manufactured domestically.

CUT-AND-SEW APPAREL MANUFACTURING (NAICS 3152)

The remainder of apparel manufacturing is placed in the **cut-and-sew apparel manufacturing** classification in NAICS. The concept of manufactured ready-to-wear may be traced to Elias Howe, who patented the lock-stitch sewing machine in 1846 (Great Idea Finder, 2004). Some people credit Isaac Singer with this invention, but his activities were related to the development of sewing machines for home use.

Discussion of cut-and-sew apparel manufacturing is further complicated by the issue of whether a firm previously recognized as a manufacturer actually produces the finished products that bear its name now or if it contracts the production to outside vendors. NAICS has separated these two divisions, but the categories are becoming increasingly blurred, as many firms previously recognized as apparel manufacturers in the United States have farmed out so much of their actual production to other vendors that they now might be better identified as brand managers or brand vendors.

Cut-and-Sew Apparel Contractor (Vendor) (NAICS 31521)

As defined in Chapter 1, CMT (cut-make-trim) and full-package vendors are those firms that provide production services and produce apparel products for other firms, including branded label goods for other manufacturers or private label goods for retailers. Typically, vendors of garments are not visible to consumers because vendors are producing products that will carry brands representing other firms. The uniqueness of the position is that vendors are paid for their production by the business that sourced the products, the products carry the sourcing firm's label in them, and the vendor does not bear the responsibility for whether the garments produced actually sell in the retail environment (the sourcing firm bears that responsibility).

One of the larger manufacturers and vendors of apparel in the United States is Kellwood Company, headquartered in St. Louis, Missouri. Kellwood became part of Sun Capital Partners, Inc., in 2008; the firm specializes in producing branded and private label apparel products for women in a number of categories. Typical consumers are not aware of Kellwood, yet they would recognize many of the products Kellwood manufactures and contracts production for under a variety of labels, including Baby Phat, Briggs New York, Democracy, Jax, Jolt, My Michelle, Rebecca Taylor, Rewind, Sag Harbor, Sam Edelmon, Sangria, and XOXO (Kellwood, 2015). In 2015, Kellwood still partnered with those-brands and described itself as follows: "Kellwood designs, manufactures, and markets a growing collection of premier fashion brands across a broad range of consumer lifestyles" (Kellwood, 2015).

Men's and Boys' Apparel Trimmings and Findings (NAICS 315211) and Women's, Girls', and Infants' Trimmings and Findings (NAICS 315212)

The other materials needed for construction of garments, beyond fabric and thread, are commonly called trims, trimmings, or findings. This term represents the product category sometimes known as *notions* in the home sewing business. **Findings** include components constructed of fabric and other materials, such as interfacings, pocket bags, and linings; *closures* include buttons, zippers, Velcro tapes, and snaps; and *trims* and decorative embellishments include lace, beading, and embroidery.

YKK is an example of a global findings manufacturer that was founded in Japan, as a zipper manufacturer, in 1934. YKK now operates 108 companies in 71 countries worldwide and is considered the world's largest maker of zippers, producing thousands of varieties for use in a multitude of consumer products, from apparel to luggage to tents and awnings. YKK produces 65,000 miles of zipper chain annually (Morris, 2014). Zippers are critical to a garment's serviceability; like thread, a zipper can either make a garment functional or render it useless. Among its many products, the firm also makes hook and loop tapes that are used in many applications, from apparel to automobile upholstery, and a large assortment of snap fasteners.

Some firms that supply findings are wholesalers that assemble assortments of closures, support materials, and trims that serve a particular segment of the apparel market, such as children's wear or bras. Most of these products require specialized equipment or processes to be manufactured, because they come in a vast variety of sizes, styles, and volume. Demand for different products in the findings category is based on fashion trends from season to season, so it remains compatible with the most current fabrics and garment designs. Other firms offering findings are more diverse, providing a variety of materials or findings to manufacturers of finished garments. One of these companies is QST Industries Inc., headquartered in Chicago, Illinois, which claims to be the world's largest supplier of innovative men's, women's, and children's apparel construction components to the international garment industry (QST Industries, 2015). This firm produces interlining products for use in men's tailored garments, such as pocket bags and curtains for the waistbands of men's slacks, and a variety of products used as closures. QST has also added a line of ecofriendly products that help make garments "green." QST has expanded its business operations into more than thirty-two countries in all regions of the world.

Men's and Boys' Cut-and-Sew Apparel Manufacturing (NAICS 31522)

The earliest forms of apparel made in factories were men's garments. Men's apparel products have always been good candidates for assembly-line production, because they are more static in terms of style than women's fashion. For this reason, men's garments also tend to be produced in fewer, larger firms than women's apparel. Boys' products are styled and constructed with techniques and fabrics similar to those used for menswear, so they are often made in the same factories. This helps explain why product data for boys' apparel have been kept as a part of men's traditionally.

Tailored apparel, such as suits and coats, were the basis of this classification for many years, but lifestyle changes in American consumers have made sportswear, active sportswear, and uniforms the current growth product categories. The manufacturing techniques for making sportswear and active sportswear tend to be quite different from those of more traditional men's tailored apparel, using a variety of innovative textile materials and encompassing an amazing breadth of end products. Because the production methods required are often the same for both men's and women's products, they are usually manufactured in the same facilities, blurring the distinction between the men's and women's manufacturing categories. Nike and the Canadian lululemon athletica are two of the most profitable sportswear firms in today's marketplace, but many others in this field are readily recognizable to US consumers, including The North Face, Patagonia, Under Armour, and Columbia Sportswear.

Cintas Corporation, Red Kap, and Superior Uniform Group are three major manufacturers of uniforms as well as related services in North America. They provide everything from shirts and pants for your local car service personnel, to suits for hotel doormen and airline personnel, to restaurant cook hats and aprons, to nurses' uniforms, hospital scrubs, and other protective garments. Cintas is the largest corporation associated with uniform manufacturing in North America with operations in both the United States and Canada. Red Kap is a part of VF Imagewear, Inc., a division of VF Corporation. Superior Uniform Group is unique in this category in that it is focused on all dimensions of providing products and services associated with uniforms. All three of these companies have developed some unique methods of product development, renovation, and distribution, including garment rental programs.

One of the legends in US menswear apparel manufacturing for more than a century was Hart, Schaffner & Marx, of Chicago, Illinois, more recently known as Hartmarx. Hartmarx expanded beyond its original focus on men's tailored suits into other areas of production; in 2008 it filed for bankruptcy. The firm was then acquired by Britain's Emerisque Brands and SKNL North America in August 2009 (Tribune Staff, 2009). Hartmarx employed about 3,000 people nationwide, with 600 of them in Des Plaines, Illinois. The firm's most prominent brands included Hickey Freeman (luxury suits), Sansabelt (casual slacks), and Hart Schaffner Marx (suits). The company also produced licensed products for numerous brands, including the Bobby Jones, Jack Nicklaus, and Austin Reed labels. In 2013, Hart, Schaffner & Marx (Hartmarx) was taken over by Peerless Clothing, a Montreal, Canada-based company with factories in Canada and overseas; thus, the brand is still available in retail stores.

Women's and Girls' Cut-and-Sew Apparel Manufacturing (NAICS 31523)

Factory production of women's wear developed later than men's, starting its climb in 1917, during World War I. One reason for the delay in factory production of women's wear compared with men's products was that women's fashions tended to go out of date more quickly than men's (and they still do). But prior to World War I, women's garments were very complex and often required hours of handwork as well as great diversity of styling. Thus, firms producing products for women tended to be smaller and had shorter production runs (fewer garments at a time) than was typical with menswear. This smaller production capacity for individual styles still remains true for the highest price points and the most fashion-oriented products in women's fashion apparel.

However, in spite of ongoing fashion change, in the latter part of the twentieth century there was a trend toward consolidation in the women's apparel market, resulting in more mass-volume production and in consumer complaints of uniformity across the marketplace caused by the homogenization of styling made possible by mass production. As a result, the volatile nature of the women's fashion business has become something of a revolving door for brands and labels available in the market over time. For example, named after the original designer for the business, Liz Claiborne, Inc. continued to grow after its namesake retired. With headquarters in New York City, the firm had 15,000 employees in 2008 and sales of more than $3,984 million (Colbert, 2009). However, those figures reflected a downturn from previous years. In 2009, the firm was restructuring and announced that it would exit the department store channel for distribution of its Liz Claiborne New York brand, designed by Isaac Mizrahi, and distribute it only through the shopping channel QVC. At that time, the firm's other brands, Liz Claiborne and Claiborne, were only to be sold in the United States by JCPenney. The design process was retained by Liz Claiborne, Inc., but the sourcing, production, and distribution of these lines was the responsibility of JCPenney (Ayling, 2009). Unfortunately, by early 2015, the decision to join with JCPenny appeared to have turned into a final disaster for Liz Claiborne.

Assembly methods for preschool children's apparel are more similar to women's than to men's apparel. Garments for young children are often constructed in unisex mode, with the only differentiations existing in color, trim, and fabric choices. Although infant apparel is categorized separately, both preschool boys' and girls' apparel volume and financial data are grouped with women's apparel. Boys' products are shifted into the men's category at about 5 years old when boys usually enter school. Products for older girls are styled and produced by methods similar to those of women's.

Other Cut-and-Sew Apparel Manufacturing (31529)

The remaining categories of cut-and-sew apparel are classified "other." The products in this area are diverse, but each grouping is developed for a very specific target market or specialized product line.

Infants' Cut-and-Sew Apparel Manufacturing (NAICS 315291)

The infants' category reflects all the apparel specially designed and produced for children from birth until they begin to walk. Products in this category are often referred to in the business as the **layette**. These products are small in size, have very specialized use and care requirements, and are subject to a number of government supervisory safety regulations. The Consumer Product Safety Commission (CPSC), under the US Federal Trade Commission in the Department of Commerce, oversees many of the products in this division, watching for flammability standards, safety issues related to choking hazards, and lead content in zippers and other closures or trims.

Two of the larger brands found in the infants' product category continue to be Gerber and Carter's, but firms like Ralph Lauren and Under Armour also entered the children's clothing business. At Ralph Lauren Children's Wear you can buy a cotton poplin shirt and pique shorts for a little boy for $125, while Under Armour's prices are more in the $20 to $40 range. Great quantities of infant apparel are developed as private label products for specific retailers, such as JCPenney, Target, and Walmart, and are manufactured by vendors throughout the globe.

Fur and Leather Apparel Manufacturing (NAICS 315292)

Both fur and leather products are traditionally made of natural animal skins and are therefore classified together. Today, many synthetic fur and leather apparel products, made of specialized fabrics produced as yardage, are found in the market. Fur products require specialized construction techniques; leather products require equipment that is typically heavier than that used for general apparel construction. The acceptability of real fur products within the consumer market varies, depending on visibility and emphasis on animal rights. However, there has been a continuing market for fine fur garments with affluent customers for centuries. These consumers tend to see their fur garments as symbols of their success, and the market for them tends to increase when the economy is strong.

Leather apparel products are available in a variety of price points. Inexpensive leather products made from cowhide or synthetic leather are readily available from many countries. Low- to moderate-price leather products are produced in locations such as China, Morocco, Cyprus, and Argentina. Pigskin has traditionally been used for budget-price products and for shoe linings (Kunz, Albrecht, Stout, & Horne, 1992). Finer leather products, such as coats and jackets, are produced at moderate to higher price points out of calfskin and lamb. Fashionable calfskin products found in the United States were traditionally imported from workshops in and around Florence, Italy, but now are also available from other sources, including China.

Apparel Accessories and Other Apparel Manufacturing (NAICS 3159)

This catchall classification contains many diverse products, from simple scarves to hats and gloves. The volume of these products seems low when compared with all the other apparel products found in the marketplace. However, many of the items in this category are specialized, and firms that produce them are very viable contributors to the overall apparel business.

Gloves are one of the largest-volume categories in this classification. Polygenex International, Inc., located in Cary, North Carolina, is a vendor for a multitude of glove types. The firm's website (www.gloves-online.com) provides an extensive listing of gloves available in the market today. In addition to the typical knit and leather gloves used for cold weather and sports, such as golf and skiing, the list includes clean-room gloves, used for precision handling and assembly work; latex gloves, including the disposable varieties used for medical purposes; rubber gloves, including those used for household cleaning; and grip gloves, including those used for gardening.

NECESSITY OF PROFITS AND ADDRESSING THE TECHNOLOGY/LOW COST LABOR PARADOX

The rate of change for apparel manufacturers from localized markets to global perspectives increased significantly in the last two decades, owing to innovations in technology and increases in capital investment. Technology made it possible for apparel markets and supply chains to become globalized. At the same time, particularly for the labor-intensive apparel production sector, the pursuit of low-cost labor has driven the textile and apparel industry worldwide.

Worldwide, the textile and apparel industry operates primarily in an environment of capitalism. In a capitalistic system, firms are privately owned and operated for a profit. Firms have to make a profit in order to have funds to invest in the growth of the firm. Growth is essential for staying even, because operating expenses tend to increase every year, even if the firm has the same physical plant, investment in materials, and number of employees. Some small level of inflation is regarded as normal, but the result of inflation is loss of buying power. So, if the inflation increase is 3 percent a year, the firm will have to buy 3 percent fewer materials, survive with 3 percent fewer utilities, and do 3 percent less maintenance, and even though employees are paid the same salaries and wages as the previous year, the employees will be forced to acquire 3 percent fewer goods and services. Thus, the firm has to grow to stay even, but it can thrive only if it is able to increase revenue faster than the rate of inflation. Of course, another option is to reduce the cost of inputs if the resulting products could continue to be sold at the same price. These are the economic challenges that every textile and apparel firm faces in today's global market.

CASE 3.3

COATS INDUSTRIAL: SEWING THREAD, YARN, AND ZIP MANUFACTURER

With a rich heritage dating back to the 1750s, today, Coats is a market leader in the production and distribution of industrial yarns, thread, and textile consumer crafts. The company is at home in more than seventy countries and employs more than 20,000 people across six continents with one of its plants in Georgia. Coats Industrial Division provides thread, yarn, zips, and trims for industrial customers in apparel, footwear, and other sewn product markets.

The pioneering history of this company has supported an innovative culture in order to provide complementary and value-added products and services to the apparel and footwear industries. In addition, it continues to invest in innovative techniques to develop technical products in new areas such as aramids, tracer threads, and fiber optics to expand opportunities for the soft-goods business. Coats is the only truly global thread supplier, with more than seventy factories and eighty other facilities around the world. It employs an unrivalled panel of sewing and yarn application experts dedicated to providing technical assistance, advice, and training.

Coats Industrial brands are well known and it seeks to support company-wide understanding of its customers and to provide the products and services that meet their current and future needs. The strong relationships with business partners and consumers, coupled with the deep expertise of its people, are necessary to build trust and certainty in the supply chain. It uses a corporate responsibility approach to underpin commitment to safeguarding people and the environment while operating globally with a goal of applying high ethical business and employment standards.

Every year Coats Industrial products go into the making of 10 billion garments, 300 million pairs of shoes, and a diverse range of products from seat belts and handbags to sports balls and tents. The strength of the business comes from its ability to work closely with customers to develop thread, yarn, and zip solutions that add significant value to their products. Annually, more than one in five garments, 75 million airbags, 300 million pairs of shoes, 1 million teabags, and thousands of surgical operations are held together with Coats Industrial thread, and the company's products are sold in more than 100 countries.

1. How is it possible that a company that originated in 1750 is still a key component of today's textile and apparel industry?
2. How has Coats Industrial managed to assist apparel firms in addressing their technology–low-cost labor paradox?
3. Try to think of yourself as an apparel manufacturing entrepreneur. What might be the advantages and disadvantages of being associated with a company like Coats Industrial?

What is the technology–low-cost labor paradox? Communication and logistics technologies have made globalization possible. In the apparel industry, globalization has made it possible for sourcing firms to chase the lowest labor cost from country to country. Other realities are now creeping in because of rising fuel costs and pressure to shorten the time line from concept to consumer for many product lines. Stay tuned to the rapidly developing multi-forms of electronic communication for developments. Take a look at Case 3.3 for a view of how one of the textile and apparel industry corporate giants became an essential long-time supplier for apparel manufacturers, how it presents itself, and how it evolved to operate in today's technology–low-cost labor paradox world.

Transportation and Logistics

Technology has profoundly influenced almost every dimension of the textile and apparel industry, from product development (including the nano fabrics mentioned earlier), transportation, and logistics, to making distant locations viable sourcing partners in supply chains. New transportation and communication tools and improvements in production as well as transportation and logistics are also influencing textile and apparel sourcing decisions. Methods of transporting textile and apparel products evolved from the camel trains out of China to sailing vessels loaded with fabrics and fashion from Europe bound for the American colonies. Today, even though air transport has become much more common, the majority of textile and apparel products are still transported in containers on fleets of steamships and transferred to rail cars and/or trucks to reach their ultimate destinations. See Figures 3.4a and b to gain some appreciation of the size of the ships and the magnitude of the difficulty of handling cargo on these monster haulers while loading and unloading as well as traveling over the water.

Costs are less when a single shipment fills an entire container, so great quantities of similar products bound for the same port are placed in a container for efficiency's sake. A smaller but growing percentage of products are shipped by air cargo to meet critical

Figure 3.4a
Loading a container ship preparing to depart.

Figure 3.4b
Think about the magnitude of
this shipping container. How
many shirts would fit inside?

deadlines for sale on the retail sales floor. **Logistics** is the science of moving products through the supply chain to their final destination in an efficient and timely manner. Use of standardized, sophisticated computer software packages and the internet for planning and tracking deliveries has compressed transportation time frames and improved efficiency for both textile and apparel firms. In addition to the use of computer and internet for scheduling and tracking the status of orders in the pipeline, the sheer volume of business has fostered the development of new technologies, for keeping track not only of containers but also of individual items included in the contents.

Universal Product Code

The **Universal Product Code (UPC)** system was developed in the 1970s and will be recognized by anyone who has examined a label on a package of food at the grocery store. It enables the tracking of products from factory to consumer. The UPC system can identify individual products for data collection at any stage of the delivery process and is most frequently used for logistics and inventory control. American companies once favored a twelve-digit configuration, but to facilitate more consistent global communication, the Uniform Code Council, a nonprofit industry group that oversees bar code standards in the United States and Canada, adopted the global thirteen-digit configuration beginning January 1, 2005. It was estimated that the new codes could save 10 percent of the time previously needed to harmonize product data and reconcile invoices internationally. During transit, the bar code system works adequately on any container on which the label can be seen and scanned. The universal bar code is also very good for tracking individual items at point of sale, but identifying items shipped within another container poses a problem.

Radio Frequency Identification

Radio frequency identification (RFID) is a new generation of highly dependable, wireless tracking bar code systems. By attaching RFID tags to the objects, RFID can identify, track, and locate products, cartons, containers, and can also be used on people and animals. It was introduced to help identify the location of transmitter-tagged pallets or cases of merchandise within large shipping containers, continuously monitor their location, and communicate where that specific pallet is in the facility when it is needed. RFID is now also the tool that is used to track individual pieces of inventory in retail stores.

The cost of RFID technology is relatively high initially, but the long-term savings in inventory and logistics costs are significant. RFID tags improve inventory management by allowing manufacturers to enter new goods into inventory efficiently and to readily track the flow of those goods. A boxful of goods can be entered into inventory all at once, without having to enter each individual item, because an RFID scanner can pick up the signals from all the individual chips within the box simultaneously, something bar code systems cannot do. The chips themselves are very small, and an RFID scanner sends out a radio signal in the store, and each chip on the specific scanned frequency responds by sending out a return signal. The chips can also be used to find desired items within closed boxes so that products that are needed in stock immediately or that have been misplaced can be located and restocked with ease. RFID tags also facilitate self-checking of merchandise as customers leave retail stores.

Communication

Technology may have had its most significant impact on the speed and sophistication of communication. Just 100 years ago, telephone and telex lines enabled the exchange of verbal information between continents via cables strung across the land and laid under the oceans. Within the last four decades, introduction of satellite communications, fiber optic cable networks, the internet, and other electronic communication devices has significantly improved the quality and speed of communications systems and efficiency of the users. Within the last 10 years the evolution of electronic devices allows person-to-person or person-to-equipment communication anytime and anywhere, dramatically changing how human beings communicate with each other and with the technical world.

Other Impacts of Computer Technology Applications

One of the newest apparel design applications is 3D virtual prototyping of apparel design to make photorealistic 3D garments. Virtual prototyping provides visualization of garments and fabric drape on a 3D avatar. An avatar is an icon or figure representing a particular person that is virtual. The virtual person can represent the shape of each size in a product line. Using an avatar makes it possible to see what a design will look like and how it will move on a model before a piece of fabric is cut. It can change flat patterns into 3D samples and reduce the number of samples that have to be made. This minimizes lead time and cost of producing physical prototypes and allows collaboration among globally distributed teams of designers. Consequently, there is a growing demand for apparel professionals who are competent in using 3D prototyping. Examples of US companies that are making use of this technology include Kohl's, Adidas, Lands' End, Lee, and Destination Maternity (Optitex, n.d.).

With these technologies, an apparel design can be created in one country, and patterns and samples can be made for that design on the same day in another country or several other countries. Additional style analysis can take place through computer transmission of digital photographs of the prototypes on the firm's fit models. The samples can then be modified by the product development team and returned for approval. Today's newest computer design systems provide the capability of completely bypassing the traditional sample revision process, which includes making multiple samples to achieve the right look and fit. Styles may be perfected in a matter of hours instead of weeks, without the need to have samples shipped back and forth or for the product development team to travel to distant factories.

Expansion of computer technology related to every aspect of a business has provided an avenue for transparency of real-time communication among members of supply chains, replacing and/or integrating electronic data interchange (EDI) with the internet, featuring interactive computer communications. However, **transparency of information** within the technology system can be an issue. Information that previously might have been considered proprietary, or private to an individual company, may of necessity become part of open communication among all participants within a system. **Real-time** communication means that changes in design or tracking of products are instantaneously and continuously available to all individuals involved, whether they are in the next room or across several continents.

These necessary interactive communications have now been enhanced by development of software packages dedicated to product data management (PDM) including the following:

- Computer-aided design (CAD) to facilitate creative processes for product development;
- Product life cycle management (PLM) to manage the product development process; and
- Enterprise resource planning (ERP) to manage resource planning for production.

For each individual product line, it has been a challenge to harness the full spectrum of these software components into workable, flexible systems available to all sectors involved in a supply chain. But these goals are now being realized by applying product life cycle management (PLM) systems that combine data and design components. PLM solutions have been instrumental in boosting efficiencies throughout the supply chain, from shortening product life cycle times by at least half to the addition of the management systems (MMS) and markdown optimization solutions (MOS) to manage inventories. Fully describing these computer solutions is beyond the scope of our discussion, but the development of these systems may be credited with shifts in global sourcing patterns for apparel.

Experimenting with New Methods of Producing Apparel

Mass customization of apparel requires integration of information technology, automation, and team-based flexible manufacturing to produce a variety of styles, based on individual customer demand (Lee, Kunz, Fiore, & Campbell, 2002). A few manufacturing and retailing firms have experimented with mass customization over the last 15 years, and some still are. For example, Brooks Brothers can produce customized factory-made items, such as men's sports coats from its flagship store in New York City, using a "digital tailor" to scan for measurements. The customer then selects fabric from swatches and decides among design details, via samples; finished garments are delivered to the customer's door in less than 3 weeks. Each stage of this form of product development—determining the customer's size, making the pattern, cutting the fabric, assembling the garment, delivering it to the customer—is dependent upon sophisticated communication and computerization. Some people think that mass customization is the future of the apparel industry. Google "mass customization of apparel" and you'll get some interesting results.

Flexible garment production systems, including single-ply cutters and modular systems with stand-up sewing, make it possible to ship finished garments the same day a style goes into production instead of 3 to 6 weeks later, as with traditional bundle systems. Flexible systems can respond to customer demand for greater variety of styles with more frequent introduction of new styles on the retail sales floor. "Hot" styles can be resupplied faster, in sizes and colors that complement existing inventory. Garments are shipped **floor ready**, that is, with all the labels and tickets required by the retailer and with appropriate hangers or other display devices. Because of application of technology, time can be reduced in nearly every aspect of merchandising, design, production, and distribution to improve profitability and consumer satisfaction simultaneously.

Clemson University's technical laboratory facilities have been working for more than a decade on no-sew production methods for apparel. The goal of building a seam that does not give way from thread breakage and that provides a barrier to air and pathogens, without being bulky or stiff, has been elusive. Today, wearable garments are indeed being made without sewing the seams but using adhesives and other special techniques. There is also a lot of experimenting to make fabrics easier to handle for manufacturing processes as well as to improve comfort and performance of garments.

The Ongoing Need for Low-Cost Labor

Even with the advent of computerization to aid in manufacturing and even though it is sometimes less labor intensive, overall the production of textiles and apparel remains labor intensive. In most production industries, technology has been able to replace labor and therefore reduce labor costs. Significant progress has been seen in the mechanization, automation, and, in some cases, "robotization" of textile production, especially in spinning, dyeing, weaving, and knitting processes. However, these technologies tend to be applied to high-volume basic fabrics that do not satisfy the fashion-minded customer. Therefore the challenge becomes to successfully apply the technologies to short production runs of fabrics that vary in fiber content, yarn type, and fabric structure.

As discussed earlier, the creative and technical design stages of apparel product development have benefited greatly from the development of software applications and other technology to facilitate design processes. However, apparel assembly remains one of the most labor-intensive manufacturing processes in the entire field of consumer products, even though some new specialized machines now assist with selected garment assembly processes. Most cut garment pieces must still be hand fed into sewing machines, and hand control must still be maintained throughout most of the remaining stages of production for most styles. Because of this heavy involvement of hand labor, the goal of most developers of apparel products has been to seek the location of cheapest labor in the world as a means of controlling the overall costs of producing finished goods. It has not yet been possible to develop technology that can control the materials handling processes required for sewing and also have those systems be adaptable to production of new styles six to twelve times a year for fashion goods categories.

One of the major by-products of the low-cost labor quest has been the perpetuation of the historical propensity for hiring women to construct apparel products. Looking back in time, as the Industrial Revolution progressed, apparel manufacturers sought women who had sewing construction skills because of their experience in sewing at home. As generations of women entered the job market, the practice of lower wages for women in the textile and apparel industry became prevalent in other jobs and forms of labor as well. As the overall income of a nation rises, some women have typically moved on to more lucrative positions within the economy, and rather than pay more to keep that workforce, manufacturers have usually looked elsewhere for a population of workers who could be trained easily to do the job for low wages. Many newly developing nations have an eager and hungry potential source of employees, especially women seeking any form of acceptable employment that can provide potential improvement in their families' levels of consumption. This was readily displayed in Case 1.1, in Bangladesh.

The need for apparel firms to keep costs of labor low has produced some rather diverse phenomena. When a firm contracts labor in a newly developing country, the positives may include improvement in the economy and standard of living for part of the population in that country. The downside is that segment of the population may abandon their traditional livelihoods and move to urban areas, where employment is available. In addition, because apparel production equipment is easily transportable, when problems arise such as demands for salary increases, the apparel employer may move on to a different city or country, leaving unemployment and great hardship in its wake. This causes disruption in that country's economy and the quality of life of its population. One of the more unwelcome outcomes of the quest for cheap labor occurs when employees are so desperate for any income that they continue to work for lower wages and in unsafe working conditions, even when the economy around them has progressed to a better level. This is the source of the phenomenon known as **sweatshops**, in which firms take advantage of employees by maintaining substandard working conditions and below-subsistence wages. This issue will be examined more fully in later chapters.

Summary

The interconnectedness of business activities between nations is reflected not only in the securing of finished products, but also in the conducting of production processes in diverse locations around the world. The Harmonized Commodity Description and Code Systems, generally referred to as Harmonized System or HS, are a multipurpose international product nomenclature developed by the World Customs Organization (WCO) and used by more than 200 countries. The Harmonized Tariff System (HTS) for the United States is an application derived from the overall HS, and focuses on identifying specific products for collection of import duties and data related to quantity of imports.

The North American Industry Classification System (NAICS) is an example of systems based on the HS that are used for categorizing manufactured products and industrial production methods. This six-digit system is used for documenting levels of trade and for assembling trade statistics related to production and labor issues. NAICS was developed to support the North American Free Trade Agreement (NAFTA). Global companies in the textile and apparel industry categories include American & Efird, Inc., Cone Mills, Kellwood Company, QST Industries, Cintas Corporation, Superior Uniform Group, VF Corporation, HMX (formerly Hartmarx), Polygenex International, Peerless Clothing, and YKK. Technology development has provided dramatic increases in productivity in textiles, improvements in the creative and technical design of apparel, and changes in transportation and logistics. Improvements in communications and information processing have facilitated development of global companies. Despite implementation of agile business systems for apparel manufacturing, low-cost labor is still regarded as an economic necessity for apparel production.

The result of these changes has been decreases in production of textiles and apparel in developed countries and increases in the number of countries involved and in the quantity of goods produced in developing and now even newly developing countries. As a proportion of consumption, imports into the United States continue to increase, but the picture varies somewhat, depending on whether units or values are measured. Analysis of the meaning of these trends is complex and requires careful consideration of the multiple issues; many of these will be included in future chapters.

Learning Activities

1. How might "seamless" apparel technology influence what kind of garments are made and where in the world apparel is made? Would it be more likely to increase or decrease US-based apparel manufacturing?
2. How could the technology–low-cost labor paradox affect the operation of a supply chain?
3. What is the source of the pressure to drive down textile and apparel product costs?
4. How is it possible for textile or apparel production to increase while employment decreases?
5. Working in small groups of two to three people, make an online search to find other "smart" fabric applications in the apparel industry, besides the ones discussed in Case 3.2. Share your findings with the class.

References

American & Efird. (2009). "Global Locations." Retrieved October 4, 2009, from http://www.amefird.com/contact/global-locations/

ATMI. (2004). *Textile Hi-Lights*. Washington, DC: American Textile Manufacturers Institute.

Ayling, J. (2009). "Insight: Liz Claiborne inks 'next level' deal with JCPenney." Retrieved October 9, 2009, from http://www.just-style.com/article.aspx?id=105561

Bhosale, N., Jadhav, B., Pareek, V., and Eklahare, S. (2013). "Seamless Garment Technology, Application and Benefits." Retrieved June 5, 2015, from http://www.fibre2fashion.com/industry-article/49/4854/seamless-garment- technology1.asp

Cline, W. R. (1990). *The Future of World Trade in Textiles and Apparel*. Washington, DC: Institute of International Economics.

Colbert, C. (2009). "Liz Claiborne, Inc. Hoover's Inc." Retrieved January 2011, from http://premium.hoovers.com/ subscribe/co/factsheet.xhtml?ID=ryskkfcffhstyf

Floor Biz. (June 4, 2009). "Commercial Carpet Report: Modular Sales Breathe Life into Sluggish Market." Retrieved November 15, 2015, from http://www.floorbiz.com/BizNews/NPViewArticle.asp?ArticleID=4541

Great Idea Finder. (2004). "Fascinating Facts about the Invention of the Sewing Machine by Elias Howe in 1846." Retrieved October 24, 2015, from http://www.ideafinder.com/history/inventions/story065.htm

Harmonized Tariff Schedule of the United States. (2008). "2008 HTSA Basic Edition, Official Harmonized Tariff Schedule of the United States Annotated." Retrieved November 8, 2015, from www.usitc.gov/tata/hts/bychapter/_0800.htm

INVISTA. (n.d.). "INVISTA's Shareholder—Koch Industries, Inc." Retrieved January 4, 2014, from http://www.invista.com/en/shareholder/index.html

Kellwood. (2015). "About Kellwood." Retrieved April 17, 2015, from http://www.kellwood.com/about.asp

Koch Industries. (April 22, 1998). "Saba/Koch Consortium to Purchase Hoechst's Polyester Business." Retrieved April 29, 2005, from http://www.kochind.com/articles/templates/article_file_template_print.asp? ID540

Kunz, G. I., Albrecht, J., Stout, S., & Horne, L. (1992). "Pigskin as a Component of the International Leather Market." *Clothing and Textiles Research Journal, 10*(1), 40–46.

Lee, S., Kunz, G. I., Fiore, A. M., & Campbell, J. R. (2002). "Acceptance of Mass Customization of Apparel: Merchandising Issues Associated with the Preference of Product, Process, and Place." *Clothing and Textile Research Journal, 20*(3), 138–146.

Martin, T. (May 31, 2013). "It Ain't Rocket Science, but Sock Making Comes Close." *Wall Street Journal*. Retrieved October 24, 2015, from http://www.wsj.com/articles/SB10001424127887324682204578515021407071076

Morris, L. S. (October 14, 2014). "Four Decades of Zippers, and Much More, from Macon's YKK." *The Telegraph*. Retrieved October 24, 2015, from http://www.macon.com/news/business/article30148497.html

Nano and Me. (n.d.). "Nano in Textiles and Clothing." Retrieved August 28, 2015, from www.nanoandme.org/nano-products/textiles-and-clothing/

Optitex. (n.d.). "3D Suite." Retrieved March 3, 2015, from www.optitex.com/en/3D-Suite-Create-Garments-fit-to-Avatar-Animate

QST Industries. (2015). "Home Page." Retrieved November 15, 2015, from www.qst.com/Default.aspx

Spieler, M. (August 2013). "Modest Growth Gives the Carpet Industry Hope." *Floor Covering News*. Retrieved October 24, 2015, from http://www.fcnews.net/2013/07/modest-growth-gives-carpet-industry-hope/

Tribune Staff. (June 26, 2009). "Bankruptcy Court OKs Sale of Suit Maker Hartmarx." *The Chicago Tribune*. Retrieved March 3, 2015, from http://articles.chicagotribune.com/2009-06-26/news 090625020_1_hartmarx-bankruptsy-sale

United States Trade Representative (n.d.) Harmonized System and World Customs Organization. Retrieved December 28, 2015, from https://ustr.gov/issue-areas/industry-manufacturing/industrial-tariffs/tariff-schedules

US Census Bureau. (2007). "NAICS Codes and Titles." Retrieved October 3, 2009, from http://www.census.gov/eos/www/naics/

US Census Bureau. (2014). "North American Industry Classification System." Retrieved January 2, 2014, from http://www.census.gov/eos/www/naics/

Wallander, M. (July 3, 2012). "T-Shirt Blues: The Environmental Impact of a T-Shirt." Retrieved November 8, 2015, from http://www.huffingtonpost.com/mattias-wallander/t-shirt-environment_b_1643892.html

World Trade Organization. (2010). "The World Trade Organization . . . in Brief." Retrieved October 24, 2015, from http://www.wto.org/english/res_e/doload_e/inbr_e.pdf

CHAPTER 4

SUSTAINABILITY IN TEXTILE AND APPAREL INDUSTRIES

NOT SO FUN FACT

23.8 billion pounds of textile and clothing go to US landfills every year. (Goodwill Industries International, n.d.)

It is the work of this generation to make clear we reject the status quo—a race toward the destruction of our planet and the wild places we play in and love. We cannot sit idly by while large special interests destroy the planet for profit without regard for our children and grandchildren.

—ROSE MARCARIO, PATAGONIA CEO (PATAGONIA, N.D.-A)

OBJECTIVES

- Examine the three dimensions of sustainability—social, economic, and environmental—in the context of textile and apparel production and consumption.
- Explore industry and consumer sustainability initiatives and opportunities by systematically applying reduce, reuse, and recycle strategies to the stages of the textile products lifecycle.
- Analyze the role of selected special interest groups, industry, and consumers in developing sustainable supply chains.

From a broad perspective, sustainability refers to endurance of systems and processes. If something is sustainable, it means it can exist forever without undermining other beings' needs in the present and in the future. As defined in Chapter 1, sustainability involves the corporate, government, and consumer responsibility to integrate economic, social, environmental, and cultural dimensions to promote cooperation and solidarity among people and generations.

Figure 4.1 suggests that interactions between the three sustainability dimensions (environmental, social, and economic) are essential for creating systems that are bearable, viable, equitable, and, ultimately, sustainable. Note that cultural is not specifically identified as a part of sustainability, although it is very important in the context of the global textile and apparel business. Culture is not overtly included as part of the sustainability concept because it is implicit to the social, economic, and environmental dimensions wherever they are applied. This chapter explores the three spheres of sustainability presented in Figure 4.1 with a special attention to the environmental dimension.

GLOBAL LEXICON

American Apparel and Footwear Association (AAFA) a US-based apparel-related trade association in the Americas

business a commercial enterprise or profession organized and operated for the purpose of making a profit by providing a product or service

closed-loop system system in which some or all of its output is used as input

code of conduct a statement of principles and standards by which business decisions are made

collaborative consumption a redistribution of used goods that are being passed from someone who does not want them to someone who does want them

corporate social responsibility (CSR) ethical obligation of businesses toward the communities as well as the ecological and social environments in which they operate

economic responsibility the obligations of an individual, group, or general population to assume responsibility for the value of utilized materials, services, and resources and for using them efficiently, with a minimum of waste

environmental responsibility the obligations of an individual, group, or general population for the physical conditions,

circumstances, and related resources influencing the health and comfort of current and future generations

ethics a system or code of morals of a particular person, group, or profession and its application to decisions or particular problems of conduct

Fair Labor Association (FLA) a coalition of companies, universities, and nongovernmental organizations dedicated to improving labor conditions around the world

fair trade a trading partnership, based on dialogue, transparency, and respect, that contributes to sustainable development by supporting trading conditions that secure the rights of marginalized producers and workers (World Fair Trade Organization [WFTO], 2009)

greenhouse gases (GHG) atmospheric gases (carbon dioxide, nitrous oxide, methane, water vapors, and some others) that trap heat from the sun and make the planet warmer

Higg Index an indicator-based tool for footwear and apparel that enables companies to evaluate material types, products, facilities, and processes based on a range of environmental and product design choices

morals the degree of conformity with generally accepted or prescribed standards of goodness or rightness in character or conduct

recovering the process of collecting and sorting out waste materials for processing into new forms, which will be marketed as raw materials for new products

recycling the process of taking a product at the end of its useful life and using all or part of it to make another product

sharing economy also known as collaborative consumption, is a trending business model when individuals and organizations prefer to borrow or rent products instead of buying and owning them

social responsibility the obligations of an individual, group, or general population toward the welfare and interest of the communities in which they live and operate, including fair treatment of human beings, resources, and the law

Sustainable Apparel Coalition (SAC) a trade organization of brands, retailers, and manufacturers, government and nongovernmental organizations, and academic experts with a focus on creating common metrics and approaches to reduce the social and environmental impacts of apparel and footwear

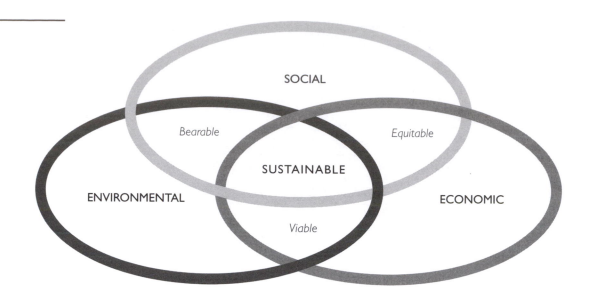

Figure 4.1
The three spheres of sustainability.

SOCIAL

Bearable

Equitable

SUSTAINABLE

ENVIRONMENTAL

ECONOMIC

Viable

SOCIAL RESPONSIBILITY

Social responsibility involves the obligations of an individual, group, or general population toward the welfare and interest of the communities in which they live and operate, including fair treatment of human beings, resources, and the law. In other words, an entity (person, organization, nation, etc.) has obligations to act for the benefit of society at large. In the business context, the term **corporate social responsibility (CSR)** is often used. CSR is the ethical obligation of companies toward the community and economic, ecological, and social environments in which they operate. In addition to the social dimension, CSR typically involves economic and environmental dimensions, which closely resembles definition and dimensions of sustainability, as presented in Figure 4.1. For future apparel industry professionals, it is important to realize that a business that is truly engaged in CSR has to sacrifice some of its profits for the social and environmental good to support and promote communities and environments in which the business operates.

During the last decade of the twentieth century, social responsibility became a watchword of business, particularly the apparel business. Reports of unjust labor practices in scenarios of labor-intensive production were common in the daily news. Exploitation was occurring with regard to pay scales below a living wage, sexual harassment, extended work hours, and child labor. Violations of human rights and poor labor conditions in toys and electronic industries were also reported, but apparel manufacturing got the most negative publicity. As discussed in Chapter 1, the apparel industry is the most labor-intensive manufacturing sector and requires a lot of manual labor to assemble products. This unique dependence on manual labor is the reason apparel production is more often associated with sweatshops than any other industry (Rivoli, 2015). As a result, in the context of the apparel industry, CSR became more commonly associated with and focused on labor conditions, treatment of workers, and human rights issues.

In response to consumers outraged by the abuses found in the United States and in many other countries, most apparel businesses moved swiftly to take steps to combat labor exploitation and communicate their efforts to the public by developing and implementing **codes of conduct**, a statement of principles and standards by which business decisions are made. A typical code of conduct outlines a company's relations with and obligations toward its employees, suppliers, customers, consumers, and communities where they operate. Development of a comprehensive code of conduct was a starting point for building a sustainable supply chain.

However, applying a code of conduct consistently throughout the complex supply chains that even small firms now operate in within the global market is extremely difficult. Refer back to Figure 1.5, representing the primary components of the global textile complex (see Chapter 1). Even small firms are often involved with individual firms in all five levels of the textile complex, and some levels, especially for large firms, may involve dozens or even hundreds of individual firms. Also, Figure 1.5 does not indicate the dozens of firms outside the textile complex that might be involved in a supply chain, for example, transportation providers. Challenges of the apparel supply chain often include multiple languages, varying cultural traditions, resource availability, and infrastructure limitations, leaving companies pressured to meet quantity and quality deadlines, financial limitations, and ethical requirements. Dedicating a company to addressing these complexities requires strong and effective executive leadership.

To deal with these complexities, it was necessary to establish a transparent and independent auditing process for manufacturing facilities, and several coalitions and nonprofit organizations were founded. One example is the **Fair Labor Association (FLA)**, which was created in 1999. FLA is a coalition of companies, universities, and nongovernmental organizations dedicated to improving labor conditions around the world. The coalition consists of close to 40 apparel companies, a dozen nonapparel brands (such as Apple and Nestle), plus 180 colleges and universities, as well as about 20 apparel factories located around the world (e.g., China, Hong Kong, Thailand, Sri Lanka, and the United States). In 2015, examples of apparel brands involved in FLA included Adidas, Fruit of the Loom, Hanes Brands, H&M, Hugo Boss, Nike, Patagonia, and Under Armour (Fair Labor Association, n.d.). Participating universities and colleges require the licensers of their trademarks and logos to be members of the FLA coalition, which includes implementation of a code of conduct focused primarily on fair labor practices. These types of organizations have improved the awareness among the general public of exploitation of people and working conditions of thousands of workers around the world.

Association of a company with human rights violations at the factories where its products are made can be very costly for the company and the image of its brands. When consumers become aware of labor exploitation blamed on a particular company, it proves very difficult to reverse public opinion. For example, in the mid-1990s, Nike was in the news for allegations that some subcontracting factories where the company's products were made had poor labor conditions. The company took the issue very seriously and implemented a number of initiatives to ensure fair labor practices. For example, in 2005, Nike was among the first apparel companies to disclose a complete list of factories around the world that produce apparel, footwear, and accessories under its brands. The company now is a member of FLA. Yet, two decades later, in 2015, almost 30 percent of 72 undergraduate students enrolled in an apparel program at a large Midwestern university named Nike as a business that could improve its social responsibility practices.

Now Nike's website provides an interactive manufacturing map that is searchable by country, brand (Nike, Converse, Hurley), and product type. A frequently updated database of almost 700 contract factories located in 42 countries around the world can be downloaded in Excel or PDF format, including addresses, number of employees, type of product and manufacturing activity, percent of female workers, and contact person information (Nike Inc., 2015).

Human rights issues are further discussed in Chapter 7 as a critical factor for making sourcing decisions when selecting a country for apparel production. The issues discussed include child labor, gender discrimination in the workplace, and human rights organizations. World regions and countries are compared using the Human Rights Risk Index.

ECONOMIC RESPONSIBILITY

Figure 4.1 indicates the inherent interconnectedness of economic, environmental, and social responsibilities associated with creating and maintaining sustainable systems. Textile and apparel businesses have always paid attention to economic responsibilities, particularly as to how they affect their bottom lines. Since the 1990s, consumers and social activist groups have been putting much pressure on corporations to also assume social and environmental responsibilities. In this text, **economic responsibility** is defined as the obligations of an individual, group, or general population to assume responsibility for the value of utilized materials, services, and resources and for using them efficiently, with a minimum of waste. Reducing use of resources and minimization of waste, whether by a consumer, business, or a nation, is also critically important from the perspective of environmental responsibility.

Another important aspect of economic responsibility is ensuring that there are equal benefits to all parties involved in any business transactions. Economically responsible organizations make business transactions fair for every company participating in an apparel supply chain, regardless of its size, wealth, and background, through providing reasonable wages and equal opportunities. Besides generating profits, many companies are truly concerned with creating long-term value for communities where they operate as well as broader economic systems. Companies involved in fair trade are a good example of integrating social and economic responsibilities to create equitable exchange of resources and contribute to developing sustainable businesses and communities.

Fair trade is closely associated with small-scale economic initiatives or partnerships among small farmers and cultural artisan producers, typically in newly developing countries, with marketers of commercial products in developed countries. The marketers provide education and opportunities to their suppliers that can change people's lives. Fair trade is supported by many nonprofit organizations whose goal is to achieve sustainability through social, environmental, and economic responsibility. In 2009, four of these organizations agreed that "Fair Trade is a trading partnership, based on dialogue, transparency and respect, that seeks greater equity in international trade. It contributes to sustainable development by offering better trading conditions to, and securing the rights of, marginalized producers and workers—especially in the South" (World Fair Trade Organization [WFTO], n.d., para 1). WFTO, the world's largest fair trade organization,

Figure 4.2a
Edna Ruth Byler, a pioneer of the fair trade movement, and the founder of Ten Thousand Villages

Figure 4.2b
Ten Thousand Villages
merchandise display featuring
unique handcrafted fair trade
products from around the world

represents over 370 member companies and 40 individual associates in 70 countries across five regions of the world.

There are numerous other entities that promote and support fair trade, most of which were founded in the late 1980s and early 1990s (e.g., Fair Trade Federation, Fairtrade International, Fair Trade Labelling—CERT, European Fair Trade Association). Ten Thousand Villages, an independent nonprofit charitable organization and a founding member of WFTO, deserves a special mention as a 1946 pioneer of the fair trade movement through the visionary work of Edna Ruth Byler (Figure 4.2a). Byler began the first fair trade grassroots campaign among her family and friends when she returned from her 1946 trip to Puerto Rico, where she witnessed striking poverty among artisans. "The seminal contribution of Byler ignited a global movement to eradicate poverty through market-based solutions. Byler believed that she could provide sustainable economic opportunities for artisans in developing countries by creating a viable marketplace for their products in North America" (Ten Thousand Villages, n.d.). Started from the trunk of Byler's car, today Ten Thousand Villages sells its products through 390 retail stores located all over the United States and a successful online business (Figure 4.2b).

Ultimately, all fair trade initiatives depend on consumers. Unless the movement of supporting small farmers and businesses, empowering artisans, and developing impoverished communities is backed by consumers, fair trade will cease to exist. From the perspective of future industry professionals, any textile and apparel company can partner with small businesses around the world and incorporate unique textiles, trims, and accessories in its product lines while supporting the fair trade mission and fulfilling economic responsibility.

ENVIRONMENTAL RESPONSIBILITY

Similar to social and economic responsibilities, environmental responsibility is a complex, multifaceted concept and can be defined in many different ways. In this text,

environmental responsibility is the obligations of an individual, group, or general population for the physical conditions, circumstances, and related resources influencing the health and comfort of current and future generations. In other words, anyone and everyone is responsible to live and operate in a way that protects the natural environment because it provides everything we need for our survival and well-being (US Environmental Protection Agency, n.d.-b).

Environmental responsibility is sometimes used interchangeably with sustainability. For example, the US Environmental Protection Agency defines sustainability as creating and maintaining "the conditions under which humans and nature can exist in productive harmony, that permit fulfilling the social, economic and other requirements of present and future generations. Sustainability is important to making sure that we have and will continue to have, the water, materials, and resources to protect human health and our environment" (US Environmental Protection Agency, n.d.-b, para 2). This same definition is sometimes used to describe environmental responsibility, but in this text we regard environmental responsibility as one of the three essential components of sustainability.

Environmental issues include climate change, protecting nature and biodiversity, and resource and waste management. These issues often pose even tougher ethical challenges than the social issues. Many of these problems develop over a long timeline, and causes are often camouflaged by acceptance of common practices and multiple sources of contributors. People around the world are becoming more aware and concerned about environmental issues, particularly with regard to preserving basic resources and limiting impact of humans on the planet's ecosystems. There are also tighter government regulations that require companies to rethink and adjust their operations to minimize impact of the environment. In addition, there is an increasing pressure from investors and consumers for sustainable practices and products and for transparent supply chains.

Historically, the process of industrialization has been a source of significant social and environmental abuses. Whether in the nineteenth, twentieth, or twenty-first centuries, countries have suffered through the development process until moderate levels of human well-being are achieved. Developed countries typically have more environmental regulations in place as well as means to enforce them than do developing and newly developing countries. When businesses from developed countries outsource operations to emerging economies, the regulations they should follow may be a gray area.

Today, with thousands of companies operating in the global environment in the presence of consumer activist organizations, attention of big business is becoming focused on corporate responsibilities and sustainability of supply chains. Time and money are being spent on social and environmental responsibilities that often, to the surprise of some, result in improvement of economic performance. As indicated in Figure 4.1, the three dimensions of sustainability are deeply intertwined.

The rest of this chapter focuses on environmental responsibilities and issues in the textile and apparel supply chain. Before diving into learning about the topic, take a couple of minutes to answer the questions below. This will help you better relate to the chapter's material, both as a consumer and future apparel industry professional. Note: Keep your responses to the questions on hand. We will refer to them as we go through the rest of the chapter.

- Within the course of the year (from today to the same date last year), how many new apparel items did you buy? How many new pairs of shoes? (Hint: If you are at home, it might be helpful to check your closet to refresh your memory.)
- How old is your oldest garment that you still wear in public?
- Why is your oldest garment so special that you have kept and used it for a long time?
- How many times a month do you do laundry and how do you dry garments after the laundry?

Environmental Problems

Many environmental issues that are global in scope are demanding our attention, such as climate change, diminishing petroleum resources, shortages of water, pollution and contamination of air, land, and water, and many others. One of the factors contributing to climate change is emission of **greenhouse gases (GHG)**, which are atmospheric gases (carbon dioxide, nitrous oxide, methane, water vapors, and some others) that trap heat from the sun and make the planet warmer. During the last 150 years, humans are responsible for almost all greenhouse gases in the atmosphere (US Environmental Protection Agency, 2013). In the United States, the major sources of GHG are electricity generation (31 percent), transportation (27 percent), and industrial activity (21 percent), as presented in Figure 4.3.

Textile-based products contribute to all of the sources of GHG. Growing natural fibers is part of agriculture. Production, or industrial activities, includes manufacturing fibers, yarns, fabrics, trims, and apparel. Transportation includes shipping raw and intermediate materials as well as final products along the supply chain and to the final consumer, typically from all around the world. Consumption stage necessitates washing and drying apparel and other home textiles, such as towels and bedding. And, finally, generation of electricity is needed to perform all of the steps of the production and consumption cycle.

Figure 4.4 shows the primary regions of the world contributing to the GHG effect with the top three contributors: China, the United States, and European Union (EU). It is no surprise that China, with almost 1.4 billion people (19 percent of the world's

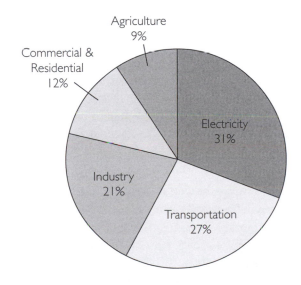

Figure 4.3
Total US greenhouse gas emissions by sector, 2013.
Source: US Environmental Protection Agency. (2013). http://www.epa.gov/climatechange/ghgemissions/sources.html

Figure 4.4

Global emissions of CO_2 from fossil fuel burning and industrial activities by country

Source: Global Greenhouse Gas Emission Data. (2008). http://www.epa.gov/climatechange/ghgemissions/global.html

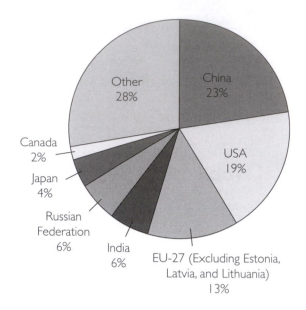

total population of 7.2 billion), is the largest contributor to climate change. The country accounts for 23 percent of global CO_2 emission. The US population of 319 million, which is 4.4 percent of the world's total, produces 19 percent of the global CO_2 emission. Just over half a billion population (511 million) of the European Union contributes only 13 percent of the global CO_2 emission. Clearly, per capita CO_2 emission rates are the highest in the United States, making the country the number-one contributor to global warming (Miret, 2014). Note that India, with 1.24 billion people, the second-largest population in the world, contributes only 6 percent of the global CO_2 emissions. Among many other consequences, climate change contributes to unstable weather patterns which result in droughts or floods in major cotton-producing countries, negatively affecting crops and cotton prices. Increases in raw material prices put significant pressure on apparel suppliers.

Besides GHG emission, manufacturing and consumption of textile-based products contribute to water and land pollution, use of nonrenewable resources, and generation of waste. Similar to being the major contributor to climate change, the United States is the world's champion in practically all of the other factors leading to these environmental problems. Accounting for 4.4 percent of the world's population, the United States consumes almost one-third of the world's resources, including 24 percent of the world's energy, and generates about 30 percent of the global waste (Global Alliances for Incinerator Alternatives, n.d.; US Energy Information Administration, 2012).

United Nations Resolution 64/292 states that "clean drinking water and sanitation are essential to the realization of all human rights." In the twentieth century, usage of water has increased at more than twice the rate of the population growth rate, and almost doubled in comparison to the nineteenth century. Yet, the amount of water on the planet has remained constant since the prehistoric days. As a result, water scarcity is the daily reality for two-thirds of the world's population. Extensive use of water in textile manufacturing and especially in cotton crop cultivation is a major environmental issue.

With respect to textile-based products, the United States is the largest apparel and footwear market in the world. In 2012, Americans spent $354 billion on new clothes and shoes (American Apparel and Footwear Association, 2014), which is slightly more than 25 percent of the world's total apparel and footwear consumption (roughly $1.2

trillion). Every person in the US market, including infants, on average purchases 62 garments and 7 pairs of shoes in the course of a year, spending approximately $900 on apparel and $230 on footwear. This translates to 20 billion garments and 2.2 billion pairs of shoes purchased annually in the US market (American Apparel and Footwear Association, 2014; Intertek, 2011).

Now, look at your answers to the questions at the end of the previous section, "Environmental Responsibility." Have you purchased more or less apparel and shoes than an average American? Are you happy with all of your purchases? How long are you planning to keep and wear them?

Scientists predict that if all 7.2 billion people on the planet consumed at the same rate as Americans do today, the present population would feel like 73 billion people lived on the planet, in terms of using all resources and generating waste. With the fast-growing middle class in China, Russia, India, and Brazil, the world's consumption rates are speeding up very quickly. Do you think we have resources to support the current and growing levels of consumption? The answer is, of course, no. Insatiable consumer appetites for more and newer products drive ever-increasing production, consumption, and disposal rates. Consumerism ideology even propagates that consumption growth is critical for a national economy's health.

Fast Fashion and Sustainability

In the realm of textile and apparel, consumer desire for new and cool trends, supported by internet technology, resulted in the fast fashion trend, which has been fueling consumerism in the twenty-first century. Fast-changing fashion trends dictate a quick turnaround of merchandise. Instead of traditional four to five seasons, fast fashion retailers offer new styles monthly or even biweekly to satisfy consumers' desire for newness and excitement. As a result, frequency of purchasing new garments and the amount of new apparel bought have increased substantially. In addition, fast fashion drives apparel prices down. Because consumers have limited disposable income, they can allocate only a certain portion of it to spend on clothing and shoes (in the United States, on average, 4.4 percent). If consumers are buying a greater quantity of clothes and more often, the prices have to be lower. With fast fashion, we as consumers buy more and more garments because

- We want to keep up with the latest fashion trends and look cool.
- Prices are low so we can afford to buy more items.
- Quality is typically low (often items have to be replaced after several washing and drying cycles due to poor construction and/or low-quality materials, or both), but we want to replace them more often anyway.

Clothing is becoming disposable: similar to plastic bags, plastic utensils, and paper plates, it is easy to dispose of low-priced last-year (or last-month) fashions and head to the mall to buy new ones. But what are the environmental consequences of apparel overconsumption? First, to make more and more apparel, businesses produce more and more fibers (natural and man-made), yarns, fabrics, and trims. More toxic chemicals are used for cotton production as well as yarn and fabric processing. More nonrenewable resources are required, such as petroleum, to produce man-made fibers. Second, to support these manufacturing activities, more natural resources are needed to generate electricity and supply water for cotton growing and textile finishing and dyeing. Third, greater amount of manufacturing activities to make more apparel contributes to greater environmental degradation, energy crisis, and climate change as a result of increasing emission rates. Finally, the amount of disposed textiles is also growing, contributing to the waste management crisis that was introduced in Chapter 2.

While many apparel companies were quick to jump on the train of fast fashion in order to increase sales, there are some that refuse to follow the trend and instead promote longevity of their products. Patagonia is one example. Besides designing and making apparel that will last decades, the company has numerous other efforts to promote and encourage garment longevity among consumers, which are discussed later in this chapter. Besides increasing production and consumption rates, there are other environmental issues associated with the textile and apparel industries. Every year more companies are attempting to address them.

Industry Environmental Initiatives

As with social responsibility, environmental responsibility is best tackled through the formation of "joint action" groups that bring different methods and priorities to the table:

- Textile, apparel, and retail firms come together with common goals.
- Trade associations collaborate with divisions of government.
- Parts of supply chains work together to improve the totality of their processes.

For example, Euratex, a European textile and clothing trade association, identified seven categories of environmental issues: sustainable raw materials, chemical usage, fossil fuel usage, volatile organic compound absorption and emissions, and water usage and waste. The Euratex mission underlines the importance of the industry's engaging regulators, policy makers, and legislators in supporting its mission. Unlike the United States, China, India, and many other countries, the EU has been a leader in implementing a battery of legislation that defines and mandates a high level of environmental and consumer safety as well as green production processes.

Sustainable Apparel Coalition (SAC) is a trade organization of brands, retailers, and manufacturers, government and nongovernmental organizations, and academic experts with a focus on creating common metrics and approaches to reduce the social and environmental impacts of apparel and footwear products around the world. One of the SAC's goals is to develop industry-wide standards for sustainable products and processes. Together, SAC brands, retailers, and manufacturers represent more than one-third of the global apparel and footwear market. In 2015, SAC consisted of close to 150 apparel and footwear companies and industry affiliates, including:

- Thirty brand managers (Adidas, Asics, Brooks, Burberry, Columbia Sportswear, Desigual, Ecco, Eileen Fisher, Esprit, Fast Retailing, Fenix, Hanes Brands, IC Group, Ikea, KEEN, Kering, Levi's, Loomstate, Lululemon Athletica, Madura Fashion & Lifestyle, Malwee, Marmot, New Balance, Nike, Patagonia, Pentland, Puma, PVH, Threads 4 Thought, and VF Corporation)
- Fifteen retailers (Ann Inc., C&A, Gap, H&M, Inditex, JC Penney, Kohl's, L.L. Bean, Macy's, Mountain Equipment Co-op, Nordstrom, REI, Target, Walmart, and Williams-Sonoma)
- Fifty-three manufacturers (1888 Mills, Allied Feather and Down, Artistics Milliners, Arvind Mills, Bayer, Charming Trim, DuPont, Gildan, Gore-Tex, Lands' End, Li & Fung, MAS Holdings, etc.)

- Twenty-three industry affiliates (American Apparel and Footwear Association, Bureau Veritas, Cotton Incorporated, International Wool Textile Association, etc.)
- Twenty-five nonprofit/government/education organizations (Danish Fashion Institute, Duke University Center for Sustainability, Fair Trade USA, Fairtrade International, Glasgow Caledonia University, US Environmental Protection Agency, The Sustainable Fashion Academy, University of Delaware, etc.)

A major SAC project is the **Higg Index**, a suite of assessment tools that standardizes the measurement of the environmental and social impacts of apparel and footwear products across the product lifecycle and throughout the value chain. The Higg Index is an indicator-based tool that enables footwear and apparel companies to evaluate materials, products, facilities, and processes based on a range of environmental and product design choices. The index was developed by SAC based on the Outdoor Industry Association's Eco Index and Nike's Apparel Environmental Design Tool.

The Higg Index consists of practical, qualitative questions to assess a company's environmental sustainability performance and suggest areas for improvement. The three core components of the index are brand, product, and facility. The index has been improved and validated through rigorous pilot testing. To better understand SAC initiatives and an application of the Higg Index, read Case 4.1 to learn about Gap Inc. initiatives on assessing the company's impact on the environment and developing strategies to minimize it. As one of SAC's founding members, Gap was involved in pilot-testing the index. Gap is a good example of a typical large apparel retailer taking on the challenge to be a more environmentally friendly business.

CASE 4.1

GAP INC.: STRIVING FOR SUSTAINABLE BUSINESS

In 2004, Gap started doing research to develop a model to tackle the company's environmental footprint systematically across the product lifecycle. The model revealed that they needed to consider environmental impact in relation to inputs, processing, and outputs as well as the levels of possible control. Take a few minutes to study the model of Gap environmental impact. Take note of the inputs, process, and outputs as well as the company's levels of control.

Figure Case 4.1

Model of Gap's environmental impact across the product lifecycle (courtesy of GAP Inc.).

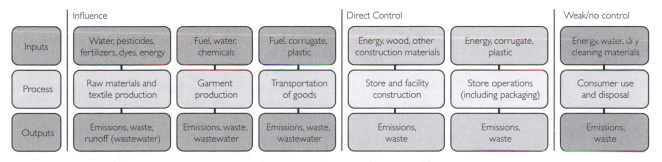

OUR IMPACT ON THE ENVIRONMENT

In 2004, we worked with CH2M Hill to assess our environmental impact throughout the product life cycle. We've confirmed that, in the short term, we should focus our efforts on the areas over which we have direct control and, therefore, the biggest opportunity to make a difference

It took a while to plan an environmentally friendly strategy, but since 2008, Gap Inc. has been measuring its environmental footprint. The company began applying the model to make its own facilities (stores and distribution centers) more environmentally friendly. In addition, Gap has selected suppliers that are willing to collaborate to support similar objectives. (More on this is later in the chapter, in the "Distribution" section.)

Gap closely relates its environmental strategy with supply chain management. The next goal is to reduce environmental footprint of the company's suppliers, specifically, cut-and-sew vendors and fabric mills. In 2012, using the Higg Index, Gap completed a pilot assessment of its 234 major cut-and-sew vendors in twenty-one countries to establish measurable goals for reducing the suppliers' water, energy, and chemical usage. During the same year, Gap held Green Manufacturing Workshops to educate 139 key vendors in Vietnam, Indonesia, India, Cambodia, and Sri Lanka about sustainability issues and corporate guidelines. The company followed with a letter to all apparel factories with explicit encouragement to issue public sustainability reports. The incentive for the vendors is to earn best practice credit on Gap's Code of Vendor Conduct ratings.

Gap's goal is to provide consumers with products they feel good about wearing. One strategy to achieve the goal is the implementation of the new Sustainable Fiber Toolkit, which was developed to help designers compare environmental and social impacts of

- different fibers;
- different manufacturing processes, including dyeing, printing, bleaching, and garment washing; and
- final product at each stage of its lifecycle.

Gap pilot-tested the Higg Index to assess environmental impact of its four high-volume products that are manufactured each season. In denim laundries, jeans are treated using large amounts of chemicals, energy, and water. Fabric mills also require a lot of the same resources for dyeing and finishing processes. Gap developed and is in the process of implementing Wise Wash manufacturing practices to reduce water, energy, and chemical usage in jeans washing by an average of 25 percent. All laundries that finish Gap's products have to comply with the company's standardized guidelines for water quality discharge, including overall water temperature, color gradations, and chemical makeup. The company has committed to working toward zero discharge of hazardous chemicals by 2020 for all products across all pathways of release (discharges, emissions, and losses) in the company's supply chain, with a full lifecycle perspective.

Source: Gap Inc. (2013). "Social and Environmental Responsibility Report." Retrieved March 7, 2015, from http://www.gapinc.com/content/csr/html/environment.html

1. How does Gap's initiative to reduce its environmental footprint affect the way the company operates?
2. You are very likely to be familiar with the Gap brand, have shopped at the company's stores many times, and/or own Gap clothes. Did you know about Gap's environmental initiatives before you read the case? Is it important for the company to inform consumers about these initiatives? Why? Why not? If yes, what would be the best way to do it?
3. Review the product lifecycle chart in the Gap's model of environmental impact. Gap has the least control over the consumer phase of the lifecycle. How could the company inform and engage its customers to be more environmentally responsible when caring for and disposing Gap's clothing?

SUSTAINABILITY MATRIX FOR TEXTILE-BASED PRODUCTS' LIFE CYCLE

What product is a sustainable product? What about manufacturing processes? How should sustainable product and manufacturing processes be defined in the textile and apparel industry? Some of these issues were introduced in Chapter 2, so this is an opportunity to have a more in-depth look on the topic. A Sustainability Matrix for Textile-Based Products' Lifecycle was developed by Elena Karpova to answer these questions and provide a foundation to systematically review the impact of textiles and apparel production and consumption on our environment. The matrix incorporates major stages in the textile and apparel lifecycle and strategies for minimizing environmental impact of products and processes. In addition we will examine strategies to make design, manufacturing, distribution, consumption, and disposal of textile-based products more sustainable. Take a few minutes to study Table 4.1.

Textile-based products' lifecycles are identified across the top of Table 4.1 and include the following stages:

1. design and product development of apparel, accessories, and home fashion;
2. manufacturing and use of all input resources;
3. distribution, transportation, and retail; and
4. consumption, including product care, and disposal.

Sustainability strategies are based on the waste management hierarchy and include:

1. avoid and reduce;
2. reuse; and
3. recycle and recover. (Zero Waste Europe, 2013; US Environmental Protection Agency, n.d.-c; Zero Waste SA, n.d.)

TABLE 4.1

SUSTAINABILITY MATRIX FOR TEXTILE-BASED PRODUCTS' LIFECYCLE

Sustainable Strategies		Major Stages of Textile-Based Products' Lifecycle			
	Most preferred / Least preferred	Design and Product Development	Manufacturing and All Input Resources	Distribution, Transportation, and Retail	Consumption and Disposal
Avoid and Reduce		Design products that last; require minimum resources to produce and minimal care. Select materials with minimal environmental impact.	Minimize waste of materials and resources (energy, water, fabrics, etc.). Reduce air, water, and land pollution (emissions, harmful chemicals).	Reduce product travel: efficient logistics; production closer to consumer. Minimize packaging for shipping and store display.	Limit purchase of new apparel (leasing and renting). Keep apparel longer (repair). Minimize impact of product care: laundry and dry cleaning.
Reuse		Design repairable and reusable products.	Reuse water in textiles and apparel processing.	Reuse packaging for other purposes.	Collaborative consumption: swapping, consignment, etc.
Recycle & Recover		Using elements of vintage apparel for new products. Design products that are easy to recover fibers from.	Upcycle products. Recover fibers to create new products.	Cardboard boxes to create new paper-based products. Plastic bags to recover fiber.	Donate to charities for recycling and recovering fiber

The sustainability strategies are listed in Table 4.1 from most to least preferred. At the top are most preferred strategies that result in minimal to no impact on the environment. While strategies at the bottom are least preferred, they are still much better than simply sending products to landfills. To effectively address current and growing environmental issues, there needs to be a shift from recycling and recovery to reuse and/or ultimately to avoid and reduce.

Avoid and Reduce Strategies

Avoiding unnecessary use of resources and generation of waste whenever possible is the most sustainable strategy. As discussed at the beginning of the chapter, the volume and rate at which resources are being channeled through the global economy have to be reduced for our planet and future generations to survive. Because clothing serves a basic human need, following right after food and shelter, people have to be clothed and cannot completely avoid apparel consumption. However, it might be possible for some people to commit to avoiding purchase of new products and instead purchase or otherwise acquire used clothing.

Reducing the amount of textiles and apparel produced and consumed translates into minimizing use of resources and generation of waste. Businesses and especially consumers have to realize that every garment and activity associated with its creation, consumption, care, and disposal have an environmental footprint "price tag" attached to the garment. If a garment was designed and produced to last three wearings and three washing cycles, after which it is no longer suitable for wearing and has to be discarded, it does not mean that it used less resources than a garment that was created to last for a decade or two. In other words, low-quality garments with short lifecycles (often associated with fast fashion) require approximately the same amount of resources to design, manufacture, transport, sell, and dispose as higher-quality, more durable garments that are made to last. Investing precious renewable and nonrenewable resources (including water, petroleum, energy, fiber, etc.) into something that will very quickly be discarded wastes these precious resources.

Reuse Strategy

Reuse is taking a product that is no longer wanted and finding a new application for it. This strategy is associated with repurposing a product when it can be utilized in a new context. Reuse strategy is more sustainable than recycling or recovery because it requires less resources and it is already part of our consumer society, so there is an existing precedent to build on. For reuse strategy to be even more successful and widely adopted, products should be designed with reusability features in mind, which means they have to be both adaptable and durable so they can retain value and function when reused. Consignment and worn clothing shopping as well as swapping are important reuse strategies. Other examples are presented later in the chapter.

Recycle and Recover Strategies

Recycling is the process of taking a product at the end of its useful life and using all or part of it to make another product. **Recovering** is the process of collecting and sorting out waste materials for processing into new forms, which can be marketed as raw materials for new products (e.g., fibers to make yarn). While it is important to recognize the difference between the two strategies, the recycling term is used more often and usually incorporates the recovering strategy. To be consistent with the industry lingo, "recycling" will primarily be used in this chapter.

The recycle and recover strategies are the last opportunity to divert products from being wasted. Recycling and recovering reduces the amount of waste, saves space in landfills, is more energy-efficient than burning waste, and conserves natural resources. The strategies are not only environmentally important but also cost effective. Almost 100 percent of textile-based products can be recycled, yet, currently, the majority of them end up in landfills. The current rate of overall waste recycling and composting in the United States is only around 34 percent (Williams, 2015).

Incineration and Landfilling

The lowest points in the waste management hierarchy are not presented in Table 4.1, but they are incineration, or burning of waste materials to generate energy, and dumping wastes in landfills. With 4.4 pounds of trash produced by every American every day, the highest rates in the world, incineration might appear to be the answer to the growing landfill problems. However, incineration does destroy resources that could otherwise be recovered and used to make new products. It also emits dangerous levels of mercury, lead, dioxins, and other harmful substances (Williams, 2015).

APPLICATION OF THE SUSTAINABILITY MATRIX

The most efficient way to demonstrate how the Sustainability Matrix for Textile-Based Products' Lifecycle can be used to systematically analyze environmental issues in the textile and apparel industries is to provide examples of best industry practices. The matrix is not an exhaustive list of all sustainable industry practices and initiatives but provides examples of the most prominent ones. Sustainable textile and apparel practices and initiatives are not static but ever-evolving, yet the matrix can incorporate all of them in one of the twelve cells in Table 4.1, as all practices can be classified under one of the three sustainability strategies as well as under one of the four lifecycle stages.

Design and Product Development

The design stage of the textile-based products' lifecycle has a tremendous impact on how sustainable products will be in the process of manufacturing, distribution, consumption, and disposal. In fact, about 70 percent of a product's environmental impact is determined during the design stage (Niinimaki, 2010). To develop sustainable products, designers can create apparel and other software goods that:

- are aimed at longevity rather than obsolescence;
- are made of materials with minimal/reduced impact on the environment;
- require manufacturing processes that minimize use of resources, waste, and pollution;
- minimize packaging needed for transportation and display of product in the store;
- are easier to repair, reuse, recycle, and recover; and
- require minimal care during consumption stage.

Figure 4.5

Unique design allows shoes to "grow" with the child by using adjustable features to regulate the length and width of the shoe.

Can the fast fashion customer become a sustainable fashion customer? Perhaps, the essence of fashion trends and the meaning of "fashionable" could be reinvented. Instead of being expressed through different colors, prints, and style elements, is it possible for fashion trends to be expressed through designs with sustainable features? Perhaps, consumer desire for newness could be channeled into creative use and reuse of garments. Would mass-market consumers support companies that produce sustainable apparel of high quality and durability, with unique design and functional features, by paying high prices? Otherwise, designing for product longevity rather than obsolescence and making profit would be a challenge for a business. For example, an accessory designer, Daniel Freitag, measures the success of his business and his own as a designer by the fact that his first bag design launched in 1993 is still in demand today and has not lost any of its contemporariness (Freitag, n.d.-b; more on this company is later in the chapter). If you are a design student, here is a challenge: next time you work on a course project, design a unique product that will be in demand not only today but also 20+ years later.

For children, creating designs that can "grow" will extend the life of a product. For example, at Gro With Me Apparel, infant and baby clothing is made with adjustable and expandable design features at legs, arms, and waist, so it can grow with the child (www.growithme.com). The clothes, all made in the US, are available in organic cotton and contain no BPA. Another example is Kenton Lee's innovative design of shoes that can expand up to five sizes (Figure 4.5). Lee's goal is to outfit children in Africa (https://theshoethatgrows.org/).

Another strategy to extend garment life is to make it easy to repair. According to industry experts, apparel companies should provide guidance and incentives for designing easily repairable products (McDonald, Turnbull, & McConnell, 2012). To maximize product repairability, design features can be used to easily replace buckles, zipper pulls, zippers, and other components and accessories.

Selection of Materials

Selecting fabric and trims is critical not only for garment aesthetics and durability but also for reducing a final product's impact on the environment. Different materials have various environmental footprints based on how they were produced and sourced, what processes they require when manufacturing apparel, type of care needed when using the garment, and whether and how easily they can be processed for recovering fiber at the end of the garment's life. To help designers make responsible material selections, Nike developed the Environmental Design Tool, based on a decade of researching hundreds of materials for the company's internal purposes (http://www.nikebiz.com/Default.aspx). The tool allows comparing multiple materials in terms of their environmental impacts: waste, energy, toxins, and water usage.

Sustainability experts suggest that the language of color should change (McConnell, 2011). Pale, pastel, and medium bright colors should mean "green" and be used for all new apparel. This will allow lower temperatures and less time and chemicals to dye fabrics while conserving water and energy. Deep and bright colors should be reserved for recycled materials only, which will allow application of a new color without stripping old colors. Finally, fluorescent colors, which require the most resources, should be used for security applications only, such as protective clothing for police and road construction workers, children's backpacks, runners' vests or stripes, etc. The sustainable language of color will help reduce the environmental impact of new fabric production and make recovering fiber from discarded textiles more efficient.

Selection of fabric fiber content also determines how easy it is to recover and recycle fiber from a discarded garment. When a fabric is made of yarn consisting of only one type of fiber (e.g., 100 percent nylon or 100 percent cotton), the fibers are much easier to recover so they can be used as raw materials for new textiles. In contrast, it is much more difficult to recover for fabrics made of a blend of fibers, such as, for example, 50 percent cotton and 50 percent polyester.

Japan-based Teijin Group operates the world's first **closed-loop system** that recovers polyester fiber from worn polyester clothing (Rodie, 2010). A closed-loop system is when some or all of its output is used as input. Patagonia, which is both Teijin's customer and supplier, collects discarded polyester garments for fiber recovery and then uses fleece fabric made of recovered fibers to create new apparel. The Patagonia vest in Figure 4.6 is made with Teijin's closed-loop recycled polyester. After its useful life, it can be dropped at one of Patagonia's stores and recycled again into new fiber to be reused in a new Patagonia garment.

Figure 4.6
Patagonia's Synchilla fleece vest made with closed-loop recycled polyester.

Manufacturing and All Input Resources

In the world of finite natural resources, long-term company sustainability depends on their ability to do more with less. Eco-efficiency—the same or greater utility from less resources—will be essential for competitive advantage and success. Some of the ways to reduce, reuse, and recover resources in the process of manufacturing apparel and input materials include:

- avoiding/reducing application of toxic chemicals in cotton growing and textile processing;
- avoiding/reducing use of virgin fibers to make fabrics and conserving land, forests, and petroleum;
- reducing and reusing natural resources (water, energy, etc.) in the production processes;
- minimizing waste of fabric through maker efficiency and reusing or recycling fabric scraps; and
- recovering fibers to create new products.

Avoid: Endangered Forests

Around the world, forests are routinely cut down, pulped, spun, and woven to make rayon, viscose, acetate, modal, and lyocell fabrics that are sewn into dresses, skirts, T-shirts, and tank tops. The amount of trees cut each year to produce pulp for making fabrics can circle the equator seven times. With the continuously growing consumer demand for more clothing, the dissolving pulp industry has been expanding. Cellulosic man-made fibers are increasingly made from the world's most ancient and endangered forests, from the tropical rainforests of Indonesia and Amazon to the great northern boreal forests in Canada. Destruction of these forests threatens the whole ecosystem and biodiversity and contributes to climate change (Figure 4.7). To address the growing

Figure 4.7

The Leuser ecosystem in Indonesia is the last stronghold of the Sumatran orangutan; the forests are being cut to make cellulose-based fabrics such as rayon.

problem, environmental organization Canopy, in collaboration with fashion designers and brands, is spearheading the Fashion Loved by Forest (Canopy, n.d.-a) initiative to build transparent supply-chain specific to forest-fabric sourcing. Among participating apparel companies are Eileen Fisher, Levi Strauss, Marks & Spencer, Patagonia, Stella McCartney, Quiksilver, and others. In 2014, two fashion giants, H&M and Inditex/Zara, joined the initiative (Apparel, 2014).

These two dozen apparel brands made a commitment to eliminate ancient and endangered forests from all of their rayon and viscose clothing. While this is definitely a very positive step and might help to curtail the problem, what about other apparel companies as well as other forests that are being cut to deliver the newest fashion trends to consumers? According to H&M's environmental sustainability manager, "H&M wants to play a strong role in ensuring a future for the planet's ancient and endangered forests. We are fully committed to exploring our supply chain and doing our utmost to avoid these fabrics within the next three years" (Apparel, 2014, para 8). How much of the endangered forests will be cut between 2014 and 2017 to make H&M tops and dresses to be sold worldwide? Check your garments' fiber content labels. How many of them are made from viscose, rayon, or acetate (cellulosic man-made fibers)? What trees were cut to make these garments? Every year more than 70 million trees are cut for fabric production alone, not including paper and furniture manufacturing needs (Canopy, n.d.-b). Production of cellulosic man-made fibers is expected to double by 2050, destroying even more trees. If the trend of cutting endangered forests continues, many species, such as the orangutan, will lose their habitat and become extinct in your lifetime. Canopy suggests the following endangered forests solutions (Canopy, n.d.-b):

- join leading brands and designers to work with Canopy on developing effective endangered forest procurement policy;
- ensure your brand is free of endangered forest fiber and support long-term conservation solutions;

- shift to eco-fabrics and support the development of agricultural residues like leftover straw as a sustainable alternative for fabric manufacturing; and

- produce and buy clothes that last and reuse and recycle fabric to capitalize on market appeal, brand benefits, and operational efficiency.

While these solutions were developed primarily with businesses in mind, they are also applicable to consumers as they are the ones that are driving demand and voting with their wallets what the industry should produce and how.

Reduce: Water and Chemicals

In the 1990s and early 2000s, governments, nongovernmental organizations, and consumers have been focused primarily on labor issues, including workers' rights and safety conditions. According to industry experts, water is becoming a priority among all the stakeholders (Horwitch, 2015). Manufacturing of fibers, yarns, and fabrics requires large amounts of water and application of chemicals with different environmental profiles. Some apparel production operations, such as laundry and special jeans finishes, also use significant amount of waters treated with chemicals. Reducing and reusing wastewater at factories and mills can reduce use of this invaluable resource, minimize environmental impact, and even potentially lower production costs (Figure 4.8).

There are a number of industry initiatives that address the availability and safety of water. AAFA and TEXbase launched VPEPxchange, an online collaboration platform that allows for supply chain transparency with respect to chemicals usage. The Voluntary Product Environmental Profile (VPEP) is a standardized supplier disclosure form containing information on the chemical makeup of products and their environmental properties relative to global standards and regulations (VPEPxchange, n.d.). VPEPxchange enables companies to make informed and educated decisions when choosing materials for producing textiles and apparel across the supply chain.

AAFA Environmental Task Force regularly updates and publishes a Restricted Substance List (RSL). RSL provides textile, apparel, footwear, and home furnishing companies with "information related to regulations and laws that restrict or ban

Figure 4.8
Reusing wastewater at textile mills is an important environmental strategy that can lower production cost in the long run.

certain chemicals and substances in finished home textile, apparel, and footwear products around the world" (American Apparel and Footwear Association, 2013, p. 3). RSL focuses on regulations, whether or not chemicals can be found in finished textile products at a certain level in different countries. It does not include regulations related to the use of chemicals in production processes. RSL helps textile and apparel professionals to make responsible decisions when choosing chemicals to manufacture textile and apparel products. Read Case 4.2 to learn about one US

CASE 4.2

VF CORPORATION'S CHEM-IQ

VF's new chemical management program, CHEM-IQ, goes beyond the RSL that every apparel company is required to use. The program is designed to detect more than 400 harmful chemicals, such as chlorinated solvents and formaldehyde, and eliminate them from the supply chains. The challenge was to create a test for 400 chemicals at a time, which would be easy and inexpensive to implement for suppliers in any country of the world.

Third-party experts were contracted to develop a list of chemicals and a coding system based on the chemicals' toxicity and potential impact on the environment. A three-color system was developed to classify all chemicals:

- green-rated chemicals contain nondetectable or trace amounts of unwanted substances and can continue to be used;
- red-rated chemicals contain unwanted substances over a specified concentration threshold and have to be replaced with a green-rated chemical from the provided preferred list within two months (VF provides assistance in finding appropriate substitutes); and
- yellow-rated chemicals require suppliers to put in place safeguards for the workers and environment and preferably replace with green-rated chemicals.

The program was first tested and implemented at VF-owned factories and key suppliers in Mexico, Turkey, and Los Angeles. A supplier collects samples of all chemicals used in its factories or mills and sends them to a certified lab for screening. The testing process takes two months from sample collection to the supplier getting back the report with color-rated chemicals. In just one year after screening more than 1,000 chemicals at 100 factories, about 100 tons of harmful chemicals were removed from manufacturing processes. You can imagine what the numbers will be after the program is implemented at nearly 2,000 of VF's suppliers in 60 countries.

According to VF, suppliers liked the simplicity of the program and its low cost (no more than $50 per chemical including shipping and lab analysis), as well as clear guidelines for how to make their facilities more environmentally friendly. The program provides specific information on which chemicals are more or less harmful and can be used to make decisions when engineering production processes. VF plans to have all its vendors across the entire supply chain participate in the program, including textile and dye mills, laundry and printing facilities, and apparel factories. Eventually, VF will use the system for scoring current and potential suppliers. In 2015, the program begins with vendors in China, India, Bangladesh, and Vietnam.

There are a number of challenges to fully implementing the program across the supply chain. First, there are a very limited number of testing labs available in the world. Samples have to be shipped internationally. VF hopes that other companies will adopt the program so the process can be further refined and eventually become an industry standard. If the chemical management program is adopted across the industry, the process will become more efficient with more labs available. The impact of proactive chemical management can be transformational for the industry.

Source: Nagappan, P. February 1, 2015. VF: Stopping hazardous chemicals from entering the supply chain. *Apparel.* http://apparel.edgl.com/news/vf-stopping-hazardous-chemicals-from-entering-the-supply-chain97930?referral type=newsletter

1. Locate and review the current RSL published by AAFA. Note countries that most often ban chemicals (substances) in textile-based products. How would you feel if these chemicals were found in your clothes and bedding? What should be done to prevent this from happening?
2. What is the relationship between RSL and CHEM-IQ?
3. What are the advantages and disadvantages for VF's chemical management program to become a standard in the industry?

company's initiative to control harmful chemicals in the apparel supply chain that goes beyond RSL.

Recycle and Recover: Materials

An increasing number of companies recycle textile-based materials to make new apparel, accessories, and other products. Only three companies, making new products from recycled tires, shoes, and truck tarpaulins, are discussed here. You are encouraged to do additional research to learn about other innovative industry practices.

In 2014, Timberland (part of VF Corporation) partnered with Omni United to create the tire-to-shoe recycling program, where tires will be used as raw material for shoe outsoles (Figure 4.9). With this program, fewer tires will go to landfill and, at the same time, less virgin rubber will be needed to make footwear outsoles (Speer, 2015). This is just one of the company's initiatives to reduce the impact of the business on the environment.

Nike's Reuse-A-Shoe program involves collecting disposed athletic shoes from any brand, recycling shoes in a scrap material to make Nike Grind used for sport surfacing such as basketball courts and tracks (Intertek, 2011). Since the 1990s, Nike has recycled 28 million pairs of shoes (Figure 4.10) and 36,000 tons of scrap material into Nike Grind that covers 630,000,000 square feet (almost enough to cover Manhattan) at more than 450,000 locations around the world (Nike Inc., n.d.-b). Read Case 4.3 to learn about a successful Swiss fashion accessories company, Freitag, that based its business model on a unique material recovery strategy.

Distribution, Transportation, and Retail

Reduce: Product Tourism

Given that 95 to 97 percent of all apparel sold in the United States (the numbers are similar for other developed economies, such as EU, Japan, Australia, Canada, etc.) is imported, it has to be shipped, often from halfway across the globe. Transportation of

Figure 4.9
Timberland signature shoes will soon have rubber outsoles made of recycled tires.

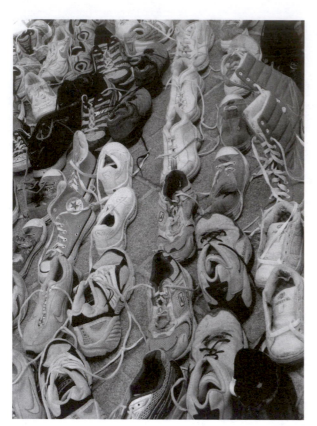

Figure 4.10
Nike's Reuse-A-Shoe program recycles worn-out sneakers into playground and sport surfaces.

raw materials, intermediates, and final apparel products all over the world is energy consuming and environmentally polluting. Extensive product tourism, while economically viable due to production in low labor cost regions, is not sustainable. When transportation is unavoidable, more environmentally friendly modes should be selected (e.g., substitute air freight for railroad).

Reduce, Reuse, Recycle: Packaging

Special attention should be given to packaging. All of the 2.2 billion shoes and 20 billion garments sold every year in the US market alone require some sort of packaging: boxes, cartons, plastic bags, hangers, etc. Most of them go straight from the store to your garbage container and sent to landfills, not even recycled. Although there are some innovative approaches to the problem, such as Puma's "clever little bag" (Figure 4.11), large-scale packaging solutions for transportation, storage, and store display are

---

CASE 4.3

FROM TRUCKS TO BAGS: A SUSTAINABLE FASHION ACCESSORIES BUSINESS

Based in Zürich, Freitag is an urban fashion company with the focus on designing and manufacturing bags and accessories. What is unusual about it is that all products are made from used truck tarpaulins (Figure Case 4.3a). Two

Figure Case 4.3a
Truck covered with tarpaulin, which is used as raw material for Freitag's bags.

Freitag brothers started this Swiss company in 1993, after one of them was looking for a durable, weatherproof, and sustainable bicycle messenger bag. The idea came when they were watching passing trucks covered with colorful waterproof material. Soon, the first Freitag bag was made out of an old truck tarpaulin with a used car seatbelt as the handle and strap. The brothers began making bags for their friends and then for friends of friends, eventually starting their own business. Now the company employs 160 people and produces 400,000 bags every year. The demand for stylish, functional, and sustainable bags and accessories is booming (Figure Case 4.3b). Design, product development, and material sourcing, as well as most of the production, is done in Zürich.

In more than 20 years of Freitag business, tons of used truck tarpaulins have been diverted from landfills and recycled into useful and unique products. The company strives to incorporate sustainable strategies in every operation. Smaller fabric scraps are used for making accessories, such as phone cases and wallets. Rainwater is used to clean huge tarpaulin sheets before sending them to production.

Figure Case 4.3b
The original Freitag messenger bag: "comfortable, expandable, unbreakable, bicyclable, laptopable"; made of truck tarpaulin.

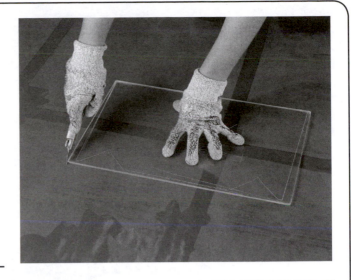

Figure Case 4.3c
Freitag's designer cuts out one bag at a time from truck tarpaulin using a pattern block and sharp knife.

Of course, Freitag's customers like the fact that by buying the company's bags they are being environmentally responsible. Even more so, they appreciate the design and functionality of the product. The key to the originality of Freitag's bags is that each of them is truly a one-of-a-kind product. Freitag's designers literally create one bag after the other, cutting special templates with a sharp knife (Figure Case 4.3c). Because truck tarps come in all colors and covered in different letters and prints that advertise companies' names and products, designers use all their creativity to carve the most beautiful and exquisite designs possible. Freitag coined the term to describe this creative design process: recycled individual products (RIP).

The company's success took it far beyond Swiss borders. It operates close to ten stores and sells products through dozens of dealerships in Europe, Asia, North America, and Australia. In 2013, it opened a store in Tokyo, Japan (Figure Case 4.3d). For its sustainability efforts and unique design, the company has been recognized with a number of awards. For example, the original Freitag model, F13 Top Cat, is in the design collection of the Museum of Modern Art (MoMA) in New York.

Source: Freitag website, www.freitag.ch

Figure Case 4.3d
Freitag has been successful selling its bags all over the world; this stand-alone Freitag's store in Tokyo has a slick and modern feel.

1. List all factors that you believe contribute to the success of this Swiss company.
2. Freitag has a successful business model that is 100 percent based on recycling materials (used tarpaulins and car seatbelts). What are the reasons that only a few companies use recyclables as their raw materials? List barriers to the business model.
3. Brainstorm other potential sources of textile-based recyclables that can be used as raw materials to make new products. Go through your daily life and think about every product that is textile-based. How can it be recycled? Develop a list of 20 potential business ideas.

Figure 4.11
Puma shoes are packaged in boxes that use 65 percent less paper, resulting in reduced usage of water and energy and GHG emission.

long overdue. In addition to reducing box waste, Puma's packaging eliminates the need for plastic bags to carry the shoe box in after purchase.

After two years of research and testing, the Sustainable Packaging Coalition released the Sustainable Packaging Indicators and Metrics Framework (Sustainable Packaging Coalition, 2009). In this comprehensive framework, indicators and metrics are organized into eight modules, covering material use, energy use, water use, material health, clean production and transport, cost and performance, community impact, and worker impact (Figure 4.12). Each module explains how indicators relate to sustainability, defines them in relation to packaging, and provides metrics and recommendations for measurements.

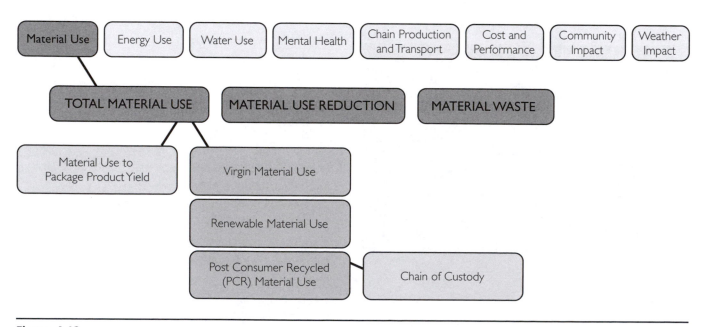

Figure 4.12
Graphical representation of the first module, Material Use, from the Sustainable Packaging Indicators and Metrics Framework.
Source: Sustainable Packaging Coalition, http://www.sustainablepackaging.org/content/?type=5&id=sustainable-packaging-metrics

Reduce and Recycle: Facility Operation

With the highest number of retail space per capita in the world, 46 square feet (Lewis, 2014), US-based retailers and brands are examining the environmental impact of their operations as this is the area where they have direct control (Figure Case 4.1). Gap's initiative is typical for any major apparel retailer. The company measured the footprint of its headquarters, distribution centers, and stores. As a result of the established 2008 benchmark, Gap has set a goal to reduce GHG emission in the headquarters and stores by 20 percent by 2015 (Gap Inc., 2013). San Francisco, where Gap is headquartered, has committed to be a zero-waste city by 2020. In support of this campaign, Gap "greened" its main building to achieve 75 percent diversion rate of the total waste generated by the employees. A comprehensive audit of the distribution center (DC) in Fresno, California, resulted in an average reduction in energy usage of 17 percent and cost savings of 30 percent. DCs in Ohio and Tennessee are undergoing the same process. The company is testing light-emitting diode (LED) technology to reduce electricity use in lighting its stores, which is the single biggest electricity usage among Gap's owned facilities.

Consumption and Disposal

Reduce and reuse are very important strategies at the consumption stage of textile-based products' lifecycle. Many examples are presented in the Table 4.1 matrix and discussed in the chapter, and still others can be added to the list. Major strategies include:

- limiting purchase of new apparel;
- leasing apparel and accessories, especially for special occasions;
- repairing products so they can be used longer;
- reducing impact of product care (laundry, drying, ironing, dry cleaning);
- collaborative consumption; and
- donating worn apparel for recycling and recovering fiber.

Reduce Strategy: New Apparel Consumption

Can sustainability and fashion go together? It appears that the two might be contradictory concepts. For apparel to become sustainable, consumption patterns have to be addressed. Patagonia, a sustainability leader in the global apparel industry, believes that its biggest contribution to the environment is extending and encouraging longevity of the clothing the company makes: "One of the most responsible things we can do as a company is to make high-quality stuff that lasts for years and can be repaired, so you don't have to buy more of it" (Patagonia, 2015). Can apparel purchasing be considered an investment? Perhaps buying classic, timeless garments of high quality? What can be done to shift consumer demand from buying greater quantities of inexpensive garments discarded quickly to buying less items that are more expensive and will last (that *are* an investment)?

Now, go back to your responses to the questions you answered at the beginning of the chapter. How many years have you been wearing the oldest garment in your wardrobe? What made this garment so special that you have kept and used it for so long? How does it make you feel? This garment must be a good investment for you, not only in the financial sense but also from the emotional perspective. Would you like to own more clothing like that and reduce your environmental footprint at the same time?

To discourage consumers from purchasing new apparel, on Black Friday 2011, Patagonia went against the mainstream culture and published an advertisement urging consumers to only buy what they need and *not* to buy the company's best-selling jacket (Figure 4.13).

DON'T BUY THIS JACKET

It's Black Friday, the day in the year retail turns from red to black and starts to make real money. But Black Friday, and the culture of consumption it reflects, puts the economy of natural systems that support all life firmly in the red. We're now using the resources of one-and-a-half planets on our one and only planet.

Because Patagonia wants to be in business for a good long time – and leave a world inhabitable for our kids – we want to do the opposite of every other business today. We ask you to buy less and to reflect before you spend a dime on this jacket or anything else.

Environmental bankruptcy, as with corporate bankruptcy, can happen very slowly, then all of a sudden. This is what we face unless we slow down, then reverse the damage. We're running short on fresh water, topsoil, fisheries, wetlands – all our planet's natural systems and resources that support business, and life, including our own.

The environmental cost of everything we make is astonishing. Consider the R2® Jacket shown, one

COMMON THREADS INITIATIVE

REDUCE
WE make useful gear that lasts a long time
YOU don't buy what you don't need

REPAIR
WE help you repair your Patagonia gear
YOU pledge to fix what's broken

REUSE
WE help find a home for Patagonia gear you no longer need
YOU sell or pass it on*

RECYCLE
WE will take back your Patagonia gear that is worn out
YOU pledge to keep your stuff out of the landfill and incinerator

REIMAGINE
TOGETHER we reimagine a world where we take only what nature can replace

of our best sellers. To make it required 135 liters of water, enough to meet the daily needs (three glasses a day) of 45 people. Its journey from its origin as 60% recycled polyester to our Reno warehouse generated nearly 20 pounds of carbon dioxide, 24 times the weight of the finished product. This jacket left behind, on its way to Reno, two-thirds its weight in waste.

And this is a 60% recycled polyester jacket, knit and sewn to a high standard; it is exceptionally durable, so you won't have to replace it as often. And when it comes to the end of its useful life we'll take it back to recycle into a product of equal value. But, as is true of all the things we can make and you can buy, this jacket comes with an environmental cost higher than its price.

There is much to be done and plenty for us all to do. Don't buy what you don't need. Think twice before you buy anything. Go to patagonia.com/CommonThreads or scan the QR code below. Take the Common Threads Initiative pledge, and join us in the fifth "R," to reimagine a world where we take only what nature can replace.

patagonia.com

* If you sell your used Patagonia product on eBay® and take the Common Threads Initiative pledge, we will co-list your product on patagonia.com for no additional charge.
© 2011 Patagonia, Inc.

TAKE THE PLEDGE

The ad informed consumers of environmentally responsible practices they can engage in and how the company can assist them. Some observers accused Patagonia of hypocrisy, stating that the company simply wanted to grab consumer attention and increase its sales.

Reduce Strategy: Leasing

Leasing apparel can be a smart alternative to buying new items because it allows

- access to a greater variety of clothing at lower cost and no storage/care requirements;
- sustainability—less apparel needs to be produced, thus reducing the use of virgin resources and pollution associated with production and disposal; and
- fulfilling consumer need for newness as well as cultural and societal expectation for outfit variety (e.g., women's office clothing).

Leasing certain types of apparel for special functions, for example tuxedos, has been around for a long time. The 2000s saw fast growth of services leasing women's apparel and accessories, with most prominent being Rent the Runway, Wear Today Gone Tomorrow, and Girl Meets Dress (the UK). Avelle (former Bag, Borrow, or Steal) offers designer accessories with no limit on the amount of renting time. The services are convenient (shipped to your door), affordable (5 to 10 percent of its retail price, or between $50 and $200), and some use organic dry cleaning only as part of environmental commitment.

Reduce Strategy: Repair

By far, most clothing is discarded way before it is beyond repair. In the era of disposable fashion, educating consumers about the benefits of repair is critical (Figure 4.14). For this strategy to be successful, public awareness and attitudes toward the activity and repaired products must change. If a patch on your favorite pair of jeans or new zipper on your jacket would become fashionable and trendy, it would give consumers bragging rights.

To encourage consumers to keep apparel longer and repair it, Patagonia joined forces with iFixit to provide step-by-step manuals for caring for and repairing Patagonia clothing and gear (iFixit, n.d). Repair requires not only knowledge of "what to do" and "how" but also appropriate tools. For busy lifestyle consumers, it must be easy to acquire and use these tools, and, of course, these tools must be there when you need them.

To promote and educate about the importance of keeping apparel longer and repairing garments when needed, in spring 2015 a Patagonia Worn Wear biodiesel truck traveled from California to New York, stopping along the way in dozens of communities and offering free clothing repair as well as teaching DIY (Figure 4.15). Overflow of tired Patagonia clothing that did not get fixed on the spot was shipped to the company's repair facility in Reno (Patagonia, 2015).

Figure 4.14
iFixit manifesto lists the benefits of repairing things that we own instead of throwing them away.

Figure 4.15
Patagonia's spring 2015 Worn Wear truck on the way from California to New York.

Reduce Strategy: Product Care

An extensive research study of textiles and clothing sustainability found that for cotton garments, the consumption stage accounts for about 60 percent of total energy use in the clothing lifecycle (Allwood, Laursen, Rodriguez, and Bocken, 2006). The major contributors to use of resources and pollution were laundry, tumble-drying, and ironing. The remaining 40 percent of energy use is divided between producing materials, manufacturing garments, and transportation. A T-shirt that is washed and tumble dried at least 25 times in its lifetime uses about 4 lb. of fossil fuel, emits 9 lb. of CO_2, and deposits 1 lb. of waste to landfill. These numbers indicate that you, as a consumer, are responsible for the environmental impact of your garments. Now, go back to your responses to the questions you answered at the beginning of the chapter. With the amount of laundry you do every month and the way you dry your clothes, is there a way to reduce the current environmental impact?

Did you know that if you simply switch from tumble drying to air drying your washed clothes, it will reduce environmental impact of your garment care by 50 percent? (Please finish reading the chapter before rushing to a store to buy a rack similar to the one in Figure 4.16.) Lowering temperatures when you do laundry (from hot to warm and from warm to cold) allows reducing environmental impact by another 10 percent (Allwood, Laursen, Rodriguez, and Bocken, 2006). Cutting down on laundry frequency and not washing your garments after only one wear, when possible, is another sustainable strategy. Finally, it is preferable to use detergents with a maximum of 5 percent of phosphates, because larger amounts result in the growth of algae, which impacts water quality and threatens various water-based organisms.

If you did not know what difference you can make by choosing environmentally responsible care of your clothing, it is likely that other consumers are unaware of their impact as well. In 2010, Levi's and Goodwill launched an initiative to educate consumers on how to reduce the climate impact of clothes they own and encourage them to extend garment lifecycle by donating used clothing (Stiska, 2010). Levi's jeans care

Figure 4.16
Air drying laundry on a rack allows for reducing apparel environmental footprint by up to 50 percent.

labels suggest using cold water for washing garments, line drying them (instead of tumble drying), and donating them to Goodwill instead of throwing them away. In 2015, Levi's Care Tag for the Planet was being sewn into every pair of their jeans (Bergh, 2015).

Reuse of Textiles and Apparel

Used clothing shopping, hand-me-downs, and swapping are some of the strategies that can be utilized to reuse apparel. These practices have been around for a long time but became less popular during the booming and wasteful decades of the late twentieth century. It appears that with the growing sustainability movement and support of information technology, these reuse practices are not only coming back to life but reinventing themselves as new business models.

Since 2000, the US used merchandise industry saw a yearly growth of 5 percent, with clothing being by far the major product category (HighBeam Business, n.d.). For example, Goodwill Industries International, Inc., a leading company in the used merchandise industry, reported 11.9 percent sales increase in 2011 (Goodwill Industries International, n.d.). In 2011, the used merchandise industry consisted of 17,866 stores and employed 144,113 workers (US Census Bureau, 2010).

Among companies that make and sell new apparel, Patagonia has been a leader in encouraging sustainable consumption practices, including reuse of worn clothing. With Patagonia's Keep Portland Worn campaign, consumers can bring used clothing to stores and receive a Patagonia gift card for half of what the clothing is sold for. The company's Worn Wear campaign advocates for using your gear to document and share the story of your life in a blog (Patagonia, 2015). Patagonia created several documentaries featuring inspiring stories of consumers showcasing their clothing's unique character accumulated through years of adventures.

Reuse: Collaborative Consumption

In addition to traditional used merchandise business models such as consignment stores, charities, and thrift markets, there are new ways to acquire, sell, and exchange preowned apparel. Since the mid-2000s, a new phenomenon known as collaborative consumption has been on the rise. Collaborative consumption, also known as sharing economy, involves individuals and organizations borrowing or exchanging products instead of buying new. **Collaborative consumption** is a redistribution of used goods that are being passed from someone who does not want them to someone who does want them. In 2011, collaborative consumption was named one of the ten new ideas that will change the world by *TIME* magazine.

There are many different models of collaborative consumption. In some cases, goods can be donated for free; in other cases, they can be swapped for different products, and they can also be sold for cash or store credit. Emerging social lending systems and peer-to-peer services are based on the concept of collaborative consumption. A number of start-ups have come up with different business models to help consumers make environmentally responsible choices easy when disposing of apparel, accessories, and other products.

The idea behind Yerdle, a swapping app (www.yerdle.com), was to come up with a way for consumers to conveniently and effortlessly trade goods that otherwise would end up in landfills. Yerdle takes exchanging clothing (and other products) to a new level.

It works in three simple steps: post a photo of an item you no longer want, ship the item to someone who wants it (items under ten pounds are shipped free), and receive Yerdle Reuse Dollars (store credit) that can be spent on anything in the Yerdle online store without spending cash.

Basically, Yerdle is a new type of virtual two-way garage sale that anyone can conveniently take part in without interrupting their lives. In addition to cleaning your closet and garage from stuff you do not need in a sustainable way (it will be reused by others who want it), you can acquire things you need without buying new goods (saving resources needed to produce them) and spending money (investing them into a better cause). Research indicates that these types of transactions also resulted in non-economic value: satisfaction of giving your things away to others and connecting with other people (Steimetz, 2014).

Another startup, Twice (https://www.liketwice.com/), is a hybrid between traditional retailers like Amazon and peer-to-peer websites like eBay. Unlike Yerdle, which trades any merchandise, Twice deals exclusively with fashion items: clothes, bags, and shoes. The rules are more specific, too: merchandise must be five years old or less; in a good condition that could be given to a friend; and only specific brands are accepted (though the list of accepted brands is very long). A payout calculator provides estimates by product (top, skirt, pants, bag, etc.) and by brand.

Twice is an easy and effective way to deal with apparel and accessories you no longer want. It is also sustainable, as your clothes will be reused. It appeals to busy consumers who are low on time: simply put unwanted clothes in a delivered selling kit with a pre-paid shipping label (or use your own box and print out a free shipping label) and mail it to the company's warehouse in San Francisco. If your clothes pass inspection, you will receive an email with a payment offer. If you accept the offer, a check is mailed to you immediately. Your clothes will be photographed, priced, and posted on the website to sell. According to Twice users, the major advantages of the service are minimal time and effort, ability to do everything from home, and receiving payment right away without waiting for your clothes to sell. Twice claims to resell 400 tons of clothing and accessories a year.

Many companies discussed in this chapter are not only examples of successful small enterprises but also exciting grassroots industry initiatives that are inspirational business models for future industry professionals and entrepreneurs. As more and more people not only realize their individual contributions to environmental degradation through high consumption and disposal rates but also take personal responsibility for their own footprints, more and more businesses offering repair, leasing, trading, and exchanging goods services of different formats and models will appear. Some of these enterprises will be small and locally owned, others will be national and international in scope. Collaborative consumption is in its infant stage and positioned for an enormous growth.

Recycle and Recover

Many consumers donate no longer wanted clothing to charities such as Goodwill, Salvation Army, REACH Caregivers, Vietnam Veterans of America, and others. Clothing donated to charities is sorted into three groups: "for sale as clothing, wiping rags, and fiber" (Rivoli, 2015, p. 220). A lot of US used clothing is exported. In 2012, 762 million kg of used clothing worth $770 million traveled from the United States to nearly every country in the world: 159 nations imported apparel disposed by US consumers (Office of Textiles and Apparel, 2013). Other used clothing will be processed to recover fiber and reuse as raw material for new products.

Summary

The three dimensions of sustainability are social responsibility, economic responsibility, and environmental responsibility. The three dimensions are deeply intertwined to create systems that are bearable, viable, equitable, and, ultimately, sustainable. In the business context, the term "corporate social responsibility" is often used to describe businesses obligations to act for the benefit of society at large. To systematically address social, economic, and environmental responsibilities, companies develop codes of conduct that outline and guide how business decisions are made. To implement code of conduct strategies and establish a transparent and independent auditing of manufacturing facilities, several nonprofit organizations that promote fair labor and fair trade as well as community development were founded.

Many environmental issues that are global in scope demand our attention, such as climate change, diminishing petroleum resources, shortages of water, pollution/contamination of air, land, and water, and many others. In the context of textile and apparel, fast fashion has been driving increased consumption rates that contribute to environmental degradation. The Sustainability Matrix for Textile-Based Products' Lifecycle can be applied to systematically analyze environmental responsibility issues in the textile and apparel industries. The matrix combines sustainability strategies (avoid/reduce, reuse, and recycle/recover) and the major stages of the textile and apparel lifecycle (design and product development, manufacturing, distribution, and consumption and disposal). The design stage of the textile and apparel lifecycle has a tremendous impact on product sustainability. Reduce and reuse are very important strategies at the consumption and disposal stage of the apparel lifecycle. Responsible consumption of textile and apparel can include limiting purchase of new apparel, leasing, repair, minimizing environmental impact of product care, collaborative consumption, and donating worn apparel.

Learning Activities

1. What is the fundamental purpose of a corporate code of conduct? Why is there a need for a corporate code of conduct?
2. Choose two of your favorite apparel brands and look them up on the internet to find the companies' statements of social and environmental responsibility. What is included in these statements? What is left out? How do the statements you found relate to sustainability?
3. Do research and find examples of two fashion-related companies (not mentioned in this chapter) that use recycle or recovery strategies. Explain how the sustainable strategies benefit the business model of these companies. Present your findings to the class.
4. How would you describe your personal commitment to social and environmental responsibility? What do you do as a consumer to make your life more sustainable? What else can you do? Come up with a feasible action plan. Hint: Review Table 4.1

and identify various sustainable activities using different strategies. Share and compare action plans with your classmates.

5. In small groups, discuss and list major impediments for moving toward sustainable supply chains. Share and compare your responses with the class.

6. What is your opinion about the feasibility of fashion becoming sustainable in the US market? What would need to happen for apparel production and consumption to become more sustainable? Write a one-page essay to present your perspective on the state of the US apparel market in terms of environmental footprint ten years from today.

References

Allwood, J. M., Laursen, S. E., Rodriguez, C. M., and Bocken, N. M. (2006). "Well Dressed? The Present and Future Sustainability of Clothing and Textiles in the United Kingdom." Retrieved October 18, 2015, from http://www.ifm.eng.cam.ac.uk/sustainability/projects/mass/UK_textiles.pdf/

American Apparel and Footwear Association. (2013). "Restricted Substance List." https://www.wewear.org/assets/1/7/RSL12english-March2013.pdf

American Apparel and Footwear Association. (January 5, 2014). "AAFA Releases ApparelStats 2013 and ShoesStats 2013 Reports." Retrieved April 29, 2015, from https://www.wewear.org/aafa-releases-apparelstats-2013-and-shoestats-2013-reports/

Apparel. (April 3, 2014). "Zara, H&M Shift Sourcing Away from Endangered Forests." Retrieved May 15, 2015, from http://apparel.edgl.com/news/Zara,-H-M-Shift-Sourcing-Away-From-Endangered-Forests91973

Bergh, C. V. (March 19, 2015). "Levi's CEO: Do the World a Favor N' Wash Your Jeans Once Every 10 Wears." *Fortune.* Retrieved October 18, 2015, from http://www.fortune.com/2015/03/19/levis-ceo-do-the-world-a-favor-n-wash-your-jeans-once-every-10-wears/

Canopy. (n.d.-a). "Fashion Loved by Forest." Retrieved May 15, 2015, from http://www.canopystyle.org/make-a-difference/

Canopy. (n.d.-b). "Forests into Fashion." Retrieved May 15, 2015, from http://canopystyle.org/assets/infographic2.png

Fair Labor Association. (n.d.). "Affiliates." Retrieved May 2, 2015, from http://www.fairlabor.org/affiliates

Freitag. (n.d.-b). "Measures of Success." Retrieved May 10, 2015, from http://www.freitag.ch/about/bros

Gap Inc. (2013). "Social and Environmental Responsibility Report." Retrieved March 7, 2015, from http://www.gapinc.com/content/csr/html/environment.html

Global Alliances for Incinerator Alternatives. (n.d.). "Consumption." Retrieved April 28, 2015, from http://www.no-burn.org/section.php?id=89

Goodwill Industries International. (n.d.). Retrieved May 2, 2015, from http://www.goodwill.org/press-releases/a-care-tag-for-our-planet-levis-care-tags-promote-donating-to-goodwill/

HighBeam Business. (n.d.). "Used Merchandise Stores." Retrieved May 10, 2015, from http://business.highbeam.com/industry-reports/retail/used-merchandise-stores

Horwitch, R. (2015). "Protecting Your Brand and Managing Risk: A Global Compliance Executive Summary." Retrieved May 2, 2015, from https://www.wewear.org/clothesline/protecting-your-brand-and-managing-risk-a-global-compliance-executive-summary/

iFixit. (n.d). "Patagonia Care & Repair." Retrieved May 18, 2015, from https://www.ifixit.com/patagonia

Intertek. (2011). "Sustainable Footwear." Retrieved October 18, 2015, from https://www.wewear.org/assets/1/7/101311McConnell.pdf

Kunz, G. I. (2010). *Merchandising: Theory, Principles, and Practice.* Fairchild Books.

Lewis, R. (March 24, 2014). "The Great Retail Demassification." *Forbes*. http://www.forbes.com/sites/robinlewis/2014/03/24/the-great-retail-demassification-part-1/

McConnell, M. (2011). "Sustainability Insights." Unpublished thesis, North Carolina State University, Raleigh, NC. Retrieved October 18, 2015, from http://repository.lib.ncsu.edu/ir/bitstream/1840.16/6819/1/etd.pdf

McDonald, M., Turnbull, E., & McConnell, M. (2012). "Environmental Metrics of Apparel and Footwear Products." Retrieved May 1, 2015, from https://www.wewear.org/assets/1/7/AAFA_Intertek_Measuring_and_Reporting_Environmental_Metrics_082112.pdf

Miret, S. (2014). "Ranking Global Warming Contributions by Country." Retrieved October 18, 2015, from http://berc.berkeley.edu/ranking-global-warming-contributions-by-country/

Niinimaki, K. (2010). "Eco-Clothing, Consumer Identity, and Ideology." *Sustainable Development*, 18(3), 150-62.

Nike Inc. (n.d.-b). "Reuse-A-Shoe." Retrieved May 18, 2015, from http://www.nike.com/us/en_us/c/better-world/reuse-a-shoe

Nike Inc. (2015). "Manufacturing Map." Retrieved May 1, 2015, from http://manufacturingmap.nikeinc.com/

Office of Textiles and Apparel. (2013). "Trade Data: US Imports and Exports of Textiles and Apparel." Retrieved May 10, 2015, from http://otexa.ita.doc.gov/msrpoint.htm

Patagonia. (n.d.-b). "Worn Wear: A Film About the Stories We Wear." Retrieved May 13, 2015, from https://www.youtube.com/watch?t=50&v=z20CjCim8DM

Patagonia. (2015). "Spring Worn Wear Tour." Retrieved May 18, 2015, from http://www.patagonia.com/us/worn-wear/

Rivoli, P. (2015). *The Travels of a T-shirt in the Global Economy*. Hoboken: John Wiley & Sons.

Rodie, J. B. (2010). "From Waste to Worth: Recycling Programs Divert Post-Industrial and Post-Consumer Waste from Landfills and Turn Them into Valuable Feedstock for New Textile Products." Retrieved October 18, 2015, from http://www.textileworld.com/Issues/2010/November-December/Features/From_Waste_To_Worth

Speer, J. K. (May 6, 2015). "Timberland Puts the Rubber on the Road." *Apparel*. http://apparel.edgl.com/news/timberland-puts-the-rubber-to-the-road99947?referaltype=newsletter

Steimetz, K. (July 24, 2014). "Recycle, Reuse, Reprofit: Startups Trying to Make Money Selling Your Stuff." http://time.com/3028066/recycle-reuse-reprofit-startups-try-to-make-money-selling-your-stuff/

Stiska, A. (2010). "A Care Tag for Our Planet: Levi's Care Tags Promote Donating to Goodwill." Retrieved October 18, 2015, from http://www.goodwill.org/press-releases/a-care-tag-for-our-planet-levis-care-tags-promote-donating-to-goodwill/

Sustainable Packaging Coalition. (2009). "Sustainable Packaging Indicators and Metrics Framework." Retrieved October 18, 2015, from http://www.sustainablepackaging.org/content/?type=5&id=sustainable-packaging-metrics

Ten Thousand Villages. (n.d.). "Our Story." Retrieved May 10, 2015, from http://www.tenthousandvillages.com/about-history/

US Census Bureau. (2010). "Database." Retrieved May 15, 2015, from http://factfinder2.census.gov/faces/tableservices/jsf/pages/productview.xhtml?fpt=table

US Energy Information Administration. (2012). "International Energy Statistics." Retrieved April 28, 2015, from http://www.eia.gov/cfapps/ipdbproject/IEDIndex3.cfm?tid=44&pid=44&aid=2

US Environmental Protection Agency. (n.d.-b). "Sustainability." Retrieved April 30, 2015, from http://www.epa.gov/sustainability/basicinfo.htm

US Environmental Protection Agency. (n.d.-c). "Waste Management Hierarchy." Retrieved May 6, 2015, from http://www.epa.gov/waste/nonhaz/municipal/hierarchy.htm

US Environmental Protection Agency. (2008). "Global Greenhouse Gas Emission Data: Emissions by Country." Retrieved April 26, 2015, from http://www.epa.gov/climatechange/ghgemissions/global.html

US Environmental Protection Agency. (2013). "Sources of Greenhouse Gas Emissions." Retrieved April 25, 2015, from http://www.epa.gov/climatechange/ghgemissions/sources.html

VPEPxchange. (n.d.). Retrieved May 10, 2015, from http://www.vpepxchange.com/

Williams, T. (January 10, 2015). "Garbage Incinerators Make Comeback, Kindling Both Garbage and Debate." *The New York Times*. Retrieved May 6, 2015, from http://www.nytimes.com/2015/01/11/us/garbage-incinerators-make-comeback-kindling-both-garbage-and-debate.html

World Fair Trade Organization. (n.d.). "Definition of Fair Trade." Retrieved May 6, 2015, from http://wfto.com/fair-trade/definition-fair-trade

Zero Waste Europe. (2013). "Waste Management Hierarchy." Retrieved May 6, 2015, from http://www.zerowasteeurope.eu/2013/04/zero-waste-hierarchy

Zero Waste SA. (n.d.). Retrieved May 6, 2015, from http://www.zerowaste.sa.gov.au/about-us/waste-management-hierarchy

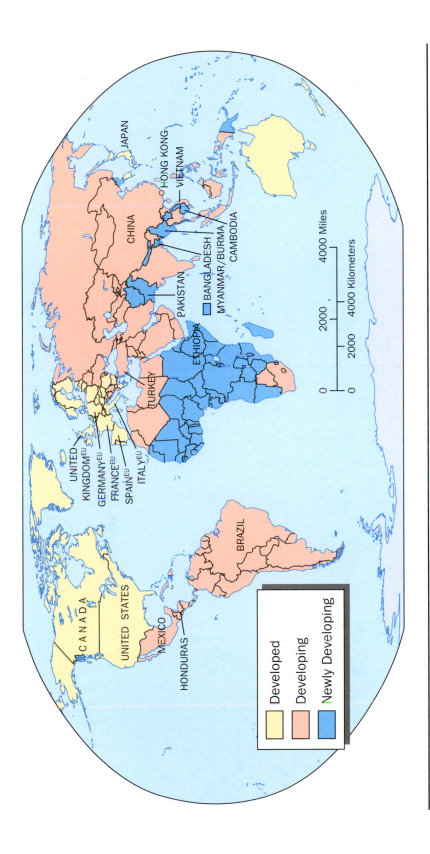

COLOR PLATE 1

Figure 1.2. World map showing locations of developed, developing, and newly developing countries in 2013 based on Gross Domestic Product per capita adjusted by Purchasing Power Parity (GDP per capita PPP) among nations.

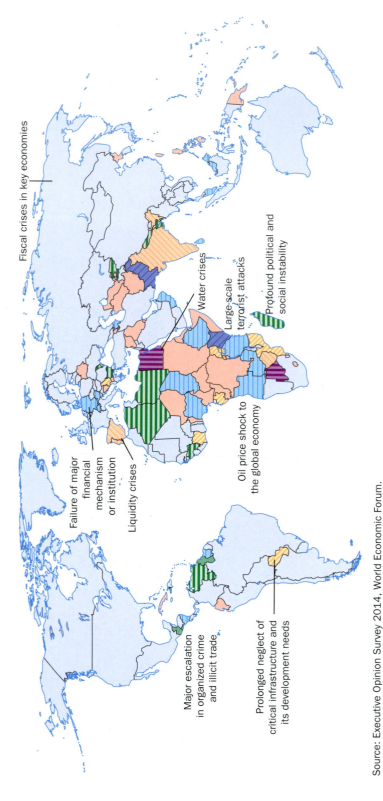

Source: Executive Opinion Survey 2014, World Economic Forum.
Notes: Only risks that are of highest concern in at least two countries are represented on the map. Other risks of highest concern: Violent interstate conflict (in Armenia). Breakdown of critical information infrastructure and networks (Cameroon). Escalation of economic and resource nationalization (Lesotho), and Greater incidence of environmentally-related events (Philippines).

COLOR PLATE 2

Figure 7.2. Global Risks of Highest Concerns for Doing Business. Note what regions have greater risk and what types of risk.

Human Rights Index 2014

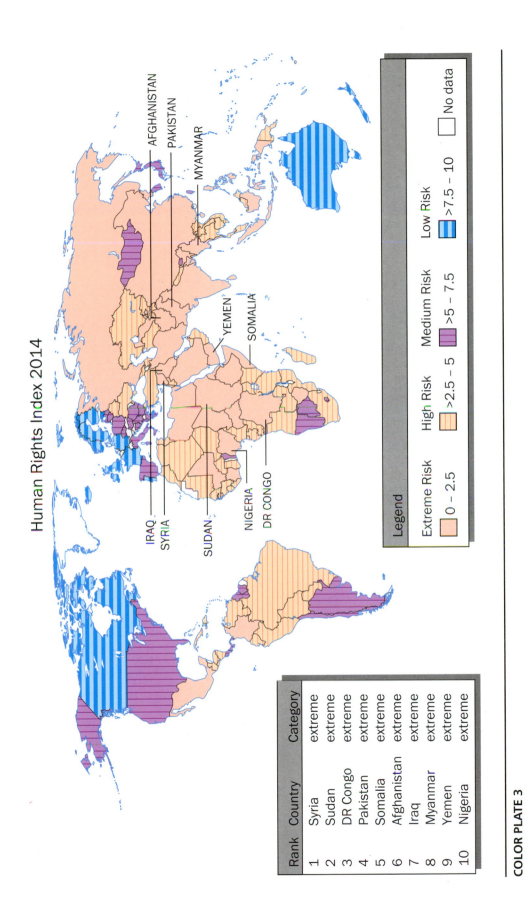

Rank	Country	Category
1	Syria	extreme
2	Sudan	extreme
3	DR Congo	extreme
4	Pakistan	extreme
5	Somalia	extreme
6	Afghanistan	extreme
7	Iraq	extreme
8	Myanmar	extreme
9	Yemen	extreme
10	Nigeria	extreme

Legend

Extreme Risk	High Risk	Medium Risk	Low Risk
0 – 2.5	>2.5 – 5	>5 – 7.5	>7.5 – 10

No data

COLOR PLATE 3

Figure 7.5. World Human Rights Risk Index, 2014

Exposure
Exposure of the population to natural hazards such as earthquakes, storms, floods, droughts, and sea level rise.

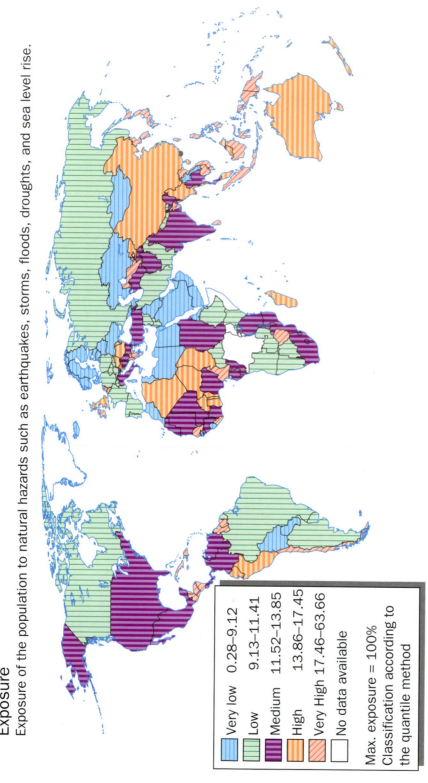

Very low 0.28–9.12
Low 9.13–11.41
Medium 11.52–13.85
High 13.86–17.45
Very High 17.46–63.66
No data available

Max. exposure = 100%
Classification according to
the quantile method

COLOR PLATE 4

Figure 7.8. United Nations University and Institute of Environmental and Human Security developed a map that classifies world countries by five levels of exposure to natural hazards.

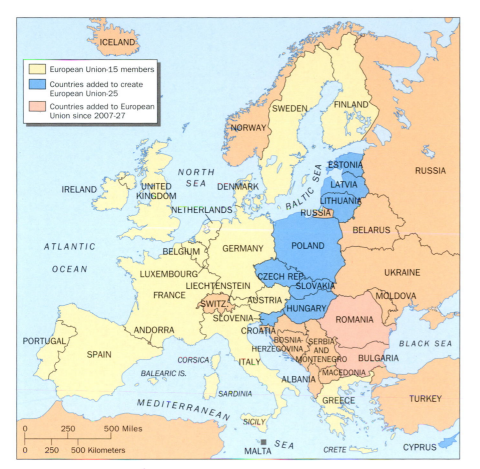

COLOR PLATE 5A

Figure 9.1. Map of Europe, indicating what countries belong to the European Union and when they were admitted to the Union

COLOR PLATE 5B

Figure 10.1. Map highlighting the Western Hemisphere trading region: North America, Central America, the West Indies, and South America.

Figure 11.1. This map highlights the four subsectors of the Asian Trade Region: East Asia, Southeast Asia, South Asia, and Oceania.

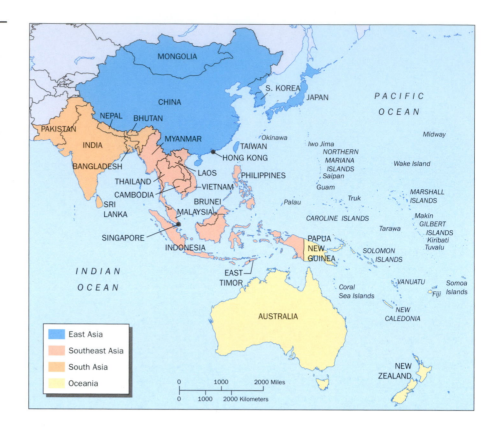

Figure 11.4 Map of East Asia

COLOR PLATE 7A

Figure 11.9. Map of Southeast Asia

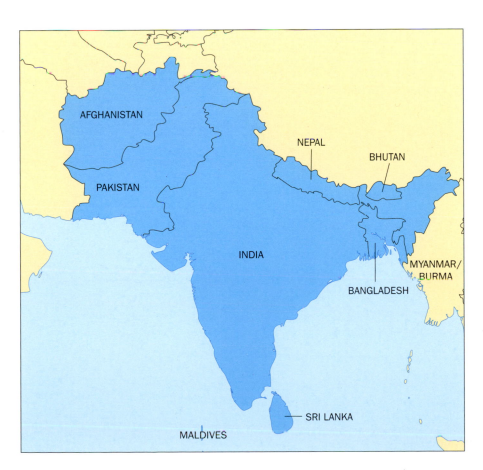

COLOR PLATE 7B

Figure 11.10. Map of South Asia

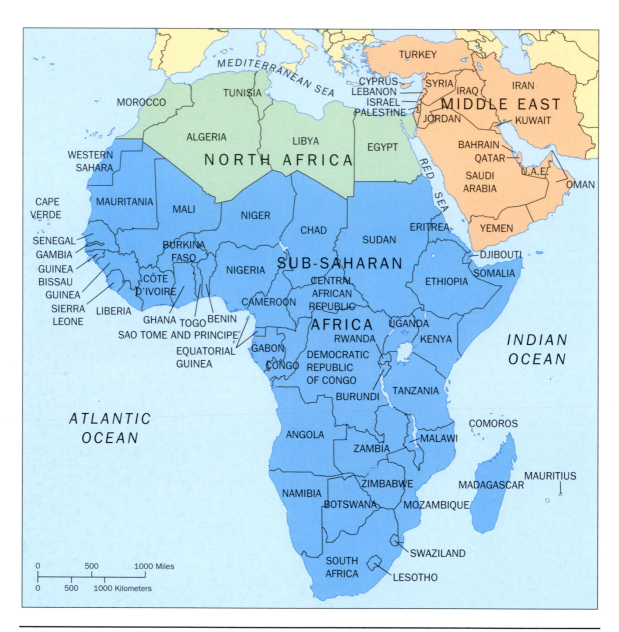

COLOR PLATE 8

Figure 12.1 Map of Middle East and Africa. Middle East is shown in the darkest beige, Sub-Saharan Africa in the dark blue, and Northern Africa is colored in light green.

THE GLOBAL SUPPLY CHAIN

PART TWO

CHAPTER 5

TEXTILE AND APPAREL TRADE
Barriers, Regulations, and Politics

FUN FACT

Instituted after the war of 1812, the first protective tariffs in the United States, intended to help boost sales of domestic goods, became a political issue when the southern states, in their resentment over having to pay more for British items, renamed Tariff 11828 the "Tariff of Abominations." (Behavioral Research and Teaching, n.d.)

OBJECTIVES

- Explore the evolution of the global textile and apparel trade.
- Examine how trade barriers limit trade and protect domestic markets.
- Discuss major international trade agreements and their intrinsic trade barriers, relevant to textiles and apparel.
- Examine political positions adopted by different segments of the textile and apparel industry, including labor activists and trade associations.
- Introduce regionalization of global trade.

Trade has many meanings in general usage—it can mean a living, an occupation, a line of business; skilled work, as distinguished from unskilled work; a craft; or an act of bargaining or exchanging. In this text the term "trade" means the buying and selling or bartering of goods and services. Trade takes place among individuals, groups, organizations, business firms, and the governments of cities, counties, states, and countries. Trade in the international and global context involves the exchange of goods and services across political boundaries. This is where protected trade, free trade, and fair trade become relevant. On the surface it seems that protected trade prevents harm, free trade does not cost anything, and fair trade provides equal value to those involved; however, that reading is much too simplistic. Fair trade was discussed in Chapter 4, and this chapter will focus on protected and free trade.

ad valorem tariff a tax set as a fixed percent of the value of an imported product

Agreement on Textiles and Clothing (ATC) a 1995–2004 World Trade Organization (WTO) trade agreement that replaced the Multifiber Arrangement (MFA)

countervailing duty a special tax that increases the price of goods to a competitive level; used against illegal trade activities such as subsidies or dumping

customs service a government agency responsible for monitoring exported and imported goods, assessing and collecting duties, and protecting the country's borders against illegal entry

dumping selling a product in another country at less than it is sold in the home country or less than it costs to produce

duty tax payment on imported or exported goods, usually based on a tariff schedule

effective tariff indicates the real amount of protection an industry has due to nominal tariff rates

embargo the prohibition of the entry of goods into a defined political area; the stoppage of trade until issues can be negotiated

exchange rates determine the ratio at which one currency can be traded for another

export policy a set of regulations that determines what products and services can leave a country for another market and under what conditions

export subsidy a payment from a government to a firm as a reward for exporting products

fabric-forward rule a trade rule that limits tariffs or provides quota-free imports, or both, for garments made of fabrics produced in one of the participating countries

free trade the unrestricted exchange of goods among nations

free trade area a region made up of two or more countries that have a comprehensive free trade agreement eliminating or reducing trade barriers on products traded among the countries

free trade zone a port or other site within a nation designated for duty-free entry of selected goods to be displayed, stored, and/or used for manufacturing

General Agreement on Tariffs and Trade (GATT) an international framework to establish ground rules for worldwide trade and promote reduction of trade barriers

government subsidy a payment from a government to a business to defray business costs

Harmonized Commodity Description and Coding System (HS) a global classification system used to describe and measure trade

import policy a set of regulations that determines what products and services can enter the domestic economy from another country and under what conditions

Item 807 a ruling that allowed garments cut in the United States to be exported and assembled in Caribbean countries and then imported with tariff based only on value added

lobbying the process of influencing the formation of legislation or the administration of rules, regulations, and policies

lobbyists paid professionals who communicate the political positions defined by their employers and try to influence formation or administration of legislation

most-favored nation (MFN) a principle that each country must treat all nations the same in terms of trade restrictions and policies, and no country should have preferential trade arrangements

Multifiber Arrangement (MFA) an international trade agreement that allowed textile and apparel trade to be regulated through quotas established in bilateral agreements between nations

multilateral trade agreement involves more than two countries

nominal tariff tax rates on imported goods published in each country's tariffs schedule

nontariff trade barriers the quota, quality standards, or other regulations or conditions that restrict the flow of goods between countries, not including taxes on imports or exports

omnichannel retailing (also spelled omni-channel) a multichannel approach to sales that seeks to provide a seamless shopping experience to customers whether they are shopping online from a desktop or mobile device, by telephone, or in a brick-and-mortar store

political strategy the general approaches used by governments, firms, other organizations, and individuals in dealing with and manipulating important and powerful components in their environments

preferential trade agreement (PTA) a form of economic integration created by reducing trade barriers

price support program purchasing and storing products from the market to reduce the supply, relative to demand, to drive up the price

production subsidy a negative trade tax; a payment of money from a government to a business to defray costs of making goods and commodities

protectionism use of trade barriers to minimize imports in order to protect domestic industry

qualified industrial zone (QIZ) a highly specialized area within an exporting country that grants a product manufactured in the zone duty-free access to participating importing countries

regionalization reducing trade barriers in selected geographic regions to facilitate trade

safeguard measures temporary action to protect an industry from fast and sudden rise of imports

specific tariff a fixed amount of tax per physical unit of imported product

technical barriers to trade (TBT) regulations, standards, and testing and certification procedures that obstruct trade

trade association a nonprofit organization formed to serve the common needs of its members

trade policy a political strategy or program designed to stimulate or control the exchange of goods between nations

trade regulation barriers and limits on types and quantities of goods

and services that cross political boundaries

trading bloc a group of countries that have created regional trade incentives and that jointly participate in trade negotiations

transaction value the price actually paid or payable for goods when sold for export

unfair competition activities defined by legal rulings and statutes that protect against unethical business practices

voluntary export restraint a self-imposed limit on the amount of product that one country can export to another country, also known as export tariff restraint agreement

World Customs Organization (WCO) a global organization whose purpose is to improve the operations and efficiency of customs services

yarn-forward rule apparel can be imported tariff- and quota-free if garments are made of yarns and fabrics from one of participating countries

THE EVOLUTION OF TRADE

"The entanglement of cultures and economies now known as globalization has been spreading for centuries and the world is smaller as a result" (Elwood, 2001, p. 8). As mentioned previously, globalization has at least three dimensions: social, political, and economic. The primary focus of this discussion is the economic aspect, or, more specifically, trade among countries and companies that are located in different countries. Comments related to the political and cultural dimensions are integrated to support and explain the development of global trade.

Friedman (2000) argued that the first era of globalization took place from 1400 to 1914, with intensive changes taking place between 1868 and 1914. The trans-Atlantic cable, connected in 1866, linked banking and financial activities from New York to London to

Paris, stimulating an era of "global finance capitalism." In that time, people freely migrated across political boundaries without passports. The invention of the steamship, the railroad, the telegraph, and the telephone was drawing the world together. According to Friedman (2000), the era before World War I (Globalization 1.0) was a globalization of countries in which the world shrank from a size large to a size medium.

The nineteenth-century era of globalization was shattered in the twentieth century by World War I, but despite the Russian Revolution, the Great Depression, and World War II, the second era of globalization emerged (Globalization 2.0), and with it, the Cold War, an international system of ideology and etiquette between the United States and the Soviet Union that lasted until 1989, when the Berlin Wall came down. Friedman (2000) described the twentieth-century era of globalization as the globalization of companies that moved the world toward a single marketplace. The world changed from size medium to size small, especially from 1980 to 2000, because of the development of electronic communication and the internet (Chanda, 2004). "Globalization 3.0 is [the] intensification of everything that was invented in Globalization 2.0—the bandwidths, the fiber-optics, the PCs, and the software capabilities that connected them. Now globalization is moving the world from size 'small' to size 'tiny' because of [the] globalization of individuals" (Chanda, 2004, p. 2).

Throughout history, a country's **trade policy** has consisted mainly of a constantly evolving series of official objectives, laws, and actions designed to influence the flow of exports and imports of goods and services (Cohen, Blecker, & Whitney, 2003). Trade policy has been primarily determined by a combination of economic perspectives and political positions and it has two primary components: export policy and import policy. **Export policy** is a set of regulations that determines which products can leave a country for another market and under what conditions. Export policy relates to efforts to sell domestically produced goods and services in foreign markets or restrict the export of selected goods to unfriendly countries. **Import policy** is a set of regulations that determines what products and services can enter the domestic economy from another country and under what conditions. The policy determines availability of foreign-made goods and services in domestic markets.

Since the end of World War II, there has been a strong movement toward eliminating trade barriers and increasing **free trade**, unrestricted exchange of goods and services among nations. Three major categories of products remain that have relatively high levels of trade protection: agriculture, steel, and textiles and apparel. **Protectionism** seeks to use trade barriers to minimize imports and protect domestic industry and/or market, whereas free trade relies on market forces to determine the volume and variety of imports (Cohen et al., 2003). Each of these strategies is fraught with controversy, because there is frequent conflict between economic logic and political and social necessity:

- There is an intricate and ever-changing relationship between trade and other economic, social, and political sectors.
- There is diffusion of authority between executive and legislative branches of government.
- Social and cultural dimensions of trade have been frequently neglected.

Political Manipulation of Trade

Politics in multiple forms influence trade every hour of every day. **Politics** are the methods, or tactics, involved in managing an organization, business, state, or government, often in a pursuit of self-interest. Power, influence, and manipulation of people and other resources tend to be the primary motivators. **Political strategy** makes it possible for governments, firms, other organizations, and individuals to deal with and manipulate important and powerful components in their environments. There is always more than one way to accomplish a specified goal; the questions are, who will benefit, and who will bear the costs? The answers to those questions represent different political positions. Change in trade policy and methods invariably improve the lot of one group while having a negative impact on other groups. Decisions are seldom simple and are consistently multifaceted.

PROTECTED TRADE

Monitoring Imports and Exports

To figure out the what, when, and who of trading, a detailed accounting system is needed to record systematically the passage of products, and recording the amounts of specific types of products is a great challenge. Measurements within the United States are still recorded in the English system, and the English system is still the primary system taught in schools (the rest of the world uses the metric system). However, serious trade protection requires accounting for products that cross international borders. The Tariff Schedules of the United States, based on the English system, were converted to the Harmonized Tariff Schedule (HTS) of the United States, based on the metric system and on the Harmonized Commodity Description and Coding System. Commonly known as the Harmonized System (HS), the Harmonized Commodity Description and Coding System, developed by the World Customs Organization, is a global classification system used to describe most trade in goods. The HS is based on ninety-seven product classifications called chapters. The product classifications break down into more than 5,000 product categories, each identified with a six-digit code, a brief description, and the standard unit of measurement.

Classifying an article under the HS is not as straightforward as it may seem. There are many rulings on HS classification. For example, a knit shirt is not necessarily a knit T-shirt or a knit blouse. Classification of textile and apparel articles is generally determined by fiber content, weight, type of product or garment, and gender and age of the end user. The HS is used by more than 200 countries in the world to monitor exports and imports, which is done by customs services.

Customs Services

The government of nearly every country in the world has a **customs service**, a government agency responsible for monitoring imports and exports, assessing and collecting duties, and protecting the country's borders against illegal entry. The names of this government agency may vary slightly in different countries, as shown below:

- Australian Customs Service
- Ghana Customs Excise and Preventive Service
- United States Customs and Border Protection (CBP)

Fundamentally, the purpose of trade protection is to prevent domestic companies from having to compete with foreign companies in their own domestic markets. Various trade barriers have been invented to allow domestic companies to charge higher prices, grow and increase the number of jobs offered, and make a greater contribution to the domestic economy. Some types of trade barriers are also used as an important source of government revenue. Obviously, this means that consumers pay higher prices and have a more limited selection of goods from which to choose. When countries erect trade barriers, the barriers have to be monitored and enforced; thus, the need for different bureaucratic structures. Trade barriers that restrict trade are commonly classified as tariff barriers and nontariff barriers.

Tariff Barriers

The most common form of trade protection is a **tariff**, which is a tax that is collected as duties on imported or exported goods. Paying duty increases the cost of imported or exported goods and therefore increases the selling price. **Nominal tariffs**, which are the tax rates published in each country's tariff schedule, are the basis of determining how much duty has to be paid for specified products. Nominal tariffs have two forms: specific and ad valorem.

Specific tariffs

- are a fixed amount of money per physical unit of product;
- are easy to apply and administer, especially on standardized goods; and
- provide a degree of protection that varies inversely with changes in import prices.

In other words, because the tariff does not change, if the import value goes up, the tariff is a smaller proportion of the revenue gained from sale of the product in the foreign country; if the import value goes down, the tariff is a larger proportion of the revenue from the sale of the goods. Thus, when the import value goes down, the tariff provides more protection for domestically produced goods of the same type. When the value goes down, it will cost proportionally more to sell the product in the foreign country.

Ad valorem tariffs are like a sales tax; they

- are a fixed percentage of the value of the product;
- can be applied to products with a wide range of product variation; and
- maintain a constant degree of protection, even when prices vary.

Sometimes, one type of tariff is applied to a single product; other times, both specific and ad valorem tariffs are applied (Table 5.1).

TABLE 5.1

EXAMPLES OF SPECIFIC AND AD VALOREM TARIFFS THAT MIGHT BE APPLIED TO DIFFERENT PRODUCTS

Product	Tariff Rates
Specific tariffs	
Chickens, ducks, turkeys	$0.02 each
Cattle, 1,550 kg or more	$0.007 per kg
Ad valorem tariffs	
Reptile leather luggage	8.5% ad valorem
Women's raincoats	8.9% ad valorem
Combined tariffs	
Baby sweaters of wool	$0.318 per kg + 14.4% ad valorem
Men's ties of man-made fibers	$0.248 per kg + 12.7% ad valorem

Determining the amount of duty that will have to be paid to import a product can be more complex than it looks. **Duty** is tax payment on imported or exported goods, usually based on a tariff schedule. Specific tariffs are relatively straightforward, because the amount of duty is dependent on physical measurements, usually the number of products or the weight of the product. The duty based on a specific tariff is calculated by multiplying the number of units of goods times the specific tariff rate.

Looking at Table 5.1, if 10,000 ducks are imported, the duty due on the flock is:

duty due = physical units of goods × specific tariff
10,000 ducks × $0.02 each = $200

According to the table, if cows are imported, the duty due is based on the total weight of the shipment rather than the number of cows. For example, if sixty cows are imported, and they weigh an average of 316.25 kilograms, the total weight of the shipment must be determined by multiplying the number of cows by the average weight of one cow and then multiplying the total by the tariff rate:

duty due = physical units of goods × specific tariff
(60 cows × 316.25 kilograms) × $0.007 per kilogram = $132.83
18,975 kilograms × $0.007 per kilogram = $132.83

If reptile leather luggage is imported, then an ad valorem tariff is applied. Remember, ad valorem tariffs are based on the value of the product rather than the number of units of the product. For example, if 1,250 pieces of reptile leather luggage were imported at a value of $340 each, the duty due on the total shipment would be:

duty due = total value of the product × ad valorem tariff
($340 × 1,250 pieces of luggage) × 8.5 percent = $36,125

When combinations of specific and ad valorem tariffs are applied to the same product, each duty has to be calculated separately and then added together. Applying both types of tariffs helps balance the inequities associated with specific tariffs. The basic calculation is:

total duty due = specific duty + ad valorem duty

An example of a combined tariff, again based on Table 5.1, is the import of 60 dozen men's man-made fiber ties at $28 a dozen. The 3 dozen ties weigh 1 kilogram. To calculate specific duty, we need to know the weight of the shipment (20 kilograms = 60 dozen ties ÷ 3 dozen per kilogram):

specific duty due = physical units of goods × specific tariff rate
(60 dozen ties ÷ 3 dozen per kilogram) × $0.248 per kilogram = $4.96

Ad valorem duty is based on the value of the total shipment:

ad valorem duty due = value of the product × ad valorem tariff rate
(60 dozen ties × $28 per dozen) × 12.7 percent = $213.36

Now we can calculate the total, or combined, duty:

combined duty due = specific duty + ad valorem duty
$4.96 + $213.36 = $218.32

These examples of tariffs and their related duties seem fairly straightforward, but a number of questions remain. For example, how is product value determined for ad valorem tariffs? The customs value of a product used as a base for ad valorem tariffs is the transaction value. The **transaction value** is the price that is actually paid or payable for the goods when sold for export. However, customs evaluators in different countries use different criteria for when the transaction value applies to the tariff. For example, US Customs and Border Protection (CBP) evaluators in the United States have traditionally used the FOB (free on board) import values, or the value when the product is loaded onto the carrier to leave the exporting country. The term FOB is misleading, because it sounds like there is no charge for freight to get the products to the carrier. There is always a cost related to transport to the carrier. From a practical, financial perspective, the cost of the freight is included in the product cost rather than listed separately. However, despite the confusing nature of FOB, for the customs product valuation the product cost is the FOB import value, without including shipping cost.

The European Union (EU) uses CIF (cost, insurance, freight) import values, the value as the product arrives in the importing country. CIF means

C = cost of merchandise
I = insurance for shipping
F = freight

The transaction value includes merchandise cost plus transport insurance and freight. Thus, even if the importing firms in the EU face the same nominal tariffs, the duty paid will be higher, because the transaction value is higher. Consequently, retail prices on imported goods will be higher in the EU than retail prices for the same goods with the same markup in the United States. The result is that US manufacturers may be less likely to export to the EU, whereas EU manufacturers may be more likely to ship to the United States. Firms in the EU have a greater protection from the same nominal ad valorem duty rate because of a difference in product valuation.

Let us go back to the luggage example in Table 5.1; when 1,250 pieces of luggage are imported at a value of $340 each, with 8.5 percent ad valorem, the total FOB duty for the United States is the same as previously calculated.

FOB ad valorem duty due = FOB value of the total product shipment
× ad valorem tariff rate
($340 × 1,250 pieces) × 8.5 percent = $36,125

To determine CIF ad valorem duty for the EU, insurance and freight have to be added to FOB value. Assume each suitcase weighs 11 pounds, for a total shipment weight of 13,750 pounds (1,250 suitcases × 11 pounds). The freight costs $4.49 per pound, and the insurance is $2 per suitcase, making a total of $2,500 (1,250 × $2).

CIF ad valorem duty due = [FOB value + freight + insurance]
× ad valorem tariff rate

CIF ad valorem duty due = [($340 × 1,250) + (13,750 lbs × $4.49 per lb)
+ $2,500] × 8.5 percent
[$425,000 + $61,738 + $2,500] × 8.5 percent = $41,585

Thus, the suitcase manufacturers in the EU have $5,460 more tariff protection on the shipment of luggage than US manufacturers just because of a difference in the way the transaction value is determined by the EU and US customs.

Another key question is what the effective rate of tariff protection is. The **effective tariff** determines the real amount of protection an industry has due to nominal tariff rates. The effective tariff also demonstrates the real impact of the nominal tariff on the prices paid by customers in the domestic market.

For example (refer back to Table 5.1 again), if you were a duck importer, would you be better off if you imported large ducks or little ducks, given a specific tariff of $.02 per duck? If you imported ducks that weighed 8 kilograms, the effective tariff rate is $.0025 per kilogram (2.5 cents ÷ 8 kilograms per duck). If you imported little ducks that weighed 1 kilogram, the effective duty rate is 2.5 cents per duck. Clearly, the effective rate of tariff protection is much less on large ducks than little ducks. The little ducks obviously have to be fed a lot of grain to become large ducks before importing, but that is another story. The point here is that the effective protection provided by a specific tariff can vary, depending on size or the value of the product imported.

What is the effective rate of tariff protection on a finished product when a tariff is applied to imported materials? Assume that three pounds of cotton are imported to make a pair of jeans. The cost of the cotton is $.43 a pound, and the tariff rate is the maximum allowed according to WTO at 56 percent. Assume also that the value of the product doubles each time it is sold from the fiber importer, through the product development and production process to the ultimate consumer. When the cotton is imported, that cost of the duty becomes part of the cotton cost, so although the cotton cost is $1.29, the importer regarded the cotton cost as $1.29 plus the duty (56 percent of the cost), a total of $2.01. The cost of the tariff is forever incorporated into the product cost when the product is priced for sale. As a result, the value of the tariff gets paid again and again, each time the product is sold (Table 5.2).

At the point of retail sale, where you buy the jeans, one-third of the retail price can be attributed to the cost of the tariffs. If there were no tariff on the cotton, with all the rest of the same assumptions, the retail price on the jeans would have been $41.28. This simplistic example demonstrates the concern about the burden put on consumers by tariffs that are intended to protect the domestic apparel industry from import competition. To learn more about the effects of tariff on product cost for companies and consumers, see Case 5.1.

TABLE 5.2

EFFECTIVE RATE OF PROTECTION ON JEANS MADE FROM THREE POUNDS OF IMPORTED COTTON WITH A 56 PERCENT DUTY RATE, ASSUMING THE PRICE DOUBLES EACH TIME THE PRODUCT IS SOLD

Transaction	Product + Duty	Total Cost Product	Duty
Import cotton	$ 2.01	$ 0.43 × 3 lbs = $1.29	$ 1.29 × 56% = $ 0.72
Yarn mill buys cotton	$ 4.02	$ 2.58	$ 1.44
Fabric mill buys yarn	$ 8.04	$ 5.16	$ 2.88
Apparel manufacturer buys fabric	$16.08	$10.32	$ 5.76
Retailer buys jeans	$32.16	$11.52	$20.64
You buy jeans	$64.32	$41.28	$23.04

ENGINEERING COST-SAVING TARIFF STRATEGIES

In the quota-free global trade, tariffs remain a major trade barrier and can drive sourcing decisions when choosing a country to manufacture apparel products. The average US tariff rate for textiles is about 8 percent and 13 percent for apparel. In fact, apparel tariff rates are one of the highest among all imported consumer product categories and can be as high as 32 percent, depending on fiber content and type of product. For example, US importers of women's knitted wool shirts from Europe pay a tax of 19.7 percent on the garment cost. It is even more expensive for companies to import man-made fiber overcoats (tariff rate of 28.2 percent) or man-made fiber T-shirts (tariff rate of 32 percent) from Italy, France, or any other European country. Ultimately, the high tariff cost is passed onto consumers who have to pay higher prices when shopping for the latest fashion trends. Likewise, US footwear tariff rates add cost to the product. It is estimated that the $54 billion US footwear industry could save up to $2.3 billion a year if import tariff rates were lowered or eliminated.

One of the strategies to lower product cost and save on import duty is to utilize US Free Trade Agreements (FTAs). While this strategy is beneficial to any brand manager or retailer, it is critical for companies that focus on delivering competitively priced apparel to their customers. To date, the United States has implemented fourteen free trade agreements (FTAs). Two of these FTAs are multilateral: NAFTA and CAFTA-DR, including eight countries. Bilateral FTAs cover twelve more countries: Israel, Jordan, Chile, Australia, Singapore, Morocco, Oman, Peru, Colombia, Panama, Bahrain, and South Korea (listed in the order these agreements were ratified). In addition, there is a special agreement, African Growth and Opportunity Act (AGOA), that allows duty-free apparel imports from qualifying Sub-Saharan African countries.

Importing high-end designer coats made in one of the European countries and paying up to 30 percent on the cost of the product can be very pricey, but a "Made in Italy" label might be worth it. At the same time, production of these designer coats could be sourced from Mexico, and while the glamour of the Italian origin would be lost, cost savings could be substantial due to duty-free import under NAFTA. In addition, production in Mexico would significantly shorten lead time. If, for example, a US retailer imports men's trousers for price-conscious consumers from China, they will be subject to a duty rate of 16.6 percent. In contrast, the same shipment of trousers would be duty free

under CAFTA if the pants were made in Honduras. For an order of 200,000 pieces at $15 per pair of trousers, the total value of the shipment will be $3 million, with duty savings of almost half a million.

Another strategy to minimize import duties is by knowing the Harmonized Tariff Schedule and smart selection of fabrics. For example, using a polyester/silk fabric to make women's shirts will result in a tariff rate of 27 percent if the silk fiber is 49 percent or less of the blend. If the silk fiber is increased by just 2 percent, to a blend of 51 percent silk and 49 percent polyester, the tariff rate will be less than 7 percent on the same shirts. The 20 percent difference in tariff rates will bring significant cost savings on pretty much the same product.

It should be noted that most FTAs have special provisions. For example, to qualify for duty-free import, at least 35 percent of product value should be added to apparel in AGOA countries, Jordan, and some others. NAFTA and CAFTA follow yarn- and fabric-forward rules. These provisions might have a significant impact on final product design and cost.

Sources: Personal communications with Kyle Madson, Sourcing Manager, Kohl's.

Muscat, S. (2014). "Lower Tariffs Could Make Quite a Difference for the High-End Fashion Industry and for Brand-Conscious Fashionistas." Retrieved May 27, 2015, from http://www.theglobalist.com/tariffs-textiles-ttip/

Platzer, M. D. (2014). "US Textile Manufacturing and the Trans-Pacific Partnership Negotiations." Congressional Research Service. R42772.

Travis, T. (2013). "Five Winning Cost-Saving Strategies for Apparel Importers and Exporters." *Apparel.* Retrieved October 24, 2015, from http://apparel.edgl.com/news/Five-Winning-Cost-Saving-Strategies-for-Apparel-Importers-and-Exporters86663

1. An average American spends $900 on apparel purchases a year. Given the average tariff rate for clothing, how much could an American save on apparel purchases a year if trade was free (no tariffs)? How much would the US government lose in revenue?

2. The Transatlantic Trade and Investment Partnership (TTIP) has been in the works for several years now. One of TTIP's proposals is to eliminate tariffs. What are the opportunities and challenges of potential free trade between the United States and the EU?

3. Despite obvious advantages of sourcing apparel production from duty-free countries, none of the current FTA countries are among the top five suppliers of US apparel imports. Why?

In sum, import tariffs are intended to reduce the volume of trade and raise the prices of imported goods. In the country that imposes the tariffs, producing firms gain, and consumers lose, because the producing firms can charge more for their products, and consumers have to pay higher prices. In the world as a whole, tariffs decrease the volume of trade and thus decrease the benefits of trade. The opposing argument is that there would be no consumers to buy the merchandise if there were no jobs to support domestic spending and that such jobs should therefore be protected by trade barriers.

Nontariff Trade Barriers

Nontariff trade barriers restrict trade by some means other than applying a tax on import or export of products. These barriers may take the following forms:

- cumbersome and/or expensive customs procedures
- distribution limits and restrictions
- exchange rates
- export quotas
- government procurement restrictions' lack of transparency
- import licensing
- import quotas
- infrastructure related to transport
- investment requirements affecting trade
- lack of intellectual property protection (copyrights, trademarks, production processes)
- price controls
- price support programs
- safeguard measures
- special and differentiated treatment (SDT) subsidies for domestic firms
- tariff rate quotas
- technical barriers to trade (TBT)
- trade preference programs
- voluntary export restraints

Of this intimidating list, exchange rates, import quotas, price support programs, subsidies for domestic firms, and voluntary export restraints are the most common nontariff trade barriers that affect textiles and apparel. Nontariff barriers tend to be controversial and divisive in trade relations because of the gap between reality and intent. Some of the nontariff barriers are considered as **unfair competition**, activities defined by legal rulings and statutes that protect against unethical business practices.

Exchange rates determine the ratio at which one currency can be traded for another (Figure 5.1). The terms *strong dollar* and *weak dollar* are sometimes used to describe exchange rates in the United States. During most of the 2000s, the US dollar has been weak against other currencies, such as the euro or British pound. Imports are commonly priced in the exporting country's currency and then quoted to a buyer in his or her domestic currency, based on the exchange rate at the time. A currency that is depreciating in value causes imports to be more expensive. Sometimes, an exporter acknowledges a depreciating currency by giving a special price to encourage importation of goods. An appreciating currency causes foreign goods to be less expensive and becomes an incentive to import goods or travel to foreign countries. There is usually a lag time between appreciation of currency and surge of

Figure 5.1
Some of the major currencies of the world, including the US dollar, the EU euro, and the Japanese yen.

imports, because new contracts have to be developed and merchandise produced, based on the change in exchange rate.

Beginning in 1944, countries that belonged to the International Monetary Fund (IMF) kept their exchange rates fixed relative to the US dollar, and the dollar was fixed relative to the price of gold. The dollar became overvalued on the gold standard, and since 1973, exchange rates have been floating and flexible. A technical explanation of the operation of exchange rates is beyond the scope of this text—other than that exchange rates are a factor in determining the relative cost of imports and domestic production.

Quotas restrict quantities of goods that can be imported or exported but are most often applied to imports. Quotas are often administered by a government that issues import licenses up to the quantity of imports that will be allowed. The licenses may be given away or sold. If the quota is sold to importing firms, it generates governmental revenue. Once the entire quota for a particular category of products is distributed, the quota may become a market in itself. In the era of textile and apparel quotas, which ended in 2005, the exporting country allocated quotas and issued the visas (licenses) for entry into the importing country. The importing country regulated the level of imports, based on the amount entered using the visas. The importing country did not allocate the quota or issue the license for entry. The ultimate consumers who bought the products paid for the products, the quota, and tariffs as well as the production and retailing processes.

Safeguard measures, or safeguards, are temporary actions to protect a domestic industry from fast and sudden rise of imports (World Trade Organization, n.d.-a). They can be imposed on a country for a specific product (e.g., apparel) or product category (e.g., cotton T-shirts) if there is evidence of fast import growth that is causing disruption in the market and/or threat to the domestic industry in the importing country. The phaseout of the MFA and its quota system in 2005 created import surges in many textile and apparel categories. As the result, safeguard quotas were imposed on Chinese imports of selected product categories by the United States and European Union until the end of 2008.

Voluntary export restraint (VER) is a self-imposed limit on the amount of product that one country can export to another country, also known as export tariff restraint agreement. VERs have commonly been regarded as "gentlemen's agreements" to restrict trade, because the agreements are not formalized into international law. When serious regulation of the textile and apparel trade began early in the twentieth century, British textiles dominated the industry internationally. However, the United States had also become a major producer. From the perspective of national security, the textile industry was regarded as critical for clothing the armed forces, but it was perceived as being unable to survive in the international market without trade protection. Therefore, by 1930 the US import tariff was 46 percent on cotton goods and 60 percent on woolen goods. After World War II, Japan became the major low-cost apparel exporter. Even though the country faced high tariffs, it was still shipping increasing quantities to the United States and Europe. The United States induced Japan to enter a voluntary export restraint agreement restricting its apparel exports.

Technical barriers to trade (TBT) include regulations, standards, testing, and certification procedures that can obstruct trade (World Trade Organization, n.d.-a). While some policies aimed to establish protection of human health and safety as well as environmental security in a country are legitimate, others might be arbitrary and an excuse for protectionism. TBT greatly vary from country to country. A special TBT Agreement was developed by WTO to provide guidelines and make sure that technical regulations are not discriminatory and do not create unnecessary obstacles for trade. The agreement stresses the importance of transparency and use of international standards when creating any policies affecting trade.

Government subsidy is a reverse tax; it is a payment from a government to a business to defray business costs. The subsidy may make it possible for a business to sell its products at a lower price in domestic markets and still make a profit. Subsidized products also may be sold in international markets at prices below the normal cost of production.

Production subsidies are an unfair form of competition, in which a government makes a gift of money to firms to defray costs of production (World Trade Organization, n.d.-a). To protect an industry from foreign competition, a country's government might impose import barriers (tariffs and quotas), but then domestic consumers would have to pay higher prices. A government subsidy might be an option to sustain a domestic industry without increasing prices; in fact, the subsidy might decrease prices. However, consumers then have to pay higher taxes to fund the subsidy program. A prolonged use of government subsidies tends to make an industry dependent on the continuing support and, therefore, less competitive globally. For example, sheep growers in the United States and other developed countries have long had a wool subsidy as part of the annual revenue. Without this subsidy, farmers and ranchers may not find wool an economically viable crop.

In the twentieth century, the majority of US-produced cotton, more than 60 percent, was consumed domestically to make yarn and fabric that was used for apparel and home furnishing manufacturing. With the growth of imports and decline of domestic textile and apparel manufacturing, domestic demand for US-grown cotton decreased significantly. As a result, in the 2000s, the majority of US production–subsidized cotton was sold on the world market at what the rest of the world regards as less than market price. According to the International Cotton Advisory Committee, US total direct support to cotton production was more than $3 billion in the 2008–2009 growing season, or 50 cents per pound of actual production. Government subsidies for large-scale cotton growers in the United States are regarded as unfair to competitors in the global market and particularly hurt small farmers in Africa and India. US cotton subsidies are greater than the GDPs of many African countries growing cotton as well as "America's entire USAID budget for the continent of Africa" (Rivoli, 2015, p. 63). A study by Oxfam, an independent, nongovernmental organization, found that with a complete removal of US cotton subsidies, the world price of cotton would increase by 6 to 14 percent, resulting in additional income for farmers in developing and newly developing countries. This additional income could feed a million children for a year or pay school fees for at least 2 million children living in extremely poor West African cotton-growing households.

While African cotton producing countries did not have the means to charge the United States on the unfair competition due to cotton subsidies, Brazil took the case to WTO that the subsidies were driving US cotton exports and kept the world prices artificially low. WTO found the US cotton subsidies violating the global trade rules. The United States ignored a 2005 WTO ruling to discontinue subsidies for cotton production. However, the WTO ruled again in 2009, and the United States had an estimated $300 million in annual sanctions as the result of failing to eliminate illegal subsidies to cotton growers. WTO estimated that US illegal cotton subsidies drove world cotton prices down an average of 9.38 cents per pound and that Brazilian farmers had to be compensated for the resulting losses (Rivoli, 2015). Finally, after years of negotiations and retaliations, in 2010 an agreement was reached that (1) the next US "Farm Bill" would discontinue cotton subsidies and (2) in the meantime, the US government would simply pay Brazilian farmers monthly subsidies of about $12 million per month (in order to continue to pay subsidies to US cotton farmers). Brazilian cotton farmers had a powerful political lobby and government support to take the case to WTO, but because African and Indian cotton farmers did not, the African and Indian cotton farmers continue to suffer from the unfair competition. The "Farm Bill" passed in 2014 continued to have cotton subsidies albeit in new formats. The Brazilian government is considering taking the case back to WTO.

Price support programs are another form of unfair competition. These programs involve government purchasing and storing products from the market to reduce the supply relative to demand and drive up the price. Price support programs are commonly applied to agricultural products in developed countries to raise the commodity price paid to farmers. In the United States some of the surplus goods are dispersed in the form of subsidies for school lunch programs. Payments to agriculture producers so they will produce less are also an option. For example, support of US agricultural producers from 2008 to 2012 was set at $58 billion a year (European Commission, 2009). Whenever negotiations to reduce textile and apparel trade barriers begin, a counterpart is always reduction of agricultural subsidies. Reduction of price subsidies increases agricultural prices in the world market, but it also makes more products available to newly developing countries, where availability of adequate food is a common problem.

Exporting goods is an important source of revenue, and some governments are alleged to subsidize their export industries. When **export subsidies** are available, a firm receives a payment from the government as a reward for exporting a product at whatever rate is specified for the product. Governments may subsidize exports to support growth of domestic industry or to increase cash flow into the country, or both. The United States, the EU, and Australia have used agricultural export subsidies since the 1970s. These subsidies were regarded as legal as long as exports did not exceed what was considered a "reasonable" market share. Although explicit export subsidies are relatively rare, indirect subsidies, such as preferential credit terms and reduced utility rates, are used throughout the world (Cohen, Blecker, & Whitney, 2003). Both production subsidies and export subsidies may provide the opportunity to sell goods abroad at less than the cost of production and less than the domestic sales price.

The intensity of global competition inspires the use of creative and sometimes unfair trade practices. In addition to nontariff trade barriers such as subsidies and price support programs, **dumping** is another form of unfair competition. Dumping is selling a product in another country at less than the domestic sales price or less than the product costs to produce. Dumping is often a companion activity to international sale of government-subsidized agriculture products. Dumping can result in an import surge that causes a dramatic drop in sales for domestic companies. Dumping, by international law, is regarded as unfair competition.

Why would a company dump products? It would appear that dumping could cause the exporting company to lose money. However, dumping can be a

- temporary strategy for establishing or maintaining market share;
- form of inventory control; or
- result of government production to provide domestic employment.

Price competition is a common means of establishing market share. For example, assume a Hong Kong–based retailer decided to enter the US retail market with stores in Los Angeles and San Francisco as well as an online store. The retailer might use intensive advertising to describe fashion-forward, upscale styling at very low promotional prices to get the attention of customers and to establish a share of the market. It may be necessary to offer products below the price that they would be sold in Hong Kong and, at least initially, below the cost of production, to sustain customer interest. Dumping is also used as a form of inventory control when a firm develops an oversupply because of a downturn in world demand or an unexpected increase in world production. Dumping may allow a company to generate cash flow when resources otherwise would be invested in unsalable inventory. Polyester fiber production has become a global activity that has flooded the market and driven down prices (World Trade Organization, n.d.-a).

Because subsidies and dumping are regarded as interference with free markets, **countervailing duties** may be used by importing countries to offset the price effect of subsidy. Countervailing duties are a special type of tariff designed to counteract subsidies and dumping. Countries importing subsidized products are empowered by the WTO to apply countervailing duties to raise the product price to what would be a normal level without the subsidy (Cohen, Blecker, & Whitney, 2003). The countervailing duty eliminates unfair competition of the subsidized low-price products' competing with nonsubsidized domestic products. Countervailing duties are not listed in tariff schedules, but rather are determined according to the level of the subsidy or the amount below the regular selling price in the country the product came from. To apply the countervailing duty, and have it approved on the global level, the importing country submits a complaint to the WTO against the exporting country. The WTO evaluates the situation and produces a ruling related to the issue.

Other safeguards against illegal trade activities include trade **embargoes** against import surges, in which trade is stopped until terms are negotiated. Sometimes, merchandise sits offshore, aboard ship for months while negotiations take place.

Developed countries increased their charges, relative to dumping of textiles and apparel, after the MFA quota system expired. As mentioned earlier, the United States embargoed the apparel shipments from China in 2008 when volume exceeded the quota limits in the Memorandum of Understanding between the United States and China. Antidumping investigations have tripled since the 1980s, involving many different types of products. For example, the United States has been accused of dumping steel. Historically, the United States and the EU have been primary users of anti-dumping duties, but now India and other developing countries are becoming just as active.

TRADE AGREEMENTS

There are several hundreds of trade agreements that impact trade in textiles and apparel. We cannot deal with all of them here, even if we wanted to; instead, this chapter gives an overview of the primary agreements that have been relevant to the textile and apparel trade during the twentieth and twenty-first centuries.

Implementation of Tariffs in the United States

You know that tariffs have two purposes: to restrict trade and to accumulate revenue for the government. In fact, the first substantive piece of legislation passed by the US Congress following the Revolutionary War was a tariff act. The tariff rate was low, an average of 5 percent, so it provided little protection to domestic industry but was an important source of revenue for the government of a fledgling country that had not yet established a tax system (Cohen et al., 2003). The battle over US trade protection had begun. Over the next 50 years, tariff rates increased in fits and starts, until they became an issue between the North and South prior to the Civil War. Some tariff rates ranged from 50 to 100 percent of the value of imports, particularly on agricultural products. States in the South thought their economies and social systems were being marginalized, because high tariffs on US imports angered countries such as Great Britain, which was the primary customer of the southern states' exports of cotton and tobacco. By 1846, Great Britain was already largely industrialized and recognized lower tariffs as a means of expanding world markets (Cohen et al., 2003).

Following the Civil War, tariffs were politicized in the United States, with one political party advocating lower tariffs, and the other supporting higher tariffs; however, a protectionist perspective remained firmly in place, for the most part. Other countries regarded the United States as isolationist. In 1930, with the Depression in progress, the Smoot-Hawley Tariff Act raised the average tariff rate to 53 percent, an all-time high. In 1932, President Franklin Roosevelt and Secretary of State Cordell Hull "deeply believed that an open trading system fostered a peaceful cooperation, and stable international political order, whereas a closed trading system produced international tension and conflict" (Cohen et al., 2003, p. 33). Hull negotiated the Reciprocal Trade Agreements Act of 1934, which became a turning point in international trade relations for the United States. The act allowed the executive branch of the US government to negotiate up to a 50 percent reduction in tariff rates as long as the other countries reciprocated the reductions. By the early 1940s, twenty-five bilateral agreements were in place, mostly with countries in the Western Hemisphere.

General Agreement on Tariffs and Trade (GATT), 1947 to 1994

After World War II, the United States became the leader in the advocacy of free trade, 100 years after Great Britain initiated the policy. After extended negotiations, in 1947 the **General Agreement on Tariffs and Trade (GATT)** was established. GATT was an international framework to establish the ground rules for worldwide trade and promote reduction of trade barriers. In 1994, it was absorbed by the WTO. GATT rules specify that a country granting a trade advantage to one country must grant the same advantage to all countries—the **most-favored nation (MFN)** principle (World Trade Organization, n.d.-b). The MFN principle means that all countries have to be treated the same, and no country will have preferential trade arrangements.

By the early 1970s, approximately 80 countries had signed GATT agreements. Several other countries had applied for membership or participated in the agreement in some manner. Countries that were GATT members held business sessions at least once a year. Frequently, topics included removal of trade barriers. These meetings reduced tariffs and other trade obstacles on thousands of products.

Tariff conferences and sessions were usually held at GATT's headquarters, in Geneva, Switzerland. Most decisions were made by simple majority vote; each country had one vote. GATT granted special privileges to developing and newly developing nations without requiring those nations to obey all of GATT's rules, which included limited use of nontariff trade barriers, such as import quotas and other restrictions on the flow of goods. Fundamentally, GATT established ground rules for worldwide trade among its signatories. The greatest achievements in trade liberalization were accomplished through GATT's multilateral negotiations, known as trade rounds. The trade rounds were time-consuming, lasting from 3 to 7 years. The trade rounds were referred to as the Kennedy Round during the 1960s, the Tokyo Round during the 1970s, and the Uruguay Round during the late 1980s and early 1990s. The Uruguay Round created a new trade management system, the World Trade Organization (WTO).

Multifiber Arrangement (MFA), 1974 to 1994

Following World War II, trade restraints between the United States and Great Britain eased somewhat but continued with Japan, Eastern Europe, and other developing countries. Japan joined GATT in 1955 and should have gained MFN status, but developed countries found ways to continue to restrict Japanese apparel exports. The source of legal authority to control imports in the United States came from Section 204 of the Agricultural Act of 1956, which gave the president the authority to enter into agreements with countries, limiting textile and apparel imports from those countries through the introduction of quota limits.

Formal textile and apparel trade regulation through GATT began in 1961, with the Short-Term Arrangement, followed by the Long-Term Arrangement, to limit imports of cotton textiles and apparel. However, between 1960 and 1970, US imports of man-made fiber textiles rose from 31 million pounds to 329 million pounds. The United States then initiated bilateral agreements extending the Long-Term Arrangement to also cover man-made textiles and apparel from primary suppliers Hong Kong, Japan, Korea, and Taiwan, who became known as the big four. The excess products not allowed to enter the United States were diverted to European countries, driving down prices there. The result was the negotiation of the **Multifiber Arrangement (MFA)**, which took effect in 1974 (Cline, 1990).

MFA was an international trade agreement that allowed textile and apparel trade to be regulated through quotas established in bilateral agreements between nations. The MFA was an exception to the GATT rules and contrary to its primary purpose of reducing trade barriers. Specifically, the arrangement violated two of the major GATT principles:

- The most-favored nation principle, requiring trade without discriminations: only multilateral agreements were allowed under GATT. Yet, MFA relied on bilateral agreements; the United States, for example, had bilateral agreements with some countries (e.g., Japan, Hong Kong, South Korea) that restricted their textile and apparel imports but not others. The European Union had the same.
- GATT stipulated that protection of domestic markets was allowed through tariffs only and no other trade restrictions should be used. Yet, MFA was based on quotas, quantitative restrictions on amount of imports (in addition to tariffs) that were different for different countries.

In addition, the MFA provided for unilateral trade restraints in the absence of bilateral trade agreements, so there was pressure on developing/producing countries to establish bilateral agreements with the developed/consuming countries. The MFA also provided for annual growth in imports of 6 percent for every country. Some flexibility was built into the MFA, via the following:

- Swing: the ability to use a portion of the unfilled ceiling of one category for another category.
- Carry over: an exporting country was allowed to use some of any unused ceiling from one agreement year to apply to the subsequent year's ceiling.
- Carry forward: an exporting country was allowed to borrow from next year's ceiling to apply to the present year's level.

There was no lack of work to administer the MFA, so bureaucracy flourished. The MFA was renewed in 1977, 1981, and 1986, each time increasing trade restraint with bilateral agreements involving more countries. By 1980, the United States had eighteen bilateral agreements; by 1990, the United States had more than sixty bilaterals. The European Community (EC) had bilateral agreements with twenty-five countries, along with unilateral restraints on Taiwan and some Eastern European countries (Cline, 1990). Yet, all the MFA efforts to restrain the growth of textile and apparel imports were not successful. In the United States and European Union, textile and apparel imports were increasing at an unprecedented rate. Despite the MFA, US imports of textiles and apparel increased from $2.3 billion in 1973 to $83.3 billion in 2004, just before the expiration of the MFA in early 2005.

The MFA did limit trade growth with countries that were major exporters where bilaterals were created. However, the primary effect of the MFA was in driving apparel production around the world. The goal was to find the next undeveloped, low-labor-cost country where apparel production could be established and where no bilateral agreement was in effect. The apparel industry was up to the task. Once apparel manufacturing was established at these new sites and imports from the new players in the textile and apparel market began to increase, the United States and EU would add a new bilateral agreement with these countries. This, in turn, stimulated search for new production sites in countries with no quotas. The MFA also encouraged diversification of supplier countries and product types.

World Trade Organization (WTO), 1994–Present

In 1994, following the 7 years of GATT trade negotiations known as the Uruguay Round, the WTO replaced the GATT, and the MFA was replaced by the Agreement on Textiles and Clothing (ATC), whose assigned task was to phase out the MFA, and thereby its quota system, by 2005. In the Uruguay Round, developing and newly developing countries requested removal of trade barriers erected by developed economies and, specifically, elimination of textile and apparel quotas limiting import quantities. The underlying argument was to bring textile and apparel trade back under ruling by GATT principles as well as the need for developing and newly developing countries to build their economies. The WTO was directed to operate on the same fundamental assumptions as GATT:

- Trade protection weakens the global economy.
- Freer trade strengthens the global economy.

Over the years, these core principles of the 1947 GATT were updated and became GATT 1994, the trade rules for the new WTO (Table 5.3).

The WTO provides a permanent forum for member countries to address their multilateral trade relations and facilitates the implementation of trade agreements. As with GATT, the WTO is primarily concerned with **multilateral trade agreements**, agreements that involve more than two countries. The highest authority of the WTO is the Ministerial Conference, which is composed of representatives of all WTO member countries and is required to meet at the ministerial level at least every 2 years (Figure 5.2). The General Council is the highest authority when a Ministerial Conference is not in session and thus directs the daily work of the WTO. Three councils and one committee group report to the General Council. Our primary interest is in the Council for Trade in Goods, which includes committees addressing subsidies, customs valuation, rules of origin, and import licensing.

TABLE 5.3

DIFFERENCES BETWEEN THE GENERAL AGREEMENT ON TARIFFS AND TRADE (GATT) AND THE WORLD TRADE ORGANIZATION (WTO)

GATT	WTO
A set of rules; a multilateral agreement	A permanent institution with its own secretariat
Applied on a provisional basis	Commitments are full and permanent
Rules applied to trade in goods	Covers trade in goods, services, and issues related to intellectual property
Rules selectively applied	Commitment of the entire membership
Disputes slow to settle, and settlements difficult to implement	Settlement system is faster, more automatic, swift to implement
System dependent on GATT 1947 until 1994	GATT 1994 is foundation of the merchandise trade system

WTO structure

All WTO members may participate in all councils, committees, etc, except Appellate Body, Dispute Settlement panels, and plurilateral committees.

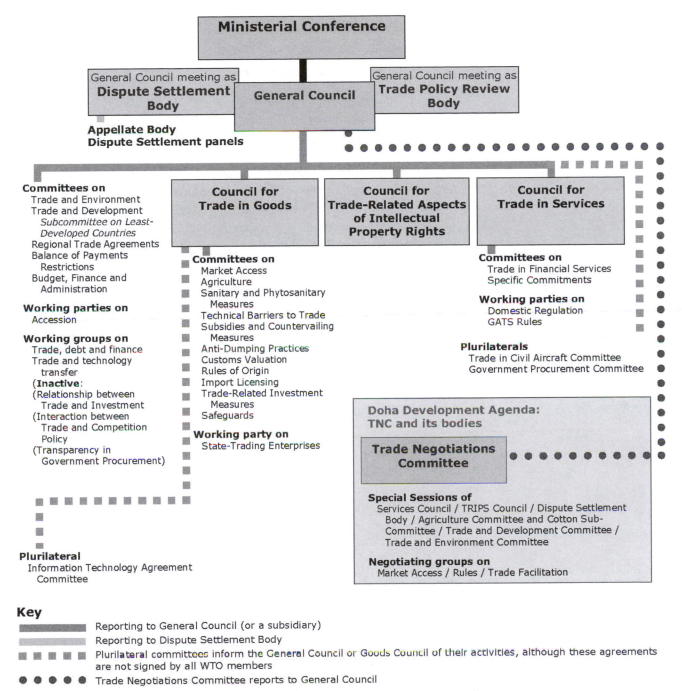

Ministerial Conference

General Council meeting as **Dispute Settlement Body**

General Council

General Council meeting as **Trade Policy Review Body**

Appellate Body
Dispute Settlement panels

Committees on
Trade and Environment
Trade and Development
*Subcommittee on Least-
Developed Countries*
Regional Trade Agreements
Balance of Payments
Restrictions
Budget, Finance and
Administration

Working parties on
Accession

Working groups on
Trade, debt and finance
Trade and technology
transfer
(**Inactive**:
(Relationship between
Trade and Investment
(Interaction between
Trade and Competition
Policy
(Transparency in
Government Procurement)

Plurilateral
Information Technology Agreement
Committee

**Council for
Trade in Goods**

Committees on
Market Access
Agriculture
Sanitary and Phytosanitary
Measures
Technical Barriers to Trade
Subsidies and Countervailing
Measures
Anti-Dumping Practices
Customs Valuation
Rules of Origin
Import Licensing
Trade-Related Investment
Measures
Safeguards

Working party on
State-Trading Enterprises

**Council for
Trade-Related Aspects
of Intellectual
Property Rights**

**Council for
Trade in Services**

Committees on
Trade in Financial Services
Specific Commitments

Working parties on
Domestic Regulation
GATS Rules

Plurilaterals
Trade in Civil Aircraft Committee
Government Procurement Committee

**Doha Development Agenda:
TNC and its bodies**

**Trade Negotiations
Committee**

Special Sessions of
Services Council / TRIPS Council / Dispute Settlement
Body / Agriculture Committee and Cotton Sub-
Committee / Trade and Development Committee /
Trade and Environment Committee

Negotiating groups on
Market Access / Rules / Trade Facilitation

Key

Reporting to General Council (or a subsidiary)
Reporting to Dispute Settlement Body
Plurilateral committees inform the General Council or Goods Council of their activities, although these agreements are not signed by all WTO members
Trade Negotiations Committee reports to General Council

The General Council also meets as the Trade Policy Review Body and Dispute Settlement Body

Figure 5.2
World Trade Organization (WTO) structure reflects the complexity of achieving and monitoring global trade agreements. The Textiles Monitoring Body is included under the Council for Trade of Goods.

There are two primary holders of a country's trade policy, rules, regulations, and laws: a country's government and the World Trade Organization (WTO). In April 2015, there were 161 member countries and 23 observer countries in the WTO. Negotiations may be in process for months or years within a country's government before the issue is ready to be presented to the WTO. All WTO decisions are made by 100 percent consensus.

WTO Agreement on Textiles and Clothing (ATC), 1995 to 2004

The Uruguay Round of trade negotiations created the WTO, the **Agreement on Textiles and Clothing (ATC)**, and the **Textiles Monitoring Body**, which were effective January 1, 1995. The primary purpose of the ATC was to complete the following:

- Phase out the MFA quota system over a 10-year period, by December 31, 2004.
- Reintegrate the textile and clothing sector into the WTO, the new world trading system.

During the operation of GATT, textiles and apparel trade was covered by the MFA and therefore was treated differently from other goods, specifically, with many imports into developed countries restricted by a system of bilateral quotas. The Uruguay Round determined that it was in the best interest of the world market to phase out the MFA. The ATC included the ground rules for the phaseout, and the Textiles Monitoring Body was created as a group within the WTO Council for Trade in Goods to monitor the process. The ATC established a four-stage system to guide countries through the phaseout. This system included time lines for categories and percentages of textile and apparel trade to be quota free.

Even though developing and newly developing countries initiated the MFA phaseout, during the ATC they began to realize that under the MFA, they actually had an artificial advantage in the guise of guaranteed market share in their negotiated quota and that they might not be capable of competing in a free trade market. When China became a WTO member in 2001, it became a real threat to all apparel producing countries in the world with no quotas. There was little industrial development in the newly developing countries to provide jobs if textiles and apparel production left. Sub-Saharan African countries as well as some Asian countries had few other opportunities. The textile and apparel industries in many of these countries were financed by China and by foreign investment from countries in which there was insufficient quota. After 2005, some of these investors decided to return to their home countries rather than continue their foreign investment.

Many firms in developed countries, including the United States and EU, feared losing their domestic production altogether. Some firms started to panic, others started to plan, and still others started to beg. The firms in panic looked for mergers and takeovers, based on the assumption that bigger is better. The planners asked the question, if we could get product anywhere in the world without the quota barrier, where would that be? Then they proceeded with arrangements to make that possible. The firms that started to beg began lobbying for extension of the quota system beyond 2005.

When the terms of the MFA expired at the beginning of 2005, the importation of apparel from China exploded. In January of 2005, US and European firms had thousands of dozens of garments produced in China stored in containers and ready to be loaded on ships when the MFA quotas expired. For example, exports from China to the United States increased from 2004 to 2005, as follows:

- cotton knit shirts increased 1,277 percent
- cotton trousers increased 1,573 percent

- cotton underwear increased 318 percent
- man-made fiber shirts and trousers increased 300 percent (Zagaroli, 2008)

The EU, which had a similar imports explosion, and the United States moved quickly to impose new import quotas on selected categories of apparel from China in June 2005. Following extensive negotiations between trade representatives, in November 2005 the United States signed a Memorandum of Understanding with China, limiting imports from China on thirty-four categories of apparel products. The agreement allowed 10 percent increases in 2006, another 12.5 percent increase in 2007, and a 15 to 16 percent increase in 2008.

When the US export limit agreement with China expired in 2008, there were ship-loads of apparel sitting offshore, waiting to be unloaded, that were included in retailers' merchandise plans to supply inventories for the spring 2009 selling period. However, the CBP did not allow the merchandise to be unloaded. Instead, it imposed "staged entry procedures" for textile and apparel goods shipped from China in 2008 that exceeded the applicable quotas. At the direction of the Committee for Implementation of Textile Agreements, the CBP limited the entry of goods as follows:

- for all shipments exported in 2008 that exceeded 2008 quotas, entry was not permitted until February 1, 2009;
- from February 1 through February 28, 5 percent of the applicable quota could be imported; and
- entry for any remaining goods was then permitted at the rate of 5 percent per month, until all shipments in excess of applicable quotas had been entered (Hong Kong Trade Development Council, 2009).

To understand the difficulty these sorts of interruptions of trade can cause, here is an example. Assume you are a retail buyer of infants' apparel for Macy's. Among the thousands of dozens of garments sitting offshore are 50,000 pairs of infants' socks that are scheduled to be for sale in Macy's stores all across the country during the month of February 2008. There would be a lot of Macy's customers' babies going barefoot or perhaps going to Walmart to get their socks, assuming, of course, that Walmart's socks are not also sitting offshore onboard the same ship.

Although the textile and apparel trade had been relatively stable during MFA, it was not uncommon for apparel producers to pack up and move across a border if lower costs or greater convenience existed in another country. In other words, there was no commitment to sustainability. Textile producers tend to be less mobile than apparel producers because of greater capital investment and the machinery and technology required.

Since the phaseout of quotas, many new trade agreements came into effect around the world. In fact, according to WTO, in 2014 there were 377 trade agreements governing the global trade. It took enormous amounts of time and resources to negotiate and ratify these free trade agreements (FTAs). Now, for companies trading across borders, it is taking even more time and resources to follow the cumbersome rules and regulations of these 377 agreements. It is not clear why so many agreements are needed to make trade free. Read Case 5.2 to learn about another agreement in the process of negotiation and its potential effects on the US and global textile and apparel industries.

CRAFTING A NEW FTA: FREE OR PROTECTED TRADE?

The year 2015 is expected to be the final point of multiyear negotiations around a Trans-Pacific Partnership (TPP), with the goal to create a free trade area for twelve Pacific countries: Australia, Brunei, Canada, Chile, Japan, Malaysia, Mexico, New Zealand, Peru, Singapore, the United States, and Vietnam (Figure Case 5.2). It would be the largest free trade area ever, accounting for 40 percent of the world's GDP. The debate over TPP involves many different levels and interest groups. The proposed FTA encounters strong support as well as fierce opposition in the participating countries.

The following rules of origin (ROO) are being debated to determine how much processing must occur within the TPP region to qualify for duty-free apparel imports to the United States and other member markets (Japan, Australia, Canada, etc.):

- Fiber-forward: man-made fibers must be extruded and natural fibers grown as well as all consequent production stages must be done within the FTA region.
- Yarn-forward: all production stages, beginning from yarn, must occur within the TPP countries; textile producers can use fibers from any country.
- Fabric-forward: all production stages, beginning from fabric, must occur within the TPP countries; textile producers can use yarns from any country.

- Cut-and-sew: only garment cutting and sewing must occur within the TPP countries; apparel producers can use fabrics from any country.

In the US textile, apparel, and retail industries, there are two major camps that have conflicting agendas with respect to TPP. On one side, there are US textile manufacturers, who oppose TPP, or, at the very minimum, demand yarn-forward ROO, which is known as "triple transformation" requirement (from fiber to yarn, from yarn to fabric, and from fabric to apparel). No other US industry has such level of protection; single transformation rule is typical for most sectors.

Textile producers' major argument is support of domestic manufacturing and jobs. In 2013, the US textile industry directly employed 230,000 workers and contributed $57 billion to the US economy. About one-third of US-made textiles are exported, primarily for apparel assembly in one of the NAFTA and CAFTA countries. TPP threatens apparel production in the Western hemisphere due to lower wages and greater production efficiencies in Vietnam, which was second only to China as the largest supplier of apparel to the US market in 2014. Even if TPP included a yarn-forward rule, US textile producers would have a hard time selling

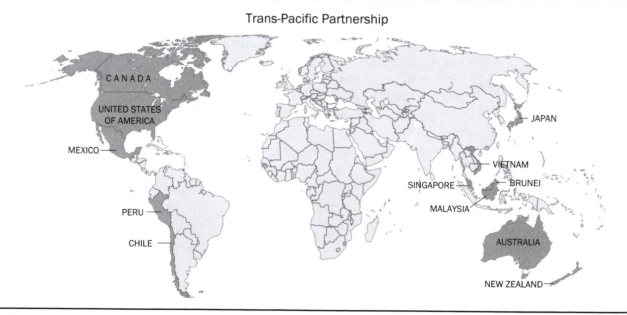

Trans-Pacific Partnership

Figure Case 5.2

Map of Trans-Pacific Partnership member countries. Note that some Pacific nations, such as Indonesia, China, and Russia, are not included in the partnership.

domestically manufactured yarn and fabric to Vietnam because of competition from Chinese mills. In addition, major textile companies from China, Japan, Hong Kong, South Korea, Australia, and Europe have invested about $1 billion to build state-of-the-art mills in Vietnam in anticipation of TPP.

On the other side, there are retailers, brands, and other companies importing apparel to the United States. The apparel and retail camp, in general, advocates for a truly free trade globally, with no restrictions or barriers, including tariffs. Specific to TPP, the group insists that as long as apparel is manufactured in one of the member countries, it should enter the US market duty-free, regardless of the origin of yarn and fabric used to make garments. For retailers and brand managers, flexibility and speed in sourcing materials and assembly to deliver the best value are often more important than savings, even significant on duty-free imports from FTA countries. Between 2003 and 2012, the number of FTA countries increased by three times, yet, their use by US apparel importers dropped by more than 25 percent. In 2012, only 20 percent of US apparel imports were from FTA countries. As a result, average apparel tariff rate has been increasing, which indicates that with a greater number of FTAs, trade actually is becoming less free. The TPP debate continues. . .

DePillis, L. (December 11, 2013). "Everything You Need to Know about the Trans Pacific Partnership." *Washington Post*.

Platzer, M. D. (2014). "US Textile Manufacturing and the Trans-Pacific Partnership Negotiations." Congressional Research Service. R42772.

Rivoli, P. (2014). *The Travels of a T-shirt in the Global Economy*. Hoboken, NJ: Wiley.

1. Do you support TPP? If yes, what ROO would you vote for, and why? If no, why not?
2. What forces were behind the final format of the adopted TPP and how did the outcome affect the US textile industry and apparel market?
3. Do you consider TPP a step toward free or protected trade? Explain.

FREE TRADE ZONES

Free trade zones, in their various formats, represent provisions within trade agreements between countries that are designed to reduce trade barriers and facilitate trade. A **free trade zone**, also known as foreign trade zone, is a port or other site within a nation designated for duty-free entry of selected goods to be displayed, stored, or used for manufacturing. The goods imported into the free trade zone may be stored or undergo repackaging or other operations before they are exported as finished goods to another country. For example, fabric can be imported duty-free in a free trade zone to manufacture apparel for re-export. The products imported into the zone are not subject to duties assessed on similar imported goods that enter commerce in the country.

Free trade zones are often established within developing or newly developing nations that are just entering into competitive participation in the global market. Their primary suppliers are sourcing companies representing firms from developed countries that seek low-cost labor and avoidance of duties on imports. At the same time, the zones provide jobs for people in developing countries who are in need of employment and lower costs to companies and consumers in developed countries in which the goods are ultimately consumed. The goods produced do not compete in the developing country's domestic market, because everything stored and processed in the zone is required to be exported. A **qualified industrial zone (QIZ)** is a highly specialized type of free trade zone that involves more than one nation, for example, Jordan and Israel or Egypt and Israel, where manufacturing can take place, similar to a free trade zone. QIZs are discussed further in Chapter 12.

Free trade area should not be confused with free trade zone. A **free trade area** is a region made up of two or more countries that have a comprehensive free trade agreement eliminating or reducing trade barriers on products traded among the countries. For example, Canada, Mexico, and United States make up NAFTA, a free trade area. Free trade zones and free trade areas require agreements between the nations involved to reduce trade barriers.

POLITICAL POSITIONING AND THE US TEXTILE COMPLEX

Trade Associations

A trade association is a nonprofit organization formed to serve the common needs of its members. Members are usually firms that are in business in the sector that the trade association represents and pay membership fees to support the services and activities of the association. Active participants in trade associations include executives of the member firms; consultants active in the field; suppliers of technology, materials, and other services; editors and writers of industry news; and educators who are specialists in the appropriate field of study.

Services provided by trade associations may include industry research, publications, seminars, trade shows, opportunities for sharing business challenges and solutions, government relations, and **lobbying**. Lobbying is the process of influencing the formation of legislation and the administration of rules, regulations, and policies. Lobbying is commonly carried out by **lobbyists**, paid professionals who communicate the political positions defined by their employers to influence formation or administration of legislation. Political positioning in the business environment requires evaluating circumstances and opportunities and determining priorities in order to best serve the interests of the industry or firm. Lobbyists employed by trade associations convey the political positions of its members to appropriate legislators.

Different segments of the textile complex often take different political positions, which are represented by their respective trade associations. Major US trade associations representing the three industries include:

- Textile industry: National Council of Textile Organizations
- Apparel and footwear industries: American Apparel and Footwear Association (AAFA)
- Retail industry: U.S Fashion Industry Association

Figure 5.3 represents the major components of the political decision-making process that creates and enforces textile and apparel trade rules, policies, and regulations for the United States. Changes in rules, policies, and regulations start in the office of the United States Trade Representative (USTR), but the final proposal has to be approved and administered by the US government. To be globally accepted, approval of the WTO is important.

The US textile complex, through respective trade associations, frequently strives to influence the formulation and administration of trade law. This is accomplished by lobbying the US Congress. The Committee for Implementation of Textile Agreements (CITA), chaired by the Department of Commerce, is responsible for implementing trade agreements. CITA also handles requests for safeguard measures against unfair competition.

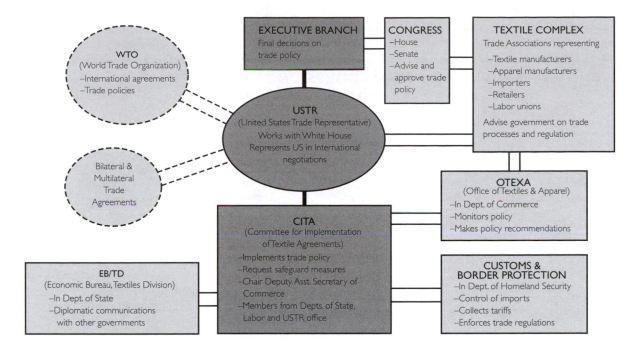

Evolution of the US Textile Complex

Table 5.4 represents the political evolution of textile, apparel, and retail firms in the US textile complex from 1950 to the present and beyond. The firms that are part of the three primary components of the US textile complex see the world differently and have different pressures and priorities. To represent the evolution of the three US industries, we used the four political perspectives that determine firms' focus and strategies to operate in the global market:

- International companies are importers and exporters (source and sell products and materials abroad) simply to support domestic operations.
- Multinational/multidomestic companies emphasize the differences among national suppliers, markets, and operating environments; they sacrifice efficiency in favor of responsiveness to local environments and customizing their products and strategies for each individual national market.
- Global companies use one common strategy and coordinated image/brand to market their products in different countries, assuming that national tastes and preferences are more similar than different. Emphasis on volume, cost management, and efficiency.
- Transnational companies are responsive to local needs in multiple countries while retaining global efficiency; they have a central corporate facility but give decision-making, R&D, and marketing powers to each individual foreign market. (Ali, 2000)

These classifications evolve from the protectionist perspective focused on the domestic market, to international trade, global free trade, and to a transnational trade perspective. When the majority of firms in a country focus on one strategy, they determine the focus of the entire domestic industry. Of course, at any given time, different firms within an industry might focus on different strategies, but the majority defines the industry's orientation. The different components of the textile complex seem to have similar perspectives in other parts of the world. In Table 5.4, the gray rows preceding each decade list major trade regulations that affected the industries' strategies during

Figure 5.3
The textile complex interacts with both the executive and legislative branches of government to influence implementation, administration, and enforcement of textile and apparel trade policies, rules, and regulations. Note in particular with which functions the textile complex tends to have direct contact.

TABLE 5.4

EVOLUTION OF THE US TEXTILE, APPAREL, AND RETAIL INDUSTRIES AND THEIR FOCUS AND PERSPECTIVES ON TRADE INTEGRATED WITH TRADE REGULATIONS IN EACH DECADE

Decade and Its Developmental Focus	Focus of Textile Manufacturing	Focus of Apparel Manufacturing	Focus of Retailing Industry
Protected Trade ⟵	Voluntary export restraints	Major trade regulations ⟶	Free Trade
1950s Entrepreneurism/ Protectionism	Domestic production Protected trade	Domestic production Protected trade	Domestic buying
Short-Term Arrangement, Long-Term Arrangement			
1960s Entrepreneurism	Domestic production Protected trade	Domestic production Protected trade	Domestic buying and moving toward international sourcing
MFA	*Item 807*		
1970s Protectionism	Domestic production Protected trade	Domestic production Protected trade	Domestic buying and international sourcing Free trade
Extended MFA		*Item 807a*	*US—Canada FTA*
1980s Verticalization/ Internationalization	Domestic production Protection with fabric-forward rules	Domestic production Protected trade Moving toward international sourcing	International sourcing Free trade
ATC (beginning of MFA phaseout)			*NAFTA*
1990s Horizontalization/ Globalization	Mostly domestic production Protection with yarn- and fabric-forward rules	Free trade International sourcing	Free trade Global sourcing International marketing
		NAFTA, CAFTA, FTAs with six other countries, AGOA	
2000s Post-quota Trade and Sourcing	Moving toward international production Protection with yarn- and fabric-forward rules	Free trade Global sourcing and marketing Social responsibility	Free trade Global sourcing and marketing Social responsibility
		NAFTA, CAFTA, FTAs with twelve other countries, AGOA	
2010s Regionalization/ Sustainability	Combination of domestic and international production Protection with yarn- and fabric-forward rules	Free trade and fair trade Moving toward transnational sourcing and marketing Emerging pockets of domestic production	Free trade and fair trade Moving toward transnational sourcing and marketing Emerging pockets of domestic production

the respective decade. Trade regulations are shown from most protective (on the left side) to least protective (on the right side).

The 1950s and 1960s: Entrepreneurism

In the 1950s, Japan was the number one apparel exporter to the US market, shipping growing quantities of inexpensive garments. The United States applied the first non-tariff trade barrier on Japan, a voluntary export restraint, in an attempt to limit apparel imports from Japan. In the 1960s, the Short- and then the Long-Term Arrangements limited quantities of cotton apparel that could be imported to the US market.

In the United States, textile and apparel manufacturing industries were close allies, focusing on increasing domestic production to satisfy the booming consumer market. On average, textile mills employed 150 people, and apparel factories employed 50 people. The textile industry had been slowly concentrating into fewer larger firms and becoming more capital intensive. Both industries were concentrated in the northeastern United States, and 80 percent of US apparel was produced there (de la Torre et al., 1978). Textile firms, apparel firms, and their trade associations all supported the protectionist perspective. Retailers began to discover the benefits of international sourcing, with a focus on Hong Kong, Japan, South Korea, and Taiwan. Retailers wanted to shop the world market to provide unique apparel for their customers. However, the majority of buying was still done domestically.

The 1970s

The United States continued to be the largest cotton-producing country, with 19.2 percent of world production (Cline, 1990). Cotton imports were limited by the Long-Term Arrangement. However, consumer preferences had changed, and in the United States consumption of man-made fibers exceeded consumption of cotton. Apparel imports were on the rise, from 6 percent of domestic consumption in 1961 to 25 percent in 1972. As the result of textile and apparel industries lobbying, in 1974, MFA established import quotas based on bilateral agreements. The United States became the largest importer of apparel in the world, with more than $3 billion annually.

The Tariff Schedules of the United States had a clause known as Item 807, which allowed garments cut in the United States to be exported for assembly and then imported, with tariff based only on value added. Value added was primarily dependent on labor cost, which kept the duty very low when products were assembled in Caribbean Basin countries. Pattern making and cutting operations were established in Miami to support 807 operations. Still, the majority of apparel in the US market continued to be supplied by domestic firms. In 1976 the United States was the largest employer of apparel workers in the world, with more than 1.3 million employees. Most apparel firms were family-owned, single plant operations. Textile and apparel industries were shifting away from urban areas into rural areas, primarily in the southeastern United States, where real estate cost less, unions were not established, and wages were lower. The number of apparel factories in the Northeast dropped by almost half.

The primary interest of apparel manufacturers was finding ways to increase the speed of garment assembly. The first major technical innovation in apparel production in 70 years was the laser beam cutter, introduced in the early 1970s. This helped the preproduction process, but sewing operators were still labor intensive and time-consuming. In the retail sector, independent retailers were still in the majority, but department store chains were growing, and discount stores had been born. Bypassing US manufacturers by sourcing apparel in Hong Kong was common. Retailers began to advocate for free trade, recognizing the benefits of lower costs available abroad.

The 1980s

By the 1980s, the MFA was a global mechanism for controlling textile and apparel trade. US retailers began to shift sourcing from the quota-restricted countries, including Hong Kong, Taiwan, and South Korea, to countries with no quotas (Glock & Kunz, 1995). As apparel production migrated to other developing countries, materials supply became an issue. Some textile producers began to establish production plants in developing countries to facilitate speed to market for the apparel plants in those locations. Imports continued to increase in developed countries at an astounding rate. Another quota avoidance strategy was to include fiber content in products that were not covered in the bilateral agreements. Quota restricted cotton, wool, and major man-made fibers, primarily nylon, polyester, and acrylic; thus, blends, including ramie, silk, and linen, became more common because they could be imported quota free, with tariffs as the only trade barrier (Glock & Kunz, 1995).

In 1986, the United States and fifty-four other nations renewed the MFA for the fourth time. At US textile and apparel industry insistence, the new agreement tightened quotas and extended product coverage to ramie, silk, and linen. Using transshipment to avoid quotas by modifying country of origin had become a known practice (Cline, 1990). The Caribbean Basin Initiative (CBI), known as Item 807a, was established, assuring US market access for Caribbean apparel products assembled from fabric made in the United States. CBI encouraged movement of apparel production out of the United States (Cline, 1990). The **fabric-forward rule** guaranteed that the domestic textile manufacturers would supply the fabric, regardless of if the apparel was assembled in the United States or Caribbean countries. The US–Canada Free Trade Agreement was approved, also including the fabric-forward rule; to qualify for duty-free, apparel had to be made of fabric produced in one of the two countries.

The size of textile, apparel, and retailing firms was exploding. Vertical mergers became commonplace. Small firms merged, were bought out, or went out of business. Yarn spinners merged with weavers and with fabric finishers. US textile manufacturers focused on mass production. They reduced the variety of fabrics produced, focused on budget- to moderate-priced goods, and increased the minimum number of yards required to make a purchase, strategies that were hurting apparel manufacturers.

Textile manufacturers continued to advocate strongly for protected trade. Apparel manufacturers remained protectionist, while developing 807 operations throughout the Caribbean Basin and experimenting with the retailers' practice of sourcing in the Far East. Apparel manufacturers bought their fabric suppliers and became vertically integrated into the retail sector. Manufacturers' outlets became the most rapidly growing form of retailing. Major manufacturers and designers developed brands that remain powerful components of the apparel industry today, such as Ralph Lauren and Calvin Klein. Retailers developed their own product development divisions so that they could go directly to CMT contractors in developing countries and avoid the apparel manufacturer's role in the traditional supply chain. Department stores were at the mercy of their branded suppliers, who determined what, how much, and when merchandise would be shipped and how it would be displayed.

The 1990s

In 1995, MFA was scheduled to be phased out within 10 years. Meanwhile, **regionalization**, reducing trade barriers in selected geographic regions, continued to develop through preferential trading agreements. In 1994, the North American Free Trade Agreement (NAFTA) went into effect, which included a **yarn-forward rule**: to qualify for free trade, yarns, as well as fabrics, had to be produced in Canada, Mexico, or the United States. Once again the benefit of the yarn-forward rule accrued to the US textile industry, because there was little textile production in Mexico or Canada.

US apparel industry employment has been declining. Apparel manufacturers began focusing on product development, closing domestic factories, and sourcing production in Mexico, the Caribbean Basin, or Asia. Consequently, apparel manufacturers abandoned their protectionist stance and joined retailers in seeking the benefits of free trade (Glock & Kunz, 2000). Branding was the name of the game, with a strong emphasis on licensing on a variety of apparel products as well as many other types of products. Many retailers, through growth, mergers, and acquisitions, became huge. Walmart became the largest retailer in the world. Price promotion became the primary mode of competition. Retailers became global in product development, sourcing, and marketing. Sourcing finished goods and apparel assembly from the low-labor-cost developing countries continued to evolve. China established itself as the primary source of choice for many brand managers and retailers.

The 2000s

Until January 1, 2005, the MFA import quotas remained in effect on most textile and apparel product categories, limiting amount of products that could be imported from major apparel manufacturing countries. China was the only country that continued to have quantitative import restrictions after safeguard measures on selected textile and apparel products were imposed by the United States and European Union in the middle of 2005. The safeguards expired at the end of 2008. By the end of the decade, a number of new free trade agreements (FTAs) were put in place, including one multilateral, Central American Free Trade Agreement (CAFTA) that consisted of six countries. Most FTAs were with countries in the Western hemisphere and included yarn- and/or fabric-forward rules to ensure the market for US-made yarns and fabrics.

In the new century US textile manufacturers and textile manufacturers in other developed countries experienced dramatic decline in demand for domestically produced yarns and fabrics due to the fast decline in domestically produced apparel. Many firms went out of business, others declared bankruptcy, and still others were merged or absorbed. Through it all, the textile industry maintained its protectionist perspective. However, by the mid-2000s, some US textile firms began expanding operations into China and other centers of apparel production to establish operations in proximity to apparel production. Less than 5 percent of apparel sold in the United States in 2009 was made domestically, with 35 percent of it coming from China. Mergers among apparel companies continued, creating "batteries" of brands. A few former apparel manufacturers closed their last factories, either domestic or abroad, and became brand managers with primary activities including design, product development, and sourcing.

Sales in the US apparel retail market reached $280 billion in 2007. Practically all major apparel retailers had their own design, product development, and sourcing teams, contracting apparel assembly directly with offshore factories. Distinction between former apparel manufacturers, who were now brand managers, and retailers disappeared as their strategies and operations became very similar, if not the same. Both were involved in global sourcing and marketing, with a strong emphasis on social responsibility. Development of private labels became a popular and profitable trend.

The 2010s

From 2009 to 2014, the number of bilateral FTAs more than doubled. The United States has been in negotiations for two multilateral large-scale FTAs: Trans-Pacific Partnership (TPP) with twelve countries and Transatlantic Trade and Investment Partnership with the EU (with twenty-eight countries). Yet many newly developing countries with preferential trade agreements have struggled during this period. Relief of duty alone does not appear to be enough to ensure competitiveness. The rules of origin rules that govern these agreements frequently dictate the sourcing of materials, increasing input costs and paperwork. With respect to US apparel market share, primary losers included Mexico, Honduras, and the Dominican Republic. Primary winners included China, Vietnam, Indonesia, India, and Bangladesh. However, increasing labor cost and tightening environmental regulations have been pushing up production costs in China. Retailers and brand managers focusing on value shifted apparel assembly to lower cost countries, such as Vietnam and Bangladesh.

Changing priorities in supply chain operation are causing buyers (the sourcing company) to impose different expectations on potential vendors (the supplier company). The trend toward faster turnover of inventory in the retail setting drives buyers to vendors with proximity to materials; reliable infrastructure for energy, transportation, and communication; and a workforce that is skilled, flexible, and dependable. Newly developing countries seldom have these resources in place.

The 2008–2009 worldwide recession and high energy costs resulted in the decline of apparel sales and overall business operations. However by 2011, the US apparel market recovered and exceeded the prerecession, 2007 level, reaching $284 billion. A primary result of the recession was that all textile and apparel firms, large and small, were finding ways to improve efficiency and reduce costs. In 2013, the US apparel industry employed 144,000 workers, down by 55,000 jobs from 2008. Partially driven by social and environmental concerns, a segment of US consumers became interested in "Made in the USA" apparel (Platzer, 2014). In response to this trend, some brands, such as Brooks Brothers, resumed limited domestic manufacturing and some new apparel companies with domestic production appeared. Both brand managers and retailers have been adopting transnational sourcing and marketing: being responsive to local needs in multiple countries, while simultaneously retaining global efficiency. While some textile manufacturers have diversified and been producing both domestically and internationally, the industry still continued the protectionist perspective to guard domestic production of yarns and fabrics as much as possible.

Other major trends included proliferation of fast fashion, greater focus on sustainability, and the rise of **omnichannel retailing**, which is a multichannel approach to sales that seeks to provide a seamless shopping experience to customers whether they are shopping online from a desktop or mobile device, by telephone or in a brick-and-mortar store.

REGIONALIZATION OF GLOBAL MARKETS

The complexity of the global market and the diversity of political climates among nations have fostered a trend to regionalization of the global textile and apparel industry, using **preferential trade agreements (PTA)**. A PTA among two or more countries extends special trading advantages by reducing trade barriers. Four primary regions form **trading blocs**, groups of countries that have created regional trade incentives and that jointly participate in trade negotiations:

1. Europe and the European Union
2. The Americas and Caribbean
3. Asia and Oceania
4. The Middle East and Africa

Each of these regions includes a combination of developed and developing or newly developing countries. The developed countries in a region provide market demand for the products produced with low-cost labor in the developing countries. This discussion introduces the basic characteristics of these four trading blocs. Chapter 6 introduces illegal and unethical activities related to textiles and apparel throughout the world, Chapters 7 and 8 focus on sourcing processes and strategies and locations around the world, and Chapters 9 through 12 discuss the nature of the textile and apparel industry in each of these four geographic regions (Figure 5.4).

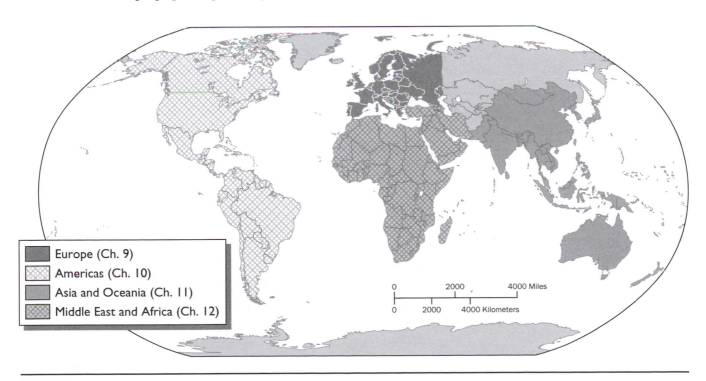

Europe (Ch. 9)
Americas (Ch. 10)
Asia and Oceania (Ch. 11)
Middle East and Africa (Ch. 12)

Figure 5.4
Four trading regions/blocks are identified on this map: Europe and the European Union (EU), the Americas and the Caribbean, Asia and Oceania, and the Middle East and Africa. All have regional distinctions in the manufacturing and distribution of textiles and apparel.

Europe and the European Union

Europe stretches from Iceland in the North Atlantic to Russia in the east, and from Scandinavia in the north to Spain and Turkey in the south. Western Europe includes many of the most developed countries in the world, whereas Eastern Europe includes a variety of developed and developing countries, many of which re-emerged in the global marketplace after the breakup of the Soviet Union in the 1990s.

Europe moved toward regionalization by creating the Common Market, beginning in 1952, followed by the European Economic Community (EEC). Then, in 1993, the EEC evolved into a twelve-nation group known as the European Union (EU). The EU has now expanded to include twenty-eight countries throughout Europe. The European trading bloc includes several western European nations—specifically, Great Britain, France, Italy, and Germany—that have traditionally been major players in the global textile and apparel industries. The region is also a major market in terms of apparel consumption. This segment of the globe is examined in Chapter 9.

The Americas

The Americas comprise Central America (seven countries), North America (three countries), South America (thirteen countries), and the West Indies (thirteen countries). Political regionalization of the Americas started in the 1980s with the Caribbean Basin Initiative. The North American Free Trade Agreement (NAFTA) then unified North America in 1994. NAFTA was followed by the US–Caribbean Basin Trade Partnership Act (CBTPA) and establishment of the Central American Free Trade Agreement, which ultimately added the Dominican Republic, to become CAFTA-DR, as well as bilateral free trade agreements with individual South American countries, including Chile, Colombia, Panama, and Peru. Mercosur, known as Common Market of the South, was established in 1991 and includes Argentina, Brazil, Paraguay, Uruguay, and Venezuela. The Andean Customs Union is comprised of four countries: Bolivia, Colombia, Ecuador, and Peru. CARICOM, the Caribbean Community, consists of fifteen countries. This part of the world is examined in Chapter 10.

Asia and Oceania

This bloc is a combination of mainland and island countries, including the two most populous nations on the globe: China and India. China is the major textile and apparel supplier in the world. Japan, South Korea, Taiwan, and India have significant production of textiles. India, Vietnam, Bangladesh, Pakistan, and Thailand are important players in apparel production and trade.

Regionalization in the Asia and Oceania area proceeded in 1977, with the creation of the Association of Southeast Asian Nations (ASEAN). The ASEAN free trade area consists of ten countries: Brunei, Cambodia, Indonesia, Laos, Malaysia, Myanmar, Philippines, Singapore, Thailand, and Vietnam. Papua New Guinea is an observer member. The major purpose of this association has been the economic development of nations within the region. ASEAN has fostered free trade agreements among mainland and island country member nations and with other countries. Japan, South Korea, and Australia are major consumer markets in the region. China and India, with fast growing middle classes, are transitioning from producer to consumer economies and rapidly increasing their consumption rates. The many changes in this region of the world are examined in Chapter 11.

Middle East and Africa

We define the Middle East region as the area stretching from Turkey, on the eastern shore of the Mediterranean, eastward through Iran. At this time, the region includes some of the more politically volatile portions of the globe, including Iraq, Iran, and Afghanistan. The Middle East has assumed much greater importance in the global textile and apparel market since establishing some apparel production sites backed by free trade agreements with United States and EU, for example, Israel and Jordan. Some oil-exporting countries have also emerged as significant consumer markets, such as United Arab Emirates (UAE).

Africa became a more significant contributor to global apparel trade through the development of CMT facilities, such as those on the island nation of Mauritius (located off the eastern coast), but many African countries have had a hard time competing since the MFA quotas were phased out in 2005. African nations have been working toward a regional presence with such international agreements as the African Growth and Opportunity Act (AGOA), first passed in 2000. AGOA has progressed through some revisions since it was originally instituted (AGOA II, AGOA III, and now AGOA IV) and as refinements were made to provide incentives for African countries to continue their efforts to open their economies and build free markets, including those related to textiles and apparel. AGOA is scheduled for renewal in September 2015. The uniqueness of this region is addressed in Chapter 12.

Summary

Trade has many meanings, but the focus in this chapter is the exchange of goods among nations. Globalization of trade has evolved in at least three phases: the globalization of countries, the globalization of companies, and, most recently, the globalization of individuals. Politics are the methods, or tactics, involved in managing an organization, business, state, or government. Power, influence, and manipulation of people and other resources may be the primary motivators. Politics exist in all organizations in which there is controversy related to objectives, use of resources, or competition for power, or a combination of these.

Protecting domestic industry from foreign competition and using trade to generate government revenue have been priorities since trade began. To operate a trade protection system, countries create customs services to monitor levels of trade and administer trade agreements. Because the GATT, and later WTO, supported reductions in trade barriers, customs services in some countries have moved their focus away from collection of duty and toward other issues, such as border protection. Trade protection is initiated by erecting trade barriers. Trade barriers have two forms: tariff and nontariff barriers. Tariffs are taxes imposed on imported or exported goods. Tariffs increase the prices of imported goods, causing domestic industry to be less efficient, raise consumer prices, and generate revenue for governments. Nontariff trade barriers take many forms, including exchange rates, price support programs, quotas, and voluntary restraints. Quotas were a critical component of the textile and apparel trade for more than 40 years. Quotas restrict trade by limiting the quantity of goods that can be imported or exported.

Unfair competition is commercial activity that tends to confuse, mislead, or deceive customers and provide unfair business advantages. Government activities, including production subsidies, export subsidies, and price support programs, are frequently regarded as unfair competition in the global market. Dumping is a form of unfair competition that involves selling products below cost of production or their normal price in the domestic market. Governments compensate for this by applying countervailing duties to reduce import surges.

The General Agreement on Tariffs and Trade (GATT) originated with the primary purpose of reducing trade barriers. However, the textile and apparel industry created the Multifiber Arrangement (MFA), a bilateral quota system to protect firms in developed countries from products made with low-cost labor in developing countries. Through multilateral trade negotiations, the World Trade Organization (WTO) absorbed the GATT in 1994. The WTO included the Textiles Monitoring body to supervise the operation of the Agreement on Textiles and Clothing (ATC), which phased out the MFA and its quota system in 2005. Quota extension agreements between China and the United States, and China and the EU, expired in 2008.

For many years, US textile and apparel manufacturers favored protectionist legislation and retailers favored free trade. Retailers have long recognized the value of the global market for giving their customers the best prices and a unique variety of goods. As US apparel manufacturers outsourced garment assembly to developing countries, they also learned the value of the global market and changed their political perspective to support free trade.

Learning Activities

1. What will Globalization 4.0 look like? Provide examples and justify your forecast. How might the textile and apparel industries be affected by the next stage of globalization?
2. Why was the textile and apparel trade allowed to operate under the MFA in ways that were contrary to GATT rules?
3. Why were tariffs unable to control the textile and apparel trade? What do quotas do that tariffs cannot?
4. Why didn't the MFA work?
5. A poultry importer has made a deal to import 1,500 young turkeys weighing 2.7 kilograms (6 pounds) each and 1,500 young chickens weighing 0.9 kilograms (1 pound) each. Considering the duty rates in Table 5.1, determine how much total duty has to be paid on the turkeys and the chickens.
6. Considering your calculations for question 5, how much increase in price per kilogram will the importer have to charge to cover the duty on the turkeys? The chickens?
7. Considering your calculations for question 6, which domestic producers have the most trade protection: the producers of turkeys or of chickens? What realities do these numbers demonstrate, relative to the effectiveness of specific tariffs?
8. You are a US importer of baseball gloves, and you want to import two groups of baseball gloves: 500 dozen, with a cost of $8.50 each, and 100 dozen, at a cost of $14.00 each. Considering a 15 percent ad valorem tariff, what is the total duty due on each group? What is the duty due on one unit in each group?
9. You did not do well with baseball gloves, so you switched over to importing designer neckties from Italy. Fourteen ties equal one kilogram. Considering potential duties of $0.0265 per kilogram and 13.5 percent ad valorem, calculate the total duty due on 900 dozen ties, at $19 each.

References

Ali, A. J. (2000). *Globalization of Business: Practice and Theory*. New York, NY: Haworth Press.

Behavioral Research and Teaching. (n.d.). "Chapter 13: The Road to the Civil War." Problem Solving Through History. Retrieved November 5, 2015, from http://www.brtprojects.org/cyberschool/history/

Chanda, N. (March 25, 2004). "Globalization 3.0 Has Shrunk the World: An Interview with Thomas L. Friedman." Global Envision. Retrieved June 22, 2004, from http://globalenvision.org/library/3/601/6/

Cline, W. C. (1990). *The Future of World Trade in Textiles and Apparel*. Washington, DC: Institute of International Economics.

Cohen, S. D., Blecker, R. A., & Whitney, P. D. (2003). *Fundamentals of US Foreign Trade Policy* (2nd ed.). Boulder, CO: Westview Press.

de la Torre, J., Jedel, M. J., Arpan, J. S., Ogram, J. S., & Toyne, B. (1978). "Corporate Responses to Import Competition in the US Apparel Industry." *Research Monograph No. 74*. Atlanta, GA: Georgia State University.

Elwood, W. (2001). *The No-Nonsense Guide to Globalization*. Oxford, UK: New Internationalist Publications.

European Commission. (February 2009). "The New US Farm Bill: Zooming In on ACRE." Retrieved November 5, 2015, from http://ec.europa.eu/agriculture/trade-analysis/map/01_09.pdf

Friedman, T. L. (2000). *The Lexus and the Olive Tree*. New York, NY: Anchor Books.

Glock, R. E., & Kunz, G. I. (1995). *Apparel Manufacturing: Sewn Product Analysis*. (2nd ed.). Upper Saddle River, NJ: Prentice Hall.

Glock, R. E., & Kunz, G. I. (2000). *Apparel Manufacturing: Sewn Product Analysis*. (3rd ed.). Upper Saddle River, NJ: Prentice Hall.

Hong Kong Trade Development Council. (January 16, 2009). "Over-Quota Apparel Imports from China Subject to Staged Entry Procedures." Retrieved November 15, 2015, from http://economists-pick-research.hktdc.com/business-news/article/Business-Alert-US/Over-Quota-Apparel-Imports-from-China-Subject-to-Staged-Entry-Procedures/baus/en/1/1X000000/1X001JXI.htm

Platzer, M. D. (2014). "US Textile Manufacturing and the Trans-Pacific Partnership Negotiations." Congressional Research Service. R42772.

Rivoli, P. (2015). *The Travels of a T-shirt in the Global Economy*. Hoboken, NJ: Wiley.

World Trade Organization. (n.d.-a). "Glossary." Retrieved September 1, 2015, from https://www.wto.org/english/thewto_e/glossary_e/glossary_e.htm

World Trade Organization. (n.d.-b). "Understanding the WTO." Retrieved September 1, 2015, from https://www.wto.org/english/thewto_e/whatis_e/tif_e/fact2_e.htm

Zagaroli, L. (December 29, 2008). "When Textile Quotas End This Week, Will Textile Jobs Go, Too?" Retrieved November 5, 2015, from http://www.mcclatchydc.com/news/nation-world/national/economy/article24518167.html

CHAPTER 6
ILLEGAL AND UNETHICAL TRADE ACTIVITY

//

FUN FACT

Eighty percent of consumers admitted that they bought fake or pirated goods regularly, with little remorse or concern for the consequences (International Chamber of Commerce (2009)). There is reason to believe a larger percentage of consumers are enjoying "fake" and/or "pirated" items today.

OBJECTIVES

- Apply concepts related to trade barriers and regulation as a framework for customs compliance.
- Examine intellectual property rights from the perspective of intellectual property law.
- Examine violations of intellectual property rights.
- Explore the many other violations of customs compliance and prevention methods.

INTRODUCTION TO INTELLECTUAL PROPERTY LAW

As has been shown in earlier chapters, regulated trade is frequently unfair; however, free trade in the global market may also be unfair. Trade regulations, lack of trade regulations, and lack of enforcement of trade regulations are all blamed for illegal and unethical activities associated with the exchange of goods between nations. Conflicting cultural traditions and standards and opportunistic human tendencies toward exploitation intensify the sometimes horrifying results. The roles of customs services in a country, for example, US Customs and Border Protection (CBP), have been addressed briefly in previous chapters, but the complexity of being customs compliant has not. The supply chain model presented in Chapter 1 (see Figure 1.6) identifies customs clearance as one of the primary segments of the supply chain. To get timely customs clearance, the merchandise and the presenting of it must be customs compliant. Any time a product is imported, the customs service of that country has to be dealt with, and every country has slightly different processes and standards to be met. The purposes and activities of customs services in each country include the following:

- protecting intellectual property rights
- monitoring and documenting identities and quantities of imports and exports

GLOBAL LEXICON

copyright a legal right gained by an author, composer, playwright, publisher, or distributor to exclusive publication, production, sale, or distribution of a literary, musical, dramatic, or artistic work

counterfeit an imitation of what is genuine, with the intent to defraud the customer

counterfeiting the act of making an imitation of an original, with the intent to defraud

customs compliant to act in accordance with customs rules and regulations

cyber crime illegal activity that uses a computer as a means of commission of a crime and as storage for the evidence of the crime

espionage the practice of observing furtively to obtain secret information especially regarding a government or a business

facilitated illegal immigration term that covers a number of serious different crimes all aimed at assisting, for financial gain, the entry into or residence in a country, in violation of the laws of that country

gray (grey) market goods original goods (they are not knockoffs) that are sold by unauthorized vendors

human trafficking facilitating the emigration of people for monetary gain

illegal transshipment shipping goods through a port or country

to facilitate the change of country of origin or to avoid quota limitations or import duties, or both, in the destination country

intellectual property (IP) copyrights, trademarks, patents, trade secrets, and semiconductor chips; inventions or other discoveries that have been registered with government authorities for the sale and use by their owner

intellectual property rights (IPR) legal protection for exclusive use by owners of copyrights, trademarks, patents, trade secrets, and semiconductor chips

intellectual property theft a crime of robbing people of their ideas, inventions, and creative expressions

knockoff an imitation of an original that does not carry the original brand, made with lower-cost materials and production methods and sold at a lower price

licensee the buyer of the right to use a merchandising property

licenser the owner of a merchandising property

licensing contract a means of transferring intellectual property rights; extending the value of a brand without having to produce the product; putting a brand name on a product produced by someone else for a contracted percentage of the sales

merchandising property the primary means of product differentiation and a source of customer loyalty

pirated a term used in the US and the EU; an imitation of the original, counterfeit

rules of origin criteria used to determine the national source of a product

seizure the act of taking control of illegal merchandise, drugs, or other products by CBP official(s) at border crossings after being legally inspected before being admitted to the United States

substantial transformation occurs when the processing of an article results in a new and different article having a distinct name, character, or use; occurs when an HS classification changes

trademark a word, phrase, logo, or other graphic symbol used to distinguish one firm's products or services from those of other firms

trademark infringement the act of misleading the public into believing the items bearing the trademark/brand name are produced and sold by the owner of the trademark, when they are not

transshipment to transfer or be transferred from one conveyance to another in order to continue shipment

transshipment center a port where merchandise can be imported and then exported without paying import duties

undocumented immigrant workers (UIWs) individuals from foreign countries without legal identification papers

- reporting imports and exports against quotas when limitations are specified
- assessing, collecting, and documenting duties
- protecting the country's borders against illegal entry

To be **customs compliant**, exporters must prepare and present the merchandise appropriately labeled and prepare and submit customs forms and reports according to customs rules and regulations in each importing country. The customs services of the World Trade Organization (WTO) member countries use the Harmonized Commodity Description and Classification System (HS) to monitor and document imports and exports. Nonmember countries may or may not use HS, but countries that aspire to become WTO members will use it. The many types of trade agreements around the world often require preparing reports about imports and exports among countries as well as reports to WTO. Using HS helps make customs' shared data useable and comparable. From these reports, WTO documents trade of all member countries and assesses trends and comparisons among countries, including scenarios in which customs compliance is missing.

Intellectual property (IP) is a wide range of creations that are products of human intellect and that have commercial value. Examples include music, literature, and other artistic works; discoveries and inventions; and words, phrases, symbols, and designs. Intellectual property law protects **intellectual property rights (IPR)** of creators/owners by ensuring exclusive use of their creations. The many dimensions of intellectual property law that protect IPR include the following:

- Copyright law covers literary, musical, and artistic works and software and gives the owner of the creative work the right to keep others from using it without permission. To be copyrightable, a creative work must be original and expressed on paper, audio or videotape, clay, canvas, or some other medium, and it must reflect some creativity.
- Trademark law covers words, pictures, symbols, industrial designs, and other forms of intellectual property used to distinguish a product from the competition.
- Patent law grants a monopoly for a limited period of time for the use and development of inventions.
- Trade secret law addresses any formula, pattern, physical device, idea, or process that provides the owner a competitive advantage and is treated in a manner to keep competitors from learning about it.

A **copyright** is a legal right gained by an author, composer, playwright, publisher, or distributor to exclusive publication, production, sale, or distribution of a literary, musical, dramatic, or artistic work. Fortunately, copyright protection rules are fairly similar worldwide, due to several international copyright treaties, the most important of which is the Berne Convention. Under this treaty, all member countries—and there are more than 100, nations—must afford copyright protection to authors who are nationals of any member country. This protection must last for at least the life of the author plus 50 years, and must be automatic without the need for any legal steps to preserve the copyright (Elias & Stim, 2003a).

A **trademark** is a word, phrase, logo, or other graphic symbol used to distinguish one firm's products or services from those of others. A trademark is the expression of the identity of the owner of the brand. A combination of copyright law and trademark law is what protects the ownership of brands, symbols, and logos representing brands in textiles and apparel as well as all other industries. Consumers use trademarks as an indicator of quality, status, beauty, durability, or desirability, or a combination of these, and therefore they can have a great deal of market value. In the United States, trademark ownership is established through use; in many other countries ownership is established through registration. Global companies have to register their trademarks in each country in which their products are sold to protect their intellectual property rights.

Trademark infringement is taking advantage of the value of a brand by applying a trademark to products without permission of the owner of the brand. The resulting products are counterfeit, described as **pirated** in EU countries. Trademark infringement is the most common violation of intellectual property rights in the textile and apparel industry as well as for consumer products in general. Trademark infringement results in counterfeit merchandise that, because the counterfeit products are often made with inferior materials and production processes, weakens the market value of original products bearing the trademark. The top fifteen most counterfeited brands seized by US Customs Service in 2013 follows. Note that about half of the brands listed are apparel-related companies (Little, 2014):

1. Nike (1,123 cases)
2. Apple (867 cases)
3. Rolex (809 cases)
4. Samsung (631 cases)
5. Adidas (532 cases)
6. Louis Vuitton (497 cases)
7. Chanel (464 cases)
8. Cialis (425 cases)
9. Viagra (365 cases)
10. Gucci (307 cases)
11. Michael Kors (285 cases)
12. Otterbox (223 cases)
13. Burberry (191 cases)
14. MAC Cosmetics (182 cases)
15. Walt Disney (182 cases)

Table 6.1 shows the relationship between intellectual property rights and the different types of creative work related to textiles and apparel. Unfair competition is also included in the table. Unfair competition is a body of law related to, but separate from, intellectual property law. The sources of US intellectual property law include federal and state legislation, statutes, and court cases. Copyright and patent laws originate in the US Constitution. The primary law related to trademarks is the Lanham Act, which was passed in 1946 and amended many times since. The Lanham Act addresses procedures for registering trademarks and lists the types of appropriate remedies when trademark infringement has occurred; it also lists remedies for unfair competition (Elias & Stim, 2003).

There is no one set of international laws that address intellectual property. The WTO has a council called Trade-Related Aspects of Intellectual Property Rights (TRIPS). TRIPS is responsible for monitoring the TRIPS agreement, which originated with the WTO in 1994. WTO members are expected to honor the agreement, which addresses categories similar to those presented in Table 6.1, including copyrights, trademarks, patents, trade secrets, and semiconductor chips. However, different countries and cultures have different laws as well as expectations for complying with laws. TRIPS is looking to the challenges associated with developing universal standards related to intellectual property rights by organizing and presenting workshops and training sessions for leaders in member countries as well as countries aspiring to become WTO members. Protection of intellectual property has continued to be a pressing problem. It was a primary issue when the admission of China to the WTO was negotiated. As you will see, China is one of the countries that is repeatedly identified among those that frequently violate intellectual property rights.

TABLE 6.1

GUIDE TO USE OF INTELLECTUAL PROPERTY PROTECTION AND UNFAIR COMPETITION LAW RELATED TO TEXTILES AND APPAREL

Creative Work	Trade Secret	Copyright	Patent	Trademark	Unfair Competition	No Rights
Advertisement (billboard, card, flyer, sign)		X		X		
Advertising copy		X				
Carpet design			X	X		
Clothing accessories and designs (belts, hats, scarves, suspenders)			X			
Comic strips		X		X		
Commercial names				X	X	
Cosmetics	X		X			
Drawings		X				
Fabric	X		X			
Fabric design		X	X	X		
Furniture design			X	X		
Garment design			Rarely			X
Jewelry		X	X	X		
Labels				X		
Logos				X	X	
Manufacturing process			X			
Method of doing business	X		X			
Names of businesses				X	X	
Names of entertainers or celebrities				X	X	
Names of famous animals				X		
Names of products or services				X	X	
Odors used in marketing				X		
Packaging			X	X		
Project designs	X	X				
Shoes			X	X		
Signs		X		X	X	
Slogans				X	X	
Songs and jingles for marketing		X		X	X	
Sporting goods designs		X	X	X		
Videotape		X				
Wallpaper design		X				
Weavings		X				
Web pages		X				
Writing articles, essays, poems, novels, short stories, nonfiction books		X				

Source: Elias, S., & Stim, R. (2003). Patent, Copyright, and Trademark: An Intellectual Property Desk Reference (6th ed.). Berkeley, CA: Nolo; Elias, S., & Stim, R. (2013). Trademark: Legal Care for Your Business & Product Name (10th ed.). Berkeley CA: Nolo.

Legal Transfer of Intellectual Property Rights

Intellectual property rights are legally transferred from the owner to another legal user via a **licensing contract**. Many intellectual properties related to apparel, in addition to trademarks, are actually merchandising properties, including brand names, logos, designer names, celebrity names, and cartoon characters. **Merchandising properties** are a primary means of product differentiation and a source of customer loyalty. For example, go to http://www.vfc.com, and click on "Our Brands." You should see a list of brands and trademarks owned or licensed by the US-based global company VF Corporation. Note that the brands are classified into categories to correspond with VF's lifestyle philosophy. It is not immediately apparent which are owned and which are licensed, as the company describes itself as the largest apparel company in the world. (Whether it actually is the largest depends entirely on what variables are used to make the calculation.) Through its growth cycle over the last 20 years, it was common for VF to buy licensing contracts for sound brands that, for one reason or another, were in financial trouble and then, after getting it re-established, buy the brand.

In a licensing contract, the **licenser** (the owner of the merchandising property) grants the **licensee**, the buyer of the right to use the merchandising property, the right to produce or source merchandise that will carry the merchandising property. The licensee pays the licenser a **royalty** or fee for the privilege, usually between 1 and 15 percent of wholesale value. A licensing contract includes the following:

- a description of the merchandising property
- a definition of the product or products that can bear the property
- the time frame for the agreement
- the responsibilities for the licenser
- the responsibilities for the licensee
- the basis of the royalty
- the amount of the royalty
- the guarantee, or minimum royalty

When a merchandising property is used without permission of the owner, via a licensing contract, it is infringement of intellectual property rights, and the product is a counterfeit. Consider Case 6.1, a description of a course on intellectual property for worldwide government officials presented by WTO and WIPO. This is an example of an ongoing series of training sessions that usually occur once a year.

Protecting Intellectual Property (IP) Rights

In 2015, the US-based "National Intellectual Property Rights Coordination Center" took on the project of examining the worldwide threats to US intellectual property rights. Here are a few of its key findings:

- Offenders consist of individuals, small groups, members of criminal organizations, and foreign government actors involved in any or all aspects of the manufacturing, distribution, and sale of offending goods.
- While most offending goods are produced overseas and cross US borders to reach US consumers, in the United States there is extensive piracy of copyrighted goods and sales of imported offending merchandise.
- Offenders in many countries pose a threat but China-based offenders are the dominant threat. (United States Trade Representative, 2015)

WTO AND WIPO HOLD FIFTH ADVANCED COURSE ON INTELLECTUAL PROPERTY FOR GOVERNMENT OFFICIALS

Twenty-five government officials from around the world will participate in the fifth joint World Intellectual Property Organization (WIPO) and World Trade Organization (WTO) Advanced Course on Intellectual Property. This advanced course represents the third and highest level of learning on intellectual property (IP) as part of the progressive learning strategy of the WTO. The main objective of the course is to update government officials on the activities and instruments of WIPO and the WTO, and to provide a forum for them to exchange information and ideas with the two secretariats as well as with a range of policymakers and organizations based in Geneva.

The course forms part of an overall strategy to build sufficient capacity within the governments of developing countries and countries with economies in transition to assess and analyze their options and to strengthen national expertise in relation to intellectual property. The course is designed to equip the participants with the necessary tools to help formulate policies that will facilitate the development process in their respective countries. In addition, it will enable participants to work together with other stakeholders in their constituencies to attain efficiency, and higher use and management of IP.

Twenty participants were selected from developing countries and countries with economies in transition. Five additional officials from developed countries were also selected and will participate at their own expense. Participants were Algeria, Bangladesh, Brazil, Bulgaria, Cambodia, Canada, China, Czech Republic, Dominican Republic, Ecuador, Estonia, Georgia, Jamaica, Kenya, Latvia, Malaysia, Myanmar, Namibia, Nigeria, Saint Lucia, South Africa, Sudan, Thailand, Ukraine, and Zimbabwe.

The course consists of a combination of presentations followed by discussion sessions, panel deliberations, and practical exercises on a wide range of issues including:

- IP law policy and development;
- the principal international treaties and conventions governing IP; and
- IP and its relation to economic development, public health, technology transfer, genetic resources, traditional knowledge, folklore, climate change, and competition policy.

The current international developments in the fields of copyrights, trademarks, industrial designs, geographical indicators, patents, and plant variety protection will also be explored. The WTO Dispute Settlement System and TRIPS, IP enforcement, as well as technical assistance and capacity building in the area of IP will also be covered. During the course, participants will benefit from sessions involving WTO TRIPS Council delegates dealing with different IP issues as well as experts from a range of intergovernmental organizations, civil society, and business and industry.

World Trade Organization. (March 11, 2013). "WTO and WIPO Hold Fifth Advanced Course on Intellectual Property for Government Officials." Retrieved October 24, 2015, from https://www.wto.org/english/news_e/news13_e/tra_11mar13_e.htm

1. Why is the understanding of intellectual property important enough to be the subject of these high-level training sessions among countries?
2. How might training sessions like this improve communication as well as understanding among apparel firms in developed and developing countries?

One of the important functions of having customs services in each country is the task of protecting the intellectual property rights of the citizens it represents. Table 6.2 shows a comparison of the value of products seized by the US Customs and Border Protection (CBP) for violation of IPR in 2013 and 2009 from countries that were the primary suppliers. A **seizure** is the act of taking control of illegal merchandise, drugs, or other products by CBP official(s) at border crossings after being legally inspected before being admitted to the United States. A seizure may consist of a single item, like a watch, or an entire shipload of products. Look carefully at the changes that occurred between 2013 and 2009; consider the countries involved as well as percentage changes in value.

VALUE OF PRODUCTS SEIZED IN 2013 AND 2009 IN MILLIONS OF DOLLARS BY US CUSTOMS AND BORDER PROTECTION (CBP)*

FY 2013 Source	Estimated MSRP**	Percent of Total Value	FY 2009 Source Economy	Estimated MSRP*	Percent of Total Value
China	$1,182.9	68%	China	$204.7	79%
Hong Kong	$437.6	25%	Hong Kong	$26.9	5%
India	$20.6	1%	India	$3.1	1%
Korea	$6.2	Less than 1%	Taiwan	$2.5	Less than 1%
Singapore	$5.1	Less than 1%	Korea	$1.5	Less than 1%
Vietnam	$4.4	Less than 1%	Paraguay	$1.5	Less than 1%
Taiwan	$3.1	Less than 1%	Philippines	$1.5	Less than 1%
Great Britain	$2.4	Less than 1%	Switzerland	$1.3	Less than 1%
Bangladesh	$1.9	Less than 1%	Dominican Republic	$0.9	Less than 1%
Pakistan	$1.3	Less than 1%	Pakistan	$0.7	Less than 1%
All Other Countries	$79.5	Less than 1%	All Other Countries	$17.2	6%
Total Value	$1,743.5	100%		$260.7	100%
Number of Seizures	24,361			14,874	

*Includes only items seized for violation of Intellectual Property Rights in countries that were the primary suppliers of a wide variety of merchandise.

**MSRP = Manufacturer's suggested retail price in millions of dollars.

Source: U.S. Customs and Border Protection. (n.d.-a). "Intellectual Property Rights Seizure Statistics." Retrieved January 12, 2014, from http://www.cbp.gov/sites/default/file/documents

The strongest trend related to violations of intellectual property rights that is obvious in Table 6.2 when comparing 2013 to 2009 is the explosion in value of CBP-seized products from China and Hong Kong. India also has a huge increase in dollar value, even though India still represents only 1 percent of the total product seized, while recent news implies that trend has continued. It is possible that it is still less than 1 percent because the total amount of illegal goods imported from the total of all countries has also become much greater. Note also that all other countries (those not listed by name), although each contributes less than 1 percent, still amounts to a total of almost $80 million in illegal merchandise. The problem with violation of IPR has clearly become a worldwide problem.

Now take a look at Table 6.3 to see a breakdown of the types of products seized by US Customs and Border Protection (CBP) in 2013. The types of commodities seized are listed from largest to smallest number of seizures by CBP for each type of product. Note that wearing apparel/accessories, handbags/wallets, watches/jewelry, and footwear are all in the top half of the list.

Patent Infringement

A **patent** is a government license that gives the holder exclusive rights to a process, design, or new invention for a designated period of time. A **design patent** is a form

TABLE 6.3

SELECTED IMPORTED COMMODITIES SEIZED IN 2013
BY US CUSTOMS AND BORDER PROTECTION (CBP)*

FY 2013 Commodities	Number of Seizures	Percent of Total Seizures	Percent of Total and Value of Seizures	
Wearing Apparel/Accessories	9,894	35%	7%	$116.2
Consumer Electronics	5,656	20%	8%	$145.9
Handbags/Wallets	2,223	8%	40%	$700.2
Pharmaceuticals/Personal Care	2,215	8%	5%	$ 79.6
Watches/Jewelry	1,729	6%	29%	$502.8
Footwear	1,683	6%	3%	$ 54.9
Optical Media	1,409	5%	2%	$ 26.8
Computers/Accessories	1,062	4%	3%	$ 47.8
Labels/Tags	788	3%	2%	$ 41.8
Other	961	3%	2%	$ 41.7

*Table includes number of seizures and the percentage of total goods seized that infringed on or violated IPR as well as the value of the top ten types of products seized in millions of dollars

Source: U.S. Customs and Border Protection. (n.d.a). "Intellectual Property Rights Seizure Statistics." Retrieved January 12, 2014, from http://www.cbp.gov/sites/default/file/documents; Frohlich, T. C. (2014). "The Nine Most Counterfeited Products in America." Retrieved November 15, 2015, from http://247wallst.com/special-report/2014/03/27/americas-nine-most-counterfeited-items

of intellectual property protection that allows an inventor or designer to protect the original shape or surface ornamentation of a useful manufactured article. Patent law grants a monopoly for a limited period of time for the use and development of inventions. Although garment designs are usually not patentable, the book *Uplift: The Bra in America* (Farrell-Beck & Gau, 2001) documented inventions relative to brassieres that were patented between the mid-1800s and the mid-1900s. *Patentable garment designs tend to be those that require creative engineering for assembly.* For example, a lawsuit was filed in Los Angeles in 2008 related to a "pants garment design product." Charming Shoppes and Lane Bryant were accused of patent infringement in a lawsuit entitled "Pants Garment and Body Profile Enhancement Features." The patent covered a pants garment with elastic components built in to allow for an improved anatomical fit. Its unique cut and assembly lifts and accentuates the wearer's buttocks and flattens the wearer's stomach (Figure 6.1).

It has not been the norm in the fashion industry to seek design patents, but some apparel firms are now very serious about protecting designs. Lululemon has been described as the "fashion industry's biggest patent troll." Lululemon is aggressively protecting its $48 sports bras and $64 tank tops by way of design patents—an unusual move in the apparel business. The maker of expensive workout gear, which famously sued Calvin Klein and G-III Apparel in 2012 for violating a design patent on its yoga pants, has since accumulated thirty-one such patents on items from bras to duffel bags, according to the US Patent Office website. The company is aiming to use the protection to deflect competitors in the increasingly popular athletic apparel space by threatening, and in some cases, pursuing litigation.

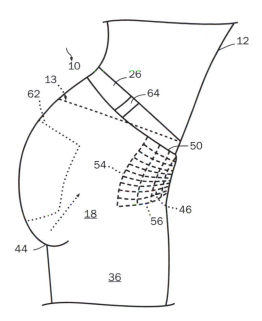

Figure 6.1
Technical drawing of pants design that was the subject of an apparel patent infringement case.

The issue of protecting fashion design was introduced in a bill in the US Congress in 2012. Although action on the bill has not been reported, among other things the bill included definitions of apparel and fashion design. In the legal document, the term "apparel" included three types of things:

a. article(s) of men's, women's, or children's clothing, including undergarments, outerwear, gloves, footwear, and headgear;

b. handbags, purses, wallets, tote bags, and belts; and

c. eyeglass frames.

The term "fashion design" means "the appearance as a whole of an article of apparel, including its ornamentation" and "includes original elements of the articles of apparel or the original arrangement or placement of original or non-original elements as incorporated in the overall appearance of the article of apparel that:

(1) is the result of a designer's own creative endeavour, and

(2) provides a unique, distinguishable, non-trivial and non-utilitarian variation over prior designs for similar types of articles." (GovTrack.com, 2012)

The language in this bill demonstrates the difficulty of defining apparel and fashion design for the purposes of legal action. In another context, part (a) of the apparel definition might be called "wearing apparel" and parts (b) and (c) might be called "accessories."

In contrast, fashion design in Europe has both copyright and design rights. Intellectual property protection is driven by the desire to maintain Europe's reputation as the center of haute couture (the business of making expensive clothes with original designs and high quality). Protection of designs is at the core of its legal regimes. Other traditional categories of apparel, footwear, and accessories can also be protected under national design and copyright laws (Montalvo, 2014). If the Copyright Act in the United States were amended to include fashion articles, similar to the national laws in France, Italy, and United Kingdom, there would likely be more cases where individual designers and inventors of new and original apparel styles could protect their intellectual property, as presented in Case 6.2.

SHOE CONNECTOR LITIGATION CASE, BY SUSAN M. MAXWELL*

When I was a senior footwear buyer at Target Stores, I learned almost on the first day on the job that separated shoes were a major source of profit loss for all shoe retailers, and especially for general merchandisers and mass merchants that sell shoes on racks. At these retail stores, most shoes were attached together in pairs using a plastic cord, similar to a plastic cord used on a garment to secure the price tag. In shoes, the plastic cord was "shot" through the instep (side) of each shoe to keep the left and right shoes paired until purchased (see Figure Case 6.2). As a result, consumers were buying new products that were permanently damaged as each shoe had a small hole on its upper side.

I was challenged to find a solution to this problem. My "moment of genius" happened one day when I saw two tags hanging on the bottom of two pieces of upholstered furniture. I have often referred to them as the "Do Not Remove Under Penalty of Law" tags. Looking at those tags, I imagined putting similar tags into the shoes at production which would allow an attaching cord to be used through the two tags (instead of through the shoe itself) and thus the left and right shoes would be attached through the point of sale with no damage to the shoe upper.

I knew I had solved the problem. I also knew that this system could be used on millions of pairs of shoes sold in the United States and other markets. I made the initial prototypes in my kitchen using my own shoes, string, and paper. After making real prototypes of sample shoes with the attaching system, I had a patent lawyer to file the paperwork. My patent was issued and I set out to market my system to mass merchandisers. As the inventor, I had the exclusive rights to make, use, and sell my patented shoe fastening system. My first licensing agreement was with Target Stores.

What I soon found out was that other retailers saw the new shoe attaching system at Target, copied it, and started using it to pair shoes in stores all over the country. When I notified these retailers of my patent and asked them to stop using my system on their shoes for free, I also offered them to legally use my system through a licensing agreement for only pennies per a pair of shoes. They all declined. I found out later that several of them have colluded against me, basically agreeing among them that if no one took a license agreement, as an individual I would not be able to stop them from using my patented system.

These retailers were multibillion dollar corporations, and I was an individual with limited funds to litigate. Moreover, I

Figure Case 6.2
Picture of pairs of shoes connected to each other for retail display so pairs cannot be separated.

was a woman in a very male-dominated footwear industry. I was forced to a point of decision: either letting the retailers to use my shoe fastening system and look the other way, or suing them for stealing my intellectual property to force them into taking a licensing agreement and paying me for the use of my patented system. I knew that this would be a monumental undertaking: a woman suing multibillion dollar companies.

I decided to litigate and asked for jury trials to make this decision. It took me fourteen years from initiating my first lawsuit to the final settlement. I prevailed in all jury trials and through settlements with all of the defendants. My shoe fastening system is still in use today. The patent expired in 2004 and the system is now "committed to the public" for use. You can see it in stores such as Target and K-Mart.

*Susan M. Maxwell specializes in import, design, and sourcing. She worked for major US apparel and retail companies and currently is president of MAX Merchandising, Inc.

Personal correspondence between Susan Maxwell and Elena Karpova.

1. Imagine that you, as a young designer and owner of a small business, invented a new and original design for a skirt. The new skirt design became popular very quickly and you are expecting to make a nice fortune and retire at the age of 30. Then, you find out that several large national retailers have begun to sell your skirt design. What will be your action if (a) in the US fashion design is protected by copyright law (similar to European Union); and (b) in the US fashion design is not protected by copyright law? Consider advantages and disadvantages of both scenarios.

CYBER CRIME, COUNTERFEITING, AND ESPIONAGE IN TEXTILES AND APPAREL

Cyber crime is a term for illegal activity that uses a computer as its primary means of commission and uses the computer for storage of evidence. The cost of cyber crime accumulates to all national and international trade activity. It endlessly affects every aspect of a supply chain. Cyber crime is a facilitator, worldwide, of illegal activity in relation to textiles and apparel and all other industries. According to STATISTA Statistics Portal (n.d.), the average annualized costs of cyber crime by affected industry sectors in the United States in 2014 were as follows:

Utilities and energy	$20.6 million
Financial services	$17.6 million
Technology	$9.2 million
Communications	$9.0 million
Transportation	$10.6 million
Services	$6.3 million
Industrial	$5.7 million
Education and research	$9.0 million
Health care	$5.0 million
Consumer products	$4.7 million

That means that cyber crime costs US business and industry almost $100 million annually. All of these industry sectors contribute to the operation of textiles and apparel industries and to the prices that consumers pay when they visit a retail store.

In 2014, worldwide, the combination of cyber crime and espionage was estimated to have cost world businesses and governments 1 percent of global income; that is $445 billion per year. **Espionage** can be defined as the practice of observing furtively to obtain secret information especially regarding a government or a business. A report funded by the security firm McAfee is one of the first efforts to analyze the costs of the combination of cyber crime and espionage based on a variety of data. According to their study, the world's largest economies suffered the most losses: United States, $100 billion; Germany, $60 billion; China, $45 billion; and Japan, $1 billion (Nakashima & Peterson, 2014). One of the purposes of espionage, of course, is the theft of intellectual property. Theft of intellectual property lessons companies' abilities to gain a full return on their inventions so they turn to other activities to make a profit. *That process depresses overall global rates of innovation* (Nakashima & Peterson, 2014).

The Value of a Brand and Trademark, and/or Patent

Globalization of production of all kinds of goods has resulted in worldwide access to popular products and technology. At the same time, ingenious marketing and receptive consumers have exploded the demand for "brands" and the benefits of "trademarks" and "patents."

- A **brand** is the name a business uses to present its products. A product sold under a brand has common law trademark rights in the state or states where it is offered. Common law means *rights are developed by use of the name* rather than by federal registration of the name. However, the "brand" is protected only in the state or states where it is sold.
- A **trademark** is a brand, symbol, label, name, device, signature, etc., which is capable of distinguishing goods and services of one business from trademarks and/or brands of others. It may include brand, label, name, color, and/or a combination of things that is registered as a symbol and that represents the product(s) and/or service(s) of its owner. Rights to a trademark arise because of federal registration of the mark.

Much of a product's worth is now tied up in the brand, a form of intellectual property, rather than in the product's quality or serviceability. It may be possible to sell a product with a brand name at five or ten times the price of a similar product without one; this is what attracts counterfeiters. Here are eight reasons why owners should file for registrations of brands/trademarks with the governments of the countries in which properties will be distributed:

1. Valuable Asset: federal registration of brand names/trademarks in all countries that are potential distribution sites provides national rights to the property.
2. Nationwide Priority: gain the right to expand business into new geographic areas without the threat of someone else registering as the owner of what you have claimed as your property.
3. Tool against Cybersquatters: if a website claims your registered property, federal registration is an element considered in legal proceedings to determine the rightful owner and allows a hold to be placed on the use of the property until the case is settled.
4. Advantages in Court: provides the legal presumption of who is the legitimate owner of the property.
5. Enhanced Remedies for Infringement: acts as a deterrent to potential infringers and triples the potential damages suffered by the owner.
6. Prevent Importation: property can be filed with customs services to prevent importation and allow seizure of infringing foreign goods.

7. Incontestable Trademark: after 5 years of continuous registration, certain grounds for cancellation of the ownership of the property are foreclosed, saving litigation expenses.
8. Cost is Low: nominal costs of registration are far outweighed by significant financial and legal advantages. (Top 10 Reasons, n.d.)

Counterfeiting/pirating is as diverse as any legal business, ranging from backstreet sweatshops to full-scale factories. Counterfeiters often get their goods by bribing employees in a company with a valuable brand to hand over manufacturing molds or master discs for them to copy. One of the most infuriating problems for brand owners, including apparel, is when their licensed vendors "overrun" production lines (produce more than was ordered by the customer) without permission and then sell the extra goods on the side.

Production overruns sold on the side are sometimes called the gray market. **Gray market goods** are the original goods (not knockoffs) but are sold by unauthorized vendors. Because they are not sold by the owner of the brand or by one of the owner's representatives, these goods are technically counterfeit. For example, during the 1990s, Target Stores stocked and sold some Calvin Klein Jeans. Calvin Klein sued Target because his company had never sold any jeans to Target. It turned out that the source of the jeans was a Calvin Klein CMT (cut-make-trim) vendor located in Florida that created production overruns to supply the Target order. Gray market goods are not a new problem, but remain a problem just the same.

Owners of brands often try to control the quantity of goods produced by supplying vendors with only the number of labels and signature snaps or buttons to cover the number of legitimate orders. Thus, there was a demand for the supply of tags and labels confiscated by the CBP. In the Calvin Klein case noted above, the vendor either managed to acquire extra labels and snaps or had copies made for the additional garments; the Target buyer probably did not know the goods were not legal. The sale to Target was very profitable for the vendor, because all it had invested in the jeans was the labor for assembly and possibly some extra fabric, probably less than 20 percent of the wholesale price. Thus, counterfeiting is profitable, even when goods are sold at a much lower price, because there is little investment in product development, and no advertising is required—the owner of the brand covers those expenses.

Distribution of counterfeit goods may involve street vendors, flea markets, or shops anywhere in the world. The internet is now believed to be the vehicle for more than $25 billion in counterfeit goods a year. Organized crime has also become involved in complex distribution networks that support large counterfeiters. There is evidence that counterfeiting is one of the funding sources used by terrorists. Sale of counterfeit T-shirts and videos in New York City are believed to be part of the funding sources for the bombing of the World Trade Center in 1993 and for its destruction in 2001. Drug dealers have turned their attention to counterfeiting, because they regard it as lucrative and low risk (Fashion Business International, 2003).

Consumers also contribute to the counterfeiting problem. Some consumers want merchandise with famous brand logos but can't afford or choose not to pay for the genuine article. Designer bags, designer shoes, and other accessories, as shown by the data in Table 6.3, have been favorite counterfeited products in the United States in recent years. Every major city has its favorite faux haunts. In the United States, these include the sidewalks of Georgetown, Baltimore's Inner Harbor, Santee Street in Los Angeles,

Figure 6.2a
Counterfeit bags are favorites of shoppers in New York.

and Chinatown in New York. Other countries also have areas known for counterfeit merchandise: Tokyo's Shibuya and Shinjuku districts and Silk Alley in Beijing, China; Bangkok, Hong Kong, and London have too many to list. Customer demand is a primary reason for the huge market and the ongoing vigorous activity of counterfeiters. Consumers both knowingly and unknowingly purchase counterfeit goods, because they want the brand, price, memory, or image, unaware of or unconcerned about the damage the practice causes legitimate businesses (Figures 6.2a and b).

Legitimate businesses lose sales, and their brands lose value, because of counterfeiting. In 2001, in the EU the counterfeit brands most frequently confiscated were Nintendo, Nike, Adidas, Nokia, and Louis Vuitton. "A study in 2000 by the Centre for Economics and Business Research estimated that the counterfeiting of clothing, cosmetics, toys, sports equipment, and pharmaceuticals within the European Union cost the region 17,120 jobs and reduced GDP by e8 billion ($7.4 billion) a year" ("Special Report," 2003, p. 53). Governments also lose revenue, because counterfeiters do not pay taxes.

The magnitude of counterfeiting worldwide has also made anticounterfeiting big business, and legitimate businesses bear the cost of implementing **anticounterfeiting** measures. Fortune 500 companies have reported that they are spending $2 to $4 million a year each on anticounterfeiting, with some spending more than $10 million (Jiminez & Kolsun, 2014). Many companies are now using hi-tech strategies similar to those used to protect dollar bills. Other strategies include unique identification numbers, holographs, and special package markings. An entire segment of business has sprung up to develop and provide anticounterfeiting technology. Anticounterfeiting experts believe that the best solution to counterfeiting is the same used to solve most other types of crime: enforcement, education, and economic growth. Illiterate and poor people are likely to be recruited to work in the production of counterfeit goods. Improving literacy and alleviating poverty reduces the opportunity for production of counterfeits as well as the customers for them. People with higher standards of living are better able to purchase branded goods than their illegal imitations.

Figure 6.2b
Customs officials sorting through counterfeit shoes, which are one of the top counterfeit products in the US market.

Counterfeiting in Textiles and Apparel

Of the more than 80 billion garments produced annually worldwide in 2004, 16 billion were T-shirts (Speer, 2004). Because the world population was approximately 6.5 billion, that means apparel producers made nearly three T-shirts for every man, woman, and child in the world that year. That surely makes a statement about apparel oversupply and the reality that the competitiveness of the apparel business is not a new phenomenon. Of that same 80 billion garments produced annually in 2004, up to 22 percent of all *branded* apparel and footwear was counterfeit.

As shown in Table 6.3, in 2013 more than $1,374.1 million in counterfeit fashion goods, including wearing apparel and accessories, handbags and wallets, footwear, watches and jewelry, were seized for attempted importation into the United States. In addition, labels and tags valued at $41.8 million were confiscated that would have been used for representing counterfeit goods as the real thing. Remember that the branded products are found to be counterfeit because of violation of trademark law. The trademark may be a brand name or logo but may also be letters, numbers, package design, color, or other aspects of a product (Elias & Stim, 2013). For example, for Levi's 501 jeans, Levi's brand name plus the double-curved arcuate stitched design on the patch pockets and the folded pocket tab are trademarks that belong to Levi Strauss & Co.

In Beijing, fake fashion goods permeated everyday life before 2000. In the Muxiyuan fabric market, merchants made a living off of fake label sales—a bag of 500 Diesel tags cost the equivalent of $6; fake Prada and Burberry were sold in batches of 10,000 or more (Lowther, 2004). Apparel companies invest millions in brand development. At the same time, legitimate tags and labels:

- only cost a few cents each
- represent the brand
- bear a company's trademarks
- are key components of product presentation

- are an important source of customer loyalty
- are very easy to duplicate

Case 6.3 reports a recent lawsuit that Under Armour launched against Nike over the use of the phrase "I Will" in advertising campaigns. Hundreds of law cases, many much more extreme than this, are launched every year, all around the world, in defense of protection of intellectual property rights.

Knockoffs

For apparel, a *counterfeit* is often an imitation of an original that illegally carries the original trademark. In contrast, a **knockoff** is an imitation of the original made by a different company, usually using lower-cost materials and production methods, and sold through legitimate retailers at a much lower price than the original. In the fashion business, imitation is the greatest form of flattery; therefore, knockoffs in themselves

---

CASE 6.3

NEGOTIATED SETTLEMENT OF TRADEMARK INFRINGEMENT LAWSUIT BETWEEN UNDER ARMOUR AND NIKE

Online advertising has become a key component of promotions and has introduced serious challenges for the protection of registered trademarks and advertising symbols for well-established companies. Rights to these trademarks and symbols are frequently the topics of lawsuits for apparel companies. Nike Inc. and Under Armour are now well-developed competitors in women's athletic apparel markets.[1]

In 2013, Under Armour launched an "I Will What I Want" campaign focused on women's athletic apparel with tag lines like "I will not be uncomfortable." The campaign included a series of ads focused on a women performing in different athletic environments. The women featured in the ads included Misty Copeland, a ballerina soloist; Gisele Bundchen in a kickboxing routine; and Lindsey Vonn in a workout routine. These adds received waves of online attention.[2] Apparently Nike noticed.

A lawsuit was brought by Under Armour against Nike charging that Nike violated the concept of Under Armour's "I Will" campaign by competing with the "Just Do It" campaign. Under Armour claimed that Nike amended their long established ads with "I will just do it." Under Armour claimed that Nike used ads like "I will swear while they sleep" and "I will finish what I started." Both brands used their "brag lines" in radio, billboards, and TV ads.

Under Armour reported that they regard their registered trademarks as "cornerstone symbols" of the company and vowed to protect "what we've worked so hard to build."[2] The brand has used the "I Will" slogan in TV ads and on billboards and in connection with hundreds of products. Nike denied infringing on the trademark claiming the words were commonly used and no infringement on Under Armour was intended. The litigation was resolved on a confidential and mutually agreeable basis.

[1]Clapp Communications. (n.d.). "Under Armour: I Will What I Want and How It Works." Retrieved September 4, 2015, from http://www.clappcommunications.com/company/blog/under-armour-i-will-what-i-want-and-why-it-works

[2]Mrabella, L. (Feb. 11, 2014). "Under Armour and Nike Settle Trademark Infringement Lawsuit." *Baltimore Sun.* Retrieved October 24, 2015, from http://articles.baltimoresun.com/2014-02-11/business/bal-consuming-under-armour-nike-settle-trademark-infringement-lawsuit-20140211_1_trademark-infringement-lawsuit-apparel-brand

1. The cost of filing a trademark infringement lawsuit is commonly over $400,000. To consumers, does it seem like lawsuits over things like "I Will" or "Just Do It" are a valid use of funds that would be likely to cause an increase in cost of products to consumers?

2. What is there about a trademark that makes it so valuable?

are not illegal. Without imitations, a new design idea would never become popular and thus become a widely accepted and profitable fashion.

According to both US and international law outside the EU, most garment designs are not protected against counterfeiting, but trademarks used on the garments are protected. Unfortunately, in the trade press it is not unusual to find the term *knockoff* used interchangeably with *counterfeit*. Thus, when reading articles about this topic it is important to have your critical thinking hat on to determine exactly what the writer means. Remember that *a knockoff is not counterfeit unless the knockoff is presented as the original, with the original brand name*. However, these laws are difficult to enforce.

Counterfeiting operations are both sophisticated and diverse, with operators keeping abreast of fashion and even ahead of consumer trends. Branded sports apparel has been a primary target, but as fashions evolve, pirating has turned to purse brands, such as Louis Vuitton, Prada, and Chanel (found at purse and shoe parties in the United States) and to knockoff athletic shoes, which are found in street markets throughout the world. The counterfeiters attend international trade fairs to steal prototypes of new products that represent heavy investment in product development but are not yet on the market. Counterfeits can then be produced so quickly that they are sometimes available before the genuine article hits the market.

OTHER CUSTOMS VIOLATIONS

There are many customs violations beyond those covered by intellectual property law. The ones commonly found in the textile and apparel industry are addressed here, including misrepresentation of country of origin, misclassification of goods, illegal transshipment, and undocumented immigrant workers.

Misrepresentation of Country of Origin

The **country of origin (COO)** of a product is determined by rules of origin. According to WTO, **rules of origin** are used

- to implement measures and instruments of commercial policy, such as safeguard measures, including tariffs, and antidumping duties
- to determine whether imported products will receive preferential treatment, based on trade agreements
- for the application of labeling and marking requirements
- for purpose of trade statistics
- for government procurement (World Trade Organization, n.d.)

The descriptions of rules of origin have evolved over the past 35 years and still leave considerable room for interpretation to individual countries. For example, according to 1985 US rules, the COO for apparel was where the fabric was cut into garment parts. During the late 1980s and early 1990s it was common practice to cut garments out of US-made fabric in the United States, export cut parts to Mexico or Central America (or both), where garments were assembled, and then return the finished garments to the United States for retail sale. However, the 1985 rules allowed the garments to carry "Made in USA" labels even though they were assembled elsewhere.

The general principles now in effect for determining the COO were included in the 1994 GATT Agreement on Rules of Origin (now the WTO Rules of Origin). These rules state that the COO is the country where goods are wholly obtained or, when more than one country is involved, the country where the last **substantial transformation** is carried out. The customs service in each WTO country is responsible for establishing regulations to carry out the COO rules and the definition of "substantial transformation." Not surprisingly, customs regulations differ considerably from one country to another, particularly with regard to this definition.

To continue with the US example, the CBP regulations published in 1996 (Section 102.21) and based on GATT 1994 required considerable adjustment for trading partners, as compared with the 1985 rules. These regulations state that the last substantial transformation for textiles occurs where the fabric is made; for apparel, it is where the garment is assembled (except for products covered by NAFTA or originating in Israel, where other rules were in effect). The lay interpretation of the 1996 US rules was as follows: The COO for fabric was determined by where it was knitted or woven, whereas the origin for yarn was determined by where the cotton was spun or the fiber extruded. The origin for apparel was determined by where the most important process of formation occurs, usually garment assembly (Elias & Stim, 2013).

Despite some efforts to clarify application of the 1996 rules of origin, WTO reports that COO disputes in the global market have continued to increase. COO disputes have continued to be a serious problem in developed countries for a number of reasons:

- increase in the number of preferential trading arrangements, including free trade areas among developed and developing countries;
- bilateral agreements, customs unions, and common markets, each with different definitions of COO; and
- increased use of antidumping laws and subsequent claims of circumvention of antidumping laws. (World Trade Organization, n.d.)

In 2008, CBP, after years of consideration and delay, proposed sweeping changes in COO rules for imported articles. CBP proposed replacing the existing system of case-by-case "substantial transformation" determinations with a uniform system of "tariff shift" rules based on the NAFTA COO marking rules codified in Part 102 of the CBP regulations. The outcomes of the application of this system to determine substantial transformation are likely to be different from those from application of the traditional rules, so serious adjustments had to be made by firms using the system (Hogan & Hartson LLP, 2008).

The EU, to accommodate the variety of practices inherent to its country members, has incorporated multiple options for determining COO by application of "last substantial transformation":

- "by a rule requiring a change of tariff (sub) heading in the HS nomenclature
- by a list of manufacturing or processing operations that do or do not confer on the goods the origin of the country in which these operations were carried out
- by a value added rule, where the increase of value due to assembly operations and incorporation of originating materials represents a specified level of the ex-works price of the product." (European Commission, 2010)

More recently (April 10, 2014), the WTO Committee on Rules of Origin agreed to implement the Decision on Preferential Rules of Origin for the Least Developed Countries (LDCs). Rules of origin determine how much processing must take place locally before goods and the materials used in the goods can be considered to be a product of the exporting country. Unfortunately no specific information about application of the rules was available (World Trade Organization, 2014). In any case, probably the only thing that is plain to see is that identifying COO is not necessarily a clear-cut process. Determining COO has been, and continues to be, a serious challenge for customs services. At the same time, COO is a key component for determining application of imports in relation to quantity limitations and/or collection of duties based on tariff schedules.

Misclassification of Goods

Another way to avoid paying of duties is misclassification of merchandise into an inappropriate Harmonized System (HS) classification. One of the important functions of HS is the classification of merchandise for export and import. The types of merchandise that are traded must be specifically matched to the appropriate description in the HS system. This allows documentation of the quantities of the numerous different classifications of merchandise that are being traded. If an exporter knows that quota for a particular classification has been exceeded in the importing country, the classification might be changed to what is known to be an open category. When import limitations are in place, it is the task of customs services to be sure that merchandise shipped for import or export is correctly classified and does not exceed quota limitations.

Customs uses a statistical, random sample selection system, such that only a few of the lots of goods are actually physically checked to see that the goods match the description (Figure 6.3). If the category of goods being shipped is one that has higher tariff rates, a different category number might be used to allow the goods to be imported under low or no tariff rates. Sometimes, misclassification happens by accident or lack of attention to the details involved in classifying goods correctly. Other times, misclassification is a method of getting merchandise into the country illegally. For example, cotton T-shirts imported to the US market are subject to 16 percent tariff rate from most countries that do not have free trade agreements with the United States (United

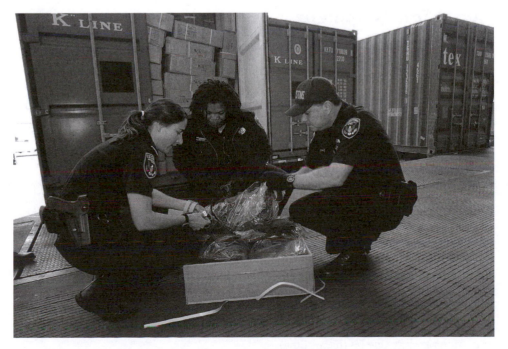

Figure 6.3
US Customs inspectors checking containers as they arrive in port to ensure security of the US borders and consumer safety as well as make sure that goods are legitimate and appropriately classified to collect import duty.

States International Trade Commission, 2015). The same T-shirts made of man-made fiber fabrics are subject to 32 percent tariff rate when imported to the United States. To reduce import duty, T-shirts might be misclassified by fiber content, which is illegal.

There are many other "creative" ways to avoid and/or reduce tariff rates and duties in our globalized world. Government lawyers have to be as creative as the shippers to keep up with newly developing methods. In 2014, in order to renew communication related to apparel trade with China, the American Apparel & Footwear Association and the China Chamber of Commerce for Import and Export of Textiles and Apparel (CCCT) signed a Memorandum of Understanding (MOU). The CCCT is the leading national trade organization, representing more than 70 percent of China's exporters and importers of textiles and clothing, with a membership of more than 12,000 companies. Among other things, it will create a forum to address apparel-related issues including product safety, labeling, retailing issues, and intellectual property rights, as well as counterfeiting. China is still the top supplier of both footwear and apparel to the US market. China is also a growing market for US-made and branded apparel and footwear (Kuhail, 2014).

Legal Transshipment

Transshipment means to transfer or be transferred from one means of transport to another to continue shipment. Transshipment is a standard and legal part of moving goods across counties, states, countries, rivers, lakes, and oceans. Transshipment is legal when goods are moved through a third country as a result of normal shipping patterns. For example, a number of small vessels may haul apparel or textiles relatively short distances to a large **transshipment center**, such as Hong Kong. In Hong Kong, the goods are consolidated onto larger vessels for more efficient shipment to distant port cities, such as Los Angeles. The goods are not modified in the third country (in this case Hong Kong), but simply travel into it and are transferred to a larger ship to then travel to other ports.

Illegal Transshipment

Because quota limitations and import tariffs vary greatly by country, one way to avoid any quotas and duties related to tariffs is to practice illegal transshipment. **Illegal transshipment** involves shipping products to a no-quota or nontariff port or country, changing the country of origin (COO), and then re-exporting to the intended importing country. The purpose of this activity is to use a COO where no quotas will be applied or tariffs assessed against the goods by the importing country's customs services.

There are often significant economic benefits (and risks) to be gained by using illegal transshipment to get products into a country in a manner in which they are accepted, but not necessarily customs compliant. As discussed earlier, the level of quota available when quota limitations are in place and the amount of duty due are determined by COO, and with it, consideration of location of production processes; types of products, as defined by HS; relevant trade agreements in effect; and origin of materials and production processes. Once COO is determined, if quota is filled, the products may be denied admission. To the country, if there is no duty or duty is waived, an additional cost of 5 percent to more than 50 percent of the value of the products may be saved. Some exporting countries, because of preferential trade agreements, may have no quota limitations or duty due on the products.

Illegal transshipment occurs when goods are shipped through a third country or port to produce counterfeit documents that illegally change the COO to avoid tariffs or quota limitations in the actual importing country. Partly because of the new COO rules, illegal transshipment of goods became a serious problem during the late 1990s. When the Multifiber Agreement (MFA) was in effect, the CBP estimated that between $2 billion and $4 billion of textiles and apparel was illegally transshipped annually, with most of it assembled in China. The goods were transshipped primarily to avoid China's MFA quota limitations in the EU and the United States.

Other countries identified as active illegal transshippers in the 1990s included Armenia, Hong Kong, Macau, Russia, and Taiwan as well as some African nations. Countries that shipped relatively few textiles and apparel to the United States were likely candidates for illegal transshipping, because they did not have bilateral agreements under MFA and therefore did not have quota limitations (Kennedy, 2003).

The 2002 US revisions of the Caribbean Basin Trade Partnership Act (CBTPA) and AGOA created new transshipping targets because they provided tangible incentives for opening their economies and building free markets. These new laws made Central American and African countries likely candidates for illegal transshipment because both import tariffs and quotas were waived (American Immigration Law Foundation, 2002). By 2004, Los Angeles—owing to its location on the Pacific Rim—became an illegal transshipment epicenter. Ninety percent of illegal transshipped goods coming into the United States were arriving in Los Angeles, and companies set up to transship goods actively continued to recruit business.

Even though MFA quotas and their extensions have now been phased out, illegal transshipment remains a significant issue, because it is also used as a tool for avoiding tariffs. Customs services have published lists of hundreds of companies, most of them Asian, that are known transshippers so that importers can avoid their services. However, the illegal transshipment problem has not been resolved. Less than 1 percent of all imported goods are actually examined by customs. If an item is flagged, perhaps because it came from a known transshipper, customs officials look at a container's packing list, pull a sample, and send it to an import specialist. If there is suspicion of transshipment or other violation, the agency can issue a detention notice and ask the importer to furnish production records within 30 days.

A month's delay in receiving fashion goods is a disaster for a fashion retailer. If illegal transshipment is determined, customs can then make a decision whether to release the goods or exclude them from consumption in the United States. Financial penalties can be assessed after the shipment has been liquidated or returned to its COO. If the COO cannot be verified, CBP can make a decision to exclude the goods from consumption in the United States. Financial penalties can be assessed under some circumstances.

Undocumented Immigrant Workers

Customs services are responsible for border protection, including preventing the transport of drugs, weapons, and other contraband, as well as illegal aliens. Providing international border security is a complex process relating to issues from terrorism, to immigration, to imported product safety. Thus, border security begins a long way from the border. For example, internationally shipped cargoes travel in various conveyances on a variety of infrastructures, through a number of places, are held in custody of numerous people and organizations, and can involve up to forty separate documents to complete the journey from source zone to the distribution zone.

If the border can be envisioned not merely as a physical boundary but rather as a flexible concept that allows for the possibility that the border begins at the point where goods or people commence their US-bound journey, a significantly wider array of options for border management policies becomes available (CSR Report for Congress, 2007). This perspective enhances our understanding of the controversy that surrounds border protection, particularly the concept of building fences around the border, as well as the inseparable role of global trade across the border. Of particular interest here is the role of legal and illegal immigrants involved in the textile and apparel industries. More specifically, about 20 percent of sewing machine operators in the United States are unregistered immigrants (UIs), so all of this is relevant to the apparel industry (ProCon .org, 2012).

Developed countries have worked toward freer trade over the last 50 years, while similar attention has not been paid to reducing barriers to immigration. Legal and illegal immigrants are blamed by many for rising crime rates and for stealing jobs that would otherwise go to native workers. Immigration is restricted by government policies, and limited numbers of people have been allowed to emigrate because of military conflict or economic catastrophe, for example, from Vietnam and Eastern Europe. Others must resort to illegal means of emigration.

Human trafficking, facilitating the emigration of people for monetary gain, developed in many places in the world hundreds of years ago. The slavery system in the early United States was certainly based on capturing people and transporting them against their will. The lure of jobs also makes poor people susceptible to gangsters dealing in human beings for forced labor and prostitution. Job seekers may pay a fee for transport, often under horrendous conditions, and end up in prisonlike environments, where they are paid little for forced labor. We still hear reports of boats sinking because they held hundreds more people than was safe, railroad cars discovered containing dozens of dead bodies, shipping containers on seagoing ships full of human beings.

Approximately 200 million standardized 40-foot and 20-foot boxes move among major ports annually; many are loaded with textiles and apparel. These shipping containers provide illicit opportunities for the transport of human beings for labor exploitation, terrorist operatives and equipment, and other contraband. In 2004, a US-based international security program, the Container Security Initiative (CSI), went into effect in the United States to prevent the use of cargo containers for smuggling or terrorism. It was estimated that CSI cost $450 to $550 per shipment, but another goal of the program was to reduce costs to companies, particularly for lost merchandise (Zarocostas, 2004). Following are the core areas of CSI:

- identify high-risk containers, based on advance information and strategic intelligence;
- prescreen and evaluate containers as early in the supply chain as possible—before they are shipped;
- use technology (large-scale x-ray and gamma ray machines and radiation detection devices) for prescreening to prevent the slowing of movement of trade; and
- achieve 100 percent container scanning by 2012.

CSI offers its participating countries the opportunity to send their customs officers to major US ports to target oceangoing, containerized cargo to be exported to their countries (U.S. Customs and Border Protection, n.d.-b). Unfortunately, the progress toward having 100 percent container scanning by 2012 was hampered by cuts in funding related to the global recession. Thus, a plan was made in late 2009 to streamline efforts to balance trade and security concerns by partnering customs with a number of US government agencies to support the port security objective (Casabona, 2009). By 2015, there were fifty-eight ports in the Americas, Europe, Asia and the Middle East, and Africa participating in CSI, accounting for 85 percent of container traffic bound for the United States (Department of Homeland Security, n.d.).

Unauthorized Immigrants in the United States

Unauthorized immigrants are another term for what historically has been referred to as *undocumented workers* or *illegal aliens*. **Unauthorized immigrants (UIs)** are individuals originating in foreign countries but now living in the United States without legal identification papers. It is estimated that about 11.6 million UIs lived in the United States in 2008. Between 2000 and 2008, the number of unauthorized immigrants increased 37 percent (Hawley, 2009). The 2012 data show a slight change in the trend with a 200,000 decline of unauthorized residents from 11.6 million in 2011 to 11.4 million in 2012 (ProCon.org, 2012).

Employment for UIs included nearly every major sector of the economy, particularly food processing, taxi services, food service, cleaning companies, farms, and apparel production (Congress of the United States, Congressional Budget Office, 2006). Many of the UIs had families in their home countries that benefited from US employment because they were able to send money home. For example, millions of families in Mexico had become accustomed to more comfortable lives supported in part by members employed in the United States. See Table 6.4 for top ten countries

---

TABLE 6.4

TOP TEN COUNTRIES OF ORIGIN AND A COMPARISON OF THE NUMBERS OF UNAUTHORIZED IMMIGRANTS (UIS) IN THE UNITED STATES IN 2000 AND 2012

2000		2012	
Country	*Number of UIs*	*Country*	*Number of UIs*
1. Mexico	4,680,000	1. Mexico	6,720,000
2. El Salvador	430,000	2. El Salvador	690,000
3. Guatemala	290,000	3. Guatemala	560,000
4. Philippines	200,000	4. Honduras	360,000
5. China	190,000	5. Philippines	310,000
6. Korea	180,000	6. India	260,000
7. Honduras	160,000	7. Korea	230,000
8. India	120,000	8. China	210,000
9. Ecuador	110,000	9. Ecuador	170,000
10. Brazil	100,000	10. Vietnam	160,000
All Countries	8,460,000	All Countries	11,430,000

Source: ProCon.org. (2012). "Demographics of Immigrants in the United States Illegally: Top 10 Countries of Origin." Retrieved March 25, 2015, from http://immigration.procon.org/view. resource.php?resourceID=000845&print=true

supplying the United States with unauthorized immigrants. Mexico, El Salvador, and Guatemala were the top three countries throughout the time period in the same order. The number of UIs varies from each country from year to year but these countries are still in the top ten.

The top four states of residence for UIs over the 2000 to 2012 time period were California, Texas, Florida, and New York, in that order. Along with the top four, some combination of Illinois, New Jersey, Arizona, North Carolina, Georgia, and Nevada were the top ten states of residence. The remaining forty states were home to about 20 percent of the undocumented immigrants. Thus, the question remains, how and what do the UIs contribute to the US economy? Employment figures show UIs employed in the broad categories of farming, building, groundskeeping and maintenance, construction, food preparation and serving, production, transportation, and materials moving. "Research shows that immigrants complement rather than compete with native-born American workers—even less-skilled workers. . . . Americans are not harmed by—and may even benefit from—immigration. This is because immigrants tend to complement the skill sets of American workers, thus helping them to be more productive" (Center for American Progress, 2014).

Immigration Reform

A recent study of the economic potential for legalizing UIs found that comprehensive immigration reform would yield $1.5 trillion to the US GDP over a 10-year period, generate billions in additional tax revenue and consumer spending, and support hundreds of thousands of jobs (Hinojosa-Ojeda, 2010). Yet the issue remains politically volatile. The production of US Social Security and green cards, for which immigrants may pay close to $600, has been described as a growth industry for more than 10 years. UIs are the most exploitable of workers. Records show they are paid less than other workers, sometimes half of minimum wage; receive no benefits; work long hours, including 12-hour days and 7-day weeks; and do not receive overtime pay. Undocumented immigrant workers (UIWs) may be hired as a "favor," in exchange for an agreement that they will not cause trouble. They are susceptible to unreasonable demands, including sexual exploitation, because they are afraid to have their illegal status revealed. Migrant workers, many of whom are UIWs, have long been regarded as essential to US agriculture, particularly for farms that grow fresh fruits and vegetables. Migrant workers are regarded as temporary residents, people who enter during the harvest season and return to their native countries when the season is over. Often, whole families migrate, and everybody works. Child labor laws do not apply to agriculture.

The apparel manufacturing business, particularly in California and Florida, has employed large numbers of documented and undocumented immigrants. During the 1970s, nearly half of the apparel workers in Southern California were Asian, mostly Korean; now nearly half are Latino, mostly Mexican. Immigration has spread across the country. For example, in 2002 a small sewing shop in Iowa had forty operators that spoke five different native languages. Apparel factories continue to be a site where pay is low but training periods are relatively short and necessary communication does not require complete understanding of one language.

Very few to none of the young generation of US citizens want to work in factories assembling apparel; like many of you, they prefer jobs with a university degree or an employment in service industry. In contrast, many migrants in many countries are attracted to apparel production jobs because of their short training periods and because the plant supervisors are accustomed to working with many nationalities and languages and like to hire people who are not afraid to work very hard. As a result, the future of the United States' and other developed countries' domestic apparel production depends, at least partially, on the availability of immigrant workers in the country.

Summary

Protected trade has long been regarded as unfair, but free trade is also unfair. Some people claim that with free trade the rich get richer, and the poor get poorer. However, just because trade can be unfair does not make it illegal or unethical; the illegal and unethical business practices addressed in this chapter include ignoring customs compliances, violating intellectual property rights, and engaging in unfair business practices. The United States has merged immigration and customs into one agency, Customs and Border Protection, but in most countries these functions are covered by different agencies.

Intellectual property rights protect creative innovations and merchandising properties with patents, copyrights, and trademark law. Products are counterfeit because of violation of trademark law. Counterfeiting is a huge global problem, with billions of dollars in counterfeit goods produced and sold every year. A licensing contract makes it possible to legally use intellectual property owned by someone else. In the apparel business the terms *knockoffs*, *counterfeits*, and *gray market goods* are sometimes used interchangeably, but they are technically different.

Customs compliance issues include transshipment to change illegally country of origin and violations of borders by undocumented workers. Transshipment has been used to avoid tariffs or other trade barriers. Undocumented workers immigrate to developed countries because of high levels of unemployment in their home countries as well as better paying or more pleasant jobs.

Learning Activities

1. What does a firm or a person gain from intellectual property rights and how does a firm or a person get intellectual property rights?
2. What are three of the reasons for the increase in the value of the goods seized by CBP in 2013 as compared to 2008?
3. What has allowed cyber crime to become a key component of illegal trade activity?
4. Why is "substantial transformation" an important factor in determining COO of an apparel product?
5. Why might an exporter purposely misclassify goods?
6. How can owners of intellectual property expect that customs services will be able to identify counterfeit/pirated products carrying their brands?

References

American Immigration Law Foundation. (2002, September). Mexican immigrant workers and the U.S. economy: An increasingly vital role. *Immigration Policy Focus, 1*(2). Retrieved November 18, 2015, from http://www.immigrationpolicy.org/sites/default/files/docs/Mex%20Imm%20 Workers%20&%20US%20Economy.pdf

Casabona, L. (2009, December 15). Customs seeks strong partners as deadlines approach. *Women's Wear Daily.*

Center for American Progress. (2014). "The Facts on Immigration Today." Retrieved October 24, 2015, from https://www.americanprogress.org/issues/immigration/report/2014/10/23/59040/the-facts-on-immigration-today-3/

Congress of the United States, Congressional Budget Office. (2006, February). Immigration policy in the United States. Retrieved November 18, 2015, from http://www.cbo.gov/ftpdocs/70xx/doc7051/02-28-Immigration.pdf

CSR Report for Congress. (2007). *Border security: The complexity of the challenge.* Retrieved November 18, 2015, from http://www.au.af.mil/au/awc/awcgate/crs/rl32839.pdf

Department of Homeland Security. (n.d.). "Container Security Initiative Ports." Retrieved March 25, 2015, from http://www.dhs.gov/container-security-initiative-ports

Elias, S., & Stim, R. (April 2003). *Patent, Copyright, and Trademark: An Intellectual Property Desk Reference* (6th ed.). Berkeley, CA: Nolo.

Elias, S., & Stim, R. (August 2013). *Trademark: Legal Care for Your Business and Product Name* (10th ed.). Berkeley, CA: Nolo.

European Commission: Taxation and Customs Union. (2010*). General aspects of non-preferential origin: Introduction.* Retrieved November 18, 2015, from http://ec.europa.eu/taxation_customs/customs/customs_duties/rules_origin/non-preferential/article_410_en.htm

Farrell-Beck, J., & Gau, C. (2001). Uplift: The bra in America. Philadelphia, PA: University of Pennsylvania Press.

Fashion Business International. (October–November 2003). "Hitting the Pirates Where It Hurts." *Fashion Business International, 25,* 27.

Frohlich, T. C. (2014). "The Nine Most Counterfeited Products in America." Retrieved March 28, 2015, from http://247wallst.com/special-report/2014/03/27/americas-nine-most-counterfeited-items

GovTrack.com. (2012). "Text of the Innovative Design Protection Act of 2012." Retrieved October 24, 2015, from https://www.govtrack.us/congress/bills/112/s3523/text

Hawley, C. (2009, July 11). Dreams fade as money from U.S. dries up. *The Des Moines Register,* p. 9A.

Hinojosa-Ojeda, R. (2010). "Raising the Floor for American Workers: The Economic Benefits of Reform." Retrieved May 15, 2010, from http://www.americanprogress.org/issues/2010/01/pdf/immigrationeconreport.pdf

Hogan & Hartson, LLP (July 2008). "CBP Proposes Sweeping Changes to Country of Origin Rules." *Customs Update.* Retrieved February 1, 2010, from http://www.hoganlovells.com/files/Publication/988dc1a2-0f16-4645-b97b-89b16e79af48/Presentation/PublicationAttachment/7bee5283-89fe-4351-aa12-9342d97f99d4/Customs2.pdf

International Chamber of Commerce (2009). Business action to stop counterfeiting and piracy. Retrieved from http://www.iccwbo.org/advocacy-codes-and-rules/bascap/consumer-awareness/consumer-perceptions/

Jiminez, G. C., & Kolsun, B. (2014). *Fashion Law: A Guide for Designers, Fashion Executives, and Attorneys.* New York, NY: Fairchild Books.

Kennedy, S. (2003). *China Cross Talk: The American Debate over China Policy Since Normalization.* Lanham, MD: Rowman and Littlefield Publishers, Inc.

Kuhail, R. (October 22, 2014). "AAFA and CCCT Forge Partnership at Washington DC Seminar." Retrieved October 24, 2015, from http://www.wewear.org/aafa-and-ccct-forge-partnership-at-washington-dc-seminar/

Little, T. (June 30, 2014). "Nike Named the Most Counterfeited Brand, but Statistics Don't Give the Full Picture." World Trademark Review. Retrieved October 24, 2015, from http://www.worldtrademarkreview.com/blog/detail.aspx?g=c085ce3e-8f80-486c-a50f-026f55d39a23

Lowther, B. (October 11, 2004). No end for China's counterfeiting contagion. Women's Wear Daily, 20-21

Montalvo, F. (September 19, 2014). Protecting Fashion: A Comparative Analysis of Fashion Design Protection in the U.S and Europe. Retrieved November 18, 2015, from http://www.cardozoaelj.com/2014/09/19/protecting-fashion-a-comparative-analysis-of-fashion-design-copyright-protection-in-the-u-s-and-europe/

Nakashima, E., & Peterson, A. (June 9, 2014). "Report: Cybercrime and Espionage Costs $445 Billion Annually." Retrieved October 24, 2015, from https://www.washingtonpost.com/world/national-security/report-cybercrime-and-espionage-costs-445-billion-annually/2014/06/08/8995291c-ecce-11e3-9f5c-9075d5508f0a_story.html

ProCon.org. (2012). "Demographics of Immigrants in the United States Illegally." Retrieved March 25, 2015, from http://immigration.procon.org/view.resource.php?resourceID=000845

Special Report: Counterfeiting: Imitating property is theft. (2003, May 17). The Economist, 52–54. Retrieved November 18, 2015, from http://www.economist.com/node/1780818

Speer, J. K. (2004, April 1). A label-conscious world: Tagless labeling, shorter cycle times drive product ID trends. Apparel. Retrieved November 18, 2015, from http://connection.ebscohost.com/c/articles/13297601/label-conscious-world-tagless-labeling-shorter-cycle-times-drive-product-id-trends

Statista Statistics Portal. (n.d). "Average Annual Costs Caused by Cyber Crime in the United States by Industry Sectors (in Millions of Dollars)." Retrieved October 24, 2015, from http://www.statista.com/statistics/193436/average-annual-costs-caused-by-cyber-crime-in-the-us/

Top 10 Reasons to Register Your Trademark (n.d.). Retrieved November 18, 2015, from http://smallbusiness.findlaw.com/intellectual-property/top-10-reasons-to-register-your-trademark.html

United States International Trade Commission (2015). Official Harmonized Tariff Schedule. Retrieved November 18, 2015, from http://www.usitc.gov/tata/hts/index.htm

United States Trade Representative (2015). 2015 Special 301 Report. Retrieved November 18, 2015, from https://www.iprcenter.gov/reports/ipr-center-reports/2015-special-301-report/view

US Customs and Border Protection. (n.d.a). "Intellectual Property Rights Seizure Statistics." Retrieved May 17, 2015, from http://cbp.gov/linkhandler/cgov/trade/prioritytrade/ipr/pubs/seizure

U.S. Customs and Border Protection (n.d.b). CSI Container Security Initiative. Retrieved November 18, 2015, from http://www.cbp.gov/border-security/ports-entry/cargo-security/csi/csi-brief

World Trade Organization. (n.d.). "Agreement on Rules of Origin (209–219)." Retrieved June 8, 2010, from http://www.wto.org/english/docs_e/legal_e-22-roo.pdf

World Trade Organization. (April 10, 2014). "Steps Agreed on Implementing Bali Decision on Rules of Origin for LDCs." Retrieved October 24, 2015, from http://www.wto.org/english/news_e/news14_e/roi_10apr14_e.htm

Zarocostas, J. (2004, March 16). Officials warn new security will be costly. Women's Wear Daily,

CHAPTER 7

SELECTING LOCATIONS FOR GLOBAL SOURCING

FUN FACT

There are about 200 countries in the world; nearly 180 of them exported apparel to the US market in 2013, for a total value of US $82 billion. (Office of Textiles and Apparel, 2014)

OBJECTIVES

- Examine factors that must be considered when evaluating potential sites for apparel production.
- Critically evaluate forces affecting sourcing decisions, including political, economic, social, and cultural forces, and trade and government regulations.
- Evaluate domestic and international sourcing locations for different types of companies and products.

Fifty years ago, when the majority of merchandise sold to consumers in a particular country was manufactured domestically, supply chains were much simpler. An apparel manufacturer assessed customer needs; planned, designed, and developed products; purchased materials, the majority of which were made domestically; produced garments in its own factories; and sold the finished goods to retailers at wholesale markets. That process seems pretty straightforward compared with today's global supply chain. Today, the supply chain requires attention to many complex components linked to the sourcing of materials and apparel production explored in this and the next chapters, to social responsibility and sustainability issues that were examined in Chapter 4, to the politics of trade barriers and regulations in Chapter 5, and to illegal and unethical trade activities in Chapter 6.

This chapter and the next focus on exploration of the supply chain components that support the processes required to produce and deliver finished textile and apparel products and utilize today's expanded global sourcing options, including design, product development, vendor compliance, materials and factory sourcing, manufacturing control, and logistics. (The framework for this discussion was first introduced in Chapter 1, Figure 1.6.) Some firms manage all the needed supply chain components themselves; other firms may contract with outside sourcing specialists who can provide the required services when expertise in these areas is not available within the firm. Somewhere between the merchandise plans and the arrival of finished styles at a retail store near you, an incredibly complex set of tasks and processes occur.

GLOBAL LEXICON

agile manufacturing an operational strategy focused on inducing velocity and flexibility in a made-to-order production process with minimal changeover time and interruptions

bureaucracy administrative system leading any large institution or government

child labor employment of children in any work that interferes with their ability to attend regular school, and that is mentally, physically, socially, or morally dangerous and harmful

consolidator a person or firm that combines cargo from a number of shippers going to the same destination into one container for the purpose of reducing shipping rates

corruption abuse of public office for private gains (World Bank, n.d.)

customer in the sourcing world, the sourcing company that contracts for delivery of services, materials, product development, or finished goods

customer a person or organization that receives or consumes goods or services from a vendor (supplier) and can choose between different products and vendors

full container load (FCL) refers to a standard 20- or 40-foot shipping container loaded with merchandise from one consigner; it is a common measure for calculating shipping rates and typically is less expensive than the same weight of loose cargo

Human Development Index (HDI) a composite index measuring average achievement in three basic dimensions of human development: a long and healthy life, knowledge, and a decent standard of living

human rights basic rights and freedoms to which all humans are entitled, often held to include the rights to life, liberty, equality, and a fair trial; freedom from slavery and torture; and freedom of thought and expression

import agent or agent, is a professional who assists a business in a foreign country and acts as intermediary between the customer and the vendor; is paid on a commission basis by the company they represent

infrastructure fundamental physical and organizational facilities and systems needed for operation of a country, city, or area; includes transportation and communication systems and power supply

labor exploitation taking advantage of employees because of poverty, gender, age, opportunity, or a combination of these

labor union an organization that bargains with employers on behalf of workers about terms and conditions of employment; lobbies for the interests of workers

LCL a shipping term for cargo that is less than full container load

lean manufacturing a philosophy of production that emphasizes efficiency and economy of scale

legal system a system of interpreting and enforcing the laws in a country

living wage the level of income that covers a family's basic needs, including maintenance of good health

manufacturing the entire process of transforming raw materials into finished goods for use or sale, using machines, tools, and labor

morals the degree of conformity with generally accepted or prescribed standards of goodness or rightness in character or conduct

sourcing calendar a time line related to the sequence of design, product development, production, and delivery to the retail sales floor

vendor a company that supplies services or products to other companies, commonly known as customers

Worldwide Responsible Accredited Production (WRAP) an independent nonprofit corporation dedicated to the promotion and certification of lawful, humane, and ethical manufacturing throughout the world

The two sourcing chapters are designed to clarify the broad categories of these tasks and processes, exploring the competencies essential to succeed in the multifaceted world of global sourcing. As stated in the Fun Fact at the beginning of this chapter, almost every country in the world has apparel industry that manufactures products domestically and exports them to the United States. Many of these products imported to the US market were conceptualized, developed, and procured by US companies that worked with mills and factories in foreign countries to acquire materials for apparel production and distribution.

As you now know, there are many steps required to manufacture a garment that occur before it can actually be sewn together. When US-based apparel professionals make decisions about where to source apparel assembly, they have 180+ countries to choose from, including the United States. How do they decide which country will have an apparel factory that can manufacture products they need, at the specified price, desired quality, and within the acceptable time frame? Countries and regions specialize in different products and services, and every country has certain advantages and disadvantages that determine how easy, safe, and expensive it is to do business there. Some countries might be a good choice for your company, whereas others might not be. What factors do apparel companies consider when deciding what country to have their apparel lines manufactured? This chapter focuses on the aspects of sourcing decisions involved when evaluating and selecting a *country* where apparel assembly and other related services will be sought. Chapter 8 examines factors that apparel professionals consider when selecting a *factory* to partner with for producing apparel.

ROLE OF GLOBAL SOURCING

Significant changes have occurred in the merchandise acquisition process in the United States and other developed countries over the last few decades. One only has to consider that the growth of the percentage of imported apparel sold in the United States went from approximately 5 percent 50 years ago to more than 95 percent today. Since the founding of the United States, textile and apparel products have been brought into the country from Europe. Settlers requested fabrics and looked to European suppliers for accessories and fashion ideas, but they were soon producing cotton fabrics and apparel domestically. The concept of sourcing has been a part of the business environment for centuries for both domestic and international acquisition of goods and services. Our purpose here is to examine the role of *sourcing* in the supply chain.

From the outset we know that a minimum of two firms will be involved in any sourcing process. One entity (the **customer**) desires some material, product, or service, while the other provides it (the **vendor**). Retail merchandise buyers (the customer) have traditionally purchased finished goods directly from manufacturers (the vendors) at wholesale. In addition to that traditional method of sourcing, an exploration of the rapidly emerging discipline of apparel sourcing also includes numerous other methods of acquiring products. To comprehend the complexity of the sourcing process today we must

- Acquire an understanding of the structure of all the interconnected, yet flexible components of the merchandise planning, product development, production, and distribution pipelines.
- Gain awareness of the myriad processes that impact garment production and distribution decisions.

- Comprehend the multitude of legal, political, economic, and cultural barriers that restrict or encourage sourcing activity.
- Consider the criteria for identifying appropriate sourcing partners, from suppliers of materials to vendors providing services and sourcing agents.
- Recognize current technologies that facilitate these processes.

Although some parts of this list have already been introduced, it will take this chapter and the next, the rest of this text, and beyond to understand fully the decision making that is involved in carrying out the sourcing process as a part of a firm's supply chain.

One simple definition of sourcing is researching and obtaining materials, trimmings, and finished garments. Another straightforward definition of sourcing that only addresses the beginning of the sourcing process is choosing the suppliers, domestic or international, that will deliver the desired goods and services. This text has already defined sourcing as a process of finding, evaluating, and partnering with a vendor or vendors to secure services, materials, production, or finished goods, or a combination of these, at a specified cost, quality, and service level, for delivery within an identified time frame. In this chapter and the next one, we are going to examine this process in-depth.

Today, most apparel firms employ specialists whose job is to make sourcing-related decisions. These sourcing specialist positions exist in addition to the more traditional positions of merchandisers, designers, product developers, and quality assurance specialists. In some large firms with expanded sourcing needs and responsibilities there may be teams of sourcing specialists responsible for acquiring diverse product categories, all working under someone in a leadership position with a title such as vice president of sourcing. The sourcing responsibilities for a small firm may fall to an individual designated the product developer, product manager, or sourcing manager. These individuals or teams make sourcing decisions for a firm after weighing all the criteria—what to buy, from where and from whom, importance to how much it will cost and level of product quality, and, ultimately, when and how finished goods will be delivered.

Retail merchandisers also benefit from sourcing competencies, because the merchandising divisions of many retailers include product development and global sourcing components. Sourcing involves a close collaboration among all departments within a company: technical design, merchandising, legal, finance, and others. Sourcing specialists work directly with domestic and international vendors who provide materials, apparel assembly, and other services related to manufacturing products; they often communicate daily with mills and factories in many different countries around the world and frequently travel to negotiate contracts, assure quality and compliance, or evaluate potential new vendors. One goal of this text is to facilitate professional preparation for expanded avenues of employment within the textile and apparel industry, going beyond the traditional roles by examining competencies and opportunities as sourcing specialists.

CHARACTERISTICS OF COUNTRIES THAT IMPACT SOURCING DECISIONS

As we look to the decisions required for sourcing apparel production, we begin by selecting a country where apparel assembly operations can be outsourced. It is typical to have cost of production be at the forefront of attention when considering where to make apparel.

Indeed, in the apparel industry—the most labor-intensive manufacturing sector—the cost of products is dependent on the cost of labor. However, the majority of the world's apparel production is not taking place in the countries with the lowest labor cost. This illustrates that many other factors are at play when a company selects a country for manufacturing its products; political, economic, social, and cultural dimensions must be considered.

Determining which sourcing option is best for a business at any given time is influenced by numerous factors that are constantly in flux and dependent not only on the type and quantity of products needed, but also on the monetary costs of acquisition and the time required to produce and deliver the products. Other factors that have to be considered concern the following:

- the overall stability and safety in a country,
- the customs requirements in different countries,
- effectiveness of infrastructure and communication,
- sophistication and effectiveness of legal and bureaucratic systems,
- level of education and technology,
- cultural norms and values, and
- trade regulations.

This list is extensive, but not exhausting considering the magnitude of specific information that must be evaluated by sourcing specialists to ensure timely delivery of desired products. It should be clear by now that deciding in what country to source has become almost as much of a driving force in this business as deciding what to buy. Make no mistake, successful firms address all the factors listed above.

To provide a framework for considering the myriad characteristics of a country that must be evaluated by sourcing professionals, all factors can be grouped into two categories (Figure 7.1): factors related to level of country development and factors related to country's geographic location. The two categories and individual factors are discussed below in

Figure 7.1
Factors impacting sourcing apparel assembly.

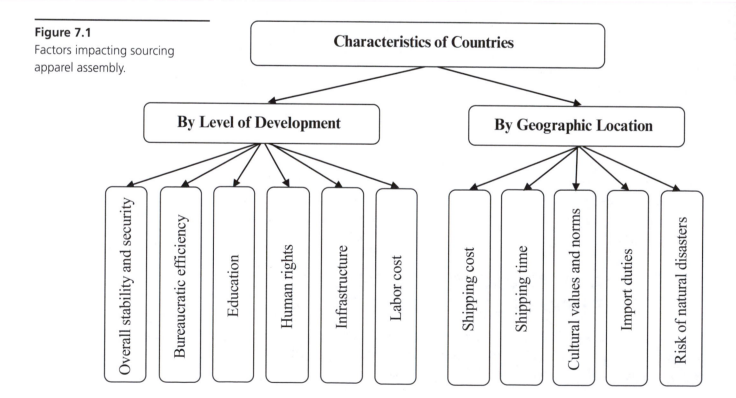

relation to making apparel sourcing decisions. The concept of country's level of economic development and the three groups (developed, developing, and newly developing countries) discussed in Chapter 1 will be employed to evaluate each country. To illustrate and discuss applications of country characteristics to selecting locations for sourcing apparel assembly in this chapter, some of the same countries presented in Tables 1.1 and 1.2 in Chapter 1 were used. Note that in the Tables 7.1 through 7.5 on the following pages, the countries are listed in the same order as in Tables 1.1 and 1.2, from highest to lowest GDP per capita (PPP), or from developed to developing and newly developing.

Factors Related to Levels of Development

Characteristics of countries in relation to levels of economic development include overall stability and security, education, infrastructure, status of the apparel industry, human rights, and labor cost (see Figure 7.1). In general, a higher level of economic development corresponds to more favorable characteristics. However, for sourcing professionals, it is critical to understand what effect each of these factors might have on sourcing apparel assembly and in general doing business with vendors in the country of interest.

Overall Stability and Security

Stability relates not only to an even and established business environment in a country but also to the safety of people who travel there. Examples of stability- and safety-related questions that sourcing specialists should consider include the following:

- Is the country's government politically stable enough to sustain planned transactions to their completion?
- Has there been any social unrest?
- How safe are shipments in transit, including materials and finished products?
- What about security for sourcing specialists who travel to the country to work with the factory?

The US Department of State monitors situations around the world, posts travel warnings and travel alerts, and provides a searchable database by country on its website (http://travel.state.gov/content/passports/english/alertswarnings.html). Travel warnings are issued when the US government does not recommend traveling to a country. Among the reasons for travel warning are unstable governments, civil war, recurrent terrorist attacks, or continuing violence. Travel alerts indicate short-term events that are important to consider when preparing to visit a country. Alerts might be issued in case of disease outbreaks, social unrest, or elevated risk of terrorist attacks. Being aware of what is happening in the country of interest by checking travel warnings and alerts (and paying attention to daily news) is important not only for the safety of sourcing professionals when they visit potential or current vendors in this country, but also to avoid disruptions in the production schedule and ensuring timely shipment and delivery of finished goods.

Political and economic instability might arise in the event of electing a new government or in the case of extensive economic, legal, or social reforms. Such changes in a country might not pose threats to personal safety, and therefore, would not result in a travel warning or alert. Yet they might significantly alter legal and economic environments and cause temporary disruptions for businesses and the flow of trade. If the rewards outweigh the risks, companies doing business in politically unstable countries must be flexible and prepared to adjust their operations and business strategies on a very short notice.

As discussed in Chapter 5, the currency exchange rate is important to consider for across border transactions in order to know in which country the US dollar can buy more. The stability of the currency exchange rate in a country is an indicator of the country's economic stability. A volatile exchange rate might result in drastic changes in production and material costs. In contrast, overly stable exchange rates might indicate that currency value is not determined by its real market value but regulated by government. For example, for decades the Chinese government maintained undervalued currency, making products from China comparatively less expensive to retailers in the developed world. Should China revalue its currency upward, as demanded by political pressure from several developed countries, its products could become more expensive, but the market would become more favorable for China to purchase and import product categories from developed nations, such as the United States and the EU. It will also be very instructive to see if China's current number one status as the world's largest apparel exporter could be maintained as its own consumer population prospers and makes further demands for access to the world's products.

Typically, more developed countries tend to have a more stable and predictable political, economic, and social environment that is favorable for doing business in these countries. In contrast, it is common for newly developing countries, such as Pakistan, to experience long-term conflicts stemming from tribalism, ethnic or religious divide, or social unrest due to poverty and inequality, inefficient democracy, or corrupt and incompetent governments. Volatility and uncertainty make it difficult to do business in these countries, causing further stagnation of their economic and social development. Many developing countries, for example China or Jordan, have been able to create a fairly stable and safe business landscape to attract foreign investments and partnerships.

Figure 7.2 provides examples of global risks that pose threats to business operations that might disrupt supply chains in different regions of the world. Global risk is "an uncertain event or condition that, if it occurs, can cause significant negative impact for several countries or industries within the next 10 years" (World Economic Forum, 2015, p. 53). In Figure 7.2, different patterns represent different types of risk. For example,

Figure 7.2

Global risks of highest concerns for doing business; note what regions have greater risk and what types of risk.

Source: World Economic Forum. (2015). "Global Risks Report 2015." Retrieved October 24, 2015, from http://www.weforum.org/reports/global-risks-report-2015

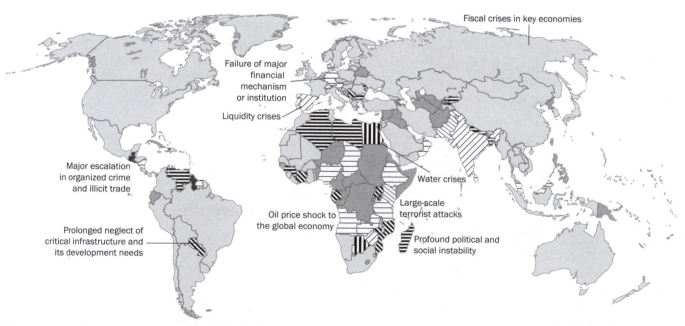

Source: Executive Opinion Survey 2014, World Economic Forum.
Notes: Only risks that are of highest concern in at least two countries are represented on the map. Other risks of highest concern: Violent Interstate conflict (in Armenia). Breakdown of critical information infrastructure and networks (Cameroon). Escalation of economic and resource nationalization (Lesotho), and Greater incidence of environmentally-related events (Philippines).

dark horizontal stripes represent profound political and social instability in Algeria, Libya, Madagascar, Venezuela, Bangladesh, and Nepal. Countries with major escalation in organized crime and illicit trade are filled with wide horizontal lines (Nigeria, Chad, Ethiopia, Tanzania, Angola, Zambia, Nicaragua, etc.). Dark diagonal stripes in Paraguay, South America, and Cote d'Ivoire indicate prolonged neglect of critical infrastructure. Two countries that have especially high threat of large-scale terrorist attacks are Kenya and Pakistan (white diagonal stripes). Only major risks are presented for every country. Regions of the world differ by major type of risk. Detailed countries' assessments in terms of risk are available at the World Economic Forum, www.weforum.org/risks.

Bureaucratic Efficiency

Efficient **bureaucracy**, the administrative system leading any large institution or government, determines how easy it is to do business in a country. Effective bureaucracy ensures clear and transparent procedures for exporting and importing materials and products, starting a new venture, and receiving required permits and certifications. Legal systems regulate business transactions, protect property rights including intellectual property, enforce laws, and resolve judicial disputes. Excessive bureaucracy results in unnecessary delays, stagnation of business operations, and increased costs.

Several world organizations have developed indices and have been tracking changes in government and bureaucracy efficiency in countries across the world, which speaks to the importance of this sourcing factor. For example, in its annual "Doing Business" report, World Bank Group (2015) measured business regulations and their enforcement in 189 countries and ranked them in terms of how easy it is to do business in each. In Table 7.1, rankings for the ease of doing business for twenty-two selected countries is displayed. The rankings show it is easier to do business in developed nations and tends to be the most difficult in newly developing countries. In agreement with the government efficiency index, Italy was ranked the lowest on the business regulations and their enforcement (number 56).

World Economic Forum (2014) assessed government efficiency in 144 countries for its annual "Global Competitiveness Report." A government efficiency index was used to measure wastefulness of government spending, efficiency of legal framework, transparency of government policymaking, and burden of government regulations. Indices for government efficiency, ethics, and corruption for selected countries are presented in Table 7.1. The ethics and corruption index is calculated based on measuring bribes, obtaining favorable judicial decisions, awarding of public contracts and licensing, and so on in 144 countries (World Economic Forum, 2014). The indices range from 1 to 7, with highest number meaning the highest level of efficiency. In Table 7.1, most developed nations tend to have more efficient governments (range from 3.1 to 5.3, not counting Italy) than developing (2.7–4.2) and newly developing countries (2.6–3.1). Italy, at 2.1, has the lowest government efficiency index among all countries.

Companies might incur additional costs not only due to interruptions in production schedule and late shipments but also because of unofficial payments, known as bribes. Bribes are part of the culture in many developing and newly developing nations, where companies and individuals often have to provide additional incentives to corrupt state officials to do what they are supposed to and/or to speed up the process of simple procedures such as receiving a driving license, activating an internet connection, completing paperwork for exporting goods, and so on. While unethical and illegal, **corruption**, which is abuse of public office for personal gains, is deeply rooted in bureaucratic and

TABLE 7.1

INDICATORS OF GOVERNMENT AND BUREAUCRATIC EFFICIENCY

Countries	Ease of Doing Business Rank/189[1]	Government Efficiency[2]	Ethics and Corruption[2]	Intellectual Property Protection[2]
Developed				
United States	7	4.0	4.3	5.4
Hong Kong	3	5.3	5.5	5.8
Germany (EU)	14	4.5	5.2	5.4
United Kingdom (EU)	8	4.7	5.4	5.9
Japan	29	4.5	5.4	6.0
France (EU)	31	3.7	4.5	5.6
South Korea	5	3.1	3.4	3.7
Italy (EU)	56	2.1	2.8	3.7
Developing				
Mexico	39	3.2	2.7	3.5
Brazil	120	2.7	2.4	3.3
China	90	4.1	4.0	4.0
Jordan	117	4.2	4.0	4.6
Indonesia	114	4.0	3.5	4.1
Honduras	104	3.4	2.8	3.5
India	142	3.7	3.4	3.7
Vietnam	78	3.2	3.2	3.1
Newly developing				
Pakistan	128	3.1	2.7	2.9
Cambodia	135	3.0	2.6	2.8
Bangladesh	173	3.0	2.2	2.5
Haiti	180	2.6	2.4	2.2
Ethiopia	132	3.1	3.1	3.1
Zimbabwe	171	2.9	2.6	2.9

[1]*World Bank Group. (2015). "Doing Business Report 2015." Retrieved October 24, 2015, from http://www.doingbusiness.org/rankings#*
[2]*World Economic Forum. (2015). "Global Competitiveness Report 2014–2015." Retrieved October 24, 2015, from http://reports.weforum.org/global-competitiveness-report-2014-2015/rankings/*

political institutions in many countries around the globe (World Bank, n.d.). While there is less difference between the groups, developed countries scored the best, with the indices ranging from 3.4 to 5.5, with the exception of Italy (2.8). Newly developing countries have the lowest indices (2.2–3.1), indicating pervasive problems with government ethics and corruption.

For apparel sourcing professionals, it is also important to consider potential counterfeit issues and the level of intellectual property protection in a country (Table 7.1). Developed countries (again, with the exception of Italy) have significantly better mechanisms in place to protect intellectual property rights than developing nations. Newly developing economies have the lowest indices.

Government inability and/or unwillingness to enforce environmental and human rights regulations create a business culture conducive to labor and environment abuses. Inefficiency of government operations not only imposes significant economic costs to businesses and slows down a country's economic development, but might add a lot of stress to the life of the sourcing professional.

Infrastructure

Infrastructure is defined as fundamental physical and organizational facilities and systems needed for operation of a country, city, or area and typically includes transportation and communication systems and power supply. Sourcing professionals must consider a number of questions in relation to the country's infrastructure support of manufacturing and delivery of the desired products. For example, consider whether the following categories are adequate:

- electricity and water for requested production
- transportation to docks
- warehouse facilities
- dock facilities
- technology and communication

Transportation infrastructure is measured by quality of roads, railroads, ports, and air transport. Adequate transportation infrastructure is necessary to deliver fabrics and findings to the factory and then finished products from the factory to port or airport for exporting to the customer's domestic market, not to mention FedEx-ing multiple samples for approval overnight. As shown in Table 7.2, developed countries have well-established transportation means, with indices in the range of 5.6–6.5, with the exception of Italy, which is 4.8 (Figure 7.3). Developing countries' transportation indices fall

Figure 7.3
Developed countries have sophisticated and well-maintained transport infrastructure, including roads, seaports, and airports. These greatly facilitate business activities, including trading across borders.

TABLE 7.2

INFRASTRUCTURE INDICATORS

Countries	Transport Infrastructure	Transport Infrastructure Rank/144	ICT Use	ICT Use Rank/144	Electricity and Phone Infrastructure	Electricity and Phone Infrastructure Rank/144
Developed						
United States	5.8	9	5.7	20	5.8	26
Hong Kong	6.5	3	6.6	6	6.9	1
Germany (EU)	6.0	7	6.0	14	6.1	12
United Kingdom (EU)	5.6	14	6.8	2.0	6.4	6
Japan	6.1	5	5.6	24	6.2	11
France (EU)	6.0	8	6.1	12	6.0	18
South Korea	5.7	10	5.6	23	5.7	31
Italy (EU)	4.8	28	5.4	26	6.1	17
Developing						
Mexico	4.5	41	2.2	88	3.9	88
Brazil	3.5	77	3.6	57	4.5	70
China	5.0	21	2.6	76	4.3	73
Jordan	3.6	70	2.2	90	4.6	66
Indonesia	4.5	39	2.1	94	4.2	77
Honduras	3.2	91	1.6	112	3.2	102
India	4.5	42	1.3	125	2.6	118
Vietnam	3.5	76	2.3	86	4.0	81
Newly developing						
Pakistan	3.4	82	1.3	127	1.9	130
Cambodia	2.8	111	1.5	114	3.3	100
Bangladesh	2.7	115	1.2	131	2.1	127
Haiti	2.2	138	1.2	128	1.9	134
Ethiopia	3.1	100	1.0	141	1.9	133
Zimbabwe	2.8	114	1.9	99	2.3	122

Source: World Economic Forum. (2015). "Global Competitiveness Report 2014–2015." Retrieved October 24, 2015, from http://reports.weforum.org/global-competitiveness-report-2014-2015/rankings/

in the range of 3.2–4.5, with the noticeable exception of China (index of 5.0), which has built sophisticated highways, ports, and airports to support the booming economy. Newly developing countries' transportation indices are the lowest, from 2.2 to 3.4, indicating poor quality and/or insufficient availability of roads, ports, and airports to effectively support business activities (Figure 7.4).

Internet and communication technology (ICT) use in a country is measured by number of internet users in a country, fixed broadband internet, internet bandwidth, and active mobile broadband subscriptions (World Economic Forum, 2014). The apparel business is very detail-oriented and requires a lot of back-and-forth communication between the customer and the factory to approve fabric and samples, fine-tune

Figure 7.4
Newly developing countries have primitive transport infrastructure, especially in rural areas. Lack of and/or poor condition of roads and ports delay merchandise delivery and discourage business.

the fit of a garment, troubleshoot construction or production problems, or address any other quality issues. If a country does not have a sufficient ICT structure to support instant communication and exchange of information, including technical specifications for materials and apparel products, timely delivery of orders might be difficult.

Similar to transportation, ICT use rate is the highest in developed countries, with indices ranging from 5.4 to 6.8 (Table 7.2). In developing countries, ICT use indices are substantially lower and fall primarily in 2s range, with Brazil being more advanced (3.6) and India and Honduras having less developed communication means (1.3 and 1.6). Newly developing countries have the lowest use of internet and mobile communication: all of the newly developing nations presented in Table 7.2 have ICT indices lower than 2.0.

Growing up in a developed nation, it is easy to take electricity supply for granted, and all the amenities it powers, such as refrigerator, electric stove, heat or air conditioner, TV, ICT, and the country's infrastructure in general. With respect to apparel assembly, electricity is essential to operate sewing machines and other equipment. No matter how excellent workmanship might be, if it is not supported by a machine, no garment can be manufactured on an industrial level. Developed nations have a reliable supply of electricity, available anywhere in the country, which is reflected in very high indices for electric and phone infrastructure in the range of 5.7–6.9 in Table 7.2. In the developing economies used here as examples, the indices are significantly lower (2.6–4.6), indicating that electricity and phone service might not exist everywhere and/or may be an intermittent supply. In the group of developing countries, India has a notably lower electricity and phone infrastructure index of only 2.6, whereas for the majority of the countries in this category the index is above 4.0. Newly developing nations have the least established infrastructure for providing electricity and phone service, with indices in the range of 1.9–3.3 in Table 7.2.

The level of infrastructure available in a country is closely related to the level of the country's economic development. In comparison with developing countries, developed countries have significantly more established infrastructure with modern and well-maintained highways, advanced information and communication technology means, and affordable and stable electricity supply available throughout the nation. Many newly developing economies have not yet established adequate and reliable infrastructure, especially, in the areas outside of major cities. It is important to note that more developed economies also have better infrastructure repair and maintenance systems, and when things go wrong, they can be addressed quickly and effectively. For example, if there is a power outage or loss of internet or phone connection, how fast will they be repaired? In most developed countries, it is a matter of several days or often several hours, depending on the severity of the problem. In many developing and especially newly developing countries the same problem might take several weeks, delaying production schedules. While not reflected in Table 7.2, developing and newly developing countries typically have substantially more expensive ICT, electricity, and phone services, which is reflected in factories' overhead costs in these countries.

Education

According to David Birnbaum, renowned apparel sourcing expert and author of several books on sourcing, education is the most important characteristic for sourcing professionals to take into account when they are selecting a country to outsource apparel assembly to. Birnbaum (2005) explained, "You can overcome anything, but if people with whom you must work cannot understand what you are saying, cannot understand what you need, or lack the technical skills to translate those needs into actual production, do not bother unpacking your bags. Any effort spent in that place will be a very costly waste of time" (p. 17).

As discussed in Chapter 1, developed countries have higher literacy rates than developing countries, while newly developing countries have the lowest literacy rates among the three groups (Table 1.2). Higher literacy rates indicate a better educated population. Almost all adults in developed countries (close to 100 percent) are literate. For the developing countries presented in Table 1.2, the literacy rates are a bit lower and range from 75 percent to 97 percent, with the exception of women in India, only half of whom are literate. In developing countries, a significant portion of adult population cannot read (between 30 percent and 70 percent). Also note that in developed economies, literacy rates are the same for males and females, whereas in some developing (like India) and all newly developing countries, significantly more males are literate in comparison with females.

Beyond the basic ability to read and write, a more advanced level of education is necessary for the factory to collaborate with sourcing professionals in producing high-quality garments. Questions to consider include: Are trained sewing machine operators available? Does the factory have a well-trained patternmaker and graders? Is there a production engineer with the knowledge of apparel construction, seams, and stitches to establish and control product quality as well as proper sequence of assembly operations for high productivity? What about textile science knowledge to account for fabrics and threads properly? Is the factory prepared to invest and handle the latest technology and software?

While there is no data available to answer these questions, the expected and average years of schooling presented in Table 7.3 for selected countries provide an idea of the level of education beyond basic literacy. Expected years of schooling (the number of years of schooling that a child of school entrance age can expect to receive) are very high for developed economies (15.3–17.1), lower but still high for developing nations

(11.6–15.2), and the lowest in newly developing countries (7.6–10.9). Actual completed mean years of schooling (average number of years of education received by people ages 25 and older) is lower than expected years of schooling but follows exactly the same pattern for the three groups of countries (Table 7.3). Many developing countries in the Americas and newly developing countries in Asia and Africa have not yet invested in the training, education, and technology necessary to compete in producing high-quality complex garments, although they might offer decent skills for manufacturing lower-end basic apparel.

TABLE 7.3

EDUCATION INDICATORS, 2012

Countries	Expected Years of Schooling	Mean Years of Schooling, Females Aged 25 Years and Above	Mean Years of Schooling, Males Aged 25 Years and Above
Developed			
United States	16.5	13.0	12.9
Hong Kong	15.6	9.8	10.3
Germany (EU)	16.3	12.6	13.3
United Kingdom (EU)	16.2	12.8	11.8
Japan	15.3	11.2	11.8
France (EU)	16.0	10.9	11.4
South Korea	17.1	11.1	12.5
Italy (EU)	16.3	9.7	10.6
Developing			
Mexico	12.8	8.1	8.8
Brazil	15.2	7.3	7.2
China	13.3	6.9	8.2
Jordan	13.3	9.4	10.4
Indonesia	12.7	6.9	8.1
Honduras	11.6	5.3	5.7
India	11.7	3.2	5.6
Vietnam	11.9	5.2	5.7
Newly developing			
Pakistan	8.5	3.3	6.1
Cambodia	10.9	3.2	5.0
Bangladesh	10.0	4.6	5.6
Haiti	7.6	3.2	6.7
Ethiopia	8.5	1.4	3.6
Zimbabwe	9.3	6.7	7.8
World	**12.2**		

Source: United Nations Development Programme. (2012). "Human Development Reports." Retrieved October 24, 2015, from http://hdr.undp.org/en/content/table-1-human-development-index-and-its-components

Human Rights

Another question a sourcing specialist must consider is: Does the country support the humanitarian and environmental conditions that are considered appropriate by the sourcing company and the ultimate consumers? Some of the effects of the textile and apparel industries on environment were discussed in Chapter 4. In this section, we will focus on **human rights**. Unfair treatment of workers in apparel industry is not only the matter of morals, it might permanently damage a company's reputation and brand image.

In 1948, the United Nations adopted a Universal Declaration of Human Rights. It asserts that all people are equal in dignity and have the right to life, liberty, and security. However, because of the multiple political, religious, and cultural perspectives on human rights around the world, no single code of human rights exists, and many people are deprived of life, liberty, and security as well as certain social and cultural rights. Sometimes businesses, including those engaged in textiles and apparel, contribute to the abuse of human rights, either knowingly or unknowingly, especially in the form of **labor exploitation**.

Labor Exploitation

Human exploitation is possible because certain segments of the population are vulnerable, allowing others to take advantage of them. Factors that contribute to vulnerability include poverty, gender, age, and ethnic or racial origin. These same factors contribute to labor exploitation in the context of employment.

Previously, we defined poverty as lack of enough income and/or resources, or both, to satisfy minimum needs. Accurately defining what constitutes a level of poverty is very complex. Beginning with Table 1.1, throughout this text we have used GDP per capita (PPP) as an indicator of resources available to people in a defined population. Resources available, in turn, are used as an indicator of well-being and level of economic development. However, other resources besides GDP also contribute to well-being. For a more complete picture of the presence of poverty, United Nations (2013) has devised the **Human Development Index (HDI)**, which incorporates three variables: GDP per capita, life expectancy at birth, and adult literacy. Life expectancy at birth is determined by a number of factors related to well-being, including nutrition and availability and quality of medical care. Adult literacy contributes to the ability to make appropriate and efficient use of whatever resources are available in a particular environment. Human development for selected countries is presented in the first column of Table 7.4:

- countries with very high HD have an index between 0.8 and 1.0
- countries with high HD have an index between 0.7 and 0.79
- countries with medium HD have an index of 0.55–0.69
- countries with low HD have an index lower than 0.54

The index presented in the second column of Table 7.4 is the International Human Rights Rank Indicator (IHRRI). It illustrates the relationship between the level of well-being, measured by HDI, and human rights issues. IHRRI is developed by an independent group of human rights defenders, formed and supported by the International NGO Global Network for Rights and Development (IHRRI, 2015), who claim that the indicator accurately reflects a real, bias-free state of human rights in each country of the world. They register actual cases of violations and then calculate the indicator based on the rates of respect for twenty-one human rights in a country.

TABLE 7.4

2013 HUMAN DEVELOPMENT INDEX (HDI) AND 2015 INTERNATIONAL HUMAN RIGHTS RANK INDICATOR (IHRRI)

Country	2013 HDI Value	IHRRI, %
Developed	.87–.91	37–72
United States	**0.914**	**68.43**
Hong Kong	0.891	37.40
Germany (EU)	**0.911**	**69.41**
United Kingdom (EU)	0.892	71.74
Japan	0.889	68.19
France (EU)	0.884	68.71
South Korea	0.891	47.62
Italy (EU)	0.872	63.01
Developing	.59–.76	28–53
Mexico	0.756	51.32
Brazil	0.744	53.58
China	0.719	53.24
Jordan	0.745	45.53
Indonesia	0.684	29.01
Honduras	0.617	41.10
India	0.586	42.86
Vietnam	0.638	27.81
Newly developing		
Pakistan	0.537	38.53
Cambodia	0.584	35.07
Bangladesh	0.558	47.3
Haiti	0.471	45.41
Ethiopia	0.435	24.60
Zimbabwe	0.492	40.3
World	**0.702**	

Sources: IHRRI. (2015). "International Human Rights Rank Indicator by Country." Retrieved January 13, 2015, from http://ihrri.com/country.php; United Nations Development Programme. (2012). "Human Development Index and Its Components." Retrieved October 24, 2015, from http://hdr.undp.org/en/content/table-1-human-development-index-and-its-components

All developed countries have high levels of human development (HDI ranges from 0.872 to 0.914) and the highest human rights ranks (37.40–71.74 percent)—all higher than 50 percent, with the exception of Hong Kong and South Korea. Developing countries in Table 7.4 are split equally between a high and medium level of human development. The four developing countries (Mexico, Brazil, Jordan, and China) that have a high level of human development (0.719–0.726) also score higher on human rights (45.53–53.58 percent) than the other four developing countries (Indonesia, Vietnam, Honduras, and India) that rank lower in IHRRI (27.81–42.86 percent) and have a

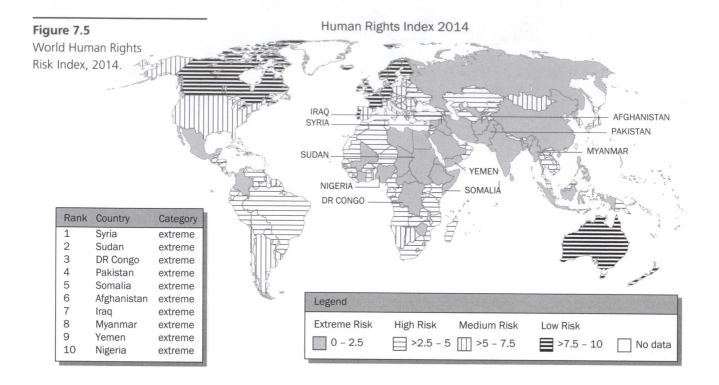

Figure 7.5
World Human Rights Risk Index, 2014.

Human Rights Index 2014

Rank	Country	Category
1	Syria	extreme
2	Sudan	extreme
3	DR Congo	extreme
4	Pakistan	extreme
5	Somalia	extreme
6	Afghanistan	extreme
7	Iraq	extreme
8	Myanmar	extreme
9	Yemen	extreme
10	Nigeria	extreme

Legend

Extreme Risk	High Risk	Medium Risk	Low Risk	
0 – 2.5	>2.5 – 5	>5 – 7.5	>7.5 – 10	No data

medium level of human development (0.586–0.684). Finally, the group of newly developing countries has the lowest human development index (0.435–0.584) but the human rights ranks are similar to developing countries (24.60–47.3 percent).

For example, Ethiopia has the lowest human development index of 0.435 and the lowest rank in human rights (24.60 percent) of all countries in Table 7.4. In contrast, the United States and Germany have the highest human development (0.914 and 0.911) and the highest human rights ranks (68.43 percent and 69.41 percent). Clearly, the more developed a nation is, the greater opportunities for its people to develop and better themselves, the less poverty and people desperate for any kind of work in any conditions, and the less conducive such an environment is to violations of human rights. In addition, as you just learned, more developed countries tend to have more efficient and effective governments, which helps to prevent work-related abuses and labor exploitation. Maplecroft, a consulting company assessing various risks around the world to businesses, developed a world map where different patterns indicate levels of human rights risk by country (Figure 7.5). Note that many countries in Africa, Asia, and the Middle East have extreme human rights risks. The top ten human rights risk countries are ranked and noted individually in Figure 7.5. In contrast, Western European countries, Canada, Australia, and New Zealand have low human rights risk.

Gender

Even in developed countries, with more transparent and effective systems to ensure human rights, women experience gender-based discrimination. In the United States it is very clear that, regardless of whether employed as executives in global corporations, faculty in schools or universities, or as production floor employees, men get paid approximately 20 percent more than women for doing the same jobs. Women also are still not rising into executive ranks at the same rate as their male counterparts, although during the economic downturn in 2009, more men lost jobs than women. Perhaps that was because the men at the same rank were paid more than women and thus provided greater savings to the company.

Around the globe, women are exploited in many ways in addition to discrimination relative to salaries or wages and promotion. The apparel industry has always been predominantly female because sewing does not require much physical strength but it does require attention to details, patience, and persistence. Apparel factory owners prefer to hire young women as sewing machine operators because they represent a docile workforce that can be easier to manage and sometimes to abuse (Rivoli, 2009).

Child Labor

Children around the world still mine for gold and diamonds, weave carpets, sew apparel and footwear, pick cotton, and work in leather tanneries. According to the United Nations statistics, one in seven children in the world can be classified as working in **child labor** (United Nations, n.d.). In 2008, there were approximately 215 million child laborers between the ages of 5 and 17 around the world. In addition, although not captured in these statistics, an unknown number of children are working in drug trafficking, prostitution, and pornography. A comprehensive report by International Labour Organization (2010) cited Argentina, Bangladesh, Bolivia, Brazil, China, India, Mexico, and the Philippines as countries where child labor is more commonly employed (Figure 7.6).

There has been an increase in awareness of child labor throughout the world and the commitment to eliminating its worst forms appears to be gaining momentum. However, there are many barriers to implementation, the primary ones being poverty, lack of financial government resources, and government corruption. Governments are also reluctant to enforce laws when large numbers of a population are desperate for any source of income.

Most countries have laws with a minimum work age of 14. However, in many countries the laws are not enforced; in addition, when people are poor and unemployed, they will often misrepresent their age. Sometimes children are the only ones available to work and are a family's only source of income. Citizens of developed countries are frequently and rightly accused of inappropriately applying our standards to scenarios in which they are not appropriate. How many of you worked as teenagers? How many of you worked in situations in which you had little training and unsafe conditions? It is easy for us to point the finger at other cultures and other countries that seemingly exploit children and, of course, sometimes they do, but so do we; what are our standards, and what are our justifications for our violations of child labor laws?

Read Case 7.1. The case presents a real story shared by a successful apparel professional, Susan Maxwell, and addresses the issue of child labor in the apparel industry. Although the events in the case date to the 1980s, in some parts of the world child labor remains a concern and is a reality even today. Sourcing specialists should be prepared to appropriately address violations of human rights, unsafe working conditions, or unethical treatment of workers, which they might witness in some factories not only in

Figure 7.6

A child laborer protests child labor exploitation in Asia.

SHOE PRODUCTION IN BRAZIL, BY SUSAN M. MAXWELL*

In the mid-1980s, I was a senior footwear buyer for Target Stores. As part of my responsibilities, I traveled to overseas factories to develop shoe samples and inspect production. On a trip to a remote rural town in Brazil, I was accompanied by an independent **import agent** working for Target on a commission basis. As we approached the rural town, the sides of the road were crowded by children in uniforms, scurrying in a direction out of town. I assumed school had recessed, and the children were headed home. At the factory, the manager explained that the workers went home for lunch. The agent and I decided to go to the town to have lunch and come back later to see the production.

Upon return to the factory, we headed directly to the production areas. I was shocked when I saw 8–12 year old children making the shoes. I recognized that these were the children in uniforms on the sides of the road when we first approached the town. It was the factory uniforms, not school uniforms. Prior to this trip, I had toured close to 1,000 factories around the world on behalf of Target Stores and never had seen child labor used in production.

I asked immediately to be taken to a phone to place an international call. I spoke with merchandise vice president and, subsequently, with the chief legal counsel for Target. I told them that I was totally stunned seeing children making the shoes and needed to know what to do. I learned, at that time, there was no policy regarding child labor at Target. I was told I should follow my gut instinct and take appropriate action, which both officers would support regardless of what decision I made. The agent explained to me that in "third world" countries, in poor areas, child labor was an absolute economic necessity: everybody was put to work at

early age so that families would not starve. The agent told me that child labor is "culturally accepted and economically required" for the children and their families to survive.

I canceled the order and told the factory owner that under NO condition would Target Stores accept a shipment of shoes made by children. The decision put me in a high jeopardy position as I was responsible for procuring these shoes for an upcoming ad and not having ad merchandise was not tolerated at Target Stores. The factory owner and the agent objected to canceling the order as both would not receive payment for the shoes. The factory owner had a substantial investment in materials and labor to produce the shoes.

I then challenged the agent to find another factory which did NOT use child labor to make these shoes and still get them shipped on time. This was a difficult task as the factories were booked and production space was hard if not impossible to find. I made the business decision I could morally live with and that I thought Target Stores would make given knowledge of such a situation. Looking at this from a larger perspective, I felt any US company should make the same decision based on our values and laws.

*Susan M. Maxwell specializes in import, design, and sourcing. She worked for major US apparel and retail companies and currently is president of MAX Merchandising, Inc.

Personal correspondence with Susan Maxwell.

1. How were the children and their families in the case affected by not getting paid for their work?
2. Think of yourself as the sourcing agent in this case. How might your company and you personally be affected when the products were not delivered on time for a selling season (e.g., Christmas)?

newly developing countries but in some developed countries as well. While reading the case, imagine yourself in similar circumstances and ponder the questions that follow. Keep in mind that in the 1980s, in the early era of apparel and footwear assembly outsourcing to lower wage countries, there had not been much publicity about child labor and human rights, and companies in developed countries did not have codes of conduct or other policies addressing these issues.

Human Rights Organizations

Human rights abuses have led to the creation of organizations that defend human rights. A union (*labor union* in American English; *trade union* in British English) is a group of workers who act collectively to address common issues. More specifically, a **labor union** is an association of workers with the purpose, in whole or in part, of bargaining with employers on behalf of workers about terms and conditions of employment. Unions may have legal rights to negotiate with management over wages, overtime, holiday pay, timing and length of working hours, health and retirement benefits, and safety- and security-related issues, depending on laws in individual countries. Collectively, workers can threaten to strike to get the attention of employers and force them to negotiate. Power and autonomy of unions vary greatly among countries. For the most part, in North America and Western Europe, unions are organized democratically, with elected officials. In other countries—China and Cuba, for example—unions may be run by the government. Other human rights organizations include various nonprofit entities committed to advancing labor conditions in specific industries.

In the apparel industry, **Worldwide Responsible Accredited Production (WRAP)**, formerly known as Worldwide Responsible Apparel Production, is a prominent nonprofit corporation dedicated to the promotion and certification of lawful, humane, socially responsible, and ethical manufacturing throughout the world. WRAP originated within the **American Apparel and Footwear Association (AAFA)**, but it soon became independent of the companies it was evaluating. WRAP is the world's largest independent certification program mainly focused on the apparel, footwear, and sewn products industries. To become WRAP certified, a five-step process is required that can take several years:

1. Application: the factory submits a completed application form and pays an application fee (US $1,195 in 2015).
2. Self-Assessment: based on the WRAP Handbook, the factory conducts a 90-day self-assessment and submits it to WRAP.
3. Monitoring: upon approval of the self-assessment, the factory selects WRAP-accredited monitoring organization to audit the facility. The audit must be passed within six months.
4. Evaluation: WRAP will review the monitor's audit report and notifies the factory if it earned the certification, or that it must correct certain procedures before it can be certified.
5. Certification: three levels of certification can be awarded, depending on the level of the factory compliance with WRAP principles: Platinum, Gold, and Silver. (WRAP, 2015)

Labor Cost

Table 7.5 presents minimum monthly wages for twenty-two selected countries that are listed from the highest to the lowest GDP per capita (refer to Table 1.1, Chapter 1). Similar to GDP per capita, developed countries have the highest minimum wages ($728–$1,833 per month). In most developing countries, minimum monthly wages are in the range of several hundred dollars, with the exception of Vietnam and India. In fact, India has the lowest minimum monthly wages of all the countries presented in Table 7.5. Newly developing countries have the lowest minimum wages, most of which are below $100. In Zimbabwe and Kenya, the wages are highest in the developing countries group. However, they might not necessarily be enforced.

Typically, when considering different countries as potential locations for sourcing apparel production, labor cost is the first thing that comes to mind. Labor cost is very important in the highly labor-intensive apparel industry. To review, refer to the discussion in Chapter 1. The high labor cost in developed nations has caused assembly lines to

TABLE 7.5

LABOR COST, 2014

Countries	Minimum Wage per Month, US$*
Developed	
United States	1,244.56
Germany (EU)	1,139.93
United Kingdom (EU)	1,355.07
Japan	1,833.59
France (EU)	778.07
South Korea	727.78
Italy (EU)	1,778.98
Developing	
Mexico	128.08
Brazil	441.97
China	242.42
Jordan	256.92
Indonesia	232.02
Honduras	430.06
India	28.37
Vietnam	73.08
Newly developing	
Pakistan	41.59
Cambodia	43.00
Bangladesh	38.57
Haiti	72.30
Zimbabwe	246.46
Kenya	117.08

*Note: The minimum wage rate applies to the worker used in the case study: a cashier, age 19 with one year of work experience.

Source: Doing Business. (2014). "Labor Market Regulation, Minimum Wage Data." Retrieved October 25, 2015, from http://www.doingbusiness.org/data/exploretopics/labor-market-regulation

relocate to developing and newly developing countries in many industries, from apparel to furniture, electronics, and steel. Yet labor cost alone does not determine the cost of apparel production, or the final cost of the product when it arrives at the sourcing company's distribution center. For example, it is important to take into account a factory's overhead costs, which are typically significantly higher in developing and newly developing countries due to higher rates of utilities, internet and phone service, bank loan rates, and so on. Among the factors that contribute to the final cost of the product are exporting and shipping costs and import duties (discussed below). While intangible factors, such as bureaucratic efficiency or cultural values, are not included in costing sheets, if the product is late, of poor quality, or manufactured with violations of human rights, ultimately, it might be too costly for the company to save pennies on lower labor cost.

Factors Related to Geographic Location

As introduced in Figure 7.1, factors related to geographic location of a potential site for sourcing apparel assembly include shipping cost and time, cultural values, import duties, and risk of natural disasters. These characteristics primarily depend on where countries are located around the world. Shipping cost and time are related to the distance and/or difficulty of travel between the production sites in exporting country and distribution center in importing country. Import duties, set by the government of the importing country based on the imported type of product and its fiber content, are subject to trade agreement (or lack thereof) between the exporting and importing countries. Cultural values are largely shaped by the region of where the country of interest is located (e.g., African cultures or European cultures) with further regional differences (e.g., Northern vs. Sub-Saharan Africa, US North vs. US South). Cultural values are important to consider because they influence things like frequency and timing of religious holidays, reliability of attendance at work, communication style and pattern, and so on. The same is true for natural disasters—different regions experience different climatic or weather-related catastrophes with varied frequencies.

To illustrate the discussion of these factors, we will use the same twenty-two countries that were used in the above discussion of the sourcing factors related to level of economic development. The countries in Tables 7.1 through 7.5 were organized in three groups by level of economic development: developed, developing, and newly developing. In the sections below, the same countries are grouped by the world's regions: Americas, Europe, Asia, Middle East, and Africa.

Shipping Time and Cost

When choosing a country to manufacture apparel lines, sourcing specialists need to consider the following questions:

- How far is the country from the market where apparel will be shipped and sold to consumer?
- How long will it take to get products from the factory to their destination?
- What are the shipping costs from the production site to the destination?
- Who is paying the expenses, including exporting apparel from the country of manufacturing, shipping to the country of destination, import duties, and custom clearance?

Shipping Time

Shipping time depends on the distance and the mode of transport between the vendor's factory and the customer's distribution center (DC). There are some online tools available to calculate shipping distance and time between two points, initial place and final destination, for most countries in the world. For example, searates.com can help you calculate distance and time in transit by air, land, sea, or rail from any place in the world to any place in the world, with the exception of some countries (SeaRates, n.d.).

Considering the ports of countries selected from those discussed earlier in the chapter, let's assume we are shipping apparel to the United States and compare distance and shipping times. Table 7.6 presents distance in kilometers and transit time in days

TABLE 7.6

DISTANCE, TRANSIT TIME, AND SHIPPING RATES TO LOS ANGELES, US, FROM SELECTED PORTS OF ORIGIN IN DIFFERENT REGIONS OF THE WORLD

Country and Port of Origin	Distance, km [1]	Transit Time, Days[1]	Shipping Rates, US$[2]
Americas			
Mexico, Mazatlan	1,926	3	555–613
Guatemala, Puerto Quetzal	3,873	7	562–621
Haiti, Cap Haitien	7,063	12	2,211–2,443
Brazil, Rio de Janeiro	13,456	22	1,609–1,778
Europe			
France, Rouen	14,217	23	1,846–2,040
United Kingdom, London	14,347	23	1,757–1,942
Germany, Hamburg	14,895	24	1,742–1,926
Italy, Genoa	15,159	25	2,760–3,051
Asia			
Japan, Tokyo	9,026	15	2,034–2,248
South Korea, Pohang	9,657	16	1,972–2,180
China, Shantou	11,509	19	2,397–2,650
Hong Kong, Hong Kong	11,823	19	2,448–2,485
Vietnam, Hanoi	12,715	21	2,712–2,997
Cambodia, Sihanoukville	13,870	23	3,446–3,809
India, Mumbai	13,870	23	2,675–2,957
Indonesia, Jakarta	14,775	24	2,675–2,956
Bangladesh, Chittagong	17,005	28	2,693–2,976
Pakistan, Karachi	19,586	32	3,029–3,404
Middle East			
Jordan, Aqaba	17,858	29	3,295–3,642
Africa*			
Cameroon, Douala	15,578	25	4,905–5,422
Kenya, Mombasa	21,603	35	4,893–5,414

*Note: Data for the two African countries included in Tables 7.1–7.5, Ethiopia and Zimbabwe, were not available. Instead, Cameroon, located in West Africa, and Kenya, located in East Africa, were used as an example of shipping transit times from the African continent to the United States.

[1]Source: SeaRates.com, retrieved January 31, 2015, from http://www.searates.com/reference/portdistance/

[2]Source: World Freight Rates.com, retrieved January 31, 2015, from http://worldfreightrates.com/freight

from twenty-one countries to the Los Angeles terminal in the United States. Multiple ports are available in most of the twenty-one countries; distance and transit time vary slightly depending on the exact location of the origin port. Note that the shipping times in Table 7.6 do not include:

- loading,
- time for preparing paperwork and completing procedures required for exporting,

- transferring shipments to a warehouse for consolidation with other orders before shipping
- unloading, and
- customs clearance.

The distance and transit times in Table 7.6 are calculated from a port of loading to a port of discharge and therefore reflect travel across water only. If the factory in the exporting country and the distribution center in the importing country are located inland, some distance from the ports, then additional time will be needed to ship product across land. In landlocked countries, shipping time increases substantially due to additional across-land travels and customs clearance in at least two countries (the exporting one and in the country where freight is loaded on boat). This is especially true for land-locked African countries with inadequate infrastructure support.

Obviously, when products are shipped to the United States, it will take longer for them to arrive from Asian countries than Central America. Consider the following shipping times:

- East Asia (Japan, South Korea, Hong Kong, and China) to Los Angeles takes just a little over two weeks (15–19 days).
- Europe to Los Angeles is 23–25 days, while it takes only 10–11 days to New York City.
- Mexico and Central America to Los Angeles takes about 3–7 days.

Depending on the exporting country, the time to export a container—the amount of days needed to file and get approved all necessary exporting paperwork in a country—differs significantly and can take between only 6 days in Hong Kong and 53 days in Zimbabwe (Table 7.7). For example, the number of days to export products from Bangladesh is 29. Time in transit from Bangladeshi Port Chittagong to Los Angeles is an additional 28 days, adding up to 57 days total. As discussed above, it is also critical to take into consideration the infrastructure of the country where the production is to take place, for if roads are bad and the factory is some distance from the port, additional delays will ensue, and it should be abundantly clear by now that time is money in this business.

Shipping Cost

It is intuitive that costs for transportation of products are closely related to the shipping distance and time in transit. The transportation costs must be factored into the overall product costs beyond labor and materials to determine which location and contractor will provide the sourcing firm with the best overall cost advantage. World Freight Rates (www.worldfreightrates.com/freight) is an excellent tool for calculating freight estimates for different shipping methods (ocean, rail, truck, and air), commodities, shipment values, load and container types, and additional charges, such as insurance and hazardous goods.

To compare ocean freight rates from different countries, let's assume we are still shipping apparel to the United States, and Los Angeles is the port of destination. Most international shipping is now done in 20- or 40-foot shipping containers. Filling the container, known as **full container load (FCL),** is the most cost-effective overall, as per-unit shipping costs are lower when the container is full. FCL commands lower

TABLE 7.7

NUMBER OF DOCUMENTS, DAYS, AND COST ASSOCIATED WITH EXPORTING GOODS FROM SELECTED COUNTRIES

Countries	Number of Days to Export	Number of Documents to Export	Cost to Export (US$ per Container)
Americas			
Mexico	11	4	1,600
Honduras	12	5	1,450
Brazil	13	6	1,925
Haiti	28	8	1,200
Europe			
United Kingdom	8	4	1,005
Germany	9	4	1,015
France (EU)	10	2	1,335
Italy	19	3	1,195
Asia			
Hong Kong	6	3	590
South Korea	8	3	670
Japan	11	3	915
India	16	7	1,320
Indonesia	17	4	555
Pakistan	20	8	800
Vietnam	21	5	610
China	21	8	620
Cambodia	22	8	795
Bangladesh	29	6	1,325
Middle East			
Jordan	12	5	825
Africa			
Ethiopia	44	8	2,380
Zimbabwe	53	7	4,265

Source: World Bank Group. (2015). "Doing Business Report 2015." Retrieved November 5, 2015, from http://www.doingbusiness.org/data/exploretopics/trading-across-borders

prices than **LCL** (less than container load). A 40-foot container is more expensive than the 20-foot container used in the example. The calculations presented in Table 7.6 are based on the following input data:

- Commodity type: Apparel
- Commodity value, USD: $250,000
- Load type: FCL (full container load)
- Container type: 20 ft
- Accessorial charges: add insurance

Similar to transit time, the least expensive shipping is from Guatemala and Mexico ($500–600 per container). Freight rates for a 20-foot container from European countries to Los Angeles range from $1,700 to $2,000, with the exception of Italy ($2,760–$3,051). Shipping merchandise from Europe to New York City, instead of Los Angeles, not only will be almost twice as fast but about $400 less per container, so figuring out the best route is important to save time and money. Freight from Asian countries in Table 7.6 ranges from $2,000 to $3,800. Shipping merchandise from Africa to Los Angeles is the most expensive: $5,000 and up per container. Unlike European countries, the freight rate from the African countries is only $100 less if the port of destination is changed from Los Angeles to New York City.

Ocean freight does not include other expenses associated with shipping merchandise from overseas. As you know, the importer pays duties on apparel imported from majority of countries, which is discussed below. Additional costs include inland transportation from the factory to the port of origin, loading, unloading, inland transportation from the port of destination and customer's distribution center (DC), custom clearance fees, and exporting fees.

Consider the *cost to export* per container (Table 7.7), which includes the costs of all procedures associated with exporting goods from a country, such as costs of documents, administrative fees for customs clearance and technical support, customs broker fees, terminal handling charges, and inland transportation (World Bank Group, 2015). Asian countries have the lowest cost to export per container ($600–900), with the exception of India and Bangladesh ($1,300). In the European countries the cost to export ranges from $1,000 to $1,300 per container. You would pay between $1,200 and $1,900 in the countries in the Americas presented in Table 7.7. And again, African countries are the most expensive, with cost to export merchandise at $2,400–$4,300 per container.

Shipping costs and costs to export (Tables 7.6 and 7.7) vary significantly, depending on the location of the production facilities and the types of access available. It is a common practice for the vendor to pay for transport to the ship or airplane, which is typically included in the price quote provided by the factory. The customer pays for transportation to the new port, although other arrangements are available. It becomes imperative that the costs of delivering products from the factory to the distribution center are factored into final contract decisions and that the overall costs of goods from diverse locations and contractors are carefully compared.

If a customer runs a relatively small business and is thus involved with relatively small orders that constitute less than container load (LCL), the firm might benefit from the use of a consolidator at the port where the goods are to be loaded. A **consolidator** is a person or firm that combines cargo from a number of shippers going to the same destination into one container for the purpose of reducing shipping rates. A partially filled shipping container costs more per unit to ship than does a full container, hence the need for a consolidator.

Sometimes, garments are shipped by air. The containers for air travel are smaller, and the costs are significantly higher, but it is much faster, so determining which form of transport is best depends on the type of sourcing calendar in use. Not having garments available for sale according to the merchandise plan is very costly for a retailer. Air transport is more likely to be used for fashion items or high-price-point products. Occasionally, air transport is used for basic products, when the vendor is behind schedule and risks losing money for the entire contract if he or she does not get all the completed goods to the sourcing firm by the delivery date on the contract.

Importance of Shipping Time

When choosing a country for apparel assembly, sourcing specialists consider how critical time is in delivering a product to the market, also known as speed-to-market, or quick response. The decision is primarily based on the type of product: basic or fashion apparel. For basic goods, time might not be an issue. In contrast, if your company produces fashion goods, then time to market is essential to offer your consumer the latest fashion trends. In this case, the time needed to export goods and time in transit might be essential.

When building a supply chain and making sourcing decisions, sourcing specialists should choose between two manufacturing philosophies: lean manufacturing or agile manufacturing. **Lean manufacturing** emphasizes efficiency, economy of scale, and reducing costs throughout the entire process, while also improving quality. **Agile manufacturing** focuses on production flexibility and speed, small runs, and quick change-over from one product to another. Based on the two manufacturing philosophies, the concept of the lean vs. agile supply chain was developed.

Lean manufacturing strategies lend themselves to the production of basic products, whereas agile strategies are better suited to fashion products. Refer back to Table 2.1 to review the characteristics of basic and fashion merchandise. Basic products are more functional and have longer retail selling periods and less frequent changes in styling. Fashion goods have much shorter retail selling periods and more frequent changes in styling (Bhatia, 2004). Demand for basic goods is more predictable; demand for fashion goods is more volatile. Assortment forecast error is also much lower for basic goods, and markdowns are much higher for fashion goods, because it is more difficult to predict the exact quantities of styles, sizes, and colors that will be needed. Menswear has a higher proportion of basic styles, and women's wear has a higher proportion of fashion merchandise.

Sourcing Calendars

The overall result of the application of agile and lean manufacturing philosophies, including the associated changes in technology and production methods to apparel manufacturing processes, has been the opportunity for compression of the sourcing calendar. A **sourcing calendar**, as presented in Table 7.8, is based on the merchandising calendar that sets the classifications of merchandise and the retail selling periods and provides a time line related to the sequences of merchandise development. These include design, product development, production, and delivery to the retail sales floor. As with the merchandising calendar, timing of the sourcing calendar is planned backward from the projected retail sales date. Putting the sourcing calendar into a time line is helpful for gaining understanding of the processes necessary as a product line progresses from concept to retail selling floor.

Table 7.8 presents three different time lines; the traditional time line is followed by more currently recognized time lines for two different types of merchandise. The traditional sourcing time line that had been in place for more than three decades took approximately 54 weeks, from start to finish. That time line meant that making decisions about the styles, sizes, and colors to be offered at retail had to be made more than a year before the merchandise arrived at the store. This schedule was accepted as customary, yet it was burdened with considerable redundancies in processes and a somewhat overblown belief that production labor costs were where the time and money issues were centered. That concern motivated the movement of production to offshore locations in a quest for lower cost labor. Unfortunately, many did not consider that getting the finished garments delivered from these far-off locations also heavily impacted the overall time line.

As shown in Table 7.8, today's basic/core merchandise sourcing calendar of about 25 to 35 weeks is considerably shorter, allowing styling and fabric decisions to be made much closer to point of sale to the ultimate consumer, as compared with the traditional model. Basic merchandise is sometimes called staple merchandise. It is stocked continually at retail, refilling similar spaces with the same sizes and colors. Men's white underwear and socks are classic examples. Lean manufacturing is generally applied to the production of more basic apparel products that have long selling periods at retail (26 to 56 weeks or more, with no style or color changes). Innovations in product development and communications technology contributed to the initial shortening of the sourcing time line. These improvements made it possible to shorten the total sourcing time line while still taking advantage of low-cost labor.

Today's fashion goods sourcing calendar provides 16 to 20 weeks, and in some cases even less, from merchandise plan to retail store, and a retail selling period of only 2 to 4 weeks. In the case of domestic production, or near-shoring production, lead time can be even less, down to 2–3 weeks. Problems inherent to the current "fast-fashion" calendar seem to be centered on availability of fabrics and other materials. Where this calendar

TABLE 7.8

COMPARISON OF THE TRADITIONAL SOURCING CALENDAR WITH TODAY'S MODELS, IN TOTAL WEEKS, UNTIL DELIVERY TO RETAIL STORE

	54	50	45	40	35	30	25	20	15	10	0
Traditional											
		Trend & Color									
			Design & Sampling								
						Buy					
								Production			
										Logistics	
											Set Floor
Today's Basics/Core Merchandise											
					Trend & Color						
						Design & Sampling					
							Buy				
									Production		
										Logistics	
											Set Floor
Today's Fashion Goods											
							Trend & Color				
								Design & Sampling			
									Buy		
										Production	
										Logistics	
											Set Floor

Source: Olivier, S. (2008). "The Value of Fast: Speed to Market Through the Glass Pipeline." Retrieved October 25, 2015, from http://archive.wewear.org/UserFiles/File/Presentations/SLC_spring_08/susan_oliver.pdf

has garnered criticism is in the risk of sacrificing quality in materials and garment assembly to achieve rapid fashion change, resulting in fashion that is almost disposable.

Logistics

Logistics is the science of moving products through the manufacturing and distribution system to their final destinations in a timely manner (see Chapter 3). Many transformations in logistics have occurred since handwritten transactions accompanied textiles transported on the Silk Road from China to Europe. Centuries later, typed transactions sent by telegraph and undersea cables in the form of telex communications directed the loading of cartons or barrels of products onto trains, steamships, and trucks.

Today, the logistics process is controlled and monitored by complex computer networks involving inputs from consignees, shippers, carriers, consolidators, and external sources as well as government agencies. To comprehend the complexity of today's logistics information flow, consider the Voluntary Interindustry Commerce Standards Association's VICS Logistics Model. Figure 7.7 provides a model of one phase in the complex logistics process. Keep in mind that any component of the process could be located anywhere in the world.

The technological options regarding logistics seem astonishing by previous standards: containers of garments are packed by machines, moved on conveyor belts controlled by computers, and placed on board trucks destined for distribution points,

Figure 7.7

One page of the VICS Logistics Model, reflecting part of the interlocking decision-making process required to achieve movement of goods from one location to another.

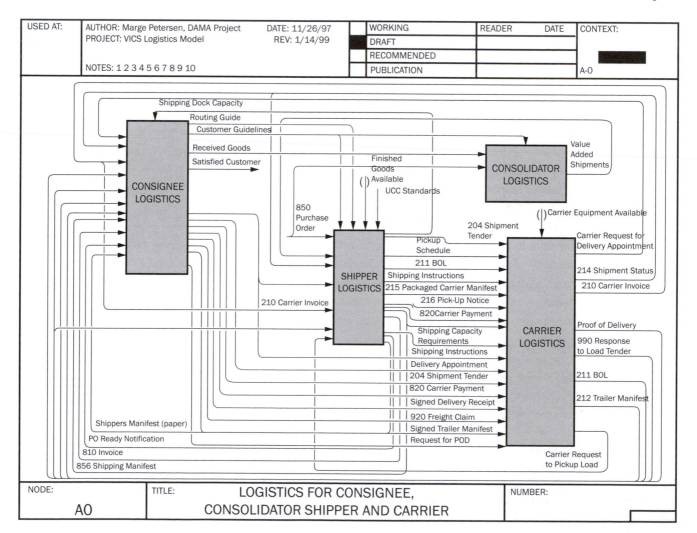

where they are then loaded aboard a ship or plane headed for delivery anywhere in the world. The new system inputs we discussed previously, including the new bar codes and radio frequency identification (RFID) tags, are scanned into a computer network. Containers and their contents can be tracked at each stage of the trip.

Import Tariffs

Another aspect to consider when deciding in what country to assemble apparel is the duty that the importing company will pay on merchandise at US Customs. You know from Chapter 5 that duty is calculated based on tariff rate. In the United States, as well as in other countries, tariff rates vary significantly, depending on the type of garment, material fiber content, and where the garment was manufactured (country of origin). Tariff costs are commonly paid by the buyer.

The tariff rates applied by US Customs are established by application of the Harmonized Tariff Schedule (HTS). The official HTS is published by the United States International Trade Commission (USITC) on January 1 of every year (http://www.usitc.gov/tata/hts/index.htm). To use HTS effectively, you need to know the Harmonized System (HS) code for your product category (http://www.foreign-trade.com/reference/hscode.htm). In both HS and HTS you will be working with Chapter 61 for knitted apparel and Chapter 62 for not-knitted apparel and clothing accessories. Each classification of garments is given a ten-digit HS code.

To find tariff rates (or rates of duty), go to the USITC website (http://usitc.gov), follow the Tariff Search Tool link on the left, and then locate either Chapter 61 or 62. For example, if you specialize in and import simple T-shirts, the garment falls under the HS category of 6109 "T-shirts, singlets, tank tops and similar garments, knitted or crocheted" in the HTS. For importing cotton T-shirts, HS code 61091000, the tariff rate of 16.5 percent applies for most countries of the world, with the exception of those that have special trade agreements with the United States, such as NAFTA, CAFTA, and free trade agreements (FTA) with Australia, Bahrain, Chile, Colombia, Israel, Jordan, Morocco, Oman, Panama, Peru, and Singapore (United States International Trade Commission, 2015). South Korea has a special tariff rate of 9.9 percent under the KORUS FTA (Korea–US). If you want the same cotton T-shirts produced in North Korea or Cuba for the US market, the tariff rate is 90 percent. This is only for cotton T-shirts. For man-made fiber T-shirts (HS code 61099010), the tariff rate, or rate of duty, is 32 percent. Note that the list of countries covered under FTAs with the United States are still free of duty. The tariff rate for long-sleeve T-shirts of wool (HS code 61099015) is only 5.6 percent. And for T-shirts containing 70 percent or more by weight of silk or silk waste, the rate of duty is even less: 2.6 percent.

When developing a product and considering fabric choices, checking tariff rates is an important costing step. The final approval of entry of the products into the country and the amount of duty ultimately assessed is at the discretion of the customs officer at the port of entry. The duty levied by customs must be paid before the importer can take possession of the goods, so it is critical to know what the rate on the products will be prior to their arrival at port.

Cultural Values and Norms

Culture is a very complex phenomenon. Many researchers have attempted to explain how culture influences people's attitudes, decisions, and behaviors. Books have been written on the topic from many different perspectives. In this section of the text, we can only outline what cultural aspects sourcing specialists have to consider and research before traveling to a foreign country and deciding whether it might be a suitable site for apparel production. Some of the questions to consider in relation to culture include:

- What are the general attitudes toward the customer's country and people?
- What is the perception of time and importance of deadlines in this country?
- How do communication patterns work?
- What are the absolute "dos" and "don'ts"?

It is essential to look into historical and contemporary relationships between the customer's country and the vendor's country. Has there been any long-standing conflict between the two countries and is there any residual? Assuming that the customer is a US-based company, is there any anti-US movement or attitudes in the country? It might be challenging to do business in an overall unwelcoming environment.

Perception of use of time is critical because it affects vendor and customer interaction and communication patterns as well as production schedule. In many regions of the world the concept of time is approached in a much less rigid way than in the United States, Canada, or some European countries (Westcott, 2007). For example, being late one hour for a meeting in some countries is a norm. Taking time to respond to an urgent inquiry by sending a quick email, or shipping orders a week later is not seen as a problem but a way of life. If you are not flexible enough to deal with such realities, contemplating more punctual cultures for your sourcing needs might be a better option.

An expert in human perception of time, Stefan Klein (2007) argues that Protestant countries are the strictest on time. Many Asian countries, such as Japan, China, Korea, are "on time" cultures because of the "saving face" (avoiding embarrassment, preserving dignity) concept. In contrast, other countries are known as *mañana* cultures: Latin America, India, Philippines, some Mediterranean countries, and others (Birnbaum, 2005; Westcott, 2007). Direct translation of *mañana* from Spanish is "tomorrow," but it usually means sometime later, at some future, unspecified time, which in reality means nothing is done on time. Similarly, there is a notion of "African" time, which means "Maybe later. Or maybe not" (Rivoli, 2009).

To effectively interact and collaborate with suppliers and vendors in different cultures, it is beneficial not only to know basic etiquette and norms, but also to understand the reasons behind the differences in thinking, decision making, and communication. For instance, pseudo-harmonism, or pretending that harmony exists in a situation when it does not, is a common conflict-avoiding strategy in many Asian cultures. In negotiations, for example, it might manifest when a vendor says "yes" to a tight schedule in order to "save face," when in reality she or he knows that it is not possible to meet the deadline. While there are some similarities between cultures based on geographic location—Asian cultures, European cultures, Middle Eastern, or Central American cultures—each country in the same region has its own cultural values, beliefs, traditions, and norms. Assumptions, generalizations, and ignorance might prove to be embarrassing and costly.

There are many excellent resources available. Denslow's (2005) *World Wise: What to Know Before You Go* focuses on business culture in countries around the world. A fascinating YouTube video, "West and East, Cultural Differences" (Bueno, 2012), features cultural experiments and research studies that delve into the specifics of Asian vs. Western thinking and help explain, for example, why the importance of adhering to a contract is perceived differently in the two cultures.

Natural Disasters Risk

Natural disasters are extreme climate-related events and include earthquakes, hurricanes, flooding, cyclones, drought, wildfires, landslides, and so on. Besides posing a safety risk to people, natural disasters can be very disruptive for business and trade. Neither vendor nor customer has any control over natural disasters that might happen in a country. In that sense, it is the same as with all other countries' characteristics discussed in this chapter—it would be very difficult, if not impossible, to change cultural norms, corrupt government, or primitive infrastructure, at least not overnight.

While nothing can be done about natural disasters, some regions and countries are more prone to them than others. Southeast Asia, Central America, the Pacific islands, parts of West Africa and Southeastern Europe, and the countries along South America's Pacific Coast are more prone to natural disasters (Figure 7.8). The World Risk Report (Alliance Development Works (2013) provides an exposure index for world countries (Table 7.9). The index measures the level of risk to population, buildings, infrastructure components, and environmental areas in a country from one or more natural disasters (higher percent indicates higher risk). According to the report, the highest risk countries were Vanuatu (67 percent chance of natural disasters), Tonga (55 percent), and Philippines (53 percent). In addition to the exposure index, the World Risk Report provides information on how well countries are prepared to deal with the disasters.

Exposure
Exposure of the population to the natural hazards earthquakes, storms, floods, droughts, and sea level rise.

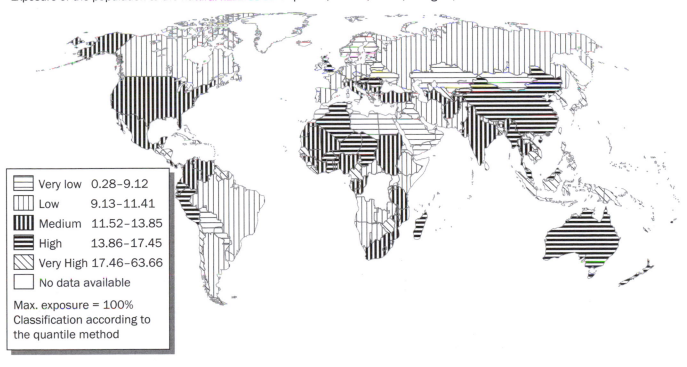

Very low	0.28–9.12
Low	9.13–11.41
Medium	11.52–13.85
High	13.86–17.45
Very High	17.46–63.66
No data available	

Max. exposure = 100%
Classification according to the quantile method

Figure 7.8
United Nations University and Institute of Environmental and Human Security developed a map that classifies world countries by five levels of exposure to natural hazards.

TABLE 7.9

RISK OF EXPOSURE TO NATURAL HAZARDS

Region and Country	Exposure Risk, Percent
Americas	
United States	12.25
Mexico	13.84
Honduras	20.01
Haiti	16.26
Brazil	9.53
Europe	
France	9.25
United Kingdom	11.60
Germany	11.41
Italy	13.85
Asia	
Japan	45.91
South Korea	14.89
China	14.43
Hong Kong	N/A
Vietnam	25.35
Cambodia	27.65
India	11.94
Indonesia	19.36
Bangladesh	31.70
Pakistan	11.36
Middle East	
Jordan	10.53
Africa	
Ethiopia	11.12
Zimbabwe	14.96

Source: Alliance Development Works. (2013). "World Risk Report 2013." Retrieved November 15, 2015, from http://worldriskreport.entwicklung-hilft.de/uploads/media/WorldRiskReport_2013_online_01.pdf

TRENDS IN GLOBAL SOURCING: EFFECTS ON SELECTING COUNTRIES FOR APPAREL ASSEMBLY

Regionalization

There is some evidence of regionalization resulting from the worldwide recession, increases in transportation costs, and consumer concerns with environmental and social issues stemming from manufacturing products in sites located far away from the consumption market. Some experts are predicting further growth in regional trade and sourcing in which smaller, more frequent shipments could be available, with lower shipping costs and decreased shipping time. Regional preferential trade agreements promote regional trade by providing tariff free access of goods to domestic markets and reducing nontariff trade barriers. Examples of such free trade agreements are NAFTA and CAFTA. Similar trade agreements are in place in other regions of the world.

Reshoring

Since the early 2000s, cases of returning apparel production to the United States (reshoring) began making the news stories. Still more of an exception than the norm, some US apparel companies are beginning to look for opportunities to manufacture products domestically. The trend is driven by several factors. First, companies look for opportunities to increase response to changing consumer preferences and fashion trends by reducing the time from designing a product to having it in the stores. Second, companies want more control over when and how apparel is being produced to minimize frustrations caused by late shipments, unreliable, or unethical foreign suppliers. Third, labor cost in China, the world's leading apparel supplier, has been rising. Fourth, the American public has been growing uneasy about dependence on foreign manufacturing.

Traditionally, primarily high-end companies, like designer Nanette Lepore, whose lines of dresses and tops are sold at Saks Fifth Avenue and Bloomingdale's, were able to afford making garments in factories located in New York City's Garment District. Recently, even lower-end retailers have started looking for "Made in USA" goods. For example, in 2013 Walmart started a campaign to increase American-made goods in its stores by $50 billion in 10 years. While apparel will not be a large portion, Walmart already sells domestically produced towels at the premium price of $9.47 (overseas made towels cost $1.97), socks, and other selected clothing and accessories (Clifford, 2013).

With increasing advertisement claims for products manufactured in the United States, from cars to electronics and appliances, the Federal Trade Commission (n.d.) has been tightening regulations on what goods can carry the "Made in the USA" label. To prevent false and misleading claims that a product is of US origin, "all or virtually all" of the product must be assembled and sourced domestically. Still, despite the manufacturers' hopes and many polls indicating that US consumers express support for American products, the majority is not willing to pay premium prices for clothes. Read Case 7.2 and think about US-based apparel manufacturing. Do you know any other examples of apparel made in the USA?

WHAT FACTORS ARE THE MOST CRITICAL WHEN SELECTING LOCATIONS FOR APPAREL SOURCING?

How can we make sense of all of the countries' characteristics reviewed in this chapter? Which characteristics are more important? What determines which country is the best choice?

Ironically, with 180+ countries in the world capable of apparel assembly, there is no "perfect" country. If a country is developed enough and has advanced infrastructure, stable government, and efficient bureaucracy, it also has high labor cost. If the labor cost is affordable

THE REEMERGENCE OF US APPAREL MANUFACTURING?

With 250 associates, Boathouse Sports designs and manufactures performance apparel in Philadelphia, PA. Team sports gear for rowing, ice hockey, lacrosse, rugby, track, and more is "built with pride in the USA" (Figure Case 7.2a). The company employs several strategies that contribute to its success: products are customized to specific sports and teams, are high quality and high performance, and are produced in small and flexible production runs that allow fast speed-to-market. According to Boathouse founder and owner John Strotbeck, it takes only 3.5 days from the time a customer orders until the finished apparel product is packed in boxes and on the way to the client. Strotbeck notes, "To manufacture apparel in the US and make a profit, you need a niche, a unique audience and a specific skill set or core competency. Ours is mass customization of athletic wear, short runs, and speed. We offer mass customization at its best" (Wang, 2015, para 4).

Another US-based manufacturing company, Keff NYC, in 2012 began to design and produce knit apparel in the heart of New York City's Garment District. The two veteran apparel executives and coowners, Eric Schiffer and Leonard Keff, believe that the company can compete with Chinese lower labor cost products because state-of-the-art Stoll's robotic, computerized machines do not require much manual labor (Friedman, 2012a). In addition, they do not pay for ocean freight and import duties because apparel is produced domestically. Similar to Boathouse, Keff NYC's competitive advantages are high-quality products and quick turnaround for higher-end retailers, like Anthropologie or Ralph Lauren, that cater to fashion-conscious consumers.

Since 2002, All American Clothing Co. has supported American jobs, families, and communities by "producing high-quality clothing in the USA at an affordable price" (n.d., para 1). The company's website features a completely transparent and environmentally friendly supply chain consisting of six to seven American companies that contributed to producing the "traceable handcrafted tee" that consumers can buy for $19.99 (Figure Case 7.2b).

The pattern repeats across other companies that work on bringing back American-made apparel—high-quality products, customized craftsmanship, durability, performance, and speed-to-market. However, this formula is not a guarantee for success. For example, a 112-year-old apparel manufacturer, Fessler USA from Pennsylvania, closed down in 2012 (Friedman, 2012b). Fessler's key strategies were quick replenishment and small orders of quality products for companies like Lucky Brand, Urban Outfitters, Nordstrom, and Michael Stars.

The average price of a garment sold in the US market is between $14 and $19, depending on source (Clifford, 2013; Statista, n.d.). Apparel retail prices are pushed down by mass market retailers, such as Walmart and Target, as well as lower-end specialty retailers, like H&M and Old Navy. According to a New York Times poll, two-thirds of American consumers check "Made in" labels to see where the product was manufactured and almost half are willing to pay 10 to 40 percent more for US-made apparel (Clifford, 2013). Yet, not many Americans are willing to pay what it costs to make apparel in the USA, and when consumers make actual purchase decisions, the majority go for lower-cost garments of the same quality produced overseas.

Figure Case 7.2a
An image from the Boathouse Sports website featuring the company's high-performance gear manufactured in the United States for men, women, and youth (http://www.boathouse.com/).

All American Clothing Co. (n.d.). "Traceable Tees." Retrieved February 17, 2015, from http://www.allamericanclothing.com/ABUS.html

Boathouse Sports. (n.d.). "About." Retrieved February 10, 2015, from http://www.boathouse.com/

Clifford, S. (November 30, 2013). "That 'Made in USA.' premium." New York Times. Retrieved January 30, 2015, from http://www.nytimes.com/2013/12/01/business/that-made-in-usa-premium.html?pagewanted=1&_r=0&src=recg

Clifford, S. (November 30, 2013). "That 'Made in USA' Premium." New York Times. Retrieved October 25, 2015, from http://www.nytimes.com/2013/12/01/business/that-made-in-usa-premium.html?pagewanted=1&_r=0&src=recg

Friedman, A. (2012a). "Fessler USA, Made in America Proponent, Closing Down." Women's Wear Daily. Retrieved February 17, 2015, from http://www.wwd.com.proxy.lib.iastate.edu/markets-news/textiles/fessler-usa-made-in-america-proponent-closing-down-6470835

Friedman, A. (2012b). "Keff NYC Up and Running." Women's Wear Daily. Retrieved February 17, 2015, from http://www.wwd.com.proxy.lib.iastate.edu/markets-news/textiles/keff-nyc-up-and-running-6557500

Statista. (n.d.). "Facts on the Apparel Market in the US." Retrieved February 17, 2015, from http://www.statista.com/topics/965/apparel-market-in-the-us/

Wang, J. (January 13, 2015). "Small Runs, Big Gains: Reshoring US Apparel Manufacturing." Apparel. http://apparel.edgl.com/news/small-runs,-big-gains-reshoring-u-s-apparel-manufacturing97649?referaltype=newsletter

1. If an apparel product suits a US customer's needs and wants, why does it matter whether it is made in the United States or elsewhere?

2. To US consumers, what could be the greatest advantages and disadvantages of producing customized apparel in the United States? What about consumers in the rest of the world that would like to acquire the products?

Figure Case 7.2b

All American Clothing website featuring traceable T-shirts. Consumers can follow the link to track T-shirts' journeys and see what US businesses and communities have contributed and benefited in the process (http://www.allamericanclothing.com/traceabletees.html).

for the product price point, then the country's location might be too far from the destination market, or the overall environment might not be conducive to doing business there.

Further, some characteristics are relative rather than absolute. For example, Northern Africa is an attractive apparel assembly site for European companies because of the proximity to the market. However, the region is less attractive for US companies for the same reason. While some country characteristics can be easily included in the product cost calculation spreadsheet (e.g., shipping cost or import duty), most of them are not (human rights, culture, infrastructure, etc.). Yet, they must be carefully considered when making sourcing decisions because the ultimate cost might be too high (for example, when the product is not delivered on time for the selling season due to corrupt bureaucracy, or the reputation of the company and brand image are damaged because of the vendor's violation of human rights).

In the end, the type of product will determine what country characteristic(s) carries more weight. For a fashion-forward company that competes on delivering consumers the latest styles and colors, speed-to-market is essential. In this case, when selecting the location for sourcing apparel assembly, cultural values (in the sense of perception of time and treating deadlines), shipping time, and time required to export the product from the country of manufacturing will have more weight than other factors. For an upper-end market company that primarily competes on delivering timeless, highest quality garments, education level and overall development of the apparel industry will be important, but not labor cost. For a company that competes on delivering basic products at affordable prices, labor cost and other costs associated with import duties, shipping and exporting costs, and so on, will be more important than factors determining speed-to-market.

Informed decisions regarding whether to develop and produce materials and garments in-house, purchase finished garments, or contract a vendor to develop and/or produce the garments cannot be made without a basic understanding of what each of these sourcing avenues entails, including

- identifying all the specific product development tasks that must be accomplished and who is to do them
- determining how to evaluate and contract vendors of materials, product development services, and production, including evaluating their quality and output capabilities
- deciding who will be responsible for specific sourcing tasks, including vendor compliance, logistics, and customs clearance
- assessing and comparing the factors that impact the final costs of sourcing option decisions

It is important to remember that even though countries' indices and rankings give an idea what the country in question is like in comparison with other countries in the region or the world, no indices are perfect nor 100 percent reflect the reality one would face in a country when visiting it or doing business there. In addition, the world changes constantly, making it necessary to supplement indices and rankings with the latest news and updates.

Summary

This chapter focuses on evaluating potential locations for sourcing apparel assembly. With almost all countries in the world having capabilities for apparel manufacturing and with a myriad of factors that must be considered when deciding where to have your apparel line produced, the evaluation and selection process can be overwhelming. To systematically approach this complex process, a framework that classifies all factors into groups was introduced. The framework (Figure 7.1) organizes all countries' characteristics relevant to sourcing apparel assembly into: (1) characteristics based on level of country development, and (2) characteristics based on geographic location.

Characteristics by level of development include:

- Overall economic, social, and political stability and security
- Infrastructure
- Level of education
- Human rights issues
- Labor cost

These characteristics are explained and illustrated using various indicators from multiple world trade and economic organizations (Tables 7.1–7.5). The data are analyzed for twenty-two selected countries that are grouped into developed, developing, and newly developing categories.

Characteristics by geographic location include:

- Shipping cost and time
- Cultural values and norms
- Import duties
- Natural disasters

The same twenty-two countries are used to illustrate application of these characteristics to the process of evaluating countries for sourcing apparel production (Tables 7.6–7.9). The countries are grouped by four major regions—Americas, Asia, Europe, and Middle East and Africa—laying a foundation for Chapters 9 through 12, where the same regions will be examined in depth in relation to textile and apparel production and trade.

Sourcing involves much more than simply finding the country that has the lowest labor costs. Much depends on what types of merchandise are needed as well as on whether the environment in the country is favorable to conducting business. Determining the overall cost of an apparel garment can be far more complex in global sourcing environments than when it is produced domestically.

Learning Activities

1. Examine Figure 7.1, which lists country characteristics important to consider for sourcing apparel assembly. Which characteristics do you believe are the most critical for making sourcing decisions, and why?

2. In this chapter, eleven country characteristics relevant to sourcing apparel production are presented and examined (Figure 7.1). Can you think of other factors that might affect selection of country for sourcing apparel production?

3. Free trade agreements between countries eliminate import tariffs, thus reducing final product cost. Compile a list of countries that currently have free trade agreements with the United States.

4. Look up the most recent "Doing Business" report (released annually) to determine five countries with the lowest and five countries with the highest ranks in terms of "ease of doing business." Classify each of the ten countries according to its level of development (refer to Chapter 1) as a developed, developing, or newly developing economy. Identify in which of the four regions (Americas, Asia, Europe, or Middle East and Africa) each country is located. Fill all the information in the table below. Analyze and explain the relationships between the ease of doing business rank and (a) level of development and (b) geographic region.

Countries	Level of Development (Developed, Developing, or Newly Developing)	Geographic Region (Europe, Asia, Americas, Middle East, and Africa)
Five highest "ease of doing business" ranks		
1.		
2.		
3.		
4.		
5.		
Five lowest "ease of doing business" ranks		
1.		
2.		
3.		
4.		
5.		

5. Examine the countries' characteristics in Tables 7.1–7.9. In groups of three to four people, discuss and select the top three countries for apparel assembly of the following apparel products:

- High-end basic goods
- High-end fashion goods
- Low-end basic goods
- Low-end fashion goods

Complete the table and justify your sourcing decisions. Be prepared to share your decisions with the class.

Type of Product	Two Examples of Companies (Company or Brand Name)	Top Three Countries	Countries' Characteristics Critical for the Decision
High-end basic goods			
Low-end basic goods			
High-end fashion goods			
Low-end fashion goods			

References

Alliance Development Works. (2013). "World Risk Report 2013." Retrieved November 15, 2015, from http://worldriskreport.entwicklung-hilft.de/uploads/media/WorldRiskReport_2013_online_01.pdf

Alliance Development Works. (2013). "World Risk Report 2013." Retrieved November 15, 2015, from http://worldriskreport.entwicklung-hilft.de/uploads/media/WorldRiskReport_2013_online_01.pdf

Bhatia, S. (January 1, 2004). "'Lean' vs. 'Agile' Considerations Shape Supply Chain Strategies." *Apparel*. Retrieved November 5, 2015, from http://apparel.edgl.com/news/-Lean-vs-Agile-Considerations-Shape-Supply-Chain-Strategies-65861

Birnbaum, D. (2005). *Birnbaum's Global Guide to Winning the Great Garment War*. New York, NY: The Fashiondex.

Bueno, C. (2012). *West and East, Cultural Differences*. Retrieved January 30, 2015, from https://www.youtube.com/watch?v=ZoDtoB9Abck

Clifford, S. (November 30, 2013). "That 'Made in USA' Premium." *New York Times*. Retrieved January 30, 2015, from http://www.nytimes.com/2013/12/01/business/that-made-in-usa-premium.html?pagewanted=1&_r=0&src=recg

Denslow, L. (2005). *World Wise: What to Know Before You Go*. New York, NY: Fairchild.

Dickerson, K. (1999). *Textiles and Apparel in the Global Economy*. Upper Saddle River, NJ: Pearson Education.

Federal Trade Commission. (n.d.). "Complying with the Made in USA Standard." Retrieved February 2, 2015, from http://www.ftc.gov/tips-advice/business-center/guidance/complying-made-usa-standard

IHRRI. (2015). "International Human Rights Rank Indicator by Country." Retrieved January 13, 2015, from http://ihrri.com/country.php

International Labour Organization. (2010). "Accelerating Action Against Child Labour." International Labour Conference, 99th Session, Geneva.

Klein, S. (2007). *The Secret Pulse of Time: Making Sense of Life's Scarcest Commodity*. Cambridge, MA: Da Capo Press.

Office of Textiles and Apparel. (2014). "US Imports of Textiles and Apparel, by Country." Retrieved February 15, 2015, from http://otexa.trade.gov/scripts/tqads2.exe/ctrypage

Rivoli, P. (2009). *The Travels of a T-shirt in the Global Economy*. Hoboken, NJ: Wiley.

SeaRates. (n.d.). "Distances and Times." Retrieved January 31, 2015, from http://www.searates.com/reference/portdistance/

United Nations. (2013). "Development Programme: Human Development Index and Its Components." Retrieved January 23, 2015, from http://hdr.undp.org/en/content/table-1-human-development-index-and-its-components

United Nations. (n.d.). "Child Labour: Vital Statistics." Retrieved January 22, 2015, from http://www.un.org/en/globalissues/briefingpapers/childlabour/vitalstats.shtml

United States International Trade Commission. (2015). "Harmonized Tariff Schedule of the United States 2015." Retrieved February 1, 2015, from http://hts.usitc.gov/

Westcott, K. (2007). "Bidding Adios to 'Manana.'" BBC News. Retrieved January 30, 2015, from http://news.bbc.co.uk/2/hi/6405379.stm

World Bank. (n.d.). "Helping Countries Combat Corruption: The Role of the World Bank." Retrieved January 28, 2015, from http://www1.worldbank.org/publicsector/anticorrupt/corruptn/cor02.htm

World Bank Group. (2015). "Doing Business Report 2015." Retrieved January 22, 2015, from http://www.doingbusiness.org/rankings#

World Economic Forum. (2014). "The Global Competitiveness Report 2014–2015." Retrieved January 26, 2015, from http://reports.weforum.org/global-competitiveness-report-2014-2015/rankings/

World Economic Forum. (2015). "Global Risks 2015 Report." Retrieved January 26, 2015, from http://www3.weforum.org/docs/WEF_Global_Risks_2015_Report.pdf

WRAP. (2015). "Certification Program: The Certification Process." Retrieved January 22, 2015, from http://www.wrapcompliance.org/certification

CHAPTER 8

SELECTING VENDORS FOR GLOBAL SOURCING

FUN FACT

Eighty billion garments are produced worldwide in a year, the equivalent of more than eleven garments for every person on the planet. (Greenpeace International, 2012)

OBJECTIVES

- Discuss types of companies engaged in sourcing apparel production and importing products.
- Evaluate the advantages and disadvantages of contracting with different types of factories for apparel production.
- Identify the criteria for selecting and evaluating vendors to provide appropriate apparel production capacity and related services for desired products.
- Examine methods for sourcing textile and apparel products, production, and related services.

APPAREL IMPORTERS

There are three major types of companies that are involved in importing apparel: private brand retailer, **brand manager**, and apparel intermediary. While there are significant differences between the three groups, the distinctions are becoming blurred as companies expand their core businesses, form alliances, and cross the borders of traditional business categories and functions.

Private Brand Retailer

Many retailers have expanded their merchandising activities to include development of their own products. Traditionally, a retailer would seek out and purchase finished apparel products from a manufacturer or through a wholesale market. Today, many retailers do part or all of their own product development and source apparel production to put their exclusive private labels, or brands, on these products. **Private brand** reflects the ownership of an exclusive label by a retailer. This strategy allows retailers to reduce merchandise costs by bypassing the manufacturer or brand manager and sourcing directly with a production contractor for finished apparel products.

cost, insurance, freight (CIF) reflects the cost of goods as well as shipping and insurance to the requested port

export processing zone (EPZ) tariff-free trade zone that is set up by governments in developing countries to promote export through simplified import and export procedures

first quality or **"firsts"** product that meets materials, design, and production, appearance, and fit standards

first sample prototype of a product made for approval of the desired design features and garment fit

free on board (FOB) reflects the cost of goods and the cost of loading them on board a vessel at the foreign port of export

intermediary a company that has expertise in design, product development, acquisition of materials, logistics, and importing as well as an established network of apparel factories they contract with

joint venture shared ownership of a business or facility by two or more firms

LDP (landed duty paid) covers the costs of goods, insurance, freight, and import duty in the destination country

letter of credit a guarantee to the seller that the buyer has the funds to complete the purchase and that they are reserved for the seller

manufacturing control a process in which expected performance is compared with actual performance

package factory in addition to apparel assembly to customer specifications, the factory can source and finance all materials and deliver goods on board; they do not offer any product development services

preproduction stage of apparel manufacturing that involves all product development activities performed before the garment is approved for production; includes design, patternmaking, grading, making first and production samples, and development of technical specifications for materials and production processes

private brand a brand owned and marketed exclusively by a brand manager or retailer

product life cycle management (PLM) the process of managing a product's life cycle from inception, design, development of related materials, manufacturing, delivery, distribution, marketing, sale, and in some cases, service and disposal

production sample garments made at the factory where the order will be mass produced to check for quality and any potential production issues; typically produced in all ordered sizes

pro forma invoice an estimate cost of goods or services sent by vendor

to customer, no a request for payment; includes description of products such as quantity, value, weight, transportation charges, etc. that can be used for customs purposes

quality assurance a commitment to product quality that utilizes the concept of error prevention as integral to the entire product development process

seconds garments that are not first quality when they come off the production line, also known as irregulars because they do not meet materials, design, production, appearance, or fit standards

sourcing agent individual or firm that provides services to procure and deliver products

specifications detailed graphic and written descriptions of styling, materials, dimensions, production procedures, and finishing instructions for a garment

standards basic characteristics used to determine acceptability of products and services

trade fair massive, usually regular trade event where producers display products and services to wholesalers and retailers

vendor compliance performance standards or rules established by the customer related to things like working conditions, wages, and age of workers that a vendor must follow in order to do business with that customer

Most US and European retailers, whether a department store, specialty store chain, or mass merchant, have created private brands. The department store Macy's describes itself as "a retail industry leader in developing private brand merchandise that differentiates the assortments in our stores and delivers exceptional value to the customer" (Macy's Inc., n.d., para 1). In 2015, the company had seventeen private brands matched to customer lifestyles, including Alfani, for "today's career-minded customer"; American Rag, for the "young, fashion-forward" customer; Epic Threads, for "tweens and kids who want cool, original clothing that expresses their personality"; and First Impressions, "classic line for newborns, infants and toddlers" (Macy's Inc., n.d.).

Gap Inc. is an example of a specialty retailer that designs, sources, imports, and sells four private brands (Gap, Banana Republic, Old Navy, and Athleta) "in more than 90 countries worldwide through about 3,300 company-operated stores, almost 400 franchise stores, and e-commerce sites" (Gap Inc., n.d.). One example of a mass merchant with private brands is Walmart. The company's merchandise mix includes private apparel brands George and Faded Glory, which are exclusive to Walmart stores.

Brand Manager

Traditionally, apparel manufacturers design, produce, and distribute products under their own brands. Today, especially in the United States, the majority of traditional manufacturers outsource production to offshore vendors. This may be for the simple reason that the products can be manufactured more easily, or that materials are more readily available, or that production costs are less when the manufacturing is completed offshore. Some manufacturers own apparel factories overseas, while others formed joint ventures with vendors in foreign countries; still others contract with factories directly or through sourcing agents to produce apparel under their own brands.

One example of this sourcing practice is Levi Strauss & Co., headquartered in San Francisco, California. For more than a century Levi's jeans were manufactured in the United States. Then production was gradually moved into Mexico. Today, all of the company's domestic production facilities have been closed, and most Levi's jeans are now produced outside both the United States and Mexico and imported into the Americas from other locations. Even though the company no longer owns any factories, it designs and develops products and is engaged in continuing innovations of materials, construction, and design of its legendary denim. Levi's are sold in many countries around the world. Its trademark is registered in more than eighty countries.

Other firms that began as manufacturers but currently outsource most of their products still own some manufacturing facilities. VF Corporation, the owner of JanSport, Lee, Nautica, The North Face, Wrangler, 7 for All Mankind, SmartWool, Timberland, and many other brands, is one such firm. The company has $11 billion in annual revenues, employs 57,000 associates around the world, and sells its products in 150+ countries through 47,000 retailers (VF Corporation, n.d.). Annually, VF Corporation produces about 450 million items in more than 1,900 owned or contracted factories across the globe. The company produces about 30 percent of these products in the factories it owns (Nagappan, 2015). Almost half of all products are manufactured in the Americas, primarily in Mexico, Dominican Republic, Honduras, Nicaragua, and Argentina. For example, Mexico specializes in jeans production, where VF Corporation owns some factories. The company's global sourcing office is based in Hong Kong. The team of 1,500 professionals manages development and sourcing of nearly 45 percent of VF's products from some 1,000 factories in China, Bangladesh, Vietnam, Indonesia, Thailand, Cambodia, Pakistan, and India. A lot of apparel produced in Asian countries does not leave the region and instead is sold to consumers in Japan, South Korea, Taiwan, Malaysia, Singapore, China, and other countries.

Apparel Sourcing Intermediary

An apparel sourcing **intermediary** is a company that has expertise in design, product development, acquisition of materials, logistics, and importing as well as an established network of factories they contract with. Intermediaries are operated by former apparel manufacturers that no longer have manufacturing capacity *and do not own brands* but have extensive expertise from design to delivering finished products to retailers or brand managers' distribution centers. These companies tend to specialize in one product category, for example, knit dresses, men's shirts, sleepwear, hosiery, intimate apparel, gloves, and so on. They often operate under licensing contracts with brand managers.

One example of an intermediary is Komar (http://www.komarbrands.com/komar -about-us/). Founded in 1908 in New York City, it produced apparel domestically for more than a century. Today Komar's niche is "design, marketing, sourcing and distribution of sleepwear, intimates, kids and layering brands" (Komar, n.d.-a). The company has licenses to develop, source, and import sleepwear for twenty-two brands, including Betsey Johnson, Oscar de la Renta, Anne Klein, Tommy Bahama, Donna Karan, DKNY, and Steve Madden. In kids' sleepwear, Komar holds almost forty licenses for such cartoon brands as Barbie, Disney, Hello Kitty, Toy Story, Scooby Doo, and many others. Striving to offer leading edge intimate apparel, Komar is known for innovative product development and manufacturing processes such as carbon sueding, sheering, and enzyme washing for a softer touch. The company has a global production management team that specializes in "quality control and assurance, product development, merchandising, factory compliance, logistics and inventory management" (Komar, n.d.-b). To diversify its portfolio, Komar has recently developed its own private brands (e.g., Planet Sleep, Cottonista, and Cuddl Duds) and acquired well-known intimate brands Carole Hochman and OnGossamer.

APPAREL MANUFACTURERS

After an apparel company selects a country for sourcing apparel assembly (refer to Chapter 7), it looks for a factory, or vendor, within this country to manufacture products. When considering vendors for apparel production, it is important to distinguish between factories capable of offering different services. There are two major types of vendors that can be used for contracting production of finished garments:

- CMT (cut-make-trim) factory
- Full-package, also known as full-service factory

The main difference between the two types is the level of service the vendor (factory) can provide to the customer, the sourcing firm.

CMT Factories

A **CMT** factory provides services listed in its abbreviation: C—cutting fabric; M—making (sewing) garments; T—providing trims, as well as cleaning and packaging finished products (Figure 8.1). The trim portion of CMT usually includes garment labels, hangtags, price ticketing, and packaging, such as plastic bags and hangers. The vendor (the CMT factory) is responsible for garment production and packaging only, and the customer is responsible for all preproduction activities and postproduction activities.

The **preproduction** stage of apparel manufacturing involves all product development activities performed before the garment is approved for production, including:

- design,
- patternmaking,
- grading,
- making first and production samples, and
- developing technical specifications for materials and production processes.

First sample is the first prototype of a product made for approval of the desired design features and garment fit. **Production samples** are garments made at the factory where the apparel line will be mass produced, to check for quality and any potential production issues; they are typically produced in all ordered sizes. **Specifications**, or specs, are detailed graphic and written descriptions of styling, materials, dimensions, production procedures, and finishing instructions for a garment.

The sourcing firm, the customer that is contracting services with the CMT factory, has already developed a merchandise plan, designed the garments, developed products, and planned for packaging, logistics, and delivery of finished goods from the CMT

Figure 8.1

The "M" part of the CMT process, making garments, is the most labor-intensive part of apparel manufacturing. Typically CMT factories are large facilities with hundreds and even thousands of sewing machine operators.

factory to the customer's distribution center. The sourcing firm is also responsible for acquiring and supplying all fabric and findings for the apparel line and also for paying exporting and importing duties, insurance, and transportation costs. Often materials required for apparel production have to be imported to the country where the factory is located, which increases the cost of the finished products. Along with the materials, the sourcing firm provides samples of garments that will be manufactured, patterns graded in all sizes, and specifications outlining requirements for garment assembly (description of all production operations, seams, stitches, etc.).

When contracting with a CMT factory, sourcing firms bear all the costs, whereas vendors provide the expertise and equipment for the production of garments. CMT vendors do not own the garments; they simply contract to produce them and are paid for that service. The customer owns the materials and finished garments throughout the transaction, while the vendor provides the necessary services for producing and packaging the garments. Some CMT factories are paid a processing fee for the order, whereas others charge a price per unit, or garment. CMT contractors are often concentrated in **export processing zones (EPZs)**, which is a tariff-free trade zone that is set up by governments in developing countries to promote export through simplified import and export procedures.

When evaluating a CMT factory before signing a contract, sourcing specialists should consider the following:

- Does the vendor have the necessary equipment and production capacity to produce the needed assortment of styles, sizes, and colors and the specified quantities of each?
- Does the vendor require minimums? Are maximums limited by available materials? Is there reorder capability?
- Does the quality level match the specifications?
- Will the quality level be adequate to warrant the cost?
- What percentage of production can be expected to be **first quality**, which is a product that meets materials, design, production, appearance, and fit standards? What happens to **seconds**, garments that are not first quality?
- Can the vendor be depended upon to deliver on time? What happens if the vendor is late or can only provide partial orders?
- What about security of the products? Intellectual property rights to first quality and seconds?
- What are labor conditions at the factory?
- Is there an adequate supply of water for the workers?
- What are the safety and sanitation conditions?
- How does the factory handle overtime work?
- What is the maximum number of hours workers can work per week?
- Are the workers paid minimum wage?

Contracting a CMT factory enables the sourcing firm to control the product development process, but the firm also must bear most of the responsibilities and costs. This method of sourcing became more complex as sourcing firms began to use multiple CMT vendors in varied international locations. As the amount of offshore sourcing increased, the complexity of government regulations and the costs of logistics and importation escalated; thus, labor costs became a smaller part of overall product cost. Sourcing customers then sought ways to push more and more of the costs and responsibilities onto the vendors.

Full-Package Factories

At the other end of the sourcing spectrum for apparel manufacturing services is **full-package** sourcing, when the vendor, in addition to cutting, making, trimming, and packaging garments, provides a full range of preproduction and postproduction services, including:

- design;
- product development including patternmaking, grading, developing specifications, making samples, and shipping them for approval to the customer;
- sourcing, purchasing, and inspecting all necessary materials including fabrics;
- providing or contracting out any specialized embellishments such as embroidery, beading, printing, and so on; and
- logistics and delivery of finished goods.

Full-package production requires higher levels of management expertise and technology, more fully developed infrastructure, and financial resources to assume the majority of manufacturing expenses. The sourcing firm requests price quotes from vendors covering all materials and services the customer will require. A price quote from a full-package vendor reflects a much more comprehensive view of the overall cost of the product, but each final contract must be very specific, with all the criteria firmly established in advance of production, to ensure **vendor compliance**, which are performance standards or rules established by the customer (including things like working conditions, wages, working hours, and ages of workers) that a vendor must follow in the process of developing, producing, and delivering the quality and quantity of the merchandise ordered.

In addition to the questions that sourcing specialists have to consider when evaluating a CMT contractor (refer to the section above), the following terms must be established prior to signing a contract to ascertain the true full-package cost of the product from a vendor and to achieve satisfactory products delivered on time:

- How much of the overall product development process is covered by the vendor's quoted price? Design? Patternmaking? Grading? Sample making? Fabrics? Findings? Delivery of finished products?
- Does the vendor have the technical expertise to write the materials specifications necessary to source the fabrics, trims, and findings the customer prefers?
- Does the vendor have the technology and expertise to perform the specified product development processes?

No purchase decision should be made until all these components are identified and compared with alternative vendor options for the same or similar product.

CHOOSING BETWEEN FULL-PACKAGE AND CMT VENDORS

There are many variations of the two models of factory operating, CMT and full-package, dependent on business conditions and product needs. Another type of factory, known as **package factories**, can source and finance all materials and deliver finished goods onboard in addition to assembling apparel to customer specifications (Platzer, 2014). However, unlike full-package factories, package factories do not offer

TABLE 8.1

OPERATIONS PERFORMED BY CMT, PACKAGE, AND FULL-PACKAGE FACTORIES

Type of Activity	Operation	Type of Factory		
		CMT	Package	Full-Package
Acquisition of fabrics, trims, and packaging materials	Sourcing materials	No	Yes	Yes
	Purchasing materials	No	Yes	Yes
	Inspecting materials	No	Yes	Yes
	Delivering materials to the factory	No	Yes	Yes
Product development	Design	No	No	Yes
	Patternmaking	No	No	Yes
	Sample making	No	No	Yes
	Grading	No	No	Yes
	Developing specifications	No	No	Yes
Apparel assembly	Cutting fabric	Yes	Yes	Yes
	Sewing garments	Yes	Yes	Yes
	Trimming and packaging	Yes	Yes	
Delivery of goods onboard	Transportation from the factory to the loading port	No	Yes	Yes
	Exporting procedures and duties	No	Yes	Yes
	Loading onboard	No	Yes	Yes

any product development services. These factories are sometimes referred to as normal-service factories (Birnbaum, 2005). CMT factories, which offer no other services beyond apparel assembly, are referred to as zero service vendors, while full-package factories are referred to as full-service contractors. Table 8.1 summarizes differences between CMT, package, and full-package factories. The table shows what types of activities and operations each type of factory is capable of completing. Note that if a cell indicates "no", it means that the corresponding operation will be the responsibility of the sourcing firm to complete.

To streamline their sourcing operations, customers increasingly began to outsource more services to factories, starting with logistics coordination and acquisition of materials. Some customers rely on factories to perform all stages of technical design. Other customers prefer to keep these operations of product development and preproduction stages in-house. This strategy gives companies a greater control over design and fit of the garments and in some cases enables them to shorten the cycle time and increase speed-to-market (Thomas & Burns, 2014). Even if a factory offers a full range of services, depending on the sourcing company's needs, the vendor can be contracted to perform only selected services. How do you determine what type of factory, CMT or full-package, is a good fit for a sourcing company? For a better understanding of the vendor selection process, complete Case 8.1.

After completing Case 8.1, you have a more in-depth understanding about the decision process a sourcing company goes through when evaluating its sourcing needs and matching them with vendors' capabilities. In the case, the company was making

CHOOSING A FACTORY

Let's imagine that you have a successful start-up apparel business designing and sourcing trendy junior tops. Your tops have become very popular because of unique design features, quality materials and construction, and smart styling. You sell your product lines through a number of fashion-forward boutiques, several online stores, and have scored an exclusive deal with a large retailer for one of its private brands. You have been doing the design work yourself and have hired several people to do technical design and sample making. Salaries and rent for your technical design department add to about $180,000 a year. To produce your garments, you have been contracting with a sourcing agent.

Given the growing business as well as your experience in sourcing and importing, you want to start contracting directly with a factory, without the agent services, to streamline the sourcing process and cut the agent fees. You are considering two vendors: one in China and another in Vietnam. You have visited the factories and like the working conditions, facilities, and locations for both of them. Each factory completed several samples of your tops and provided you a quote. The Chinese factory is full-package, and the quoted price, $6.00 per top, includes the following services: sourcing and payment for all materials, patternmaking, grading, making samples, and delivering finished goods onboard of a ship. The Vietnamese factory offers some services beyond CMT but it does not have the staff to do technical design; the $5.00 per top quote includes sourcing and purchasing all materials and then delivering finished garments onboard. The quality of samples from both factories is very good, and the estimated shipping time and costs as well as import duties are the same from both locations. Both factories are reliable and appear to be easy to communicate with.

If you contract the Vietnamese factory, you continue to do all technical design in-house: patternmaking, grading, making first samples, approving fit, preparing technical specification packages for the vendor, and then approving production samples sent to you from the factory. If you work with the Chinese factory, you can outsource most of the technical design functions to the vendor and save about $180,000 a year. You will still need to have fitting sessions in-house to approve first samples made in the factory, but you can trust the factory with the production samples and skip the approval. Calculate all the costs in the table below for both factories.

1. What factory will you choose to place your orders? Justify your sourcing decision. Compare your decision and justifications with your classmates.

2. For the company in the case, what would be the advantages and disadvantages of working with Chinese vs. Vietnamese factories?

	Cost for Chinese Factory	Cost for Vietnamese Factory	Cost Difference
Average price per top			
Cost for 100,000 tops			
Cost of technical design department			
Total preproduction and production cost			

a strategic decision of either keeping technical design in-house (including pattern-making, grading, making samples, and development of specifications), or outsourcing it to the factory that will be performing apparel assembly. In general, sourcing companies can outsource to factories three major components:

1. acquisition of materials;
2. product development, primarily technical design; and
3. delivery of finished goods onboard of a vessel, which involves transportation logistics and exporting procedures.

We are ready to explore advantages and disadvantages of outsourcing these three major components of pre- and postproduction tasks to the vendor.

Outsourcing Acquisition of Fabric

CMT factories do not have capabilities to source, pay, and inspect fabrics. If a sourcing company does not want to supply fabric, it has to contract with a package or full-package factory. Let's consider advantages and disadvantages of outsourcing acquisition of fabric to a vendor. Think about why it would be a good business decision to let the factory source, inspect, and pay for fabrics to produce your apparel line.

The following are reasons the customer might want the factory to be responsible for acquiring the fabric:

- Sourcing company does not need extra people on staff to source, purchase, and coordinate delivery of fabric to the factory in time for apparel assembly (this service is a part of the quote provided by a full-package factory).
- Sourcing company does not need to invest in fabric several months before the finished products are selling.
- Sourcing company does not need to pay for shipping fabric to the factory, which can be expensive, especially if fabric has to be imported from other countries.
- Factory can utilize its network of local textile mills suppliers to order fabrics and trims and secure best available quality and price.
- Factory is responsible for inspecting all materials for quality and negotiating with local mills if problem arises.
- Factory is responsible for delivery of all materials in time for production and negotiation with local mills in the case of late deliveries.
- Factory is responsible for making up time during production in case of late delivery of materials.
- When the factory invests money in your order and owns materials, and then later finished garments, then any negotiations about quality or late shipments become easier.

Package and full-package factories prefer to order and purchase fabrics and findings because they might make a profit when acquiring the materials. Typically, it is beneficial for both the customer and the vendor if the latter handles acquisition of materials. An exception would be mass market retailers that compete on price. These companies have very large orders of fabrics, findings, and trims, and can negotiate better prices with textile mills and findings and trims suppliers. Ordering materials allows these companies to save money and keep product price low.

Sourcing professionals should remember that the materials used in apparel production are produced on a different time line than that used for apparel production. Textile mills typically operate on a calendar where fabrics are not produced in production-run quantities until after they are ordered by apparel companies from samples marketed at trade shows during the design phase of the merchandising calendar (Table 7.8 in Chapter 7). As a result, there is a time lag between when apparel lines were designed and when production run quantities of the selected fabrics would be available for garment production.

Findings and trims are also designed and produced as samples and marketed at trade shows scheduled to coincide with the trending and designing phases of the merchandising calendar. Basic findings are typically produced in anticipation of sales at textile trade fairs. Because the variety of trims is nearly infinite, their selection and availability often will impact not only production schedules, but also what finished products will look like if substitutions must be made during production in order to complete the garments on a contract schedule (Figures 8.2a, b, and c.).

Textile mills sometimes establish minimums as to the size of the orders they will produce. If an apparel company is going to produce garments that require 1,500 yards of fabric, and the textile firm has an order minimum of 1,800 meters, fabric sourcing specialists must recognize that first, meters are longer than yards, and second, there will be a significant amount of leftover fabric that must either be factored into the overall cost of a garment as waste, or used to produce additional garments. Both factors are going to make the overall cost of the order go up.

There is also the issue of exclusivity. If an apparel company purchases a fabric or findings from a textile mill and does not want anyone else to be able to use the same designs, then a special contract has to be established with the textile or trim supplier and the cost of the fabric or trim design will go up to ensure the exclusivity right. Sometimes, apparel companies will purchase an original fabric under the condition that it will have exclusive rights to the fabric's production for a specified period of time (such as a year) and that the textile producer may sell the fabric to someone else after that time period has elapsed. All these things have to be spelled out in the contracts with the vendor.

Outsourcing Technical Design

As shown in Table 8.1, CMT factories focus on apparel assembly and do not have the skills or equipment for completing any preproduction activities. If sourcing companies want to outsource technical design services, they have to contract with full-package factories. What are potential advantages and disadvantages of outsourcing technical design to a vendor instead of completing all the preproduction activities in-house?

Advantages

From Case 8.1 you know that outsourcing technical design to the factory is typically attractive from the cost perspective and allows the customer to save money. This is because patternmakers and sample makers in developing countries (where apparel assembly typically takes place) cost less than patternmakers in developed countries such as the United States. You are familiar with the relationship between labor cost and a country's level of development from Chapters 1 and 7. In addition, the cost of facilities in developing countries is usually less than renting an office for technical design department in New York City or Los Angeles (see Figure 8.3).

Transferring sample making from the sourcing firm into a factory setting can result in significant savings for the sourcing firm. Buying fabrics and findings for samples can

Figure 8.2a
A great variety of fabrics is available for apparel producers. Not only aesthetic features should be considered (color, motif, pattern, etc.) when selecting fabric but also type (knit or woven), weight, structure, and finishing. The fabrics presented here feature unique African motifs.

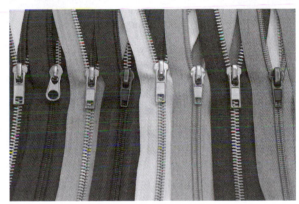

Figure 8.2b, c
The assortment of findings and trims might be even greater than the variety of fabrics, and care must be exercised when selecting them for specific garments to ensure the functional and aesthetic needs of a garment are met.

be very costly, depending on the product type. Obviously, in the T-shirt business the fabric—simple jersey—won't be expensive, but if you need silk, wool, or special performance polyester fabric, buying yardage for a hundred of samples and sewing them adds up in the course of a year. Further, only 40 percent to 60 percent of all original samples will actually translate into orders and will be mass produced. For one reason or another, many samples never make it into production. If the factory makes samples, it sources fabric and bears all associated costs in the hope to get the orders, and the cost of making samples at the factory is much lower than making them in-house.

Another advantage of outsourcing technical design services is that when a full-package factory makes patterns and samples, it can anticipate any potential issues that

Figure 8.3

Even though in the twenty-first century a lot of patternmaking is done on computer, a patternmaking department takes a significant amount of space, with large tables for checking and measuring patterns and samples as well as pattern blocks from current and past seasons stored for reference.

may arise later in the production process. For example, the factory can suggest changes in pocket or closure construction to make assembly easier and production more efficient while keeping the same look of a garment. The vendor is able to determine the most effective construction of seams, stitches, closures, and so on based on the skills of the workers and available equipment.

Disadvantages

Outsourcing technical design might result in a longer lead time needed to develop new products. In contrast, keeping pattern and sample work in-house might speed up the process. When first samples, or first prototypes of new styles, are made in the sourcing firm's headquarters, it is much easier and faster to communicate any needed changes in a garment design and fit when pattern and sample makers are located in the next room. Communicating the same changes through email to a patternmaker speaking a different language in a factory located thousands of miles away is complicated and tends to delay approval of new samples. FedEx-ing samples for fitting session and approval around the world takes time and money. The fact that factories in Asia are in a different time zone and 10 to 12 hours ahead of sourcing companies in the United States contributes to the delay in communication. In this respect, factories in the Western Hemisphere have an advantage because they are in the same time zones as the United States.

Another disadvantage of outsourcing technical design is that patternmakers in foreign countries, even though they might have exceptional skills, do not know what the product line's target consumers' preferences in styling and fit are. For example, how high or low jeans are supposed to sit in relation to the waistline? How loose and baggy sweatpants should be? How tight a top should fit around the chest and hips? In-house technical designers generally have a good understanding of the company's target market fitting preferences. Communicating these subtle yet very important fit differences to technical designers in foreign countries might be challenging and time consuming.

Finally, when a sourcing firm outsources all technical designs, it completely depends on the factory to do all the preproduction tasks. If, for whatever reason, the business relationship is discontinued (the factory went out of business or began working with another customer), the sourcing firm will have to scramble to find another full-package vendor. Getting the new vendor up to speed in understanding the company's sizing, fit, and aesthetics, not to mention following various vendor compliances, will require a substantial amount of time and resources, and is likely to result in delayed delivery of merchandise for the selling season.

Making Strategic Decisions

Given both the advantages and disadvantages of outsourcing technical design to a factory, what would be a good strategic decision for a sourcing firm? Under what circumstances do retailers and brand managers outsource technical design to vendors? And when do they prefer to keep technical design tasks in-house? Three factors are critical to consider when making this important strategic decision:

- type of apparel,
- company's competitive advantage in the market, and
- company's philosophy.

First, if the sourcing firm specializes in tailored or fitted apparel, such as formal suits, dresses, or jeans, where the right fit is critical and might require several samples for approval, it makes sense to keep technical design in-house. In contrast, pattern and sample work for simple and/or loose-fitted garments, such as lounge wear or sweaters, can be outsourced to a factory. Next, if the sourcing firm competes in the market on price, then garment cost is critical, but fit might be less of a priority. In this case, outsourcing technical design might allow the sourcing firm a lower product price, as was suggested in Case 8.1. However, when garment fit is a retailer's or brand manager's signature, then keeping technical design in-house allows for a greater control over fit and sizing, especially when the apparel line is produced at different factories located in different countries, which is very typical. For example, assume an apparel specialty retailer might manufacture knit tops in Honduras, tailored jackets in Vietnam, silk dresses in China, jeans in Mexico, and cashmere cardigans in Italy. When all the garments come together in a store, all the garments in size 6 must fit a model perfectly as well as all the other sizes.

Finally, the company's philosophy might weigh into the decision whether to outsource jobs in technical design or keep them in the country. In other industries, such as electronics, it is becoming common to indicate not only country of manufacturing but also country of design. Some of you might have seen on products, such as iPhone, the label "Designed in the USA." It is likely to be a growing trend, when more and more products will have a designation that they were designed to generate support for white-collar jobs in the domestic market.

Many companies, especially large retailers and brand managers, work with both CMT and full-package contractors. They maintain technical design in-house to complete preproduction tasks for difficult-to-fit and new, experimental styles. At the same time, they let factories handle technical design for styles that have minor changes from previous season(s) or are relatively simple to fit. That's why CMT factories are preferred for basic apparel that has simple construction and low number of materials.

Outsourcing Delivery of Goods

As shown in Table 8.1, CMT contractors do not offer any services beyond apparel assembly. If contracting with a CMT factory, the sourcing company is responsible for delivering fabric to the factory as well as all operations associated with exporting and delivery of finished products. In contrast, package and full-package contractors are in charge of delivering finished apparel products onboard of a ship or to an airplane (Table 8.1). In addition to arranging transportation of goods from the factory to a port of origins, the contractor is responsible for completing all paperwork needed for exporting the products and loading them onboard. Package and full-package contractors also bear all the costs associated with exporting and inland delivery of goods. These costs are a part of the quote provided by vendors to customers (Case 8.1).

As described in Chapter 7, depending on a country, it takes between two and eight documents to export goods and costs between $600 and $4,200 per container. Needless to say, it is much easier for local factories to navigate the bureaucracy associated with transportation and exporting of goods. Similar to the discussion of outsourcing acquisition of materials, it makes more sense to engage in delivery of goods for large companies that utilize economies of scale and compete on price. These companies can negotiate better rates because of the high volumes they export and import. For small- and medium-size companies it might be more efficient to outsource delivery of products onboard to factories.

Regional CMT and Full-Package Capabilities

When selecting a contractor, sourcing professionals need to keep in mind that, depending on the level of apparel industry sophistication, a majority of factories in a country tend to be either full-package or CMT. The level of industry maturity is closely related to a country's level of development. Developing countries are more likely to have relatively advanced apparel industries with factories upgraded to full-package capabilities. In newly developing countries, most factories tend to offer basic CMT services. Some examples of a countries' product specialization and dominant type of factories are provided below. A more detailed review of regional and country specialization in apparel manufacturing is presented in Chapters 9 through 12.

Most countries in the Western hemisphere, notably in Central America and the Caribbean, have "ample cut, make, and trim apparel assembly capacity" (Platzer, 2014, p. 10). US retailers, brand managers, and intermediaries supply factories in Honduras, Dominican Republic, El Salvador, and Guatemala with US-made fabrics and yarns to knit and cut-and-sew basic apparel such as underwear, T-shirts, and socks. The majority of the factories are not capable of offering any other services beyond CMT. Similarly, factories in Mexico work primarily on a CMT basis and are known for producing high volumes of commodity denim (Gereffi & Frederick, 2010).

In Asia, India has an excellent reputation for strong design skills and intricate embellishments such as embroidery and bidding on cotton apparel; most factories are full-package. Sri Lanka's factories have full-package capabilities and specialize in women's underwear and bras as well as knitted intimate apparel. For apparel assembly in Bangladesh and Cambodia, almost all materials have to be imported from China, India, or Taiwan. CMT or package contractors specialize in cotton knit and woven apparel; few factories offer full-package services. China, as the world's lead apparel supplier, has a broad range of vendors in both textile and apparel and a capacity to produce any garment at any price point. Most factories offer sophisticated full-package services.

COSTING

Because the basic purpose of a business is to make money for the firm, it follows that in order to remain in business the firm must acquire its goods for less than the price they will ultimately charge their customers. Remember that the firm will also be paying for numerous business expenses in addition to the cost of the goods it sells, so the overall anticipated markup is definitely not just profit. Major components that constitute the cost of a product include:

- labor cost,
- factory overhead,
- cost of materials (fabric, findings, trims, packaging, etc.),
- sourcing agent fees (if applicable),
- freight and insurance,
- import duty paid at customs based on tariff rate,
- customs clearance fees, and
- inland transportation to the customer's distribution center.

These cost components are inherent to all apparel products, but the actual costs vary greatly by type of garment, number of garments ordered, materials and construction methods used, and the country where the garments are sourced. Table 8.2 presents examples of how cost of the same jacket can differ depending on location of manufacturing.

CMT Cost

CMT cost covers all production processes, which are the labor and overhead required to manufacture one garment. Labor cost is calculated as the hourly wage rate multiplied by the amount of time needed to make one garment, which depends on available equipment and machinery as well as the skills of the workers in the factory. Both components of labor cost differ significantly by country. In Table 8.2, a factory in Indonesia has a much lower hourly rate but requires 50 percent more time to make a jacket than factories in China or the United States. Complicated styles require more time and result in higher labor costs. Factory overhead includes costs of electricity, phone and internet, utilities, loan payments, and any other factory expenses. Overhead cost, calculated as percent of labor cost (Table 8.2), tends to be higher for developing and newly developing countries, as you learned in Chapter 7. If a sourcing firm contracts with a CMT vendor, it owns all the materials and goods and simply pays a quoted fee (CMT) to the vendor for performing cut, make, and trim operations.

TABLE 8.2

COMPONENTS OF JACKET COST FOR SELECTED COUNTRIES

Cost Component	Direct Cost, by Country			
	China	Mexico	Indonesia	USA
Hourly rate	$1.8 8	$2.17	$0.44	$10.00
Labor cost (hourly rate × time to make a jacket)	$1.88 (1 hr per jacket)	$2.71 (1.25 hr per jacket)	$0.66 (1.5 hr per jacket)	$10.00 (1 hr per jacket)
Overhead (percent of labor)	$1.88 (100%)	$2.71 (100%)	$1.65 (250%)	$3.00 (30%)
CMT cost (labor + overhead)	**$3.76**	**$5.42**	**$2.31**	**$13.00**
Fabric cost	$15.00	$15.00	$15.00	$15.00
FOB cost (CMT + materials)	**$18.76**	**$20.42**	**$17.31**	**$28.00**
Freight and insurance	$0.50	$0.20	$0.65	0
Customs clearance	$0.75	$0.75	$0.75	0
CIF cost (FOB + insurance and freight)	**$20.01**	**$21.37**	**$18.71**	**$28.00**
Duty (tariff rate 20% of FOB)	$3.75	0 (tariff rate 0% under NAFTA)	$3.46	0 (no import duties)
LDP Cost (FOB + duty + freight + customs)	**$23.76**	**$21.37**	**$22.17**	**$28.00**

Based on Birnbaum (2005); Gereffi & Frederick (2010); Ha-Brookshire (2014); World Freight Rates (n.d.).

Fabric Cost

The single largest cost of apparel production is the fabric, which can be 50 to 70 percent of the total cost of a product. The basic price will be dependent on the fiber content, the type of fabric, and the quality and quantity required for the style. In some products this cost may be as high as 70 percent of the total when

- the fabric is unique (e.g., made of luxury fibers, has special finishes or design);
- the fabric has to be acquired some distance from the garment production site and requires additional transportation and tariff charges;
- there is significant fallout (wasted fabric), owing to large fabric design motifs or garment styling requirements (e.g., cut on bias); or
- the size range includes more large sizes.

The same discussion applies to findings, where costs vary greatly. For example, special lace or buttons made of rare materials might add significant cost to a garment.

Fabrics are purchased by the total amount of yardage needed for production of the entire order for a particular style. Note that the costs are calculated for only one garment in Table 8.2 and that the total yardage required will be dependent on the overall number of garments to be constructed, the size range that is being served, plus the addition of approximately 6 percent to allow for potential seconds or irregulars; that is, garments that are not first quality when they come off the production line.

In Table 8.2, fabric cost is the same for all countries. However, depending on what fabric and findings are needed, most likely they will need to be imported for apparel assembly in Indonesia and Mexico because only a limited selection of fabrics and findings is produced and available domestically. In this case, transportation and import duty will increase the cost of materials. In contrast, practically any materials can be purchased in China and the United States for apparel assembly domestically.

FOB Cost

FOB (free on board) reflects all materials and production costs as well as loading the goods on board a vessel at the foreign port of export (Table 8.2). Package and full-package factories work on an FOB basis and are responsible for all operations that the FOB quote covers. The customer takes responsibility for all remaining costs: shipping charges, insurance, import duty and customs clearance fee at the port of destination, and inland transportation to the customer's distribution center. In the case of the FOB contract, the vendor owns the materials that it purchased and the products up to the point when they are loaded on board of a vessel. After that, the ownership of the goods is transferred to the sourcing firm.

CIF Cost

CIF (cost, insurance, freight) is another way a factory can quote product cost. CIF reflects the cost of goods as well as insurance and freight to the port of destination (Table 8.2). For example, CIF Los Angeles is the price for the cost of the garments, shipping, and insurance until the goods reach the port of Los Angeles. The sourcing firm is responsible for paying import duty and customs clearance fees at the port of destination and inland transportation to the customer's distribution center. In the case of the CIF contract, the vendor owns the finished products up to the point when they reach the destination port, where the ownership of the goods is transferred to the sourcing firm.

LDP Cost

Another alternative is to quote **LDP (landed duty paid)**, which includes the cost of goods, insurance, freight, duty, and customs clearance. In the case of the LDP contract, the vendor owns the products and is responsible for all costs and operations until the goods are cleared by the customs at the port of destination. After that, the sourcing firm takes possession of the merchandise and is only responsible for delivering goods to its distribution center.

Important Considerations

Factory overhead for FOB, CIF, and LDP quotes typically include product development services such as purchasing and inspecting fabrics and trims, patternmaking, sample making, grading, and development of specifications. Thus, if the vendor is a full-package contractor, the quotes will be higher, but if the sourcing firm does much of the product development steps, the quotes will be lower. However, the sourcing firm must then provide a larger margin within its own overhead to cover these shifts in product development costs, as you learned in Case 8.1.

The size of the order can also impact costs. For example, if the production run is small (few in number), the costs will escalate per item because of the time and effort involved in setting up, which may require adding or removing machines from the production line, changing their sequence, or adjusting machines for different types of fabrics or assembly methods. Conversely, if the order is large, the setup costs can be spread over more garments, and the cost of each garment will go down.

Before making a decision among vendors, the sourcing firm should consider prior experience with them and reliability in meeting contract deadlines for delivery of goods. Making a decision between vendors depends on a company's strategic priorities and its competitive niche in the market. If the company competes primarily on price, which is the case for mass market retailers, then the cost of products will be the major factor when choosing a vendor. For fashion-forward companies that draw consumers by being the first in the market to offer the latest fashion trends, speed-to-market is the critical factor. For companies that specialize in highest quality of materials and garment construction, the driving factor will be the factory's capability to manufacture products of great craftsmanship, which requires highly skilled workers and sophisticated machinery and equipment.

METHODS OF SOURCING

There are several ways a company can approach the process of sourcing textile materials, finished apparel goods, and apparel production. The primary methods of developing sourcing programs include the following:

- going factory direct,
- establishing a joint venture,
- using sourcing agents,
- developing licensing agreements, and
- attending trade shows and trade fairs.

Factory Direct Sourcing

As the name suggests, with this approach to sourcing textile materials and/or apparel assembly, customers contract directly with factories or mills. Depending on the type of apparel product sourced, the sourcing firm (retailer, brand manager, or sourcing intermediary) makes a strategic decision of whether to work with a CMT, package, or full-package factory. All types of companies engaged in sourcing apparel production described earlier in the chapter (private label retailers, brand managers, and intermediaries) utilize the factory direct sourcing method. The main advantages of contracting directly with a factory are:

- eliminating the need for a middleman or sourcing agent and
- saving money.

Because there is no middleman, the customer can directly negotiate the cost of products and services with the vendor. In addition, factory direct sourcing allows a streamlined communication process that can facilitate faster speed-to-market when developing and manufacturing new products.

With advantages come risks. A sourcing firm that works directly with the vendor is fully responsible for evaluating the manufacturing facilities as well as crafting a contract outlining all the expectations and potential consequences of violating compliance related to working and environmental conditions, product quality, and so on. The process might be overwhelming for a novice apparel importer and too complicated and risky for a smaller-size business. If the sourcing firm is unfamiliar with production methods or assessing the capacity of vendors, contracting through a sourcing agent might be more appropriate than direct-to-factory sourcing.

Large-size brand managers and some retailers utilize factory direct sourcing because they operate on economy of scale and have the expertise, staff, and resources to support the operations. Mass market retailers use factory direct sourcing strategies to obtain apparel to be sold under their private brands. For example, Walmart sources approximately 20 percent of apparel, footwear, and home furnishings directly from factories in China, Mexico, Bangladesh, Jordan, and other countries (Gereffi & Frederick, 2010). Sears relies more extensively on a factory direct strategy and sources approximately 60 to 70 percent of merchandise through its sourcing and quality assurance offices worldwide.

Similarly, some specialty retailers contract directly with factories to source apparel assembly and other related services. For example, Gap Inc. relies primarily on factory direct sourcing, working with 900 vendors in sixty countries, with the majority of merchandise sourced from China (27 percent) as well as Bangladesh, Sri Lanka, Pakistan, Philippines, Jordan, Vietnam, Cambodia, Morocco, Turkey, and India (Gereffi & Frederick, 2010). Note that a lot of apparel manufactured in these far-flung locations from the Gap's home country, the United States, is destined to foreign markets. The company has 3,700 stores worldwide and sells its products in ninety countries (almost half of the total number of countries in the world today!). For instance, a significant portion of the apparel Gap sources from Chinese factories stays in China and is sold in one of the company's more than forty stores in the country to satisfy the burgeoning Chinese middle class's quest for American fashion (see Figure 8.4). Likewise, a lot of apparel for Gap's stores in South Africa are produced within the African continent to minimize product travel (Figure 8.5).

All apparel intermediaries that source products for customers (retailers, designers, or brand managers) work directly with factories. This is one of the intermediaries' primary expertise areas and a major service they can offer to companies of any size. More detailed discussion is provided in the "Sourcing Agents" section.

Figure 8.4
The classic American look that Gap represents is very popular in China. This huge poster, featuring a Western model in a denim outfit, informs Chinese consumers about a Gap store to open in Beijing.

Figure 8.5
When developing and sourcing apparel production for different countries, it is important to keep in mind that the seasons in the Northern and Southern Hemispheres are different. In this photo taken in January, a Gap storefront in an upscale mall in Pretoria features the summer collection because it is mid-summer in South Africa.

Joint Venture

Some of the reasons a company might want to establish an offshore manufacturing presence include having a manufacturing base in a close proximity to a major foreign consumer market, lower labor costs, and/or local availability of unique skills or resources. Offshore facilities can improve speed-to-market and operational costs, but they also carry considerable risk. Even though a firm may find labor costs and taxes are lower in overseas countries, the investment in facilities and equipment can be high, and locking capital into a fixed asset in another nation can be risky if the political or business climate in that nation is unstable.

A **joint venture** is shared ownership of a facility with a local business. The positive aspects of joint ventures include a sharing of the financial risks and a better understanding of the culture and business legalities that local offshore partners can provide. Also, the initial investment can be lower. It is more typical for large and medium-size retailers and brand managers to form a joint venture to manufacture products in a foreign country than it is for small apparel businesses.

Sourcing Agent or Sourcing Intermediary

The concept of sourcing agents is not new, but their role is typically not apparent to the retail consumer. Because of the exceptional growth of international sourcing in the apparel business since the 1990s, the importance of sourcing agents has increased significantly as a critical link in the overall supply chain. A **sourcing agent** is an individual or a company that provides services to procure and deliver products. "Sourcing agent" is sometimes used interchangeably with "intermediary," but their roles are quite different.

A sourcing agent's services are limited and can be as simple as being the customer's representative located near the factory to facilitate communication and negotiate contracts between the vendor and the customer. Other services might include inspection of product quality and vendor compliance. Often, familiarity with the sourcing country's language and knowledge of local culture, business environment, and factories are the primary reasons to enlist the services of sourcing agents. Sourcing agents do not own products and are paid a commission based on a percentage of the total order cost purchase, which can be between 4 and 12 percent, depending on the amount of services provided by the agent.

Intermediaries are medium- to large-size companies with a global presence through offices in different regions of the world. In contrast to sourcing agents, intermediaries own all input materials and finished products until their ownership is transferred to a retailer or a brand manager at a wholesale price. Apparel intermediaries are capable of providing a wide range of services from product ideation and development (including pattern and sample work and technical specifications) to obtaining all necessary fabrics and findings, contracting with factories, to delivering finished products to the customer's distribution centers or stores. For example, Komar, described at the beginning of this chapter, does exactly that for many of its retail clients and brand managers: it specializes in design, product development, sourcing input materials, contracting apparel assembly with factories, and delivering intimate apparel to its customers, which are leading US brands.

Large retailers might own an intermediary that performs all sourcing functions. Associated Merchandising Corporation (AMC), founded in 1918 and acquired by Target Corporation in 1998, provides all sourcing services for its parent company. AMC operates from more than fifty offices in forty countries worldwide. Apparel intermediaries can hire independent sourcing agents in different countries of the world to monitor apparel products quality and other vendor compliances.

Reflecting the importance of intermediaries in the global market is the fact that the second-largest supplier of apparel to the world after China is not an individual nation, but a firm, Li & Fung. Perhaps the distinctiveness of Li & Fung's position can best be understood when one considers that it has achieved this status without owning any factories or employing any factory workers. The largest retailers in the world use the company to develop, produce, and deliver consumer goods. Li & Fung has evolved from a sourcing agent to the leading global supply chain manager. The company orchestrates sourcing activities for many of the world's largest retailers, acting as a sourcing intermediary. In the US market, the company supplies the majority of apparel, footwear, and toys sold at Walmart. Kohl is one of the largest Li & Fung customers, and others include Liz Claiborne, Inc., Levi Strauss & Co., and Gymboree (Gereffi & Frederick, 2010). Examples of European companies collaborating with Li & Fung are Tesco and Talbots. Read Case 8.2 to learn more about Li & Fung and its role in the global apparel and other consumer goods industries.

Licensing

Licensing, as discussed in Chapter 6, is a means of extending the value of a brand without actually having to develop and produce a new product. Typically, the name of a brand, sports team, cartoon character, or celebrity is placed on the product developed and produced by another firm, and the owner of the brand or name is paid a percentage of the sale of any items sold under the name. This is how Ralph Lauren can have his name on a perfume made by someone else, or a cartoon character can appear

LI & FUNG

Li & Fung, a US$19.3 billion leading consumer goods sourcing company, manages supply chains for retailers and brands worldwide. Headquartered in Hong Kong, the company employs some 25,000 people in 300+ offices in more than forty different countries (Figure Case 8.1a). Li & Fung has an established global sourcing network of about 15,000 suppliers that provide "quality-conscious, sustainable and cost-competitive, consumer goods for our customers around the world" (Li & Fung, n.d.). The company specializes in the design, product development, sourcing, logistics, and distribution of consumer goods such as apparel, home furnishings, footwear, toys, furniture, accessories, and health and beauty products, among others.

In addition to the Hong Kong headquarters, Li & Fung has strategically positioned offices in every major consumer market to serve local retailers and brand managers as well as offices in major apparel producing centers next to these major consumer markets. Li & Fung has a presence in the world's fashion centers of Paris, London, Tokyo, and New York City. Within the company there are teams of product specialists who manage the entire supply chain, from product design and development, to raw material and factory sourcing, to production planning and management, to quality assurance and export documentation, to shipping arrangements.

Across the Atlantic, the main sourcing country offering European retailers speed-to-market and flexible production is Turkey, with the coordinating office in Istanbul. The main Latin American office offering the same to US retailers is based in Guatemala City. In addition, Li & Fung has offices in every epicenter of apparel production:

- The Ho Chi Minh City office in Vietnam coordinates apparel assembly and logistics for North American and European brands.
- The Dhaka office in Bangladesh focuses on manufacturing apparel and home furnishings.
- The Shanghai office in China coordinates complete in-country logistics services to support sourcing apparel, hardgoods, and beauty categories.
- A major office in Bangkok as well as five other locations in Thailand support sourcing garments, furniture, beauty, and personal care products.
- The Philippines hosts operations and distribution centers in fourteen cities to support garment manufacturing through extensive in-country logistics.
- The Phnom Penh office in Cambodia focuses on apparel and footwear manufacturing.
- Four offices in India (New Delhi, Bangalore, Chennai, and Tirupur) deal with apparel, textile, and hardgoods categories.

Figure Case 8.2a
Li & Fung's global employees make a diverse group, which is essential for successful communication and teamwork across borders and cultures.

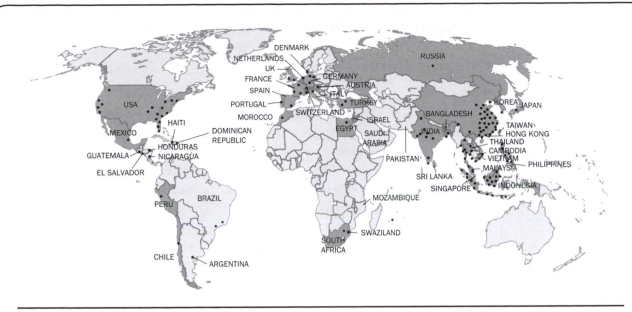

Figure Case 8.2b
Li & Fung is a global network of offices and suppliers that represents the world's centers of apparel production and distribution.

To comprehend the vast presence of Li & Fung's offices and suppliers, study Figure Case 8.1b, which presents some locations of this sourcing giant. Given its size, the company has the best available technology to support instant communication and data interchange within the global network, coordinating all aspects of product design and development, materials supply, manufacturing, and logistics.

Apparel. (March 26, 2014). "Li & Fung Spins Off Global Brands Group as Separate Licensing Unit." Retrieved February 27, 2015, from http://apparel.edgl.com/news/Li-Fung-Spins-Off-Global-Brands-Group-as-Separate-Licensing-Unit91814

Gereffi, G., & Frederick, S. (2010). "The Global Apparel Value Chain, Trade and the Crisis." Policy Research Working Paper 5281. The World Bank.

Li & Fung. (n.d.). "About." Retrieved February 25, 2015, from http://www.lifung.com/about-us/our-global-network/

1. What are some advantages and disadvantages of using Li & Fung as sourcing intermediary for small vs. large apparel retailers and brand managers?

2. What effect can giant transnational sourcing intermediaries such as Li & Fung have on the future of the global apparel industry? What are possible implications for apparel businesses of different sizes located in developed and newly developing countries?

on children's pajamas. Licensing contracts specify the responsibilities of each partner involved, and strict guidelines and product specifications are generally a part of the agreement.

International licensing is an alternative to exporting that enables well-known brands to establish a presence in another country without having to manufacture or distribute there. A brand owner contracts (as the licensor) with an intermediary (the licensee); the licensee then produces and may distribute the branded products. This is how some designers gain a presence in a distant nation. Apparel intermediaries have evolved as large players in the licensing business. Earlier in this chapter you learned about multiple brands that Komar licenses from designers, brand managers, and movie studios. In 2014, Li & Fung spun off its department managing global brands in a subsidiary, Global Brands Group, which holds licenses for dozens of fashion, footwear, accessories, and character brands (Global Brands Group, n.d.). Some of the brands in the fashion category include Calvin Klein, Jennifer Lopez, Sean John, Tommy Hilfiger, Under Armour, Nautica, and New Balance.

Trade Fairs

Trade fairs, or trade shows, are designed to get textile and apparel manufacturers and retailers together to facilitate efficient transfer of ownership of products and services. These events are very popular with textile and apparel businesses because the cost of a face-to-face presentation of a product to potential customers is less than 50 percent of a personal sales visit. The shows serve as the conduit for locating fabrics and other materials, for identifying locations and firms that provide CMT and full-package manufacturing, for finding intermediaries that can offer various services in developing and sourcing products, and for selling apparel product lines at wholesale to retailers.

Trade shows are held periodically throughout the year to showcase new products and services. Consumers may become aware of these trade fairs when fashion show photos from these events are distributed through the internet and other media. However, the real business of these market events occurs on the floor of the market itself, where vendors present their wares to their customers, including retail buyers and other trade representatives, to generate orders for materials, technology, machinery, finished products, and services. Calendars and locations for trade shows are available online and published in trade papers, such as *Women's Wear Daily*, as well as numerous websites that feature these events.

The number of international trade fairs has mushroomed since the mid-1990s, keeping pace with the overall market trend of purchasing materials, products, and services from offshore locations. The prêt-à-porter and couture shows in Paris, Milan, and London are notable, because they have been traditionally scheduled to introduce retailers and the consumer market to the newest trends in ready-to-wear products coming from the major designers of Europe. In terms of volume of product sold for breadth of distribution, today's buyers are being enticed to travel to other areas of the world to conduct business. For example, China's longest running trade fair is the Canton Fair in Guangzhou, China. This marketplace is enormous and, when in session, is teeming with activity as buyers from all over the world gather to order all manner of products produced in China, including apparel.

SOURCING TECHNOLOGY

Many companies offer different software packages to help businesses manage sourcing operations and build an effective and efficient supply chain. For example, the online magazine *Apparel* offers its "Buyer's Guide," a searchable database of companies providing technology solutions for all aspects of the apparel business (Apparel, n.d.). Some of the categories in the Buyer's Guide related to sourcing are:

- color management
- design and product development
- manufacturing and production solutions
- product ID/labeling
- supply chain, sourcing, and logistics
- warehousing and distribution

Further, there are forty-six subcategories under the "supply chain, sourcing, and logistics" category, offering software solutions. Some of them include:

- EDI (electronic data interchange) (23)
- ERP (enterprise resource planning) software (23)
- Master data management (MDM) (23)
- Quality management/vendor scorecard (25)
- Sourcing management software (27)
- Transportation/logistics software (18)

The number next to the software indicates how many companies that offer solutions and services related to these functions are listed in the Buyer's Guide database. All listed companies have product descriptions and related links. To learn more about software capabilities and related services and stay on par with the latest technological advancements, apparel companies often attend trade shows to network with software providers and participate in seminars and workshops.

Product Lifecycle Management Systems (PLM)

In an increasingly competitive environment, delivering the right product at the right cost and on time has become more and more challenging. To solve the problem, companies turn to technological solutions, such as **product life cycle management (PLM)**, one of the most widely used types of software related to supply chain management. In the apparel industry, PLM refers to the process and software for managing a product's life cycle from inception, design, development of related materials, manufacturing, delivery, distribution, marketing, sale, and in some cases, service and disposal. In recent years, apparel and footwear companies have been investing millions into software to address these challenges.

What exactly does PLM do? PLM is a web-based platform, which allows everyone who works on designing and developing a product to virtually collaborate in real time, thus reducing the amount of paperwork, communication time, and possible errors as well as saving money. For example, when a designer wants to make modifications to a garment, she or he enters the changes in the PLM system. Everyone else involved in the process is able to see the changes immediately and take necessary actions. The sourcing department is able to make changes in the required materials; the factory is able to adjust patterns, cut fabric, and sew a sample that is sent to the designer for approval. After a fitting session, the designer enters any needed adjustments in the fit or design features so the factory can make a new sample if necessary.

With fast-changing fashion trends, the number of product lines retailers deliver in their stores has increased from the traditional four to five per year to ten to twelve on average. This has increased the number of styles a company is working on simultaneously at a given time. PLM helps to bring together the multiple documents needed to develop a technical specification to one place that is accessible to everyone involved in the supply chain. Instead of having multiple files in different formats (e.g., technical flat in Adobe Illustrator, costing sheets in Excel, and patterns in special software) that have to be emailed back and forth between the customer and the factory as well as within the customer's organization between different departments, all information is stored in one place and updated seamlessly.

Potentially, PLM is capable of bringing together all of the company's internal operations as well as external, or vendor's functions, including:

- product planning,
- product development,
- sourcing materials, assembly, and other services,
- marketing,
- sales,
- compliance,
- sustainability,
- distribution, and
- finance.

For example, Rocky Brands, an Ohio-based innovative footwear company that produces work, hunting, and military boots, among other products, was able to reduce the time for approval of new samples for production from four to five days to several hours as a result of PLM integration (Zager, 2015). In addition, the new system decreased redundant work: the company's accounting department now needs to approve a sample only once, whereas before it had to handle sample purchase order data at least three times.

Rocky Brands further expanded the use of PLM to centralize all marketing and e-commerce data related to a product. The company's VP of strategy, execution, and process improvement, Mary Lorenz, explains that now all related product information, including its story, search criteria, description, and photographs, are located in one place, when previously it "was maintained on people's hard drives in spreadsheets, Word, and little databases. It was a horror story to get it all pulled together. We were always scrambling when it was time to put it up on the website" (Zager, 2015, para 11).

Using PLM can help accomplish the following:

- reduce time required for product development by at least 50 percent; companies that have implemented PLM system across their supply chains report decreased time in the product lifecycle from 120 to 60 days or less;
- decrease direct materials spending by 5 percent to 10 percent;
- streamline supply chain by eliminating redundant operations;
- standardize products and processes to minimize development costs and financial losses due to mistakes;
- increase gross margin by 5 percent to 25 percent; and
- decrease inventory level. (Just-style, n.d.; Kern, 2014; Suleski & Draper, 2014)

According to *Apparel*'s 2014 survey of apparel and fashion companies, the major benefit expected from PLM implementation was the standardization of processes (Suleski & Draper, 2014). Standardization of processes leads to lower costs, reduced risk, and increased reliability of processes when developing and bringing new products to the market. Plus, not only product developers and manufacturers but also retailers can benefit from PLM. Because garment information can be available to all supply chain participants, from a brand manager to factory, logistics firm to retailer, PLM allows the latter to replenish best-sellers faster and in some cases even cancel merchandise that is not selling before it gets produced.

Industry experts predict that the next big step in PLM application will be analytics to identify successful vs. ineffective products and processes. The software potentially can be used for postseason review of best-selling and poor-selling products. Gartner's research indicates that in the apparel industry "50 percent of new products fail to meet their key metrics," yet, companies tend not to track "what percent of products hit their targets" (Suleski & Draper, 2014, p. 26). As a result, often line planning for next season is not based on a systematic postseason performance review of products and supply chain processes to identify successful designs, materials, vendors, logistics, and other operations to eliminate inefficiency. PLM will allow these companies to achieve better performance by identifying effective products and processes.

MANUFACTURING CONTROL AND VENDOR COMPLIANCE

The sourcing company has to have an established set of rules by which it will do business with its vendors, whether the vendors are providing materials, product development, production, quality assurance, logistics, or customs clearance. The customer's set of rules provides the basis and defines the standards for vendor compliance and for manufacturing control.

Manufacturing control is a process in which a vendor's expected performance is compared with actual performance. **Vendor compliance** is performance standards or rules established by the customer that a vendor must follow in order to do business with that customer. The standards for vendor compliance are included in the contract that the vendor signs when hired to provide services. A vendor might have multiple customers, so it needs to be prepared to deal with a wide variety of standards. The vendor compliance contract establishes the areas of manufacturing control desired by the customer related to quality and performance of materials and finished goods, their quantities, and timing of delivery, as well as manufacturing processes including working conditions and environmental regulations. Knowing the factory conditions where the products are to be produced is also important to ensure that employees are being paid a reasonable wage, are not working under sweatshop conditions, and that the vendor's record of ethical practices is appropriate. The conduct of vendor firms needs to be monitored throughout the production cycle to ensure that they are meeting their contractual obligations related to product quality and country of origin and care labeling.

Quality Assurance

Quality assurance is a commitment to product quality that utilizes the concept of error prevention as integral to the entire product development process. The overarching concept is that making it right the first time is more cost-effective than deciding what to do with defective garments. The issue of quality is complicated by the fact that fabrics that are often sourced in one part of the world have to be compatible with trims sourced elsewhere. The result is the need for development of quality and product standards followed by constant monitoring of their application in product specifications and production.

Standards are the basic characteristics used to determine acceptability of the quality and resulting performance and appearance of products and services. Specific standards are usually established for thread, fabrics, findings, fit, and garment assembly for all the products sourced by a firm. These standards provide the parameters for business decisions related to development of a firm's product specifications and a baseline for consistency of product offerings. To ensure that they contribute to making a profit, product developers ultimately determine which product characteristics will be desired by their customers and will comply with regulations imposed by the government. Determining the appropriate standards to apply to a particular product depends on the type and length of use a product might receive in the hands of a consumer.

The United States utilizes voluntary standards developed by industry members working within ASTM International to establish criteria related to performance of textiles, stitch and seam classifications, and measurements for sizing. Voluntary standards developed by the American Association of Textile Chemists and Colorists (AATCC) are used as criteria for evaluating product performance related to colorants (dyes) and chemical finishes. Note that government restrictions came into effect in the United States in 2009, stemming from application of the Consumer Product Safety Improvement Act (CPSIA) governing products sold to children. These restrictions include tighter regulations on lead content of items for children aged 12 and under and can impact the selection of findings and trims used in garments for this age group. In recent years, the lead content of consumer products has become a global safety issue.

There are also some US government–mandated standards related to flammability and product safety, which are overseen by the Consumer Product Safety Commission (CPSC) within the Department of Commerce. However, in an increasingly global environment, the movement has been toward using mandates from the International Organization for Standardization (ISO) for determining product standards. Organizations in the United States and abroad have worked with the ISO to select or develop recognized methods for evaluating textile materials in numerous categories. There are now ISO standards for evaluating textiles for such properties as crocking (color transfer by rubbing), shrinkage, fading, and pilling. Methods for testing tensile strength of yarns have been developed but vary by fiber and yarn type. Standards for laboratory ovens used for drying lab dips for color matching remain an issue. Among the few areas of standards that are mandated by governments are two categories that appear to have a greater impact on apparel producers and consumers than others: labeling standards, including country of origin (COO), and product care and maintenance. Sizing standards, because of the lack of mandated oversight, have flexible application and potential ongoing annoyance to ultimate consumers.

Country of Origin (COO) Labeling

COO labeling rules help establish the tariff rate for duties charged on imported products; also, consumers like to know where products come from. Consumers active in social responsibility often use COO as a primary selection criterion. The complexity of international sourcing increases the difficulty in determining the COO of a product. When an apparel product's fiber comes from one country, the textile used for it is produced in another country, trims are sourced from a third country, the garment is constructed in a fourth country, and finished in a fifth country, it is not that easy to determine the actual source of that product.

If a product or its components originated from different countries, the country of origin is determined based on the place of the product's last "substantial transformation." Commonly used rules for determining a product's substantial transformation are:

- the country where product transformation resulted in a change of tariff category (e.g., from fabric category to apparel category); or
- the country where the greatest value was added to the product.

The label stating COO must be permanently attached to the garment. That permanence may be established by a sewn-in label or by marking the fabric in a manner that the mark will not come off during wear or care.

Care Labeling

The issue of care labeling also intensified with the increased global trade, especially the issue of whether care instructions should be provided in multiple languages. ISO solved that problem by selecting a series of pictograms to express the cleaning and pressing requirements for apparel products. For the EU those diagrams eliminated the necessity of using all the different languages spoken in its twenty-seven countries on products sold throughout Europe.

ASTM went to the ISO and requested that it be able to use the ISO care labeling pictograms on products to be sold in the United States, Canada, and Mexico. A French company owned the rights to the ISO pictograms, and ASTM worried that it might have to pay for the privilege of using them (Dowling, 1997). Also, some of the European care labels included water temperature, and US washing machine controls only indicate hot, warm, and cold. The result was that ASTM developed its own set of pictograms that are similar to but not exactly the same as the ISO care label standards. The care label issue persists in that the ASTM symbols used in North America are not compatible with the symbol system developed by the ISO and required of products sold elsewhere. The dilemma continues.

SOURCING DOCUMENTS

Product Specifications, Cost Sheets, and Vendor Bids

Technical specifications, or specs, are the detailed graphic and written descriptions of styling, materials, dimensions, production procedures, and finishing instructions for a garment style. Written specifications for garment styles are used not only to ensure that final products will meet overall customer's quality standards, but also to provide the detailed criteria necessary for the production and ultimate acceptance of individual products. Specifications are used by everyone involved with a product, including those that develop, produce, promote, and sell the product and those suppliers and vendors that will provide materials and distribution. Specifications are an integral part of the contracts between a sourcing firm and production contractors.

Clarity of language is often an issue, so great care must be taken so that specification sheets are clear and easily understood. Providing photos, technical sketches, or actual samples can prevent many misunderstandings. Textile and apparel firms take great care in the development of specifications because incomplete instructions or mistakes in communication can be disastrous in terms of cost. The specification (spec) sheet package for a garment style is usually prepared by the technical designers who are most familiar with translating the apparel designs from either sketches or samples into written instructions.

The amount of detail in written specs will vary significantly, depending on the sourcing option selected. CMT sourcing requires very detailed specs, whereas with full-package sourcing, the factory is responsible for product development, including specs. However, the more meticulous the spec package is, the more likely the final products will satisfactorily meet the requirements of the customer. At a minimum a specification package should have a style summary sheet, including a drawing of the garment, its brief written description, and a preliminary cost sheet for comparing bids provided by potential contractors. More detailed instructions become part of the compliance standards discussed earlier in this chapter. Figure 8.6 shows a preliminary cost sheet for a single garment.

The cost sheet, and any other available specification information for the garment style, provides the stepping-off point for a vendor to prepare a bid quotation for consideration by the customer. The bidding process moves the cost quotations from a single sample garment to the costs of an entire production run for a specified number of garments. Negotiations continue until vendors provide all the information needed by the customer to make the final decision. At this point, bids from potential vendors, including all factors that might impact the final selection, have to be considered, and additional paperwork and contracts may be initiated. Certainly, the overall product costs will be of great importance in the final selection of vendor, but other considerations must also be weighed.

It is critical that the specification packages provided by the sourcing firm and the contract bids provided by the potential vendor contain all the information needed for completion of the garment and that they spell out who will be responsible for each of the identified functions related to production and delivery to ensure that both parties

Figure 8.6

Cost sheet used to establish garment design and CMT cost estimates for a pair of women's slacks.

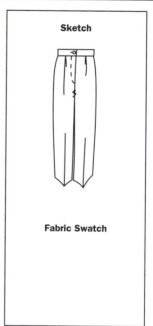

Alex Cameron
New York, NY 10012
212-555-7367
Cost Sheet

Style #: 9807 — Description: tailored, pleated front slacks — Date: 1/10/2010
Division: Women's Sportswear — Size Category: Miss — Season: F2010
Sample Size: 10 — Technical Designer: Beth Hale
Fabric: 12 oz. Polyester/rayon blend suiting — Color: Heather gray

Size	6	8	10	12	14	16
Size Set	1	2	3	3	2	1

Fabric	Yardage	Price	Cost
Suiting, 60" wide	1.5	3.90	$5.85
Lining, 60" wide	1.5	1.20	$1.80
Interfacing	.125	.90	$ .11
Total Fabric			$7.76

Trim/Findings	Quantity	Price	Cost
Zipper, 7"	1	.45	$ .45
Button	1	.09	.09
Thread	1	.20	.20
Brand Label	1	.08	.08
Care Label	1	.02	.02
Hang tag/price ticket	1	.06	.06
Packaging	1	.17	.17
Total Trim			$1.07

Labor	Cost
Cutting	$1.10
Sewing	$1.85
Total Labor	$2.95

	Description	Cost
Shipping	$10.00 per dozen	$ .83
Duty	16% of labor/material	$1.88
Overhead	18% of cost	$2.61

Sketch

Fabric Swatch

Total Manufacturing Cost: $17.10
Markup: 62%
Retail Price: $45.00

understand who is responsible for which operation. The trend is for the customer to push as much of the cost and responsibility onto the vendor as possible, and, in doing so, it becomes ever more critical for all tasks to be accounted for in the bid contracts.

Payment for Goods

After receiving the quotes and deciding which bid to accept, the customer requests a **pro forma invoice** from the selected vendor that includes all information for the sale; this serves as confirmation of the total cost of the goods (Figure 8.7). A final invoice is provided by the vendor when the merchandise is shipped.

Payment for imported merchandise is often done by a **letter of credit**, which is a guarantee to the vendor that the customer has the funds to complete the purchase and that they are reserved for the seller by the buyer's bank. This letter usually has an expiration date close to the date of expected delivery in the contract; if the delivery date is not met, the letter of credit may need to be amended or in extreme cases allowed to expire, preventing payment. Other methods of payment include wire transfers, whereby the customer's bank sends money electronically to the vendor's bank when confirmation is received that the order has been shipped.

Insurance

Decisions about insurance are another area of consideration. As discussed in Chapter 7, international business involves various risks, and insurance coverage can ameliorate problems the importer might encounter should anything happen to merchandise while

Figure 8.7
Example of a pro forma invoice for Alex Cameron slacks.

Pearl River Enterprise Salisbury Road Kowloon, Hong Kong Tel: 852 5555 00000 Email: Kwon@pearlriver.com		Bankers: Bank of China Admiralty Center Hong Kong	
Buyer: Alex Cameron New York, NY 10012 USA	Pro Forma No.: 201 Order No.: PDS1-2010 Payment Mode: LC Terms: FOB	Date: 15/Feb/10 Date: 15/Feb/10 Port: Hong Kong	

Ref. No.	Description	Packing	Quantity	Port	Ship Date	Rate US$	Amount
9807	Tailored, pleated front slacks	12/24	3,600 Ea	Hong Kong		14.39	51,804.00

TOTAL CBM: 131.25   TOTAL FOB: $51,804.00

it is en route to its destination. The two basic types are marine insurance, which protects the merchandise when it is in port or being shipped, and inland marine insurance, which covers the shipment at other times, such as on a truck, airline, or other conveyance used to get the goods to their final destination. Depending on a customer's needs, policies are available to cover loss from fire, bad weather, or theft, but coverage is not available for political instability or war.

Shipping Issues

Prior to signing a contract with a vendor, both the customer's and the vendor's customs agencies, as well as any other countries where merchandise will be shipped, should be consulted to avoid potential problems regarding legal issues that might exist with the product in the country of import. Also, precise contract language will help ensure that packing regulations required at the destination country have been followed by the vendor. Most of this is about paperwork, but it must be handled properly to avoid having merchandise held by the customs in the importing countries.

For novice importers, it is recommended that a customs broker be selected early in the sourcing process to ensure that goods can ultimately enter the desired arrival port and that necessary documents will be available when needed. In the United States, customs brokers are licensed by the US Customs and Border Protection. The information derived from the customs broker becomes a part of the vendor compliance standards.

Clearing Customs

Clearing customs is mostly about paperwork; different goods can require different types of documentation, but there are three forms the shipper must always present at the customs.

- The bill of lading is issued by the carrier or shipper. It is basically a receipt of the goods, acknowledging they have been received on the vessel for shipment and spelling out their destination and the terms for transporting them to their final destination.
- The commercial invoice is used as a customs declaration by the vendor that is exporting the goods and is required to determine their value for assessment of duties and taxes.
- The packing list provides an itemized listing of the merchandise in the shipment and is attached to the outside of the shipping container.

To avoid storage fees at the dock, arrangements can be made for a freight forwarder or other transporter, such as a trucking firm, to facilitate the shipment of goods to the final destination.

Summary

Private brand retailers, brand managers, and sourcing intermediaries are three major groups of firms that import apparel products. A number of methods for sourcing textile materials, finished products, and apparel production are available to apparel importers, including factory direct sourcing, joint ventures, licensing, trade shows, and the utilization of sourcing agents. Apparel manufacturers operate under two major models: CMT factories and full-package, or full-service, factories. When contracting with full-package factories, sourcing firms tend to outsource preproduction and postproduction activities to the vendors. When apparel importers make strategic decisions which type of factory to contract with, they consider the advantages and disadvantages of outsourcing technical design, acquisition of materials, and delivery of finished products to the vendors. Costing of finished apparel products depends on the types of services provided by manufacturing contractors and the country where production takes place.

Sourcing involves much more than simply finding the vendor that has the lowest labor costs. Much depends on what types of merchandise are needed as well as on whether the vendor has the capability to make merchandise to quality specifications in the volume required and in an ethical manner. In addition, attention must be paid to the level and degree of sophistication of communication capabilities and to potential variations in the time line for delivery, dependent upon the types of desired end products and the distance between production and final distribution to consumers.

Sourcing in the global environment is a complex and multidimensional process that heavily relies on sourcing technology such as product lifecycle management (PLM). Much of the sourcing process itself is embodied in the paperwork involved in its financial forms and contracts, beginning with product specification and cost sheets. Vendor selection is made through a bidding process, using pro forma invoices and identification of forms of payment for vendor services.

Learning Activities

1. Why do sourcing firms tend to lean more toward full-package contracts?
2. What is the purpose of vendor compliance contracts?
3. Using the data in Table 8.2, calculate the percentages of (a) labor cost and (b) fabric cost in the total product cost (LDP) for each of the four countries. What is the percent range for the fabric cost in the jacket's total cost? What is the percent range for the labor cost in the jacket's total cost? What are the reasons for the significant ranges?
4. Let's imagine that JCPenney (mass merchant) and J.Crew (at a higher price point) want to produce a tailored wool jacket. Using the data in Table 8.2, justify what country you will recommend for each of the two retailers to have jackets produced. When making your decision, take into account what is more important for each company to compete in the market (price point, quality of garment construction, craftsmanship, lead time to deliver latest trends, etc.). Compare your decision with your classmates.
5. Identifying major knowledge and skills necessary for sourcing apparel professionals:

   a. Based on what you have learned about sourcing apparel assembly in Chapters 7 and 8, what knowledge and skills should sourcing professionals have to be successful in the industry? First, make a list of knowledge and skills working individually (or in small groups), and then compare and discuss them as a class.
   b. Follow up with an internet search to identify job postings for sourcing professionals (sourcing managers, assistant sourcing managers, sourcing directors, etc.). Use *Women's Wear Daily, Sourcing Journal Online,* and other sources. Compile a list of knowledge and skills listed in advertised positions and compare it with your own list.
   c. What are the major job requirements for sourcing professionals and why? Do you believe your program's curriculum helps students develop the required knowledge and skills?

References

Apparel. (n.d.). "Buyer's Guide." Retrieved February 27, 2015, from http://apparel.edgl.com/buyers-guide/

Birnbaum, D. (2005). *Birnbaum's Global Guide to Winning the Great Garment War*. New York, NY: The Fashiondex.

Dowling, M. (July 1997). "New Care Labels for Textiles." *Catalog Age, 14*(7), 18.

Gap Inc. (n.d.). "About: Brands." Retrieved February 22, 2015, from http://www.gapinc.com/content/gapinc/html/aboutus/ourbrands.html

Gereffi, G., & Frederick, S. (2010). "The Global Apparel Value Chain, Trade and the Crisis." Policy Research Working Paper 5281. The World Bank.

Global Brands Group. (n.d.). "Licensed Brands." Retrieved February 28, 2015, from http://www.globalbrandsgroup.com/brands

Greenpeace International. (November 22, 2012). "Window on the World." Retrieved March 5, 2015, from http://greenpeace.tumblr.com/post/36286411529/80-billion-garments-are-produced-world-wide-the-equivalent-of-over-11-garments-a-year-for-every-person-on-the-planet/

Ha-Brookshire, J. E. (2014). *Global Sourcing in the Textile and Apparel Industry*. Upper Saddle River, NJ: Pearson.

Just-style. (n.d.). "About PLM: How Does PLM Work?" Retrieved February 26, 2015, from http://www.just-style.com/plm/how-does-PLM-work.aspx

Kern, S. (August 1, 2014). "PLM: Is Out of the Box a Reality?" Retrieved February 26, 2015, from http://apparel.edgl.com/news%5CPLM—Is-Out-of-the-Box-a-Reality-94273

Komar. (n.d.-a). "About Us: Komar Today." Retrieved February 25, 2015, from http://www.komarbrands.com/komar-about-us/

Komar. (n.d.-b). "Sourcing: Komar Sourcing." Retrieved February 25, 2015, from http://www.komarbrands.com/komar-sourcing/

Li & Fung. (n.d.). "About." Retrieved February 25, 2015, from http://www.lifung.com/about-us/our-global-network/

Macy's Inc. (n.d.). "Private Brands." Retrieved February 22, 2015, from https://www.macysinc.com/macys/private-brands/default.aspx

Nagappan, P. (February 1, 2015). "VF: Stopping Hazardous Chemicals from Entering Supply Chain." Retrieved March 19, 2015, from http://apparel.edgl.com/news/vf—stopping-hazardous-chemicals-from-entering-the-supply-chain97930?referaltype=newsletter

Platzer, M. (2014). *US Textile Manufacturing and the Trans-Pacific Partnership Negotiations*. Washington, DC: Congressional Research Service.

Suleski, J., & Draper, L. (2014). "PLM for Apparel 2014: The Next Stage for Alignment Begins to Take Place." Retrieved February 26, 2015, from http://apparel.edgl.com/reports/plm-for-apparel-2014—the-next-stage-of-alignment-begins-to-take-shape93059?referaltype=newsletter

Thomas, C., & Burns, A. (2014). "Strategy Shift: Collaboration, Tech Advancements Pave Path to Decentralized Sourcing." Retrieved November 5, 2015, from http://apparel.edgl.com/reports/Strategy-Shift—Collaboration,-Tech-Advancements-Pave-Path-to-Decentralized-Sourcing-94226

VF Corporation (n.d.). "About VF: Global Presence." Retrieved February 6, 2015, from http://www.vfc.com/about/global-presence

World Freight Rates (n.d.). "Ocean Freight." Retrieved January 31, 2015, from http://worldfreightrates.com/freight

Zager, M. (February 1, 2015). "Rocky Brands Steps Up to PLM Platform." Retrieved February 26, 2015, from http://apparel.edgl.com/news percent5CRocky-Brands-Steps-Up-to-PLM-Platform97929

TRADING PARTNERS

PART THREE

CHAPTER 9

EUROPE AND THE EUROPEAN UNION

FUN FACT

The European Union (EU) is the largest economy in the world, the top trading partner for eighty countries, and the world's largest trading block for manufactured goods and services. (European Commission, n.d.)

OBJECTIVES

- Explore the evolution of economic and political organization in Europe as related to the textiles and apparel business.
- Investigate trade and economic development regulations in the region.
- Examine the roles of textiles and apparel-producing and apparel-consuming countries and their areas of expertise.

The continent of Europe encompasses multiple ethnicities; frozen and tropical environments; diverse cultures; and developed and developing countries ranging from miniscule to large in size. It incorporates part of the former Soviet Union as well as part of Turkey. Throughout history, these countries have struggled with ethnic conflicts and efforts to unify the territory. The European Union (EU) consists of twenty-eight countries, accounts for 28 percent of the world's exports and imports, and is the world's largest trading block for manufactured goods and services. The EU imports more from developing countries than the United States, Canada, Japan, and China combined. Europe also has a long history in textiles and apparel and includes many of the leading fashion centers in the world. In response to competitive challenges, the textile and apparel industry in Europe has undertaken a lengthy process of restructuring, modernization, and technological progress.

POLITICAL AND ECONOMIC OVERVIEW: EFFORTS TO UNIFY EUROPE

Examine Figure 9.1, a map of Europe. The region is often described as having two parts: Western Europe and Eastern Europe. Note the locations of large countries and consider which might generally be described as northern, western, eastern, and southern Europe. Because geographical sources differ in how they describe the locations of countries, we

GLOBAL LEXICON

adversarial relationships common behaviors between suppliers and customers; in the textile complex, belief that success of one is dependent on costs to another

cost center a department within an organization that is essential to the operation of the company but does not produce a profit

euro European Union common currency, initiated in 2001 by fifteen countries of the EU

European Commission a politically independent institution

responsible for proposing EU legislation, implementing it, and monitoring compliance

European Union (EU) an organization formed in 1993 to expand cooperation regarding trade, social issues, foreign policy, security, defense, and judicial issues

extra EU trade with nations that are not members of the EU

intra EU trade among nations that are members of the EU

supranational organization requires that members give up a portion of their control over selected policies and allows the organization to compel compliance with its mandates

technical textiles textile products designed for thermal and/or mechanical performance and durability including those made for protective clothing and medical use

---

are not going to pick one system; however, it is useful to know the general location of the nations on the continent and their relationships to one another. As you work your way through the following discussion, be sure to locate each country on the map as it is mentioned.

People in Europe have long sought to create economic and industrial—if not political—unity beginning as early as the ninth-century empire of Charlemagne, which included much of Western Europe. During the early 1800s, the French empire of Napoleon I encompassed much of the European continent. During World War II, in the early 1940s, Adolph Hitler nearly succeeded in uniting Europe under Nazi domination. In between these events, many other European dynasties developed and fell. Table 9.1 provides a summary of the continuing evolution of European economic and political organization over the last 60+ years. This evolution required dozens of years of negotiations and dozens of treaties among European countries. You can use this table as a point of reference as these countries are discussed throughout the chapter.

Early collaborations among European countries were international or intergovernmental organizations that depended on the voluntary cooperation of their members. Following World War II, requests for supranational organization became frequent. A **supranational organization** requires that members give up a portion of their control over selected policies and allow the organization to compel compliance with its mandates. European countries recognized the need to take common political positions and command resources comparable with the organization of the United States. They believed that larger markets would promote competition and lead to greater productivity and higher levels of living. Because countries were reluctant to surrender control over political affairs, supranational organization began with economic and industrial integration.

Figure 9.1

Map of Europe, indicating what countries belong to the European Union and when they were admitted to the Union.

Belgium, Luxembourg, and the Netherlands were leaders in trade integration. In 1948, they created a free trade area encompassing the three small countries by forming the Benelux Customs Union (BCU). Trade within the area was tariff and quota free. Then France and West Germany proposed industrial unification of the coal and steel industries, creating the European Coal and Steel Community (ECSC). They invited other nations to participate, and the members of BCU responded. In 1957, the ECSC nations carried unification one step further through formation of the European Economic Community (EEC), widely known as the Common Market. The EEC treaty included a gradual elimination of import duties and quota among member nations and a common external tariff system. Member nations implemented common policies regarding transportation, agriculture, and social insurance and permitted free movement of people and financial resources among the member countries. The UK and other

TABLE 9.1

EVOLUTION OF EUROPEAN POLITICAL AND ECONOMIC ORGANIZATION

Year	Event	Countries Involved
1948	Benelux Customs Union free trade area formed	Belgium, Luxembourg, the Netherlands
1950	European Coal and Steel Community (ECSC) formed	Belgium, France, Italy, Luxembourg, the Netherlands, West Germany
1957	European Economic Community (EEC) Common Market formed by ECSC	Belgium, France, Italy, Luxembourg, the Netherlands, West Germany
1960	European Free Trade Association (EFTA) formed	Austria, Denmark, Norway, Portugal, Sweden, Switzerland, United Kingdom
1967	European Community (EC) formed by merger of EEC and ECSC	Belgium, France, Italy, Luxembourg, the Netherlands, West Germany
1973	EC expanded	Denmark, Ireland, United Kingdom
1981	EC expanded	Greece
1986	EC expanded	Portugal and Spain
1993	European Union (EU) officially formed when EC member legislatures ratified Maastricht Treaty, became known as European Union–12 (EU-12)	Belgium, Denmark, France, Germany, Greece, Ireland, Italy, Luxembourg, the Netherlands, Portugal, Spain, United Kingdom
1994	EU and EFTA joined to form European Economic Area (EEA)	Austria, Belgium, Denmark, France, Germany, Greece, Ireland, Italy, Luxembourg, the Netherlands, Norway, Portugal, Spain, Sweden, Switzerland, United Kingdom
1995	European Union–15 (EU-15) created by adding three countries to EU-12	Austria, Finland, Sweden
2001	EU-15 adopted the euro	Currency used in everyday transactions in twelve European countries
2004	EU-15 added ten countries, became EU-25	Cyprus, Czech Republic, Estonia, Hungary, Latvia, Lithuania, Malta, Poland, Slovakia, Slovenia
2005	Countries identified for potential EU membership	Belarus, Bulgaria, Romania, Russia, Turkey
2005	EU constitution rejected by France and the Netherlands, raised questions about use of euro	France and the Netherlands
2005	EU import quotas phased out, according to the Agreement on Textiles and Clothing	EU-15 and all countries with bilateral agreements
2005	EU initiated new quotas on apparel from China	EU-25 and China
2007	EU-25 added two countries, to become EU-27	Romania and Bulgaria
2007	EU extended import quotas with China expired	EU-27 and China
2009	New EU constitution went into effect; Treaty on EU-27 involved the Functioning of the European Union (TFEU)	
2013	EU-27 added one country to become EU-28	Croatia

Source: Data collected from the World Trade Organization (WTO) and the European Commission.

nations wanted a free trade area instead; therefore, they formed the European Free Trade Association (EFTA), which provided for elimination of tariffs on industrial products only. However, the UK soon recognized the success of the EEC and, overcoming considerable internal resistance, sought membership but was denied twice because of vetoes by President Charles de Gaulle, of France. In 1967, the ECSC and the EEC joined to form the European Community (EC). The EC gradually implemented the economic features of the EEC, but France blocked expansion of membership until 1973, when the UK, Ireland, and Denmark joined. Within the UK, considerable resistance to EC participation continued.

The European economy passed through a deep recession in the late 1970s and early 1980s. The combined profit of Europe's 100 largest corporations was zero. Unemployment, especially among the young, was very high. Growth in productivity lagged behind wage increases. Social costs (health care, unemployment and disability compensation, education, and so on) were twice that of either Canada or the United States (Stone, 1994). It was very apparent that changes had to be made to revitalize the European economy. The effort became focused once again on attempting to create a unified Western Europe.

In 1991, the twelve EC members signed the Maastricht Treaty and in 1993 became the **European Union (EU)**. The primary goal of EU was to expand cooperation regarding trade, social issues, foreign policy, security, defense, and judicial issues. Another major goal was to implement a single currency for EU members. In a move toward these goals, the European Union–12 (EU-12; the original group of EU countries) and EFTA joined in a cooperative arrangement, to form the European Economic Area (EEA). EEA's purpose is to promote a continuous and balanced strengthening of trade and economic relations among the contracting parties, with a view toward creating a homogenous European trade area. Accomplishments include the development of common product standards and the reduction of trade barriers among countries, to institute a so-called single-document structure. For example, truck drivers previously had to carry more than thirty-five documents, which had to be processed when crossing the border from one country to another.

Another problem was that nationalistic policies within countries had created internal monopolies in services, particularly in telecommunications. These monopolies were in a position to continue to charge their customers for the inefficiencies that had become common in their operations. Monopolies were abandoned in favor of competition. Government procurement also was opened up to all countries in the group instead of being confined to individual countries. It became possible to access the whole Western European market and take advantage of economies of scale (Stone, 1994).

In 1995, the EU-12 became the European Union–15 (EU-15) when Austria, Finland, and Sweden were admitted. In 2001, the EU-15 implemented the use of a single currency, the **euro**, thereby accomplishing one of the EU's primary goals. Of the fifteen countries, twelve adopted the euro. In 2004, the EU-15 was enlarged to include ten new member states, forming the European Union–25 (EU-25). These new nations also participate in the EEA. Some of the new nations are located in Eastern Europe and emerged from communist rule, in part as a result of the demise of the Soviet Union. In 2007, with the admission of Bulgaria and Romania, the EU-25 became the European Union–27 (EU-27). At this time, a revised constitution was sought, via development of the Treaty of Lisbon (which was based on a previous version, the Reform Treaty), and nations within the union began to sign the newly developed constitution. In late 2009, the Treaty of Lisbon became the Treaty on the Functioning of the European Union (TFEU), providing a new constitution for the EU. The **European Commission**, which is the politically independent institution responsible for proposing EU legislation, implementing it, and monitoring compliance, considers the single market one of the EU's greatest achievements (European Commission, 2009a).

By 2010, a financial crisis that originated in 2008 forced EU nations to adopt a $950 billion package to aid financially troubled Eurozone nations and support the euro; additional measures were adopted and additional funds were set aside in 2011 and 2012. That forced several EU nations to adopt severe austerity measures. The austerity measures hit many EU nations hard and, as a whole, EU unemployment increased to record levels. In 2013, the EU became the EU-28 with the joining of Croatia.

Economic and Industrial Standing of Selected European Countries

The last four chapters of this text focus on four different regions of the world and their involvement in textiles and apparel. In order to gain a better understanding of the role of working conditions and the environments for businesses in different countries in the world, we will use the Global Competitiveness Index (GCI) in the last four chapters. The GCI provides a measure of national competitiveness "defined as the set of institutions, policies and factors that determine the level of productivity of the country. The level of productivity, in turn sets the level of prosperity that can be reached by an economy" (World Economic Forum, 2015). The GCI is an indicator of how much support and/or opposition a company has to deal with to do business in a particular country. Basically, *the higher the GCI number, the less productive the country is.*

Many of the indicators used to calculate GCI were introduced in Chapter 7 in Table 7.1 in the discussion about selection of countries for sourcing textiles and apparel. The two primary factors for sourcing are (1) level of development and (2) geographic location; these are also key contributors to GCI rankings. The GCI has three components related to the characteristics of a country:

1. The Basic Requirements Subindex includes factors related to institutions, infrastructure, macroeconomic environment, and health and primary education.
2. The Efficiency Enhancers Subindex includes factors related to higher education, efficiency of goods markets, labor markets, financial market development, technological readiness, and market size.
3. The Innovation and Sophistication Subindex considers factors related to business sophistication and innovation.

For each country being presented in tables and discussed in this and the following chapters, the Global Competitive Index (GCI) is presented as a number in parentheses next to the names of the countries in the table (the lower the number, the more competitive the country). The GCI provides an indicator of the ability of each country to compete in the world market, of the environment businesses operate within, and of how much help or hindrance the country provides to companies doing business there.

Table 9.2 itemizes the characteristics of the European countries that are most active in the textile and apparel trade, sorted into three categories by time of EU membership and listed in alphabetical order in each category. In addition, the table includes a selection of European countries that are active in textiles and/or apparel but are not members of the EU. This table provides a foundation for the discussion in this chapter. Take a few minutes to look over the range of GCIs next to the name of the country and think about what that number means.

TABLE 9.2

CHARACTERISTICS OF SELECTED EUROPEAN COUNTRIES THAT ARE ACTIVE IN THE TEXTILE AND APPAREL TRADE[1]

European Union (EU) Countries with 2014–2015 Global Competitiveness Index (GCI) for Each	Geographic Size (in Thousands of km)	Population (in Millions)	Life Expectancy (in Years)	Adult Literacy Rate	GDP[2] (in Billions of US Dollars)	Per Capita GDP (in US Dollars)	Inflation Rate[3]	Labor Force (in Millions)	Unemployment Rate	Internet Users (in Millions)
EU-15 (1995)										
Finland	338.2	5.3	79.7	100.0%	$ 221.5	$ 34,900	1.2%	2.67	8.6%	4.39
Germany (5)	357.0	81.0	80.4	99.0%	$ 3,621.0	$ 34,200	0.8%	44.76	5.0%	65.13
Netherlands (8)	41.5	16.9	81.1	99.0%	$ 798.1	$ 39,000	0.3%	7.89	7.2%	14.87
United Kingdom (9)	243.6	63.7	79.6	99.0%	$ 2,435.0	$ 35,400	1.5%	32.59	5.7%	51.44
Sweden (10)	450.3	9.7	81.9	99.0%	$ 434.2	$ 36,800	-0.2%	5.12	7.9%	8.40
Denmark (13)	43.1	5.6	79.1	99.0%	$ 248.7	$ 36,200	0.3%	2.77	5.7%	4.75
Belgium (18)	30.5	10.5	79.9	99.0%	$ 467.1	$ 36,600	0.5%	5.22	8.5%	8.11
Luxembourg (19)	2.6	0.5	80.1	100.0%	$ 50.7	$ 77,600	0.7%	0.25	7.1%	0.43
Austria (21)	83.9	8.2	80.2	98.0%	$ 386.9	$ 45,400	1.5	3.78	4.5%	6.14
France (23)	643.4	66.3	81.7	99.0%	$ 2,587.0	$ 32,800	0.6%	29.87	9.7%	45.26
Ireland (23)	70.3	4.8	80.6	99.0%	$ 224.7	$ 42,200	0.3%	2.17	11.3%	3.04
Spain (35)	505.4	47.7	81.5	97.9%	$ 1,534.0	$ 33,700	-0.2%	22.93	24.3%	28.12
Portugal (36)	92.1	10.8	79.0	93.3%	$ 276.0	$ 21,700	-0.9%	5.27	14.2%	5.17
Italy (49)	301.3	61.7	82.3	98.4%	$ 2,066.0	$ 32,200	0.2%	25.51	12.5%	3.04
Greece (81)	131.9	10.8	80.3	96.0%	$ 284.3	$ 32,100	-1.4%	3.91	26.8%	4.97
EU-25 (2004)										
Estonia (29)	45.2	1.3	74.1	99.8%	$ 35.4	$ 18,800	0.5%	0.67	8.6%	6.68
Czech Republic (37)	78.9	10.6	78.3	99.0%	$ 299.7	$ 25,100	0.4%	5.42	7.9%	6.0
Lithuania (41)	65.3	3.5	76.0	99.6%	$ 79.0	$ 15,000	0.2%	1.45	11.1%	1.96
Latvia (42)	64.6	2.2	73.4	99.7%	$ 48.6	$ 14,500	0.7%	1.01	9.5%	1.50
Poland (43)	312.7	38.3	76.7	99.8%	$ 941.4	$ 17,800	0.1%	18.26	12.7%	22.45
Malta (47)	0.3	0.4	80.1	92.8%	$ 13.4	$ 23,800	0.2%	0.19	5.9%	0.24
Cyprus (58)	9.3	1.2	78.3	97.6%	$ 24.9	$ 21,200	-0.3%	0.36	15.9%	0.43
Hungary (60)	93.0	9.9	75.5	99.4%	$ 239.9	$ 18,800	0.0%	4.39	7.1%	6.18
Slovakia (75)	49.0	5.4	74.9	99.6%	$ 149.9	$ 21,100	-0.1%	2.73	12.7%	4.06
Slovenia (70)	20.3	2.0	77.8	99.7%	$ 60.54	$ 28,200	0.4%	0.91	13.6	1.1

European Union (EU) Countries with 2014–2015 Global Competitiveness Index (GCI) for Each	Geographic Size (in Thousands of km)	Population (in Millions)	Life Expectancy (in Years)	Adult Literacy Rate	GDP[2] (in Billions of US Dollars)	Per Capita GDP (in US Dollars)	Inflation Rate[3]	Labor Force (in Millions)	Unemployment Rate	Internet Users (in Millions)
EU-27 (2007)										
Bulgaria (54)	110.9	6.9	74.3	98.2%	$ 123.3	$ 12,600	–1.6%	2.51	5.1%	1.40
Romania (59)	238.4	21.7	74.7	97.3%	$ 386.5	$ 11,500	1.4%	9.95	7.0%	7.79
EU-28 (2014)										
Croatia (77)	56.6	4.5	76.4	98.1%	$ 128.5	$ 17,600	0.2%	1.71	21.0%	2.23
European Countries Outside the European Union										
Switzerland (1)	41.3	8.1	82.4	99.0%	$ 444.7	$ 41,600	0.0%	5.15	3.2%	6.15
Norway (11)	323.8	5.1	81.6	100.0%	$ 339.5	$ 53,300	1.9%	2.72	3.4%	4.43
Turkey (45)	783.6	81.6	73.3	79.2%	$ 1,512	$15,300	8.9%	27.56	9.4%	27.23
Russia (53)	17,098.2	142.5	70.2	99.4%	$ 3,568.0	$15,200	11.9%	75.25	4.8%	40.85
Ukraine (76)	603.6	44.3	69.2	99.4%	$ 373.1	$ 6,400	16.5%	22.11	8.8%	7.77
Belarus[4]	207.6	9.5	72.2	99.6%	$ 171.2	$ 18,631	18.3%	5.00	1.0%	2.64

[1] Table is sorted by the three stages of development of the European Union (EU) membership plus European countries not in the EU in 2014. The Global Competitiveness Index 2014–2015 (GCI) ranking for each country is in parentheses following each country name. The time frame indicated in the header in each of the four sections of the table indicates when groups of countries became a part of the European Union.

[2] Gross domestic product (GDP), in purchasing power parity.

[3] The rate at which the general level of prices for goods and services is rising and, subsequently, purchasing power is falling.

[4] Belarus is not yet included in the Global Competitiveness Index.

Source: Based on estimates of 2014 data from Central Intelligence Agency (CIA). "The World Factbook." Retrieved December 28, 2015, from https://www.cia.gov/library/publications/the-world-factbook/

Scan down the first two columns of data in Table 9.2 (geographic size and population). Look for the countries that are the largest in size and have the largest populations. Then look at the last section of the table. Russia, not a member of the EU, is by far the largest country in the world (more than 17 million square kilometers) and has the largest population. Russia is physically nearly twice as large as the United States and spans eleven time zones. Western Russia is less than a fourth of the size of the total country of Russia and is located east of the Ural Mountains, in Europe. Eastern Russia makes up northern Asia. Russia is being discussed in this chapter, because its population density is concentrated in the western part of the country, it has become closely associated with the EU, and it is a potential EU member. Also, Russia is a primary participant in the textile and apparel trade with EU countries. Turkey is the second-largest country in Europe, a little bigger than Texas, and has the third-largest population. Turkey is split between Europe and Asia and has been trying for many years to gain membership in the EU. You should be aware of the location of Turkey as well as its importance in the textile and apparel industry; however, much of our discussion of Turkey takes place in Chapter 12, as part of the Middle East.

Examine the *life expectancies* and *literacy* as listed in Table 9.2. Note that most of the countries in the EU-15 have life expectancies exceeding 78 years and literacy exceeding 98 percent. In contrast, most of the newer members of the EU have life expectancies that are considerably shorter, in the mid 70s, while literacy remains similar. What does that tell you about the levels of development of these three groups of EU member countries? Now look at GDP per capita. This is a good indicator of the *current* well-being of the population in each country. EU-15 countries, with the exception of Portugal, have per capita GDP of over $32,000. Note that Luxembourg, an extremely small but wealthy country, has a per capita GDP of over $77,000. In contrast, new members of the EU have significantly lower GDP per capita. Note, too, that Germany has the largest gross domestic product (GDP), even though Russia has by far the largest population. What does that say about the level of industrial development in each country? It is dangerous to examine GDP outside the context of the other characteristics of a country. Geographic size, population, and literacy all contribute to GDP; this is why GDP per capita is a better measure of overall well-being in a country than is GDP alone. Per capita GDP helps explain the relationship between GDP and the size of the population.

The inflation rate of a country is another indicator of trends in the well-being of the population. **Inflation** is the rate at which the general level of prices for goods and services is rising and subsequently purchasing power is falling. If the inflation rate is negative, the purchasing power is increasing. According to some standards, inflation of 3 percent or less is regarded as acceptable or normal. Negative inflation rates are unusual, but, in general, inflation rates are low because of the worldwide economic recession in 2009. Rapidly rising inflation is often a part of economic recovery. The highest inflation rates in Table 9.2 are in countries outside the EU: Belarus at 12.5 percent, Russia at 11.9 percent, and Ukraine at 16.5 percent. The high rates of inflation put serious pressure on the choices consumers have to make to obtain basic goods and services. EU members all have inflation rates of at or less than 5 percent. The highest inflation rate among the EU countries is Romania, with 5 percent; the lowest is Ireland, with -3.9 percent.

In Chapter 1, based on 2012 data, we used GDP per capita (PPP) as an indicator of a country's overall level of economic and industrial development (refer back to Table

1.1) and the discussion of how countries are classified by level of economic development, using world's average GDP per capita. According to that distribution, of the EU members included in Table 9.2, most countries can be classified as developed and some countries, such as Romania, as developing economies. Of the European countries listed in Table 9.2 that are outside the EU, Switzerland and Norway have remained independent of the EU by choice. Some other European countries such as Turkey and Ukraine are trying to gain membership or likely will in the future.

For firms seeking new countries for sourcing textile and apparel production, the size of a country's labor force and the unemployment rate are of particular interest. Obviously, countries with larger populations have larger labor forces. Average age of population may also be of interest; it might suggest whether a large portion of the population is very young or very old and therefore unemployable. Some small countries, such as Luxembourg, which is smaller than Rhode Island, have thousands of workers who commute from surrounding countries daily to work there. Unemployment rate is a statistic that countries do not like to report, and the numbers can be very misleading. Many footnotes tend to be attached to employment and unemployment data. For example, some countries report low unemployment rates but note that large portions of the population are "underemployed," that is, are doing jobs for low pay that do not make use of people's capabilities. There is a question as to whether transient labor should be counted. Thus, it is not appropriate to take employment data at face value and seek out explanations from alternative sources. For example, if you Google "Luxembourg unemployment data," multiple choices will pop up to give an opportunity for comparisons.

The "Internet Users" column is included in the table as an indicator of two things. First, the number of customers that might be using websites for business purposes, including retail sale and purchase of merchandise, is established. Second, the number of internet users as a percentage of the population is an indicator of the level of overall technology development and adoption within a particular country.

Another issue facing the European Union and many other countries is the aging of their populations. Aging populations change distribution of wealth, types of products purchased, availability of funds for medical care, and other needs; more specifically to this text, it will change the types of textiles and apparel people need, want, and/or can afford to buy. This concern has grown to the point that the EU funded a research project that was published in 2014 titled "Population Ageing in Europe: Facts, Implications and Policies." Read the following concept statement and then read Case 9.1.

Longevity is one of the biggest achievements of modern societies. In the last 20 years, people all over the world have, on average, gained 6 years of life expectancy. Children born after 2011 have a one in three chance of reaching their 100th birthday. Europeans are living longer than ever before and this pattern is expected to continue due to unprecedented medical advances and improved standards of living. By 2020, a quarter of Europeans will be over 60 years of age. Combined with low birth rates, this will bring about significant changes to the structure of European society, which will impact on our economy, social security and health care system, the labour market and many other spheres of our lives. (European Commission, 2014a)

DOES THE WORLD NEED MORE BABIES?

Much has been written about Europe's debt and financial crises, but it faces many other challenges. Many European countries' populations are rapidly aging, while potential parents are having few babies. "Thus, governments and advocacy groups are becoming increasingly creative about getting their citizens to procreate" (Noack, 2015). This trend was noted in the United States when the *National Review* reported "as a general rule people have fewer babies as their societies become more affluent and urbanized" and "the US birth rate in 2011 was 63.2 per 1,000 women ages 15 to 44, the lowest ever recorded" (Barone, 2013). Sex education classes are being blamed, in part, for the decline in the birthrates around the world. Twenty-one US states now have laws related to the medical accuracy of sex education classes, but no guidance seems to be applied across state lines or within states related to the general content of sex education classes (National Conference of State Legislatures, 2015).

In contrast, in Europe and in particular in Denmark, schoolchildren are being taught in class that they should have more babies. Fertility rates lag far behind other countries even though the Scandinavian country comes out on the top of many other international rankings. The Association Sex and Society, which produces Denmark's sex education guides, says unwillingness to raise children is only part of the problem. Sex education has focused on using contraceptives and preventing diseases, while not including the benefits of having babies and raising healthy children. Now Denmark's teachers are addressing the need to include the entire life cycle process (Figure Case 9.1).

Other European governments are also addressing this problem. For example, an employed parent of a newborn child in Sweden has a total of 480 days of paid time to care for the child. When the parent returns to work, he or she is entitled to receive previous salaries. Parents also get other benefits, including subsidized gym memberships. Children in France can participate in many types of entertainment and activities for free or for a discounted price. France, Germany, and some other European countries pay families a monthly allowance for children who are younger than 20 (Noack, 2015). These benefits are examples of the recognition that aging of the population has dramatic impacts on each country's economy and the businesses that operate within it. It can also mean dramatic changes for the textiles and apparel industries that operate in each country and around the world.

Noack, R. (April 11, 2015). "Please Make More Babies, Europe Urges Its Residents." *Star Tribune*, p. 2.

Barone, M. (February 4, 2013). "More Jobs and More Babies, Please." Retrieved October 25, 2015, from http://www.nationalreview.com/article/339654/more-jobs-and-more-babies-please-michael-barone

National Conference of State Legislatures. (2015). "State Policies on Sex Education in Schools." Retrieved August 27, 2015, from www.ncsl.org/research/health/state-policies-on-sex-education-in-schools.aspx

1. How might the increasing elderly population relate to a growing problem of lack of available jobs for teenagers and young adults?
2. How might the ideas presented in Case 9.1 relate to the growing demand for designer apparel for children?
3. In what ways might aging of populations cause changes in the mode of operation of the textiles and apparel industry?

Figure Case 9.1
Sex education class in Copenhagen.

ROLE OF THE EUROPEAN UNION IN TEXTILES AND APPAREL

In general, in Europe as well as around the world, countries have used production of textiles and apparel as a means of industrialization. During the last 50 years, developed countries have seen their textile and apparel industries' employment decline, while domestic consumption became dependent on imports. (Note: Most of the reports related to European countries use the term "clothing" instead of "apparel," so you will see "clothing" used more in this chapter than in previous chapters.)

The textile and apparel industry in the EU comprises the following segments:

- treatment of raw materials, that is, the preparation or production of natural and man-made textile fibers and yarns
- production of knitted and woven fabrics
- finishing activities, to give fabrics visual, physical, and aesthetic properties
- transformation of fabrics into products such as garments, carpets, home textiles, and technical or industrial textiles

In June 2014, the European Commission reported as follows:

- "The EU textile and clothing sector is a SMEs (small and medium enterprises) based industry as companies of less than fifty employees account for more than 90 percent of the workforce and produce almost 60 percent of the value added."
- In the EU-28 the biggest producers in the textile and apparel industry are the five most populated countries, i.e., Italy, France, UK, Germany, and Spain, accounting for about three-quarters of EU-28 production of textiles and clothing. Southern countries such as Italy, Greece, and Portugal, some of the new member states such as Romania, Bulgaria, and Poland and, to a lesser extent, Spain and France, contribute more to total clothing production, while northern countries such as the UK, Germany, Belgium, the Netherlands, Austria, and Sweden contribute relatively more to textile production.
- As regards the textiles and clothing external trade performance, about 20 percent of EU-27 production in value is sold in the external market despite limited access to many third country markets. However, [there] remain significant impediments to trade in textiles and clothing, especially in some of the largest and more competitive exporters in the sector, and the European industry has the potential to increase production and exports to those parts of the world when trade barriers [are] lifted. By comparison with manufacturing as a whole, it is worth noting that external markets are the higher importance for the textiles and clothing industry. (European Commission, 2014b)

The industry has seen a series of radical transformations since the early 1990s, owing to a combination of technological changes, higher production costs, the emergence of significant global competition, and the elimination of the quota system. The response to these challenges has been considerable shifts in the industry's overall approach. In general, the industry has reduced its focus on mass production and fashion basics to concentrate on a wider variety of products, especially technical/industrial textiles and nonwovens and on high-quality garments with high design and/or performance content.

Distribution is the last element of the textile and apparel supply chain and is made up of all the activities involved in selling the product to the final consumer through various distribution networks, including retail. This element is reported separately from the textile and apparel industry itself. To appreciate the magnitude and diversity of this process, we need to briefly explore European retail. What may be a surprise to some is that the eight top retailers in the world, after the global leaders, Walmart and Costco, are European:

- Carrefour—France
- Tesco PLC—UK
- Metro Ag—Germany
- Schwartz—Germany
- The Kroger Co.—Germany
- Aldi—Germany

These firms are all involved in the sale of general merchandise, with a heavy focus on food, but they also have expanded to clothing sales in recent years.

The top ten fashion retailers based in Europe are reported in Table 9.3. Many of these retailers are also leaders in sourcing for their own brands, engaged in producing their own brands, and/or have expanded far beyond Europe to assert a global presence. The country's GCI (1-144) follows each name in the description.

TABLE 9.3

TOP TEN EUROPEAN FASHION RETAILERS IN 2013, RANKED BY SALES IN BILLIONS OF EUROS[a]

Rank	Retailer	Retail Revenue (Billions of Euros)	Description Including Each Country's Global Competitiveness Index in Brackets[b]
1	H&M	€11.4	Sweden (10); more than 2,000 stores around the world; concept is fashion, fast fashion, and quality at best price
2	Inditex	€10.9	Spain (35); uses more than 100 other companies that design, manufacture, and distribute apparel in more than 4,530 stores in 73 countries; includes Zara, Pull and Bear, and other brands
3	Marks & Spencer	€9.4	United Kingdom (9); more than 600 UK department stores, expanding internationally; 51% of business in food, 49% in clothing and home goods
4	C&A	€6.8	Belgium (18); part of Swiss Cofra Group, with retail headquarters in Germany (5); 1,149 clothing stores, plus 214 children's stores and other specialty formats in Europe, Latin America, and China
5	Primark	€5.3	UK (9); founded in Dublin, now in eight European countries; casual and career wear, soon to be in US
6	Next	€4.4	UK (9); 500 stores in the UK and Ireland and 170 franchise stores overseas; casual women's, men's, and children's apparel and accessories
7	Debenhams	€2.8[c]	UK (9); department store group with 153 stores in the UK and Ireland and 48 stores in 17 other nations
8	Esprit	€2.8[c]	US (3); founded in San Francisco, managed now from Germany (5); 770 stores in 40 countries
9	Benetton Group	€1.6[c]	Italy (49); 6,000 stores in 120 countries; major brands include United Colors of Benetton, Sisley, and Playlife
10	Arcadia	€1.0[c]	UK (9); privately owned, with 2,500 stores in 30 countries and seven major fashion brands, including Topshop and Miss Selfridge

[a]Information in this table was derived from individual companies' websites.

[b]GPI indicators are the numbers following the country name indicating the country's ranking in the Global Production Index (GPI).

[c]Estimate.

Source: Retail-Index.com. (2010). "Top Fashion & Clothing Retailers in Europe." Retrieved April 3, 2015, from www.retail-index.com/Sectors/FashionClothingRetailersinEurope.aspx

At the end of the Multifiber Arrangement in the mid-2000s, the textile industry of Europe was still generating a surplus of exports over imports; however, EU nations as a group have now experienced a reversal in that pattern. Much of the growth in overall textile production in the region has been attributed to the automation of the spinning and weaving processes and the development of textile products beyond those used for apparel, such as industrial applications and nonwovens. During the first decade of the twenty-first century, Europe focused attention on the development of automation in a number of processes within apparel manufacturing, believing that these technological advances would contribute to mass customization in garment production and help reclaim some of the production being lost to imports coming from developing countries. The primary goal of the European apparel business has been to retain its image as a world fashion leader and contributor of high-value design.

An overall picture of imports and exports of EU textile and apparel products can be ascertained by an examination of Tables 9.4a and 9.4b. Table 9.4a addresses textile and apparel imports; Table 9.4b addresses textile and apparel exports as measured by value in square meter equivalents. The tables present the totals for EU-27, then break those

TABLE 9.4A

IMPORTS OF TEXTILES AND APPAREL BY THE EUROPEAN UNION (EU-27) AND OTHER SELECTED EUROPEAN COUNTRIES, IN MILLIONS OF US DOLLARS

Country	Textile Imports (in Millions of US Dollars)			Apparel Imports (in Millions of US Dollars)			Percentage Share in Total Merchandise Imports[a]		
	2000	2006	2012	2000	2006	2012	2000	2006	2012
EU-27	$57,422	$76,329	$74,118	$83,191	$144,448	$170,058	5.4%	4.1%	2.9%
Intra EU[b]	$41,200	$52,402	——[d]	$43,043	$ 70,078	$ 84,658	——[d]	——[d]	——[d]
Extra EU[c]	$16,222	$23,927	$27,126	$40,148	$ 74,370	$ 93,083	6.2%	5.3%	3.9%
Other European Countries									
Switzerland (1)	$ 1,326	$ 1,800	$ 2,050	$ 3,160	$ 4,654	$ 5,721	5.4%	4.4%	2.9%
Norway (11)	$ 509	$ 772	$ 906	$ 1,287	$ 1,977	$ 2,668	5.2%	4.2%	3.1%
Russia (53)	$ 1,316	$ 3,613	$ 4,661	$ 2,688	$ 8,103	$ 9,218	8.9%	9.2%	2.9%
Ukraine (76)	$ 450	$ 916	$ 1,280	$ 60	$ 342	$ 1,157	3.6%	2.2%	1.4%
Croatia (77)	$ 249	$ 484	$ 416	$ 278	$ 518	$ 609	8.3%	4.4%	2.9%
Belarus[d]	$ 256	$ 427	$ 639	——[e]	——[e]	$ 240	3.0%	1.5%	0.5%

Note: Textiles and apparel are given as a percentage of each country's total merchandise imports along with the Global Competitiveness Index for each country.

[a]*Total: total textile plus apparel imports in the world.*

[b]*Intra EU: trade among EU-27 nations.*

[c]*Extra EU: trade with countries other than EU-27 nations.*

[d]*Belarus is not listed in the GCI.*

[e]*Data not available.*

Source: World Trade Organization. (2009). "Merchandise Trade by Product." Retrieved January 16, 2010, from http://www.wto.org/english/res_e/statis_e/its2009_e/its09_merch_trade_product_e.pdf; World Economic Forum. (2015). "Global Competitiveness Report 2014–2015." Retrieved October 25, 2015, from http://reports.weforum.org/global-competitiveness-report-2014-2015/

TABLE 9.4B

EXPORTS OF TEXTILES AND APPAREL BY THE EUROPEAN UNION (EU-27) AND OTHER SELECTED EUROPEAN COUNTRIES, IN MILLIONS OF US DOLLARS

Country	Textile Exports (in Millions of US Dollars)			Apparel Exports (in Millions of US Dollars)			Percentage Share in Total Merchandise Exports[a]		
	2000	2006	2012	2000	2006	2012	2000	2006	2012
EU-27	$56,737	$73,846	$69,366	$56,240	$91,437	$80,356	4.6%	3.3%	1.9%
Intra EU[b]	$41,170	$52,310	$46,992	$43,286	$70,538	$84,658	5.1%	3.5%	2.2%
Extra EU[c]	$15,567	$21,536	$22,394	$12,954	$20,899	$27,717	3.7%	2.7%	1.3%
Other European Countries									
Switzerland (1)	$ 1,503	$ 1,593	$ 1,175	$ 607	$ 1,620	$ 1,922	2.7%	1.9%	0.6%
Norway (11)	$ 173	$ 233	$ 208	——[e]	——[e]	——[e]	0.3%	0.2%	——[e]
Russia (53)	$ 430	$ 537	$ 657	——[e]	——[e]	——[e]	0.4%	0.1%	0.1%
Ukraine (76)	$ 127	$ 244	$ 232	$ 417	$ 682	$ 719	3.8%	2.1%	2.1%
Croatia (77)[f]	$ 87	$ 113	$ 110	$ 469	$ 538	$ 604	12.6%	5.3%	4.2%
Belarus[d]	$ 410	$ 504	$ 727	$ 262	$ 350	$ 449	9.2%	3.2%	1.2%

Note: Textiles and apparel are given as a percentage of each country's total merchandise exports along with the Global Competitiveness Index for each country.

[a]Total: total textile plus apparel exports in the world.

[b]Intra EU: trade among EU-27 nations.

[c]Extra EU: trade with countries other than EU-27 nations.

[d]Belarus is not listed in the GCI.

[e]No data available.

[f]Croatia was in the process of joining the EU in 2012, so it is included in this table.

Source: World Trade Organization. (2009). "Merchandise Trade by Product." Retrieved January 16, 2010, from http://www.wto.org/english/res_e/statis_e/its2009_e/its09_merch_trade_product_e.pdf; World Economic Forum. (2015). "Global Competitiveness Report 2014–2015." Retrieved October 25, 2015, from http://reports.weforum.org/global-competitiveness-report-2014-2015/

figures down into intra EU and extra EU, and finish with selected non-EU European nations.

- **Intra EU** refers to trade among countries that are members of the EU.
- **Extra EU** refers to trade with European countries that are not members of the EU.

The countries included in addition to EU members are those identified by the WTO as European countries ranked among the largest textile and apparel traders in the world. Note in particular that, in almost every country, apparel imports rise more consistently than textile imports. (Note: The data related to GCI are in parentheses after each country name.)

The last three columns of Tables 9.4a and 9.4b identify the percentage of each nation's total merchandise trade that is made up of textiles and apparel. These percentages may be associated with a number of things related to dependence on the textile and apparel trade, such as:

- level of domestic consumption,
- availability of materials for domestic production,
- level of economic or industrial development, or both

Note that EU-27 had steady increases in the value of both textile and apparel imports and exports but that the dollar value of apparel trade was consistently much higher than the textile trade. During the given time periods, the dollar value of textile imports and exports remained similar, whereas the dollar value of apparel imports and exports more than doubled. Remember, this is the time period in which trade adjustments were being made to the ending of the MFA quota system, which had long limited low-cost apparel imports from developing countries. That is reflected in the $87 billion increase in extra EU apparel imports from 2000 to 2012.

Now look at intra EU textile and apparel imports and exports. These data show a dramatic increase from 2000 to 2006 followed by a slowdown to 2012. It appears that extra EU sources caused some slowdown of intra EU trade. The data reported for imports and exports are similar to each other in each time frame, because they reflect reports of the same goods being traded across borders within the EU system of countries. Compare intra EU and extra EU textile imports and exports. Intra EU trade in textiles is more than double extra EU trade. In other words, EU countries were acquiring more textiles for production of finished goods from countries inside the EU than from the rest of the world. Because of missing intra EU data for 2012, it is difficult to make a judgment, but given the slight decline in the EU-27 for 2012 textile imports, intra EU must have also had a decline. Now compare extra EU apparel imports and exports. Apparel exports were far lower than imports throughout the period. The majority of apparel being consumed was coming from outside the EU. At the beginning of the period, extra EU apparel imports were already more than double apparel exports; at the end, they were triple, showing a rapid increase from outside countries.

Consider the other European countries. As with the EU, both textile and apparel imports and exports increased throughout the period for those countries for which data were available. The greatest changes occurred for Russia, whose trade with the EU increased dramatically. Russia was a primary European player in the textile trade as well as a primary importer of apparel, due to its large population (Table 9.2). Now turn your attention to the last three columns of the tables. These columns report the country's percentage share of textiles and apparel in the country's total merchandise trade. This is an indicator of the dependence of a country's economy on the textile and apparel trade. Related to imports, all except Russia show the same or slight declines of participation; Russia shows a slight increase followed by a dramatic decline. In terms of exports, all the countries show declines in participation in textile and apparel trade.

The EU liberalized trade with China, based on normal trade relations principles, when China joined the WTO in 2001. Trade was also liberalized with countries in Central and Eastern Europe, many of which had previously been part of the former Soviet Union or Socialist Bloc. Quotas were established until 2005 and more liberal safeguards were in effect until 2008. Free trade agreements also were developed between the EU and Egypt, Tunisia, Morocco, Chile, Mexico, and Sub-Saharan African nations. However, many of these agreements have had to be renegotiated as the EU expanded and old agreements expired. To be competitive, manufacturers and retailers in high-wage countries increasingly outsourced CMT (cut-make-trim) production to Eastern Europe and northern Africa to reduce garment costs because of the availability of preferential trade agreements. Despite outsourcing, some EU domestic manufacturing firms went out of business and others were gobbled up in mergers and acquisitions.

In 2003, the EU collectively was considered the largest trader of textiles and apparel in the world. In 2005, the EU faced a surge in imports from China when the Multifiber

Arrangement expired. As mentioned earlier, the EU immediately initiated a series of extended quotas on selected apparel categories that, to the fury of importers and retailers, resulted in a refusal to release more than 80 million Chinese-made sweaters, trousers, and bras that were being held in European ports. Importers could not fill orders, and retailers could not fill their shelves. European governments were blamed for issuing too many import licenses (Fuller, 2005). By the end of 2007, all those extended quotas on Chinese goods had expired, and the influx of goods from that country resumed. By 2009, China provided more apparel to the world market than the EU. Overall, the EU internally is still producing large quantities of many product categories. Its members are also their own best customers while Russia is one of the best external customers.

The EU has trade agreements with numerous nations throughout the world. Some are with other European nations, such as Norway, Iceland, and Switzerland. Of particular interest here is the Cotonou Agreement, which provides free trade in goods with seventy-nine nations from Africa, the Caribbean, and the Pacific and will be in effect until 2020. Between the changes in the membership of the EU itself, the involvement of the WTO, and ongoing negotiations, understanding the full gamut of trade agreements in force for this continent can be somewhat daunting. At the same time, due to the activity of the European Free Trade Association, a total of twenty-five free trade agreements with thirty-five different countries were operating in 2015 (European Free Trade Association, (n.d)). In general, these trade agreements provide for trade preferences, which may include the provision for reduced or nonexistent tariffs on goods traded between the participating nations and the EU.

Beginning in 2009, Germany (GCI = 5) has established a role as the biggest trade partner of Vietnam (GCI = 68). Vietnam and Germany have built a foundation for a long-term trade cooperation relationship. Germany also provides a gateway for Vietnamese products to be exported to European markets. In 2013, the bilateral trade between the two countries increased by 18 percent compared to that of 2012 and reached a value of US$7.7 billion. Vietnam's exports to Germany increased by 15.5 percent and achieved a value of US$4.7 billion, creating a trade surplus of US$1.77 billion. In 2014, trade with Germany increased by another 7.32 percent. Textiles and garments are 15.1 percent of the total export value. Many different types of footwear were third in export value and increased by 40 percent in 2014. Other Vietnamese exported products include telephones, mobile phones and parts, and coffee (Vietnam Trade Promotion Agency, 2014). In 2014, Germany stood at 22nd out of 101 countries and regions investing in Vietnam. Trade included 232 effective projects and total registered capital of $1.25 billion invested. About 250 different enterprises, including many leading corporations such as Siemens, Bosch, Bilfinger, and many others, are also operating effectively in Vietnam. See Table 9.5 for a financial comparison of the growth of trade between Vietnam and Germany.

ROLES OF INDIVIDUAL EUROPEAN COUNTRIES IN TEXTILES AND APPAREL

For the most part, in Europe the textile and apparel business is operated by companies rather than by governments. Trade regulations and economic incentives are developed and managed by governments. Manufacturing and retailing of textiles and apparel are planned and managed by companies based in individual countries and doing business

TABLE 9.5

EXAMPLES OF VIETNAM'S EXPORTS TO GERMANY IN NINE MONTHS OF 2014 IN US DOLLARS[1,2]

Products	Export Value (Nine Months of 2014)	Export Value (Nine Months of 2013)	Rate of Growth
Total export value	$3,761,221,747	$3,504,662,832	7.32%
Telephones, mobile phones, and parts	$1,015,883,479	$1,242,583,720	−18.24%
Textiles and garments	$ 570,094,281	$ 463,842,171	22.91%
Footwear	$ 414,469,137	$ 296,855,075	39.62%
Computers and electrical parts	$ 208,156,130	$ 234,198,711	−11.12%
Fishery products	$ 174,859,583	$ 146,004,169	19.76%
Machines, equipment, tools, instruments	$ 130,447,540	$ 88,712,785	47.04%
Handbags, purses, suitcases, headgear	$ 101,995,899	$ 96,631,678	5.55%

[1]World Economic Forum, 2015.
[2]Vietnam Trade Promotion Agency, 2014.

in one or more other countries. In the EU-28, the eleven countries that are the biggest producers in the textile and apparel industry include the following (GCIs are given as indicators of how much support and/or opposition a company has to deal with to do business in that country):

- Both textile and clothing production: Germany (5), United Kingdom (9), France (23), Spain (35), Italy (49)
- Mostly textile production: Belgium (18), Netherlands (8), Austria (21), Sweden (10)
- Mostly apparel production: Portugal (36), Greece (81)

About 20 percent of the textiles and apparel production in EU countries is sold to firms outside the EU-28; thus, 80 percent is sold within the EU.

Levels of labor costs and social costs are some of the primary factors that have determined which countries have continued to have primary roles in the textile and apparel complex. Labor costs are associated with production and/or services that are assigned to individual products or to a cost center. An individual product might be a selected component of a product line that a customer wants to purchase. A cost center is a department within an organization that is essential to the operation of the company but does not produce a profit. Social costs include health care, unemployment and disability compensation, retirement plans, education, and so on. In developed countries it is common to have laws that require payment of both labor costs and social costs. In developing countries, not only are labor costs consistently lower but social costs may not be required by law or be included in wages of employees. Because of the necessity of intense human involvement in textile and apparel production, lots of labor hours are commonly required. Thus, costs of labor are primary considerations when determining locations for textiles or apparel production businesses.

The textile production costs presented in the following discussion as well as in similar tables in the following three chapters are based on all production activities in the textile industry, including spinning, weaving, dyeing, and finishing. Apparel manufacturing labor costs on a per hour basis are generally proportionally lower than textile labor costs. The current common practice of producing apparel in developing countries tends to be more fragmented, sometimes hundreds of tiny businesses with fewer than fifty operators, up to many huge ones with thousands of operators. Apparel production is also less automated and more labor intensive than textile production, and total labor costs are very difficult to measure. That is why we have not presented comparable wage data for apparel production.

Some of the Western European countries that were early members of the EU were leaders in the textile and apparel trade for hundreds of years. Because there is relatively little data available from the WTO about trade by individual members of the EU today, other sources of data have to be used to explore the roles of the European countries selected for discussion in this text. Table 9.6 demonstrates the range of labor and social costs for textile manufacturing in EU countries using Gross Global Competitiveness Index 2014–2015 rankings and US labor costs and as a point of comparison. Similar types of comparisons are appropriate for other dimensions of the textile complex, including apparel production and retailing.

TABLE 9.6

LABOR, DIRECT WAGES, AND SOCIAL COSTS PER HOUR FOR TEXTILE PRODUCTION IN EUROPEAN COUNTRIES ACTIVE IN TEXTILES PRODUCTION

Country and GPI Ranking	Total Labor Costs as a Percentage of US Labor Cost[a]	Total Labor Costs (in US Dollars)[b]	Total Labor Costs (in Local Currency)	Direct Wages[c] (in Local Currency)	Social Costs[d] (in Local Currency)	Social Costs as a Percentage of Direct Labor Costs[e]
United States (3)	100%	$17.41	$17.41	$13.52	$ 3.89	29%
Germany (5)	146%	$25.42	18.05 €[e]	13.46 €	4.59 €	34%
UK (9)	102%	$17.70	12.21 £[f]	9.16 £	3.05 £	33%
Belgium (18)	209%	$36.39	25.84 €	14.90 €	10.94 €	73%
France (23)	175%	$30.39	21.58 €	11.10 €	10.48 €	94%
Spain (35)	106%	$18.39	13.06 €	8.79 €	4.27 €	49%
Portugal (36)	54%	$ 9.45	6.71 €	4.21 €	2.50 €	59%
Poland (43)	28%	$ 4.81	14.14	10.85	3.29	30%
Italy (49)	128%	$22.31	15.84 €	9.66 €	6.18 €	64%
Bulgaria (54)	11%	$ 1.85	2.55	1.84	0.71	39%

Note: Costs presented as a percentage of US textile production costs, with Global Competitiveness Index rankings for 2014–15 in parentheses beside the country name.

[a]In US dollars, total labor cost per hour as a percentage of US labor cost per hour = a country's cost per hour / US labor cost per hour × 100.

[b]Total labor cost per hour = direct wage per hour + social cost per hour.

[c]Direct wage: the amount paid per hour for a specified time period.

[d]Social costs: include health care, unemployment and disability compensation, retirement plans, education, and so on. In local currency, social costs as a percentage of labor costs = social costs / direct wages × 100.

[e]€ = EU euro.

[f]£ = British pound

Source: Based on Werner International Management Consultants. (2009). "Primary Textiles Labor Cost Comparisons 2008." Retrieved May 25, 2010, from http://texnet.ilgstudios.net/files/2009/08/Werner_International_-_Labor_Cost_Study_2008.pdf

The total labor cost per hour in EU countries, converted to US dollars, ranges from $36.39 in Belgium to $1.85 in Bulgaria. The dollar cost, of course, is based on the US exchange rate for the local currency in the appropriate year. The ratio of other countries' cost to US costs—from 209 percent in Belgium to 11 percent in Bulgaria—provides important insight into overall well-being and levels of consumption and living in the EU. It would be interesting to see a similar comparison among US states.

The relationship between direct wages and social costs is also indicative of levels of development. Social costs related to the production of goods and services, such as textiles and apparel, are the result of the social responsibility component of supply chain sustainability. In general, developed countries tend to provide higher rates of social costs, because standards of living include greater expectations for medical care and retirement benefits, both primary elements of social costs. Social costs also include deduction for income taxes, which varies greatly among countries. To an employer, social costs represent what it costs to have an employee beyond paying a wage. For example, according to Table 9.6, in France a firm's financial plan must include a level of sales/revenue that will support a relatively high level of wages for employees, plus nearly an equal additional amount for social costs.

Note that US social costs are not nearly as high as those of most of the EU countries listed, even though social costs are relatively high for all the countries. The difference is that, in the EU basic healthcare services are provided to citizens free of charge, and employers are responsible for providing funds to support the government program. In the United States, many employee benefits plans include some medical coverage, but employees are personally responsible for the rest—the result being that wages need to be relatively higher in the United States to provide the same level of living.

Social costs are a primary contributor to the decline of textile and apparel manufacturing in the EU and other developed countries. When products can be sourced from developing countries instead, not only are the wages less, but the social costs are sometimes much less or nearly nonexistent. Unfortunately, social costs can be used for worker exploitation. Social costs are sometimes deducted from employees' salaries and used by the employers for their own benefit.

The countries that follow have been selected to represent European nations with major participation in textiles and apparel. Some were members of EU-15, others became members of the EU in 2004 and 2007, and still others are potential members of the EU, but all are involved in textiles and apparel. Many other European countries are also important participants. We encourage you to explore their contributions on your own.

Germany (GCI = 5)

Germany now has Europe's largest economy as well as the largest population, over 81 million people. Modern Germany emerged after World War II, when the military zones created by the Allies were merged to form two separate states: the Federal Republic of Germany and the German Democratic Republic (known outside of the country as West Germany and East Germany, respectively). West Germany became embedded in the economics and politics of Western Europe, while East Germany was aligned with the communist Soviet Union. The end of the Cold War allowed for the unification of Germany in 1990. Germany's affluent and technologically powerful economy is currently the fourth largest in the world. Review Germany in Table 9.2 for a demographic perspective and current textile and apparel trade activity.

Germany has a highly regulated labor market and a skilled workforce, which favored development of outsourcing for apparel production during the early 1980s. Low-wage markets in central Europe were the target, particularly Hungary. German apparel manufacturers used CMT contractors, exporting materials and importing the finished goods. Trade regulations were in place to reduce import tariffs, based on value added in the foreign country rather than on total product value (Taplin & Winterton, 2004). Consequently, apparel production in Germany began to decline, while the apparel firms themselves started to grow in terms of sales numbers.

Effective management has resulted in rapid growth of some apparel firms, placing a few German firms among Europe's largest. As shown in Table 9.3, two of the largest German-based fashion retail groups are C&A, ranked number four in Europe, and Esprit (originally from San Francisco, but now based in Ratingen, Germany), ranked number eight. One well-known German clothing brand is Bogner, which specializes in leisure wear and active sportswear and is particularly known for its skiwear. Bogner was one of the first German apparel firms to export clothing to the United States. It was also the outfitter of the 2010, 2012, and 2014 German Olympic teams (Bogner, n.d.; Figure 9.2). See Case 9.2 to get a taste of operating a global apparel company in a multicultural world.

German textile manufacturers have been focused on increasing their market share of high-quality fabrics. For decades, Italian competitors have had a monopoly on this market because of close collaboration with the strong brands created by Italian apparel designers. As shown in Table 9.6, Belgium and France are the only European countries that have higher textile manufacturing labor costs than Germany, so focusing on production of high-end, luxury products increases profitability potential. German textile manufacturers have also been exploiting opportunities for the development of new innovative textiles that satisfy needs beyond traditional end uses, including health care,

Figure 9.2

German athletes in official Winter Olympic 2014 Games in Sochi, Russia. The uniform is designed and manufactured by Bogner.

HUGO BOSS, A GERMANY-BASED VENDOR OF APPAREL AND ACCESSORIES, MODIFIES ITS ORGANIZATIONAL STRATEGIES

Hugo Boss AG is an example of a high-profile, Germany-based design group known around the world (Figures Case 9.2 a, b). Hugo Boss is a vendor of fine tailored suits as well as sports and leisure wear for men and women, including Berlin brand handbags and a variety of other apparel related items. In 2015, Hugo Boss operated 388 stores, 531 shops, and 122 outlet locations, a wholesale business of about 1.4 billion euros (about $1.5 billion).[1] It has a flagship store on New York's Fifth Avenue where the company presents all of its fashion group collections under one roof, including classic lines. It also has stores and outlets in many US states and had a men's suit production plant in Brooklyn, Ohio, until it was sold in 2015.[1]

Stores and production facilities are located in many countries around the world, including Canada, France, Japan, Korea, Singapore, and Mexico. One business practice that Hugo Boss has used in many countries is called franchising. Franchising involves granting the right to other companies to use its business model and brand for a prescribed period of time. The franchise is a privilege granted by a manufacturer (in this case Hugo Boss) to a dealer (in this case a retailer) for distribution of the manufacturer's products. The franchised store pays the franchisor a percentage of sales for the use of the Hugo Boss name on the store. When fashion retail sales in Germany declined in the fourth quarter (2014), Hugo Boss made plans to "take over 17 franchise stores in South Korea, set up its own distribution company in Dubai, and take over all its stores in China, where it planned to operate 140 outlets."[2] Because European shoppers have been forecast to curtail high-end purchases, Hugo Boss has planned to take over more of its franchised stores in Asia and the Middle East to capitalize on rising luxury clothes and accessories demand in those locations.[3]

[1]Ricadela, A. (April 8, 2015). "Hugo Boss Forecasts Profit Gain on Outlet Takeovers." Retrieved October 25, 2015, from http://www.businessoffashion.com/articles/news-analysis/hugo-boss-forecasts-profit-gain-outlet-takeovers

[2]Aliyu, W. (March 20, 2015). "Hugo Boss Leaving Country, but 300 Local Jobs Are Here to Stay." Retrieved October 25, 2015, from www.wkyc.com/story/news/local/cuyahoga-county/2015/03/19/hugo-boss/25058991/

[3]Loeb, W. (March 3, 2015). "Why Hugo Boss Is So Successful." Retrieved October 25, 2015, from http://www.forbes.com/sites/walterloeb/2015/03/23/why-hugo-boss-is-so-successful/

1. What might be some advantages and disadvantages of using franchising in the apparel industry?
2. What might be four advantages and four disadvantages of apparel firms operating in multiple countries around the world?
3. Identify three or four ways global technology is essential to operate global apparel companies.

Figure Case 9.2 a and b
Hugo Boss stores.

environmental protection, road building, packaging, and so on (Adler, 2004). Prices of these products are not limited by the high levels of competition that are common in the apparel market.

Technical textiles are textile products designed and produced for their thermal or mechanical performance and durability, including those made for protective clothing and medical use (University of Cambridge, 2009). Technical textiles amounted to approximately 40 percent of total textile production in Germany and this area was recognized as the most promising in the textile industry as early as 2005 (US Department of Commerce, 2005). This was the beginning of the rapid growth of some types of special textile products, discussed primarily in Chapter 12. Germany is also a global leader in the development and export of textile and apparel production machinery, focusing on sewing machinery, laundry and textile cleaning equipment, and machines for processing and finishing technical textiles. In 2008, production value of this equipment was 1 billion euros, with exports accounting for 773 million euros (Just-style.com, 2009b).

One of the major trade shows in Germany is the International Trade Fair for Sports Equipment and Fashion (commonly known as ISPO), held in Munich. ISPO is considered the world's largest sporting goods trade show, and it reflects the industry's strength in specific product lines. In addition to active sport apparel, especially apparel products related to winter sports, this fair also features safety products, such as helmets and protectors. To expand its horizons, in 2015 ISPO entertained nearly 30,000 participants featuring 434 exhibitors with 656 brands associated with outdoor, action sports, ski, sport style, and fabrics and fibers segments in Beijing (ISPO 2015).

United Kingdom (GCI = 9)

The United Kingdom (UK) was formally known as the United Kingdom of Great Britain (England, Wales, and Scotland) and Northern Ireland. The Industrial Revolution that began in Great Britain during the early 1700s had, by the mid-1800s, made it the richest country in the world. By then, the British Empire controlled one-fourth of the world's surface, including colonies in India, Africa, and the Americas. During the 1900s, the two World Wars seriously depleted British resources, and the empire was dismantled. The UK is now a member of the EU but has not adopted the euro; it has maintained the pound as its currency. Review "United Kingdom" in Table 9.2 for a demographic perspective.

Great Britain's Industrial Revolution had spread to the Americas and other parts of Europe by the early 1800s, moving production out of homes and into factories, where power-driven machines and their operators replaced handwork. Some historians argue that the greater availability of goods did more to increase levels of living than political and trade union activities. Other historians focus on the disruption of family life; crowded and unsanitary conditions in housing; and terrible working conditions for men, women, and children. The majority agree that most of the Western world was changed from a rural and agrarian society to an urban and industrial society as a result of the Industrial Revolution.

The textile and apparel industry was a major contributor to Great Britain's Industrial Revolution. For thousands of years there had been few changes in the techniques for making cloth. European spinners had borrowed and adapted the Indian spinning wheel and weaving looms, but the speed of producing yarns and cloth remained largely the same (Baity, 1942). Then, in 1733, John Kay invented the flying shuttle, which carried the filling yarn through the warp, speeding the pace of weaving. Suddenly, yarn spinners who spun by hand could not keep up with the mechanized weaving process. In the 1760s, James Hargreaves's spinning jenny allowed multiple yarns to spin at the same time, and in the 1780s a steam engine was created to drive power looms. Spinning and weaving became a thousand times faster than they had been 100 years before. Industrial espionage made it possible for US spinners and weavers to use machines copied from the English inventions. **Industrial espionage** is conducted for commercial purposes to illegally acquire trade secrets and/or technological or commercial research data, formulas, strategic plans, pricing plans, and so on. It was not until 1840, however, after several tries by European inventors, that the sewing machine came into being, through the work of Thomas Howe. A. B. Wilson and Isaac Singer later added features to make it more efficient. Clearly, the textile industry was well established before the making of apparel became a factory system.

The wool industry was established as a cottage industry, but the explosive growth of the cotton industry in the early 1800s was dependent on import of raw cotton. With cotton from the United States and India, Great Britain became the largest producer of cotton cloth in the world, but not without conflict. Wool was domestically produced, and woolen fabrics were regarded as staples for apparel. Wool producers, spinners, and weavers demonstrated against what they regarded as unfair competition from the imported cotton fiber. But the fashion for Indian-style cotton calico prints won the day. By 1913, Great Britain was responsible for 60 percent of world trade in cotton goods. As recently as 1969, textiles and apparel provided 21 percent of jobs for the employed segment of the British population. Great Britain is still known for fine quality cotton and wool fabrics. Its success has been dependent on anticipating trends in the consumer market and on using international suppliers. Internationalization of the textile pipeline has always been the case in the UK (Jones, 2002). Liberty of London, originally a textile brand known for fine woolen and cotton fabrics, flourished through the middle of the twentieth century. More recently, it struggled through vertical mergers and takeovers, but the firm is still a factor in the London retail scene.

Adversarial relationships among specializations in the textile pipeline were established early. The textile pipeline was made up of a series of companies, each having a special part of the many processes that are required to change a bale of fiber into a finished textile product. *Each member of the pipeline had to deal with at least one supplier and customer, the source of the conflicts and frustrations leading to adversarial relationships among necessary components of the pipeline.* For example, spinners of yarn, weavers of cloth, and producers of garments each developed their own trade associations, did not know one another, and had little knowledge of one another's businesses. There was little understanding that collaboration could make business better for both suppliers and customers. Instead, managers of firms believed that for a firm to make more profit, its suppliers and customers had to make less profit. These attitudes carried over well into the twentieth century. Jones (2002) proposed that the failure to achieve collaboration between the UK textile manufacturing and apparel manufacturing segments was a major factor in the recent decline of those two parts of the industry. The same attitudes that have been a detriment to the growth of the textile industry are reflected in the still-present adversarial relationships between apparel manufacturers and retailers. These problems suggest a dysfunctional trade matrix whose participants have not been able to engage in the collaboration necessary for effective supply chain business systems.

Today, the UK manufacturing base and employment are still eroding after an already lengthy decline. Imports now dominate; thus, the majority of apparel sold in the UK is imported. Activity in textile and apparel manufacturing in the UK is now focused on design and product development more than production. Potentially, the UK may also serve as a source of innovation in niche or high-quality products, such as state-of-the-art wool production. The UK is also focusing on nanotechnology coatings and smart functions, to be applied to clothing and textiles, and on the design and manufacture of technical textiles introduced in the discussion of Germany.

Table 9.7 demonstrates a historic example of the relationship between UK output and employment between 1978 and 2002. It is a reflection of twenty-four annual business cycles and their relationships to each other, although every year isn't included in the table. The trends reflected by these statistics are also representative of apparel production trends in many other developed countries in Europe as well as the Americas. Those trends continued well beyond 2002. Unfortunately, comparable, more recent data are not available. The table presents output and employment in the form of an Industrial Production Index (IPI). (Be careful not to confuse this index with the Global Competitiveness Index introduced earlier.) In the IPI, the level of employment and output in 1995 is treated as 100 percent; each of the other numbers represents the differences from 100 percent backward and forward through time.

Focus on the Output column. Note that output decreased almost every time period ending up in 2002 at about half of what it was in 1978. That doesn't necessarily mean that UK citizens were wearing half as many new clothes; it means that domestic apparel production was becoming less competitive due to high costs or less expensive apparel was being sourced outside the UK. That trend in output of apparel in the UK and in other developed countries has continued rather consistently to the present. At the same time production was declining, employment also steadily declined, but at a much faster rate. The IPI for employment started out nearly double the IPI for output but ended up almost the same IPI. That suggests that productivity nearly tripled from 1978 to 2002.

TABLE 9.7

OUTPUT AND EMPLOYMENT IN THE UNITED KINGDOM CLOTHING INDUSTRY FROM 1978 TO 2002, ACCORDING TO THE INDUSTRIAL PRODUCTION INDEX (IPI)

Year	Output	Employment
1978	108.8	202.8
1980	99.9	178.1
1985	109.4	151.9
1990	106.2	129.2
1995 (IPI = 100%)	100.0	100.0
2000	72.5	72.0
2001	62.6	65.6
2002	56.0	55.5

Source: Based on Jones, R. M., & Hayes, S. G. (2004). "The UK Clothing Industry: Extinction or Evolution?" Journal of Fashion Marketing and Management, 8(3), 262–278.

That trend has also continued with applications of high technology to everything from design and pattern making to garment assembly and packaging. By 2004, the overall UK clothing and textile industry employed approximately 182,000 people, divided evenly between clothing and textiles (University of Cambridge, 2009).

During the 1998 to 2002 time period in the UK, overall consumption expenditure increased, as did consumption expenditure on clothing and footwear. The consumer clothing market in the UK was more than £26 billion in the mid-2000s (Jones & Hayes, 2004). Clothing as a percentage of total consumption expenditure also increased, from 6.5 percent to 8 percent, so lack of demand would not seem to be an explanation for reduction in clothing production. By 2006, consumers in the UK were spending about £780 per person per year on textiles and apparel, £625 of which were on clothes (University of Cambridge, 2009). Even with overall production declines, however, some textile and apparel firms continue to be successful, focusing on design, product development, brand management, and retail.

Between 1990 and 2012 the UK economy grew by about 60 percent and clothing manufacturing declined by over 60 percent, while UK designers were thriving. The UK contributes heavily to the global market in high-end designer and brand recognition. UK fashion apparel designers, such as Stella McCartney, Vivienne Westwood, Alexander McQueen, and Victoria Beckham, and UK brands, such as Burberry, Aquascutum, and Dewhirst Group Limited, continue to be known throughout the world. Burberry products, such as its famous raincoats, trademarked plaid scarves, and other fashion items, are sold in stores in fifty nations. These major firms focus on product development and sourcing apparel production from offices scattered across the globe. Some of them provide merchandise for their own stores as well as other leading brands, such as Marks & Spencer and Nike.

According to House of Commons Library (2014), in 2012 the UK fashion industry

- contributed 14.3 billion pounds to the economy,
- directly employed 470,000 people,
- involved 17,600 businesses, and
- had a turnover of 50.4 billion pounds.

Because the UK is an EU member, UK policy is subsumed in EU policy, which covers such areas as trade, innovation, competition, and employment. The EU focus on trade liberalization is reflected in UK trade practices, including the removal of barriers to imports. Despite the exit of most manufacturing in apparel and textiles from the UK, the industry continues to be highly valuable in the retail and branding portion of the supply chain, and many of those well-known retailers are backward vertically integrated into some aspects of apparel manufacturing. In general, the UK apparel industry is characterized by potential for high profit from innovation, marketing, and retailing, but low return from production.

Some of the UK's traditional apparel retailers have found their markets eroded by competition from mass merchants that rank among the world's 250 largest Global Powers of Retailing (GPR). The merchandise assortments in these supercenters include a lot of textiles and apparel. UK-based Tesco is a hypermarket/supercenter (ranked fifth in GPR) and focuses on value-priced merchandise. Dominant UK-based apparel and footwear specialty retailers include Next (ranked 163rd in GPR), with stores in seventy-four countries, and Arcadia Group Limited, known for its Topshop and Miss Selfridge brands (ranked 213th in GPR), with stores in forty-six countries

Figure 9.3

Two UK-based apparel retailers, Next and Topshop (a division of Arcadia Group), "surround" Zara, a Spanish fast fashion retailer (a division of Inditex Group).

(Figure 9.3). Among the designer-level apparel institutions in the UK is Aquascutum London, serving men, women, and juniors. It was established in the 1850s and is still going strong today. Aquascutum is renowned as the inventor of the trench coat during the 1800s and is still adapting the style to meet the needs of today's customers. Its website (www.aquascutum.com) provides an excellent display of designer apparel priced from $100 to $2,000 each.

Italy (GCI = 49)

A democratic republic replaced dictatorship after Italy's alliance with Germany resulted in defeat in World War II. Economic revival followed. Persistent problems in Italy include illegal immigration, low income, and low technical standards in the welfare-dependent agricultural south. In contrast, the prosperous industrial north is dominated by private, flourishing companies. Take note that Italy's GCI is 49, while Germany's is 5. That is a strong suggestion that it is much more difficult to do business in Italy than it is in Germany. As shown in Table 9.6, Italy's labor costs are less than those of France and Germany, but more than those of the UK and Spain. Review Italy in Table 9.2 for a demographic perspective. Textiles, apparel, footwear, and accessories are all regarded as essential industries in Italy, which employs approximately 800,000 people and is home to 30,000 distribution companies (Zargani, 2009). Production of high-value garments tends to be spatially concentrated around sources of high-quality fabric production near Milan and Florence.

One of Italy's largest textile trade fairs is the Pitti Immagine Filati, held in Florence. This trade show features the latest in yarns and knit fabrics produced by Italian yarn mills. The ITMA Industrial Fair features fabric, leather, as well as textile and apparel machinery. Milano Unica is held twice a year, representing "the three essential characteristics of the textile fair: singular, exclusive, united" (TradeShows.com, 2015). In total,

Figure 9.4

Italian trade shows are known for unique ambience, creative displays, and original products.

there were over fifty textile, clothing, accessories, and manufacturing equipment trade shows in 2015 in Italy (Figure 9.4).

Italy has an industrial organizational model in which small firms are formed into industrial districts that support the production of certain types of finished goods. The industrial districts receive government support and have therefore proliferated. The Italian textile complex has been able to evolve into a scenario in which major apparel firms have multiple domestic textile firms supplying materials and many small domestic as well as international retailers as their customers, as indicated in Model A, in Figure 9.5. Retail distribution in Italy continues to be extremely fragmented, but the system is protected by extensive regulations and the powerful influence of shopkeepers' organizations.

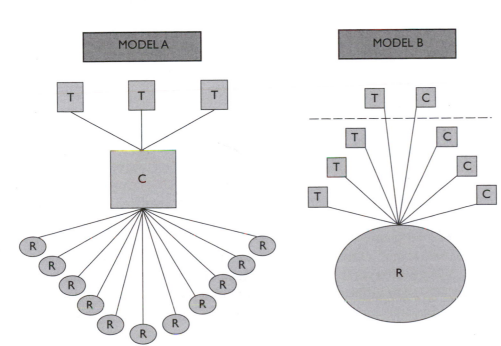

Figure 9.5

Evolution of the textile and apparel industry. The Italian textile and apparel industry has moved from a central manufacturer model (Model A) to the central retailer model (Model B). In the diagram, *T* represents textiles, *C* is clothing, and *R* is retailers. (Based on Guercini, 2004, p. 331)

Figure 9.6a

A model wearing extravagantly decorated jacket walks the runway during the Versace show as part of Milan Fashion Week Menswear Spring/Summer 2015.

The Italian strategy for competing with low-wage countries has been differentiation and niche marketing related to high-value-added products consistent with its designer image and extensive use of domestic subcontracting. Italy is now the leading exporter of upscale, fashion-forward apparel and shoes, with the United States as one of its primary customers. The demands of sophisticated Italian consumers and the Italian fashion sense perpetuated by brands such as Giorgio Armani, Versace, Prada, Brioni, and many others have solidified Italian dominance in the high-value market (Figure 9.6a and b). However, recognizing these brands individually as Italian in origin can be tricky; for example, the Italian firm Fendi is part of the LVMH (Moët Hennessy–Louis Vuitton) ownership group of France.

Referring back to Figure 9.5, Model B shows that there has also been a strong trend toward the growth of huge, powerful retailers. This trend is making dramatic changes in the organization of the apparel business in Italy. These huge firms have come about through a combination of vertical and horizontal integration. These retailers are absorbing merchandising, design, and product development responsibilities that used to be the exclusive functions of apparel manufacturers. When retailers absorb these tasks, textile and apparel firms produce the materials and garments ordered by the retailers. The dotted line in the model shows that pressure from industrial retailers on their suppliers to reduce wholesale prices has increased the tendency of textile and clothing manufacturers to locate production plants outside of Italy, especially in low-wage countries.

Italy has some of the largest apparel companies in Europe. Some of these companies have grown through mergers with suppliers, others through mergers with their retail customers, and still others through both. Sometimes, a company will grow by merging with a competitor. However, by 2014, the industry was working toward recovery after a two-year period of recession-related decline. For example, the Benetton Group, known as the United Colors of Benetton for women and Sisley brand for men, is still one of Italy's and the world's primary vertically integrated apparel firms, with manufacturing and retailing in 120 countries, but changes were being made in products and processes for companies large and small.

Figure 9.6b
Final walk-through of models at the Prada Ready to Wear Fall/Winter 2014–2015 runway show as part of Milan Fashion Week Womenswear.

The fast fashion phenomenon made a serious dent in sales for the traditional upscale fashion manufacturers and retailers. Consumers were developing different priorities related to quality and frequency of fashion change. Some consumers are trading upscale, carefully made fashion products for lower cost, frequently changing, appealing styles, and this is a worldwide trend. Fashion producers have to modify sourcing decisions to meet a shorter production period while making low-cost, appealing designs available every few weeks. These trends are impacting sales in Italy and in developed countries around the world (Binnie, 2014).

France (GCI = 22)

France suffered extensive losses in its empire, including wealth, manpower, and rank among world powers, despite being on the winning side in both World War I and World War II. In more recent years, France's reconciliation with Germany has contributed to the economic unification of Europe. France is the world's sixth-largest economy, closely following the UK. As with Germany, the French government is focusing on problems of high-cost labor and an inflexible market with restrictions on layoffs in the face of an economic slowdown. To deal with unemployment issues, a 35-hour workweek was instituted, allowing businesses to hire more people to get work done (Denslow, 2005). Review France in Table 9.2 for a demographic perspective.

Textiles and apparel have been among France's major industries. In 2002, the textile and apparel industry in France employed 200,000 people and generated sales of $30.2 billion, with exports of $13 billion. Today, production has gone down and the focus has shifted to imported goods for domestic distribution and the export of high-value-added garments. The bulk of France's fashion exports today are in prêt-à-porter (ready-to-wear) products manufactured and sold under the names of recognized designers or fashion houses, such as Karl Lagerfeld, for Chanel; John Galliano, for Christian Dior; and Hermès (a brand, not a designer). The collections of these brands are sold globally in their own nameplate boutique stores and also by other retailers. The semiannual prêt-à-porter trade shows in Paris are among the marketing highlights of the fashion business calendar. With mergers and acquisitions a consistent part of the industry, it is of interest to take a closer look at one of the more visible ownership groups: Moët Hennessy–Louis Vuitton (LVHM), with headquarters in Paris, represents not only Louis Vuitton, but also Marc Jacobs, Fendi, Céline, Kenzo, Givenchy, and Donna Karan.

France also maintains leadership in the marketing of fashion-forward fabrics. Fashion fabrics are featured at the Première Vision textile trade shows held in Paris. An estimated 700 weavers present collections to some 50,000 professional visitors from nearly 100 different countries when they come together in Paris twice each year to view the latest in fabric designs. Haute couture (high fashion), which was once the undisputed empress of Paris fashion, now sustains itself through hosting Hollywood celebrities and their stylists at fashion shows and through the sale of very high price, unique fashion products to individual customers. The royalties earned on sales of designer prêt-à-porter and other licensed products provide financial support for the smaller haute couture businesses. Many French designers and manufacturers have had to take action to protect their designer status as the world's leaders in high fashion and their meaning in the global marketplace. To achieve that, every fashion season, fashion houses have to come up with new ideas for haute couture and prêt-à-porter collections (Figures 9.7a and b).

Legal actions to protect designs, brands, logos, and any other identifications of brands have become commonplace in the textiles and apparel industry. A French court has ordered eBay, the online auction giant, to pay damages to LVMH Moët Hennessy–Louis Vuitton SA for allowing the sale on its site of counterfeits of the French luxury goods company's fragrances. eBay was ordered to pay 80,000 euros, or $117,820 at current exchange rates, for allowing a key word search for Christian Dior, Kenzo, Givenchy, and Guerlain perfumes on its site without authorization. The ruling marked LVMH's second court victory against eBay. The auction site was ordered to pay 38 million euros, or $55.7 million, for allowing the sale of fake LVMH merchandise. In contrast, eBay has

Figure 9.7a

An exhibition by French fashion designer Jean-Paul Gaultier at the Grand Palais in Paris is a showcase of creative ideas, techniques, and craftsmanship of haute couture fashion.

petitioned the European Union to stop luxury goods companies from blocking online sales of their products, as regulators prepare to adjust antitrust rules on distribution deals to take into account the stronger power of large retailers because of the popularity of e-commerce. eBay lawyers have become regular courtside fixtures on both sides of the Atlantic as the internet auction site has locked horns not only with LVMH, but also L'Oréal and Tiffany & Co., with mixed results. At one point, eBay was ordered to pay Hermès (a fine jewelry retailer) a fine of 20,000 euros, or $31,058, for failing to monitor the authenticity of goods sold on its site. However, in a case that pitted eBay against Tiffany, a US court ruled that eBay does not have the legal responsibility to prevent the sale of counterfeit goods (Berton, 2009).

Many developed countries, including France, experienced a wave of mergers and acquisitions among textile and apparel manufacturers early in the twenty-first century. As with Italy, these mergers and acquisitions were much more intense in retailing than in manufacturing, resulting in fewer, more powerful retailers. The large vertical retailers greatly increased their outsourcing to optimize their financial resources with more favorable production terms (Taplin & Winterton, 2004). Paris is the principal import, marketing, and distribution center in France; Lyon is its primary commercial and industrial center. The Avenue des Champs-Elysées in Paris is the most luxurious and expensive retail space in Europe. Until the late 1980s, imports came primarily from other European countries, including Italy, Germany, and Belgium; CMT production came from Turkey and northern African nations. Then, as Eastern European production centers became available after the breakup of the Soviet Union, some production was sought in that region in the 1990s. In the early 2000s, most production was outsourced by Russian companies to China as well.

Today, China supplies much of France's moderately priced goods. Couture houses and major retailers also develop bridge and moderately priced lines of ready-to-wear apparel carrying designer names to increase sales volume. Large department stores in France include the landmark Galleries Lafayette and Printemps flagship stores on the Boulevard Haussmann in Paris. The emergence of mass merchandisers in France has paralleled their growth in other developed nations. Today, the third-largest retailer in the world is the French Carrefour (Figure 9.7c), following US-based Costco Wholesale Corporation and Walmart Stores, Inc., the two largest retailers in the world. An intriguing recent retailing development is that stores in Paris, Marseille, Lille, and some of the tourist areas across France will be able to trade on Sunday, while the rest of the nation will continue its long-maintained policy of closing for a noon hour on weekdays and all day Sunday.

Figure 9.7b

Givenchy's 2015 prêt-à-porter fashion show at Pier 26 in New York City.

Figure 9.7c
France-based Carrefour is the
third-largest retailer in the world.

Spain (GCI = 35)

Southern and eastern EU countries have historically had high unemployment rates, particularly for women, with Spain and Greece at about 31 percent. By 2014, the EU unemployment rate for women, on average, was 10.3 percent, with unemployment in Germany at 4.6 percent and Austria at 10.3 percent. Spain, which is about the size of California, was slower to embrace the Industrial Revolution than the Northern European countries; therefore, its economic development was also slower than that of the UK, Germany, and France. However, Spain's per capita GDP expanded until the early 2000s, peaked in 2008, then suffered from a recession, but was partially recovered by 2014. As shown in Table 9.6, total labor costs in Spain are now similar to the UK and United States. Despite relatively slow industrial development, Spain is a major producer of textiles and apparel, and the country's economy relies heavily on this industry, which provides close to 10 percent of its employment. Review Spain in Table 9.2 for a demographic perspective.

The spinning and fabric industries are highly concentrated in the Catalonia and Valencia areas, representing significant employment in those areas. Markets are joined by two major hubs: Madrid and Barcelona. High-quality imported or locally produced foreign apparel is usually sold effectively by small, specialty chain stores. However, Spain and other lower-cost European apparel producers faced a lot of pressure from lower-cost imports in the 2000s, when the quota system expired. Zara, however, is an example of a bright spot in the Spanish fashion scene. A member of the Inditex Group, Zara has become known as a vertical international fashion leader. The first Zara shop opened in La Coruña, Spain, which is now home of the headquarters. The company is credited for pioneering the concept of fast fashion, which was partially possible due to ongoing communication from stores to more than 300 design professionals for accurate fashion forecasting and speedy delivery of desired styles, colors, and prints.

Poland (GCI = 43)

Poland, slightly smaller than New Mexico, joined the EU in 2004 and became one of the most productive of the newer EU members. During World War II, Poland was invaded by Germany and the Soviet Union. As a Soviet satellite state after the war, Poland was relatively tolerant and progressive. Cotton, wool, and silk textile mills were important industries. During the 1990s, after the dissolution of the Soviet Union, the country transformed its economy into one of the most robust in central Europe. Review Poland in Table 9.2 for a demographic perspective.

Referring back to Table 9.2, examine the numbers for Poland. Poland's determination to join the EU shaped many aspects of its economic policy. The country spent most of the 1990s privatizing former state-owned companies and encouraging investment. Apparel production within Poland was estimated at $1.5 billion, from 44,000 small factories, in the first decade of the twenty-first century (US Department of Commerce, 2005). The Polish apparel industry was expecting intensified competition from Asia when the quota system ended, even though, as shown in Table 9.6, Poland's labor costs were some of the lowest in the EU. In the early 2000s, Polish companies began moving apparel assembly to Asia, Belarus, and Ukraine (Ukrainian wages were significantly lower than Polish wages). As Poland prepared to become a member of the EU, the textile and apparel industry remained an important part of the economy, representing 15 percent of manufacturing employment (Larsen, 2004); however, many Polish apparel firms joined other European countries and outsourced to China.

Today, the Polish apparel industry also focuses on developing and promoting some of its domestic brands. A number of local designers have been successful in the global fashion market. One example is Eva Minge's fashion house. Since 2008, the designer has been presenting her collection at Paris Haute Couture Fashion Week and received numerous prestigious awards, including Oscar in Fashion and Luxury Brand of the Year (Eva Minge, n.d.). Capitalizing on the success, Eva Minge expanded her brand to non-apparel products, such as sunglasses, luxurious furniture, and shoes. Based in Poland, Eva Minge fashion house recognizes the importance of Western Europe as the center of high fashion and maintains a showroom in Milan.

Of note is Intermasz, a four-day event showcasing products from apparel, textile, and clothing industries. This is one of Poland's largest business platforms devoted to modern machinery, devices, and computer-aided production preparation systems for textiles, apparel, and shoes as well as design and decoration studios for upholstered products (Intermasz, 2015). This trade fair and several others, such as the Fast Fashion Exhibition, reflect the nation's continuing activity as a textile and apparel producer. In 2009, Weyerhaeuser NR Company, a North American firm, announced that it intended to build a new cellulose fiber–processing plant in Gdansk, Poland, to produce cellulose for use in hygiene products, such as diapers, household wipes, and nonwoven fabrics (Fibre2Fashion, 2009). The plant officially opened in 2013 with the goal of producing 67,000 tons of nonwoven fabric annually (Polish Information and Foreign Investment Agency (n.d.))

The growth in the economy over the past decade has resulted in a dramatic change in retailing. The Polish retail apparel industry was valued at $8 billion in 2013. The apparel industry is forecast to reach $10 billion by 2018 (Report Linker, 2014). Foreign retail chains were quick to take advantage of opportunities in the Polish market—most of the largest retailers in Europe have established sites in Poland. Foreign retailers now hold over 50 percent market share, resulting in some decline in small domestic retailers. While US sporting and denim brands are popular, they are subject to a high duty rate to get them into the EU, which results in considerable cost disadvantages.

Romania (GCI = 59)

Romania, which is slightly smaller than Oregon, is a country in southeastern Europe bordered by Bulgaria and Ukraine. Romania was under communist control and textile and apparel industries were government operated until 1996. Romania had to overcome rampant corruption and lagging economic and democratic reforms before it achieved its goal of becoming a member of the EU in 2007. Review Romania in Table 9.2 for a demographic perspective.

In 2005, trade sanctions changed and China was allowed unrestricted access to the Romanian market, which provided strong competition. As the country has developed and labor costs have increased, employment in Romania steadily decreased from 2005 to 2009, with more than 300,000 textile workers losing their jobs. Close to 20 percent of apparel firms were closed down (Radio Romania International, 2009). Although Romania is still considered a major producer of tailored apparel, including suits and blazers, it is a relatively small player in the global market. During the same time, it was reported that there were still 2,100 footwear producers and 6,000 textile and garment producers operating in Romania. The firms that had been moving from CMT toward full-package methods were the ones that appeared to be meeting with the most success in surviving the competitive environment. There was also a movement toward Romanian companies opening their own retail shops, initially in shopping centers in major cities, such as Bucharest.

Russia (GCI = 53)

Russia, formally known as the Russian Federation, is nearly twice as large as the United States and is located west of the Ural Mountains partially in Eastern Europe, with the remainder of the country in northern Asia, bordering the Arctic Ocean. The Russian empire was formed in the late 1600s, after nearly 500 years of gradual unification. More than 200 years of expansion followed, until 1917, when the communists seized power, and the Union of Soviet Socialist Republics (USSR; also known as the Soviet Union) came into being. In 1991, after prolonged stagnation of the economy, the Soviet Union splintered into fifteen independent republics, Russia being by far the largest. Russia and other countries have struggled to build democratic political systems and market economies to replace the strict social, political, and economic controls of the communist period. Russia negotiated for 18 years for admission to the World Trade Organization and was finally admitted in 2012. Review Russia in Table 9.2 for a demographic perspective.

Russia has more farmland than any other country in the world, but much of it is too cold or too dry. Following a financial crisis in 1998, the country experienced economic growth averaging 7 percent annually, resulting in doubling of real disposable income and the development of a middle class, but was hit hard by the worldwide economic recession. Former state-run large textile and apparel factories were privatized in the 1990s and for about a decade manufactured products for European brands. Following

Figure 9.8

A small independent store in downtown St. Petersburg features a variety of American denim brands.

the fast economic development and labor cost growth in the early 2000s, the majority of Russian apparel firms began to outsource assembly to Asia. As a result, as shown in Tables 9.4a and 9.4b, Russia now is importing far more textiles and apparel than it is exporting.

Retailing has undergone a profound change since the late 1990s. Street markets, a common form of retailing during the transition years from socialism to a market economy, declined significantly. Today, many major brands and designers have established significant presence in Moscow and St. Petersburg as well as other major cities, catering to the insatiable appetites of the new Russian elite and growing middle class. Retail sales experienced a significant increase in the early 2000s. In addition, these years saw the emergence of a thriving luxury market: "Russia—in particular, Moscow—has shaped up as an El Dorado for many of Europe's leading luxury players" (Women's Wear Daily, 2007). US sport and active wear brands as well as jeans are very popular in the country (Figure 9.8).

For now, the overall economic picture in Russia is mixed. The Russian recession has disrupted traditional commerce and could remain volatile for some time. The impact of falling oil prices (oil is the historic foundation of the Russian economy) from $150 a barrel in mid-2008 to about $50 today, as well as the collapse of domestic credit, combined to seriously damage Russia's economy. Another exacerbating factor was that Russia alienated foreign investors by nationalizing many companies, which kept away a lot of foreign capital. "Russia has been unique in the way its assets are distributed. A lot of wealth accumulated among the young who have an appetite for conspicuous consumption, which is why you often see Russians spending abroad, especially in London. The Russian boom is over, but it is still an economy that has a lot of potential to grow over time" (Ellis, 2010).

Summary

Examination of the economic and industrial standing of European countries reveals a wide range of geographical sizes, populations, and levels of economic well-being. Of those examined, Russia is the largest in size and population, but more than half of it is located in

Asia. Malta is the smallest, smaller than twice the size of Washington, DC, with a population of fewer than half a million people. Europe's per capita GDP ranges from $77,600 in Luxembourg to $6,400 in the Ukraine. The Global Competitiveness Index is introduced to contribute to understanding how different organizational structures and business activity contribute to the ability of a country to grow in the world market.

The formation of the EU profoundly changed the relationships among countries and it continues to do so as new members are added. Members of the EU-15 are the most developed countries in Europe, not counting Switzerland and Norway, which have chosen not to join. All but two of the ten countries that joined in 2004 are in the "developing" category. Their addition unifies rich and poor countries into a powerful trading organization.

In 2003, Europe was the largest trader of textiles and apparel in the world, but by 2009 it had slipped to second place, behind China. Intra EU trade was nearly double extra EU trade in textiles, whereas extra EU trade exceeded intra EU trade in apparel. The WTO reports trade numbers for all EU nations as one set of numbers and participation of individual countries is not identified, just as trade figures for individual states within the United States are typically not treated individually. Most countries have some form of textile and apparel manufacturing, and all have retailing. Among European countries, total costs for textile production ranged from the equivalent of $36.39 per hour, in Belgium, to $1.85, in Bulgaria. Social costs are a serious concern and range from 73 percent of labor costs, in Belgium, to 30 percent, in Poland, as compared with 29 percent in the United States. These may be a reflection of the socialist political systems that long dominated Europe.

Many of the largest clothing manufacturers are located in four Western European countries: France, Germany, Italy, and Spain. These EU representatives were also historical leaders in the textile and apparel trade in Europe. In addition, Poland and Cyprus joined the EU in 2004; Romania is one of the EU's newest members, having joined in 2007. All have heavy involvement in textiles and apparel. Significant changes have occurred in Russia in recent years, and it has given a roller coaster performance as a major market for EU-produced textiles and apparel.

Learning Activities

1. In what ways is the EU different in organization and purpose from the United States?
2. Within the EU-27, which countries are likely to be importers for consumption of textiles and apparel?
3. Which countries are more likely to be the producers and exporters of textiles and apparel? Why did you select these countries?
4. If you were a retail telemarketer, would you be more interested in the number of internet users or the percentage of internet users in a country? Why?
5. Given what you know now, if you were in charge of sourcing for a moderately priced, private label line of casual, young women's apparel to be imported by Macy's, would you consider a firm in a European country as a supplier? Why or why not?

6. If, as a sourcing professional, you were required to use a European country for your product line, what are four or five factors that you would consider in making the decision?

7. What is the meaning of extra EU versus intra EU? What difference does it make in terms of trade relationships?

8. From your consumer perspective, does it make a difference whether a label says "Made in Europe" or "Made in Italy"? Explain your perspective.

9. Does your image of French fashion allow France to be the home of the second-largest mass merchant in the world? Explain.

10. Spain might be regarded as a latecomer to the fashion business. What advantages does Spain currently hold over France and Italy?

References

Adler, U. (2004). "Structural Change: The Dominant Feature of the Economic Development of the German Textile and Clothing Industries." *Journal of Fashion Marketing and Management*, 8(3), 300–319.

Baity, E. C. (1942). *Man is a Weaver*. New York, NY: Viking Press.

Barone, M. (February 4, 2013). "More Jobs and More Babies, Please." *National Review*. Retrieved October 26, 2015, from http://www.nationalreview.com/article/339654/more-jobs-and-more-babies-please-michael-barone

Berton, E. (September 21, 2009). "LVMH Wins eBay Suit." *Women's Wear Daily*. Retrieved October 26, 2015, from http://www.wwd.com/business-news/lvmh-wins-ebay-suit-2301885/

Binnie, I. (January 10, 2014). "Italy Fashion Industry Back to Growth in 2014 - Trade Bodies." *Business News*. Retrieved November 5, 2015, from uk.reuters.com/article/2014/01/10/uk-italy-fashion-growth-idUKBREA0912220140110

Bogner (n.d.). Sponsoring. Retrieved December 27, 2015, from http://en.bogner.com/Sponsoring

Central Intelligence Agency. (n.d.). *The World Factbook*. Retrieved February 6, 2010, from http://www.odci.gov/cia/publications/factbook/index.html

Denslow, L. (2005). *World Wise: What to Know Before You Go*. New York, NY: Fairchild Publications.

Ellis, K. (January 28, 2010). "Emerging Nations: The Year Ahead." *Women's Wear Daily*. Retrieved October 26, 2015, from http://www.wwd.com/business-news/emerging-nations-the-year-ahead-2437851//?full=true

European Commission. (2009a). "Textiles and Clothing, External Dimension." Retrieved January 30, 2010, from http://ec.europa.eu/enterprise/sectors/textiles/external-dimension/index_en.htm

European Commission. (2009b). "Textiles and Clothing, Single Market." Retrieved May 28, 2010, from http://ec.europa.eu/enterprise/sectors/textiles/single-market/index_en.htm

European Commission. (2014a). "Population Ageing in Europe: Facts, Implications and Policies." Retrieved October 26, 2015, from ec.europa.eu/research/social-sciences/pdf/policy_reviews/kina26426enc.pdf

European Commission. (2014b). "The EU-28 Textiles and Clothing Industry—Enterprise and Industry." Retrieved May 16, 2015 from http://ec.europa.eu/enterprise/sectors/textiles/single-market/eu27/index_en.htm

European Free Trade Association. (n.d.). "Free Trade Agreements." Retrieved May 16, 2015, from http://www.efta.int/free-trade-agreements

Eva Minge. (n.d.). "History." Retrieved May 12, 2015, from http://www.evaminge.com/en/homepage/history

Fibre2Fashion. (November 6, 2009). "Poland: Weyerhaeuser to Build Cellulose Fibers Processing Facility in Gdansk." Retrieved February 10, 2010, from http://www.fibre2fashion.com/news/fibre-news/newsdetails.aspx?news_id=78894

Fuller, T. (August 29, 2005). European trade commissioner pledges to end quota dispute. The New York Times. Retrieved December 28, 2015, from http://www.nytimes.com/2005/08/29/business/worldbusiness/european-trade-commissioner-pledges-to-end-quota-dispute.html?_r=0

Guercini, S. (2004). "International Competitive Change and Strategic Behavior of Italian Textile-Apparel Firms." *Journal of Fashion Marketing and Management, 8*(3), 320–339.

House of Commons Library. (September 17, 2014). "Dressed for Success?" Retrieved October 26, 2015, from http://www.commonslibraryblog.com/2014/09/17/dressed-for-success

ISPO. (2015). "ISPO Beijing 2015: Asia's Strongest Sporting Goods Show Posts New Record Numbers." Retrieved October 26, 2015, from http://press.ispo.com/en/ISPO-Services/ISPO-BEIJING/ISPO-BEIJING-Press-releases-detail_1664.html

Jones, R. M. (2002). *The Apparel Industry.* Osney Mead, UK: Blackwell Science.

Jones, R. M., & Hayes, S. G. (2004). "The UK Clothing Industry: Extinction or Evolution?" *Journal of Fashion Marketing and Management, 8*(3), 262–278.

Just-style.com. (June 29, 2009a). "Fast Fashion Designer Freesoul Turns to PLM." Retrieved May 26, 2010, from http://www.just-style.com/plm/ITALY-Fast-fashion-denim-designer-Freesoul-turns-to-PLM_n104594.aspx

Larsen, P. E. (July, 2004). "Poland Ready for a Wild 2005." *Women's Wear Daily,* 16.

National Conference of State Legislatures. (February 13, 2015). "State Policies on Sex Education in Schools." Retrieved August 27, 2015, from http://www.ncsl.rg/research/health/state-policies-on-sex-education-in-schools.aspx

Noack, R. (April 11, 2015). "Please Make More Babies, Europe Urges Its Residents." *Star Tribune,* 2.

Polish Information and Foreign Investment Agency (n.d.). Factory of Weyerhaeuser Poland already opened. Retrieved December 27, 2015, from http://www.paiz.gov.pl/index/?id=967c2ae04b169f07e7fa8fdfd110551e#21

Radio Romania International. (October 6, 2009). "The Textile Industry in Romania." Retrieved February 10, 2010, from http://www.rri.ro/ art.shtml?lang=1&sec=10&art=22392

Report Linker. (August 2014). "Apparel Retail in Poland." Retrieved April 14, 2015, from http://www.reportlinker.com/p0151658-summer/apparel-retail-in-Poland.html

Stone, A. (1994). "What Is a Supranational Constitution?" *The Review of Politics 56*(3), 441–474.

Taplin, I. M, & Winterton, J. (2004). "The European Clothing Industry: Meeting the Competitive Challenge." *Journal of Fashion Marketing and Management, 8*(3), 256–261.

TradeShows.com. (2015). "Milano Unica." Retrieved October 26, 2015, from http://www.ntradeshows.com/milano-unica

University of Cambridge. (2009). "Well Dressed? The Present and Future Sustainability of Clothing and Textiles in the United Kingdom." Retrieved October 26, 2015, from http://www.ifm.eng.cam.ac.uk/resources/sustainability/well-dressed/

US Department of Commerce. (January 5, 2005). "EU: Local Industry and Market Information for Member Countries." Retrieved January 5, 2005, from http://web.ita.doc.gov/tacgi/overseas.nsf

Vietnam Trade Promotion Agency. (November 17, 2014). "Germany—The Biggest Trading Partner of Vietnam in the EU." Retrieved October 26, 2015, from http://www.vietrade.gov.vn/en/index.php?view=article&catid=203Anews&id=2234%3Agermany-the-biggest-trade-partner-of-vietnam-in-the-eu&catid=20:news&Itemid-287

Werner International Management Consultants. (2009). "Primary Textiles Labor Cost Comparisons 2008." Retrieved May 25, 2010, from http://texnet.ilgstudios.net/files/2009/08/Werner_International_Labor_Cost_Study_2008.pdf

Women's Wear Daily. (May 16, 2007). "To Russia with Love." *Women's Wear Daily,* 12.

World Economic Forum. (2015). "Global Competitiveness Report 2014–2015." Retrieved April 12, 2015, from www3.weforum.org/WEF_GlobalCompetitivenessReport_2014-15.pdf

World Trade Organization. (2009). "International Trade Statistics 2009. Section 2: Merchandise Trade by Product, 107–114." Retrieved January 16, 2010, from http://www.wto.org/english/res_e/statis_e/its2009_e/its09_merch_trade_product_e.pdf

Zargani, L. (March 6, 2009). "Italian Government to Boost Fashion." *Women's Wear Daily*. Retrieved February 7, 2010, from http://www.wwd.com/business-news/italian-government-to-boost-fashion-2042397/

CHAPTER 10
THE AMERICAS AND THE CARIBBEAN BASIN

//

FUN FACT

Nearly three hundred apparel and textiles trade shows are held in the United States annually and there are hundreds more held all around the world. (Expodatabase, n.d.)

OBJECTIVES

- Examine the evolution of economic and political organization in the Americas.
- Describe the roles of selected countries in textile and apparel production and consumption, areas of expertise, and specialization.
- Explore industrial development and trade regulations in the different sectors.
- Identify primary countries participating in the textile and apparel business.

North, Central, and South America span the globe vertically, from the Arctic Ocean, across the equator, almost to the Antarctic continent. The combination of these continents is sometimes referred to as the New World. From the old-world perspective—that of Europe, Asia, and Africa—the Americas were unknown for thousands of years. Once the Americas were discovered, northern Europe colonized primarily the northern areas, whereas southern Europe focused more on the southern areas. The industrial technology developed in Europe migrated to the early American colonies through industrial espionage. The influences of European and some Asian and African cultures are still reflected in different sectors throughout the Americas and in the textiles and apparel found there.

POLITICAL AND ECONOMIC OVERVIEW

Examine Figure 10.1, a map of the Americas. Many names are given to the combined land areas of North, Central, and South America as well as the West Indies. These are the primary land areas in the region of the world commonly called the Western Hemisphere or historically called the New World. Sometimes, these land areas are referred to as North and **Latin America**, which separates Canada and the United States from Mexico and Central and South America. In textile and apparel literature, Central America and the West Indies are commonly referred to as the Caribbean Basin countries. The terms *America* and *the Americas*, as used in this text, refer to the combination of North,

Andean a term that originated with early archaeologists that studied the civilizations in the mountains of Peru and Bolivia in western South America

Andean Trade Preference Act (ATPA) the primary trade agreement between the United States and northern South America, established in 1991

Andean Trade Promotion and Drug Eradication Act (ATPDEA) an agreement among the United States, Peru, and Bolivia in 2002 that made those countries eligible for duty-free treatment on exports of US goods for the first time

Caribbean Basin Economic Recovery Act (CBERA) commonly known as the Caribbean Basin Initiative (CBI), a trade preference program initiated by the United States in 1983 that expanded the use of Item 807 by eliminating quota restraints

Central America–Dominican Republic–United States Free Trade Agreement (CAFTA-DR) (2002) an agreement intended to solidify the United States as the leading supplier of goods and services to Central America and Dominican Republic and to provide these countries with duty-free access to the US market

charge-back a financial penalty imposed by the customer on a vendor for noncompliance with established vendor compliance rules

Free Trade Area of the Americas (FTAA) the most comprehensive free trade agreement under discussion since the early 2000s, involving thirty-four countries in North, Central, and South America

Latin America a term applied to all Spanish- and Portuguese-speaking nations south of the United States

Mercosur (Common Market of the South) (1991) free trade within, and a common external tariff for, Argentina, Brazil, Paraguay, Uruguay, and Venezuela; accounts for 70 percent of South America's total economy

North American Free Trade Agreement (NAFTA) (1994) eliminated tariffs and quotas among Canada, Mexico, and the United States

Organization of American States (OAS) (1948) has the purpose of a Pan-American Union for closer economic, cultural, and political relations within the Americas

Pan-American Union (1910) a union with the purpose of closer economic, cultural, and political relations within the Americas

Middle, and South America. All these terms are used as appropriate to the discussion that follows. As each sector or country is discussed, be sure to locate it on the map.

Efforts to Unify the Americas

In 1776, following the Revolutionary War, thirteen North American colonies gained independence from Great Britain and formed the United States. During the early 1800s, the first Pan-American Conference was held, with the purpose of uniting new Latin American republics that had also recently gained independence from European monarchies. In the mid-1800s, Mexico ceded Texas to the United States, and Canada retained ties to the British crown but became self-governing. Table 10.1 provides a list of key political and economic events that influenced the textile and apparel business in the Americas during the second half of the twentieth century and the beginning of the twenty-first century. Many of these agreements and trade programs are still in effect and

Figure 10.1

Map highlighting the Western Hemisphere trading region: North America, Central America, the West Indies, and South America.

can be drawn upon under appropriate conditions. Use this table as a point of reference as these events are discussed throughout the chapter.

Numerous free trade agreements have occurred since 2010 to promote free trade between and among countries in the Americas and with other nations. Since 2009, US exports to free trade agreement (FTA) partners have increased more rapidly (64 percent) than US exports to the rest of the world (45 percent). FTA partners are especially important to the small- and medium-size exporters including textiles and apparel (US International Trade Administration, 2014). The Pan-American Conference created the **Pan-American Union** in 1910, with the purpose of closer economic, cultural, and political relations within the Americas. Almost 40 years later, following World War II, while three European countries were forming their first free trade area, the ninth Pan-American Conference created the **Organization of American States (OAS)**. The original members included the United States and twenty democratic Latin American republics.

TABLE 10.1

EVOLUTION OF THE POLITICAL AND ECONOMIC ORGANIZATION OF THE AMERICAS SINCE 1948

Year	Event	Countries/Sectors
1960	Economic programs begin to improve living conditions in Latin America	United States, Latin America
1962	OAS expels Cuba's communist government	OAS members
1973	Caribbean Community and Common Market (CARICOM) formed to foster trade	17 West Indies countries
1982	Canada becomes completely independent of Great Britain as a confederation with a parliamentary democracy	Canada and Great Britain
1983	Caribbean Basin Economic Recovery Act (CBERA) enacted to stimulate industrial development; includes Item 807	United States and Caribbean Basin countries
1988	US–Canada Free Trade Agreement eliminates trade duties and quotas	United States and Canada
1988	Andean Pact, a free trade area with a common external tariff	Bolivia, Ecuador, Peru, Venezuela
1991	Andean Trade Preference Act (ATPA)	United States, Bolivia, Colombia, Ecuador, Peru
1994	North American Free Trade Agreement (NAFTA)	Canada, Mexico, United States
1994	Southern Common Market (Mercosur, in Spanish, or Mercosul, in Portuguese); free internal trade; a common and external tariff	Argentina, Brazil, Paraguay, Uruguay; Bolivia and Chile have agreement
2000	Caribbean Basin Trade Partnership Act (CBTPA) and African Growth and Opportunity Act (AGOA) implemented	United States, Caribbean Basin, and Africa
2000	Textile and Enforcement Operation Division of US Customs and Border Protection (CBP) created to control shipping contraband	United States
2001	Free Trade Area of Americas (FTAA) proposed by United States	United States, 34 democracies in Western Hemisphere
2002	Trade Act, including Andean Trade Promotion and Drug Eradication Act (ATPDEA), expands ATPA	United States and Andean countries
2003	US–Chile Free Trade Agreement	United States and Chile
2005	US approves Central American Free Trade Agreement (CAFTA)	United States and 6 Central American countries
2006	United States reaches CAFTA agreements	United States and El Salvador, Honduras, Nicaragua, Guatemala
2007	United States reaches CAFTA-DR agreements	Dominican Republic
2009	United States reaches CAFTA agreements	Costa Rica
2009	US–Peru Trade Promotion Agreement	United States and Peru
2010	United States pending free trade agreements	United States, Colombia, Panama

Source: Data collected from the World Trade Organization (WTO) in 2010.

The Pan-American Union held the First Summit of the Americas in 1994. The members established broad political, economic, and social development goals and entrusted the OAS with the responsibility of advancing their shared vision:

- defending democracy through an Inter-American charter, which defines essential elements of democracy and guidelines for responding effectively if it is at risk;
- protecting human rights by addressing problems, including police abuse and violations of due process, by applying regional law to human rights;
- strengthening security to prevent financing of terrorism, tightening border control, and increasing cooperation among law enforcement agencies;
- fostering free trade by creating a hemisphere-wide trading zone, the Free Trade Area of the Americas (FTAA);
- combating illegal drugs by strengthening antidrug laws, enhancing prevention programs, and taking steps to stem trafficking of illegal narcotics, related chemicals, and firearms; and
- fighting corruption by adopting the Inter-American Convention against Corruption, the first treaty of its kind in the world. (Organization of American States, n.d.)

All thirty-five independent countries of the Americas have ratified the OAS charter and belong to the organization. The OAS also passed a resolution to allow the Republic of Cuba to participate, at Cuba's request. One has only to check the news each day to realize that much remains to be done to meet the goals established by the OAS, but the challenge is great, given the diversity of perspectives that the goals must address. The OAS has four official languages (English, Spanish, Portuguese, and French), and sociocultural perspectives and values differ among North, Central, and South America. As a result, there are some differences in family, education, employment, and lifestyle practices. The roots of these ideas, customs, and skills have passed from one generation to the next and still exist in Europe and parts of Asia, the source of much of the Americas' emigrated population. These contrasting cultural perspectives are ongoing challenges among the primary regions of the Western hemisphere as they are in many other parts of the world. The cultural values related to time, work, frugality, education, merit, community, and ethics cannot be judged in terms of right and wrong; rather, they should be recognized as various perceived realities, judged case by case (or culture by culture).

The **Free Trade Area of the Americas (FTAA)** is the most comprehensive free trade agreement now under discussion, involving thirty-four countries in North, Middle, and South America. It was hoped that negotiations on an FTAA would be completed by 2005, but there was no closure on the matter by 2015. The planned focus of FTAA would be industrial development through reduction of trade barriers. One of the reasons development is difficult is the number of trade agreements with conflicting terms already in existence among the participating countries. North Americans see FTAA as an extension of NAFTA, and South Americans see FTAA as an extension of **Mercosur (Common Market of the South)**.

Economic and Industrial Standing of Selected American Countries

The Americas include some of the richest and poorest countries in the world. Table 10.2 itemizes characteristics of countries in the Americas that are the most active in the textile and apparel trade, sorted by geographic sector. The countries in the table are listed in alphabetical order in each section to make it easier to refer back to the table for information about individual countries. By scanning the first two columns of the table, it quickly becomes apparent that Canada has the largest geographic size, with nearly 10 million square kilometers, although the United States and Brazil are only a little

TABLE 10.2

CHARACTERISTICS OF COUNTRIES LOCATED IN THE AMERICAS THAT ARE ACTIVE IN TEXTILE AND APPAREL TRADE

Country with GCI[a] for each	Geographic Size (Square Kilometers in Thousands)	Population (in Millions)	Life Expectancy (in Years)	Adult Literacy	GDP[b] (in Billions of US Dollars)	GDP per Capita	Inflation Rate[c]	Labor Force (in Millions)	Unemployment Rate	Internet Users (in Millions)
North America										
Canada (15)	9,984.7	34.8	81.7	99.0%	$ 1,579.0	$44,500	2.0%	19.2	6.9%	25.1
Mexico (61)	1,964.4	120.3	75.4	94.2%	$ 2,143.0	$17,900	3.8%	52.9	4.7%	23.3
United States (3)	9,826.7	318.9	79.6	99.0%	$17,460.0	$54,800	2.0%	156.0	6.2%	231.0
Caribbean Basin										
Costa Rica (51)	51.1	4.8	78.2	97.4%	$ 71.2	$14,900	4.7%	2.3	8.5%	1.5
Dominican Republic (101)	48.7	10.3	77.8	90.9%	$ 135.7	$12,800	3.3%	5.0	14.6%	2.1
El Salvador (84)	21.0	6.1	74.2	85.5%	$ 50.9	$ 8,000	1.5%	2.8	6.2%	0.8
Guatemala (78)	108.9	14.7	71.4	78.3%	$ 118.7	$ 7,500	3.5%	4.6	4.1%	2.0
Haiti (137)	27.8	10.1	63.2	48.7%	$ 18.5	$ 1,800	4.3%	4.8	40.6%	1.0
Honduras (100)	112.1	8.6	70.9	85.4%	$ 39.0	$ 4,700	6.2%	3.6	4.3%	0.7
Jamaica (86)	11.0	2.9	73.5	87.5%	$ 24.3	$ 8,700	8.8%	1.3	13.6%	1.5
Nicaragua (99)	130.4	5.9	72.7	78.1%	$ 29.9	$ 4,800	6.1%	3.1	7.4%	0.2
South America										
Argentina (104)	2,780.4	43.0	77.5	97.9%	$ 927.4	$22,010	36.4%	17.3	7.7%	11.2
Brazil (57)	8,514.9	202.7	73.3	91.3%	$ 3,073.0	$15,200	6.3%	110.9	5.5%	65.0
Chile (33)	756.1	17.4	78.4	95.1%	$ 410.3	$14,700	2.1%	8.5	6.5%	5.5
Colombia (66)	1,138.9	46.2	75.3	93.6%	$ 410.3	$13,500	2.9%	23.7	12.0%	17.1
Peru (65)	1,285.2	30.2	73.2	93.8%	$ 376.7	$12,000	3.3%	16.6	9.2%	7.1
Uruguay[d]	176.2	3.3	76.8	98.4%	$ 69.8	$12,600	8.8%	1.7	6.7%	1.3
Venezuela (131)	912.1	28.9	74.4	93.5%	$ 545.7	$17,900	69.8%	14.4	7.8%	7.2

Note: Table includes the Global Competitiveness Index (GCI) for each country in brackets following the country's name.

[a]GCI = Global Competitiveness Index

[b]GDP adjusted by purchasing power parity

[c]Consumer prices

[d]Global Competitiveness Index was not available

Source: Based on estimates of 2014–2015 data from Central Intelligence Agency (CIA). "The World Factbook." Retrieved October 29, 2015, from https://www.cia.gov/library/publications/the-world-factbook/index.html.

smaller. However, the United States has by far the largest population, with an estimated 318.9 million, followed by Brazil, with 202.6 million, and Mexico, with 122.3 million. Canada, although very large in size, has a population of only 36.2 million. Argentina has a slightly higher population than Canada but is less than one-third of Canada's size. Most of the West Indies, islands in and around the Caribbean Sea, are tiny in comparison with countries in North and South America. Table 10.2 is intended as a reference as you work your way through the rest of the chapter.

First of all, notice the range of GCIs in each region. Remember, the GCIs go from 1 to 144 and are defined as the set of institutions, policies, and factors that determine the country's level of productivity. The smaller the GCI number, the greater ability of the country to compete in the world market. Notice that North America has quite a range of GCIs from 3 to 61; the Caribbean Basin has a range from 51 to 137; and South America has a range from 33 to 131. Examine the life expectancies and literacy rates. Canada has the longest life expectancy, 81.7 years, followed by the United States, Costa Rica, and Chile. Haiti has by far the lowest level of life expectancy, at 63.2 years. Canada and the United States report high literacy rates, at 99 percent, followed closely by Uruguay and Argentina. Haiti has the lowest literacy rate, at 48.7 percent; Nicaragua is second lowest, at 78.1 percent.

The United States has by far the highest per capita GDP in the Americas, at $52,800, but that is not the highest in the world, because Luxembourg (in Europe) has $92,400. Canada is second in the Americas, with per capita GDP of $44,500. Canada and the United States are the only countries in the Americas that can be regarded as developed countries, according to the criteria presented in Chapter 1 (significantly higher than the world's average GDP per capita of $16,100). Most of the countries' GDPs per capita fall within the range of Uruguay ($12,600) and Jamaica ($8,300). Developing countries' per capita GDP is around the world's average of $13,100, with a range of $3,000 to $20,000. Only Haiti, with the lowest per capita GDP at $1,800 (significantly less than the world's average), is classified as a newly developing country.

Inflation rates across the Americas in 2012 ranged from -0.7 percent in the United States to 69.8 percent in Venezuela. Only nine countries have reported inflation rates of less than 4 percent, suggesting most of the economies in the Americas are unstable. The Americas suffered from the uncertainties of the global recession. The size of the labor force and unemployment rates are indicators of opportunities for economical labor costs, although labor pools seem relatively small. Only Brazil, Colombia, Mexico, and the United States exceed 20 million workers. Jamaica had the smallest labor force, with 1.3 million; the United States had the largest, with 155 million. Unemployment rates range from 3.2 percent, in Guatemala, to 40.6 percent in Haiti. Several of the countries of the Americas have less than 2 million internet users, so current opportunities for e-tailing are limited in those countries.

TRENDS IN TEXTILE AND APPAREL TRADE IN THE AMERICAS

The American countries included in Tables 10.3a and b are those identified by the WTO as ranking among the largest textile and clothing traders in the world. Each country name is followed by its GCI. The tables report the value of imports and exports of textiles and clothing in US dollars for selected years in 2000, 2006, and 2011. The last two columns of each table include each country's percentage share of textiles and apparel in each country's total merchandise imports. Because of recent growth and/or the developing nature of some of these countries, there is some missing data. You may want to put a tab on some of these pages to make it easy to refer back to these tables as you work through the rest of this chapter. The tables begin with North American NAFTA countries, followed by the other regions of the Americas.

A quick scan of the numbers in Tables 10.3a and 10.3b shows the leadership of the United States, Canada, and Mexico (the NAFTA countries) in the textile and apparel trade in the Americas. NAFTA was a primary player in developing that leadership in the last decade of the twentieth century, but once the quota system expired, exports from Canada, Mexico, and Caribbean Basin countries to the United States decreased as imports from China and other Asian nations increased. This created some hard times for the Caribbean Basin countries. For the United States, there was a huge increase of

TABLE 10.3A

IMPORTS OF TEXTILES AND APPAREL IN SELECTED AMERICAN COUNTRIES[1] AND THE VALUE OF TEXTILES PLUS CLOTHING[2]

Regions and Countries with Global Competitiveness Index	Textile Imports			Apparel Imports			Percent Share of T&C in the Economy's Total Merchandise Imports	
	2000	2006	2011	2000	2006	2011	2005	2011
North America (NAFTA)								
United States (3)	15,985	23,498	25,359	67,115	82,969	88,588	5.2	4.3
Canada (15)	4,126	4,472	4,502	3,690	6,987	9,532	3.3	3.1
Mexico (61)	5,822	5,951	5,859	3,602	2,517	4,086	3.7	2.3
Caribbean Basin (CBERA)								
Costa Rica (51)	184	232	338	592	239	291	5.9	4.1
Dominican Republic (101)	1,173	941	1,010	—	—	225	6.8	6.8
El Salvador (84)	325	672	1,035	713	333	1,782	16.4	13.5
Haiti (137)	—	—	—	—	—	716	—	—
Honduras (100)	501	1,239	1,654	2,275	423	3,808	73.2	68.8
South America (Andean; Mercosur)								
Argentina (104)	653	820	1,282	333	559	—	7.5	2.5
Brazil (57)	1,045	1,599	4,303	173	442	2,066	0.9	1.8
Chile (33)	431	522	1,192	501	1,003	2,519	3.7	5.0
Colombia (66)	558	864	1,530	80	239	644	5.0	4.0
Peru (65)	165	358	1,245	59	134	487	3.5	2.6
Venezuela (131)	286	644	665	390	736	533	4.3	2.9

[1] In millions of US dollars.

[2] As a percentage of each country's total merchandise imports.

Source: World Trade Organization (WTO). (2009 and 2013). "International Trade Statistics 2009. Section 2: Merchandise Trade by Product, 107–114." Retrieved January 16, 2010, from http://www.wto.org/english/res_e/statis_e/its2009_e/its09_merch_trade_product_e.pdf and May 4, 2013, from https//www.wto.org/english/res_e/statis_e/its2013_e/its13_merch_trade_product_e.pdf

TABLE 10.3B

EXPORTS OF TEXTILES AND APPAREL BY SELECTED AMERICAN COUNTRIES[1] AND THE VALUE OF TEXTILES PLUS CLOTHING[2]

Regions and Countries with Global Competitiveness Index	Textile Exports			Apparel Exports			Percent Share of T&C in the Economy's Total Merchandise Exports	
	2000	2006	2011	2000	2006	2011	2005	2011
North America (NAFTA)								
United States (3)	10,952	12,580	13,791	8,629	4,885	5,223	2.0	1.3
Canada (15)	2,204	2,369	2,024	2,077	1,798	1,289	1.2	1.7
Mexico (61)	2,571	2,192	2,140	8,631	6,323	4,638	4.4	1.9
Caribbean Basin (CBERA)								
Costa Rica (51)	—	—	—	660	235	172	6.7	1.7
Dominican Republic (101)	—	—	309	2,555	1,734	645	31.8	11.5
El Salvador (84)	79	80	284	1,673	1,814	1,830	52.6	39.8
Haiti (137)	—	—	—	245	432	677	83.6	88.0
Honduras (100)	—	—	—	2,275	2,613	3,808	55.3	52.9
South America (Andean; Mercosur)								
Argentina (104)	258	219	300	—	—	193	1.0	1.2
Brazil (57)	895	1,365	1,108	—	—	193	1.4	0.5
Chile (33)	114	112	213	—	—	—	2.6	3.7
Colombia (66)	268	383	486	520	962	650	6.0	2.6
Peru (65)	128	199	374	504	1,204	1,402	7.0	4.1
Venezuela (131)	—	—	—	—	—	—	—	—

[1]In millions of US dollars.

[2]As a percentage of each country's total merchandise imports.

Sources: World Trade Organization (WTO). (2009). "International Trade Statistics 2009. Section 2: Merchandise trade by product, 107–114." Retrieved January 16, 2010, from http://www.wto.org/english/res_e/statis_e/its2009_e/its09_merch_trade_product_e.pdf; World Trade Organization (WTO). (2014). "International Trade Statistics 2012." Retrieved May 4, 2013, from https//www.wto.org/english/res_e/statis_e/its2013_e/its13_merch_trade_product_e.pdf

imports of both textiles and apparel between 2000 and 2006, with an additional increase in 2011 supported by NAFTA. In contrast, exports of textiles (Table 10.3b) increased only slightly, and export of apparel decreased from 2000 to 2011. Many US apparel brands were being sold around the world, but few of those garments were actually produced in the United States; instead, they were being sourced and sold elsewhere by US firms.

Consider the Caribbean Basin countries. Comparison of textile imports with textile exports suggests that imports are intended either for domestic consumption or for inputs into production of apparel for export. Apparel imports had even less in value than textile imports, supporting that proposition. Considering apparel exports, Costa Rica and Dominican Republic show some increases over the time period, whereas El Salvador, Haiti, and Honduras have recorded increases. South America shows considerable activity in both textile imports and exports and also in apparel imports. Brazil, the most populous in the region, shows the largest quantity of textile imports and exports (with the exception of Chile, which has slightly higher apparel imports). Brazil grows large quantities of cotton and manufactures significant amounts of fabric and apparel. Apparel exports from the reported South American countries are typically lower in comparison with the Caribbean Basin countries.

A comparison of the labor costs for producing textiles in selected nations in the Americas in Table 10.4 provides us with some insight as to why some have met with more success than others in the global trading of their textile materials. Few textiles are produced in Caribbean Basin countries. Unfortunately it was not possible to find more recent data for the table, but it demonstrates well the differences among countries related to levels of payment for work.

All the nations in Table 10.4 have lower labor costs for fabric production than the United States. Many of the nations in the Caribbean do not have the expertise and the equipment to make good quality textiles. The South American countries also show significant levels of social costs. This may contribute to the lack of textile and export activity for these countries as well. Peru, the South American nation with the lowest total cost, has taken a different approach by seeking out a niche market for fine alpaca sweaters and fabrics that appeal to consumers in many countries.

Historically, companies in the Caribbean Basin have been primarily involved with apparel production, with labor rates lower than those of the lowest South American countries. The Caribbean Basin companies originally competed for a share of the US market by using 807-type production. Item 807 involved exporting US cotton textiles in the form

TABLE 10.4

TOTAL LABOR COSTS PER HOUR FOR TEXTILE PRODUCTION IN SELECTED AMERICAN COUNTRIES COMPARED WITH US LABOR COSTS[a]

Country	Total Labor Costs per Hour (in US Dollars)	Total Labor Costs as a Percentage of US Labor Costs[b]	Total Labor Costs (in Local Currency)	Direct Wages (in Local Currency)	Social Costs (in Local Currency)	Social Costs as a Percentage of Direct Wages[c]
United States (3)	$17.41	100%	$ 17.41	$13.52	$ 3.89	28.8%
Uruguay (80)	$ 6.20	36%	151.11	114.70	36.41	31.7%
Argentina (104)	$ 4.48	26%	15.41	10.76	4.65	41.2%
Brazil (57)	$ 3.41	20%	7.90	4.80	3.10	64.6%
Colombia (66)	$ 2.45	14%	5,484.00	3,775.00	1,709.00	45.3%
Mexico (61)	$ 2.17	12%	30.01	20.14	9.87	49.0%
Peru (65)	$ 2.02	12%	6.32	3.41	2.91	85.3%

[a]Considering direct wages and social costs with the Global Competitiveness Index for each country following each name; total labor costs per hour = direct wages per hour + social costs per hour

[b]In US dollars, total labor cost per hour as a percentage of US labor costs per hour = a country's labor cost per hour ÷ US labor cost per hour × 100

[c]In local currency, social costs as a percentage of direct wages = social costs ÷ direct wages × 100

Source: Werner International Management Consultants. (2009). "Primary Textiles Labor Cost Comparisons 2008." Retrieved May 25, 2010, from http://texnet.ilgstudios.net/files/2009/08/Werner_International_Labor_Cost_Study_2008.pdf

of cut garment parts, assembling the garments in one of the countries, and exporting finished apparel back to the United States. The 807 method of garment assembly was fundamental to helping apparel production move from the United States to Central American countries with lower labor costs. With the implementation of the Central American Free Trade Agreement (CAFTA-DR), apparel production in most countries converted from 807 to CMT (cut, make, trim). Under CMT, US garment firms delivered fabric and patterns so both cutting and assembly could be accomplished at lower labor cost.

ROLE OF NORTH AMERICAN COUNTRIES IN TEXTILES AND APPAREL

The United States and Canada have one of the longest unprotected but shared borders in the world, and almost nine of every ten Canadians live within 100 miles of it. In 1985, 80 percent of trade was already free between the two countries. Among the products that still had tariffs were textiles, apparel, and automobiles. Trilateral negotiations (among the United States, Canada, and Mexico) began for the **North American Free Trade Agreement (NAFTA)** in 1991. NAFTA went into effect in 1994. NAFTA is focused primarily on trade and investment rather than on political or economic unity. Based on country of origin (COO) qualification, the following went into effect following ratification of NAFTA:

- 50 percent of duty was removed from US-made goods imported into Mexico;
- 90 percent of goods traded among Mexico, Canada, and the United States would be tariff free within a 10-year period;
- textiles and apparel had a 15-year transition period to eliminate tariffs;
- nontariff barriers, such as quotas, were removed immediately;
- restrictions on direct foreign investment were eliminated;
- national environmental standards were to be upheld; and
- workplace health and safety, the minimum wage, and child labor laws were to be upheld.

Average hourly wages at that time were $2.32 in Mexico, $14.31 in the United States, and $14.71 in Canada. There was fear, especially by states in which apparel manufacturing was still a major employer, that low-wage jobs would move to Mexico (Taplin, 2003). By 2002, in part because of NAFTA, the United States was by far the largest trading partner and foreign investor in both Canada and Mexico. Total trade between the United States and Canada was more than $450 billion a year, almost two-and-a-half times more than in the early 1990s: 70 percent of Canada's imports were from US suppliers, and more than 85 percent of Canada's exports went to US firms; nearly two-thirds of Canada's foreign investment came from the United States (Hakim & Litan, 2002).

Trade between Canada and Mexico also increased five times, to $9 billion, nearly the same as trade between Brazil and Argentina. Despite these trade gains, the effect of NAFTA on the industrial well-being of the participating countries has been controversial. From a textile and apparel perspective, NAFTA represented a break with the protectionist perspectives that had been in effect for more than a century, and trade among the NAFTA members increased. However, since the demise of the global quota system, competition from China and other nations, such as Vietnam, has become too great, and Mexico has suffered significant setbacks in its overall trade numbers in textiles and apparel.

The United States (3)

For decades, the United States has been the world's largest economy. Review Table 10.2 for an overview of the status of the United States and Americans. The country has a market-oriented economy in which private individuals and business firms make most of the decisions, and federal and state governments buy most needed goods and services in private markets. The economy had steady growth, low unemployment and inflation, and rapid advances in technology. The September 11, 2001, terrorist attack on New York City's World Trade Center dramatically changed perspectives on safety, security, and patriotism. The subsequent war between the United States–led coalition and Iraq, and US-NATO supported military interventions in Afghanistan and Syria required significant economic resources. Long-term problems include rapidly rising medical costs, pension costs of the aging population, sizable trade and budget deficits, and stagnation of family income for lower-income groups. In late 2008 and early 2009, the United States led the world into the global economic recession, with unemployment figures rising to more than 10 percent, an increasingly heavy debt burden, and a crisis in the banking sector. Recovery was mostly achieved by 2014.

Domestic Production of Textiles and Apparel

With growing imports and the implementation of NAFTA, manufacturing employment in textiles and apparel continued to decline. Employment in the US textile industry peaked in 1950, and by 1980 textile employment had decreased by 33 percent. During the same time, the number of apparel employees increased by 5 percent. This loss of textile and apparel industry jobs is even more significant when measured against a growth of 11.3 percent in overall manufacturing jobs in the United States during this period. The decline in employment in textiles from 1950 to 1980 was largely related to application of new technology, resulting in increased productivity and less manual labor required for production of yarns and fabrics. As employment dropped, fewer people were producing more goods until production peaked, in 1997.

The decline in apparel workers began after 1980; between 1980 and 2002, the workforce was cut by a total of 56.6 percent. In 2013, the apparel industry employed only 144,000 workers, down from almost a million in the 1980s. These job losses were concentrated in the southeastern United States: North and South Carolina, Georgia, Alabama, and Virginia. US apparel production continued its decline through 2008, down to 582 million garments, and import penetration, or the percentage of the US market that is supplied by imports, reached record levels of 97 percent in 2008 (American Apparel and Footwear Association, 2009).

Between the implementation of NAFTA in January 1994 and May of 2007, the US textile and apparel manufacturing sector lost more than one million jobs, reflecting a 65 percent decrease in employment in the industry (Fibre2Fashion, 2007). This drop cannot be solely blamed on NAFTA. Overall market trends, including the end of the MFA quota system among WTO members; the implementation of numerous bilateral free trade agreements between the United States and other, individual nations; and the implementation of the Central America–Dominican Republic–United States Free Trade Agreement (CAFTA-DR) all exerted an influence as well. The pattern of sourcing textile and apparel products offshore parallels similar patterns found in other developed nations in Europe and in Japan and should really come as no surprise, yet for those whose livelihood depended on this industry, it was a severe blow. (See Figure 10.2.)

Figure 10.2

Evolution of the level of employment in textiles and apparel manufacturing jobs in relation to all other manufacturing jobs in the United States from 1940 to 2005.

US Department of Agriculture. (n.d.). "US Textile and Apparel Industries and Rural America." Retrieved October 26, 2015, from http://www.ers.usda.gov/ topics/crops/cotton-wool/background/ us-textile-and-apparel-industries-and-rural-america.aspx

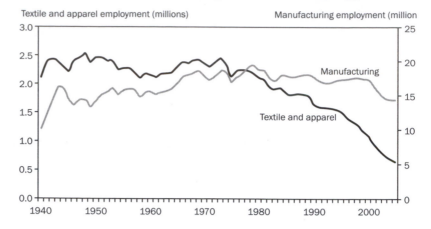

TEXTILE AND APPAREL JOBS, 1940–2005
The decline in textile and apparel jobs has been greater than for all manufacturing jobs

Textile and apparel employment (millions)   Manufacturing employment (million

There are some bright spots in the US textile and apparel industry. During recent years, textile production has become automated and computer controlled and more textiles can be made with fewer employees. In 2013, the US textile industry generated nearly $57 billion in shipments and directly employed about 230,700 Americans. More than one-third of textile production continues to be exported mostly to NAFTA countries (Platzer, 2014). United States-based apparel manufacturers, such as VF Corporation and Levi Strauss & Co., have closed dozens of jeans plants in the United States and moved them to low-wage countries. VF produces about half of its jeanswear in locations throughout the Americas, such as Mexico and Argentina; the remainder is produced in other locations throughout the world. Many US manufacturers have foregone any manufacturing activity and are now considered brand managers. We have discussed many of these as examples elsewhere throughout this text.

New York, once the most prominent fashion center in the Americas, and the largest production center up through the mid-1900s, has been feeling a significant downturn in its role. But not all apparel manufacturers have left the United States. In fact, in the early 2010s, there have been signs of reshoring, or pockets of domestic apparel production reemerging in the country, as discussed in Chapter 8. Read Case 10.1 for insight into the growth and development of a long-established, family-owned, US-based apparel company, Carhartt.

California Apparel Centers

Major manufacturers also seemed to be abandoning the San Francisco area as a production center. Levi Strauss & Co. still has headquarters there, but its products are sourced offshore. Esprit moved its financial headquarters to Hong Kong and now has its marketing arm in Germany. However, we would be remiss not to mention The North Face (owned by VF), which is located across the Bay from San Francisco, in Berkeley, and has become a leader in performance sportswear for hiking and mountaineering. Gap Inc. is also headquartered in San Francisco.

Since the mid-1980s, Los Angeles County, California, has become the largest apparel production center in the United States, specializing primarily in women's wear, specifically juniors, denim apparel, and niche sportswear such as surfing apparel. The area was already a main center for design and fashionable sportswear as well as home to the most visible means of presenting emerging styles: the entertainment industry. Many high-end

WHAT MAKES CARHARTT GO?

About 125 years ago, Hamilton Carhartt & Company was born. After experimenting unsuccessfully in a number of employment venues, Hamilton Carhartt discovered a need for work clothing for railroad employees. "Union-made" bib overalls were created, and they became standard work-wear for thousands of people that worked with their hands and their backs. (During that time, "union-made" meant the garments were manufactured by members of a labor union.) By 1910, Carhartt had fabric mills in South Carolina and Georgia as well as garment production plants in both the United States and Canada.[1]

Hamilton Carhartt died in 1937 and his son Wylie took over the company. Wylie was very concerned about the poverty and distress related to the Great Depression and set priorities on better working conditions and improved pay scales. He also expanded into Super Dux and Super Fab hunting product lines. Robert Valade, husband of Wylie's daughter Gretchen Carhartt, assumed leadership of Carhartt in 1959. In 1976, the "hard-finish duck Active Jac" was introduced in a "hoodie" form, and the style remains the top-selling jacket for Carhartt today.[2]

One of Carhartt's growth strategies has long been supporting nonprofit trade, sports, and heritage organizations to enhance growth and effectiveness in their endeavors. Here are a few examples of organizations that Carhartt supports:

- National Sponsor for FFA (Future Farmers of America), beginning in 1997
- SkillsUSA, an organization devoted to preparing high-performance workers, enhancing educational experiences, and developing leadership, beginning in 2000
- Helmets to Hardhats, an organization that helps military service members transition back into civilian life, beginning in 2014

- Union Sportsmen's Alliance, a nonprofit conservation organization of AFL-CIO current and retired members with a goal of conserving healthy wildlife habitat

During the same time frame, Carhartt also developed retail stores in the United States as well as parts of Europe and Australia. The goal in opening stores in these regions was to open opportunities where they didn't already have retail distribution and to create "exposure to the brand."[2] The most recent addition to Carhartt's retail empire is a flagship store in downtown Detroit in 2015.[3] To introduce the press to the new store and to one of Carhartt's newest designs, Carhartt flew the publicity crew to a Detroit baseball game so they could be introduced to the grounds crew that were wearing Carhartt's newest design at the baseball park. It was described as a "Full Swing Sandstone Jacket," a roomy and well-insulated model that incorporates trademark technology to offer more comfort and a greater range of movement for the wearer. "It has the Freedom Gusset, the Mighty Back, and the Flex Elbow . . . these mean you're going to be plenty comfortable wearing this jacket."[4]

[1]Carhartt. (n.d.). "About Carhartt/Carhartt History." http://www.carhartt.com/content/carhartt-history

[2]Burgess, Z. (June 22, 2014). "After 125 Years, Carhartt Rolls Up Its Sleeves for the Future." *Crain's Detroit Business*. Retrieved October 29, 2015, from http://www.crainsdetroit.com/article/20140622/NEWS/306229972/after-125-years-carhartt-rolls-up-its-sleeves-for-the-future

[3]Carhartt. (n.d.). "Carhartt: Born in Detroit in 1889. Reborn in 2015." http://www.carhartt.com/query/Carhartt+Born%20in%20Detroit%20in%201889%20Reborn%20in%202015

[4]Mueller, L. (August 31, 2015). "Carhartt Took Us to a Detroit Tigers Game to Show Us a Jacket You Need This Fall." Retrieved October 29, 2015, from http://newsroom.carhartt.com/in_the_news/carhartt-took-us-to-a-detroit-tigers-game-to-show-us-a-jacket-you-need-this-fall-by-gus-turner-complex-com

1. How has Carhartt managed to remain vital to apparel consumers over their 125 years of business?
2. How might other companies benefit from these strategies?

fashion jeans, including Rock & Republic, 7 for All Mankind, Citizens for Humanity, paperdenim&cloth, and True Religion are made in Los Angeles. Employment in the Los Angeles apparel industry nearly doubled while textile and apparel employment in the rest of the nation declined by half. Since the 1990s, Los Anegeles has been the nation's largest apparel employer; New York City was second. There are still many surviving pockets of apparel production in other areas throughout the country, including the Hart Schaffner Marx men's tailored suit facility near Chicago.

Los Angeles is a major center for immigration, especially from Asia, Central America, and Mexico; therefore, it has a ready supply of low-cost labor as well as apparel manufacturing expertise. By 2000, Los Angeles County had 144,000 textile and apparel jobs, 60 percent of which were held by Korean Americans. Los Angeles had the largest Korean community outside of Korea, with more than 186,000 residents (The USA Online, n.d). Many emigrating Koreans were experienced in the textile and apparel industry and were able to establish firms with relatively few resources. The result was the growth of a Korean subset of the Los Angeles textile and apparel industry that includes family-owned firms, such as Forever 21. There is also an apparel market center, San Pedro Mart, where the first language is Korean, the second language is Spanish (because many Koreans migrated to the United States via South America), and the third language is English (The USA Online, n.d). Los Angeles provides retail buyers with over 100 fashion brands representing a variety of price ranges.

One of the most well-known California apparel brands is Guess. It began as a small jeans manufacturer in Berkeley, California, and evolved into a global brand, doing more than $2 billion in business annually. Guess was established in 1981 by the Marciano brothers. Their first style was stone-washed, slim-fitting jeans, and Bloomingdales was their first department store customer. Guess became a representative of a young, sexy, and adventurous lifestyle. Guess is now available in more than eighty countries around the world (Guess.com, n.d.). In Los Angeles, American Apparel, which is a vertically integrated manufacturer, distributor, and retailer, continues to be one of the most globally visible apparel manufacturing companies that call the city home (Figures 10.3 and 10.4). In the 2000s, this firm employed thousands of workers in the Los Angeles area and sold its products in over 250 stores worldwide. In 2014, the board of directors fired the controversial founder and former CEO of the company, Dov Charney, for multiple cases of business misconduct (Wahba, 2015). In 2015, the company announced that it may have to go out of business, following declining sales and the drop in the company's shares by 87 percent.

Figure 10.3

American Apparel headquarters located in downtown Los Angeles, California. For many years, the company has represented a possible comeback for US apparel manufacturing.

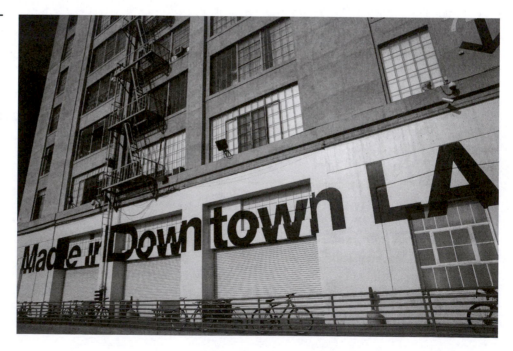

Figure 10.4
Employees sew garments at the American Apparel factory. The company uses modular manufacturing, by which a group of five to six people produce the entire garment.

US Retailing

Many US apparel retailers are involved in design and product development and nearly all large retailers provide online shopping for ultimate consumers. Of the top fifteen largest retailers in the world (based on new retail revenue in 2013), eight of them were based in the United States, including Walmart Stores Inc. (number 1) and Costco Wholesale Corporation (number 2). One of them (number 15) was a nonstore giant, Amazon; however, Amazon is now also moving on to in-store retailing. As an example of how large these retailers are, in 2015, under the name 71 Banners, "Walmart operated 11,000 retail units in 27 countries; employed 2.2 million associates around the world—1.3 million in the United States alone" (Walmart.com, n.d.). Other countries outside the United States that provide homes for the largest apparel retailers in the top fifty include France, Germany, and the UK. The largest apparel/footwear retailer is TJX Companies, Inc. (number 36) United States, followed by Inditex, S.A. (number 44) Spain, and H&M (number 49) Sweden. Three department store retailers are also in the top fifty: IKEA (number 28) Netherlands; Sears (number 29) United States; and Macy's, Inc. (number 34) United States (Deloitte, 2015).

Huge retailers require huge quantities of merchandise, limiting the ability of small- and medium-sized apparel producing firms to become suppliers, which has been a problem for apparel entrepreneurs worldwide. However, internet-enabling technologies provided unprecedented opportunities for these small businesses to target ultimate consumers directly. The landscape for apparel products acquisition has changed significantly as the percentage of imports has increased. Retailers still source at the major trade fairs in the United States, such as in New York and the MAGIC shows in Las Vegas, but they continue to move toward developing private label merchandise and sourcing offshore. They have moved toward direct-to-factory sourcing either through their own sourcing offices or electing a sourcing agent to do the job for them. Many of the largest retailers from other areas of the world, such as H&M and Zara, are opening shops in the United States, whereas many US-based brands are opening stores elsewhere. Walmart has expanded internationally, into Argentina, Brazil, Canada, Central America, Chile, China, Japan, India, Mexico, Puerto Rico, and the UK. Gap Inc. owns and operates more than 3,300 stores worldwide, with stores throughout the United States as well as in ninety countries.

The United States has been notoriously overstored at times, with vacancies available in many malls across the nation. Specialty retailers are finding themselves welcomed as tenants for some of these vacant storefronts. In early 2015, several mall-based fashion retailers, including Wet Seal, Houlihan Lokey, and Coldwater Creek, Inc., declared bankruptcy. "The continuing fundamental shift in consumer behavior away from traditional mall shopping toward online-only stores and increased competition throughout the specialty retail fashion industy have created a difficult operating environment," Thomas Hillebrandt, Wet Seal's chief financial officer, said in the company's Chapter 11 filing in US Bankruptcy Court (McCarty & Pearson, 2015).

Internet shopping has been integrated into in-store shopping with constant customer electronic checking of pricing and selections online in comparison to in-store options. Most US retail stores today have been driven to having websites for shopping, and do a significant amount of their overall business through this venue. The marketing of fashion is also in an era of change as the nation and the world live with the online social networking environment. This has changed the ways that designers introduce their new lines to directly reach ultimate consumers.

Role of the United States in the Textile and Apparel Trade

According to the American Apparel and Footwear Association (AAFA), the trend in US apparel sourcing since the expiration of the quota system in 2005 has been consolidation among the top few supplier countries and a loss of market share for smaller countries (American Apparel and Footwear Association, 2009). Between 2004 and 2008, market share of the top ten apparel suppliers rose from 57.5 percent to 77.2 percent, whereas the next group of ten suppliers lost market share, dropping from 25.3 percent to 14.4 percent during the same time period. Data on 2009 imports indicated that China, Vietnam, Indonesia, Bangladesh, India, Pakistan, Haiti, and Sri Lanka were benefiting from no-quota trade (Birnbaum, 2009). Sufferers included Mexico, the Philippines, Jordan, Sub-Saharan Africa, Cambodia, and CAFTA-DR nations.

By 2014, the United States had many free trade and trade preference programs with countries around the world. Table 10.5 reports the top countries that were sources for the US apparel retailers in 2008 and 2014, with each country's Global Competitiveness Index in parentheses. Note that Mexico, Honduras, and El Salvador are the only major supplier countries to the United States located in the Americas. China took the top spot from Mexico in 2003; however, since the early 2010s, rising production costs in China have slowed down the growth as many mass market retailers switched apparel assembly to lower-cost countries, such as Vietnam and Bangladesh. Note, too, that Mexico has now moved from being the number six US supplier, in 2008, to the number eight, in 2014; thus, it still has an active role.

The dominance of China in 2014 still remains very apparent with a 42 percent market share; Vietnam has made a significant increase of about 4 percent to nearly an 11 percent market share. Cambodia and Bangladesh have also achieved slight increases. Other suppliers appear to have given up market share. The percent change from 2013 to 2014 is interesting because it suggests new trends are developing. Major increases in the US

TABLE 10.5

COMPARISON OF MAJOR SUPPLIERS' MARKET SHARE IN US APPAREL IMPORTS IN 2008 AND 2014

Source of Imports	Rank 2008	Market Share 2008	Rank 2014	Market Share 2014	Percent Change 2013 to 2014
World		100.00%		100.00%	3.2%
China (28)	1	34.32%	1	42.03%	4.0%
Vietnam (68)	2	6.73%	2	10.73%	13.2%
Bangladesh (109)	3	6.33%	3	6.28%	4.9%
Honduras (100)	4	5.87%	5	4.23%	1.1%
Indonesia (34)	5	4.84%	4	4.86%	−1.2%
Mexico (61)	6	4.56%	8	3.58%	0.9%
Cambodia (95)	7	3.92%	6	3.98%	−4.2%
India (71)	8	3.89%	7	3.73%	8.1%
El Salvador (84)	9	3.68%	9	3.08%	−1.0%
Pakistan (129)	10	3.05%	10	2.29%	0.4%
Thailand (31); Nicaragua (99)	11[a]	2.16%	15	1.88%	0.9%
Philippines (52)	12	1.70%	13	1.32%	−2.7%
Sri Lanka[b]	13	1.67%	12	1.61%	4.7%
Dominican Republic (101)	14	1.58%	17	1.03%	2.4%

[a]In 2014 Nicaragua took over at number 11 with 1.88 percent market share and Thailand dropped out of the top fourteen suppliers of apparel to the United States. Thailand has lower labor costs, but Nicaragua's proximity to the United States could be a factor in this change.

[b]GCI is not available.

Source: US Department of Commerce. (n.d.). "US General Imports, Office of Textiles and Apparel." Retrieved May 4, 2015, from http://www.otexa.ita.doc.gov

apparel market share include Vietnam (13.2 percent), India (8.1 percent), Bangladesh (4.9 percent), and Sri Lanka (4.7 percent). These countries bear watching to see if they can maintain growth over time.

Canada (15)

Since World War II, with vast distances and rich natural resources, Canada has been transformed from a largely rural economy into an industrial and urban one. The country, with ten provinces and three territories, became completely independent of Great Britain in 1982. Economically and technologically, Canada has developed in parallel with the United States. Review Table 10.2 for an overview of the status of Canada and Canadians.

Besides NAFTA, Canada also established free trade agreements with Chile, Costa Rica, Israel, and Peru. As a result of free trade with Chile, Canada more than doubled its textile exports, but apparel imports declined. The Israeli agreement has had little impact on the textile trade, but Canadian apparel exports to Israel tripled right after the agreement was signed. Canada also participates in the European Free Trade Agreement

(EFTA). A number of other trade agreements are under discussion, but the largest is the thirty-four-nation Free Trade Area of the Americas (FTAA).

Canadian textile and apparel companies hoped FTAA would resolve inequities implicit in the United States–Caribbean Basin Trade Partnership Act (CBTPA). Canada required all apparel labeling and marking to be in both English and French, and imported products must have country of origin labels. CBTPA has required use of US-made yarns and fabrics; it was a yarn-forward rule that precluded participation from the Canadian textile industry. More recently, CBTPA was replaced by CAFTA-DR, the Dominican Republic and Central American Free Trade Agreement. Clearly, negotiation of textile and apparel trade agreements is an active, ongoing process that sees no end because changes in technology, economies, and consumer expectations fuel endless changes to products and services.

Today, Canada is very similar to the United States' market-oriented economic system, patterns of production, and high living standards. The two countries are so closely aligned that a downturn in the US economy has an immediate effect on Canada's. A key strength of the Canadian economy is a substantial trade surplus, something the United States does not have. One of Canada's internal political issues continues to be the relationship with the province of Quebec, with its French-speaking residents and unique culture.

Textiles and Apparel in Canada

Canada has three very active trade associations: the Canadian Textiles Institute, the Canadian Apparel Federation, and the Retail Council of Canada. Canadian Retail Apparel Market is scheduled 2015 to 2019 in Toronto. The National Apparel Bureau provides apparel vendors with credit information on Canadian retailers. In the mid-1990s the Canadian textile industry included about 1,100 plants and employed 62,000 people. The apparel industry was producing industrial applications, military uniforms, and a range of garments for consumers. Overall, the apparel industry had 94,850 employees in 2002, but that number had decreased to about 65,000 by 2006 (Industry Canada, 2009) and has continued to decline since then.

In 2011, the Canadian apparel manufacturing sector included approximately 3,000 establishments, mainly small- to medium-sized companies, mostly Canadian owned and operated primarily in Quebec, with some others in Ontario and British Columbia. Most apparel firms have off-shored their production to control costs but some also operate short run and replenishment facilities in Canada in order to respond to fast-changing trends (fast fashion), and to produce high-end apparel. Nonmanufacturing, high-value-added activities such as design, R&D, branding, merchandising, marketing, logistics, and distribution have remained in Canada (Industry Canada, 2015).

The majority of Canadian apparel exports, almost 90 percent, are destined for the United States, but the overall amount of exports has been declining steadily as Canada competes for the US market share with Asian powerhouses. At the same time, apparel imports have been increasing. China continues to be the largest source of import increases, reaching 50 percent in 2006, followed by Bangladesh and the United States, with contributions of a mere 7 percent each (Industry Canada, 2009). By 2015, nearly ten times more apparel was imported than exported (Industry Canada, 2015). According to the Canadian Apparel Federation, the Canadian apparel industry has many features that, compared with the US industry, are unique:

- Canada has [only] about 10 percent of the US population. Canadians believe they have a stronger sense of regional identity whereas the United States subscribes to the "melting pot" theory. They believe their regional identities influence the way they dress. Canadian apparel often reflects a "mid-Atlantic/Western European" influence in its textile and apparel design.
- Canadian garment makers have become experts at producing small runs of their products since the domestic market is small. This has become an asset when producing "fast fashion" merchandise. US firms are better at supplying mass retailers because their domestic markets are large. Canadian apparel firms have the systems in place to effectively produce and market small runs, and that gives them a leg up on American companies when it comes to filling niche markets. Canadian apparel manufacturers are fast and deliver good quality.

Canada's textile and apparel manufacturers have faced pressures similar to those that have decimated European and US industries, prompting Canadian survivors to focus on high-end products and highly automated systems. Canadian firms that continue doing well include:

- Canada Goose: global headquarters in Toronto, Ontario, home to its new 96,000-square-foot factory to meet the demand for made in Canada outdoor products selling at premium retailers in more than fifty countries
- lululemon athletica: headquarters in Vancouver, British Columbia; design, sourcing, and quality assurance teams are based in Vancouver; production is outsourced around the world; now in hundreds of stores across Canada, the United States, Australia, and Hong Kong
- Roots: headquarters, design center, and leather goods factory in Toronto; privately held since 1973; product lines focus on active sportswear and leather goods, including footwear, bags, jackets, accessories, and natural fiber clothing, with 120 locations in Canada and the United States
- Tribal Sportswear: a Montreal-based manufacturer known for superior quality women's pants, jackets, tops, sweaters, and other sportswear; acquired by Haggar, based in Dallas, Texas, in 2013 to provide a women's line to complement the men's wear established by Haggar in 1926

Retailing in Canada

In Canada, both the population and 60 percent of retail sales are concentrated in Ontario and Quebec and so are the retailers. As experienced in other developed countries, Canada has had massive retail consolidation over the past three decades, leading to fewer, larger retailers. In the process, these large retailers have tended to augment their global sourcing capabilities and eliminate many Canadian apparel suppliers from their supply chain. Walmart arrived in Canada in 1994 and spread rapidly; consumers began to understand the concept of everyday low prices. Costco and Sam's Club are now both also well established. These larger retailers have exerted tremendous price and performance pressures on traditionally smaller Canadian apparel companies, increasingly levying **charge-backs** on suppliers and requiring sharing in advertising costs (co-op advertising) and other discounts.

There are seven Canada-based retailers listed in the 2013 Top 250 Global Retailers but only one, Hudson's Bay Company (HBC), a department store, is directly associated with the textiles and apparel industry. Affectionately referred to by locals as "the Bay,"

Figure 10.5

Hudson's Bay flagship store in downtown Toronto, Canada.

this department store is Canada's best known and has been a part of Canadian history for more than three centuries (Hudson's Bay Company, 2010). Over the past ten years, internet shopping has grown as a retail channel, with consumers buying goods and services online. In the early 2010s, similar to the United States, there has been a rise of small independent retailers offering unique merchandise online and, in some cases, through brick-and-mortar stores in reviving Main Street areas of small towns. See Figure 10.5 and Case 10.2.

Mexico (61)

The site of advanced Amerindian (American Indian) civilizations, the area that would become Mexico gained independence in the early 1800s, following three centuries of Spanish reign. Mexico is a federal republic with thirty-one states. The country has a mixture of modern and outmoded industry and agriculture, with a growing private sector. Infrastructure has improved, particularly in the north, because of increased trade with the United States and Canada since NAFTA was established. "'You trust your blood, and that's it,'" reflects the Mexican perspective on the advantages of family-owned businesses and a lack of faith in other institutions, including academic and financial (Economist Staff, 2004, pp. 63–64). That tradition still dominates business operations in Mexico. Review Table 10.2 for an overview of Mexico and Mexican citizens.

The Mexican government is aware of the need to modernize the tax system and labor laws, but progress is slow. Government eradication efforts to control cultivation of opium poppy and cannabis, production of heroin and methamphetamine, and trans-shipment of cocaine from Central America have been essential for any progress to be made. In 2004 it was estimated that 70 percent of the US cocaine supply came through Mexico; in 2007, it was the largest foreign supplier of marijuana and methamphetamine

THE DEVELOPMENT OF HUDSON'S BAY COMPANY, CANADA'S MERCHANT SINCE 1670[1]

During the 1600s, a pair of resourceful Frenchmen discovered a wealth of fur in the interior of the North American continent—north and west of the Great Lakes—accessible via the great inland sea that is Hudson's Bay. Despite their success, French and American companies would not back their business. It took the vision and connections of Price Rupert, cousin of King Charles II, to acquire the royal charter, which in May 1670 granted the lands of the Hudson's Bay watershed to The Governor and a Company of Adventurers of England, trading into Hudson's Bay.

In its first century of operation, Hudson's Bay Company (HBC) was ensconced in a few forts and posts around the shores of James and Hudson's Bays. Natives brought furs annually to these locations to barter for manufactured goods such as knives, kettles, beads, needles, and blankets. By the late 1700s, competition forced HBC to expand into the interior of the continent. A string of posts grew up along the great river networks of the west, foreshadowing the modern cities that would succeed them: Winnipeg, Calgary, and Edmonton.

In 1821, HBC merged with its most successful rival, the North West Company based in Montreal. The merger also set the pattern of the company's growth, being the first of a series of notable acquisitions. By the 1890s, changing fashion tastes contributed to the fur trade losing importance. Western settlement and the Gold Rush quickly introduced a new type of client to HBC—one that shopped with cash and not skins—and the retail era began. The company's focus shifted as it concentrated on transforming trading posts into "saleshops" stocked with a wider variety of goods than ever before.

In 1913, HBC opened its first modern department stores in Calgary and Edmonton. During the next 80 years stores were established across Canada; new divisions were created and competitors were absorbed. In 1970, the company's 300th year of existence, Queen Elizabeth granted the company a new charter and HBC formally became a Canadian company, with headquarters in London and Winnipeg. Then, the company set out to establish stores coast to coast. One of the strategies was intense acquisition of competitors over the next 20 years.

In 1994, Walmart Stores, Inc. entered the Canadian market, quickly becoming a fierce competitor to some of the HBC divisions, and tougher times ensued. To better support its divisions that most closely competed with Walmart, HBC increased the size of some of its stores to offer more diverse assorts in an effort to improve the opportunity to compete. Hiring executives from competing stores resulted in lawsuits that required the company's time as well as money. The twenty-first century found HBC well into its fourth century of retailing in Canada. Its major divisions include Bay, Zellers, Home Outfitters, and Fields—together providing for more than two-thirds of the retail needs of Canadians. In 2012, HBC began an aggressive modernization program to catch up with sourcing methods and technology applications.

[1]Encyclopedia.com. (n.d.). "Hudson's Bay Company." Retrieved November 1, 2015, from www.encyclopedia.com/topic/Hudsons_Bay_Company.aspx.

1. Take a few moments to think through how apparel production and distribution would have evolved during each century of Hudson's Bay's existence. Identify two or three things that would have made production of apparel and acquisition of finished goods by a retailer different in each of the four centuries.

(Central Intelligence Agency, 2010). One has only to check the news to hear of trouble on the US–Mexico border related to the drug trade. However, Bolivia, Colombia, Jamaica, and Peru are also very active suppliers.

According to the World Bank's vice president for Latin America, NAFTA (North American Free Trade Agreement) has had positive effects in Mexico, but they could have been better. The benefits across the country were unequal. The most developed and competitive sectors of the north and central regions clearly gained from trade liberalization, whereas less developed areas in the south, with largely Amerindian populations, have not. Moreover, large firms benefited from access to US capital markets, whereas small and medium-sized firms did not. Without NAFTA, Mexican global exports would be roughly 25 percent lower, direct foreign investment would be approximately 40 percent less, and per capita income would be approximately 5 percent lower. The modest gains in per capita income were attributed to underinvestment in education, innovation, and infrastructure. Institutional failures in improving accountability, regulatory effectiveness, and control of corruption moderated the gains provided by NAFTA (World Bank, 2003). Energy reform was put into law in August 2014. It is expected to transform Mexico's hydrocarbon and electricity sectors. These innovations already have benefited business and industry and the general population by providing opportunities for better paying jobs across the country. By 2007, in addition to NAFTA, Mexico had negotiated thirteen free trade treaties with more than forty nations, making more than 90 percent of its exports and imports under free trade agreements (Workman, 2007). As shown in Table 10.2, Mexican GDP per capita is the highest among the Caribbean Basin countries, but per capita income is about 30 percent of the US per capita income. Mexico has highly unequal income distribution across the population and high levels of unemployment.

Free trade created demand for a more skilled Mexican workforce, a challenge the educational system was not prepared to meet (World Bank, 2003). Mexican business schools began catering to a rising demand for courses specifically focused on the problems and exigencies of running a family-owned business, including conflict resolution and familism, which results in having too many family members who do not serve a real purpose on the payroll (Economist Staff, 2004). Mexico has the lowest school enrollment rate (56 percent) among 15- to 19-year-olds of any of the thirty-four countries that are members of OECD (Organization of Economic Cooperation and Development). When young people are in school, attendance is inconsistent. When young people do get training, the new abilities of the graduates seem to be inconsistent with the needs of the available jobs. OECD also indicates that nearly 30 percent of 25- to 29-year-olds are neither employed nor in education or training (Urrietta, 2014).

Textiles and Apparel in Mexico

Following implementation of NAFTA, in 1994, Mexico's share of the US textile and apparel market grew dramatically, but China became dominant in 2003, and Mexico has lost market share ever since. Some of the textile jobs that were added after NAFTA was instituted were at plants owned by US-based firms, including Burlington, Cone Mills, Dan River, DuPont, Guilford, and Tarrant. These companies, as well as some major apparel companies, established ultramodern production plants in Mexico. The apparel plants were established first, and textile production followed because efficiency increases when textile plants are located close to apparel plants. The goal was to reduce the established 34- to 40-week apparel supply chain to 15 to 20 weeks in order to compete with escalating imports from Asia (Kurt Salmon Associates, 1999). It appeared that NAFTA was working well for Mexico. But with the elimination of quotas, the majority of US retailers and brands switched the sourcing of apparel production to China.

In 2004, the apparel industry employed 563,000 people. However, by 2009 the textile and apparel sector only generated approximately 300,000 direct jobs in Mexico, which was about 2 percent of national employment (Maquila Solidarity Network, 2009). The majority of these jobs were held by women, with the key states for textile and garment production being the state of Mexico, the Federal District, Puebla, and Guanajuato. Within Latin America, Mexico remained the largest exporter of apparel to the US market. However, by 2008 Mexico had dropped to sixth place as a supplier to the US market, a drop of more than 14 percent from the previous year. In 2014, Mexico supplied only 4.5 percent of US textile and apparel imports.

The results of economic and industry changes in Mexico during this period were that in early 2009 thousands of additional jobs were lost and 666 more businesses closed. Labor groups reported the following:

- more production is destined for the national market with declining orders from international brands;
- more precarious employment conditions, production slowdowns, and withholding of salaries;
- extended work hours and intensified production goals to make up for decrease in personnel; and
- plant closures. (Maquila Solidarity Network, 2009)

The Mexican federal government instituted measures to help the industry cope with the downturn in the form of a fiscal stimulus package, but it has been heavily criticized. Of the business that remains, the United States still receives more than 90 percent of Mexico's textile and apparel exports. Mexican textile and apparel exporters are now almost entirely dependent on US retail market demand.

The World Bank reports the belief that NAFTA would be more effective with certain modifications in the agreement itself, with regard to COO (country of origin): Mexican industries, such as textiles and apparel, should have easier access to the US market; COO rules should be less of a barrier. Many US apparel firms disagreed strongly because of the essential need to control transshipment and counterfeiting.

In Mexico, by 2012, textile and apparel industries accounted for 4.7 percent of GDP (textiles 1.3 percent, apparel 2.5 percent), but textiles and apparel also accounted for nearly 20 percent of all manufacturing employment. The majority of these jobs were held by women working for 8,614 companies. Most of the textiles and apparel firms are located in Guadalajara, Monterrey, and above all Mexico City where luxury brands have a greater presence (Montano, 2013).

Retailing in Mexico

From 1999 to 2003, both the manufacturing and retailing sectors suffered lack of growth because of the flat economy in the United States. Nonetheless, retailing in Mexico developed two distinct parts. One part is a growing, modern retail sector with specific target markets, operational efficiencies, and advanced technology. Many retail formats are available, from limited selection warehouses to more service-oriented hypermarkets, which stock more than 30,000 SKUs. The other part is the traditional retail sector, a sizable segment of which is in the informal economy, with open markets in which prices are bartered, and taxes are not paid. Traditional, owner-operated, neighborhood stores and markets (Figure 10.6) now rely on extensive distribution networks for merchandise, similar to convenience stores in the United States. Shopping patterns have also changed. More women are now employed, so men take on some shopping responsibilities. Working families are more likely to shop once a week instead of shopping every day, as their parents still do. Cash payments are predominant, as most consumers do not have credit cards.

Figure 10.6

Traditional apparel market in
Mexico: piles of traditional
cotton apparel with handcrafted
elements.

Walmart became a big retail factor in 1997, when it bought a chain of stores
in Mexico. It raised the fury of activists by planning to build a store next to
2,000-year-old, pre-Columbian treasures just north of Mexico City. There were
marches and protests, similar to events related to the building of Walmart stores
in the United States. However, there were already several other businesses in the
same area, and Walmart was eventually granted the permits to build (Case, 2004).
Walmart is now Mexico's largest retailer and the largest private sector employer,
with 105,000 employees on the payroll. Walmart is able to sell at lower prices than
competing retailers because of its centralized distribution system and technology.
The rest of Mexico's retail industry is rushing to adopt Walmart's cost-cutting
techniques. Domestic producers and retailers are feeling the pressure from the

Figure 10.7

Storefront of German high-end
shoe manufacturer and retailer
Birkenstock.

abundance of Chinese and Indian imports that are being carried in the stores. It is not surprising that Walmart has put many small, family-owned retailers out of business. Sam's Club is also very successful in Mexico.

More recently, more multinational retailers have established stores in Mexico, including luxury brands Michael Kors, Hermes, and Bulgari. Construction of premium retail shopping centers continues and is expanding beyond Mexico City to other large and mid-sized cities and resort areas. Between 2011 and 2014, dozens of retailers opened up stores around the country. Retail growth of 3 to 4 percent per year is regarded as sustainable in Mexico (Euromonitor International, 2014). Figures 10.7 and 10.8 present examples of brands available in Playa del Carmen, a town of less than 150,000 people in a provincial touristy area of the country. Note the difference in the price points for the two examples in this small- to mid-size town: Birkenstock is known for one of the most expensive casual (and very comfortable) shoes, whereas Forever 21 competes primarily on delivering the latest inexpensive, medium- to lower-end quality fashions to younger consumers.

Figure 10.8
Forever 21, a US-based fast fashion retailer, in a Playa del Carmen mall.

CARIBBEAN BASIN (CBERA) COUNTRIES

Caribbean Basin countries include nations that are located in Central America and the West Indies. The earliest residents of what is now Central America were the Mayan Indians, who built one of the first known civilizations in the Western Hemisphere more than 2,000 years ago. Spanish invasions in the 1500s destroyed the Indian societies. In 1821, the Central American area was freed from Spain, and five states were formed: Costa Rica, El Salvador, Guatemala, Honduras, and Nicaragua. One hundred years of efforts toward unification of the states resulted in the formation of Central American Union, in 1923. The Central American Union nations became members of OAS and in the 1960s formed the Central American Common Market. Shortly thereafter, political and military conflicts broke out and continued sporadically well into the 1980s, at times with US intervention.

The West Indies is a 2,000-mile chain of dozens of islands that separate the Caribbean Sea from the Atlantic Ocean. The West Indies consists of three major groups of islands: the Bahamas, in the north; the Greater Antilles, near the center; and the Lesser Antilles, in the southeast. The islands are actually the peaks of an underwater chain of mountains. Their mild winters make the islands one of the world's most popular resort areas. Some islands are independent countries, such as Barbados, Cuba, Haiti, the Dominican Republic, and Jamaica. Others are territorial possessions of the United States or several European countries. The people represent many races and nationalities. Most people speak English, French, or Spanish, along with many local dialects.

Caribbean Basin countries are transshipment points for cocaine and heroin from South America as well as for arms for drug dealing. Illicit production of opium poppy

TABLE 10.6

US TRADE PROGRAMS THAT FAVOR CARIBBEAN BASIN COUNTRIES

Program	Benefits
Tariff Schedules of the United States (1963), Harmonized Tariff Schedules of the United States (HTSUS; 1989), Item 807	US fabric-forward rule of origin for cut garment parts to be exported, assembled, and imported, with tariff based only on value added
Caribbean Basin Economic Recovery Act (CBERA or CBI; 1983)	US fabric-forward rule of origin for duty-free access to US markets
Caribbean Basin Trade Partnership Act (CBTPA; 2000)	US yarn-forward rule of origin for duty-free access to US market
The Central America–Dominican Republic–United States Free Trade Agreement (CAFTA-DR; negotiated 2002; rolling implementation until all countries approved, January 2009)	Sectoral rule of origin for yarns and fabrics for products cut and sewn in the sector, for duty-free access to regional markets

United States–Panama Trade Promotion. (2012). "Increased Textile Access for US Textile and Apparel Companies Agreement." Retrieved from https://ustr.gov/trade-agreements/free-trade-agreements/panama-tpa

and cannabis is mostly for local consumption. For the most part, poverty still prevails because of unequal distribution of income. Review the locations of the countries in Figure 10.1 and the descriptive demographics in Table 10.2. The growth of the textile and apparel industry in the Caribbean Basin is largely the result of US economic development legislation and trade preference programs. Table 10.6 provides summaries of some of the recent programs. Many other trade programs are also in existence, including numerous free trade agreements among different Caribbean Basin countries.

The United States has had trade economic incentive programs with Caribbean Basin countries for more than 40 years. For example, Item 807 of the United States Tariff Schedules was established in 1963 and replicated as Chapter 9802 of the Harmonized Tariff Schedules of the United States in 1989. Item 807 has a fabric-forward rule that allows cut parts of garments to be exported, assembled in a foreign country, and imported with tariff assessed only on value added if the parts were cut from US-made fabric. Item 807 allows US apparel production to leave the country but benefits US textile production because use of US-made fabrics is a requirement.

Many Caribbean Basin countries established apparel industries because of the demand for sewing services for 807 by US manufacturers and retailers. The use of 807 exploded during the 1980s because of escalating apparel production costs in the United States. Huge cutting services developed in Miami to process cut parts for export to Caribbean Basin countries, where they were assembled. In 1983, the United States initiated the **Caribbean Basin Economic Recovery Act (CBERA)** (commonly known as the Caribbean Basin Initiative [CBI]), a trade preference program intended to stimulate industrial growth in initially twenty-two, and later twenty-seven, Caribbean countries in Central America and the West Indies. CBERA expanded the use of Item 807 by eliminating quota restraints.

The Central America–Dominican Republic–United States Free Trade Agreement (CAFTA-DR) includes seven signatories: the United States, Costa Rica, the Dominican Republic, El Salvador, Guatemala, Honduras, and Nicaragua. The US Congress approved the CAFTA-DR in July 2005. The United States implemented the CAFTA-DR on a rolling basis as countries made sufficient progress to complete their commitments under the agreement. The agreement was fully implemented in 2009 (Export.gov, n.d.). However, the controversy over CAFTA-DR has been significant, and many continue to question its efficacy in light of other economic issues in the marketplace and the massive competition for market share coming from Asia. The 2012 United States–Panama Trade Promotion Agreement was intended to allow US textile and apparel firms greater access to textile-related products and services in Panama, but the agreement has not yet been realized.

If you are in the textile and apparel business and want to source products from the Caribbean Basin, the greatest challenge is to decide which trade preference program is most appropriate for your products. The second most difficult thing is to decide which country is the best source. The following discussion provides basic information about many of the countries and their roles in textiles and apparel. Apparel professionals had been expecting that the elimination of the long-standing quota system would reduce demand for textiles and apparel from Mexico and Caribbean Basin countries, and this proved to be the case.

Central American Countries

Costa Rica (51) is a Central American success story. Since the late 1800s, only two brief periods of violence have interrupted its democratic development. Although still a largely agricultural country with widespread land ownership, Costa Rica has expanded its relatively stable economy to include strong technology and tourism industries. As shown in Table 10.3a and b, Costa Rica's level of living, as measured by per capita GDP, is the highest in the Caribbean Basin region. Foreign investors are attracted to the country's political stability and high education levels; in addition, tourism brings in foreign exchange. Costa Rica was among the top twenty-five countries exporting apparel to the United States in 2003, but the amount declined significantly for several years, especially when quotas were removed globally. Costa Rica also lost market share to CAFTA-DR members as they implemented the agreement gaining access to the US market (Costa Rica did not sign until early 2009). In the interim, numerous factories closed. Also, because of Costa Rica's economic and industrial success in other areas, production costs have increased, so sourcing companies have looked elsewhere. Costa Rica is a member of the Central American Common Market (CACM).

El Salvador, Guatemala, Honduras, and Nicaragua have continued to be relatively unstable politically and economically. The governments are striving to open new export markets, encourage foreign investment, modernize the tax and health care systems, and stimulate their sluggish economies. El Salvador adopted the US dollar as its currency and now concentrates on maintaining a disciplined fiscal policy, as reflected in its low inflation rate. Embracing the dollar has benefits but also caused problems, because it was common practice for Latin American countries to devalue their currencies against the dollar in order to take business away from neighboring countries and the United States (Lyons, 2005). Honduras and El Salvador have been active in providing US apparel imports but, according to Table 10.5, both lost some market share in 2014 compared to 2008.

Guatemala is the largest and most populous country in Central America, but as shown in Table 10.2, has a per capita GDP less than half of Costa Rica's. Guatemalan apparel producers were concerned about the United States' 2002 legislation requiring that fabrics be dyed and finished in the United States to qualify for CBTPA preferences. The producers believed it would make it more difficult to change over to full-package production. Korean-based investors accounted for about 65 percent of Guatemala's apparel production during the middle of the first decade of the twenty-first century. They made some significant inroads in apparel trade with the United States with the implementation of CAFTA-DR, but when China and Asia unleashed their competitive blitz at the end of quotas, the Guatemalan industry began a downward spiral. In spite of that, textiles and apparel is still the second-largest source of export earnings. One of the success stories in Guatemala is Denimatrix, which focuses on the high-fashion jeans market. The firm was formed when Carlos Arias teamed with the Texan cotton-making cooperative Plains Cotton Cooperative (PCCA) to purchase the family-owned Koramsa, and in early 2010, the firm was producing 140,000 garments a week (Freeman, 2010). Denimatrix is a leaner firm than those in the past, but it has a faster turnaround time, which makes it highly competitive in its niche market.

Honduras is one of the poorest countries in the Americas, with extraordinarily unequal distribution of income and massive unemployment. Honduras is the leading apparel producer in Central America, and apparel is its largest source of export earnings. Implementing CBTPA is changing Honduras from being an 807/9802 supplier to importing US fabrics (instead of cut garment parts). Production of knit fabrics and apparel is an important part of the industry. Despite its problems, Honduras has attracted investment both by US companies looking for less expensive offshore opportunities and by Asian firms seeking a spot for speed-to-market production for the Americas. As shown in Table 10.5, in 2008 Honduras secured the rank of fourth in US apparel imports and dropped to fifth in 2014.

Nicaragua, also one of the poorest Central American countries, slowly rebuilt its economy through the 1990s but was hard hit by Hurricane Mitch in 1998. Unfortunately, Nicaragua continues to be dependent on international aid and debt relief. The textile and apparel sector consists mostly of assembly operations in government-sponsored free trade zones outside the capital, Managua (Figure 10.9). The country's apparel industry specializes in basic cotton men's and women's knit shirts. In 2014, the country exported to the US 1.5 billion dollars of apparel, a slight increase from 2014 (OTEXA, 2015). The growth of the industry is largely attributed to the low-cost and high-quality workforce.

Figure 10.9

Maquilas apparel factory employs 30,000 workers in the free trade zone outside of Managua, Nicaragua.

The West Indies

The Dominican Republic shares one of the larger islands of the West Indies with Haiti. Its economy, however, is more developed than Haiti's. The Dominican Republic has had one of the fastest growth rates in the Western Hemisphere, although political problems have persisted and growth slowed in 2013. The service sector, which includes tourism and free trade zones, has taken over as the nation's largest employer. Growth slowed in the early 2000s, largely because of the sluggish US economy. In 2004, the unequal distribution of income meant that the poorest half of the population received less than 10 percent of national income, while the richest 10 percent received nearly 40 percent of the national income. The Dominican Republic was the seventh-largest apparel exporter to the United States in 2003; however, the end of quotas brought much stronger competition for the US market, which, combined with a weakened global economy in 2008 and 2009, greatly affected the country's US market share. In 2009, the Dominican Republic had dropped to fourteenth in imports into the United States.

Haiti, in a space slightly smaller than Maryland, is the poorest country in the Western Hemisphere. Early in its history, it was a French colony dedicated to forestry and sugar-related industries, and became the richest in the Caribbean through heavy importation of African slaves and environmental degradation. In the late 1700s, half a million slaves revolted. After a prolonged struggle, independence was gained, but political violence continues to the present day. Despite the turmoil, Haiti has a small but vital apparel industry. In 2001, Haiti exported $217 million in apparel to the United States, but production was reduced after that because of political unrest. Efforts in the US Congress to provide additional aid to Haiti have proven to be uneven. The United States has made significant efforts to impact the local economy, since the devastating earthquake that hit in January 2010, but recovery has been slow (see Case 10.3).

SOUTH AMERICA

South America's political history is similar to that of the Caribbean Basin: through most of the 1500s, South America was occupied by Spain or Portugal, and the continent has struggled with military dictatorships and rebellions ever since. Some countries are further along than others in developing market economies. South America has huge deposits of natural resources, including minerals and petroleum that are not fully commercialized, but some resources are being exploited in ways that are highly destructive to the environment. These natural resources, along with agriculture, are responsible for the majority of GDP. Both oil and agriculture are subject to wide fluctuations in world market prices. The countries suffered through the US and global recessions from 1999 to 2003 and again from 2008 to 2010 but have been persevering.

For most countries, privatization of utilities, banking, and trade is still in progress. In general, the less developed the market economy, the greater the poverty level and the more unequal the distribution of income. Many of the countries have the same problems as the Caribbean Basin, with trafficking of drugs and money laundering. Colombia, Peru, and Bolivia are the world's largest cultivators of coca and cocaine, which are exported mostly through Argentina, Brazil, and Chile to European and US drug markets. Promotion of alternative crop programs has been unable to keep pace with farmers' attempts to increase cultivation of products for the drug market.

HAITI MINIMUM WAGE INCREASE IGNITES COMPETITION ROW IN APPAREL INDUSTRY

Port au Prince, Haiti: The issue of the minimum wage is inflaming employment relations in Haiti, as garment factory owners and workers unions argue about the optimum rate amid fears that the country's apparel exports may become uncompetitive if the bar is set too high. Garments constitute 90 percent of Haiti's exports, earning $800 million a year, the biggest source of foreign revenue. The sector employs 31,000 people, a significant if small contribution to organized jobs in a poor, predominantly young workforce beset by unemployment rates of more than 40 percent.

Ironically, the dispute was triggered by attempts to formally raise the minimum wage. On December 10, 2013, a few hundred people took to the streets of the Haitian capital, Port au Prince, in protest against a scheduled increase in the minimum wage on January 1, 2014. It might have been another demonstration against President Michel Martelly's government, except for what came next. Furious at the marginal 12 percent pay increase for an eight hour day (from 200 to 225 Haitian gourdes, or about $0.40 an hour) some protesters vandalized garment factories in the main industrial park, prompting the owners to close them for a few days. The Association des Industries d'Haiti warned that the closure and an increased reputation of instability risked grave damage to the garment sector. The 12 percent increase in minimum wage was recommended by Haiti's high wage council, a recently constituted body mandated by law and comprising the government, private sector, and trade unions. But the increase is considered derisory by the more militant and vocal of Haiti's seventeen textile sector unions. Some of the unions were asking for a 150 percent increase, to 500 gourdes per day.

The demand has been dismissed as absurd and irresponsible by factory owners, government officials, Haitian economists, and foreign observers. Haiti's minimum wage, they say, is already four times that of textile workers in Bangladesh. In an attempt to explain their opposition to too high a minimum wage, garment factory owners recently wrote an open letter exhorting workers to "keep Haiti competitive" in the race against "big rivals": Bangladesh, Cambodia, and Vietnam. The apparel industry says it is a struggle to sell

Haiti as a garment hub because energy costs are high and workers are less skilled and productive compared with rival locations in Asia.

"I'm amazed we still have a garment industry at all in Haiti. We are already so much less competitive than other countries," said a businessman speaking on condition of anonymity. Haiti's enviable advantage lies in a unique US gift called the Hemispheric Opportunity through Partnership Encouragement (HOPE) Act, which was signed into law in 2008 and provides duty-free export for apparel and textiles products. In the year starting December 20, 2012, Haiti was allowed to export as much as 306,742,329 square meters equivalent (SME) to the United States duty-free so long as 50 percent of the garment was assembled in Haiti. From December 20, 2013, the annual duty-free quota rose to 322,629,971 SME. But Haiti found it hard to meet last year's quota, exporting just 259 million SME to the United States up to October. Critics say this comes down to Haiti's inability to rise to the challenge of "scoring an open goal."

But there are no easy answers. The cost of living is comparatively high in Haiti, with the consumer price index increasing 124 percent in the past decade, according to economists. Yet the minimum wage has barely gone up threefold in the same period. According to some estimates, the typical Haitian family spends half its budget on food. It may be compassionate common sense to align basic pay with a living wage. But that would mean fewer orders, even for the low end of the apparel sector, such as T-shirts. Some observers say it may be better to lower the cost of living rather than raise the minimum wage unsustainably. But they know that may be easier said than done.

Lall, R.R. (December 21, 2013). "Haiti Minimum Wage Increase Ignites Competition Row in Textile Industry." Retrieved November 1, 2015, from http://www.theguardian.com/global-development/poverty-matters/2013/dec/31/haiti-minimum-wage-increase-ignites-row-textile-industry

1. Using Case 10.3 as an example, how have US trade programs contributed to the development of Caribbean Basin countries?

2. What can foreign-based apparel companies do to help stabilize apparel production opportunities in Haiti and other countries with similar problems?

South American countries fall into two trade groups: Andean countries, in the north, and Mercosur countries, in the south. The term **Andean**, a reference to the Andes Mountains, includes Bolivia, Colombia, Ecuador, and Peru. The United States established the Andean Pact, a trade preference program, in 1960 and updated it in 1991 and 2002. *Mercosur* is a trade name for the Southern Cone Common Market, which includes Argentina, Brazil, Paraguay, Uruguay, and Venezuela. These five Mercosur countries account for 70 percent of South America's total economy. The EU is in the process of developing more trade agreements with South America. An EU–Mercosur trade agreement has been in the works since 2010.

Andean Countries: Bolivia, Colombia, Ecuador, Peru

The Andean countries are a relatively small source of US imports of textiles and apparel. The Andean sector became eligible for duty-free treatment for the first time with enactment of the **Andean Trade Promotion and Drug Eradication Act (ATPDEA)**, Division D of the Trade Act of 2002. Peru and Colombia account for most of the US textile and apparel imports from Andean countries. The two countries were considered price competitive by sourcing countries when the quota system increased the costs of sourcing from Asian countries, but both found themselves affected by the rise in Asian competition after quotas were removed. However, the allowance in ATPDEA for use of sectoral yarns and fabrics was expected to help keep Andean products competitive, by qualifying them for tariff reductions. These nations have been having a bumpy ride between the demise of quotas and the recent global economic downturn. In 2012, the EU signed a comprehensive trade agreement with Colombia and Peru. It is intended to open up markets on both sides as well as increase the stability and predictability of the trading environment. In 2014, negotiations were concluded for accession of Ecuador to the trade agreement. Efforts are also being made to include Bolivia. The EU is one of the largest trading partners with the Andean countries and one of its primary investors (European Commission, n.d.).

Colombia suffered a 40-year insurgent campaign to overthrow the government, supported in part by funds from the drug trade that escalated during the 1990s. The country is the third-largest economy in Central and South America. A United States–Colombia trade agreement is now in force. The agreement eliminates tariffs and other trade barriers and promotes economic growth for both countries. The two economies are largely complementary in that Colombia is a large importer of grains from the United States and exports tropical fruits to the United States. In addition, US cotton, yarn, and fabric exports are used in many apparel items that Colombia exports back to the United States. Trade barriers were reduced to the benefit of both countries. The agreement also provides greater protection for intellectual property rights and will eliminate tariffs when fully implemented (Office of the United States Trade Representative, 2015).

Colombia is one of the more successful apparel producers in South America with forty-five textile and 10,000 apparel manufacturers. Most are small factories since 50 percent of them have between twenty and sixty sewing machines; key products are jeans for men and boys, cotton trousers for women and girls, and bras. Over 50 percent of Colombian-produced clothing is sold to the international market (Swiss Colombian Chamber of Commerce, 2012). Colombia's textile and apparel sector is concentrated in two major cities: Medellín focuses on apparel production and some textiles, and Bogotá generates more textiles, especially knitted fabrics and knit apparel. Much of Bogotá's

Figure 10.10

A worker fabricates textiles in Textiles Romanos mill in Bogotá, Colombia.

knitwear companies are family run and vertically integrated, producing for exports on a full-package basis (Figure 10.10).

Colombia produces a range of fabrics but has to make up for shortfalls with imported fabrics from China and the United States. Venezuela had been Colombia's biggest customer, receiving more than half its exports (the United States was the second-largest customer and Mexico was third). Colombia has become one of the main fashion centers in Latin America with its successful trade shows Colombiatex and Colombiamoda (Figure 10.11). These are international trade shows with hundreds of exhibitors from throughout the Americas, from Brazil to the United States, and thousands of international buyers and visitors. Colombiatex features everything from fiber innovations to finished textiles and supplies, from buttons and zippers to machinery. Colombia specializes in high-quality fashion apparel and its facilities meet ISO 9000 and ISO 9002-4 certification, internationally recognized standards for world-class production. Colombia is a good source for quick-turn business, for which customers are willing to pay a premium.

Ancient Peru was the seat of Andean civilizations, most notably that of the Incas, whose empire was captured by the Spanish in 1533. Peruvian independence was declared in 1821. After many years of military rule, Peru returned to democratic leadership in 1980. A decade of dramatic turnaround in the economy was followed by significant progress in curtailing guerrilla activity. Peru's economy grew rapidly in 2002 and 2003, but at the same time, allegations of government corruption continued to arise. Textile and apparel exports from Peru to the United States rose 21.5 percent in 2003. However, lack of infrastructure deterred continued expansion in trade and investment. Despite its internal problems, Peru developed an integrated textile and apparel sector, from the production of raw material inputs (cotton, alpaca, llama, and vicuña) and textile processing through apparel manufacturing. The Zarate Industrial Zone, in Lima, became the center of several leading apparel manufacturers and suppliers of textile inputs. Peru produces high-quality apparel products, including combed cotton knit tops. Some suppliers believe Peru could compete in high-end knit shirts.

Many of Peru's leading textile manufacturers have become vertically integrated, eliminating the need to import raw materials or outsource sewing. They produce

Figure 10.11
A model presents a creation by Colombian designer Hernan Zajar during the Colombiatex fair on January 28, 2015, in Medellín, Colombia.

high-quality knit fabrics made from domestically produced long staple cotton fiber. These excellent fabrics and high garment production standards drew high-end brands like Polo Ralph Lauren, Theory, Lacoste, and Burberry to Peru. Companies in Peru are also getting into elastomeric yarns, an area that was experiencing explosive growth in 2013. At PeruModa, Peru's primary trade show, the recent success of its textile industry was attributed to 2,000 years of textile heritage (Donaldson, 2014).

Southern South American and Mercosur Countries

Chile is the success story of South America, much like Costa Rica is the success story of Central America, and yet it is not yet a member of Mercosur. Sound economic policies maintained consistently since the 1980s have contributed to Chile's steady growth and have helped secure the country's commitment to a democratic system of government. Chile has increasingly assumed sectoral and international leadership roles benefiting its status as a stable, democratic nation. Chile is considered the most stable economy in Latin America (Hall, 2009). Chile and the United States signed a free trade agreement in 2003, the first such pact with a South American country. Chile already had free trade agreements with Bolivia, Canada, CACM, Colombia, EFTA (European Free Trade Association), Ecuador, the EU, Mercosur, Mexico, South Korea, and Venezuela. Chile's retail sector has also been very active. Walmart, Topshop, and Zara all have a presence there.

After Argentina gained independence from Spain, in 1816, periods of political conflict limited growth until a return to democracy in 1983. Argentina began to build on rich natural resources, a highly literate population, an export-oriented agricultural sector, and a diversified industrial base. Rapid-growth economic problems have persisted in the form of inflation, external debt, and budget deficits. Argentina is a member of Mercosur, which supports duty-free trade of apparel among member countries. Textile and apparel companies are located mainly in the city of Buenos Aires and in the surrounding area. The Argentinean textile market is heavily dependent upon import of synthetic fibers, fabrics, and novelty items, such as accessories. Argentina is one of the fastest-growing markets for Indian textiles. It also concentrates heavily on niche products. Argentina's apparel industry is fragmented, and more than 65 percent is run by small family units employing, on an average, fifty people. Argentina has become a fashion-conscious nation and is a magnet for international retailers. Zara, Harrods, Calvin Klein, Lacoste, Nike, and Yves Saint Laurent have locations here. The leading retailer in Argentina is the French retailing giant Carrefour-Promodes. Forecasts are optimistic for the near future.

Brazil is by far the largest country and has the largest population in South America. Brazil became independent of Portugal in 1822 and has recently overcome 50 years of military rule to pursue industrial and agricultural growth. Today, Brazil is South America's major economic power and regional leader. Its economy is larger than all the other South American countries, and it is expanding its presence in world markets. Brazil's strong economy is based on a floating exchange rate, an inflation-targeting regime, and tight fiscal policy. Problems include increasing domestic and foreign debt and the challenges of increasing employment. Strength in the textile and apparel sector had made Brazil the sixth-largest textile and apparel producer in the world by 2006, but achieving that status had been an uneven road.

The major strength of Brazil's textile market has been cotton, and there has been expansion into production of polyester. Unifi, a North Carolina–based textile manufacturer, has operations in Brazil, and Santana Textiles is a Brazilian fabric giant that has launched an eco-friendly stretch denim, with Creora elastane fibers in the yarns. Creora, a registered trademark, is a dry-spun spandex yarn for specialty textile fabrics made in Korea. Brazil is one of the world's leading denim producers. Brazil has been leading South America out of the economic crisis and is considered one of the fastest-growing consumer markets in the world. *Women's Wear Daily* identified Brazil, with its $94 billion apparel market, as the top-ranked nation with potential for retail expansion (Hall, 2009). There is a high level of fashion consciousness here, compared with other emerging markets. International retailers currently in Brazil are Zara, 7 for All Mankind, C&A, and Timberland, while luxury firms are working to enter this market. Walmart also has a significant presence there.

The following Newswire provides an interesting overview of and forecast related to the future of the apparel industry in the Americas and the rest of the world in coming years.

> **London, Nov. 4, 2014; PRNewswire**—The expansion of the global apparel industry is forecast to reach 3.6 percent per year in coming years. Between 2007 and 2013 the market increased with an average annual growth of 5.1 percent. Currently, womenswear accounts for 50.0 percent of the global demand while the remaining market share is divided between menswear (34.5 percent), clothing accessories (3.9 percent), babies' garments (2.8 percent), gloves and mittens (2.3 percent), headgear (2.0 percent), other garments (4.1 percent) and parts of garments and clothing accessories (0.5 percent). Brazil, China, Italy, Japan, and the United States represent the largest apparel markets. The strongest annual growth is forecast to occur in Tanzania (17.5 percent), Bangladesh (14.3 percent), Ethiopia (13.4 percent), Cambodia (13.1 percent), and Yemen (12.6 percent) (PR Newswire, 2014).

Summary

The Americas consist of four primary land areas: North America, Central America, the West Indies, and South America. The United States economically dominates the area, much as the EU dominates Europe. The ranges of measures that describe the economic and industrial standing of countries in the Americas also have much in common with countries in Europe: countries are very large and very small, very rich and very poor.

The Organization of American States (OAS), formed in 1948, was the first effort to unify the political, social, and economic goals of the Americas. The challenge, in part, is the numerous agreements, all with different terms, already in place among countries in the Americas. Another challenge is the difference in cultural values between North American progressive and Latin American traditional cultures. The contrasts in these cultural values continue to be a challenge to the progress of economic development in several countries.

The discussion of the roles of countries in textiles and apparel is divided into three parts: North America, Caribbean Basin, and South America. The Global Competitiveness Index is used throughout the chapter as a reminder of development of each country as it is discussed. From a textile and apparel perspective, Canada and the United States have negative trade balances in both textiles and apparel, because they are importing for production and consumption more than they are producing for export. Los Angeles County is the largest apparel production center that remains in the United States. Imports of less expensive Asian textiles have made serious inroads into apparel production in the Americas.

The North American Free Trade Agreement (NAFTA) initially increased the flow of textile and apparel production to Mexico, but some of that growth has almost evaporated, owing to the end of quotas and the poor economy in 2008 and 2009. Mexico is still sixth in rank of importers into the United States. NAFTA also rapidly increased trade among the three countries, such that they are each other's largest customers and suppliers. Modifications in trade rules have changed opportunities for Central and South American countries to export products into North America. Apparel production in Central America and the Caribbean was developed and continues to be supported by US-initiated trade programs, but some of these countries were also hard hit with the end of the quota system. The Dominican Republic and Honduras remain major suppliers. The tropical environment of the Caribbean Basin—the combination of Central America and West Indies—has made it one of the most famous tourist areas in the world.

South America has two politically unified areas: the Andean sector, in the north, and the Mercosur sector, in the south. Colombia is in the Andean sector and is a major apparel supplier, especially to neighboring nations; it is also the site of a primary apparel trade show. The Mercosur sector represents 70 percent of South America's GDP. Brazil now has one of the world's strongest economies. Brazil and Colombia are primary sites for apparel trade shows in Latin America.

Learning Activities

1. Assume you are ready for a global adventure and are seeking a job in which you could be employed at least part of the time in a foreign country. Which of the data presented in Tables 10.1 and 10.2 would help you in deciding the countries you might like to consider?

2. How many American countries generate a per capita GDP that is higher than the United States? What is the fundamental meaning of this observation?

3. Why are Caribbean Basin countries more likely to be involved in textile imports and apparel exports?

4. Some industry observers believe that the enclosed shopping mall with department store anchors will soon be a thing of the past. What kind of things might speed that up and what might slow the process down?

5. Explain why apparel manufacturing in the United States and Canada has declined, particularly in the 1990s.

6. Why are more Central American countries more involved in apparel manufacturing than North American or South American countries?

References

American Apparel and Footwear Association. (2009). "Trends: An Annual Statistical Analysis of the U.S. Apparel and Footwear Industries." Retrieved November 17, 2015, from https://www.wewear.org/assets/1/7/Trends2008.pdf

Birnbaum, D. (March 10, 2009). "Economic Headwinds Take Toll on US Apparel Imports." Retrieved October 14, 2009, from http://www.just-style.com/comment/economic-headwinds-take-toll-on-us-apparel-imports_idro3541.aspx

Burgess, Z. (June 22, 2015). "After 125 Years, Carhartt Rolls Up Its Sleeves for the Future." *Crain's Detroit Business*. Retrieved November 1, 2015, from http://www.crainsdetroit.com/article/20140622/NEWS/306229972/after-125-years-carhartt-rolls-up-its-sleeves-for-the-future

Case, B. M. (2004). "Welcoming Walmart to Mexico." *Dallas Morning News*. Retrieved November 9, 2004, from http://www.dallasnews.com

Central Intelligence Agency. (2010). "The World Factbook." Retrieved November 6, 2010, from http://www.odci.gov/cia/publications/factbook/index.html

Deloitte. (2015). "Global Powers of Retailing 2015: Embracing Innovation." Retrieved November 1, 2015, from www2.deloitte.com/content/dam/Deloitte/global/Documents/Consumer-Business/gx-cb-global-powers-of-retailing.pdf

Donaldson, T. (2014). "Peru Textile and Clothing Exports up 7%, US Leads Growth." Retrieved November 1, 2015, from http://www.sourcingjournalonline.com/peru-textile-clothing-exports-7-u-s-leads-growth-td/

Economist Staff. (March 20, 2004) "Still Keeping It in the Family." *The Economist*, pp. 63–64.

Euromonitor International. (2014). "Executive Summary: Retailing in Mexico." Retrieved November 1, 2015, from www.euromonitor.com/retailing-in-mexico/report.

European Commission. (n.d.). "Trade Policy, Andean Community." Retrieved May 1, 2015, from ec.europa.edu/trade/policy/countries-and-regions/regions/Andean-community/

(Expodatabase, n.d.). Trade fairs USA apparel fashion, textiles, jewelry. Retrieved December 15, 2015 from http://www.expodatabase.com/trade-shows-america/usa/apparel-fashion-textiles-jewellery/

Export.gov. (n.d.). "Dominican Republic-Central America-United States Free Trade Agreement (CAFTA-DR)." Retrieved June 1, 2010, from http://www.export.gov/FTA/cafta-dr/index.asp

Fibre2Fashion. (June 2, 2007). "Post-NAFTA Job Loss in Textiles and Apparel Exceeds 1mm." Retrieved November 1, 2015, from http://www.fibre2fashion.com/news/daily-textile-industries-news/newsdetails.aspx?news_id=35976

Freeman, I. C. (2010, January 19). Speaking with style: Carlos Arias, president, Denimatrix. just-style.com. Retrieved February 21, 2010, from http://www.just-style.com/interview/carlos-arias-president-denimatrix_id106466.aspx

Guess.com. (n.d.). "Heritage: The Guess Story." Retrieved September 21, 2015, from shop.guess.com/en/OurStory/

Hakim, P., & Litan, R. (2002). "The Future of North American Integration: Beyond NAFTA." Washington, DC: Brookings Institution Press.

Hall, C. (July 2, 2009). "WWD List: Windows of Opportunity." *Women's Wear Daily*. Retrieved November 17, 2015, from http://wwd.com/globe-news/trends-analysis/wwd-list-windows-of-opportunity-2199757/

Hudson's Bay Company. (2010). "Our History." Retrieved May 31, 2010, from http://www.hbc.com/hbcheritage/history/overview.asp

Hudson's Bay Company. (2015). "Our History." Retrieved April 29, 2015 from https://www2.hbc.com/hbc/history

Industry Canada. (2009). "Overview of the Canadian Apparel Industry: Industry Profile." Retrieved February 18, 2010, from http://www.ic.gc.ca/eic/site/apparel-vetements.nsf/eng/ap03295.html

Industry Canada. (2015). "Canadian Consumer Products Industry: Apparel Industry Profile." Retrieved April 27, 2015, from https://www.ic.gc.ca/eic/site/026.nst/eng/h_00070.html

Kurt Salmon Associates. (1999). *Moving to Mexico—The Battle against Low Cost Asian Imports*. New York, NY: Author.

Lyons, J. (2005, March 8). El Salvador faces costs of taking the U.S. currency as its own. The Wall Street Journal.

Maquila Solidarity Network. (October 2009). "The Crisis and Its Effect on Mexico's Textile and Apparel Industry." Retrieved June 3, 2010, from http://en.maquilasolidarity.org/sites/maquilasolidarity.org/files/MSN-Crisis_and-Garment_Sector_in_Mexico-2009-10.pdf

McCarty, D., & Pearson, S. (2015). "Wet Seal Joins March of Mall Retailers into Bankruptcy." Retrieved November 1, 2015, from http://www.bloomberg.com/news/articles/2015-01-16/wet-seal-joins-parade-of-clothing-retailers-filing-bankruptcy

Montano, S. (2013). "The Mexican Textile and Apparel Market." The US Department of Commerce. otexa.ita.doc.gov/Pdfs/Sylvia/Montano.pdf

Office of the US Trade Representative. (2015). "US–Colombia Trade Agreement." Retrieved May 1, 2015, from https://ustr.gov/uscolombiatpa/facts

Organization of American States. (n.d.). "About the OAS." Retrieved February 15, 2005, from http://www.oas.org/documents/eng/oasinbrief.asp

OTEXA. (August 31, 2015). "Major Shippers Report." Retrieved September 24, 2015, from http://www.otexa.ita.doc.gov/msrcty/v2190.htm

Platzer, M. D. (August 28, 2014). "US Textile Manufacturing and the Trans-Pacific Partnership." Congressional Research Service. Retrieved December 27, 2015, from https://www.fas.org/sgp/crs/row/R42772.pdf

PR Newswire. (2014). "Apparel Markets in the World to 2018—Market Size, Trends, and Forecasts." Retrieved May 6, 2015, from http://www.prnewswire.com/news-releases/apparel-markets-in-the-world-to-2018-market-size-trends-and-forecasts-281428231.html

Roshan Lall, R. R. (2013). "Haiti Minimum Wage Increase Ignites Competition Row in Textile Industry." Retrieved November 1, 2015, from www.theguardian.com/global-development/poverty-matters/2013/dec/31/Haiti-minimum-wage-ignites-row-in-textile-industry

Swiss Colombian Chamber of Commerce. (2012). "Colombia Textiles." Retrieved November 17, 2015, from www.s-ge.com/en/filefield-private/files/55030/field_blog_public_files/14553

Taplin, I. M. (2003). "The Politics of Industrial Restructuring: NAFTA and Beyond." *Journal of Fashion Marketing and Management*, 7(2), 111–118.

The USA Online (n.d). Los Angeles, California. Retrieved December 27, 2015, from http://www.theusaonline.com/cities/losangeles.htm

Urrietta, L. (July 28, 2014). "Texas Perspectives: Mexico's Education System Not Up for the Challenge that Energy Reform Brings." *UTNews*. Retrieved November 1, 2014, from http://www.news.utexas.edu/2014/07/28/mexico's-education-system-not-up-for-the-challenge-that-energy-reform-brings

US International Trade Administration. (2014). "Trade Agreements Benefit US Exports." Retrieved May 5, 2015, from www.trade.gov/mas/ian/build/grops/public/,tg_ian/documents/webcontent/tg_ian_005310

Wahba, P. (August 17, 2015). "American Apparel Says It May Have to Go Out of Business." *Fortune*. Retrieved September 14, 2015, from http://fortune.com/2015/08/17/american-apparel-bankruptcy/

Walmart.com. (n.d.). "Where in the World Is Walmart?" Retrieved May 3, 2015, from http://www.corporate.walmart.com/our-story/locations/Mexico#

Werner International Management Consultants. (2009). "Primary Textiles Labor Cost Comparisons 2008." Retrieved May 25, 2010, from http://texnet.ilgstudios.net/files/2009/08/Werner_International_-_Labor_Cost_Study_2008.pdf

Workman, D. (February 7, 2007). "World's Top Free Trade Country: Mexico Leading Nation with Most Privileged Export-Import Deals." Retrieved June 3, 2010, from http://free-trade.suite101.com/article.cfm/worlds_top_free_trade_country

World Bank. (December 17, 2003). "NAFTA: Positive for Mexico but Not Enough." Retrieved June 1, 2010, from http://web.worldbank.org/WBSITE/EXTERNAL/NEWS/0,,contentMDK:20146201~menuPK:34457~pagePK:34370~piPK:34424~theSitePK: 4607,00.html

CHAPTER 11
ASIA AND OCEANIA

FUN FACT

The 2015 China Keqiao International Textiles, Fabrics & Accessories Exhibition had 20,455 registered professional purchasers including 4,246 overseas buyers from more than 90 countries during the four day exhibition period, with sales of 3.9 trillion yuan ($635,166,181.80). (China Keqiao International Textiles, 2015)

OBJECTIVES

- Establish the magnitude of Asia as a political and economic region and its connections to Oceania and the world.
- Compare the economic and political positions of individual countries within Asia and Oceania.
- Examine the status of the textile and apparel business in selected Asian countries.

Asia is the largest continent, both in terms of size and population, covering almost one-third of the world's landmass, with countries ranging from fully developed to newly developing. Oceania, located in the Southern hemisphere, includes the entire region between the continent of Asia and the Americas. It is small by comparison but is closely connected to Asia economically. Political systems in the regions range from democratic and communist governments to those ruled by kings, sheikhs, and sultans. Civilization in Asia is ancient compared with that of Europe, the Americas, and Oceania. Yet, when the Industrial Revolution occurred in Europe and the Western hemisphere, the result was rapid economic development that left Asia's traditional cultures intact.

GLOBAL LEXICON

Asia-Pacific Economic Cooperation (APEC) a forum for twenty-one member nations to facilitate economic growth, cooperation, trade, and investment in the Asia-Pacific region, established in 1989

Association of Southeast Asian Nations (ASEAN) established to enhance the trade options for its ten member countries with a goal of establishing an ASEAN Economic Community

guanxi the importance of connections and personal relationships when working within China or other Asian nations

socialist-capitalist economy a more privatized market-oriented economy that promotes trade and growth, while still restricting the freedoms of individuals

The world's two most populous nations, China and India, each with more than a billion individuals living within their borders, are located in Asia. In 2013, as measured by the sum of exports and imports, China took over the role of being the biggest trading nation in goods from the United States. That was a surprising development given that the US economy was more than double the economy of China. However, the Chinese economy is now expanding at more than double the rate of the United States. China grows at about 7 percent a year and the United States at about 3 percent (Yueh, 2014). Half of the Asian continent's countries have populations smaller than that of New York City.

POLITICAL AND ECONOMIC OVERVIEW

Figure 11.1 is a map of the geographic regions and subsectors that are discussed in this chapter. For our purposes, Asia and Oceania have been subdivided into the following four groups of nations:

- East Asia, represented by China, Hong Kong, South Korea, Taiwan, and Japan
- Southeast Asia, including eight of the ten **ASEAN (Association of Southeast Asian Nations)** countries

Figure 11.1

This map highlights the four subsectors of the Asian trade region: East Asia, Southeast Asia, South Asia, and Oceania.

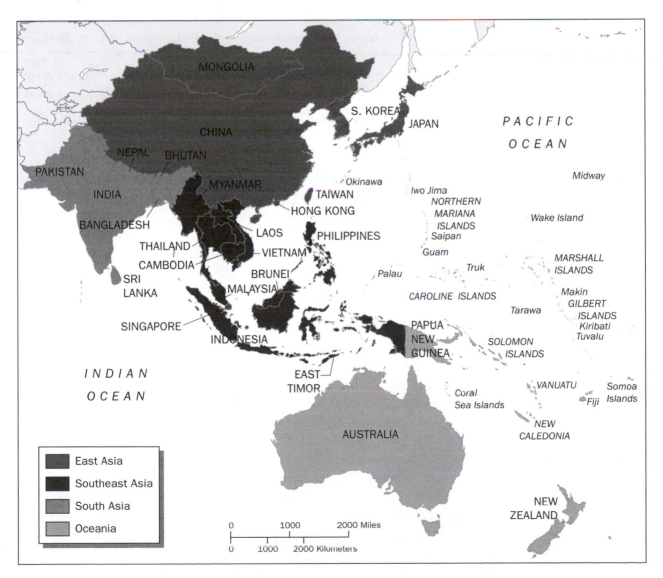

- South Asia, from Pakistan to Bangladesh
- Oceania, made up of Australia and New Zealand

Note: Russia and Turkey have land areas in both Europe and Asia and the Middle East. Discussion of Russia was introduced with Europe, because most of the population of Russia is located primarily in Europe, while Turkey is discussed with the Middle East in Chapter 12. As we progress through this chapter, please refer back to the map in Figure 11.1 as each region or nation is introduced, to clarify its location in your mind and identify its neighbors.

Asian Regional Collaboration

The **Asia-Pacific Economic Cooperation (APEC)** was established in 1989 as a forum for facilitating economic growth, cooperation, trade, and investment in the Asia-Pacific region. APEC has twenty-one member nations that extend beyond Asia to North and South America and Oceania. Table 11.1 provides a list of member nations. The region served by APEC is sometimes called the Pacific Rim, an area very deeply involved in the trade of textiles and apparel. APEC's member economies account for more than 40 percent of the global population, 58 percent of the world GDP, and about 58 percent ($20 trillion) of global trade (White House Office of the Press Secretary, 2014). As with earlier chapters, names of countries presented in tables are followed by the Global Competitiveness Index (GCI) to help orient readers thinking in terms of level of competitiveness and productivity of each country. Take special note of the range of GCIs of countries that are members of APEC, from Singapore (2) to Papua New Guinea (144).

TABLE 11.1

MEMBERSHIP IN ASIA-PACIFIC ECONOMIC COOPERATION (APEC) ALONG WITH GLOBAL COMPETITIVENESS INDEX (GCI)

East Asia	Southeast Asia
Japan (6)	Singapore (2)
Taiwan (Chinese Taipei) (14)	Hong Kong, China (7)
South Korea (26)	Malaysia (20)
China (28)	Thailand (31)
North Asia	Indonesia (34)
Russia (53)	The Philippines (52)
North America	Vietnam (68)
United States (3)	Papua New Guinea (144)
Canada (15)	Brunei[a]
Mexico (61)	*Oceania*
South America	New Zealand (17)
Chile (33)	Australia (22)
Peru (65)	

[a]*Not included in GCI.*

Source: World Economic Forum. (2015). "The Global Competitiveness Index, 2014–15 Rankings." Retrieved November 1, 2015, from http://reports.weforum.org/global-competitiveness-report-2014-2015/

The current purpose of APEC is to build a twenty-first century model of economic integration that could combine trade liberalization "at the border," improve the business environment "behind the border," and enhance supply chain connectivity "across the border." Priorities for moving forward included the following:

- Bolster the economies in the region by boosting supply chain performance.
- Reduce tariffs to enhance trade within and outside of the region.
- Support implementation of technology throughout the region.
- Promote environmentally friendly technology, manufacturing, and transportation.
- Move toward achieving a free trade area of the Asia/Pacific region.
- Raise awareness of trade secret protection and enforcement.
- Reduce the threat that terrorism poses for the region. (White House Office of the Press Secretary, 2014)

APEC is similar to the OAS (Organization of American States), in that dialogue among APEC members does not produce treaty obligations or binding commitments; rather, members reach consensus and make commitments on a voluntary basis. APEC's first efforts were to increase trade by reducing trade barriers, including tariffs in countries located on the Pacific Rim. APEC's goal of free and open trade and investment not only fosters economic growth, but also creates jobs and helps lower costs of goods and services. Furthermore, this goal helps create an environment for the safe and efficient movement of goods, services, and people across borders in the region. However, many countries still resist a comprehensive agreement that extends across the regions and that could greatly simplify the trade process.

Among Asian and Oceania countries, across-the-border connectivity in the form of regional and bilateral trade agreements is already in place, with many more on the horizon. By one count, in 1991, there were just six regional/bilateral agreements; in 2009 there were 166, with more than sixty others in various stages of negotiation. However, this multitude of trade agreements did not generate the increases in trade that were anticipated. Trade barriers (primarily in the form of tariffs) within Asia were, for the most part, already relatively low, and many of the new trade agreements conflict with each other. Because of the conflicts, these trade agreements may be used only about 20 percent of the time (World Trade Organization, 2009).

In November 2014, APEC (Asia-Pacific Economic Cooperation) met in Beijing, China, with a goal to move toward a new free trade zone. The APEC summit agreed to launch a study into the Free Trade Area of the Asia-Pacific (FTAAP). During the same time period the United States was negotiating a separate Trans-Pacific Partnership (TPP) that involved twelve countries in the region, but did not include China or Russia. President Obama rejected suggestions by news commentators that the TPP was a way of countering growing Chinese influence in the area. The desired outcome was to promote more regional integration conducive to long-term development. They are regarded as rival agreements. The Trans-Pacific Partnership

- involves twelve Pacific Rim countries;
- is backed by the United States, includes Japan, excludes China and Russia; and
- could account for more than one-third of the world's economic output.

The Free Trade Area of the Asia-Pacific

- is a longer-term project, first proposed in 2004;
- is backed by China and includes major economies; and
- would provide a greater economic boost than TPP, according to China. (BBC News, 2014)

One or some combination of both agreements could make considerable change in the well-being of developing countries in the region and the role of textiles and clothing in that process.

Economic Standing of Countries in Regions of Asia and Oceania

Table 11.2 presents a detailed breakdown of the characteristics of countries in Asia and Oceania that are active in the textile and/or apparel industry. Focus on the first two columns of Table 11.2, geographic size and population. China wins the world population race, with by far the largest population. India is second to China in population. Russia is the largest nation geographically, but since part of its area is in Europe, we look to China as being the largest Asian nation discussed here. Australia is second in size but has a comparatively small population, somewhat similar to Canada in both measures. Two of these nations are very tiny: Hong Kong, in East Asia, and Singapore, in South Asia.

In Table 11.2, focus on life expectancy and adult literacy. Note that, as with other parts of the world, longer life expectancies tend to be associated with higher levels of literacy. In general, East Asia and Oceania have longer life expectancies and higher literacy rates than do Southeast Asia and South Asia. Less than 60 percent of the population is literate in three of the five countries in South Asia, the exceptions being India and Sri Lanka. Oceania and Japan have the highest literacy rates among the countries in the table, comparable to developed countries in the EU and Americas.

Consider gross domestic product (GDP). Based on GDP, China has the second-largest economy in the world (the United States has the largest), followed by Japan, Germany, and France. Recall the system presented previously for ranking countries according to level of development, using the world's average per capita GDP (see Chapter 1). Each of the regions of the world reviewed so far exhibit different patterns of economic development and overall well-being. Most of the European countries examined are developed countries, with some relatively well-off developing countries. Only two American/Caribbean Basin countries are developed, the United States and Canada, and one, Haiti, newly developing, with the rest being developing countries.

Within the Asian/Oceania region, according to the per capita GDP, there are eight countries that can be considered developed nations: Hong Kong, Japan, Macau, South Korea, Taiwan, Singapore, Australia, and New Zealand. All the countries of East Asia are in the "developed" category, with per capita GDPs significantly higher than the world's average of $16,000, except China, which is a developing country, with per capita GDP of $17,630. In Southeast Asia and South Asia, only one country, Singapore, is developed, with the majority of nations being newly developing countries, with per capita GDPs significantly less than the world's average.

Unemployment rates appear similar to what we have seen for other parts of the world, with higher rates for some of the poorest countries. Labor force displays the number of people available to generate the GDP. China's 800 million potential laborers make it easy to see how it has become the manufacturer to the world. Overall, for Asia and Oceania, East Asia and Oceania are well developed except for China. Southeast Asia and South Asia are less developed, except for Singapore. In fact, comparing the world regions we have examined so far, South Asia is by far the most underdeveloped.

TABLE 11.2

CHARACTERISTICS OF SELECTED COUNTRIES IN ASIA AND OCEANIA THAT ARE ACTIVE IN THE TEXTILE AND APPAREL TRADE, WITH GLOBAL COMPETITIVENESS INDEX (GCI)

Country	Geographic Size[a]	Population (in Millions)	Life Expectancy[b]	Adult Literacy (%)	GDP (in Billions US Dollars)[c]	GDP Per Capita[d]	Inflation Rate (%)	Labor Force (in Millions)	Percent Unemployment Rate	Internet Users (in Millions)
East Asia										
Japan (6)	377.9	126.8	84.5	99.0%	$ 4,807.0	$37,800	2.8%	65.6	3.6%	109.3
Hong Kong (7)	1.1	7.3	82.8	93.5%	$ 400.6	$55,200	3.7%	3.7	3.1%	5.2
Taiwan/Taipei (14)	36.0	23.5	79.8	98.3%	$ 1,022.0	$43,600	1.5%	10.9	3.8%	17.7
South Korea (26)	99.7	50.6	79.8	97.9%	$ 1,786.0	$35,400	1.5%	26.1	3.3%	45.3
China (28)	9,596.9	1,355.7	75.2	95.1%	$17,630.0	$12,900	2.1%	793.3	4.1%	641.6
Macau[e]	0.03	0.7	95.6	95.6%	$ 51.9	$88,700	6.0%	0.4	1.9%	0.4
Southeast Asia										
Singapore (2)	0.7	5.6	84.4	96.4%	$ 445.2	$81,300	1.5%	3.1	1.9%	4.0
Malaysia (20)	329.8	30.5	74.5	93.1%	$ 746.8	$24,500	3.1%	13.0	2.9%	19.2
Thailand (31)	513.1	68.4	74.2	96.4%	$ 990.1	$14,400	2.1%	39.7	1.0%	17.8
Indonesia (34)	1,904.6	255.5	72.2	92.8%	$ 2,554.0	$10,200	6.3%	120.3	5.7%	38.2
Philippines (52)	300.0	103.0	72.5	95.4%	$ 694.6	$ 7,000	4.5%	42.3	7.2%	37.6
Vietnam (68)	331.2	91.8	73.0	93.5%	$ 509.5	$ 5,600	4.6%	53.7	3.1%	36.1
Cambodia (95)	181.0	0.4	63.8	73.9%	$ 50.25	$ 3,300	4.2%	8.6	1.6%	0.07
South Asia										
India (71)	3,287.3	1,299.5	67.8	74.0%	$ 7,277.0	$ 5,800	8.0%	481.2	8.6%	243.6
Sri Lanka (73)	65.6	20.9	76.4	91.2%	$ 217.1	$10,400	3.8%	8.4	4.2%	1.2
Nepal (102)	147.2	28.0	67.2	57.4%	$ 66.9	$ 2,400	8.4%	15.1	46.0%	3.3
Bangladesh (109)	144.0	158.8	70.7	58.8%	$ 535.6	$ 3,400	7.2%	77.6	5.0%	10.2
Pakistan (129)	796.1	191.8	67.1	54.7%	$ 884.2	$ 4,700	8.6%	65.6	6.8%	18.5
Oceania										
New Zealand (17)	267.7	4.2	80.9	99.0%	$ 158.7	$35,000	1.4%	5.9	5.6%	3.1
Australia (22)	7,741.2	21.3	82.1	99.0%	$ 1,100.0	$46,600	2.7%	6.0	6.4%	15.2

[a]Square kilometers, in thousands

[b]In years

[c]GDP (Gross Domestic Product) in purchasing power parity

[d]Gross Domestic Product per capita in purchasing power parity

[e]Not included in the Global Competitiveness Index (GCI)

Sources: Central Intelligence Agency. (2015). "The World Factbook." Retrieved November 1, 2015, from https://www.cia.gov/library/publications/the-world-factbook; World Economic Forum. (2015). "The Global Competitiveness Index, 2014–15 Rankings." Retrieved November 1, 2015, from http://reports.weforum.org/global-competitiveness-report-2014-2015/

OVERVIEW OF ASIAN TEXTILE AND APPAREL TRADE

As discussed previously, a significant portion of production capacity in textiles and apparel has moved from developed nations, countries in Western Europe and the Americas, to developing and newly developing countries (refer back to Chapters 9 and 10 for a review). The migration toward the textile and apparel production to areas with lower labor costs in Asia began more than 60 years ago, when Japan first assumed the role of low-cost producer of many products, including textiles and apparel. During the 1970s, as Japan developed and production costs increased, Hong Kong, Taiwan, and South Korea took over the position of leading exporters of low-cost apparel.

At their peak in the early 1980s, despite quotas, Hong Kong, Taiwan, and South Korea (the "big three") supplied almost 30 percent of world exports of textile and apparel products. However, wages began to increase in the big three as these countries developed, again making room for production in nations with lower labor costs. Then a new generation of low-cost exporting countries emerged. China was the leader. India, Pakistan, Indonesia, the Philippines, and Thailand also became major suppliers. More quotas were imposed by importing nations on the new exporters, creating opportunities for another wave of emerging suppliers, including Bangladesh, Pakistan, and Sri Lanka. This movement toward lower-labor-cost nations is referred to by economists like Pietra Rivoli (2009) as the "race to the bottom," that is, the bottom of labor costs.

For many newly developing and developing Asian nations, their textile and apparel industries are a significant source of employment and export earnings. However, when China gained membership in the WTO in 2001 it became the dominant apparel supplier in the world. In 2005, the WTO-mandated termination of the MFA brought the end to most quotas, and caused considerable apprehension among participating nations. The EU and the United States got quota extensions on some apparel categories from China, but by the end of 2008 those quota extensions also ran out. Vietnam entered the picture during the decade, and as a new WTO member in 2007 benefited from the end of quota restrictions on their textile and apparel products.

Tables 11.3a and 11.3b are similar in structure to those presented in Chapters 9 and 10 (see Tables 9.4a and b, 10.4a and b). They show, for 2000, 2006, and 2013, textile and apparel imports (Table 11.3a) and textile and apparel exports (Table 11.3b). The last two columns of each table present the share of total textile and apparel imports or exports in each country's total merchandise trade. These tables are organized by region: East Asia, Southeast Asia, South Asia, and Oceania.

In Table 11.3a, consider the countries in East Asia. Between 2000 and 2013, China increased both its textile and apparel imports. Textile imports almost doubled, from almost $13 billion in 2000 to $22 billion in 2013. During the same time period, apparel imports increased more than four times, from $1.2 billion in 2000 to $5.3 billion in 2013. Growing apparel imports indicate that China is becoming a consumer society: while still being the world apparel production leader, the country is beginning to import more apparel, even though the amounts are very small in comparison with developed nations such as the United States, Japan, or the European Union. You can see that in 2013 textile imports were four times higher than apparel imports. Despite enormous domestic textile production capabilities, China still imports a lot of yarns and fabrics to support apparel manufacturing. The share of Chinese textile imports in the world's total

TABLE 11.3A

VALUE OF IMPORTS OF TEXTILES AND APPAREL* BY COUNTRY IN ASIA AND OCEANIA AND THE PERCENTAGE OF EACH COUNTRY'S TOTAL MERCHANDISE IMPORTS**

Region and Country	Textile Imports (in Millions of US Dollars)			Apparel Imports (in Millions of US Dollars)			Percentage Share of Textile and Apparel Imports	
	2000	2006	2013	2000	2006	2013	2000	2013
East Asia								
Japan (6)	$ 4,935	$ 6,176	$ 8,766	$19,709	$23,831	$33,632	6.5%	5.1%
Hong Kong[a] (7)	$13,716	$13,975	$10,420	$16,008	$18,852	$16,458	13.4%	4.3%
Taiwan/Taipei (14)	$ 1,630	$ 2,059	$ 1,246	$ 978	$ 1,223	$ 1,610	3.3%	1.1%
South Korea (26)	$ 3,359	$ 4,909	$ 5,218	$ 1,307	$ 3,744	$ 7,535	2.9%	2.5%
China[a] (28)	$12,832	$16,358	$21,563	$ 1,192	$ 1,724	$ 5,335	6.2%	1.4%
Southeast Asia								
Singapore[a] (2)	$ 1,275	$ 1,101	$ 1,072	$ 1,881	$ 2,497	$ 2,916	2.3%	1.1%
Malaysia[a] (20)	$ 1,114	$ 1,063	$ 1,454	$ 148	$ 359	$ 1,012	1.6%	1.2%
Thailand (31)	$ 1,630	$ 2,059	$ 3,059	$ 131	$ 276	$ 789	2.8%	1.5%
Indonesia (34)	$ 1,251	$ 730	$ 5,788	$ 39	—[c]	$ 570	2.9%	3.4%
Philippines[a] (52)	$ 1,250	$ 1,244	$ 907	—[c]	—[c]	—[c]	3.4%	1.4%
Vietnam (68)	$ 1,379	$ 3,988	$10,643	$ 450	$ 271	$ 687	11.7%	8.6%
Cambodia (95)	$ 432	$ 1,202	$ 3,080	—[c]	—[c]	—[c]	22.3%	23.7%
South Asia								
India (71)	$ 578	$ 1,972	$ 3,579	$ 22	—[c]	$ 522	1.1%	0.9%
Sri Lanka (73)	$ 1,483	$ 1,540	$ 1,960	—[c]	—[c]	—[c]	20.7%	10.9%
Bangladesh (109)	$ 1,350	$ 1,538	$ 6,217	$ 174	$ 168	$ 293	17.2%	17.9%
Pakistan (129)	$ 130	$ 551	$ 1,245	—[c]	—[c]	—[c]	1.2%	2.8%
Oceania								
New Zealand (17)	$ 369	$ 506	$ 631	$ 401	$ 740	$ 1,176	5.6%	4.6%
Australia (22)	$ 1,632	$ 2,051	$ 2,617	$ 1,858	$ 3,279	$ 6,257	4.9%	3.8%

*In millions of US dollars

**With the Global Competitiveness Index for each country in parentheses

[a]Includes imports into processing zones

[c]Data is not available

Source: World Trade Organization. (2014). "International Trade Statistics 2014." Retrieved May 13, 2015, from https://www.wto.org/english/res_e/statis_e/its2014_e/its14_toc_e.htm; World Economic Forum. (2015). "The Global Competitiveness Index, 2014–15 Rankings." Retrieved November 1, 2015, from http://reports.weforum.org/global-competitiveness-report-2014-2015/

textile imports was almost 7 percent in 2013, the third largest after the EU (24 percent) and the United States (8.4 percent; World Trade Organization, 2014).

With $107 billion in textile exports, China was the number one textile supplier to the world, accounting for almost 35 percent of the world's total exports. As shown in Table 11.3b, textile exports exploded during the same time period, and were more than three times greater in 2013 than in 2000. Chinese textile exports reflect the

TABLE 11.3B

VALUE OF EXPORTS OF TEXTILES AND APPAREL* BY COUNTRY IN ASIA AND OCEANIA AND THE PERCENTAGE OF EACH COUNTRY'S TOTAL MERCHANDISE EXPORTS**

Region and Country	Textiles Exports (in Millions of US Dollars)			Apparel Exports (in Millions of US Dollars)			Percentage Share of Total Merchandise Exports	
	2000	2006	2013	2000	2006	2013	2000	2013
East Asia								
Japan (6)	$ 7,023	$ 6,934	$ 6,841	$ 534	$ 485	$ 487	1.6%	6.1%
Hong Kong[a] (7)	$13,441	$13,910	$ 10,718	$24,214	$28,391	$ 21,937	18.5%	1.1%
Taiwan/Taipei (14)	$11,891	$ 9,780	$ 10,246	$ 3,015	$ 1,410	$ 888	7.1%	3.7%
South Korea (26)	$12,710	$10,110	$ 12,043	$ 5,027	$ 2,183	$ 2,100	10.3%	2.6%
China[a] (28)	$16,135	$48,678	$106,578	$36,071	$95,579	$177,435	21.0%	12.8%
Southeast Asia								
Singapore[a] (2)	—[c]	—[c]	—[c]	$ 970	$ 1,798	$ 5,095	69.8%	54.8%
Malaysia[a] (20)	$ 1,270	$ 1,437	$ 1,851	$ 2,257	$ 2,842	$ 4,586	3.6%	2.8%
Thailand (31)	$ 1,958	$ 2,873	$ 3,874	$ 3,759	$ 4,247	$ 4,100	8.2%	3.5%
Indonesia (34)	$ 3,505	$ 3,614	$ 4,632	$ 4,734	$ 5,760	$ 7,692	9.9%	6.7%
Philippines[a] (52)	$ 297	$ 239	$ 172	$ 2,536	$ 2,624	$ 1,558	0.7%	3.0%
Vietnam (68)	$ 299	$ 1,058	$ 4,786	$ 1,821	$ 5,579	$ 17,230	14.7%	13.0%
Cambodia (95)	$ 907	$ 911	$ 891	$ 1,825	$ 1,983	$ 1,272	2.0%	0.5%
South Asia								
India (71)	$ 5,570	$ 3,614	$ 18,907	$ 5,960	$ 9,499	$ 16,843	8.8%	11.6%
Sri Lanka (73)	$ 244	$ 154	$ 236	$ 2,812	$ 3,046	$ 4,511	56.3%	47.7%
Nepal (102)	$ 182	$ 157	$ 284	—[c]	—[c]	—[c]	22.7%	32.1%
Bangladesh (109)	$ 393	$ 1,494	$ 1,893	$ 5,967	$ 8,318	$ 23,501	74.1%	87.2%
Pakistan (129)	$ 4,532	$ 7,469	$ 9,341	$ 2,144	$ 3,907	$ 4,549	74.0%	55.2%
Oceania								
New Zealand (17)	$ 142	$ 262	$ 253	$ 116	—[c]	$ 225	1.1%	1.2%
Australia (22)	$ 347	$ 312	$ 227	—[c]	—[c]	—[c]	0.5%	0.1%

*In millions of US dollars
**With the Global Competitiveness Index for each country in parentheses
[a]Includes imports into processing zones
[c]Data not available
Source: World Trade Organization. (2014). "International Trade Statistics 2014." Retrieved May 13, 2015, from https://www.wto.org/english/res_e/statis_e/its2014_e/its14_toc_e.htm; World Economic Forum. (2015). "The Global Competitiveness Index, 2014–15 Rankings." Retrieved November 1, 2015, from http://reports.weforum.org/global-competitiveness-report-2014-2015/

buildup of production capacity that resulted from the opportunity to supply fabrics for many other countries that were becoming involved in clothing production. Textile imports and exports of other East Asian countries are comparatively level, with some increases and decreases. It is important to remember that business success is measured by *increases*.

In 2013, China exported apparel worth $177 billion, a fivefold increase from $36 billion in 2000, overtaking the EU, with "only" $118 billion (keeping in mind that almost $87 billion of that was among EU members). The number three apparel exporter in 2013 was Bangladesh, with $24 billion; followed by Hong Kong, with $22 billion; India and Vietnam, both at $17 billion; and Turkey at $15 billion. Note: Of the $22 billion exported by Hong Kong, $21 billion was for re-exports. Re-exports include merchandise exported in the same state as it was imported. The purpose of the import is often to reassort the merchandise and/or to make a change in shipping carriers.

All the East Asian countries show increases in apparel imports, whereas exports for Hong Kong, South Korea, and Taiwan decreased rather dramatically. The growth of their economies had increased production costs, so these countries moved to producing capital- and technology-intensive goods such as electronics and autos.

Among Southeast Asian nations, Singapore is unique, a tiny developed country actively engaged in the textile and apparel trade. Between 2000 and 2013, Singapore had increases in apparel imports but decreases in textile and apparel exports and textile imports, a pattern consistent with other developed countries. Other Southeast Asian nations had textile imports increases, with the exception of the Philippines, indicating increasing domestic apparel production that led to the growth in apparel exports. All countries recorded larger apparel imports in 2013. Vietnam shows dramatic increases in textile imports and exports as well as almost a tenfold increase in apparel exports between 2000 and 2013. As these developing countries (with the exception of Singapore) are industrializing, apparel consumption is going up. In 2012, Vietnam was ranked number two in the world, showing a 14 percent annual growth rate (Beron, 2014).

Similar to Southeast Asian countries, all South Asian countries had booming apparel manufacturing and recorded increases in textile imports and apparel exports. All countries, with the exception of Sri Lanka, also had surges in textile exports. Apparel exports for Bangladesh increased almost four times and doubled for other countries.

Oceania is represented by a pair of developed countries, Australia and New Zealand, both of which have increasing textile and apparel imports. These countries are exporting textile products, primarily in the form of wool, but reflect no exports of apparel in amounts comparable to the other nations included here. Both countries exhibit the typical import and export patterns of developed countries.

Considering percentage share of textile and apparel imports, look at the exports table first; the numbers indicate the level of economic dependence a country has on the textile and apparel industries. All the countries in East Asia were less dependent on textiles and apparel in 2013 than they were in 2000: the shares of textile and apparel exports in the total merchandise imports were less than 5 percent, with the exception of China at almost 13 percent. This suggests that industries in those countries have become more diversified. In Southeast Asia, most countries also have low shares, with the exception of Cambodia at 55 percent. Dependence on these exports in South Asia is the highest for the region and range from 11.6 percent for India to 87 percent for Bangladesh.

Since the removal of MFA quotas, brand managers and retailers in many developed countries, including the United States, have consolidated their purchasing activity to fewer nations as a way of simplifying their tasks and achieving benefits of economy of scale. For example, at one point a few years ago, Liz Claiborne was sourcing from more than sixty countries. That number was reduced to about thirty as quota restrictions were lifted.

PARTICIPATION OF ASIAN COUNTRIES IN TEXTILES AND APPAREL

By early 2005, some minor reductions in prices had manifested themselves in China, along with an explosion of its exports into the world's markets. Then, when quota was reinstated on many categories until 2008, the impact of elimination of the costs involved was delayed. When the quota system was eliminated, the competitiveness of nations as sources of textile and apparel production shifted from quota-based restrictions to other factors, including the following:

- tariff structures
- social responsibility
- security of shipping
- the country's overall business climate
- infrastructure conditions and logistics
- proximity and access to major import markets
- availability of low-cost, skilled workers
- effective management
- appropriateness of product quality
- access to reliable supply of competitively priced materials
- reliability of delivery, according to specifications
- levels of supplier service (US International Trade Commission, 2004)

Figures 11.2 and 11.3 provide a 2014 labor cost comparison among countries that were active in textile manufacturing, including spinning, weaving, and dyeing and finishing. Remember that we are looking at textile wages, which are higher than apparel wages. Apparel labor cost is not covered by the report, so cut-and-sew operations are not part of these comparisons. Labor cost is a strong indicator of the well-being of the nation. The higher the labor cost, the better off the population tends to be.

Labor cost gaps remained huge among major textile producing countries. Within the forty countries covered by this report, in 2014 the textile labor cost in Switzerland was the highest, at $51.36/hour. That is eighty-two times higher than in the lowest wage countries, Bangladesh and Pakistan, at $0.62 per hour. The labor cost in Western European countries remained the highest in the world. Textile labor cost per hour in Asia ranges from $30.81 in Japan to $0.62 in Bangladesh. For five countries, labor cost is lower than $2 an hour, which seems to be too low for a living wage. (It is important to remember that many people in the United States are paid the US minimum wage for work, including apparel production processes and retail sales, that is not a comfortable living wage in the United States either.) Figure 11.3 illustrates labor cost evolution by considering the percentage change from 2000 to 2014 for each country.

Consistent with statistics from other sources, Werner's report also mentions the remarkable labor cost increase in China, which is approaching $3.00 per hour, up from only $0.69 in the year 2000, a 275 percent increase over a 14-year period. From 2000 to 2014, the labor cost in the US textile industry went up about 25 percent. However, in terms of absolute difference, in 2014, China's labor cost per hour was still only 15 percent of the level paid in the United States (Werner International, 2014). Take note that only Brazil, Japan, and Argentina had no increases in labor costs (due to recessions in these countries) and the United States had the least increase.

The high and increasing domestic labor costs shown in Figures 11.2 and 11.3 have forced many firms in developed nations to source manufacturing in countries with lower labor

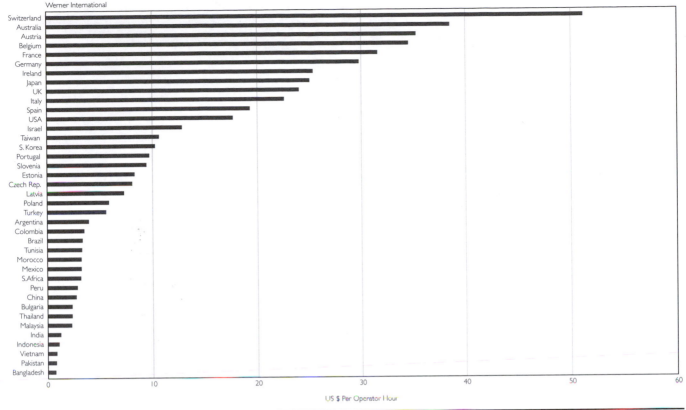

Figure 11.2

Textile industry labor cost for selected countries.

Source: Werner International. (2014). "A 2014 World Textile Industry Labor Cost Comparison." Retrieved November 5, 2015, from http://www.werner-newtwist.com/en/newsl-vol-011/index.htm

costs. As you now know, looking only at wage rates severely underestimates total labor costs as well as distorting the actual perception of labor costs. Social responsibility costs also have to be considered including health insurance and other benefits for employees as well as taxes, training costs, and other things like uniforms for workers. Social costs range from 70 percent of total wage cost down to 11 percent in newly developing countries.

Beyond the wage rates and social costs, many other things factor into the cost of production. Rates of productivity, including sewing skills, culturally influenced work patterns, and availability of viable production equipment are also factors contributing to labor costs. These factors vary significantly among countries and influence not only the amount, but also the types and quality of products that can be produced. Asia, most particularly China, is considered to have a highly skilled labor force that can provide complex sewing and construction details appropriate for diverse apparel goods. This makes the nation a highly desirable source for export products.

Availability of cost-competitive and high-quality fabrics and trim within a country or region is another important factor in determining where importing nations will go to secure apparel assembly. China has the advantage in availability of fabrics, trims, and findings, because most materials needed to construct garments are produced there. If the fabrics must be imported, most are available in surrounding Asian countries. As discussed in Chapter 7, shipping time and other logistics issues, such as customs service practices and especially tariff rates, can affect the lead time required for delivery and the costs of finished apparel products.

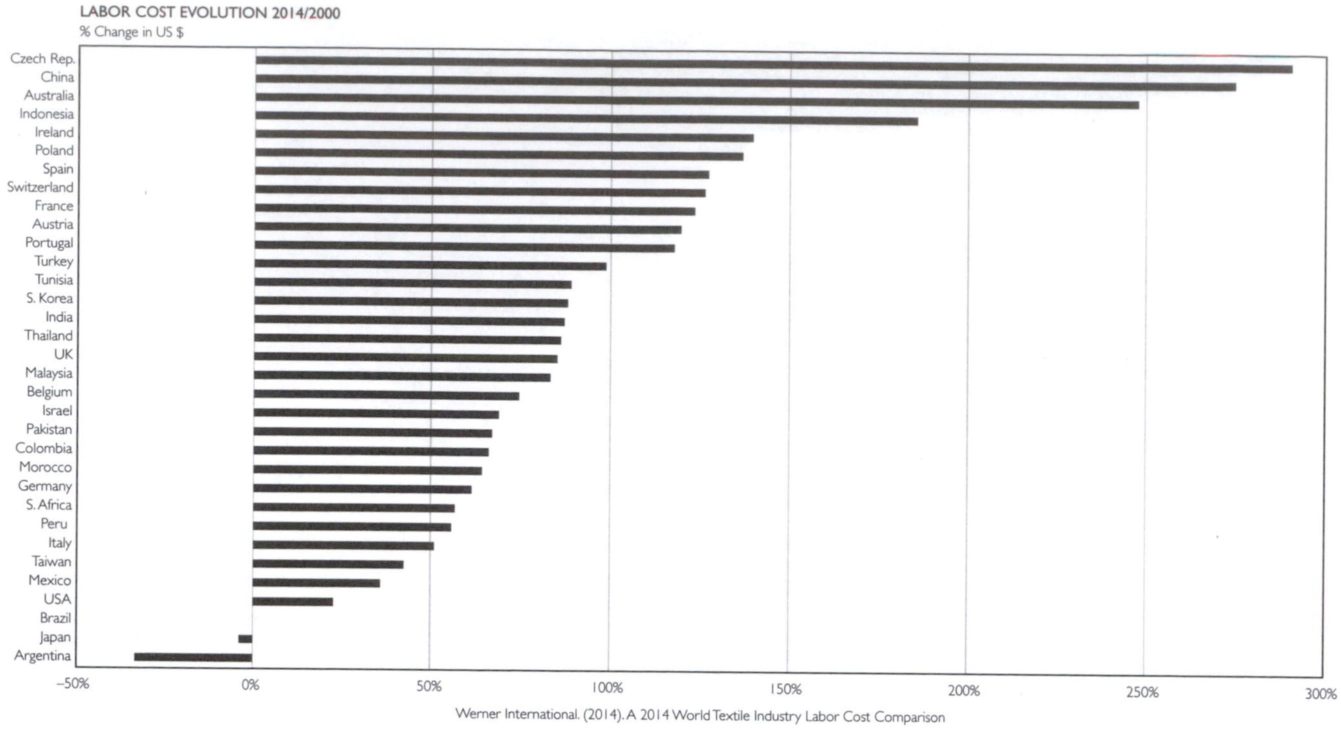

LABOR COST EVOLUTION 2014/2000
% Change in US $

Werner International. (2014). A 2014 World Textile Industry Labor Cost Comparison

Figure 11.3

Textile industry labor cost percentage change from 2000 to 2014.

Werner International. (2014). "A 2014 World Textile Industry Labor Cost Comparison." Retrieved November 5, 2015, from http://www.werner-new twist.com/en/newsl-vol-011/index.htm

The level of service required by suppliers is also a consideration in the selection of a country for procuring products. Countries in East Asia, in particular, tend to have high levels of service, including comprehensive product development and pattern-making services, customized packaging, and reliable quality control and logistics arrangements. At the other end of the spectrum are nations in which political unrest and security issues have become increasing threats to doing business.

The textile and apparel industry is a key source of output and job growth in many developing countries and provides them with capital to foster further economic gains in other areas. One of the by-products of innovation within the industry as a whole has been that in some developing countries, employment figures may have dropped, but productivity has increased because of technical advancements, just as it did years ago in developed countries. Even with these advancements, however, the apparel industry remains a labor-intensive sector and a major employer in many developing nations.

David Birnbaum (2009) divided Asian countries into three groups. At the top were the strategic suppliers, the inner critical core: China, Vietnam, and Indonesia. Below the favored few are the second line suppliers, still preferred, but not at the same level of support. This group includes India, Pakistan, and Sri Lanka. At the bottom are the marginal suppliers, the national equivalents of subcontractors. When business is good, this group does well, but when business goes bad, they feel a sense of crisis. Birnbaum goes on to identify the marginal suppliers as CAFTA-DR (see Chapter 10) and Cambodia.

There are many differences in the viewpoints of Eastern and Western cultures, from the type of logic used for self-expression to the sense of time. Table 11.4 gives a brief summary of these different views and may provide readers with a platform

TABLE 11.4

SUMMARY OF THE WORLD VIEWS OF EASTERN AND WESTERN CULTURES

World Views	Eastern Culture	Western Culture
Thinking patterns	Spiral (holistic)	Linear, purpose oriented
Communication	Implied and subtle	Explicit and direct
Goals/success	We/us-oriented; meeting group goals and working for group success	I/me-oriented; focusing on individual achievement
Self-expression	Subtle and nonverbal	Overt; people are asked to "speak their mind"
Time sense for meetings	Appointments less driven by exact start and end times	Arrive on time, and end on time
Business relationships	Taking time to develop sound relationships; hard to form but usually long-lasting	Written agreement is important; easy to form but not necessarily long-lasting relationships

Source: Jung, J. (February 2009). "Doing Business the Chinese Way: Eastern and Western World View and Business Practices in China." Fiber. Retrieved February 16, 2009, from http://www.udel.edu/fiber/issue3/researchbriefs

for understanding the two contrasting viewpoints that may be present when seeking sourcing agreements between firms from these different cultures.

Tony Liu, the director of external relations and international programs at Beijing University, indicates that respect for authority carries over into business negotiations and that "just call me James" when introducing oneself will not work in China, where formality is embedded in business practices (Jung, 2009). In addition, it is helpful for foreign businesses to utilize **guanxi**, the importance of connections and personal relationships, when working within China or other Asian nations. The goal of being considered a part of the group, and not an outsider, may be achieved through informal dinner meetings and the exchange of favors. These behaviors often lead to long-term business relationships within this culture.

EAST ASIA

East Asian nations are diverse in their political and economic structure, ranging from Japan, one of the most advanced nations in the world, to China, the most populous nation on the planet and a communist country that is moving toward a more open economy (Figure 11.4). We begin with a discussion of China, owing to its role as the largest producer of textile and apparel products in the world; followed by three East Asian nations that have developed beyond their apparel production peak: Japan, South Korea, and Taiwan; and complete the discussion of East Asia with the contributions of Hong Kong. Note: For your convenience, the Global Competitiveness Index rating of each country accompanies the country's name as a reminder of its productivity level.

China (28)

US trade with China began in 1785, when a ship carrying Chinese products landed in New York with tea, porcelain, and 3,200 pounds of nankeen, a cotton fabric used to make men's trousers (CNN.com, 2005). In the late 1800s, China still had active trade in Asia and Russia but withdrew from trade with much of the rest of the world until the Nixon administration reopened trade with China in the late 1970s. A giant with 1.36

Figure 11.4

Map of East Asia.

billion people, which constitutes about one-fifth of the world's population, China has been undergoing enormous changes in recent years. After decades under a sluggish, centrally planned communist system, China began moving into a "**socialist-capitalist**" economy in 1978. This revised system is a more privatized market-oriented economy that promotes trade and growth, while still restricting the freedoms of individuals. As the current global leader in the export of textile and apparel products, the country has gained its competitive edge because of a favorable economic environment, government support through tariffs and tax incentives, and low labor and raw materials costs. See Table 11.5 for a current picture of the growth of China's market share in providing textiles for world markets. Note that China's market share has increased in every part of the world.

China is not only a big producer, but also a huge consumer market. In 2004, the country had more than 100 million people who were considered middle class. A Chinese family could live a life comparable to a US middle-class family for a fraction of the cost, when measured in US dollars (Fishman, 2004). The number of people living in urban centers in China rose dramatically, from 19 percent in 1976 to 30 percent in 1996 (Fashion Business International, 2004). As part of the population continued to shift away from rural lifestyles, the number of urban centers rose from 223 to 666. There were 100 cities with more than a million in population in China (Fishman, 2004). By 2014, Shanghai was one of the largest cities in the world, with over 23 million people, well ahead of New York City's population of approximately 8 million.

TABLE 11.5

CHINA'S MARKET SHARE OF WORLD TEXTILE EXPORTS, BY DESTINATION, 2005 AND 2013*

	China's Market Share in 2005	China's Market Share in 2013
World	47.1%	59.8%
Asia	22.6%	28.4%
Europe	8.1%	9.3%
North America	7.8%	9.3%
Africa	2.5%	4.4%
Middle East	3.2%	3.7%
South and Central America	1.8%	3.2%
CIS (Commonwealth of Independent States)	1.0%	2.3%

*World Trade Organization. (2013). "International Trade Statistics." Retrieved November 9, 2015, from https://www.wto.org/english/res_e/statis_e/its2014_e/its2014_e.pdf

Through direct foreign investment from Hong Kong alone, more than 11 million Chinese were employed in apparel factories at the beginning of the twenty-first century, many of them in the Pearl River delta region between Guangzhou and Shenzhen. However, years of economic expansion have placed enormous pressures in some of these areas, not only on the economy, but also on the infrastructure. Foreign investors were dealing with issues such as energy shortages, escalating raw material and labor costs, and limited availability of land. As the pressures increased, growth of urbanization began shifting from the southern region to the north, spreading from the Guangzhou area, in Guangdong province, to the coastal provinces, to the northeast, including Fujian, Shanghai, Jiangsu, and Zhejiang. China is also developing the Yangtze River from Shanghai into its heartland.

Although China's leaders have been trying to move away from manufacturing toward an economy based on innovation, basic production remains very strong, with the textile and apparel industry being significant contributors to the country's GDP. Consumption rates have risen fast and many domestic producers began focusing on Chinese consumers (Women's Wear Daily Staff, 2010).

More recently, Chinese consumers may value price over quality, and younger generations are increasingly willing to pay premiums for higher-end products and brands. The under-20 generation is the most like US shoppers, who seem endlessly open to new products. They significantly influence their parents' decisions on food, clothing, electronics, and other purchases (Figure 11.5). Social media is an effective marketing tool for the under-20 age group (Qiu & Zhao, 2011).

Textile Manufacturing in China

In 2008, China was the world's third-largest importer of textiles, after the EU and the United States, reflecting its use of these products not

Figure 11.5
Young Chinese, who have more discretionary income and brand awareness, will become the main body of consumers in the next decade.

Source: Elena Karpova, 2011

only for producing apparel for export, but also for serving its domestic market. Being the world's largest cotton producer, China still imports significant amounts of cotton because domestic supply is insufficient to meet the demand of the textile industry. The country is the number one destination for US cotton exports. Besides cotton, China has abundant supplies of other natural fibers, such as ramie, silk, and Angora rabbit hair.

In recent years, China has focused heavily on improving its textile production capabilities. By 2003 it was exporting about two times more textiles than it was importing; by 2008 it was exporting four times more textiles than it was importing, while still remaining a significant global importer. China is now the world's largest producer of man-made fibers and also competitive in supplying any kind of yarns, fabrics, and trims at any price and quality. China alone represented 20 percent of the total global trade in textiles in 2005, but by 2013 that percentage had risen to 35 percent (World Trade Organization, 2014). In 2013, according to Table 11.3b, China was exporting $107 billion of textiles, slightly more than one-third of the world's total textile exports ($307 billion). Read about one of China's largest textile-producing regions in Case 11.1.

CASE 11.1

KEYS TO KEQIAO'S SUCCESS

Keqiao, China—Keqiao is one of the most vibrant, bustling textile manufacturing, trade, and distribution hubs in the world. With China Textile City as its biggest competitive edge, the area has the competition sewn up and is leading the way to an optimistic future for China's textile industry. Strategically located to the south of the Yangtze River delta and close to the international airport and Shanghai, the entire textile district consists of twelve towns with a population of nearly 700,000 permanent residents and 650,000 migrants. Keqiao is fully connected and easily accessed by a comprehensive network of railways and expressways linking the network together. In the 20 years since Keqiao in Shaoxing County was designated China Textile City, tax breaks and political support have helped boost its development as the main textile hub in the world's largest fabric-producing country. With the manufacturing industry as the backbone of its economy, Keqiao is one of the largest textile production bases on the Chinese mainland. More than 3 million tons of chemical fibers were produced in Keqiao, in addition to 10 billion meters of printed and dyed fabrics and about 300 million garments. Together, these generated annual exports of textile fabrics worth more than US $10 billion.

China Textile City provides a fine collection of different types of fabrics for garments, home textiles, and industrial textiles. It functions as a textile distribution center on a huge scale, supplying the most varied textile products in the world. Founded in the 1980s, China Textile City is the first national professional textile market with "China" as part of its name. China Textile City has five distinctive textile trade areas covering 3.6 million square meters with more than 25,000 companies. More than 6,000 overseas buyers and more than 1,000 overseas representative agencies are based there. Textile City is also the first place in China to implement intellectual property protection, facilitate access to modern financial services, guide and foster technological innovation, build domestic brands, and create fashions. Efforts are being made to build the world's most comprehensive textile information database and the most convenient trade transaction process of any e-commerce platform in the textile industry.

Sources: HKTDC. (n.d.-b). "About HKTDC." Retrieved May 18, 2015, from http://aboutus.hktdc.com/en/#home; Movius, L. (November 24, 2009). "China's Textile City Grows in Stature." *Women's Wear Daily*. Retrieved February 17, 2010, from http://www.movius.us/articles/WWD-ShaoxingKeqiao.html

1. It is hard to imagine a textile and apparel manufacturing center with 700,000 permanent residents and 650,000 migrants. What might be the role of permanent residents versus migrant residents in this type of community?
2. What would be the value of availability of intellectual property protection for buyers in a setting like this?
3. Think of yourself as a sourcing agent for an apparel manufacturing company. What might be three or four key components of your shopping plan for taking on Keqiao?

Apparel Manufacturing in China

There are about 110,000 apparel companies in China, 10 percent of which are very large and employ more than 5,000 workers each. Much of the country's production is regarded as high quality, at least high enough to satisfy critical sourcing managers from around the world. As shown in Table 11.5, the WTO reported that between 2000 and 2008, the market share of clothing exports from China into other nations increased. We know that Chinese production increased significantly over this period.

Table 11.6 identifies some of the largest textile and apparel companies currently operating in China and their organizational structures and major strengths. These companies have been in business from 25 to 35 years. Examine the descriptions of the companies, their business strategies, the variety of types of goods, and the quantities they produce. Note that these companies are all still successfully operating in China, but specific updated output information is seldom available; we do know that Youngor is now producing 10 million suits a year instead of 2 million—that's 5,480 suits produced each day of the year! Making suits is a very labor-intensive process. Thousands of people are employed by this company in order to produce 10 million suits a year.

As described in Case 11.1, there has been a trend for larger China-based companies to consolidate their production within self-contained cities, in which factory buildings that employ several thousand people are combined with accommodation blocks (including housing) for both workers and management. There are also design rooms, research and development facilities, finishing plants, printing and embroidery, and even company hotels for visitors. However, the availability of labor has become an increasing problem in some of the areas supporting factory towns. As shown in Table 11.2, China reported an unemployment rate of about 4.1 percent in 2013. However, other sources report a very different picture. In developing countries the rural population is attracted to entry level positions; thus, the migration of people from rural areas into cities in search of work is continuing, but at an unpredictable pace. However, workers are not reliably available at the time and place in which needs arise, and then they must be trained before becoming productive.

> One of the key predictors of level of unemployment in developed and developing countries is *level of education*. According to data reported by a China Household Finance Survey (2012), higher educated Chinese youth are more likely to be unemployed than less educated Chinese youth. . . . This observation is perhaps not that surprising; China's economic miracle has insofar been driven by three sectors: export-driven manufacturing [like textiles and apparel] and construction and large energy and capital intensive heavy industries dominated by the state, none of which offer a large number of white-collar jobs suitable for university graduates. . . Put differently, there appears to be an inverse correlation between educational attainment and ease of finding employment . . . This is contrary to [developed countries like] the US and the UK where a higher level of education helps young people secure jobs . . . Low-skilled youth may find jobs easily right now, but if the country's economic development slows, many social problems will follow (Tse & Esposito, 2014).

Wage rates and turnover rates of employees have both risen in China, exceeding those of lower-cost, newly developing rivals, including Vietnam, Bangladesh, and Indonesia. Skilled Chinese workers are attracted to higher-paying positions elsewhere in the industry or in other sectors, such as electronics. Chinese apparel manufacturers are now addressing the same economic challenges that have been faced by firms in the developed world, such as

TABLE 11.6

MAJOR TEXTILE AND APPAREL PRODUCERS IN CHINA

Company	Date Established	Business Strategy	Output per Year
Youngor Group Co.	1979	Fully vertically integrated, from yarn to finished garments, in one "city" Market leader in shirts and business suits Mostly men's and women's wear; children's wear is ancillary	2 million suits 10 million shirts 30 million knitted leisure wear and children's wear $1.2 billion in sales; 50:50 textiles and clothing 50% exported
Jiangsu Sunshine Group	1986	Largest wool textile producer in Asia Imports much of wool fiber from Australia Produces own power for spinning, weaving, dyeing, finishing, and garment production Uses integrated system of advanced technology Retail shops in Shanghai and Qingdao	350,000 men's suits 20 million meters of worsted wool fabrics 20 million meters of denim 15,000 tons of tops 2 million meters of roving fabrics 1.5 million suits $785 million in sales in 2003
Dalian Dayang Trands Co.	1979	Better men's suits, women's fashion, casual and sportswear One suit factory a joint venture with Israel's Bagir One of largest garment manufacturers in China	10 million pieces per year, including 450,000 suits from joint venture with UK's Marks & Spencer $2 billion in sales; 95% exported
Baoxiniao Group	1996	Moderate men's suits Operates 550 retail stores in China Pioneered franchise operations in China	Produces 800,000 suits, 90% domestic $120 million in sales
Bosideng Group	—	World market leader in down apparel One of China's biggest clothing manufacturers and retailers	Products sold around the world, majority sold domestically Has stores in UK Exports $40 million annually

Ever Glory International Group	1993	High- to middle-priced casual wear and sportswear for men, women, children
		
		Joint-venture factories in Cambodia and Vietnam
		
		Operates three wholly owned subsidiaries:
		
		    Goldenway Nanjing Garment Co.
		
		    New-Tailun Garments Co.
		
		    Nanjing Catch-Luck Garments Co.
			18 million garments per year
			
			$80 million in sales
			
			Traded on NASDAQ in the United States

Zhejiang Shouwang Group	—	Based in Hangzhou, the world's largest production base for leather and fur garments Produces cashmere sweaters Has twelve garment factories 360 company–owned retail shops in China	4 million fur and leather garments $120 million in sales, 95% exported
Shenzhen H&S Garment Co.	1990	Casual clothing, sportswear, uniforms Uses state-of-the-art CAD/CAM systems	Gross production capacity more than $5 million

Source: Based on Tait, N. (June–July 2004). "China: This Giant Is Not Sleeping." Fashion Business International, pp. 28–35.

how to maintain an appealing selling price while meeting time lines and covering all costs. According to Figure 11.3, China's labor costs in 2014 had increased by 275 percent since 2000 to nearly $3 an hour, the second-highest increase rate, only to Switzerland. Because of lower labor costs elsewhere, China is now outsourcing production to other countries to meet demand for finished goods from less developed countries in the rest of the world.

In 2013, Chinese apparel exports were about $177 billion, which is 38 percent of the total world's apparel exports of $406 billion (refer back to Table 11.3b for a closer look). Despite rising labor and production costs due to tightening environmental regulations, China is still producing and exporting massive amounts of textile and apparel products throughout the world, and no other country comes close to competing with the giant.

Retailing in China

In the twenty-first century, especially with the surge in the size of its middle class, China has become an advantageous retail market. There has been a significant increase in retail offerings, further facilitated by changes in government regulations. Restrictions were lifted in December 2004 on foreign-invested retail, allowing companies to enter and expand into the Chinese market much more easily. Today, all major retailers and brands, from mass-market to luxury, from around the globe have opened stores in China's major cities, especially Shanghai and Beijing. There is a growing number of retail chains based outside the country but operating successfully in China, with Walmart ranking as number two in sales compared to many other foreign retail chains. By 2013, China was the world's second-largest retail market—second only to the United States—and was expected to exceed the United States within 5 years. Chinese retailers were beginning to launch their own private label lines and social media was having a growing impact on preferred brands and retail sales.

Another recent change is in the visibility of Chinese apparel designers in the retail scene. They are working toward increased input into the overall design of apparel products, by moving into technical design and creative design areas. To this end, enrollment in apparel programs in China's universities has increased the supply of trained personnel in these fields. One apparel firm of note is Li-Ning Co., Ltd., a leading sports brand enterprise. Li Ning focuses on the midmarket consumer and is a vertically integrated company that manufactures, distributes, and retails its own products related to sport and leisure uses (Figure 11.6).

Figure 11.6
A customer exits a Li-Ning Co. Store in Beijing, China.

Textile and Apparel Producing Countries in East Asia

Hong Kong, Japan, South Korea, and Taiwan have developed their economies beyond the point at which low-cost apparel production is feasible, so they have turned to outsourcing most apparel production and developing technical textiles. See Table 11.2 to review the demographics of these countries and Tables 11.3a and 11.3b for a review of their textile and apparel trade. These countries have no domestic supply of natural fibers, so most firms have focused on research and development of synthetic materials.

Hong Kong (7)

Hong Kong is an island that is about six times the size of Washington, DC, and is located just off mainland China. It was occupied by the UK in 1841. Hong Kong developed under European occupation and became a special administrative region (SAR) of China in 1997. Hong Kong has a free market economy that is heavily dependent on international trade. Hong Kong is one of the leading global exporters of textiles and clothing, right behind China, the EU, and Bangladesh (World Trade Organization, 2014). During the 1970s, Hong Kong moved production to Southeast Asian countries to gain preferential export access to the European market and was already beginning to provide sourcing services to US department stores. In the late 1980s, when textile and apparel export quotas were introduced in many additional nations, Hong Kong, which had entered into these arrangements early and therefore had larger quota allotments than many newer entries into the market, was able to continue to expand overall production (Au & Yeung, 1999).

During much of its industry development, Hong Kong initiated considerable foreign direct investment (FDI) into other countries, including the Association of Southeast Asian Nations (ASEAN) and China. Hong Kong especially sought production capacity in the Guangdong Province of China, focusing on the Pearl River delta region. By investing heavily in production facilities in areas where low-cost labor was readily available, garments destined for the United States were initiated with origin-conferring operations in Hong Kong but frequently moved to Chinese factories for partial assembly, such as especially labor-intensive operations. The products were then re-exported through Hong Kong, under quota.

With the end of quotas, Hong Kong had to compete directly with Chinese factories that were no longer hampered by quota limitations. Because Hong Kong often owned the Chinese facilities, its involvement as a middleman between China and developed countries continued. In 2013, out of $22 billion of Hong Kong's apparel exports, it was estimated that practically all of them were re-exports. Indeed, with a very small population of only 7.3 million, one of the world's highest per capita GDP of $55,000 (higher than Japan or the United States), and very high real estate prices, apparel factories would not be feasible in this new financial center of Asia (Figure 11.7). For example, sweater panels (front, back, sleeves) could be knitted in a Chinese factory, then exported to Hong Kong, where they are put together using automatic equipment that reduces involvement of manual labor, and then re-exported to the United States or EU.

Hong Kong's unique role of connecting Western buyers with Chinese, and now the world's, apparel factories evolved over the years not only because English is one of its national languages but also due to Hong Kong's companies understanding both Western as well as Eastern business practices and cultures. These companies initially facilitated

Figure 11.7
Hong Kong is one of the most modern and expensive cities in the world and is a financial center of Asia.

business transactions but soon began to offer a variety of high-quality services in design, product development, branding, sourcing, and so on. Much of Hong Kong's attention in textiles and apparel now focuses on broker activities. Many apparel firms coordinate everything from product development to shipping. As has been discussed, businesses such as Li & Fung excel in this venue. As early as 2006, Li & Fung was using Southeast Asia and Bangladesh for sourcing rather than China. The goal has been to use management of materials and borderless manufacturing to reach its value-added sourcing goals and the measure of the company's success can be seen almost daily as updates of its activities are reported in the industry trade papers. See Chapter 1 to review the Li & Fung supply chain model and Chapter 8 for further information on Li & Fung.

Other supply chain management or sourcing firms of note include Connor (officially known as William E. Connor & Associates), which began as a small purchasing office in Tokyo but has since moved to Hong Kong, and two other Hong Kong–based firms, Linmark Group and Newtimes International Trading, which have headquarters in Hong Kong, China, and Taipei. The Newtimes Group specializes in the sourcing and supply chain management of apparel and home products for export to the United States, Europe, and Japan. Two apparel firms headquartered in Hong Kong are Fountain Set Limited and TAL Group. These successful firms are very different in their organization. Fountain Set is recognized as one of the world's largest circular knitted fabric manufacturers and has vertically integrated operations, from spinning through finishing. Fountain Set's product range includes dyed yarns, sewing threads, and knit garments. It is a public firm, listed on the stock exchange in Hong Kong, and has facilities in Canada, China, South Korea, Sri Lanka, and Indonesia. The TAL Group is a private, family-owned firm and one of the world's largest clothing manufacturers. It produces a variety of garments for a number of global brands and is considered the world's largest dress shirt manufacturer. The firm employs approximately 23,000 people in garment plants in China, Hong Kong, Indonesia, Malaysia, Mexico, Taiwan, and Thailand.

Hong Kong is home to one of the largest global trade shows, Hong Kong Fashion Week (Figure 11.8), which runs concurrently with the World Boutique trade show.

Figure 11.8
Models prepare for the runway
at Hong Kong Fashion Week.

These events offer wholesale buyers the opportunity to include the latest in garments
and accessories from high-end fashion to mass merchandise in their collections. Multiple venues are available to see samples of fabrics, apparel, and accessories from elaborate fashion shows to sit-down discussions with vendors to examination of samples of
the newest fabrics and garment designs (HKTDC, n.d.-a).

Japan (6)

Japan's rapid economic development after World War II moved it through the "developing country category" into a developed nation. Japan has matured and shifted its
industrial focus to high technology on a wide range of products, including specialized
textiles and apparel. The country now has the world's third-largest economy, following
the United States and China. In 2013, Japan was ranked by the WTO as tenth in global
exports of textiles and third in global apparel imports, after the EU and the United
States. Japanese textile exports of $7 billion constituted only 2.2 percent of the world's
total textile exports in 2013, which was down from 5.6 percent in 1990. In 2013, Japan
imported $9 billion of textiles, or 2.7 percent of the total world's textile imports (World
Trade Organization, 2014).

Japan's apparel imports increased from $9 billion in 1990 to $34 billion in 2013,
almost four times (World Trade Organization, 2014). Despite the significant growth,
the country's apparel share in the world's total imports has not changed much: it was
7.8 percent in 1990 and went down to 7 percent by 2013. Interestingly, Japanese apparel
exports remained relatively stable. In 1990, the country exported apparel worth $568
million. In 2011, Japanese apparel exports increased to $595 million, and then dropped
to $487 million in 2013. Japan exports a majority of textiles to East Asia (WITS, 2015).

Partially because Japan has very limited natural resources, including fresh water and
land, the country has been at the forefront of sustainability. Japan's newest textile pas-
sion is technical textiles and Germany is a primary competitor. Technical textiles is
reported to be the fastest-growing segment of the textile industry worldwide. The Japanese textile industry now has a focus on the development and production of high-tech
synthetic fibers, fabrics, and related products, including microfibers. This is reflected

in a Japanese textile industry that focuses on innovative processes and applications, such as intelligent fibers and fabrics that respond to atmospheric as well as wearer's conditions, biodegradable products, detergent-free laundry, and pollution-free manufacturing. Mentions of technical textiles are frequently showing up in advertising new lines of active sportswear. Technical textiles is a growing field that is expected to keep developed countries involved in design and development of textiles and apparel. Technical textiles produced in Japan and elsewhere are providing special opportunities in many locations around the world (see Case 11.2).

CASE 11.2

JAPANESE HIGH-TECH TEXTILES CIRCLE THE WORLD, AND BEYOND

The integration of centuries-old textile arts with cutting-edge scientific technology—both impressive in themselves—has given rise to high-tech Japanese fabrics that have made a powerful mark on global industry. These materials protect spectators at the racetrack and in the stadium from wind, rain, and blazing sun, and they also provide ecological solutions for greening barren land and mitigating water shortages. Japanese companies have found ways to mass-produce an "artificial spider silk" that is stronger than steel and high-tech textiles developed in Japan are playing a major role on the frontiers of space exploration.

Dream Fiber Changes the World

The area around Tsuruoka in Yamagata Prefecture, otherwise a pastoral town in the Tohoku region and one of Japan's leading producers of rice, is the surprising home of one of the most cutting-edge man-made fibers in the world. Stronger than steel and more elastic than nylon, the "artificial spider silk" produced here meets the needs of an array of industries that need fibers that are light, yet strong. This includes materials for automotive parts, artificial blood vessels, and human hair, as well as thread for clothing.

Although a great many scientists had attempted to create artificial spider silk with these special properties, no one had been able to successfully mass-produce the man-made fiber until a venture firm formed by a group of young researchers from Keio University came along. The start-up utilized the latest biotechnology to enable a different organism to create a protein resembling spider silk. The scientists then collected this protein and processed it into fiber. The experimental facilities for mass production were completed in December 2013, and research and development is now being fast-tracked in anticipation of full-scale mass production within a few years.

Textiles Restore Life to Barren Land

In the suburbs of Johannesburg, South Africa, farmers are working hard to reclaim land laid to waste by mining. Central to these efforts are long fabric tubes manufactured using a method jointly developed by Japanese knit and fiber manufacturers. Farmers fill the tubes with soil and fertilizer, lay them in long rows on the ground, and plant crop seeds between them. Before long, corn and other plants take root in the tubes, and the fields gradually expand. At the same time, the tubes also help keep wind from scattering sand in the air. Knit from biodegradable polylactic acid fiber that will decompose into soil, these tubes are produced using *maruami*, a circular knit technique developed by Japanese knit manufacturers for outstanding elasticity. The tubes are easy to set up, and they also retain a great deal of water. This superior water retention allows farmers to grow crops even with a small amount of water and fertilizer. People will now be able to grow crops in the desert—even on concrete, so the idea is attracting a lot of attention.

Source: Niponica. (2013). "Japanese High-Tech Textiles Circle the World, and Beyond." Retrieved July 10, 2015, from www.web-japan.org/niponica/niponica11/en/feature/feature05.html

1. What are three or four common *apparel problems* related to strength of fiber that technical textiles might be able to solve?
2. What characteristics and qualities would the textiles have to have in order to solve the problems you have identified?
3. How might technical textiles be able to contribute to the ongoing challenge of reducing waste of textiles and apparel?

Retailing in Japan

Japan is home to nine of the Top 250 Global Retailers in the world that are textile and apparel oriented, and many others focused on electronics and technology. The textile and apparel oriented retailers include the following:

#74. Isetan Mitsukoshi Holding LTD, department stores operating in nine countries, and

#76. Fast Retailing Co., LTD, apparel/footwear specialty stores operating in thirty countries.

Isetan is the largest department store group, with twenty-six stores nationwide in Japan. "Each of these stores is an all-genre department store, offering high-end goods from Japan and around the world spanning all categories from clothing to food" (Isetan Mitsukoshi Group, n.d.).

Japanese consumers have traditionally demanded high-quality products and fashionable apparel and European and US luxury brands have continued to open flagships there. Japanese consumers have been described as having a "seemingly insatiable appetite for luxury goods." It was estimated that Japanese citizens consumed "41 percent of the world's luxury goods" earlier in the decade (Socha, 2004, p. 14). In 2014, Japanese consumers, with expenditures close to $30 billion, were second only to the United States in luxury goods expenditures (Deloitte, 2014).

Taiwan (Taipei) (36)

Taiwan's textile industry has developed into a major seat of manufacturing in the region. With little access to local natural fibers, Taiwan has focused on becoming the synthetics capital. Because the Taiwanese textile industry is continually investing in new machinery and developing new products, it has built a comprehensive production system that has enabled it to become a major supplier of textile products. In 2013, Taiwan was ranked eighth worldwide in textile exports, thanks to its production of synthetic fibers and yarns and functional textiles for the sports industry. Textile exports were valued at $10.2 billion vs. imports at $1.2 billion in 2013. Most apparel production has been shifted to other countries, such as Vietnam and Cambodia, while textile production is expected to continue to grow (Chalupsky, 2014).

Taiwan focuses on development and production of the newest of technological performance fabrics. For example, many of the materials that are needed to produce Nike and other firms' athletic shoes were developed and produced here. Taiwan has also become a major supplier of functional apparel fabrics. Mainland China received 21.4 percent of Taiwan's textile export volume. It must be noted that Taiwan lives in the shadow of China, because China does not recognize Taiwan as a sovereign nation, but rather considers it one of its territories. The United States also does not officially recognize the government of Taiwan as a separate nation; however, the United States and most of the world treat it as such and are involved in significant investments and trade with the country. The WTO keeps Taiwan's trade figures separate from China's under the Chinese-recognized name Taipei.

SOUTHEAST ASIA (ASEAN COUNTRIES)

The nations to be explored here are countries selected from members of the Association of Southeast Asian Nations (ASEAN). The ASEAN members are Brunei, Cambodia,

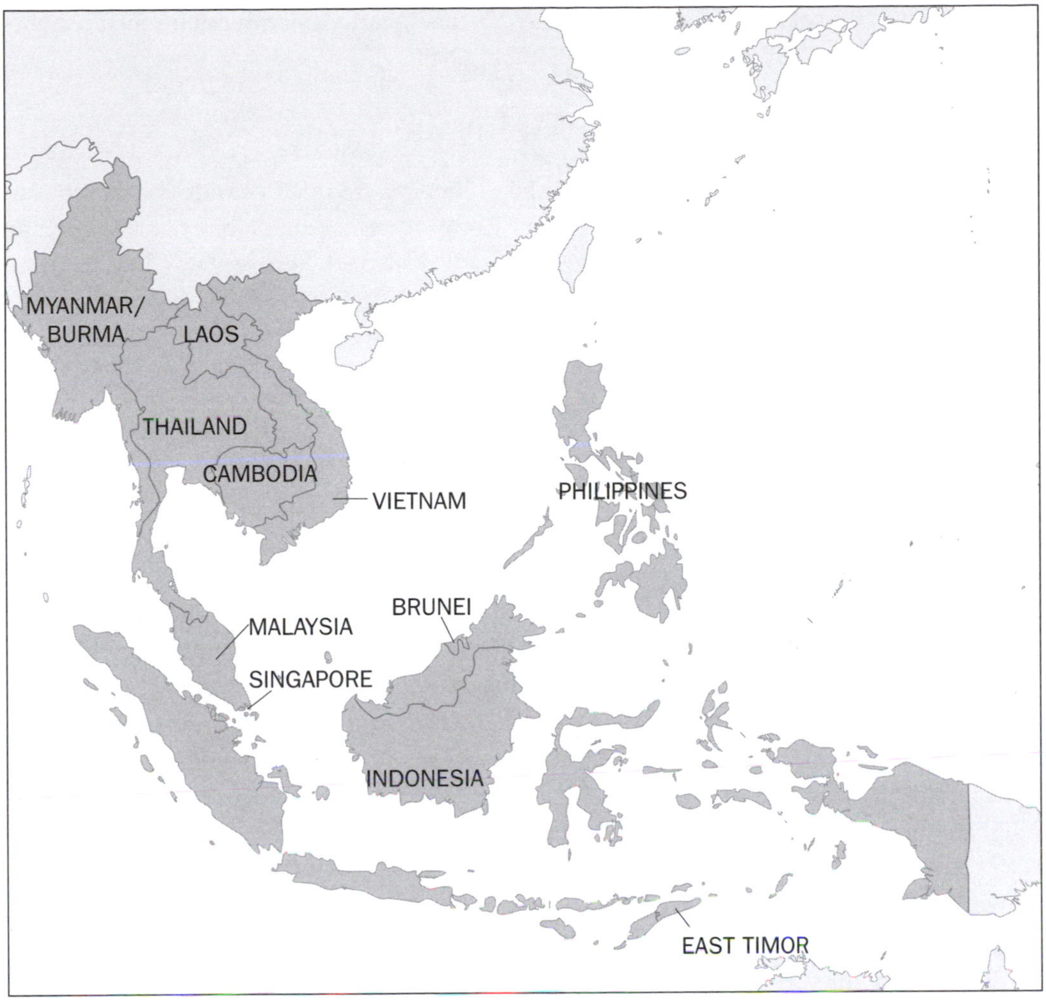

Figure 11.9
Map of Southeast Asia.

Figure 11.9
Map of Southeast Asia.

Indonesia, Laos, Malaysia, Myanmar (formerly Burma), the Philippines, Singapore, Thailand, and Vietnam (Figure 11.9). A major function of ASEAN is to enhance trade options for its ten member countries. A significant decision announced at its summit conference in Bali, in October 2003, was the intention to "establish an ASEAN Economic Community as a single market and production base with free flow of goods, services, investment, and skilled labor as well as freer flow of capital by 2020" (Association of Southeast Asian Nations, 2004). In early 2010, a new free trade agreement between ASEAN nations and China came into full effect. This new "ASEAN plus one" agreement means that 94 percent of the products traded in the area will be tariff free (Just-style.com, 2010). Under this agreement, more Chinese companies set up factories in Vietnam and Cambodia.

In 2004, about 1 million people lost their jobs in Indonesia and Sri Lanka because of the tsunami, and a significant number of those were related in some way to the textile and apparel industry (Zarocostas, 2005). Unfortunately, some Southeast Asian countries also have been home to terrorist activities. Attacks have occurred in the Philippines (Manila) and Indonesia.

The following discussion begins with island countries and Malaysia—countries on a peninsula and surrounding islands in the South China Sea—including Singapore, Malaysia, Indonesia, and the Philippines. Southeast Asian countries share the Southeast

Asian peninsula; for example, Thailand, Vietnam, and Cambodia share the area bordered by the Gulf of Tonkin and the Gulf of Thailand.

Island Countries and Malaysia

Singapore, Malaysia, Indonesia, and the Philippines were all colonized by European countries at about the same time as Hong Kong. These countries were occupied during World War II, and their economies were greatly disrupted. Recovery was accomplished sporadically and at different rates. The GCI for each country is an interesting indicator of the level of recovery and development since World War II.

Singapore (2)

A small island nation, Singapore is about three times the size of Washington, DC, and is located at the end of the Malay Peninsula. As shown in Table 11.2, Singapore is one of the wealthier nations in Asia, with the highest per capita GDP ($81,300) in the trading block, low unemployment, and a high literacy rate. Since the return of Hong Kong to the Chinese, some of the financial and marketing activities of Southeast Asia have shifted to Singapore. Because of its strong economy and small population of 5.6 million, much of the emphasis is on marketing and consumption of apparel products rather than production. Singapore has become a significant fashion capital for the region, actively marketing products to buyers around the globe through international trade fairs.

In May 2003, Singapore and the United States entered into an ambitious free trade agreement, breaking new ground in emerging areas such as e-commerce, and establishing high standards for intellectual property, transparency, and customs. This agreement included a yarn-forward rule that requires yarns for apparel products to be made in one of the two countries to qualify for duty-free imports to the US market.

Malaysia (20)

Malaysia's territory is slightly larger than New Mexico. It shares the Malaysian peninsula with Thailand and the island of Borneo with Indonesia in the South China Sea. Malaysia's largest city is Kuala Lumpur. The nation has transformed itself since the 1970s from a producer of raw materials into an emerging multisector economy with relatively high per capita GDP of $24,500 and low unemployment. Malaysia has been working toward providing more diverse product development services and the creation of indigenous brands. Industry is focusing its efforts on producing for the higher-value-added upscale market and on licensing branded goods. Because it produces petrochemicals, Malaysia also exports synthetic fibers and yarns. According to Table 11.5, Malaysia only had an 88 percent increase in labor costs since 2000 and was one of the early users of electronic data interchange (EDI) to improve the timely clearance of cargo at several of its ports.

The textile and apparel industry now employs more than 13 million workers. The industry has declined in relative importance during recent years, owing to the buildup of other industries, especially in high-tech and other capital-intensive industries. Between 2000 and 2013, Malaysia's textile exports increased and apparel exports nearly doubled (see Table 11.3b). Textile and apparel imports also grew between 2000 and 2013.

Indonesia (34)

Indonesia is a group of dozens of islands between the Indian and Pacific Oceans. The total landmass is about three times the size of Texas. With 255 million people, Indonesia is the world's third-largest democracy, after India and the United States. Indonesia suffers from significant political and social instability, so doing business there can be a challenge; one of the major reasons for concern is Indonesia's unpredictable court system. Despite these problems, Indonesia was number 12 globally in textile exports and number 8 in apparel exports by dollar value (World Trade Organization, 2014). Indonesia used to be the largest producer of textiles and apparel in the ASEAN region. However, Vietnam has surpassed it, and Indonesia is now the second-largest producer and exporter. In 2012, the United States was Indonesia's largest importer of textiles and apparel, accounting for 36 percent of the total exports followed by the EU at 16 percent and Japan at 5 percent. Indonesia continues to be the leading textile and apparel producer but has not been able to sign any trade agreements that would allow for goods to enter the United States or EU at special tariff rates. Thus, it can be difficult for Indonesia to compete with other producer countries (Textile World Asia, n.d.).

The Philippines (52)

The United States established military bases in the Philippines during World War II; the last ones were closed in 1992. The Philippines has had a difficult time sustaining continued economic growth to alleviate poverty; it has a high annual population growth rate and unequal distribution of income. Like Indonesia, the Philippines is a developing country, with a per capita GDP of $7,000. Refer to Table 11.2 for other characteristics of the country. The textiles and apparel trade declined in importance in the Philippines during the 2000s. Its textile sector remained small, but the apparel sector became quite large, with 1,200 factories employing about 400,000 workers in the middle of the decade (US International Trade Commission, 2004). Yet by 2013 apparel exports had dropped by almost half in comparison with 2000, to only $1.5 billion a year. In 2014, the International Showcase in London featured Manila Wear from the Philippines, created by six designers that incorporated indigenous sustainable materials into their designs. While Manila is not generally known as an international fashion capital, it would like to become a leader in sustainable design processes. Designers from the Philippines are looking to combine inspiration from the tropical landscape that surrounds them with Western design aesthetics (De Leon, 2014).

The Philippines is appreciably closer to markets in the Americas than other ASEAN nations; however, this advantage was tempered by manufacturing costs, which were much higher in the Philippines than in China and other developing countries. In addition, the Philippines has few locally produced raw materials, making production lead times longer than those of other nations in the region.

South China Peninsula Countries

Thailand is the only Southeast Asian nation never to be taken over by a European power. Cambodia was invaded by Vietnam during the Vietnam War and occupied for 30 years afterward. Political disruption continues to the present day. The three countries are all about the same size, similar to New Mexico. You will notice, based on the GCIs of these three countries, that there is a wide range of global competitiveness among them.

Thailand (31)

Thailand has a free enterprise economy and welcomes foreign investment. A popular government pushed expansionist policy, including support for village economic development, until late 2009, when citizen unrest resulted in protests and riots. Thailand also has had multiple ongoing border conflicts and serious problems with cultivation and production as well as illicit transit of drugs. As shown in Table 11.2, Thailand's per capita GDP is more than double the combined per capita GDP of Vietnam and Cambodia, at $14,400. The textile and apparel sector is concentrated mainly in Bangkok. Thailand maintains a full spectrum of operations, from spinning yarns and making fabrics through apparel design and production. The country has a well-developed textile industry that is well known for production of silk and special techniques such as batik. In the 2000s, there were about 3,500 textile mills, most of which were small- and medium-sized businesses (Watchravesringkan et al., 2010). In 2013, Thailand's textile exports were $4.8 billion, a 50 percent increase from 2000.

The apparel industry has a large number of firms, ranging in size from small, ten-person operations to those with a thousand machine stations; about half of these are large integrated operations. Apparel production in Thailand tends to be of better quality than that of some neighboring countries, with shorter lead times, owing to the use of locally produced materials and full-package capabilities. However, apparel exports have been stagnating since 2000 and remained in the range of $4 billion (refer back to Table 11.3b). Despite the Thai government efforts to support the industry, it has been losing its market share to lower-cost countries, such as Cambodia and Bangladesh. As shown in Table 11.4, Thai hourly wages were higher than those of competing nations throughout southern and southeast Asia. The Bangkok International Fashion Fair (BIFF) and Bangkok International Leather Fair (BIL) showcase the ASEAN fashion industry. The Thai textile and apparel industry focuses on promoting long-standing traditions in silk fabrics and apparel design by developing its own national brands (Watchravesringkan et al., 2010).

Vietnam (68)

Vietnam was seriously disrupted by both the Vietnam War, in the 1970s, and the conservative government that followed. Vietnam took advantage of the low capital investment requirements and availability of low-cost labor within its country, establishing a significant garment industry during the final decade of the twentieth century. The country saw this avenue of industrialization as a means of gaining a more sound economic footing after several decades of political unrest. Vietnam began by supplying low-cost T-shirts and other simple garments to the Soviet Union and Eastern Europe in the 1980s. Through trade relations with Europe, Vietnamese textile and apparel manufacturing flourished, with shipments to Europe and development of skilled laborers. Today, Vietnam's producers have significantly upgraded their production capabilities. In doing so, the nation has become an attractive source of exports to the EU and the United States.

Vietnam's success is evident. In 2000, the country's exports were $2.1 billion in textiles and garments (refer back to Table 11.3b). By 2006, that figure increased significantly to $10.6 billion, ranking Vietnam number seven globally in apparel exports when compared with other producers around the globe (World Trade Organization, 2009, p. 112). In 2013, Vietnam exports reached $23 billion. As shown in Table 11.3b, apparel exports, at $17.2 billion, were much higher than textile exports, at $4.8 billion. In 2013, the country was ranked the number five apparel exporter globally, surpassing India (World Trade Organization, 2014). As was discussed in Chapter 5, major textile corporations from the EU, the United States, Japan, and China have invested in fiber, yarn, and fabric production facilities in Vietnam in anticipation of Trans-Pacific Partnership, a trade agreement that would allow duty-free apparel made in Vietnam into the US market. Vietnam's plan to increase its market share in the global apparel market was successful. The country was able to achieve the three following goals:

- transition from primarily CMT-based apparel manufacturing to full-package production;
- increase domestic production of cotton to reduce dependency on cotton imports; and
- increase domestic spinning and weaving capacities to have more fabric produced domestically and shorten delivery time.

Read Case 11.3 to learn more about Vietnam's textile and apparel industries.

CASE 11.3

VIETNAM IS ON THE MOVE

Vietnam's textile and apparel industries have had three components. In the early 2000s, all state-owned textile and apparel companies belonged to Vinatex (Hayes, 2004). By the end of 2008, Vinatex completed its privatization, and the company had five big subsidiary companies: Phong Phu Textile, Dong Xuan Knitting, 8.3 Knitting, Dong Phuong Garment, and Vietnam Fashion (Tuan, 2008). Other enterprises were privately owned and family run, some belonging to municipal government agencies. The third group of companies consists of foreign-owned companies.

About 4,000 businesses make up the textile and garment industry that employs about 9 percent of the population of nearly 91 million. The United States, Japan, and South Korea as well as countries in the EU are the primary export targets, absorbing about 80 percent of total textile and apparel exports. Vietnam's textile and garment sector is a key contributor to its economic growth and one of the country's largest industries. In 2013, Vietnam's textile, garment, and accessory exports accounted for 15 percent of the country's gross domestic product, 18 percent of its total exports, amounting to about US $20 billion (Thomasson, 2014).

Today, Vietnam's largest textile and garment producer and exporter is Vinatex. It is a state-owned and controlled conglomerate that includes mother company Vietnam Textile Garment Group, research and training centers, some

120 subcompanies, and 2.5 million employees. Vinatex does business with more than 400 companies from 65 countries and regions (Thomasson, 2014). One of the industry's goals is to reduce dependency on imported materials. Many government subsidized projects are under way related to cotton farming, yarn spinning, and weaving. A goal is in place for domestically supplying 70 percent of materials for garment production. Currently, China is Vietnam's primary outside source of raw materials and other inputs.

Vietnam has benefited from being a member of the Association of Southeast Asian Nations (ASEAN). Nearly a dozen trade agreements are in the negotiation stage that would provide better access for materials for production and duty-free access for the sale of apparel and accessories. Vietnam's apparel industry has attracted considerable foreign investment made in anticipation of free trade agreements that will facilitate industry growth (Thomasson, 2014).

1. What might contribute to Vietnam's opportunities for having reliable export opportunities to the United States?
2. What might be the disadvantages of being dependent on the United States as Vietnam's primary export customer?
3. Vinatex is a "state-owned" conglomerate. What does that mean in terms of operating a business?

Cambodia (95)

Mirroring the history of many other nations, Cambodia established a significant garment industry during the 1990s. Cambodia saw this avenue to industrialization as a method of putting its nation on sounder economic footing, after several decades of political unrest. Cambodia negotiated a trade agreement with the United States in 2001, based on Cambodia's commitment to improving labor conditions, such that they conformed to international labor standards, in exchange for liberalized quota in the nation's textile and apparel sector. After the phaseout of quotas, the growth in Cambodia's apparel business has been significant, although more modest than in Vietnam or Bangladesh. In 2000, apparel exports were less than $1 billion, and, together with textiles, represented almost 70 percent of the entire country's merchandise exports; by 2006 apparel exports almost doubled, and by 2013 reached $5 billion (refer back to Table 11.3b). Even though the country's dependence on textile and apparel exports decreased, it still represented more than half of total national exports in 2013. This heavy dependence on apparel exports during a volatile economy can be quite risky, yet indications are that China may

---

CASE 11.4

FORMULATION OF THE ASEAN ECONOMIC COMMUNITY

A collaboration to reduce trade barriers that originated in 1967 by five of the neighboring Southeast Asian nations has contributed to the economic development of the region. That effort gradually became the ASEAN (Association of Southeast Asian Nations) now including ten countries listed here according to the GCI of each: Singapore (2), Malaysia (20), Thailand (31), Indonesia (34), Philippines (52), Vietnam (68), Cambodia (88), Laos, also known as Lao PDR (93), Myanmar, also known as Burma (139), and Brunei.[1] ASEAN has now evolved into the ASEAN Economic Community (AEC), with a potential dynamic open market of 600 million customers and a production base that is expected to compete with the world's largest economies. AEC is regarded as Southeast Asia's equivalent to the European Union, because it makes up the world's seventh largest economy. Over the past 10 years, international trade has tripled and foreign direct investment is flowing into the region.[1]

One of the challenges of the AEC is to remove the remaining barriers among countries for the movement of capital, services, and goods to allow ASEAN to acquire a larger share of manufacturing from around the world. Barriers include convoluted licensing and land requirements, problems related to airplane traffic, and complex trade policies. Local companies will then have the revenue to expand beyond their local markets. Since wages in China are on the rise, the low cost of labor in some AEC countries could provide the opportunity to provide a new, accessible region for apparel production.[2,3] Another challenge, of course, is the need to build up the skills of labor forces, improve local infrastructure, and modernize equipment. Restrictions on foreign investment that were put into place to protect domestic businesses will have to be removed so the firms use that resource to grow.

[1]Brunei is not included in the Global Competitiveness Index but is often described as "very tiny and very rich because of oil and gas."

[2]Romulo, G. D. (January 5, 2015). "Preparing for the ASEAN Economic Community of 2015." Retrieved November 1, 2015, from http://www.mb.com.ph/preparing-for-the-asean-economic-community-of-2015/

[3]Wei Han, W. (May 21, 2015). "Call to Asean states: Clear non-tariff barriers soon." *The Straits Times.* Retrieved November 1, 2015, from http://www.nationmultimedia.com/aec/Call-to-Asean-states-Clear-non-tariff-barriers-soo-30260613.html

1. What types of things will the group of countries in the ASEAN Economic Community (AEC) be able to accomplish that wouldn't be possible with the countries as individual economies?

2. What are the primary ways the apparel industry in that region should benefit from the AEC?

3. Identify three major adjustments apparel companies in the region will have to make to serve foreign customers.

outsource some of its CMT here to compensate for increasing domestic labor and production costs.

Case 11.4 presents some of the issues and challenges that must be overcome to unify the Southeast Asian countries for further economic development.

SOUTH ASIA

The textile and apparel sector is believed to be the largest source of manufacturing jobs in South Asia (Figure 11.10), and its labor costs for textile and apparel production are the lowest in Asia. India has been by far the most invested in the textile and apparel industry in this region. However, there are concerns that the productivity rates of laborers in India, Pakistan, and Bangladesh are about 20 to 25 percent below those in China. One of the most difficult issues in transporting products from South Asia is the distance from major markets. It takes about 45 to 60 days to ship from India to the East Coast of the United States. The EU is considerably closer and provides India with its biggest market for products.

Figure 11.10
Map of South Asia.

India (71)

India's population reached more than 1 billion in 2000 and was growing at a startling rate of nearly 2 percent per year. By 2015, it reached 1,250,000,000 and is expected to exceed the population of China by 300 million in 2050 (Internet World Stats, n.d.). One of India's strengths in global trade is competency in the English language, initiated in part by a long history as a part of the British Empire. India was a major provider of raw cotton to the British long before much of Asia was focused on the global market. Cotton is such a significant part of Indian culture that when the nation gained independence from Britain, in 1947, it placed a blue spinning wheel on its flag—appropriate for a country that used to derive 30 percent of its export earnings from the textile sector (Krznaric & Schmidt-Whitley, 2003). However, in 2013, the textile and apparel share in the Indian total merchandise exports dropped to 11.6 percent (refer to Table 11.3b).

Textiles have always played a crucial role in Indian history and were the second-largest industry in the country in 2003 (Krznaric & Schmidt-Whitley, 2003, p. 31). According to Table 11.4, India still has a very low labor cost, at only about $1 dollar an hour; however, it is higher than most other countries in the South Asian region, such as Pakistan, Bangladesh, and Nepal. In 2013, India was the world's third-largest textile exporter ($19 billion) following China ($107 billion) and the EU ($72 billion). India had a significant textile trade surplus, with textile imports being only $3.5 billion. Between 2000 and 2013, Indian textile exports more than tripled (refer to Table 11.3b). In 2010, India became the world's top organic cotton producer, ranking as the second-largest overall cotton producer following China. In the past, the industry also relied heavily on production of other natural fibers, such as wool, silk, and jute. Production of man-made fibers has been increasing in recent years, and man-made fibers now constitute close to 30 percent of all yarn produced.

The Indian apparel industry consists of 29,000 firms, most of which are small- and medium-sized (Lu & Karpova, 2011). Apparel manufacturing alone employs 18 percent of the national labor force. In 2013, India was ranked as the number six apparel exporter globally. Interestingly, in 2000, India and Bangladesh both exported apparel worth $6 billion, and in 2006, India ($9.5 billion) was slightly ahead of Bangladesh ($8.3 billion). However, by 2013, Bangladeshi apparel exports almost tripled, to $23.5 billion, whereas Indian apparel exports less than doubled, to $16.8 billion (refer to Table 11.3b). Much of the Indian apparel industry focuses on production for domestic consumption. The middle class is increasing remarkably in size, and tastes are turning away from the traditional sari or shalwar kamiz forms of dress to Western tastes in apparel design.

Production facilities are scattered throughout the country, but the headquarters of India's most powerful companies are divided among three locations: Mumbai (Bombay), considered the economic heart of India; New Delhi, the capital; and Bangalore (considered the nation's Silicon Valley), where the more temperate weather has lured manufacturers seeking to modernize their production processes. These firms cater to the mass-produced market (Figure 11.11).

A lesser-known benefit of India's industry is its fashion culture. India's apparel producers seem to have the ability to make things that do not look ethnic; "they simply look special" (Birnbaum, 2000, p. 90). One of the serendipitous outcomes of having

Figure 11.11
Workers in an apparel manufacturing facility prepare cut garment parts for transfer to the garment assembly area of the factory.

rather antiquated loom capabilities in some locations is that they can turn out unique fabrics that are used by couture designers throughout the world. One local firm, TCNS, decided to capitalize on decades of experience manufacturing for export to customers such as JCPenney, Target, Levi Strauss & Co., Gap, and Banana Republic, to cater to a promising local market. To this end, TCNS focused on more traditional clothes for its domestic brand W but incorporated Western influences (Krznaric & Schmidt-Whitley, 2003). Foreign brands are coming to India, not only to manufacture for their own markets, but also to establish a commercial presence in the retail market.

To enable Indian firms to compete with China, the government provides them with some assistance by allowing import of raw materials duty-free. India's duties on other products range from 15 to 35 percent. Also, India's rigid labor laws, which prevent companies from laying off workers if business slows, are a major worry. In response to these industry concerns, the government is setting up China-style special economic zones in various parts of the country, where factories are expected to have somewhat greater flexibility in their hiring and firing practices.

Although India is considered a major alternative source to China for apparel products, the nation is also seen as suffering from a weaker infrastructure and inefficiencies posed by the country's bureaucracy. Some firms indicated difficulty working with India because of a lack of transparency in legal requirements and complicated paperwork that increases costs and necessitates the use of a broker, rather than dealing directly with manufacturers. These factors affect timely deliveries and may impact India's competitiveness. However, India has a very large pool of workers, and Indian firms tend to have well-educated management and technicians.

Volume is no longer seen as the main goal of the Indian garment exporter community, which is now focusing on higher-value products, including more fashionable items and accessories. Because India is known for its capability for providing labor-intensive embellishments on apparel, such as hand embroidery and beading, "Indians think that they should capitalize on designs, embellishments, embroideries, and details" (Krznaric & Schmidt-Whitley, 2003, p. 35). The Indian fashion industry is globally competitive on price and quality and has the added dimension of being able to provide innovative design.

Sri Lanka (73)

Sri Lanka (formerly Ceylon) is an island nation located off the southeast tip of India. Sri Lanka won its independence from Britain in 1948. The country maintains strong links with the UK, and many people continue to speak English. Sri Lanka suffered a prolonged civil war for more than 25 years, but in 2009 it finally drew to a close. The garment industry became an engine for Sri Lanka's economy, providing more than 300,000 jobs and almost half of the nation's foreign earnings (Burtin & Ergüney, 2003). Sri Lanka lacks a significant textile industry and depends on textile imports to supply much of its apparel production, causing lead times of 90 days rather than the 60-day standard of many Asian neighbors. Sri Lanka imports most of its fabrics and yarns from Hong Kong, China, and India. To ensure quick delivery times of these materials, the country has focused on closer links with India and Pakistan. To that end, Sri Lanka instituted a free trade agreement with India in 2000 that was to provide local suppliers with tariff-free fabrics (Roy, 2004). A similar agreement was developed with Pakistan. Sri Lanka produces only 10 percent of its textile needs locally and hopes to increase that level. Its processing facilities are technologically advanced.

During the application of the quota system, the garment industry grew significantly between the mid-1980s and mid-2000s, and it was anticipated that many of the 850 major companies active in the apparel-manufacturing sector would disappear with the dismantling of quotas (Burtin & Ergüney, 2003). However, as shown in Table 11.3b, when you look at the figures for apparel exports during the period from 2000 to 2013, they continued to reflect a slow but steady climb. Much of Sri Lanka's production was for discount stores, and its present goal is to increase its presence in the higher-end market. One of Sri Lanka's particular product strengths has been lingerie. The garment industry has given rise to an impressive accessory industry. Among these firms is Mainetti, one of the largest garment hanger suppliers in the world, with operations in twenty-five countries. The company's local facility, Mainettech, is the island's leading supplier of hangers and is the regional hub for supplying these to the Indian subcontinent.

In the past, Sri Lanka was known for compliance with international standards in labor, environmental protection, and respect for human rights. However, in February 2010 the EU withdrew the country's GSP (Generalized System of Preferences) trade benefits for 6 months to encourage Sri Lanka to address problems with its poor human rights record. This meant apparel exports would have tariffs added to some apparel categories of up to 9.6 percent, effectively a price hike on products imported into the EU (Barrie, 2010).

In response the Sri Lankan apparel industry went beyond improved human rights into the concept of the ecofriendly "green" garment factory, which cut energy use in half and water consumption by 70 percent. These factories have found business sustainability through the practice of lean manufacturing, with lowered overhead and faster return on investment. LEED Platinum and Gold Certified entities practice international standards of recycling, effluent treatment, and waste management practices. In 2014, Sri Lanka was the only apparel manufacturing country in Asia to ratify all 27 ILO (International Labour Organization) conventions (Sri Lanka Export Development Board, n.d.).

Bangladesh (109)

After gaining independence from Pakistan in 1971, Bangladesh has been on a bumpy road to economic development. It is a newly developing country with a per capita GDP of $3,400, a large population of 160 million (about half of the US population), a literacy rate lower than 60 percent, and only 10 million internet users. The country's territory is slightly less than the size of Iowa, making it extremely densely populated.

In the 2010s, Bangladesh was in the center of the global news because of building collapses and fires in factories producing apparel for major Western brands. Despite all these issues, in the 2010s Bangladesh has been the fastest growing center of apparel production, along with Vietnam. Because the country does not have an established textile industry, Bangladesh imports large quantities of fabrics and uses them to produce the garments that it exports. According to Table 11.3a, textile imports rose slightly from 2000 to 2006, but then increased four times between 2006 and 2013. In 2000, Bangladesh was importing $1.35 billion in fabrics; in 2006 that had risen to over $1.5 billion, but by 2013 fabric imports were $6.2 billion. Textile exports, even though they increased substantially between 2000 and 2013, remained quite low, at $1.9 billion. During that time period, according to Table 11.4, Bangladesh had the lowest textile industry labor cost, less than $1 an hour.

Of great interest is that during that same time period, apparel exports almost quadrupled, from $5.9 billion, in 2000, to almost $23.5 billion in 2013. This made Bangladesh the third-largest apparel exporter in the world, following China ($177 billion) and the EU ($118 billion). One of the reasons that explains the impressive growth of the Bangladeshi apparel industry, despite the poor infrastructure, has been stable and predictable bureaucracy in the country and the government that is committed to a nonintervention policy with respect to the garment sector (Ahmen, Greenleaf & Sacks, 2014); however, the nonintervention policy also resulted in the very low wages in the industry and poor working conditions. It is important to note that Bangladesh is one of the safest Muslim countries to travel to and do business with. You can also see in Table 11.3a the country's heavy dependence on textile and apparel exports as a source of income: they constituted 87 percent of the Bangladeshi total merchandise exports. Note that in comparison to 2000, Bangladesh has increased its dependence on textile and apparel industries, in contrast to all East and Southeast Asian countries reviewed in this chapter.

Pakistan (129)

Pakistan provides a more limited range of products than India but is considered a good source of cotton goods, especially home textile products and fabrics. Pakistan is the world's fourth-largest producer of cotton after China, India, and the United States. The country is recognized as providing consistent quality and having large capacity for producing spun yarn and unfinished cotton fabrics. In 2013, Pakistan ranked ninth in textile exports and twelfth in apparel exports globally: the country exported textiles on $9 billion and apparel on $5 billion (World Trade Organization, 2014). Both textile and apparel exports doubled between 2000 and 2013, indicating industry growth. The share of textile and apparel exports in total Pakistani merchandise exports has decreased from 74 percent in 2000 to 55 percent in 2013, meaning a greater diversification of the overall industrial activity in the country.

The business climate in Pakistan can be more difficult to deal with, as discussed in Chapter 7. Energy problems, underdeveloped infrastructure, and security and safety issues all contribute to business being diverted to other countries (Mehta, 2013). In late 2009, the government of Pakistan began to intervene in industry activities by monitoring, and finally, blocking, some of the country's cotton yarn exports (Abdullah, 2010a). The rationale was that this would ensure availability of raw materials for value-added textile and apparel industry activities within the country. Cotton yarn exports had been increasing from year to year and made it difficult for the producers of ready-made cotton garments to secure raw materials for their work.

The garment cities in Pakistan are Karachi, Lahore, and Faisalabad. In early 2010, plans were announced to set up the nation's largest garment city at Hyderabad, in Sindh province, in the hope of attracting foreign investors. Little information has become available about development of that. Labor issues surfaced in early 2010, as textile workers staged protests calling for workers' rights and an increase in minimum wages; problems continued into 2013. It is estimated that approximately 3.5 million people are employed as textile workers in Pakistan, and most work on daily wages, without job security or social security benefits (Abdullah, 2010b). In 2014, the International Labor Organization assisted in organizing a round table to:

- Develop an understanding of the current situation of the Pakistani textile sector; and
- Identify areas of technical support that would be required to make the Pakistani textile sector compliant with international standards.

More than fifty delegates including senior diplomats, government officials, representatives from textiles and garment producers associations, workers and employers federations, as well as from academia and civil society, attended the round table discussion (International Labour Organization, n.d.). Only time will tell whether the efforts of this group can improve the effectiveness of the Pakistani textile sector and improve the opportunities of the people who live there.

OCEANIA

Oceania, which is made up of Australia, New Zealand, Papua New Guinea, and smaller islands. The region is unique because of its location as an economically developed set of developed island nations in the Southern hemisphere that also has strong ties to Europe. Until now, all the developed countries we have looked at have been in the Northern hemisphere. The British, first following the US Revolutionary War and later, World War II, populated Oceania with immigrants. Before the Revolutionary War, Great Britain had sent many convicts to the American colonies; after losing those colonies, it shipped prisoners to Australia instead. The prisoners included criminals, but also political prisoners, petty lawbreakers, and poor people who had been imprisoned for not being able to pay their debts. They first established a settlement in Sydney in 1788, and during the 80 years that Australia served as a penal colony, nearly 200,000 people were sent there. The natives of the region were pushed back into the central part of the country. Free settlers also migrated to the colony, most often family members of the convicts.

Following World War II in 1945, "Europe was in chaos. Germany was crushed and the map of Europe was being carved up by the United States and the Soviet Union. Western Europe was supported by the United States while Eastern Europe was invaded by the Soviet Union. Migrants began streaming out of Eastern Europe to places like Australia and the United States to get away from oppression in the homelands by the Soviet Union. The Cold War between the United States and the Soviet Union meant that nuclear war was a real threat and some people saw Australia as a safe place to live" (NSW Migration Heritage Center, n.d.).

Several European governments began programs to encourage people to migrate to Oceania and, throughout a 30-year period, generated more than 3.5 million additional immigrants. Japanese investors soon enhanced the development of Oceania's natural and industrial resources. New Zealand's and Australia's textile and apparel exports are small (review Table 11.3b) and account for 1 percent or less of the total merchandise exports in both countries. Textile and apparel imports are substantially higher than exports and have been continuously increasing in the twenty-first century, similar to other developed nations. The textile and apparel share in the total countries' imports is around 4 percent for both countries.

New Zealand (17)

New Zealand consists mainly of two islands in the Pacific Ocean located east of Australia. The center of the domestic apparel industry is Auckland, the capital. Domestic production within the country is increasingly limited but of very high quality and mostly for domestic consumption. Like Australia, New Zealand has moved into the realm of consumption of textile and apparel products, rather than production. New Zealand imports a large portion of its apparel. The retail market operates approximately a season behind Europe and the United States, and local importers use this to their advantage, purchasing end-of-season surplus goods and selling them at the start of the season in New Zealand. Residents are heavy users of the internet and online shopping is gaining popularity.

Australia (22)

Australia is a developed nation with per capita GDP of $46,600, high literacy, and low unemployment rates (refer back to Table 11.2). Its population is slightly larger than Sri Lanka's. Australia's textile and apparel industry has moved its focus from production to consumption, following the pattern of developed nations in other parts of the globe. Australia remains the world's top producer and exporter of wool fiber and fabric. In 2013 Australia's 71 million sheep produced more than 341 million kilograms of wool, accounting for almost 60 percent of the global total (Government of South Australia, 2014). The two largest wool-producing states are New South Wales and Western Australia. Tasmania also produces wool. The wool industry has formed the Wool Carbon

Figure 11.12
Textile and Fibre Technology Division at Commonwealth Scientific and Industrial Research Organisation, Geelong, Australia.

Alliance to work with the Australian government to research the role wool can play in the future. The premise is that a household can reduce its carbon emissions by living with wool products, a planet-friendly fiber that is renewable, biodegradable, and recyclable and that takes less energy to produce than man-made fiber products. The Australian Commonwealth Scientific and Industrial Research Organisation (CSIRO) has a special division dedicated to research and application of innovative wool technologies from fiber to finished garments (Figure 11.12).

Australia is also researching the use of insect silk and is moving a step closer to making lightweight fabrics from this biomimetic material. The nation's scientists have managed to produce an artificial version of threads made by honeybee larvae and are currently looking at potential applications for these fine threads, including medical use (sutures and artificial tendons and ligaments). Australia's apparel industry is relatively small and focused on fashion goods, and just a few apparel lines are produced for export. One apparel manufacturer is Pacific Brands. This firm has found very difficult market conditions in the past few years that have affected its international sales. The firm has had to cut its workforce and close several of its factories since the end of the quota system, yet its top-performing brands have maintained market share.

Like most developed nations, the majority of apparel sold within the country is imported. However, we would be remiss if we did not mention UGG boots, for they are distributed throughout the world. Australia has been credited with their origin, but their earliest identification was with pilots in World War I, who were said to have worn them for warmth in unpressurized airplanes. Reportedly, sheep shearers in rural Australia wore the boots during shearing season in the 1920s, and surfers and competitive swimmers wore them during the 1960s and 1970s for keeping warm while out of the water. The boots are made from sheepskin tanned with the wool attached, and assembled with the wool side inside (imitations are made of synthetic materials). The wool provides warmth and comfort by absorbing moisture and retaining heat. The boots also have a sensible rubber sole. The brand has a long and complicated history involving multiple ownerships in several countries. In the early 2000s, UGGs became a fashion trend in the United States, leading to increased global production and sales.

Signage in Sydney reflects the role of the Japanese in its development, as street signs are bilingual, in English and Japanese. Today, after a long flight from the United States to Australia, one can turn on the TV and not miss a single day of the "soaps"; however, when conducting business in this area, it is important to remember that it is on the other side of the international dateline, a day ahead of the United States—be sure to check your calendar.

Summary

Asia is the largest trading bloc of the global textile and apparel industry. Taken individually, China and India produce massive quantities of textile and apparel products for their own huge populations, but also for export to the rest of the world. Some of the poorest nations, including Bangladesh, Cambodia, Nepal, and Pakistan, are also in this bloc. Some perceive these four nations as the most vulnerable in this region to changes in trade patterns brought about by the disappearance of apparel quotas.

APEC (Asia-Pacific Economic Cooperation) assists with facilitating economic growth, cooperation, and trade in the Asia-Pacific region. The Global Competitiveness Index (GCI) is a useful tool providing perspective on each country's level of development. The Textile Industry Labor Cost Comparison is another indicator of a country's role in the textile and apparel industry as well as the well-being of each population.

The pattern of growth for textile and apparel industries reflects the overall economic development of the individual nations. While beginning with a population in which the labor force was needed to fill basic survival needs, attention has shifted to more advanced technologies and, finally, to consumption as overall economies grew. Japan and Australia were primary producing nations after World War II, and as they developed, other locations, including Taiwan, South Korea, and Hong Kong, took up the production banner. Now some countries are moving past the focus on apparel and textile production toward more focus on marketing and retailing of finished goods.

The pattern continues today as each developing nation repeats the cycle by participating in basic apparel production, followed by rising wage demands and shifting production to more advanced products that bring about a higher overall economic productivity, and, ultimately, predominance of marketing and consumption of textile and apparel products. China is still riding the pinnacle of the production wave, but Bulgaria, Thailand, Malaysia, and a few other nations are poised to take advantage if China's economy heats up and costs accelerate there. The application of sophisticated technologies and more effective management systems focused on sustainability can improve the efficiencies of supply chains while doing a better job of meeting and exceeding consumer needs and wants.

Learning Activities

1. Consider the overall functions of the EU, OAS, and APEC. Which one contributes the most to the opportunities for development of the textile and apparel business? Explain your answer.

2. Using Tables 11.1 to 11.3, identify which nations are primarily consumer/importer nations within each region of Asia and Oceania. What criteria did you use to make your choices?

3. Identify which nations are primarily exporter/producer nations economically dependent on textiles or apparel, or both, within each region. What criteria did you use to make your choices?

4. Identify three ways Hong Kong is unique, as compared with South Korea, Taiwan, and Japan.

5. In what ways are the ASEAN countries different from the East Asian countries?

6. Pick the two Southeast Asia countries that you think will be most active in textiles in 10 years. Explain your choices.

7. Pick two Southeast Asia countries that you think will be most active in apparel in 10 years. Explain your choices.

8. Put on your Macy's sourcing hat. You are sourcing a moderate-priced, private brand line of casual young women's apparel. Given what you now know, which region would you select—Europe, the Americas, Asia, or Oceania? Why?

References

Abdullah, A. (February 12, 2010a). "Pakistan: Customs Authorities Block Cotton Yarn Shipments." Retrieved March 5, 2010, from www.just-style.com/news/customs-authorities-blockcotton-yarn-shipments_id106725.aspx

Abdullah, A. (February 23, 2010b). "Pakistan: Protests Held Over Workers' Rights." Retrieved March 5, 2010, http://www.just-style.com/news/protests-held-over-workers-rights_id10641.aspx?lk=rap

Ahmen, F., Greenleaf, A., & Sacks, A. (2014). "The Paradox of Export Growth in the Area of Weak Governance: The Case of the Ready Made Garment Sector in Bangladesh." *World Development, 56*, 258-271.

Association of Southeast Asian Nations. (January 30, 2004). "Joint Press Statement: 17th ASEAN-US Dialog." Retrieved February 5, 2004, from http://www.asean.org/15982.htm

Au, K., & Yeung, K. (1999). "Production Shirt for the Hong Kong Clothing Industry." *Journal of Fashion Marketing and Management, 3*(2), 166–178.

Barrie, L. (February 17, 2010). EU: Retailers Brace as Sri Lanka Loses Trade Benefit. Retrieved March 5, 2010, from http://www.just-style.com/new/retailers-brace-as-sri-lanka-loses-trade-benefit_id106786.aspx

BBC News. (November 11, 2014). "APEC Summit: Chinese Trade Pact Plan Backed by Leaders." Retrieved November 1, 2015, from www.bbc.com/news/world-asia-29999782

Beron, R. (2014). "2014 Outlook on Asia Apparel and Textile Sourcing." Retrieved November 1, 2015, from https://www.sourcingjournalonline.com/2014-outlook-asia-apparel-textile-sourcing/

Birnbaum, D. (2000). *Birnbaum's Global Guide to Winning the Great Garment War.* Hong Kong: Third Horizon Press.

Birnbaum, D. (August 21, 2009). "Sourcing: Marginal Suppliers Need a Radical Re-Think." Retrieved February 25, 2010, from http://www.just-style.com/comment/marginal-suppliers-need-a-radical-re-think_id105103.aspx

Burtin, A., & Ergüney, O. (April–May, 2003). "Sri Lanka: A Prospect of Peace. Special Report." *Fashion Business International*, pp. 24–35.

Central Intelligence Agency. (2015). "The World Factbook." Retrieved November 1, 2015, from https://www.cia.gov/library/publications/the-world-factbook

Chalupsky, M. (February 10, 2014). "Texfact of the Week: Taiwan's Textile and Apparel Industry Set for Growth." From www.techtexil-blog.com/en/texfact-of-the-week-taiwans-textile-and-apparel -industry-set-fc. Retrieved December 16, 2015, from http://www.techtextil-blog.com/en/texfact -of-the-week-taiwans-textile-and-apparel-industry-set-for-growth/

China Keqiao International Textiles. (2015). "About Textile Expo." Retrieved May 9, 2015, from www .ctcte.com/autumn/en/index-aboutFbh.html

CNN.com. (2005). "The Story of Porcelain." Retrieved January 25, 2005, from http://www.cnn. com/2004/TRAVEL/12/21chinaware.ap/index.html

De Leon, C. (March 4, 2014). "Fashion Designers Benefit Communities in Philippines with Indigenous Textiles." Retrieved November 1, 2015, from www.theguardian.com/sustainable-business/ sustainable-fashion-blog/fashion-design-philippines-textile-innovation

Deloitte. (2014). "Global Powers of Luxury Goods 2014." Retrieved November 1, 2015, from http:// www2.deloitte.com/content/dam/Deloitte/it/Documents/about-deloitte/GP_Luxury_2014.pdf

Fashion Business International. (October–November, 2004). "China: The World's Factory." *Fashion Business International*, pp. 30–32.

Fishman, T. C. (July 4, 2004). "The Chinese Century." *The New York Times Magazine*. Retrieved from http://www.nytimes.com/2005/07/04/magazine/04China.html?pagewanted=all

Government of South Australia. (2014). "South Australian Sheep and Wool Industry Scorecard Overview 2013–14." Retrieved November 18, 2015, from http://pir.sa.gov.au/__data/assets/pdf _file/0005/255137/PIRSA_Sheep_and_Wool_Scorecard_2013-14_vFLR.PDF

Hayes, D. (February–March, 2004). "The Chinese Century." *The New York Times Magazine*.

HKTDC. (n.d.-a). "Hong Kong Fashion Week for Spring/Summer." Retrieved September 22, 2015, from www.hktdc.com/fair/hkfashionweekss-en/s/1867-General_Information/HKTDC-Hong-Kong-Fashion-Week-for-Spring-Summer/Fair-Details.html

HKTDC. (n.d.-b). "Keys to Keqiao's Success." Retrieved May 18, 2015, from http://www.hktdc.com/wet

International Labour Organization. (n.d.). "Pakistani Textile Sector in International Arena." Retrieved May 24, 2014, from http://www.ilo.org/islamabad/whatwedo/publications/WCMS_245786/lang --en/index.htm

Internet World Stats. (n.d.). "Usage and Population Statistics." Retrieved July 9, 2015, from www. internetworldstats.com

Isetan Mitsukoshi Group. (n.d.). "About Isetan Mitsukoshi Group Department Stores." Retrieved July 10, 2015, from www.globalblue.com/brands/specials/isetan-mitsukoshi/isetan-mitsukoshi-department-stores

Jung, J. (2009). "Doing Business the Chinese Way: Eastern and Western World View and Business Practices in China." *Fiber: Online Journal of the International Fashion and Apparel Industry*. Retrieved November 1, 2015, from http://www.udel.edu/fiber/issue3/researchbriefs

Just-style.com. (2010). "Asia: Region Awaits Effects of New China Trade Deal." Retrieved February 25, 2010, from http://www.just-style.com/pap.aspx?id=106309

Krznaric, A., & Schmidt-Whitley, J. (October–November, 2003). "India: Millions in the Making. Special Report." *Fashion Business International*, 30–37.

Lu, Y., & Karpova, E. (2011). "Comparative Advantages of the Indian and Chinese Apparel Industries: An Analysis of the Global Value Chain." *International Journal of Fashion Design, Technology and Education, 4*(3), 197–211.

Mehta, M. (August 7, 2013). "The Global Economic Crisis and the Changing Pattern of Sourcing." *Apparel*. Retrieved November 1, 2015, from www.apparel.edgl.com/news/the-global-economic-crisis-and-the-changing-pattern-of-sourcing87751

Movius, L. (November 24, 2009). "China's Textile City Grows in Stature." *Women's Wear Daily*. Retrieved from http://www.movius.us/articles/WWD-ShaoxingKeqiao.html

Niponica. (2013). "Japanese High-Tech Textiles Circle the World, and Beyond." Retrieved July 10, 2015, from www.web-japan.org/niponica/niponica11/en/feature/feature05.html

NSW Migration Heritage Centre. (n.d.). "Objects through Time—New Australia, 1945 to 1965." Retrieved July 11, 2015, from www.migrationheritage.nsw.gov.au/exhibition/objectsthrough

Qiu, Y., & Zhao, J. (July 1, 2011). "Understanding Chinese Consumers." *China Business Review.* Retrieved November 18, 2015, from www.chinabusinessreview.com/understanding-chinese-consumers

Rivoli, P. (2009). *The Travels of a T-shirt in the Global Economy: An Economist Examines the Arkets, Power, and Politics of World Trade.* Hoboken, NJ: Wiley.

Romulo, B. D. (January 5, 2015). "Preparing for the ASEAN Economic Community of 2015." Retrieved November 18, 2015, from http://www.mb.com.ph/preparing-for-the-asean-economic-community-of-2015/

Roy, D. (2004). Indi-Sri Lanka trade: Hype and reality. *Asia Times Online.* Retrieved June 4, 2010, from http://www.atimes.com/atimes/South_Asia/FC12Df05.html

Socha, M. (December 8, 2004). "Big Brands Opening Bigger Tokyo Stores." *Women's Wear Daily,* 14.

Sri Lanka Export Development Board. (n.d.). "Sri Lankan Apparel." Retrieved June 2, 2015, from www.srilankabusiness.com/apparel/

Textile World Asia. (n.d.). "Country Profiles—Indonesia: Driving Ahead." Retrieved July 11, 2015, from http://www.textileworldasia.com/Issues/2013/October-November-December/Country_Profiles/Indonesia-Driving_Ahead

Thomasson, S. C. (2014). "Country Profiles: Vietnam on the Move." Textile World Asia. Retrieved November 1, 2015, from http://www.textileworldasia.com/Issues/2014/April-May-June/Features/Vietnam_On_The_Move

Tse, T., & Esposito, M. (2014). "Youth Unemployment in China: A Crisis in the Making." CNBC Breaking News. Retrieved November 1, 2015, from www.cnbc.com/id/101433696

Tuan, N. (January 25, 2008). "Vietnam: Vinatex to Complete Privatisation This Year." Retrieved February 25, 2010, from http://www.just-style.com/news/vinatex-to-complete-privatisation-this-year_id99709.aspx

US International Trade Commission. (January 2004). "Textiles and Apparel: Assessment of the Competitiveness of Certain Foreign Suppliers to the US Market." Retrieved March 16, 2005, from http://www.usitc.gov/publications/docs/pubs/332/pub3671/pub3671.pdf

Watchravesringkan, K., Karpova, E., & Hodges, N. (2010). "The Competitive Position of Thailand's Apparel Industry." *Journal of Fashion Marketing and Management, 14*(4), 576–597.

Werner International. (2014). "A 2014 World Textile Industry Labor Cost Comparison." Retrieved November 5, 2015, from http://www.werner-newtwist.com/en/newsl-vol-011/index.htm

White House Office of the Press Secretary. (November 11, 2014). "Fact Sheet: 22nd Annual APEC Economic Leaders' Meeting." Retrieved November 18, 2015, from https://www.whitehouse.gov/the-press-office/2014/11/11/fact-sheet-22nd-annual-apec-economic-leaders-meeting

WITS. (2015). "World Bank Country Profile." Retrieved May 31, 2015, from www.wits.wordbank.org/CountryProfile/Country/JPN/Year/2013/TradeFlow/Export/Partner/all/Product/50-63_TextCloth

Women's Wear Daily Staff. (January 28, 2010). "Country Focus: China." *Women's Wear Daily.* Retrieved November 1, 2015, from http://www.wwd.com/business-news/country-focus-china-2437560?navSection=package&navId=2438328

World Economic Forum. (2015a). "The Global Competitiveness Report 2014–2015." Retrieved April 28, 2015, from www.weforum.org/reports/global-competitiness-report-2014-2015

World Economic Forum. (2015b). "The Global Competitiveness Index, 2014–15 Rankings." Retrieved November 1, 2015, from http://reports.weforum.org/global-competitiveness-report-2014-2015/

World Trade Organization. (2009). "International Trade Statistics 2009. Section 2: Merchandise Trade by Product (107-114)." Retrieved January 16, 2010, from http://www.wto.org/english/res_3/statis_e/its2009_merch_trade-product-e.pdf

World Trade Organization. (2014). "Statistics: Section 4.5 Textiles, Textile Exports of Selected Regions and Economies by Destination, Table 11.52." Retrieved November 9, 2015, from https://www.wto.org/english/res_e/statis_e/its2014_e/its2014_e.pdf

Yueh, L. (April 30, 2014). "Is China About to Overtake US as the World's Largest Economy?" BBC News. Retrieved November 9, 2015, from http://www.bbc.com/news/business-27216705

Zarocostas, J. (January 2005). "ILO Study Finds One Million Jobs Lost as Result of Tsunami." *Women's Wear Daily*, 19.

CHAPTER 12
THE MIDDLE EAST AND AFRICA

FUN FACT

There are over 1,500 different languages spoken in the Middle East and Africa. (One World Nations Online, n.d.)

OBJECTIVES

- Explore the economic, political, and cultural strengths and limitations within and among individual countries within the Middle East and Africa.
- Establish the roles of textile and apparel in the economies, lifestyles, and politics of the region.
- Comprehend the necessity of global connections for success in the textile and apparel industry.

All phases of life in the Middle East and Africa, including the textile and apparel business, are impacted heavily by the cultural patterns rooted in religious affiliations. Three of the world's major religions were initiated here: Judaism, Christianity, and Islam. The tensions flourish among those who focus on a faith-based culture anchored in religious beliefs versus those who espouse a more secular orientation based on economic and political behaviors. Followers of the Islamic faith, Muslims, constitute the largest representative group throughout much of this trading bloc, which stretches from Sub-Saharan Africa (SSA) up to the Mediterranean Rim and eastward through Iran. Doing business here requires recognition of some basic patterns of behavior, such as that Sunday is a business day, Friday is the day of faith, and the workweek therefore becomes Sunday through Thursday. There are exceptions to this pattern, but it can be somewhat disconcerting to those coming from more secularly based cultures in Europe and the Americas.

Sensitivity to cultural differences must also extend to perceptions of the role of women in some of these societies. For Muslim women, the ability to work outside the home is often restricted by male relatives. This may include discouraging activities such as working for male supervisors or receiving a college education. Two geographic areas within the region, the Nile Valley of Egypt and the Mesopotamian region we now know as Iraq, are major cultural centers of the region and are foundations of their civilizations.

POLITICAL AND ECONOMIC OVERVIEW

Figure 12.1 presents a map of the Middle East and Africa. This region encompasses some of the very richest and the very poorest people in the world. We will discuss this region as three distinct areas: the Middle East, North Africa, and Sub-Saharan Africa (SSA). As with the other chapters in this part of this text, the countries selected for discussion from each sector are those most prominently involved in the textile and apparel industry. We will approach discussion of the region as follows:

- Middle East: the countries lying east of the Mediterranean and Red Seas, south through the Arabian Peninsula, and eastward, toward South Asia; includes Turkey, which straddles Europe and Asia
- North Africa: the countries on the northern border of the continent, adjacent to the Mediterranean Sea
- SSA: countries that are located south from the Sahara Desert

As we progress through this chapter, please refer back to the map in Figure 12.1 to appreciate each nation's location in relation to other countries in the region.

World Bank

The World Bank has been mentioned numerous times throughout this text, but it is particularly important to this region. It is not actually a "bank," but rather a specialized agency of the United Nations, made up of 188 member nations. The term "World Bank" is used to refer to the International Bank for Reconstruction and Development (IBRD) and the International Development Association (IDA). The mission of the World Bank is to improve the living standards of people in the developing world. It is a development institution that collaborates with many other related organizations.

The world's newly developing low-income nations typically cannot borrow money in international markets or have to pay high interest rates to do so. The World Bank is able to provide them with interest-free loans and direct contributions from developed countries, along with policy advice, technical assistance, and knowledge-sharing services.

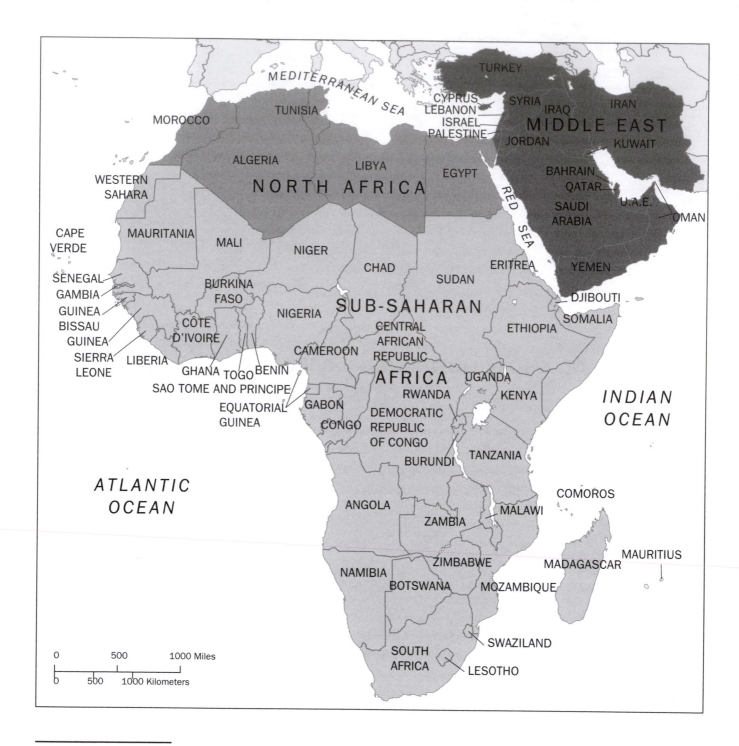

Figure 12.1

Map of Middle East and Africa. The Middle East is shown in the darkest gray, Sub-Saharan Africa in the lightest gray, and North Africa is colored in medium gray.

In fiscal 2013, the Board approved $31.5 billion in World Bank financial assistance, comprising $15.2 billion in IBRD lending and $16.3 billion in IDA support. About 1.2 billion people live in extreme poverty—about 21 percent of the population in the developing world. The goal was to reduce the number of people living in extreme poverty, defined as less than $1.25 a day. The World Bank Group works on achieving the goal in an environmentally, socially, and economically sustainable way. One of the major challenges has been Africa's underdeveloped infrastructure, which reduces economic growth by up to 2 percent each year (World Bank, 2015).

The **International Monetary Fund (IMF)** also works in tandem with the World Bank, but its role is different. The purpose of the IMF is to help integrate countries into the global economy. IMF does this through advising and assisting member countries in implementing economic and financial policies that promote stability, reduce vulnerability to crisis, and encourage sustained growth and increasing living standards. Because international trade and investments cross national borders, countries must buy and sell currencies to finance imports and exports. The IMF monitors these transactions and helps member nations work within the global monetary system. Any of the 188 IMF member nations (developed or newly developing) may call on their services.

Background and Current Conditions of the Region

Political tensions in and among some of the countries in the three areas of the region are often very pronounced and result in difficult conditions for doing business. Nevertheless, the importance of the region in the global marketplace is underscored by centuries of trade with the rest of the world. Active textile and apparel trade has extended from the ancient camel caravans traversing the Middle East and African deserts to and from India and China, to the ships that plied the Mediterranean, carrying products to Europe. Southern and West Africa also have a long history of significant cotton production and trade with other nations. Many areas of these trading regions, both in the Middle East and in Africa, were repeatedly colonized by European nations, most recently by the United Kingdom (UK) and France, in the 1800s. These areas did not gain full independence until the 1950s and 1960s.

There is some confusion as to which countries to include in which region, because there are nations that are perceived to be European, Asian, or African but that are located in the area generally considered to be the Middle East. For example, we are including Turkey in our discussion of the Middle East, even though Turkey has been actively seeking EU membership for several years. Turkey's largest city, Istanbul, is in Europe, but the bulk of the nation, including its capital, Ankara, is in continental Asia, in the region commonly described as the Middle East.

According to the United Nations Conference on Trade Development, despite a long history of regional integration, internal trade among countries in the Middle East and Africa remains low, compared with other parts of the world. The two countries most active in intraregional trade are South Africa and Nigeria, responsible for about half of total internal trade. Reasons for the extremely low internal trade include time-consuming and high-cost transport, which is a result of poor transport and communications infrastructure and overall low level of manufacturing and trade. Political instability and low levels of domestic investment result in multiple inefficient, costly, and unpredictable border procedures, hampering trade in and among the Middle Eastern, North African, and SSA sectors as well as with other regions (Perera, 2009). These persistent problems continue.

Internal trade is made up of a diversified set of manufactured goods, whereas exports to the rest of the world are concentrated primarily on natural resources, including ores, minerals, and oil, as well as agricultural products, such as cotton and coffee. There appear to be real opportunities for developing systems to facilitate internal trade as well as export of manufactured goods. Recent bilateral and multilateral trade agreements among countries in the Middle East, as well as with China and the United States, were expected to provide opportunities for both intraregional trade and exports to other parts of the world, but that continues to be slow to develop.

TABLE 12.1

CHARACTERISTICS OF SELECTED COUNTRIES IN THE MIDDLE EAST AND AFRICA

Country, with 2014–2015 GCI	Geographic Size (in Thousands of km)	Population (in Millions)	Life Expectancy (in Years)	Adult Literacy Rate	GDP (in Billions of US Dollars)	GDP per Capita (PPP) (in US Dollars)	Inflation Rate	Labor Force (in Millions)	Unemployment Rate	Internet Users (in Millions)
Middle East										
UAE (12)	83.6	5.6	77.1	93.8%	$ 605.0	$65,000	2.2%	4.9	2.4%	3.5
Saudi Arabia (24)	2,149.7	27.3	74.8	94.7%	$1,616.0	$52,800	2.9%	11.2	11.2%	9.8
Israel (27)	20.8	7.8	81.3	97.8%	$ 268.3	$33,400	0.5%	3.8	6.6%	4.5
Turkey (45)	783.6	81.6	73.3	95.0%	$1,512.0	$19,600	8.9%	27.6	9.4%	27.2
Jordan (64)	89.3	7.9	74.1	95.4%	$ 79.8	$11,900	3.0%	2.0	12.3%	1.6
Iran (83)	1,648.0	80.8	70.9	86.8%	$ 945.5	$16,400	11.0%	28.4	10.3%	25.4
Yemen (142)	528.0	26.1	64.8	70.1%	$ 106.0	$ 3,900	11.8%	7.3	27.0%	4.5
Syria (No GCI)	185.2	17.9	64.4	86.4%	$ 106.0	$ 5,100	34.8%	4.0	33.0%	2.4
North Africa										
Morocco (72)	446.6	33.0	76.5	68.5%	$ 254.4	$ 7,700	1.1%	12.0	9.6%	13.2
Tunisia (87)	163.6	10.9	75.7	81.8%	$ 125.1	$11,400	5.7%	4.0	15.2%	3.5
Egypt (119)	1,001.4	86.9	73.5	73.8%	$ 945.4	$11,100	10.1%	28.3	13.4%	20.1
Sub-Saharan Africa										
Mauritius (39)	2.0	1.3	75.2	90.6%	$ 23.4	$17,900	3.9%	0.6	8.0%	0.3
South Africa (56)	1,219.1	48.4	49.6	94.3%	$ 683.1	$12,700	6.0%	20.2	25.0%	4.4
Kenya (90)	580.4	45.0	63.5	78.0%	$ 134.7	$ 3,100	7.2%	17.7	40.0%	4.0
Lesotho (107)	30.4	1.9	52.7	79.4%	$ 5.6	$ 2,900	6.0%	0.9	28.1%	0.08
Ghana (111)	238.5	25.8	65.8	76.6%	$ 109.4	$ 4,200	15.0%	11.3	11.0%	1.3
Ethiopia (118)	1,104.3	96.6	60.8	49.1%	$ 139.4	$ 1,500	7.8%	47.3	17.5%	0.45
Nigeria (127)	923.8	177.2	52.6	59.6%	$1,058.0	$ 6,100	8.3%	55.0	23.9%	44.0
Madagascar (130)	587.0	23.2	65.2	64.7%	$ 33.6	$ 1,400	6.4%	12.2	3.6%	0.3
Uganda (no GCI)	241.2	36.8	58.7	73.7%	$ 21.5	$ 1,165	4.9%	17.4	3.8%	16.2

Note: Countries are listed according to GCIs in each region.

Sources: Based on estimates of 2014–2015 data from Central Intelligence Agency (CIA) (n.d.). "The World Factbook." Retrieved October 29, 2015, from https://www.cia.gov/library/publications/the-world-factbook/index.html; and World Economic Forum. (2015). "The Global Competitiveness Index, 2014–15 Rankings." Retrieved November 1, 2015, from http://reports.weforum.org/global-competitiveness-report-2014-2015/

Table 12.1 provides an overview of the primary countries located in the Middle East and Africa that are involved in the textile and apparel industry. The countries in each region are listed in order according to each country's GCI noted next to each name. As you now know, the GCI in use is the Global Competitiveness Index 2014–2015 rankings. Take a moment to skim through the GCIs in each region. The countries in each region include a wide range of comparative global competitiveness as well as the associated level of economic well-being. Think of this table as a reference tool as we work through the rest of the chapter.

Use the map in Figure 12.1 to appreciate the locations and the range in geographic size of the countries. You will soon find that the size of the country often has little relationship to the size of the population in these regions. Saudi Arabia, nearly one-fifth the size of the United States, is by far the largest, followed by Ethiopia and South Africa. The smallest countries in the trading bloc are Lebanon and Mauritius, both of which are somewhat smaller than Rhode Island. Nigeria has the largest population, followed by Ethiopia, Egypt, and Turkey. With a few exceptions, life expectancy and literacy are among the world's lowest compared with the other regions of the world we have examined.

It is important to keep in mind the entire region has a population close to 1.3 billion (almost 18 percent of the world's total population). The African continent has almost 1.1 billion people, and 205 million people populate the Middle East. Moreover, Africa's population is the fastest growing in the world, primarily because most women do not have access to family planning. At the current population growth rate of 2 percent, the African continent is expected to have 1.9 billion people by 2050, making it the most populous region of the world. Table 12.1 presents the characteristics of countries that are active in textile and apparel trade in the Middle East and Africa. (Note: The countries are listed according to GCI for each country in each region in tables throughout the chapter.)

Factors such as oil reserves heavily influence the overall economic health of some nations within the region, including United Arab Emirates (12), commonly known as UAE, and Saudi Arabia (24). This is reflected in their GCIs, GDPs (gross domestic products), and per capita GDPs. According to Table 12.1, the most developed nations in the region in terms of annual per capita GDP are the UAE (with $65,000), Saudi Arabia (with $52,800), and Israel (with $33,400). At the other end of the spectrum, three nations included in Table 12.1 are considered among the least developed in the world, with per capita GDPs of less than $2,000: Ethiopia (with $1,500), Madagascar (with $1,400), and Uganda (with $1,165). All of them are located in SSA. High inflation rates and high unemployment rates in most countries provide additional dimensions of the levels of poverty. The miniscule number of internet users, in relation to the population, is a strong indicator of lack of technological development. Ironically, the African continent is the richest in natural resources, yet it has the greatest number of poor economies in the world. This is primarily due to the long history of European colonization, uneven distribution of wealth, and corruption.

TEXTILE AND APPAREL TRADE ACTIVITY

As we discovered with the other geographic regions discussed in Chapters 9 through 11, developed nations, such as the UAE, tend to focus on the consumption of textile

TABLE 12.2A

IMPORTS OF TEXTILES AND APPAREL BY MIDDLE EASTERN AND AFRICAN COUNTRIES

Country	Textile Imports			Apparel Imports			Percent of Total Imports	
	2000	2006	2013	2000	2006	2013	2000	2013
Middle East								
UAE (12)	$2,055	$3,567	$3,460	$832	$3,055	$3,921	3.7%	3.0%
Saudi Arabia (24)	$986	$1,204	$2,145	$813	$1,649	$3,447	13.2%	3.3%
Israel (27)	$759	$718	$710	$471	$788	$1,555	3.3%	3.0%
Turkey (45)	$2,124	$4,686	$6,789	$264	$1,098	$3,140	4.4%	3.9%
Jordan (64)	$172	$725	$829	$61	$247	$399	5.0%	5.6%
Iran (83)	$298	$730	$745	—[1]	—[1]	—[1]	2.9%	1.5%
Syria (no GCI)	$399	$353	$153	—[1]	—[1]	—[1]	10.5%	2.8%
North Africa								
Morocco (72)	$1,364	$1,945	$2,455	$232	$274	$340	12.8%	6.2%
Tunisia (87)	$1,207	$1,594	$1,710	$438	$550	$486	14.6%	8.9%
Egypt (119)	$526	$1,094	$2,390	$404	$411	$530	6.7%	5.0%
Sub-Saharan Africa								
Mauritius (39)	$411	$266	$270	—[1]	—[1]	—[1]	19.6%	5.0%
South Africa (56)	$570	$975	$1,369	$223	$1,123	$1, 901	2.9%	3.1%
Kenya (90)	$47	—[1]	$346	—[1]	—[1]	—[1]	4.1%	2.1%
Lesotho (107)	—[1]	—[1]	—[1]	—[1]	—[1]	—[1]	—[1]	—[1]

Note: Amounts given in millions of US dollars and as a percentage of each country's total merchandise imports
[1]Data not available

Source: World Trade Organization. (2014). "Merchandise Trade by Product." Retrieved November 2, 2015, from https://www.wto.org/english/res_e/statis_e/its2014_e/its14_merch_trade_product_e.pdf

and apparel products; developing nations, such as Jordan and Mauritius, tend to use the textile and apparel industry as an industrial engine to fuel their development; and newly developing nations, such as Kenya (90), Ethiopia (118), Egypt (119), and Nigeria (127), are looking to make use of apparel production as an avenue to economic development. Tables 12.2a and b present nations that are tracked by the World Trade Organization (WTO) for activity in textiles and apparel. Notice the tables are laid so Table 12.2a shows textile and apparel imports and Table 12.2b shows textile and apparel exports.

In Table 12.2a (imports), UAE (12), Saudi Arabia (24), and Turkey (45) are the most active in both textiles and apparel. In Table 12.2b (exports), Turkey is by far the most active. The North African countries are all involved in some textile and apparel exports, with slightly more apparel exports and textile imports. North African countries are importing around $2 billion in textiles and exporting around $3 billion in apparel (with the exception of Egypt, which exports $1.3 billion). The Sub-Saharan countries are less active in the textile and apparel industry than their northern neighbors.

TABLE 12.2B

EXPORTS OF TEXTILES AND APPAREL
BY MIDDLE EASTERN AND AFRICAN COUNTRIES

Country	Textile Exports			Apparel Exports			Percent of Total Exports	
	2000	2006	2013	2000	2006	2013	2000	2013
Middle East								
UAE (12)	$3,137	$4,567	$ 2,736	$ 971	$ 2,400	$ 1,599	8.2%	1.1%
Saudi Arabia (24)	$ 114	$ 315	—[1]	—[1]	—[1]	—[1]	0.1%	—[1]
Israel (36)	$ 490	$ 744	$ 701	—[1]	—[1]	$ 155	1.6%	1.3%
Turkey (45)	$3,672	$7,585	$12,157	$6,533	$12,052	$15,408	46.7%	18.2%
Jordan (64)	—[1]	—[1]	$ 111	$ 115	$ 1,257	$ 1,150	6.1%	15.9%
Iran (83)	$ 766	$ 766	$ 950	—[1]	—[1]	—[1]	2.7%	1.2%
Syria (no GCI)	$ 158	$ 820	$ 105	$ 129	$ 864	$ 60	6.2%	8.2%
North Africa								
Morocco (72)	$ 123	$ 242	$ 361	$2,401	$ 3,238	$ 3,122	34.0%	16.0%
Tunisia (87)	$ 154	$ 349	$ 413	$2,227	$ 3,018	$ 2,802	40.7%	18.8%
Egypt (119)	$ 412	$ 650	$ 1,489	$ 710	$ 1,138	$ 1,365	23.9%	10.0%
Sub-Saharan Africa								
Mauritius (39)	$ 81	$ 78	$ 114	$ 948	$ 772	$ 761	66.1%	30.5%
South Africa (56)	$ 240	$ 306	$ 425	—[1]	—[1]	$ 503	0.8%	0.9%
Kenya (90)	$ 26	—[1]	$ 61	$ 9	—[1]	$ 279	6.8%	5.8%
Lesotho (107)	—[1]	—[1]	—[1]	$ 161	$ 478	$ 418	73.1%	49.3%

Note: Amounts given in millions of US dollars and as a percentage of each country's total merchandise exports

[1]Data not available

Source: World Trade Organization. (2014). "Merchandise Trade by Product." Retrieved November 2, 2015, from https://www.wto.org/english/res_e/statis_e/its2014_e/its14_merch_trade_product_e.pdf

The dominant countries involved in apparel imports are the developed countries in the Middle East: Israel, Saudi Arabia, Turkey, and the UAE. For these countries, apparel imports range from $1.5 billion (Israel) to almost $4 billion (UAE). South Africa, the most developed nation on the African continent, also has relatively high apparel imports, at almost $2 billion. Between 2000 and 2013, the dominant textile trader in both imports and exports was Turkey. Apparently, the textile imports were supporting their rather substantial apparel exports. In 2013, Turkey, at $15.4 billion, was ranked the number seven apparel exporter in the world, following India and Vietnam, both at $17 billion (World Trade Organization, 2014). Turkey's relatively high level of apparel imports ($3 billion) indicates that as the country gets more developed, consumption level increases. All the countries, except Israel, UAE, and South Africa, show a positive trade balance in apparel, which suggests they produce more than they consume. Having a negative trade balance, in which apparel imports exceed exports, is a common condition for developed countries.

Look at the last two columns in Table 12.2a. From 2000 to 2013, all countries, with the exception of Jordan and South Africa, had substantial declines in imports of textiles and apparel. If the economy remains on about the same level, that suggests more textiles and apparel are being made domestically. Check the levels of exports in Table 12.2b. As compared to many other nations we have explored, there is a higher proportion of nations within this geographic region that are more dependent upon textile and apparel products as a major share of their total merchandise exports. The dependence of an economy on merchandise exports was extremely high for some countries in these sectors in 2000, but had fallen by 2013 for all the economies in the tables. The most dramatic reductions were the following:

- Mauritius, 66.1 percent down to 30.5 percent
- Turkey, 46.7 percent down to 18.2 percent
- Tunisia, 40.7 percent down to 18.8 percent
- Morocco, 34.0 percent down to 16.0 percent
- Egypt, 23.9 percent down to 10.0 percent

Lesotho reported in 1995 that 94 percent of its total merchandise trade was in export of textile and apparel products (US International Trade Commission, 2004), indicating that there was little industry there besides textile and apparel production. One would like to think that the dependence on the textile and apparel industry declined because the economy in the country improved and diversified. However, two factors have probably made greater contributions to this decline: the worldwide recession, which slowed demand for textiles and apparel in developed countries, and the end of the MFA quota system, which abolished limits on imports from Asia's big exporting countries. These developments have greatly affected the textile and apparel industry throughout this trading bloc; development of trade over the next decade will be very interesting to watch.

Overall, the region's participation in the global textile and apparel trade remains low. In 2013, the value of the world's total trade reached $460 billion in apparel and $306 billion in textiles, for a combined $766 billion (World Trade Organization, 2014). All Middle Eastern and African countries together contributed no more than 10 percent to the total textile and apparel global trade, with Turkey accounting for more than half of the region's textile and apparel trade. Recall that the region's population is 1.3 billion, or 18 percent of the world's total.

PARTICIPATION OF INDIVIDUAL COUNTRIES IN TEXTILES AND APPAREL

The Mediterranean Rim nations, including Morocco (72), Tunisia (87), and Egypt (119), have specific advantages for production and export of products that should put them on the right path for protecting their competitive edge, including the following:

- availability of indigenous raw material supplies, such as Turkish cotton;
- an abundant supply of low-cost labor; and
- close proximity to important markets in the EU.

However, the GCIs for these countries indicate a relatively low level of global competitiveness. Table 12.3 presents the textile industry labor cost comparison for African and Middle Eastern countries active in textile production, which was introduced in Figure 11.2. Interestingly, the wage rates are consistently lower with the countries' decreasing levels of global competitiveness.

TABLE 12.3

LABOR COSTS, IN US DOLLARS, FOR TEXTILE PRODUCTION IN SELECTED MIDDLE EASTERN AND AFRICAN COUNTRIES, COMPARED WITH US LABOR COSTS

Country	US Dollars per Hour	Labor Cost Increase 2000–2014
United States (3)	$18.00	25%
Israel (27)	$12.25	75%
Turkey (45)	$ 4.75	105%
Morocco (72)	$ 3.25	70%
South Africa (56)	$ 2.50	60%
Tunisia (87)	$ 2.75	90%

Source: Werner International. (2014). "A 2014 World Textile Industry Labor Cost Comparison." Retrieved November 5, 2015, from http://www.werner-newtwist.com/en/newsl-vol-011/index.htm

CASE 12.1

A GLIMPSE OF TEXTILE PRODUCTION IN NIGERIA

Cultural heritage related to Sub-Saharan textiles often describes men as weavers and women as thread spinners, using wool or other fine animal hair. Some of these traditional textiles are still being produced, but modern textile production began in the early 1950s. Kaduna Textile Mills came into being in the 1950s and Nigerian Textile Mills in the 1960s. These companies tended to be vertically integrated, starting with locally grown high-quality cotton and proceeding to weaving, dyeing, printing, and finishing. By 1995, synthetic fiber production had been added along with a wide variety of fabric types, but the industry continues to be labor intensive.

Beginning in 1990, African Textile Manufacturers LTD in Kano, Nigeria, created a specialization in production of African and wax print textiles. These products have long been favorites in traditional African culture. Now they are becoming popular for fashionable dress fabrics and are being seen on runways of upscale fashion venues around the world. This opportunity presents new challenges to producers to modify operations to deal with the global market. The World Export Development Forum was held in Rwanda in 2014 to support development of global business opportunities.

African Textile Manufacturers Ltd. (n.d.). "The Company." Retrieved November 1, 2015, from www.atmltdonline.com/aboutus.aspx

MBendi Information Services. (n.d.). "Textiles and Clothing in Nigeria: Overview." Retrieved August 31, 2015, from www.mbendi.com/indy/txtl/af/ng/p0005.htm#5

MBendi Information Services. (n.d.). "World Export Development Forum: Africa is Open for Business." Retrieved September 17, 2014, from www.mbendi.com/a_sndmsg/news_view.asp?l=155180&PG=295

1. Do you think there are markets in developed countries for these types of products? Why or why not?

2. If you answered "yes" to question 1, what will be the greatest challenges in that endeavor?

3. If you answered "no" to question 1, what are the barriers that could be the causes of failure?

Referring back again to Figure 11.2, compare China's labor cost (the major textile and apparel producer in Asia and the world) with Turkey's labor costs (the leading producer in the Middle East–Africa region). You can see that between 2000 and 2014 China had a 275 percent increase in labor cost whereas Turkey had only a 100 percent increase. Yet China's labor cost, approaching $3 an hour, still is much lower than Turkey's labor cost of $4.75 an hour. For additional comparison of wages between Asian and African countries, refer to Table 7.5. It provides another perspective because it includes minimum monthly wages. Nigeria (see Case 12.1), the most populous African country, with 173 million people, was not included in the labor cost study but it is involved in textile production.

As we discuss individual nations within the Middle East–Africa region, we explore some bilateral agreements with the EU and the United States for tariff reductions, which were put in place to help industrialize these economies. Some of these trade agreements and preference programs with the United States include the following:

- African Growth and Opportunity Act (AGOA)
- Bahrain Free Trade Agreement (FTA)
- Israel Free Trade Agreement
- Jordan Free Trade Agreement
- Morocco Free Trade Agreement
- Oman Free Trade Agreement
- Qualified Industrial Zones (QIZ) in Jordan and Egypt

The **African Growth and Opportunity Act (AGOA)**, a component of US Trade and Development with the purpose to assist SSA in achieving economic self-reliance, has gone through five updates since its inception in 2000. Under AGOA, duty-free imports of textile and apparel materials are allowed into the United States from thirty-seven African countries granted beneficiary status. In 2014, forty-one Sub-Saharan African countries were eligible for AGOA benefits (Office of the United States Trade Representative, n.d.). Of special importance to suppliers is the "third-country fabric provision" which enables apparel made in these newly developing countries to have duty-free access to the US market.

A **Qualified Industrial Zone (QIZ)** is a special area within an exporting country that grants a product manufactured in the zone duty-free access to the US market (USAID, 2006). This means that apparel produced in Egypt is subject to tariffs when it enters the US market, unless it was made in the factories located in a QIZ. Egyptian textile and apparel industries were dominated by large state-owned and -controlled enterprises throughout the 1980s, but Egypt has significantly opened up its industries to the private sector and foreign investment since that time. Tunisia and Morocco have been highly dependent on foreign investment to finance their industries, and Jordan is also heavily dependent on direct foreign investment in factories built within its QIZ areas. Some of the small entrepreneurial business activities and manufacturing startups being initiated in newly developing nations, especially in Africa, are being supplemented by financial assistance from the World Bank and the IMF. As mentioned previously, these two global institutions provide key resources to many of the poverty-stricken countries of the Middle East and Africa as well as other parts of the world.

THE MIDDLE EAST

The Middle East is a region that stretches from Turkey (46) south throughout the Arabian Peninsula and east through Iran (83). Much of the Middle East is desert. People live crowded along the sea coasts and in river and mountain valleys that have enough water to grow crops. The region is the birthplace of civilization and its history can be traced back thousands of years, and three of the world's major religions were born in this region: Islam, Christianity, and Judaism. Ongoing economic, political, and religious struggles continue between the Palestinians and Israelis. Conflicts also continue within Arab monarchies, such as Saudi Arabia, and Arab republics, such as Iraq and Syria. Other conflicts continue between people who want to keep traditional ways of life and those who want to change in order to keep up with a more secular, modern world.

When oil was discovered in several Middle Eastern countries, industrial development began, creating a great dichotomy between the rich and poor. As a result of oil exports and industrialization, most countries in the region have high per capita GDP (PPP) and are considered to be more of a market for textile and apparel products than producers. Take note of the scenario in the following paragraph, which still applies today:

> With the war in Iraq, unstable politics in Iran and the ongoing unrest in the occupied territories bordering Israel, luxury retailing may not be the first thing that comes to mind when thinking of the Middle East. However, for the six Persian Gulf states that comprise the Gulf Cooperation Council—Saudi Arabia, Kuwait, United Arab Emirates, Bahrain, Oman and Qatar—huge oil riches, relative sociopolitical stability and recent drives to modernize and diversify their economies have led to growing pools of wealthy consumers and a booming demand for status brands. (Lipke, 2007, p. 26)

The Middle East has a long and colorful history of trade in textile and apparel products, but currently is not a major player in global textile and apparel production and trade. As the countries in the region became more developed, for example UAE, they decreased involvement in textile and apparel production and export (refer to Table 12.2b). Developing countries, with the exception of Turkey, have difficulty competing with more efficient and productive Asian textile and apparel manufacturers.

Only several Middle Eastern nations made the 2013 WTO list of leading textile and apparel traders in the world market. The WTO (2014) reported that Turkey, with $12 billion, had moved up globally in textile exports, from a ranking of tenth in 2003 to seventh in 2013. At $7 billion, Turkey was also ranked seventh in textile imports in 2013. The only other country from the Middle East region included on the list of leading textile exporters and importers was the UAE. The country moved down from tenth in 2008 to fourteenth in 2013 as a textile exporter (World Trade Organization, 2014). The country was not a major textile importer in 2013.

Nations in the Middle East that achieved world rank as top exporters of apparel products in 2013 included only Turkey, at number seven, which was down from number four in 2008. Three countries were major apparel importers in 2013 (World Trade Organization, 2014):

- the UAE, with $4 billion, was number eleven, following China;
- Saudi Arabia, with $3.5 billion, was number twelve; and
- Turkey, with $3 billion, was number fourteen.

Developed Countries of the Middle East

Despite a wealth of oil in many Middle Eastern countries, only a few approach the status of developed country, based on per capita GDP. Three countries have per capita GDP

Figure 12.2
Male shoppers wearing traditional Middle Eastern and Western clothing outside Graff Diamonds Ltd., a luxury jewelry store, in one of Dubai's malls.

of more than $30,000, placing them as developed nations. The UAE, Israel, and Saudi Arabia are discussed here.

The United Arab Emirates (UAE) (12)

During the early 1970s, seven small states in the Middle East, formerly under protection of the UK, joined to form the United Arab Emirates (UAE), a country about the size of Maine, located on the edge of the Persian Gulf. The UAE's prosperity is due to oil revenues, a moderate foreign policy, and a trade surplus, which have allowed it to play a vital role in the affairs of the region. The tiny country's oil and gas reserves are expected to last another 100 years. As shown by the imports and exports of textiles and apparel in Tables 12.2a and b, firms in the UAE are importing slightly more textiles than they are exporting, indicating activity in production of apparel and/or other textile-based products. It should be noted that both textile exports and imports decreased in 2013 in comparison with 2006, pointing to a possible decline in textile and apparel manu-facturing. On the other hand, in 2013 these firms were importing more than twice as much apparel as they were exporting. They are also importing nearly five times as much as they were importing in 2000. These increases indicate a booming consumer market during this time period.

Even though the UAE is considered to have a relatively small apparel manufacturing component, it does produce some woven and knitted apparel for export. Most labor in these factories is from other countries. Because of its high per capita GDP—up from $23,200 in 2003 to $41,800 in 2009, and to $65,000 in 2014—the UAE has become a target market for upscale apparel retailers from around the globe, especially from the EU. Some have even labeled Dubai as the "Hong Kong of the Middle East" because of the strength of presence of fashion retailers from Europe and other markets, including the United States (Moin, 2004). The UAE, along with Bahrain, is a major customer of US industry in the area of fashion goods and industrial fabrics. As early as 2009, Tom Ford opened a store in Dubai, joining another he had opened earlier in Abu Dhabi, UAE. The made-to-measure suiting salon within the store is a testament to the level of the

Figure 12.3
The Kingdom Center shopping mall in Riyadh, Saudi Arabia, looks like an upscale US mall, with the only difference that by far most female shoppers are covered from head to toe in black traditional attire.

consumer experience for men in this area. European designer boutiques have thrived there (Figure 12.2).

Saudi Arabia (24)

As with UAE, most of the industrial wealth of this nation comes from oil rather than manufacturing. At the same time, Saudi Arabia is a major market for women's and children's clothing. With a relatively high overall per capita GDP of $52,800 in 2014 (up from $11,800 in 2003), the apparel market is distinctly divided between the upper, high-end consumer market and the lower-priced apparel sector. The growth in this economy is probably a solid reflection of oil prices in the late 2000s. The high-end sector is dominated by imports from Europe and the United States. Retailers from around the globe, including Gap, Banana Republic, and Cole Haan, are among US brands that have already opened stores here. H&M and Zara have entered the fast-fashion market and seem to be doing well, owing to the size of the youth market. The lower end of the market is dominated by imports from Asia and by small tailor shops.

Saudi Arabia's retail apparel sales calendar tends to follow a seasonal pattern paralleling Saudi religious holidays and summer breaks, when sales are highest. The mall in the capital city of Riyadh is a testament to Western retailing. In public, women are covered by the abaya, an everyday women's dress for outside the home that tends to be somewhat conservative. However, in private many of these consumers, especially the young and those from the higher end of the market, dress in the latest global fashions (Figure 12.3).

Israel (27)

Despite an ongoing Israeli–Palestinian conflict and limited natural resources, Israel has intensively developed its agricultural and industrial sectors over the last 25 years. It is also considered a developed country, because in 2014 its per capita GDP reached $33,400 (up from $19,800 in 2003). Substantial transfer payments and foreign loans, particularly from the United States, are major sources of economic aid. A considerable portion of Israel's population is concentrated in the metropolitan areas of Tel Aviv and Haifa. The transportation system in Israel is considered excellent, and most imported and exported goods pass through the Mediterranean Port of Haifa. As might be expected from its higher per capita GDP, Israel is home to considerable retail activity—shopping malls, specialized chain stores, and franchises.

Israel's textile and apparel industry is ongoing, despite relatively high labor costs. Israel's labor force is highly educated and trained, so high productivity rates partially offset the higher labor costs. Israel is known for its use of advanced technology and production of high-quality products. Industry is highly automated and has a reputation for offering good service and rapid turnaround of orders. However, terrorism, in the form of the ongoing intifada with the Palestinians (*intifada* is a term used to define the overt conflict between the Palestinians and Israelis), makes for an intimidating atmosphere at times. As a result, some firms have moved much of their production to more cost-competitive countries, including Jordan and Egypt, which have QIZ programs. Qualified Industrial Zones (QIZ) are areas in Jordan and Egypt that receive duty-free trade status with the United States on the condition of Israeli participation in at least part of the production process.

For example, the Israeli-based firm Bagir Group Ltd. is a maker of technologically innovative men's and women's suits that are "washable, flexible, crease resistant, stain proof and even recycled" (Bagir Group, n.d.). The company claims that one in six men in the UK own a suit made by Bagir. Its headquarters are in Kiryat Gat, close to the Gaza Strip, where conflicts often arise. The firm maintains offices there but offers "global production and vertical supply chain" with manufacturing sites in Jordan, Egypt, Turkey, Romania, China, Vietnam, and Myanmar (Burma) for a total production capacity of 4 million units (Bagir Group, n.d.).

Developing and Newly Developing Countries in the Middle East

One country in the Middle East still falls in the "developing country" category: Turkey, which in 2013 had a per capita GDP of $19,600 (up from $6,700 in 2003). Due to the country's fast economic growth in the last decade and substantially increased GDP per capita, it soon will be considered a developed economy if it continues on its current development path. Jordan is a developing nation, with a per capita GDP of $11,900 in 2013 (up from $5,300 in 2009). Each has some unique aspects to the operation of its textile and apparel industry. Syria is also a developing country in this area, with per capita GDP of $5,100 in 2013 (refer back to Table 12.1 for the status of these nations).

Turkey (45)

Turkey outclassed all other countries, except China, in developing a highly effective global textile and apparel business. Turkey is slightly larger than Texas and its western extension, including Istanbul, lies in southeastern Europe; the larger portion of the country, including the capital, Ankara, is in Asia, between the Black Sea and the Mediterranean. Because of a complex and turbulent history, Turkey reflects the influence of Greek, Roman, Byzantine, Arabic, and Turkish cultures. This predominantly Muslim country is the most Westernized of this group; women do not have to cover up their bodies and enjoy the same rights as men, especially younger generations. Some political turmoil continues as a result of cultural conflicts. Turkey has a close trade relationship with Western European countries and is negotiating admission into the EU. Turkey provides an example of the benefits of trade liberalization to developing countries.

Despite accelerating inflation, rising unemployment, labor unrest, and political violence, beginning in the mid-1980s Turkey became a successful apparel exporter, with production centralized in Istanbul; in 2001 Turkey became and remained until the time of this writing the seventh-largest apparel exporter in the world as well as the top apparel exporter to the EU. Turkey's apparel industry benefited from the country's export-led industrialization strategy and close association with the EU. A customs union, established with the EU in 1996, removed barriers to EU imports from Turkey and to Turkey's imports from the EU (Neidik, 2004).

Another key benefit to Turkey's apparel industry is a strong domestic textiles industry. Turkey, a major producer of cotton yarns and fabrics since the 1960s, is also a leading producer of wool and the third-largest mohair producer in the world. In addition, Turkey is reported to have the sixth-largest synthetic textile production capacity in the world. Because of domestic textile availability in the 1980s, Turkey became one of the few low-wage, full-package apparel vendor countries that evolved into branded manufacturing capabilities. Apparel plants became larger, with product development, cutting, sewing, and finishing in the same facility. Quality control was improved to meet the standards of moderate and better manufacturers and retailers around the world. By the end of the twentieth century, Turkey's major apparel producers were outsourcing production in Eastern European and Central Asian countries, where labor costs were lower (Neidik, 2004).

In the late 1990s, foreign direct investment, particularly from the United States and the EU, made major contributions to upgrading and specializing both textile and apparel production facilities. The two largest US jeans makers (VF Corporation and Levi Strauss & Co.) are prominently represented in their efforts to globalize their brands. VF is the largest apparel firm in the world and the maker of Lee, Wrangler, and Rustler jeans, among its many branded products.

Questions remained as to whether the Turkish textile and apparel industry would be able to sustain growth over the next decade, but, as shown in Table 12.2b, as of 2013 textile exports had increased 150 percent since 2006, and apparel exports continue to increase. Direct foreign investment has positioned Turkey for a stronger position, relative to other European countries; it can continue to be a hub for foreign brand access as Eastern Europe develops. Textile and apparel represented 46.7 percent of Turkey's overall merchandise exports in 2000 but had dropped to 18.2 percent of overall exports in 2013, even though the volume of exports had increased significantly. This reflected a general strengthening of other segments of the nation's economy.

As a reflection of the continued strength of Turkish industry, in January 2010, Li & Fung opened a new hub in Istanbul. This hub is to enable the firm to do sourcing business in Europe, the Mediterranean, the Middle East, North Africa, and the former republics of the Soviet Union. Li & Fung will serve as the interface between suppliers in Turkey and the company's worldwide customers, collaborating closely with Turkish vendors and supporting them in the fields of textile export, logistics, merchandising, and quality assurance.

In addition to its production expertise, Turkey is now seen for its potential as a retail market. For example, to broaden its worldwide business, Kenneth Cole Productions, Inc., entered a retail licensing agreement with the Park Bravo Group, the Turkey-based firm that operates Park Bravo and Park's stores and that has licensing partnerships with other brands, including Nine West, Enzo Angiolini, AK Anne Klein, and La Senza, for the Turkish market. Park Bravo will distribute and market Kenneth Cole New York men's and women's clothing, footwear, and accessories in Turkey. Jill Granoff, the chief executive officer of Kenneth Cole Productions, emphasized that "Turkey has a young, dynamic population and is one of the leading emerging markets of the world" (Karimzadeh, 2010). Trends in apparel import data support this statement, as shown in Table 12.2a. In 2000, the country imported only $2.1 billion worth of clothing, but by 2013, the number increased more than three times, to $6.8 billion.

Jordan (64)

"'Jordan is the eye of a hurricane,' says Constanzi Yaghnam, a Jordanian apparel factory owner. 'We're surrounded by turmoil, but then you have an oasis that's calm and beautiful'" (Greene, 2003, p. 10). With Israel on one side and Iraq on the other, Jordan is indeed in the center of unrest. Yet, as shown in Table 12.2b, in 2000 Jordan exported only $115 million in apparel; in six years that figure had risen ten times, to $1.25 billion. In 2013, apparel exports remained strong at $1.15 billion, despite concerns that the country might lose some apparel production to competition from Asia after removal of quotas. In 2013, Jordan's share of textile and apparel exports in the country's total merchandise exports was 15.9 percent, up from 6.1 percent in 2000, a reflection that Jordan's economy depends more on textile and apparel industries.

Jordan has a free trade agreement with the United States that came into effect in 2001. Under the US–Jordan FTA, at least 35 percent of apparel value has to be added in Jordan to qualify for duty-free access to the US market. Much of the impetus for growth in CMT activities came in the QIZs, in collaboration with Israel, since 1996. The Jordan–Israel trade zone combined the production activities of two nations of rather dissimilar development levels in a trade scenario with the United States. In addition to the US–Jordan Free Trade Agreement and the QIZ program, Jordan has free trade agreements with the EU, the Greater Arab Free Trade Area, Morocco, Turkey, Singapore, and Canada.

Most of the factories in the QIZ zones have been built with foreign investment funds from countries such as Hong Kong, Israel, and South Korea, and the management and production expertise needed to initiate production is sent from the originating country. Jordan also has had to import workers from Bangladesh, India, and Sri Lanka to function at the line management level. With Jordan's total population of 7.9 million and only 2 million in the labor force, there are not enough workers for labor-intensive apparel manufacturing. In 2012, Jordan's textile and apparel industries employed 60,000 workers, two-thirds of whom were guest workers from Asian countries (Thomasson, 2012).

Shipping times from Jordan to the United States are better than from many Asian countries. Jordan has low overall manufacturing costs because of low wages, no income tax, and inexpensive rent and electricity. Persistent problems with adequate water supply prevent the development of a textile industry, but Jordan is close to regional fabric suppliers, such as Egypt, Turkey, Israel, and Pakistan. The Jordanian apparel industry therefore depends on importing components for apparel production, from fabrics to trims to packaging. Factories operate on a CMT basis and are not capable of providing full-package services such as patternmaking, grading, and sample-making (Madson, 2015).

Jordan believed that its firm stance on ethical employment and human rights issues would hold it in good stead. "These are not sweatshops.. . .They're fully equipped garment manufacturing facilities, and they have very strict requirements regarding human rights standards" (Greene, 2003, p. 10). Unfortunately, some rather grievous labor issues surfaced at a few of the plants within the QIZ zones, especially related to migrant workers from outside of Jordan, and it has since been working diligently to correct these problems.

In October 2009, officials from the US trade representative's office, the US Labor Department, and the US State Department convened a meeting in Jordan with the labor subcommittee of the US–Jordan Free Trade Agreement to discuss labor issues, including alleged child labor, forced labor, trafficking of migrant workers from Asia, and enforcement of the rules written into existing agreements. Representatives visited garment factories in the QIZ zone to observe and assess local working conditions (Casabona, 2009). It is believed that many of the labor abuses can be attributed to a combination of factors, including heavy dependence on migrant labor and rapid expansion of foreign-owned factories within the QIZ zone. The sector simply became a magnet for these problems as firms overreached in their quest to complete more orders. To improve workers' conditions, in 2013 Jordan's Ministry of Labor raised the minimum wage from 150 Jordanian dinars (US $211) per month to 190 Jordanian dinars (US $267) per month.

NORTH AFRICA

On a continent with many contrasts in culture and level of development, North African nations benefit from close proximity, across the Mediterranean Sea, to the developed countries of Europe. We are limiting our discussion of this sector to the developing countries of Tunisia, with $11,400 per capita GDP; Egypt, with $11,100 per capita GDP; and Morocco, with $7,700 per capita GDP.

Tunisia (87)

Tunisia went through a 30-year period with a one-party political system in which the president repressed Islamic fundamentalism and established rights for women unmatched by any other Arab nation. Tunisia had a diverse economy and, over the past decade, the government moved toward increasing privatization. The result has been growth in GDP at a faster rate than most other African nations (Central Intelligence Agency, 2015). Tunisia's secular system of government means there is a greater openness toward Western ways of doing business than in many other countries in the region. Arabic is the primary language. Tunisia has been a WTO member since its inception. Tunisia was the country where the Arab Spring, an uprising against totalitarian regimes in Middle Eastern countries, originated in early 2011, which resulted in new leadership for the country.

Tunisian imports of textiles have been continually growing since 2000, when the country imported $1.2 billion. The value of textile imports increased to $1.7 billion in 2013. This activity indicates that fabrics are being imported into the country to manufacture apparel and other textile-based products. Apparel imports have remained relatively low and stable in the twenty-first century, around $500,000. However, some of these apparel imports are likely to be for re-export. Tunisia built its apparel export market on its outward processing trade with the EU, where companies in developed countries export fabrics or parts of garments to Tunisia, then reimport them as fully formed garments, similar to the US Item 807 system.

The textile and apparel industry used to be a more prominent contributor to Tunisia's economy, accounting for 40.7 percent of the country's total industrial goods exports in 2000, but it dropped significantly to 18.8 percent in 2013 (refer back to Table 12.2b). The value of apparel exports has decreased slightly from $3 billion in 2006 to $2.8 billion in 2013. Textile exports have been relatively small, at $413 million in 2013. This indicates that other changes were occurring in the economy to decrease the dependence on this industry and increase overall exports.

Tunisia's major customers were historically France, Italy, Germany, Algeria, Belgium, and the United States (Textile and Clothing in Tunisia, n.d.). However, it became very hard to compete with Asian countries such as Bangladesh or Pakistan, for example, whose labor costs of $0.62 an hour are only a fraction of the Tunisian labor cost of $2.75, which is also higher than the labor cost in China (see Figure 11.2). Tunisia was looking for ways to safeguard its industry from Asian competition; the apparel industry provided 210,000 jobs in more than 2,000 companies in 2011, with the majority of businesses being small- and medium-sized (Textile and Clothing in Tunisia, n.d.). Almost half of all textile and apparel businesses have foreign direct investments, and more than 1,600 companies produce apparel entirely for export markets. Overall, the textile and apparel sector contributes 46 percent of all manufacturing jobs in the country.

The industry embraced newer technology, such as computer-aided design (CAD), computer-aided manufacturing (CAM), and computer-integrated manufacturing (CIM), to reduce costs per unit, and developed quick response (QR) strategies, including just-in-time (JIT) methods. Major exported apparel product categories include jeans, women's underwear, and work wear. One of Tunisia's largest employers is the denim wear maker Sartex, based in Tunis. The company has advanced manufacturing technologies and a testing lab to complete various product certifications. This firm had 3,000 workers in the middle of the first decade of the twenty-first century, and customers included Marc Jacobs, Hugo Boss, Ralph Lauren, and Levi Strauss & Co. (Textile and Clothing in Tunisia, n.d.).

Proximity to Europe allows for a quick shipping time, with truck delivery being the fastest, most preferred, and reliable method. Delivery time takes no more than 7 to 10 days anywhere in Europe (Textile and Clothing in Tunisia, n.d.). Tunisia has many trade agreements with its neighboring nations and is a driving force in the Union of Arab Maghred (UAM), which aims to strengthen cooperation among Algeria, Morocco, Tunisia, Libya, and Mauritania. Broader privatization and further liberalization of foreign investment are among the challenges for the future.

Egypt (119)

The regular flooding of the Nile River, providing fertilizer and water to the region, and the semi-isolation created by surrounding deserts set a scene for the development of one of the world's greatest civilizations. Over nearly 2,000 years, Egypt was repeatedly overrun and seized by legions of jealous neighbors, including Greeks, Romans, Byzantines, and Arabs. It was not until after World War II that Egypt acquired full sovereignty. The government has struggled since then because of a rapidly growing population and overtaxed resources. Lack of substantial progress on economic reform limited foreign direct investment in Egypt and limited growth of GDP, until recently. As a result of the 2011 Arab Spring, also known as the Egypt Revolution, there was a temporary setback in economic activity in the country; however, the textile and apparel industries recovered quickly as the country moved on the path of democratic development. The Egyptian per person GDP increased from $4,000 in 2003 to $11,100 in 2013. Review the country's other economic indicators in Table 12.1.

Egypt is the producer of the finest long-staple cotton in the world. The textile complex includes the full spectrum of cotton processing operations, including spinning, weaving, converting, knitting, and garment manufacture. It also has some linen production from domestic flax crops. The textile and apparel industry continues to be a major employer in the country; however, the sector's contribution to the nation's total merchandise export has decreased from 24 percent in 2000 to only 10 percent in 2013. This indicates that the Egyptian economy has been diversifying and depends less on textile and apparel production. From 2000 to 2013, as shown in Tables 12.2a and b, Egypt more than tripled its textile exports from $412 million per year to $1.5 billion per year. The country's textile imports increased at an even greater rate, from $526 million in 2000 to $2.4 billion in 2013, indicating that the country required more fabric for apparel production than it was able to produce itself. During this same period, apparel exports almost doubled, from $710 million to $1.4 billion. The textile and apparel industry employs almost half a million workers, accounting for 25 percent of the country's manufacturing employment (Apparel.com, 2014).

Since 2008, seven QIZs were created in Egypt to provide duty-free access to the US market if textile and apparel products included some Israeli content (Apparel.com, 2014). This forced Egypt and Israel to work together, similar to the Jordanian QIZ agreement with the United States. The provision established free trade areas in Cairo, Alexandria, and the Suez Canal zone. Egypt and Israel began shipping cotton underwear, knit shirts, and pants to the United States duty free through this arrangement. Hardliners in Cairo complained that they had to work with Israel but seemed to accept the plan as they saw Egyptian exports and incomes increase. A unique aspect of Egypt's involvement is that a 10 percent cap was placed on foreign workers to ensure that Egyptians would benefit from the creation of new jobs (Tucker, 2008). This strategy helped Egypt avoid the types of labor abuses that were alleged at factories in Jordan, which has a similar QIZ trade agreement but relied more on foreign workers. One impediment to continued growth in these production facilities has been the lack of skilled local labor. In 2015, textile authorities from Egypt and Israel announced a plan to double duty-free exports to the US market within three years and reach the $2 billion mark (Textile Industry Portal, 2015).

In 2014, QIZs had 260 apparel companies, some of which were vertically integrated (Apparel.com, 2014). Manufacturing facilities were capable of providing full-package services and delivering high-quality garments at a relatively low labor cost. Another advantage of apparel producers in Egypt is their ability to deal with complex designs and provide safe labor conditions. The combination of these factors attracted many Western brands to source apparel manufacturing in these QIZs, including Aeropostale, Calvin Klein, Disney, Gap, Hanes, JCPenney, Macy's, Nautica, Timberland, and Zara. It appeared that operational efficiency and record-keeping capabilities to meet the needs of US clients were at issue, and the government established teams to work with smaller factories to help them get up to speed.

By 2008, medium- to large-scale companies dominated the industry, with a strong public sector in spinning and weaving (Just-style.com, 2009). The textile sector had been lagging behind in application of new technology; however, the latest technologies—CAD, electronic data interchange (EDI), supply chain management (SCM), and

TABLE 12.4

ARAFA HOLDING SUPPLY CHAINS FOR ITS THREE MAJOR DIVISIONS

Product Line	Textiles	Apparel and Tailoring	Retail and Distribution
Luxury	(sourced)	ETC (Egypt Tailoring Co.)	Pal Zileri, Forall Ermenegildo Zegna
Formal	Golden Tex	SGC (Swiss Garments Co.)	Egypt and Portugal BMB Group Limited
Casual	(sourced)	SGC Crystal	United States

Source: Arafa Holding. (n.d.). "Corporate Overview." Retrieved June 18, 2015, from https://s3.amazonaws.com/inktankir/base/s3/ecc77e95d4823c94b5d7513f27702e25.pdf

product data management (PDM)—were adopted for apparel production, including patternmaking, spreading, cutting, sewing, and packaging. They produce a complete range of apparel products from simple T-shirts to tailored suits.

In 2015, a leading global textile and clothing manufacturer and retailer, Arafa Holding, based in Egypt, announced expansion plans to European markets. The company, which already has a presence in seventy countries around the world, will be targeting German, French, Portuguese, Turkish, and Spanish retail markets (Ayyad, 2015). Table 12.4 illustrates the company's structure, supply chain, and value creation model. Reading the table going down shows its three major divisions: luxury, formal, and casual wear as well as the brand names of each. Reading the table across shows involvement from textile manufacturing through retail distribution (Arafa Holding, n.d.). To support an expansion in domestic textile and apparel production capacity, Arafa Holding plans to penetrate the European retail sector through establishing joint ventures as well as strategic acquisitions.

There has been an influx of multinational retailers into Egypt in recent years, as its large population of 87 million provides a considerable retail market, even though the overall per person GDP is within the level of a developing country. City Center Alexandria opened in 2003 and has long been home to one of the largest shopping malls in the Middle East–North Africa region (*Retailing in Egypt,* 2004). It continues to be a primary stop for both local shoppers and tourists.

Morocco (72)

With per capita GDP of $7,700, Morocco is considered a developing nation. Since winning its independence in the mid-1950s, the Kingdom of Morocco has endorsed a vigorous program to promote foreign investment in order to develop a strong textile and apparel industry. Despite programs supported by IMF and the World Bank, only modest gains have been made.

In the twentieth century, the garment industry became one of the country's crucial industrial sectors, fundamental in maintaining the economic balance of the kingdom. In 2013, Morocco imported almost seven times more textiles than it exported, and exported nine times more apparel than it imported (refer back to Tables 12.2a and b). Apparel exports decreased slightly in 2013, to $3.1 billion, in comparison with $3.2 billion in 2006. At $361 million, textile exports remain quite low. Textile imports have been on the rise since 2000 and reached $2.5 billion in 2013, indicating growing apparel production for the domestic market.

Textile and apparel factories are considered essential for employment in the country, providing jobs for more than 60 percent of employed women in the early 2000s. Yet with the country's total labor force at 12 million, Morocco is not a major player in global apparel manufacturing. The country's dependence on textile and apparel exports has decreased by more than half since 2000, to 16 percent in 2013, and so reliance on this avenue of employment and revenues has been decreasing.

Morocco also has a long tradition of production of leather and accessories. Most methods of tanning and dyeing of skins use natural materials and/or sustainable processes (Figure 12.4). The Moroccan apparel industry is also known for production of denim; the cities in which most industry activity occurs are Marrakech and Casablanca. Their proximity to the EU bodes well for maintaining some market share. The most commonly mentioned impediments to the industry include limited diversification of products, underdeveloped yarn and fabric sectors, the high price of energy, and dependence primarily on European markets, including Spain (49 percent of the total Moroccan apparel exports), France (27 percent of the total exports), the UK, and Italy (Maroc Export, 2014). Based on the apparel exports trends, the industry was able to maintain its share of the market after quota removal, despite higher labor costs in comparison with producing countries in Asia. Morocco instituted new trade agreements in an attempt to maintain industry competitiveness.

Among those agreements was the US–Morocco Free Trade Agreement, which entered into force on January 1, 2006 (Export.gov, n.d.). It was anticipated that this agreement would open up Morocco's economy to greater exports to the United States. Because of the agreement, 95 percent of the US consumer and industrial goods exported to Morocco no longer pay a tariff and tariffs on all US exports to Morocco will be phased out by 2024. The Moroccan economy has been steadily improving at an increasing rate over the last 10 years from $481 million to nearly $2 billion, including a substantial portion of textile- and apparel-related exports (Export.gov, n.d.).

In 2013, the Moroccan textile and apparel industry employed 174,000 people, contributing to 30 percent of the country's manufacturing employment and 6 percent of the national GDP (Maroc Export, 2014). The industry consisted of 1,200

Figure 12.4
Traditional leather processing and dyeing in Morocco has not changed much for centuries.

companies with a total production capacity of 1 billion garments a year. Major strategies employed by the industry to remain competitive included:

- investments in expertise and skill development, with a goal to educate 2,000 engineers and 30,000 operators by the end of 2015, and
- adopting the "Fiber Citizen" program to further advance the industry's ethical and sustainable practices. (Maroc Export, 2014)

SUB-SAHARAN AFRICA (SSA)

There are forty-nine nations involved in the Sub-Saharan Africa (SSA) geographic sector, many of them among the most economically disadvantaged nations in the world (Williams, 2015). Review Table 12.1 for selected SSA countries' economic and human capital indicators. Only two countries have per capita GDP greater than $10,000: Mauritius (39) and South Africa (56). Note the lowest life expectancy (as low as 52 years for Nigeria and Lesotho) and literacy rates (49 percent for Ethiopia and 59 percent for Nigeria) as compared to the other regions of the world discussed in Chapters 9, 10, and 11.

Unfortunately, SSA has been affected the most by one of the world's worst health pandemics: HIV/AIDS. According to United Nations AIDS Programme, in 2013 out of 35 million people living with AIDS/HIV worldwide, SSA accounted for 24.7 million, or 70 percent. Besides being a major humanitarian issue, the AIDS/HIV pandemic has a detrimental effect on SSA industries and economic development. For example, a manager of a leading South African producer of men's tailored wear commented that the company's major problem has been constant rotation of sewing machine operators, who are unable to continue working because of AIDS (Karpova, 2009). As a result, the company has to constantly hire and train new workers, which greatly reduces productivity and quality as well as adds to the overhead costs of training.

In the late twentieth century and early twenty-first century, a few SSA countries had worked on developing export-oriented apparel industries with the goal of industrialization, providing employment, and generating revenues. With the help of foreign direct investments, Mauritius (39), Kenya (90), Lesotho (107), and Madagascar (130) have been the most successful (Farole & Winkler, 2014). As a result, SSA apparel exports increased from $1.3 billion in 1997 to $3.2 billion in 2004. The growth, however, was not significant on the global scale: SSA exports accounted for only 1.3 percent of the world's total apparel exports in 2004.

After the removal of the MFA quota in 2005, SSA apparel industries have been experiencing declines in employment, number of companies, production, and exports (Farole & Winkler, 2014). SSA apparel exports were further hurt as a result of the global economic crisis in 2008–2009. Because of decreased apparel demand in SSA's major destination markets, the United States and European Union, apparel exports from the region declined by 19 percent in 2008 and 10 percent in 2009. In 2010, the regional market share in the world's apparel exports was only 0.6 percent, indicating an inability of new African industries to compete with Asian producers, and specifically, China. Based on exports, with the exception of Mauritius (39), South Africa (56), and Lesotho (107), there is little textile and apparel activity in Sub-Saharan Africa. Most of the area's factory ownership and management are controlled by foreign interests, and much of that investment is from Asia. With respect to apparel manufacturing, SSA countries tend to focus on longer production runs of basic products, such as trousers, T-shirts, and woven shirts.

The SSA area has higher costs to produce cotton yarn and fabrics than do China, India, and other Asian nations, such as Vietnam and Bangladesh. For this reason, SSA lost market share when the quota system expired. It was estimated that Uganda alone showed a reduction in shipments of 68 percent from 2006 to 2008 (Just-style.com, 2010). When compared with Asia, there also were concerns about the lack of variety of fabrics that could be produced. Because fashion dictates the types of fabrics used, these factors seem to put the region at an additional disadvantage over other trading regions.

One of the primary agricultural exports from nations in SSA is cotton. The cotton-growing region stretches from Côte d'Ivoire eastward through Chad. Especially fine-quality cotton comes from the area near Lake Victoria, in Uganda. After the market crash in the early 2000s, cotton production has been bouncing back at a double-digit percentage per year. Burkina Faso, the leading cotton-growing country in the region, produces nearly 800,000 tons per annum (Coulibaly, 2014). Other countries in the region—Mali, Ivory Coast, Benin, Cameron, and Senegal—experience similar growth in cotton production. Privatization of textile companies increased and enabled extension of production facilities, yet only a small portion of local cotton is processed into yarn and fabric in the region. In recent years, Ghana (111) and Nigeria (127), located on the Atlantic Rim, have developed some textile manufacturing and are producing both fashion and uniform fabrics. Unfortunately, these countries have been plagued by counterfeit apparel from China, causing layoffs of hundreds of workers in Nigeria (McGregor, 2015). Another practice that is prevalent in SSA countries is the import and distribution of used apparel products that provide competition for domestically produced goods.

East African Community

SSA countries had received trade benefits from the EU under the Cotonou Agreement, which provided duty-free and quota-free access for textiles and apparel from Africa, the Caribbean, and some Pacific countries. This agreement was initiated in 2000 and subsequently renewed until 2020. It is described as the most comprehensive partnership agreement between developing countries and the EU. It provides a framework for the EU's relations with seventy-nine countries from Africa, the Caribbean, and the Pacific (ACP). Its intent was to establish a comprehensive partnership with three goals: development cooperation, political cooperation, and economic and trade cooperation with a focus on institutions, integration, and infrastructure. According to Kimenyi and Kibe (2014):

> One of the regions in Africa that is making remarkable progress in all these "I's" [institutions, integration, and infrastructure] is the East African Community [EAC]. The EAC's original members—Kenya, Uganda, and Tanzania— have recently been joined by Rwanda and Burundi. South Sudan is expected to join the community soon. The region has fast-tracked regional integration and has seen considerable progress in institutional reforms. Moreover, East Africa boasts much greater political stability than it has at any time in its recent past and peace has been restored in most of the countries. The region has seen major investments in both national and regional infrastructure. On Nov. 28, for example, President Uhuru Kenyatta of Kenya inaugurated the commencement of construction of a rail project that will link Kenya's coast town of Mombasa

AFRICA IS EMERGING AS AN APPAREL SOURCING OPPORTUNITY

China's financial problems became national news in 2015. China's labor costs were rising while the value of its currency was declining. Consequently, apparel sourcing agents began to seriously search the rest of the world for apparel production opportunities. Africa has become an interesting possibility; there are many opportunities and challenges.

Opportunities include access to African textile materials and production resources as well as retail markets. Some regions are very poor and others are very rich, but all are part of a rapidly growing population. It has also become fashionable to recognize Africa as a fascinating place that has much to offer for business and travel opportunities (Russell, 2014). *Challenges* include barriers in communication, poor infrastructure, and slow border crossing processes. Many countries within Africa are charged with not having a "fast-paced business culture." Complicated timing systems drive the operation of global companies, thus there is a sense of urgency that is built into the operation of global markets. Also, nearly 100 different languages are spoken in Africa; seventeen of those languages are regarded as "commonly spoken." Until recently, there has been little incentive to attempt to create some sort of an agreement to establish what languages should be available for interaction with foreign business opportunities, but that scenario is starting to change.

Ethiopia is now seeking a spot on the apparel stage. "Ethiopia wants to attract foreign direct investment (FDI) in three industries in particular: the textile/apparel industry is the priority for national development, followed by the leather industry and finally the food processing industry" (Mehta, 2014). Advantages for companies investing in the apparel/textile sector include both the availability and low cost of raw materials and labor, as well as the emphasis the sector places on high-quality manufacturing as the key to remaining competitive in international markets. These factors, coupled with attractive incentive packages for foreign investors, are attracting increasing numbers of textile and apparel companies.

Mehta, M. (December 1, 2014). "The New Kid on the Block: Africa Is Vying for a Larger Share of the Global Textile and Apparel Pie." Retrieved November 3, 2015, from http://apparel.edgl.com/news/The-New-Kid-on-the-Block—Africa-Is-Vying-for-a-Larger-Share-of-the-Global-Textile-and-Apparel-Pie96802

Russell, M. (March 25, 2014). "Analysis: Is Africa the Next Frontier in Apparel Sourcing?" Retrieved November 3, 2015, from http://www.just-style.com/analysis/is-africa-the-next-frontier-in-apparel-sourcing_id120902.aspx

1. What are the primary challenges Ethiopia is trying to overcome?
2. In what ways might AGOA provide assistance for Ethiopia's apparel industry development?

to Kampala (Uganda), Kigali (Rwanda), and Juba (South Sudan). With positive growth trajectory predicted over the medium term, the EAC has a good chance of reaching a developmental tipping point.

Ethiopia (118) on the eastern edge is also making the news with opportunities related to apparel. See Case 12.2.

Kenya (90) and the Role of Cotton in the SSA

Kenya's economy is currently the largest in the region and much more dynamic than other East African countries. It has a more advanced human capital base and a diversified economy. It has adopted a new constitution with a devolved government that involves granting powers at the regional and local levels. Kenya has been the regional hub for trade and finance in East Africa, but it was hampered by corruption in its judicial system, resulting in cancellation of support from the IMF in 1997. IMF support resumed in 2000, but so did corruption. With a per capita GDP of $3,100, Kenya remains predominantly an agrarian society with a large incidence of HIV/AIDS that has affected the availability of trained labor. Being a newly developing economy, Kenya lacks the strong import/export infrastructure found in other apparel producing countries, making the movement of goods a challenge. This results in slow movement of imported fabric and trims from the port to the garment factories and finished goods back to the port for export. A possible solution might be to allow extra production lead time. This might be acceptable for basic apparel goods, but not for all retailers and brands in the business of fashion apparel products (Madson, 2015).

Following implementation of AGOA, in 2000, Kenya began to attract some foreign direct investment in apparel production for export. Fabric imports increased from $47 million in 2000 to $346 million in 2013 to support apparel manufacturing (refer to Table 12.2a). Industry utilized the third-party fabric provision from AGOA that enabled it to seek lower-cost fabrics from Asia. Some apparel factories that had closed in the 1990s reopened. As a result, apparel exports from Kenya increased *thirty* times, from only $9 million in 2000 to $279 million in 2013. These numbers are small when compared with many powerhouse producers but are much needed in this developing economy. By far the majority of Kenya's apparel companies have not yet upgraded to full-package or full-service facilities and instead work on a CMT basis (Madson, 2015; refer to Chapter 8 for discussion).

Kenya's previously active cotton-processing industry deteriorated in the 1990s to the point that it almost collapsed from a combination of bad weather and competition from foreign suppliers. There was rising unemployment during that time, causing considerable civil unrest. There was also an influx of imported used clothing for domestic use that further hampered Kenyan cotton, textile, and apparel production. As a result Kenya became a marginal performer in the cotton market. The decrease in production was blamed on inferior farming techniques, substandard seeds, and pests contaminating the plants in the field. It is hoped that introduction of pest-resistant cotton varieties from the United Nations will lead to Kenya's return to the international cotton market. But in 2014, Kenya produced only 32,000 bales, whereas its neighbor Tanzania produced 375,000 bales (Statista, n.d.).

Mauritius and South Africa are among the economically strong SSA countries, with per capita GDPs of $17,900 and $12,900, respectively (see Table 12.1 for a comparison). As with other countries developing to this level in other parts of the world, the textile and apparel industries are being threatened by production opportunities in lower-wage countries.

Mauritius (39)

The small island of Mauritius is located in the southern Indian Ocean off the southeast coast of Africa to the east of Madagascar, and has a population of 1.3 million. It seems at first an unlikely spot to discover an export-oriented apparel industry. Historically, the island had been a port of call for ships on the East Indies trade route as far back as the 1590s. A stable democracy, with regular free elections and a positive human rights record, contributed to Mauritius's rank as SSA's largest apparel producer.

Mauritius had been a large center for apparel production for some time, but political setbacks created difficulties for the tiny nation in 2001 and 2002. These setbacks caused a drop in overall economic conditions, and the United States reclassified the nation as "least developed," qualifying it for full eligibility in trade breaks through the provisions of AGOA. Previously, the per person GDP was just high enough to make

Mauritius ineligible for those incentives. This island nation has lost thousands of jobs in recent years as customers have moved their production needs to less-developed nations. According to Tables 12.2a and b, since 2000 textile imports into Mauritius have declined and apparel exports have also declined. Consequently, the country's dependence on apparel exports has increased. In 2000, 66 percent of export revenues came from textiles and apparel. In 2013, the number was 30 percent, suggesting an increasing health in the economy because of more diversity in the economy.

South Africa (56)

After South Africa gained independence from the British in 1902, it continued to operate under a policy of segregation and economic discrimination against the country's nonwhite majority, which is known as apartheid. **Apartheid** is the state of being separate, a policy of strict racial segregation and political and economic discrimination against nonwhites. The result of the 1948 election was extension of apartheid, and the existing racial segregation became institutionalized. It wasn't until the 1990s that South Africa finally saw the end of apartheid and the establishment of black majority rule. South Africa has eleven official national languages, reflecting its diverse cultural and ethnic background. By the twenty-first century, South Africa had the most advanced transportation, telecommunications, and utilities infrastructure in SSA (US International Trade Commission, 2004).

By world standards, South Africa is a middle-income country. As shown in Table 12.1, per capita GDP in 2013 was $12,900. South Africa has an abundant supply of natural resources and a population of 48 million people. However, growth has not been strong enough to reduce South Africa's high unemployment and poverty rates that remain from the apartheid era. In 2014, the unemployment rate in South Africa was 25.5 percent (Figure 12.5). The biggest recent job losses were in the manufacturing and agriculture industries (Steyn, 2014). Part of the problem is illegal immigrants, who

Figure 12.5
Unemployed men sit by the road in the township of Tshepisong, South Africa. High unemployment contributes to escalating crime rates in the country.

come from poor neighboring countries, such as Zimbabwe, Mozambique, and others, in search of job opportunities.

In the 1990s, when international antiapartheid trade sanctions were lifted, the textile and apparel business in South Africa underwent restructuring. There was an active industry, but most production was for domestic use, causing a trade deficit in textiles and apparel. The government encouraged foreign direct investment, but investors were torn between lower wages in other SSA nations and the developed export infrastructure and skilled labor found in South Africa. By 2004, South Africa produced cotton and man-made fibers, exported surplus wool, and claimed to be the world's leading producer of mohair. The country also produced short-staple cotton (lower in quality than that produced in Egypt) and relied on imports from Zimbabwe, Zambia, and Mozambique to meet its long-staple cotton requirements. South Africa is the only SSA nation producing synthetic filament yarn, a highly capital-intensive industry.

South Africa has thriving and diverse textile, apparel, and retail industries. Because of relatively high labor costs in comparison with most Asian and African apparel producing countries (refer to Figure 11.2 and Table 7.5), larger mass-market apparel companies in South Africa have been outsourcing apparel assembly instead of manufacturing the product domestically. As a result, employment in textile and apparel industries has been slowly declining, with companies closing apparel factories as early as 2010. The trend is also notable in increasing apparel imports, which in 2013 were almost four times larger than apparel exports (refer back to Tables 12.2a and b). In 2013, South African apparel exports were $1.9 billion, up from only $223 million in 2000. Textile imports also increased significantly during the same period, from $570 million in 2000 to $1.4 billion in 2013. Export of textiles and apparel is less than 1 percent of overall trade.

Because South Africa is on the path to being a developed economy, the country's apparel and retail industry represents an interesting mix of companies that successfully utilize US and European business models (focus on managing and developing brands, experiential retailing, supply chain management, fast fashion, etc.) while still having a number of small traditional businesses, primarily in rural areas. Trubok, established in 1933, is "Africa's top supplier of quality, on-trend fashion, offering value for money, impeccable design and styling, manufacturing excellence and superior customer service" (Trubok, n.d.). The company focuses on developing its own brands for specific lifestyle target markets, such as Kazzi (for "the sassy city customer who works hard and plays hard and likes to make a statement, while emanating cutting-edge influence and timeless style"), Lancetti (for "the young, techno-savvy, urban mover-and-shaker who likes to stand out from the crowd"), Jean Pierre (for "an established man of the world"), and others.

An example of a young, thriving small business is Design Team, a company owned by two female entrepreneurs who design and screen print small runs of unique African-inspired fabrics for interior and apparel design. Originally the company started designing and printing exclusive fabrics for upholstery, curtains, bedding, and pillows at high-end South African hotels and resorts. As their business grew, they hired more employees and expanded the product line designs to wallpaper and apparel and adopted digital technology. The company's website features twenty-one themed collections of fabrics in various colorways.

At the same time, rural areas of South Africa have traditional tailoring shops that offer various services, from custom-made traditional African clothing to alterations to

making curtains and other textile-based home goods. As shown in Figure 12.6, these businesses are typically quite primitive, use simple home sewing machines, and often are a one-person business who takes apprentices to learn the trade. Women business owners are skilled in sewing but lack the knowledge and resources to grow and differentiate product and service offerings and take them beyond the local market. While these businesses appear to be profitable, they are not thriving.

Similar to the differences in the types of apparel businesses in the country, the retail market of South Africa is deeply divided between those of better economic

means and those who are very poor. The divide between rich and poor in South Africa is literal: all houses and apartment buildings are behind high walls topped with electrified chicken wires, and all malls, universities, hospitals, and other public buildings are gated, with guards on duty. An exception might be primitive housing, often erected illegally, that still is likely to have fencing (Figure 12.7). These unlawful settlements are typically formed by illegal immigrants. Keep in mind that South Africa is one of the wealthiest and more developed countries on the continent. The lifestyle of the majority of the population is even more undeveloped in the majority of SSA nations.

Woolworths is another South African retailer (different from the US Woolworth's), founded in Cape Town in 1931, and now has hundreds of stores in South Africa and franchise partners throughout Africa and the Middle East. The company has made considerable efforts toward sustainability in recent years and was the first South African retailer to sponsor organically grown cotton.

In the sustainability world, the concept of a **zero-waste supply chain** is one that completely reuses, recycles, or composts all materials. This concept is sometimes referred to as a corporate take-back program, where companies that produce a good are also responsible for its disposal (Dictionary of Sustainable Management, 2015). South Africa is the home of an effort to make textile materials that can provide a zero-waste supply chain, and Case 12.3 explores how it could be possible to have a zero-waste textile supply chain.

Lesotho (107)

Lesotho is a small, newly developing, landlocked nation surrounded by South Africa, with a population of 1.9 million people. One of Lesotho's greatest plights in recent history is the prevalence of HIV/AIDS. In 2008, it was estimated that 23.2 percent of the adult population of Lesotho was infected, and 18,000 deaths were attributed to the

Figure 12.8
Big Blue's store, a South African lifestyle retailer.

SOUTH AFRICA PROJECT TO GROW GRASS FOR RECYCLABLE TEXTILES

An initiative was launched in 2015 in South Africa to grow a new type of grass that can be used to create zero-waste recyclable textiles. The project has been initiated by sustainable textile and fashion company, Dutch aWEARness, which specializes in the *closed loop supply chain*.

The new Miscanthus (elephant grass) developed by the University of Wageningen in the Netherlands contains a high amount of cellulose, which can be used to create viscose rayon—a sustainable alternative to natural materials for textiles. After use, it can be converted back to cellulose and made into viscose rayon again. The material is said to have a very limited impact on the environment, is easy to grow in a variety of climates, and can be recycled over and over again.

The "Grass for Sustainable Growth" will kick off in Johannesburg, South Africa, next month [March 2015], with the planting of 1,500 hectares of Miscanthus in South Africa's Easter Cape. The project fits within the "Black Economic Empowerment" initiative of the South African government and is supported by the Dutch Ministry of Economic Affairs.

The INGCA consortium—comprising Dutch aWEARness and the South African companies Ekcon and AlternaFruit—is behind the planting, and provides additional employment and good working conditions for local farmers. The profits are entirely reinvested in the region. Dr. Precious Mioloy-Motsepe, chairman of African Fashion International, will be invited to become the ambassador of the project.

Note: A number of projects are now in progress in the United States and other countries evaluating the potential for using Miscanthus not only for endless supply chains for textiles but also as a source for energy.

Barrie, L. (February 25, 2015). "South Africa Project to Grow Grass for Recyclable Textiles." Retrieved November 3, 2015, from http://www.just-style.com/news/south-africa-project-to-grow-grass-for-recyclable-textiles_id124476.aspx. Copyright 2015. All content copyright just-style.com.

1. Why might the concept of "endless" or "closed loop" supply chains become an essential component of the textile and apparel industry (and many other industries) in the near future?
2. What kind of fundamental changes might manufacturers and retailers have to make in their production and promotion processes to support endless or closed loop supply chains?
3. How might the priorities of textiles and apparel consumers have to change so they can endorse endless or closed loop supply chains?

---

disease (UNAids.org, 2008). Because of AIDS and other issues inherent to poverty, the average life expectancy was just 52.7 years in 2013 (refer back to Tables 12.2 a and b for more current data).

Lesotho grows jute and manufactures jute products including yarn, twine, rope, webbing, bags for packaging grain, and carpet backing, and also produces mohair fibers. Of greater importance is the country's apparel assembly sector. From almost nothing a few years previous, Lesotho exported $234 million of textile and apparel products in 2001, representing 94 percent of the nation's total merchandise exports that year (US International Trade Commission, 2004). In 2001, per capita GDP was just $558, yet by 2004, it was estimated at $3,000, even with an unemployment rate of 45 percent (Central Intelligence Agency, 2004). Unfortunately, things have deteriorated in recent years, owing to competition from Asia and the global economic downturn. In 2014 the per person GDP was $2,900 and the unemployment rate was down to 28 percent (refer back to Table 12.1).

In 2008, Lesotho was the largest AGOA apparel supplier to the United States. In 2014, Kenya had replaced it as the largest AGOA supplier of apparel, with $379 million of apparel exports. Lesotho was the second-largest AGOA importer of apparel to the US market, with $290 million (Williams, 2015). In 2013, Lesotho's textile and apparel imports as well as textile exports were too small to report (refer to Tables 12.2a and b).

Apparel exports were down from $478 million in 2006 to $418 million in 2013. The country's reliance on apparel exports (and the apparel industry) decreased from 73 percent in 2000 to 49 percent in 2013, indicating Lesotho's industrial diversification into other manufacturing sectors.

The ready-to-wear apparel industry in Lesotho is entirely foreign-owned (Farole & Winkler, 2014). In 2013, the industry consisted of thirty-one apparel firms (thirty-seven plants). The country had only one textile mill, also foreign-owned, that was producing cotton fabrics. Half of the plants were owned by Taiwanese and Chinese companies and the other half were owned by South African investors (Farole & Winkler, 2014). Locally owned apparel firms operating in Lesotho are small tailoring shops specializing in African apparel and clothes for special occasions for the domestic market. For Lesotho, the main issue continues to be the disparity between those who are improving their lives economically and those who remain destitute.

Madagascar (130)

Madagascar is a large island off the eastern coast of Africa about twice the size of Arizona, with a population of 23 million. It is a newly developing country, with per capita GDP of $1,400 and a literacy rate of 64 percent (refer to Table 12.1). Madagascar had a growing apparel industry, fueled by AGOA participation, until political turmoil erupted in 2002. Before the problems, there were 140 apparel companies in Madagascar's export-processing zone (EPZ) employing between 80,000 and 100,000 workers (US International Trade Commission, 2004). The main apparel product, accounting for almost half of output, was fully fashioned knitwear. The industry was relatively low-tech by international standards, as about 90 percent of the fully fashioned knitwear was made on hand-knitting machines. Most other products were done CMT.

A primary example of the kinds of setbacks plaguing the industry following the 2001 election was the blockade of the ports and roads, which halted clothing production for most of 2002. It was anticipated at that time that the political turmoil would inhibit future investment in the area and that competition from other markets would also inhibit recovery. Although some progress was made in the late 2000s, in 2009 the government was overthrown in a military coup. Also in 2009, the United States threatened Madagascar with removal from the list of African Growth and Opportunity Act (AGOA) beneficiary countries (Williams, 2015). Madagascar was deemed to be failing to meet the requirements necessary to continue AGOA participation in early 2010, resulting in the termination of their benefits of duty-free concessions under AGOA by US President Barack Obama (Williams, 2015).

In 2013, Madagascar's apparel exports were $381 million, up from $309 million in 2000 (World Trade Organization, 2014). The country's share of apparel exports in the total merchandise exports was cut in half between 2000 and 2013, from 40 percent to 20 percent. To support apparel manufacturing, Madagascar exports a significant amount of textiles: $279 million in 2013, up from $200 million in 2000. Also in 2013, SGS, a leading textile inspection, verification, and testing and certification company, opened a testing facility in Madagascar. Its purpose was to assist local garment manufacturers to comply with international regulations and requirements (Just-style.com, 2014b). In June 2014, the Obama administration reinstated AGOA eligibility for Madagascar (Williams, 2015).

Using the textiles and apparel industry as a means of a country's economic development presents a paradox in which labor exploitation often goes hand in hand with success, while the industry may decline for dozens of reasons during the process. It is a puzzling and frustrating phenomenon replayed in dozens of countries around the world. What is the social, economic, and environmental responsibility of the businesses involved? And what are the roles of textiles and apparel as the global market evolves? These are some of the primary questions that must be answered in order to have sustainable textile and apparel supply chains.

Summary

The Middle East and Africa trading region is linked by a centuries-old tradition of trade with other regions, an emphasis on the use of the Arabic language, and the widespread practice of Islam. By GDP per capita (PPP), the region is home to some of the most economically developed countries, such as the UAE, Saudi Arabia, and Israel, and also many of the least economically developed nations, including Ethiopia, Nigeria, and Madagascar. This region is also home to some of the wealthier nations in the world, including the UAE and Saudi Arabia, which enjoy high per capita GDPs from the production of oil and which focus more on consumption of apparel than on its production. Life expectancies range from 81.3 years in Israel to 49.6 years in South Africa.

The effects of apartheid policies of segregation and political and economic discrimination against nonwhite groups that were initiated by American and European politics nearly 100 years ago still persist today. The average life expectancy in several of the SSA nations is fewer than 55 years, largely because of poverty and the high incidence of HIV/AIDS and other diseases.

This region is also where some of the world's finest cotton is grown, especially in Egypt and Uganda. Production and export of cotton textiles and apparel in Turkey places it in the top ten in world rankings for export of these products. Many other nations in the area are looking to apparel production as a means of improving their economic station in life, via either foreign investment in production facilities, such as in Mauritius and Lesotho, or entrepreneurial startup factories, such as those in Ghana, funded by the World Bank.

Regional trade agreements with the EU and the United States and preference programs provide free access to markets for exports to many nations in this region. One example of such a program is AGOA, which affects most SSA nations. The QIZ agreements between the United States and Jordan and Egypt also provide the incentive of tariff-free access to the US market. Nonetheless, many of these nations are truly struggling and vulnerable. At this point, we can only wait and see how they fare.

Learning Activities

1. If you were required to source apparel in the Middle East–Africa trading bloc, what country or countries would you be most likely to select? What would your decision be based on?
2. What resources are available that should contribute to textile and apparel industry development in Africa?
3. What are three or four factors that inhibit economic development in several of these countries?
4. What barriers hamper textile and apparel industry development?

5. Refer back to Case 2.1. How would that scenario of recycling and waste change if the textile industry operated with endless supply chains based on something like the opportunity with Miscanthus grass in Case 12.3?

6. Describe what types of merchandise an apparel buyer might successfully source in South Africa. Why did you make those choices?

References

Apparel.com. (January 29, 2014). "Egyptian Ready-Made Garment Industry's 'Road Show' Hits Manhattan." Retrieved June 17, 2015, from http://apparel.edgl.com/news/egyptian-ready-made-garment-industry-s—road-show—hits-manhattan90888

Arafa Holding. (n.d.). "Corporate Overview." Retrieved June 18, 2015, from https://s3.amazonaws.com/inktankir/base/s3/ecc77e95d4823c94b5d7513f27702e25.pdf

Ayyad, M. (January 24, 2015). Arafa Holding Plans European Market Entrance in 2015. Retrieved November 3, 2015, from http://www.dailynewsegypt.com/2015/01/24/arafa-holding-plans-european-market-entrance-2015/

Bagir Group. (n.d.). "About Us." Retrieved June 17, 2015, from http://www.bagir.com/html/global_production.html

Barrie, L. (February 25, 2015). "South Africa Project to Grow Grass for Recyclable Textiles." Retrieved November 3, 2015, from http://www.just-style.com/news/south-africa-project-to-grow-grass-for-recyclable-textiles_id124476.aspx

Big Blue. (n.d.). "About Big Blue." Retrieved June 26, 2015, from http://www.bigblue.co.za/about-us/

Casabona, L. (October 1, 2009). "U.S. Sends Delegation to Jordan to Discuss Labor Issues." *Women's Wear Daily*. Retrieved November 5, 2015, from http://wwd.com/search/?s=U.S.+sends+delegation+to+Jordan+to+discuss+labor+issues

Central Intelligence Agency. (2004). *The World Factbook*. Dulles, VA: Brassey's.

Central Intelligence Agency. (2015). "World Factbook: Tunisia." Retrieved November 5, 2015, from https://www.cia.gov/library/publications/the-world-factbook/geos/ts.html

Coulibaly, L. (October 16, 2014). "West Africa Cotton Producers Forecast Bumper 2014/15 Crop." *Reuters*. Retrieved November 6, 2015, from http://www.reuters.com/article/2014/10/16/cotton-westafrica-forecast-idUSL6N0S92AR20141016#uw8xwWSGi8Zk1p8G.97

Dictionary of Sustainable Management. (2015). "Closed-Loop Supply Chain." Retrieved June 12, 2015, from www.sustainabilitydictionary.com/closed-loop-supply-chainEgyptOfficial

Export.gov. (n.d.). "US–Morocco Free Trade Agreement (FTA)." Retrieved July 5, 2015, from https://ustr.gov/trade-agreements/free-trade-agreements/morocco-fta

Farole, T., & Winkler, D. (2014). "Making Foreign Direct Investment Work for Sub-Saharan Africa." Retrieved November 5, 2015, from https://openknowledge.worldbank.org/bitstream/handle/10986/16390/9781464801266.pdf?sequence=1

Green, J. (September 2, 2003). "Jordan Trades on Stability." *Women's Wear Daily*.

Just-style.com. (July 2009). "Egypt Textiles and Clothing Report Q_3 2009." Retrieved July 24, 2009, from http://www.just-style.com/market-research/egypt-textiles-and-clothing-report-q3-2009_id79155.aspx

Just-style.com. (January 15, 2010). "US: Senator Calls for Review of Uganda's AGOA Trade Status." Retrieved March 10, 2010, from http://www.just-style.com/news/senator-calls-for-review-of-ugandas-agoa-trade-status_id106432.aspx

Karimzadeh, M. (February 8, 2010). "Kenneth Cole to Reach Turkey in New Deal." *Women's Wear Daily*. Retrieved November 5, 2015, from http://wwd.com/globe-news/designer-luxury/kenneth-cole-to-reach-turkey-in-new-deal-2450238/

Karpova, E. (2009). Personal interviews. Johannesburg, South Africa.

Kimenyi, M.S., & Kibe, J. (January 6, 2014). "Africa's Powerhouse." Retrieved November 3, 2015, from http://www.brookings.edu/research/opinions/2013/12/30-kenya-economy-kimenyi

Lipke, D. (November 14, 2007). "Growth Region: Many Middle East States Offer an Unexpected and Seemingly Insatiable Market for Luxury Goods." *Women's Wear Daily*, 26.

Madson, K. (2015). Sourcing manager, Kohl's. Personal correspondence, June 2015.

Maroc Export. (2014). "Textile Industry in Morocco." Retrieved November 3, 2015, from http://www.marocexport.gov.ma/carnets/denim%20novembre%202014%20basse%20re%CC%81solution.pdf

McGregor, L. (June 5, 2015). "750 Workers Laid Off at Uganda's Textile Manufacturers." *Sourcing Journal*. Retrieved November 3, 2015, from https://sourcingjournalonline.com/750-workers-laid-ugandan-textile-manufacturer-lm/

Mehta, M. (December 1, 2014). "The New Kid on the Block: Africa Is Vying for a Larger Share of the Global Textile and Apparel Pie." Retrieved November 3, 2015, from http://apparel.edgl.com/news/The-New-Kid-on-the-Block—Africa-Is-Vying-for-a-Larger-Share-of-the-Global-Textile-and-Apparel-Pie96802

Moin, D. (July 6, 2004). "Harvey Nichols Headed to Dubai." *Women's Wear Daily*, 26.

Neidik, B. (2004). "Organization Foundations of Export Performance: The Case of the Turkish Apparel Industry." *Journal of Fashion Marketing and Management*, 8(3), 294.

Office of the United States Trade Representative (n.d.). "African Growth Opportunity Act (AGOA)." Retrieved November 5, 2015, from https://ustr.gov/issue-areas/trade-development/preference-programs/african-growth-and-opportunity-act-agoa

One World Nations Online (n.d.). "Official and Spoken Languages of African Countries." Retrieved November 5, 2015, from http://www.nationsonline.org/oneworld/african_languages.htm

Perera, K. (September 14, 2009). "Opening Statement." United Nations Conference on Trade and Development, Trade and Development Board, 56th Session, Geneva, Switzerland, September 14–15, 2009. Retrieved November 5, 2015, from http://unctad.org/sections/wcmu/docs/tdb56stat_SirLanka_en.pdf

Retailing in Egypt (September, 2004). Report of Euromonitor International. Retrieved October 9, 2004, from http://www.the-infoshop.com/study/eo23381_retailing_in_egypt.html

Statista. (n.d.). "World's Leading Cotton Producing Countries." Retrieved June 11, 2015, from www.statistia.com/statistics/263055/cotton-production-worldwide-by-top-countries

Steyn, L. (July 29, 2014). "SA's Unemployment Rate Spirals Further into the Record Books." Retrieved June 11, 2015, from www.mag.co.za/article/2014-07-29-sas-unemployment-rate-spirals-further-into-the-record-books

Textile and Clothing in Tunisia. (n.d.). "Sector Overview." Retrieved November 5, 2015, from http://www.textileintunisia.net/textile-sector.php

Textile Industry Portal. (2015). "Israel, Egypt Set Target of US$2bn Duty-Free Textile Exports to U.S. Within 3 Years." Retrieved June 18, 2015, from http://www.egytex.com/news/3102

Thomasson, S. C. (2012). "Jordon's Textile and Apparel Sector: Small but Significant." Retrieved November 15, 2015, from www.textileworldasia.com/Issues/2012/October-November-December/Country_Profiles/

Trubok. (n.d.). "About Us." Retrieved June 24, 2015, from http://www.trubok.co.za/about.html

Tucker, R. (January 8, 2008). "Egypt Hunts New Growth Path." *Women's Wear Daily*, 16.

UNAids.org. (2008). "Lesotho." Retrieved June 11, 2010, from http://www.unaids.org/en/regionscountries/countries/lesotho

USAID. (2006). "Assessing the Impact of Egypt's Qualified Industrial Zones." Retrieved November 5, 2015, from http://pdf.usaid.gov/pdf_docs/Pnadj759.pdf

US International Trade Commission. (2004). "Textiles and Apparel: Assessment of the Competitiveness of Certain Foreign Suppliers to the US Market." Retrieved November 3, 2015, from http://www.usitc.gov/publications/docs/pubs/332/pub3671/pub3671.pdf

Williams, B. R. (2015). *African Growth and Opportunity Act (AGOA): Background and Reauthorization*. Washington, DC: Congressional Research Service.

World Bank. (2015). "Global Monitoring Report 2015–2016: Development Goals in an Era of Demographic Change." Retrieved November 15, 2015, from http://pubdocs.worldbank.org/pubdocs/publicdoc/2015/10/503001444058224597/Global-Monitoring-Report-2015.pdf

World Trade Organization. (2014). "Textile Exports of Selected Regions and Economies by Destination, 2013." Statistics: International Trade Statistics 2014. Merchandise Trade. Retrieved November 15, 2015, from www.wto.org/english/res_e/statis_e/its14_merch_trade_product_e.htm

GLOSSARY

accessories handbags, jewelry, purses, wallets, tote bags, and belts as well as eyeglass frames

acquisition the act of making products available for personal use; increases inventory of goods available for consumption

active inventory garments used within a one-year period

ad valorem tariff a tax set as a fixed percent of the value of an imported product

adversarial relationships common behaviors between suppliers and customers; in the textile complex, belief that success of one is dependent on costs to another

African Growth and Opportunity Act (AGOA) a component of the US Trade and Development Act of 2000; the purpose is to assist Sub-Saharan African (SSA) countries in achieving economic self-reliance; was renewed in June 2015 until the end of 2025

agile manufacturing an operational strategy focused on inducing velocity and flexibility in a made-to-order production process with minimal changeover time and interruptions

Agreement on Textiles and Clothing (ATC) a 1995–2004 World Trade Organization (WTO) trade agreement that replaced the Multifiber Arrangement (MFA)

America's Apparel Producers' Network (AAPN) membership includes representatives of the top twelve apparel and textile producing countries in the Western Hemisphere with a strong focus on sourcing, sustainability, and social responsibility

American Apparel and Footwear Association (AAFA) a predominantly US-based apparel-related trade association in the Americas

Andean a term that originated with early archaeologists that studied the civilizations in the mountains of Peru and Bolivia in western South America

Andean Trade Preference Act (ATPA) the primary trade agreement between the United States and northern South America, established in 1991

Andean Trade Promotion and Drug Eradication Act (ATPDEA) an agreement among the United States, Peru, and Bolivia in 2002 that made those countries eligible for duty-free treatment on exports of US goods for the first time

apartheid the state of being separate; a policy of strict racial segregation and political and economic discrimination against nonwhites

apparel clothing, accessories, and/or other attire that covers, adorns, and sometimes protects the human body

apparel firm a commercial or industrial business that is engaged in some aspects of designing, merchandising, marketing, producing, and/or retailing garments and other attire

apparel industry combination of trades and businesses that contribute to designing, developing, producing, and retailing garments and other attire that covers, protects, and/or adorns the human body

apparel knitting mill a manufacturing facility that interloops yarns to produce garments without producing the fabric first; can produce sweaters, tops, scarves, hats, dresses, and underwear

apparel manufacturer firm engaged in the entire process of apparel manufacturing; might also be involved in sourcing materials and/or retailing

apparel manufacturing processes involving division of labor for designing, merchandising, developing, producing, and often wholesale marketing garments and/or other attire that adorn the human body

apparel production part of the process of apparel manufacturing that actually converts materials—including fabrics, findings, trims, and usually thread—into garments; also known as apparel assembly

apparel production vendor firm that takes orders for apparel products from other firms and that either produces or arranges for the production of those specific garments; historically called production contractors

apparel sourcing determining the most cost efficient vendor of services, materials, production, and/or finished goods at a specified quality and service level, for delivery within an identified time frame

apparent consumption an estimation of domestic consumption of people in a country or region based on levels of domestic production, imports, and exports (production + imports – exports)

Asia-Pacific Economic Cooperation (APEC) a forum for twenty-one member nations to facilitate economic growth, cooperation, trade, and investment in the Asia-Pacific region, established in 1989

Association of Southeast Asian Nations (ASEAN) established to enhance the trade options for its ten member countries with a goal of establishing an ASEAN Economic Community

basic goods goods that are standardized and utilitarian, with infrequent demand for changes in styling

brand manager a former apparel manufacturer that is engaged in design and product development but owns little or no production facilities and sources garment assembly from vendors located elsewhere in the world

bureaucracy administrative system leading any large institution or government

business a commercial enterprise or profession organized and operated for the purpose of making a profit by providing a product or service

buying power *see* purchasing power

Caribbean Basin Economic Recovery Act (CBERA) commonly known as the Caribbean Basin Initiative (CBI), a trade preference program initiated by the United States in 1983 that expanded the use of Item 807 by eliminating quota restraints

Central America–Dominican Republic–United States Free Trade Agreement (CAFTA-DR) (2002) an agreement intended to solidify the United States as the leading supplier of goods and services to Central America and Dominican Republic and to provide these countries with duty-free access to the US market

charge-back a financial penalty imposed by the customer on a vendor for noncompliance with established vendor compliance rules

child labor employment of children in any work that interferes with their ability to attend regular school, and that is mentally, physically, socially, or morally dangerous and harmful

closed-loop system system in which some or all of its output is used as input

clothing wearing apparel including men's, women's, and children's garments as well as gloves, footwear, and headgear

clothing renovation brushing, laundering, dry cleaning, ironing, and any other method used to restore garments to what is regarded as wearable condition after wearing

clothing standards criteria determining styles, sizes, and colors of garments regarded as suitable for specific occasions

code of conduct a statement of principles and standards by which business decisions are made

collaborative consumption a redistribution of used goods that are being passed from someone who does not want them to someone who does want them

complement a product purchased and used along with another; for example, shoes and socks

conglomerate business formed when firms serving multiple markets join together with common ownership

consolidator a person or firm that combines cargo from a number of shippers going to the same destination into one container for the purpose of reducing shipping rates

Consumer Price Index (CPI) a measure of the impact of inflation on consumer purchasing power in the United States

consumption commodities (goods and services), their uses, and services consumed by an individual or a family

consumption expenditure money used to support the level of consumption during a specified period

contractor firm that provides services for other businesses, often used for selected apparel manufacturing processes; in today's sourcing language these firms are called vendors

converter fabric mill that specializes in application of yarn and fabric finishes

copyright a legal right gained by an author, composer, playwright, publisher, or distributor to exclusive publication, production, sale, or distribution of a literary, musical, dramatic, or artistic work

corporate social responsibility (CSR) ethical obligation of businesses toward the communities as well as the ecological and social environments in which they operate

corruption abuse of public office for private gains

cost center a department within an organization that is essential to the operation of the company but does not produce a profit

cost, insurance, freight (CIF) reflects the cost of goods as well as shipping and insurance to the requested port

counterfeit an imitation of what is genuine, with the intent to defraud the customer

counterfeiting the act of making an imitation of an original, with the intent to defraud

countervailing duty a special tax that increases the price of goods to a competitive level; used against illegal trade activities such as subsidies or dumping

country of origin (COO) the location where an article was wholly obtained; when more than one country is involved, the location where the last substantial transformation was carried out; the location where there is a change in the product designation number, according to the Harmonized Commodity Code and Designation System (HS)

customer in the sourcing world, the sourcing company that contracts for delivery of services, materials, product development, or finished goods

customs compliant to act in accordance with customs rules and regulations

customs service a government agency responsible for monitoring exported and imported goods, assessing and collecting duties, and protecting the country's borders against illegal entry

cut-and-sew apparel manufacturing a cut-and-sew apparel production that performs both preproduction and production processes

cut-make-trim (CMT) factory or vendor apparel contractors that commonly provide apparel assembly as their primary service

cyber crime illegal activity that uses a computer as a means of commission of a crime and as storage for the evidence of the crime

department store retailer that provides a variety of product lines, including apparel for men, women, and children; soft goods for the home; and home furnishings, usually at moderate-to-higher price levels

developed country nation whose gross domestic product per capita and other measures of well-being fall well above the world average

developing country nation whose gross domestic product per capita and other measures of well-being fall near or slightly below the world average

discard the act of giving up possession and ownership of a garment; reducing inventory

discretionary income the amount of money available after all current obligations are covered

disposable income take-home pay; the amount available to an individual or family to support the level of consumption, savings, and investment at a particular time

distressed goods merchandise that is not saleable at the intended price; seconds, overruns, samples, last season's goods, retailer returns, and so on

domestic production products made in the same country in which they are sold

dumping selling a product in another country at less than it is sold in the home country or less than it costs to produce

duty tax payment on imported or exported goods, usually based on a tariff schedule

dyeing the process of combining fibers, yarns, or fabrics with a coloring substance and creating a bond

e-commerce electronic business transactions conducted by systems such as the internet

e-tailing retailers providing opportunities for ultimate consumers to purchase products or services, using electronic systems such as the internet

economic responsibility the obligations of an individual, group, or general population to assume responsibility for the value of utilized materials, services, and resources and for using them efficiently, with a minimum of waste

EDI electronic data interchange; a means of passing document information between companies

effective tariff indicates the real amount of protection an industry has due to nominal tariff rates

elastic demand when income increases consumer demand decreases; when income decreases consumer demand increases; products with elastic demand are called normal goods

embargo the prohibition of the entry of goods into a defined political area; the stoppage of trade until issues can be negotiated

environmental responsibility the obligations of an individual, group, or general population for the physical conditions, circumstances, and related resources influencing the health and comfort of current and future generations

espionage the practice of observing furtively to obtain secret information especially regarding a government or a business

ethics a system or code of morals of a particular person, group, or profession and its application to decisions or particular problems of conduct

Euratex (European Apparel and Textile Confederation) organization that leads the efforts of the European textile industry with regard to negotiating trade agreements to reduce barriers to trade

euro European Union common currency, initiated in 2001 by fifteen countries of the EU

European Commission a politically independent institution responsible for proposing EU legislation, implementing it, and monitoring compliance

European Union (EU) an organization formed in 1993 to expand cooperation regarding trade, social issues, foreign policy, security, defense, and judicial issues

exchange rates determine the ratio at which one currency can be traded for another

export policy a set of regulations that determines what products and services can leave a country for another market and under what conditions

export processing zone (EPZ) tariff-free trade zone that is set up by governments in developing countries to promote export through simplified import and export procedures

export subsidy a payment from a government to a firm as a reward for exporting products

exports goods shipped to another country for import in exchange for money, other goods, or jobs

extra EU trade with nations that are not members of the EU

fabric finishing processes that convert greige goods into completed fabric

fabric-forward rule a trade rule that limits tariffs or provides quota-free imports, or both, for garments made of fabrics produced in one of the participating countries

facilitated illegal immigration term that covers a number of serious different crimes all aimed at assisting, for financial gain, the entry into or residence in a country, in violation of the laws of that country

Fair Labor Association (FLA) a coalition of companies, universities, and nongovernmental organizations dedicated to improving labor conditions around the world

fair trade a trading partnership, based on dialogue, transparency, and respect, that contributes to sustainable development by supporting trading conditions that secure the rights of marginalized producers and workers (World Fair Trade Organization [WFTO], 2009)

fashion a style of dress accepted by the majority of a group at a particular time

fashion goods individualized, differentiated by style, color, and fit; characterized by frequent changes in styling

fiberweb fabrics made directly from fibers; traditionally called nonwovens

findings materials other than face fabric used to construct garments: interlinings, pocket bags, linings, closures, and trims

firm any for-profit business, corporation, proprietorship, or partnership

first quality or "firsts" product that meets materials, design, production, appearance, and fit standards

first sample prototype of a product made for approval of the desired design features and garment fit

flexible production system quickly and efficiently producing a variety of styles at low volume per style, with zero defects; often uses single-ply cutters and modular systems with stand-up sewing

floor ready garment producers attach retailer-specified tickets and labels to garments that are ready for display before shipping them out

free on board (FOB) reflects the cost of goods and the cost of loading them onboard a vessel at the foreign port of export

free trade area a region made up of two or more countries that have a comprehensive free trade agreement eliminating or reducing trade barriers on products traded among the countries

Free Trade Area of the Americas (FTAA) the most comprehensive free trade agreement under discussion since the early 2000s, involving thirty-four countries in North, Central, and South America

free trade the unrestricted exchange of goods among nations

free trade zone a port or other site within a nation designated for duty-free entry of selected goods to be displayed, stored, and/or used for manufacturing

full container load (FCL) refers to a standard 20- or 40-foot shipping container loaded with merchandise from one consigner; it is a common measure for calculating shipping rates and typically is less expensive than the same weight of loose cargo

full-package factory or vendor apparel production firms that not only provide production services but also assist with and finance materials sourcing and some phases of product development

garment a piece of clothing

GDP-per capita (PPP) abbreviation for gross domestic product per capita adjusted by purchasing power parity

General Agreement on Tariffs and Trade (GATT) an international framework to establish ground rules for worldwide trade and promote reduction of trade barriers

global trade interactive participation of many groups, cultures, and nations in the merchandising, design, development, production, and distribution of products and services

globalization process whereby the world's people, their firms, and their countries become increasingly interconnected in all facets of their lives

government subsidy a payment from a government to a business to defray business costs

gray (grey) market goods original goods (they are not knockoffs) that are sold by unauthorized vendors

greenhouse gases (GHG) atmospheric gases (carbon dioxide, nitrous oxide, methane, water vapors, and some others) that trap heat from the sun and make the planet warmer

greige goods fabrics whose fibers are still their natural color and texture; usually require additional processes to improve aesthetics and performance

gross domestic product (GDP) market value of the output of products and services produced within a country in a year

gross domestic product (GDP) per capita gross domestic product (GDP) of a country divided by the number of people in the population after GDP has been adjusted by purchasing power parity (PPP); hereafter referred to as GDP per capita (PPP)

gross national product (GNP) value of the average output produced by domestic residents of a nation as they labor within that nation

gross national product (GNP) per capita gross national product of a country divided by the number of people in the population

guanxi the importance of connections and personal relationships when working within China or other Asian nations

Harmonized Commodity Description and Coding System (HS) a global classification system used to describe and measure trade

Harmonized System (HS) the international Harmonized Commodity Description and Classification System, developed by the World Customs Organization

Harmonized Tariff Schedule of the United States (HTS) the classifications of goods used to determine tariffs on specific products imported into the United States

Higg Index an indicator-based tool for footwear and apparel that enables companies to evaluate material types, products, facilities, and processes based on a range of environmental and product design choices

horizontal integration when previously competitive enterprises engaged in offering similar goods or services join together under a single management organization

Human Development Index (HDI) a composite index measuring average achievement in three basic dimensions of human development: a long and healthy life, knowledge, and a decent standard of living

human rights basic rights and freedoms to which all humans are entitled, often held to include the rights to life, liberty, equality, and a fair trial; freedom from slavery and torture; and freedom of thought and expression

human trafficking facilitating the emigration of people for monetary gain

illegal transshipment shipping goods through a port or country to facilitate the change of country of origin or to avoid quota limitations or import duties, or both, in the destination country

import agent or agent, is a professional who assists a business in a foreign country and acts as intermediary between the customer and the vendor; is paid on a commission basis by the company they represent

import and export trading recently developed type of enterprise that assists textile and apparel firms in satisfying customer demand for goods and services from the global market

import penetration the amount of consumption in a country or region that is provided by imports (imports ÷ consumption)

import policy a set of regulations that determines what products and services can enter the domestic economy from another country and under what conditions

imports goods available for domestic consumption or materials available for domestic production because of exports of other countries

inactive inventory garments that have not been used for at least one year

income elasticity the relationship between change in income and resulting change in expenditure

inelastic demand when income increases consumer demand decreases; when income decreases consumer demand increases; products with inelastic demand are called normal goods

inflation an increase of general price level, causing a decline in purchasing power

infrastructure fundamental physical and organizational facilities and systems needed for operation of a country, city, or area; includes transportation and communication systems and power supply

intellectual property (IP) copyrights, trademarks, patents, trade secrets, and semiconductor chips; inventions or other discoveries that have been registered with government authorities for the sale and use by their owner

intellectual property rights (IPR) legal protection for exclusive use by owners of copyrights, trademarks, patents, trade secrets, and semiconductor chips

intellectual property theft a crime of robbing people of their ideas, inventions, and creative expressions

intermediary a company that has expertise in design, product development, acquisition of materials, logistics, and importing as well as an established network of apparel factories they contract with

International Monetary Fund (IMF) works in tandem with the World Bank; helps integrate countries into the global economy by assisting member countries; monitors international currency transactions

international trade any exchange of goods involving two or more countries

intra EU trade among nations that are members of the EU

inventory the entire stock of garments owned by and/or available for use by an individual, family, or group of people that could be used as clothing at a given time

Item 807 a ruling that allowed garments cut in the United States to be exported and assembled in Caribbean countries and then imported with tariff based only on value added

joint venture shared ownership of a business or facility by two or more firms

knit fabric fabric made by intertwining yarn or thread in a series of connected loops rather than by weaving

knit outerwear sweaters (jumpers), jackets, and coats

knockoff an imitation of an original that does not carry the original brand, made with lower-cost materials and production methods and sold at a lower price

labor exploitation taking advantage of employees because of poverty, gender, age, opportunity, or a combination of these

labor union an organization that bargains with employers on behalf of workers about terms and conditions of employment; lobbies for the interests of workers

Latin America a term applied to all Spanish and Portuguese speaking nations south of the United States

layette complete outfit of apparel for a baby from birth until he or she begins walking; may also include bedding

LCL a shipping term for cargo that is less than full container load

LDP (landed duty paid) covers the costs of goods, insurance, freight, and import duty in the destination country

lean manufacturing a philosophy of production that emphasizes efficiency and economy of scale

lean retailing effective management of inventory, based on accurate and timely information and frequent resupply

legal system a system of interpreting and enforcing the laws in a country

letter of credit a guarantee to the seller that the buyer has the funds to complete the purchase and that they are reserved for the seller

level of consumption the quantity and quality of goods and services that are available to be used by an individual or group during a given time period

licensee the buyer of the right to use a merchandising property

licenser the owner of a merchandising property

licensing contract a means of transferring intellectual property rights; extending the value of a brand without having to produce the product; putting a brand name on a product produced by someone else for a contracted percentage of the sales

living wage the level of income that covers a family's basic needs, including maintenance of good health

lobbying the process of influencing the formation of legislation or the administration of rules, regulations, and policies

lobbyists paid professionals who communicate the political positions defined by their employers and try to influence formation or administration of legislation

logistics the process of planning, implementing, and controlling the efficient, effective flow and storage of goods, services, and related information from point of origin to point of consumption for the purpose of conforming to customer requirements

manufactured fibers made from chemical compounds; examples include nylon, polyester, acrylic, polypropylene, and spandex; also known as man-made fibers

manufacturing control a process in which expected performance is compared with actual performance

manufacturing the entire process of transforming raw materials into finished goods for use or sale, using machines, tools, and labor

market week calendar time set aside for trade shows featuring manufacturers' and brand managers' lines of textile materials, apparel, or machinery, presented at wholesale to other manufacturers or retail buyers

mass customization the integration of information technology, automation, and team-based flexible manufacturing to produce a variety of products and services based on individual customer demand

mass retailer firm that offers a wide variety of consumer goods in a self-service environment with broad appeal across income ranges, ethnic groups, occupations, and lifestyles

merchandising property the primary means of product differentiation and a source of customer loyalty

Mercosur (Common Market of the South) (1991) free trade within, and a common external tariff for, Argentina, Brazil, Paraguay, Uruguay, and Venezuela; accounts for 70 percent of South America's total economy

merger combining two business entities into one larger business

minimum needs the essentials of life, defined by levels and standards of consumption and living; vary according to place and time

morals the degree of conformity with generally accepted or prescribed standards of goodness or rightness in character or conduct

most-favored nation (MFN) a principle that each country must treat all nations the same in terms of trade restrictions and policies, and no country should have preferential trade arrangements

Multifiber Arrangement (MFA) an international trade agreement that allowed textile and apparel trade to be regulated through quotas established in bilateral agreements between nations

multilateral trade agreement involves more than two countries

nano used loosely means "small" or "short-time"; nano in technology means application of extremely small things to make changes that can be used across many science fields

nanotechnology application of extremely small item, entity, or thing to make changes in performance or behavior that can be used across many science fields

natural fibers cotton, wool, silk, and linen as well as other vegetable and animal fibers

newly developing country nation whose gross domestic product per capita and other measures of well-being fall well below the world average; just beginning to be engaged in industrial development, likely to involve apparel production; some sources use term "least developed country"

nominal tariff tax rates on imported goods published in each country's tariffs schedule

nonstore retailer firm that sells goods to the ultimate consumer without use of traditional "brick-and-mortar" store presentation

nontariff trade barriers the quota, quality standards, or other regulations or conditions that restrict the flow of goods between countries, not including taxes on imports or exports

nonverbal communication uses appearance to communicate perspective, identity, age, sexual orientation, educational level, occupation, economic status, or marital status

North American Free Trade Agreement (NAFTA) eliminated tariffs and quotas among Canada, Mexico, and the United States in 1994

North American Industry Classification System (NAICS) a standardized system for collecting, analyzing, and publishing statistical data involving trade among Canada, Mexico, and the United States; NAICS data includes textiles and apparel and many other products

Office of Textiles and Apparel (OTEXA) a division of US Department of Commerce that monitors textile trade throughout the globe in terms of both quantity and value

omnichannel retailing (also spelled omni-channel) a multichannel approach to sales that seeks to provide a seamless shopping experience to customers whether they are shopping online from a desktop or mobile device, by telephone, or in a brick-and-mortar store

Organization of American States (OAS) (1948) has the purpose of a Pan-American Union for closer economic, cultural, and political relations within the Americas

origin-conferring operations processes that determine what a label on a product will state as country of origin

outsourcing contracting out specific operations outside the company to a domestic or foreign vendor with the goal to perform these operations more efficiently and/or at a lower cost; outsourced operations might include manufacturing, product development, logistics, IT, accounting, customer service, etc.

outward processing temporary exporting of goods for manufacturing processes or repair purposes; the goods are then re-imported back into the country with partial or total exemption from import duty or taxes; primarily used in European Union

package factory in addition to apparel assembly to customer specifications, the factory can source and finance all materials and deliver goods onboard; they do not offer any product development services

Pan-American Union (1910) a union with the purpose of closer economic, cultural, and political relations within the Americas

per capita by or for each individual; total is divided by the number of individuals involved and all share equally

per capita purchasing power parity measure that allows comparison of well-being among populations in different countries, as indicated by GDP; determined by adjusting GDP of a country by

the buying power of its currency using the Consumer Price Index and dividing the total by the number of people in the population

pirated a term used in the US and the EU; an imitation of the original, counterfeit

political strategy the general approaches used by governments, firms, other organizations, and individuals in dealing with and manipulating important and powerful components in their environments

politics methods or tactics involved in managing an organization, business, state, or government, often in a pursuit of self-interest; sometimes includes crafty or unprincipled methods, or both

poverty a lack of enough income or resources, or both, to satisfy minimum needs

preferential trade agreement (PTA) a form of economic integration created by reducing trade barriers

preproduction stage of apparel manufacturing that involves all product development activities performed before the garment is approved for production; includes design, patternmaking, grading, making first and production samples, and development of technical specifications for materials and production processes

price elasticity the relationship between the change in price for a product and the related change in demand for the same product

price support program purchasing and storing products from the market to reduce the supply, relative to demand, to drive up the price

primary source the most frequent means of clothing acquisition; purchased new ready-to-wear in developed countries, purchased secondhand or handed down in newly developing countries

printing the localized application of color to the surface of a yarn or fabric

private brand a brand owned and marketed exclusively by a brand manager or retailer

product development design and engineering of products to be serviceable, producible, salable, and profitable

product lifecycle management (PLM) the process of managing a product's lifecycle from inception, design, development of related materials, manufacturing, delivery, distribution, marketing, sale, and in some cases, service and disposal

product obsolescence discard of products owing to lack of interest in them rather than lack of their fundamental usability

production sample garments made at the factory where the order will be mass produced to check for quality and any potential production issues; typically produced in all ordered sizes

production subsidy a negative trade tax; a payment of money from a government to a business to defray costs of making goods and commodities

productivity a ratio of the outputs of a production process to the inputs; a measure of performance toward an established goal

progressive tax an increase in tax rate as income rises

protectionism use of trade barriers to minimize imports in order to protect domestic industry

purchasing power the amount of goods or services that can be acquired with a specified amount of currency at a given time and place; the value of money in terms of what it could buy during a specified period of time; also sometimes called buying power

purchasing power parity (PPP) measure that allows comparison of well-being among populations in different countries, as indicated by GDP; determined by adjusting GDP of a country by the buying power of its currency using Consumer Price Index

qualified industrial zone (QIZ) a highly specialized area within an exporting country that grants a product manufactured in the zone duty-free access to participating importing countries

quality assurance a commitment to product quality that utilizes the concept of error prevention as integral to the entire product development process

quota method used to restrict quantities of certain types of goods that can be imported or exported; limit on the quantity of products allowed to enter or exit a country

radio frequency identification (RFID) a new generation of wireless tracking bar code systems being used for identifying and tracking products, cartons, and containers with tags attached to the objects

real expenditure spending adjusted to reflect purchasing power, considering rate of inflation

real income earnings adjusted to reflect purchasing power, considering rate of inflation

real-time immediately available when data are collected

recovering the process of collecting and sorting out waste materials for processing into new forms, which will be marketed as raw materials for new products

recycling the process of taking a product at the end of its useful life and using all or part of it to make another product

regionalization reducing trade barriers in selected geographic regions to facilitate trade

regressive tax requires lower-income people to pay higher rates than higher-income people

retail product developer individual or team that creates product designs and develops merchandise plans and specifications for a retailer's private brands, which are ultimately sourced from production vendors

retailing sale of merchandise or services, or both, to ultimate consumers

rules of origin criteria used to determine the national source of a product

safeguard measures temporary action to protect an industry from fast and sudden rise of imports

secondary source a means of acquiring clothing other than the primary source: gifts, purchased used, handed down, rental, home sewing, custom-made, and others

seconds garments that are not first quality when they come off the production line, also known as irregulars because they do not meet materials, design, production, appearance, or fit standards

seizure the act of taking control of illegal merchandise, drugs, or other products by CBP official(s) at border crossings after being legally inspected before being admitted to the United States

sharing economy also known as collaborative consumption, is a trending business model when individuals and organizations prefer to borrow or rent products instead of buying and owning them

social responsibility the obligations of an individual, group, or general population toward the welfare and interest of the communities in which they live and operate, including fair treatment of human beings, resources, and the law

socialist-capitalist economy a more privatized market-oriented economy that promotes trade and growth, while still restricting the freedoms of individuals

soft goods products made of textiles or other flexible materials: fabrics, apparel, linens, towels, upholstery, and small fashion accessories

sourcing agent individual or firm that provides services to procure and deliver products

sourcing process of finding, evaluating, and partnering with a vendor to secure services, materials, production, or finished goods, or a combination of these, at a specified cost, quality, and service level, for delivery within an identified time frame

sourcing calendar a time line related to the sequence of design, product development, production, and delivery to the retail sales floor

specialty retailer retailer that focuses on specific classes of merchandise to the exclusion of other products

specific tariff a fixed amount of tax per physical unit of imported product

specifications detailed graphic and written descriptions of styling, materials, dimensions, production procedures, and finishing instructions for a garment

square meter equivalent (SME) a means of measuring quantities of fabric and garments that are being exported or imported

standard of consumption or living a level that is urgently desired and strived for, substantial success yielding special gratification, and substantial failure yielding bitter frustration

standards basic characteristics used to determine acceptability of products and services

substantial transformation occurs when the processing of an article results in a new and different article having a distinct name, character, or use; occurs when an HS classification changes

substitute a product purchased and used in place of another; for example, pants rather than skirts

supply chain total sequence of business processes involving single or multiple companies and countries that enables demand for products or services to be satisfied; an apparel supply chain might include some or all of the following: design and product development agencies, material suppliers, manufacturers, transporters, warehousers, retailers, and consumers

supranational organization requires that members give up a portion of their control over selected policies and allows the organization to compel compliance with its mandates

sustainability involves the corporate, government, and consumer responsibility to integrate economic, political, environmental, and cultural dimensions to promote cooperation and solidarity among people and generations

Sustainable Apparel Coalition (SAC) a trade organization of brands, retailers, and manufacturers, government and nongovernmental organizations, and academic experts with a focus on creating common metrics and approaches to reduce the social and environmental impacts of apparel and footwear

sweatshop a firm with poor working conditions, very low pay, safety violations, and often inhumane treatment of employees

takeover absorption of a weaker firm into a more successful operation

technical barriers to trade (TBT) regulations, standards, testing, and certification procedures that obstruct trade

technical textiles textile products designed for thermal and/or mechanical performance and durability including those made for protective clothing and medical use

temporary possession a means of momentary clothing acquisition from sources such as rental, borrowing, and clothing provided by an employer

textile complex combination of textile-related industries that supply soft goods to the world population; includes firms engaged in man-made fiber production, textile manufacturing (knit, woven, and nonwoven fabrics), apparel manufacturing, retailing, and product consumption and disposal

textile industry combination of trades and businesses that contribute to production, manufacturing, and retailing of fibers, yarns, fabrics, and related materials

textile materials sourcing identifying appropriate countries of origin and vendors of fabric, thread, or findings at a specified quantity, quality, and service level, for delivery within a designated time frame

textile mill a manufacturing facility where yarns or fabrics are produced

textile product mill a manufacturing facility that produces fabric and uses it to create consumable goods, including carpets, rugs, curtains, draperies, and bed and bath products

thread a special form of yarn designed for use in sewing cut fabric pieces together to form garments or other products

total income gross income or personal income

trade agreement means of encouraging, regulating, or restricting elements of trade among countries

trade association a nonprofit organization formed to serve the common needs of its members

trade balance quantitative relationship between exports and imports of a country

trade barriers means of regulating or restricting trade; examples include state trading, tariffs, quotas, and limits on foreign investment

trade deficit negative trade balance; value of imports exceeds value of exports

trade exchange of goods, services, or both; can be domestic, international, or global

trade fair massive, usually regular trade event where producers display products and services to wholesalers and retailers

trade policy a political strategy or program designed to stimulate or control the exchange of goods between nations

trade regulation barriers and limits on types and quantities of goods and services that cross political boundaries

trade surplus positive trade balance; value of exports exceeds value of imports

trademark a word, phrase, logo, or other graphic symbol used to distinguish one firm's products or services from those of other firms

trademark infringement the act of misleading the public into believing the items bearing the trademark/brand name are produced and sold by the owner of the trademark, when they are not

trading bloc a group of countries that have created regional trade incentives and that jointly participate in trade negotiations

transaction value the price actually paid or payable for goods when sold for export

transparency of information open communication among all participants within a system

transshipment to transfer or be transferred from one conveyance to another in order to continue shipment

transshipment center a port where merchandise can be imported and then exported without paying import duties

underwear and sleepwear knitting mill a manufacturing facility in which products are produced by cutting and sewing knit fabrics

undocumented immigrant workers (UIWs) individuals from foreign countries without legal identification papers

unfair competition activities defined by legal rulings and statutes that protect against unethical business practices

Universal Product Code (UPC) a bar code system for identifying and tracking products or containers

vendor a company that supplies services or products to other companies, commonly known as customers

vendor compliance performance standards or rules established by the customer related to things like working conditions, wages, and age of workers that a vendor must follow in order to do business with that customer

vertical integration combining firms that perform different stages of the manufacturing and/or retailing of similar and/or compatible types of products

voluntary export restraint a self-imposed limit on the amount of product that one country can export to another country, also known as export tariff restraint agreement

wearing apparel garments that cover the human body for comfort, protection, and adornment

well-being a good or satisfactory condition of existence; a state of being comfortable, healthy, and happy

World Customs Organization (WCO) a global organization whose purpose is to improve the operations and efficiency of customs services

World Trade Organization (WTO) an institution with more than 160 countries as members; deals with the global rules of trade among nations

Worldwide Responsible Accredited Production (WRAP) an independent nonprofit corporation dedicated to the promotion and certification of lawful, humane, and ethical manufacturing throughout the world

woven fabrics produced by interlocking two or more sets of yarns at right angles

yarn a continuous strand produced by twisting fibers together

yarn-forward rule apparel can be imported tariff- and quota-free if garments are made of yarns and fabrics from one of participating countries

zero-waste supply chain a supply chain that completely reuses, recycles, or composts all materials.

PHOTO CREDITS

Frontis, Title Page, Lucian Milasan / Shutterstock.com

Part 1, Opener, stockbyte/Thinkstock

Chapter 1, Figure 1, Courtesy of Fairchild Books (from 2nd ed)

Chapter 1, Figure 2, Courtesy of Fairchild Books (from 2nd ed)

Chapter 1, Figure 3, Jeff Holt/Bloomberg via Getty Images

Chapter 1, Figure 4, Danish Khan/Getty Images

Chapter 1, Figure 5, Grace Kunz

Chapter 1, Figure 6, Li & Funk Limited

Chapter 1, Figure 7, Bao Fan/ChinaFotoPress/Getty Images

Chapter 1, Figure 8, Boye / WWD / . Conde Nast

Chapter 1, Figure 9a, Andrew Burton/Getty Images

Chapter 1, Figure 9b, Ericksen / WWD / . Conde Nast

Chapter 1, Figure 9c, Ericksen / WWD / . Conde Nast

Chapter 1, Figure 9d, Ericksen / WWD / . Conde Nast

Chapter 1, Case 1.1, Mehul Srivastava/Bloomberg via Getty Images

Chapter 2, Figure 1a, nikitabuida/Shutterstock

Chapter 2, Figure 1b, Movius / WWD / . Conde Nast

Chapter 2, Figure 1c, Iannoccone / WWD / . Conde Nast

Chapter 2, Figure 2, Secondary Materials And Recycled Textiles (SMART) Association

Chapter 2, Figure 3a, Aquino / WWD / . Conde Nast

Chapter 2, Figure 3b, Ericksen / WWD / . Conde Nast

Chapter 3, Figure 1, US Census Bureau

Chapter 3, Figure 2, CAMERA PRESS/Charles Fox/Redux

Chapter 3, Figure 3, China Photos/Getty Images

Chapter 3, Figure 4a, China Photos/Getty Images

Chapter 3, Figure 4b, Noam Armonn/Shutterstock

Chapter 4, Figure 1, Courtesy of Fairchild Books (from 2nd ed)

Chapter 4, Figure 2a, Photo Courtesy of Ten Thousand Villages, USA

Chapter 4, Figure 2b, Cyrus McCrimmon/The Denver Post via Getty Images

Chapter 4, Figure 3, EPA

Chapter 4, Figure 4, EPA

Chapter 4, Figure 5, Kenton Lee

Chapter 4, Figure 6, Courtesy of Patagonia

Chapter 4, Figure 7, ROMEO GACAD/AFP/Getty Images

Chapter 4, Figure 8, China Photos/Stringer/Getty Images

Chapter 4, Figure 9, lenscap67/Istockphoto

Chapter 4, Figure 10, KAREN BLEIER/AFP/Getty Images

Chapter 4, Figure 11, Simon Dawson/Bloomberg via Getty Images

Chapter 4, Figure 12, Courtesy of Fairchild Books (created for this edition)

Chapter 4, Figure 13, Courtesy of Patagonia

Chapter 4, Figure 14, www.ifixit.com

Chapter 4, Figure 15, Courtesy of Patagonia

Chapter 4, Figure 16, Thinkstock

Chapter 4, Case 4.1, EPA

Chapter 4, Case 4.3a, Joel Tettamanti

Chapter 4, Case 4.3b, Peter Wurmli

Chapter 4, Case 4.3c, Joel Tettamanti

Chapter 4, Case 4.3d, Sebastian Mayer

Part 2, Figure 1, microvector/Shutterstock

Chapter 5, Figure 1, WWW / . Conde Nast

Chapter 5, Figure 2, G

Chapter 5, Figure 3, . World Trade Organization

Chapter 5, Figure 4, G

Chapter 5, Case 5.2, Q2A

Chapter 6, Figure 1, Image from U.S. Patent No. U.S. 6,543,062 B1 (Amsel et al., 2003)

Chapter 6, Figure 2a, Spencer Platt/Getty Images

Chapter 6, Figure 2b, Kevork Djansezian/Getty Images

Chapter 6, Figure 3, JOHN D. SIMMONS/KRT/Newscom

Chapter 6, Case 6.1, Guenter Schiffmann/Bloomberg via Getty Images

Chapter 7, Figure 1, Elena Karpova

Chapter 7, Figure 2, Q2A

Chapter 7, Figure 3, Alan Traeger/Getty Images Images

Chapter 7, Figure 4, Tim Makins/Getty Images

Chapter 7, Figure 5, Maplecroft/Q2A

Chapter 7, Figure 6, MANPREET ROMANA/AFP/Getty Images

Chapter 7, Figure 7, VICS logistics

Chapter 7, Figure 8, Welle, T., Birkmann, J., Krause, D., Suarez, D.C., Setiadi, N. and J. Wolfertz (2013): The WorldRiskIndex: A concept for the assessment of risk and vulnerability at global/national scale. In: Birkmann, J.: Measuring Vulnerability to Natural Hazards: Towards Disaster Resilient Societies Second Edition, pp. 219-251, United Nations University Press. ISBN-13: 978-92-808-1202-2. /Q2A

Chapter 7, Case 7.2a, Boathouse Sports

Chapter 7, Case 7.2b, Image Courtesy of All American Clothing Co.

Chapter 8, Figure 1, Elena Karpova

Chapter 8, Figure 2a, Elena Karpova

Chapter 8, Figure 2b, FlamingPumpkin/Getty Images

Chapter 8, Figure 2c, Jose Antonio Macie/Getty Images

Chapter 8, Figure 3, Elena Karpova

Chapter 8, Figure 4, FREDERIC J. BROWN/AFP/Getty Images

Chapter 8, Figure 5, Elena Karpova

Chapter 8, Figure 6, G

Chapter 8, Figure 7, G

Chapter 8, Case 8.1a, Li and Fung

Chapter 8, Case 8.1b, Li and Fung/Q2A

Part 3, Figure 1, Gallup / WWD / . Conde Nast

Chapter 9, Figure 1, Q2A

Chapter 9, Figure 2, Photo by Karina Hessland/Bongarts/Getty Images

Chapter 9, Figure 3, . Scott Hortop / Alamy

Chapter 9, Figure 4, . epa european pressphoto agency b.v. / Alamy

Chapter 9, Figure 5, Courtesy of Fairchild Books (from 2nd ed based on Guercini, 2004, p.331)

Chapter 9, Figure 6a, Jacopo Raule/Getty Images

Chapter 9, Figure 6b, Victor VIRGILE/Gamma-Rapho via Getty Images

Chapter 9, Figure 7a, Geoffroy Van der Hasselt/Anadolu Agency/Getty Images

Chapter 9, Figure 7b, MIGUEL MEDINA/AFP/Getty Images

Chapter 9, Figure 7c, . Stephane ROUSSEL / Alamy

Chapter 9, Figure 8, Elena Karpova

Chapter 9, Case 9.1, SOFIE AMALIE KLOUGART/The New Yo rk Times/Redux

Chapter 9, Case 9.2a, David Surowiecki/Getty Images for Hugo Boss

Chapter 9, Case 9.2b, John Lawson /Getty Images

Chapter 10, Figure 1, Q2A

Chapter 10, Figure 2, Courtesy of Fairchild Books (created for this edition)

Chapter 10, Figure 3, Patrick T. Fallon/Bloomberg via Getty Images

Chapter 10, Figure 4, Patrick T. Fallon/Bloomberg via Getty Images

Chapter 10, Figure 5, Hudson Bay Co.

Chapter 10, Figure 6, Elena Karpova

Chapter 10, Figure 7, Elena Karpova

Chapter 10, Figure 8, Elena Karpova

Chapter 10, Figure 9, Christopher Pillitz/Getty Images

Chapter 10, Figure 10, Alejandra Parra/Bloomberg via Getty Images

Chapter 10, Figure 11, Frazer Harrison/Getty Images

Chapter 11, Figure 1, Q2A

Chapter 11, Figure 2, Courtesy of Fairchild Books (created for this edition)

Chapter 11, Figure 3, Courtesy of Fairchild Books (created for this edition)

Chapter 11, Figure 4, Q2A

Chapter 11, Figure 5, Elena Karpova

Chapter 11, Figure 6, Keith Bedford/Bloomberg via Getty Images

Chapter 11, Figure 7, George Rose/Getty Images

Chapter 11, Figure 8, Gareth Gay/Getty Images

Chapter 11, Figure 9, Q2A

Chapter 11, Figure 10, Q2A

Chapter 11, Figure 11, Manjunath Kiran/AFP/Getty Images

Chapter 11, Figure 12, Elena Karpova

Chapter 12, Figure 1, Q2A

Chapter 12, Figure 2, Chris Ratcliffe/Bloomberg via Getty Images

Chapter 12, Figure 3, Ali Al Mubarak/Getty Images

Chapter 12, Figure 4, Julian Love/Getty Images

Chapter 12, Figure 5, Melanie Stetson Freeman/The Christian Science Monitor via Getty Images

Chapter 12, Figure 6, Elena Karpova

Chapter 12, Figure 7, Elena Karpova

Chapter 12, Figure 8, Big Blue South Africa.

INDEX

Taiwan, 64, 370

takeovers, 5, 22

TAL Group, 367

Target, 28, *29*, 32, 33, 133, 174–175, 177, 379

tariffs, 63, 221, 334, 349
  ad valorem tariffs, 129, 133, 134
  effective tariffs, 129, 135–136
  implementation in the US, 143
  import, 221
  Item 807, 129, 155, 317, 334
  nominal tariffs, 129, 133
  specific, 130, 133
  strategies, 137

taxes
  progressive, 39, 56, 57
  regressive, 40, 56–57

technical barriers to trade (TBT), 130, 140

technical textiles, 269, 290, 368

technology
  development, 85–86
  sourcing, 256–259

technology-intensive, 18, 36

temporary possession, 40, 41

Ten Thousand Villages, 97

Tesco, 253, 280, 293

textile and apparel industry, 5. *see also* labor issues; sourcing; textile complex
  the Americas and the Caribbean Basin, 308–343
  Asia and Oceania, 346–385
  business/labor/government connection, 11
  capital and technology intensive, 18
  classification of products, 66–67
  codes of conduct, 93, 94
  computer technology applications, 85–86
  developed countries, 3, 19
  in Egypt, 409
  employment in, 3
  globalization overview, 2–37
  low entry barriers, 18
  the Middle East and Africa, 390–422
  Moroccan, 411–412
  political evolution of, 153–159
  products, 16–19
  textile and apparel supply matrix, 60–88
  in Thailand, 374
  trade associations, 29, 102, 130, 152, 326
  transportation and logistics, 83–84
  in Tunisia, 408
  in Vietnam, 375